AMERICAN GOVERNMENT TODAY

CRM BOOKS Del Mar, California

AMERICAN GOVERNMENT TODAY

Advisers

Michael Lipsky
*Massachusetts Institute
of Technology*

Donald Matthews
University of Michigan

Lewis Lipsitz
*University of North
Carolina at Chapel Hill*

Jack Walker
University of Michigan

Contributors

Richard J. Barnet
*Institute for Policy Studies,
Washington, D.C.*

Edward N. Beiser
Brown University

Jonathan D. Casper
Stanford University

Harry M. Caudill
Attorney, Whitesburg, Kentucky

James W. Clarke
University of Arizona

Roger H. Davidson
*University of California,
Santa Barbara*

Barbara Deckard
University of California, Riverside

Delmer D. Dunn
University of Georgia

George Frederickson
Indiana University

Paul Halpern
*University of California,
Los Angeles*

Robert J. Huckshorn
Florida Atlantic University

Everett C. Ladd, Jr.
University of Connecticut

Harlan Lewin
*California State University,
San Diego*

Robert L. Lineberry
University of Texas at Austin

Lewis Lipsitz
*University of North Carolina at
Chapel Hill*

Michael Lipsky
*Massachusetts Institute of
Technology*

Norman R. Luttbeg
Florida State University

Grant McConnell
University of California, Santa Cruz

Mark V. Nadel
Cornell University

James K. Oliver
University of Delaware

Gary Orfield
The Brookings Institution

John C. Pierce
Washington State University

Douglas D. Rose
Tulane University

William A. Schultze
*California State University,
San Diego*

Rodney Stark
University of Washington

Brief biographies of the advisers and contributors
and attribution of their work in this text appear
on pages 501–503

What is "American" politics? What is the government's agenda? Who runs the government? Where do we come in? To these time-honored questions there are few undisputed answers. Indeed, if real answers were possible, there would be fewer books on the subject and we would not have the opportunity here to provide a fresh analysis of the basic questions of American Government Today.

A new perspective on these questions demands a new approach. The planning and execution of this book, as well as its development within, will thus be unique to many readers. The broad scope and rapid proliferation of knowledge in contemporary political science make it very unlikely that one or two authors alone can produce an introductory book that is comprehensive, equally authoritative across all topics, and current. Therefore, we set out to involve the creative energies and experience of as broad a group of political scientists as was required to achieve our goals.

PREFACE

In May 1972 a seminar was held in Washington, D.C. to hammer out the central plan and approach of the book. Among those attending the seminar were Professors Michael Lipsky, Lewis Lipsitz, Donald Matthews, and Jack Walker, all of whom became project advisers and, in the course of the book's construction, provided hundreds of hours of indispensable guidance and criticism as well as substantial portions of the final manuscript.

Following the recommendations of our four advisers, we contacted scholars with recognized expertise in the areas of our concern and commissioned them to write the chapters. Each adviser took responsibility for one of the four units and, working closely with each author, helped to develop the chapter outlines and to critique the manuscript at every stage. In addition, each chapter was submitted to an acid test early in its development: It was closely scrutinized by Byron Heilman, Fred Horn, Malcolm Moore, James Oliver, and Thomas Scism, each an experienced and perceptive teacher of American government. Their comments—and those of their students—greatly influenced the final product.

This book is unconventional in other ways—from the way it is organized, to the elements that comprise it, to the way it looks.

First, the table of contents reveals our belief that an analysis of broad public policies provides the most meaningful perspective for understanding American political life, that only in the content of public policy do we see why politics matters so much to each of us. Therefore, the Unit I chapters on American ideology, interests and institutions, and the distribution of wealth serve to define the context of American politics. They are followed in Unit II by analyses of four broad, generic problems of governance—the management of the economy, foreign affairs and national security, race, and civil liberties—problems that command the greatest share of the machinery and energy of our national government. Accompanying each of these chapters is a Perspective, in which the reader is invited to examine at closer quarters the attempts by government to come to grips with

one of the particular problems introduced in the preceding chapter.
We do not pretend that the Perspectives, or even the chapters preceding them, take an impartial, above the battle, view of American
public policy. Areas of prolonged and intense controversy are discussed, areas where policy is deeply problematic and also deeply important. The Perspectives are signed by their authors because they
represent views strongly held; their purpose is to stimulate thought
and debate rather than to seek consensus.

The chapters of Unit III examine the four national institutions that
are largely responsible for the creation and control of public policy.
Exhaustive descriptions of formal institutional powers and functions
are sacrificed to allow a focus on the patterns and behaviors of each
institution as it deals with, or attempts to deal with, the broad policy
issues that inform this book.

Unit IV analyzes the other end of the process, the devices and avenues
that serve as links between citizens and those who make and administer public policy. How effective are those links? How do we
gain access to them? Do some have privileged access? What recourse
remains for those without access to conventional political power?

Effective communication demands the use of media other than the
written word. Well-conceived and well-executed graphics can com-
plement as well as expand a text; but they can also convey great complexity with an ease and clarity that words approach only with
difficulty. As a result, the graphics in this text are designed both to
explore and to call attention to relationships; they clarify concepts,
demonstrate alternatives, and personalize material in a way that is
designed to seize and to hold the reader's interest. Indeed, had many
major concepts been portrayed verbally rather than graphically, the
book would be far longer.

There are additional elements that contribute to the effectiveness of
this text:

–The Prologue and Epilogue start and complete a process of involvement and awareness of the importance of politics in everyday life.
–Unit introductions explain how the chapters fit together and raise
  key questions of theory and interpretation to guide the student's
  reading.
–Topical Inserts are brief readings from popular sources that appear
  occasionally to provide further illustration or opinion.
–Chapter summaries tie the major concepts of each chapter together
  in capsule form in order to stress the interconnection of ideas rather
  than facts.
–Margin notes define important concepts or add interesting side-
  lights; they appear next to the text rather than within it to maintain
  a smooth flow of content.
–Suggested readings accompany each chapter, in addition to the
  complete listing of text references in the back of the book.

Above all, this book is written to involve, to inform, and to convince its readers that politics matters. Some may find it awkward or controversial; others may find it exciting, enlightening, maybe unsettling. Few, we hope, will read this book and fail to generate strong opinions; and that is our aim.

Roger G. Emblen

Publishing Director
CRM Books

CONTENTS

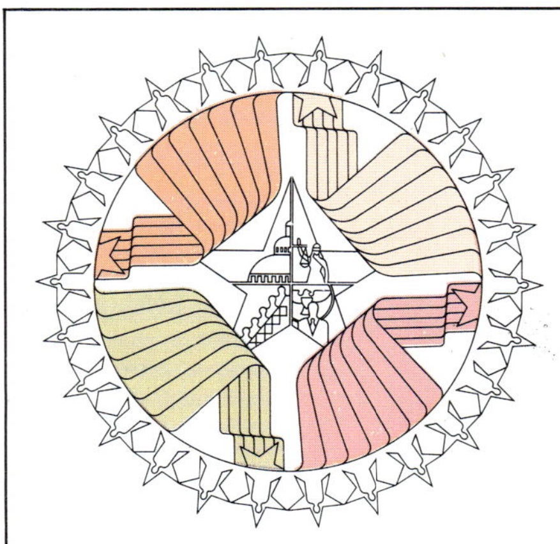

UNIT II

WHAT IS THE GOVERNMENT'S AGENDA?

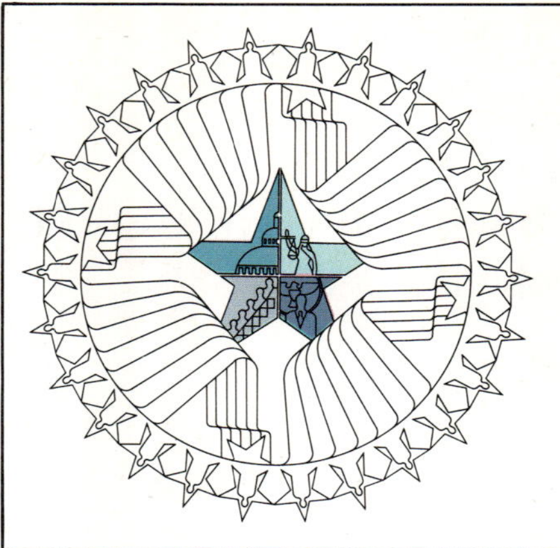

UNIT III

WHO RUNS THE GOVERNMENT?

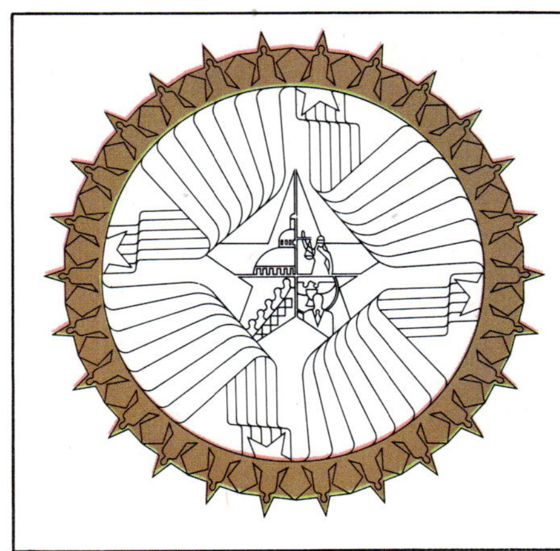

UNIT IV

WHERE DO WE COME IN?

All quoted passages in this prologue are taken either from actual interviews done by the author or from written materials based on other actual interviews. The author wishes to thank the students of his political science freshman seminar at the University of North Carolina, Chapel Hill in the fall of 1972 for their cooperation; in particular, Bill Fraiberg, Pat Fitzgerald, Liz Dixon, and Elliott Moorman. We also acknowledge the use of interview materials from *The Workers* (A Nader Report), edited by Kenneth Lasson (Grossman, 1972), a set of nine talks with people in different occupations that sheds interesting light on making do in contemporary America; Studs Terkel's *Hard Times,* a lengthy and fascinating set of interviews about the Great Depression (Pantheon, 1970); and Robert Coles, *The South Goes North*—Vol. III of *Children of Crisis* (Atlantic; Little, Brown, 1971).

PROLOGUE

POLITICS IN EVERYDAY LIFE

This book is about the meaning of politics in America. According to one definition, politics is the nuts-and-bolts workings of political institutions: How does Congress work? What are the powers of the President? What does federalism mean?

But politics is also part of life as it is lived day-to-day by most of us. It is involved in our usual undertakings: from the price of meat to the length of the lives of young men; from planning for old age to the care of the newborn; from the financing of education to getting high; from the quality of the air and water to the distribution of income.

This book is based on the premise that government is not merely a *thing* that can be understood by studying its history or its bylaws; nor is it a *structure* whose essence lies in the height of its walls, the length of its corridors, or the titles on its doors. We believe that government is a *process* that can only be understood by examining its decisions and the ways in which it reaches them. We examine our government from the view that politics is primarily about the making and executing of policies. By policies we mean the patterns of governmental decisions and nondecisions that intentionally and unintentionally affect our lives in significant ways. With such a view at the heart of our approach, we have determined that four broad areas of decision making so dominate the government agenda that they have substantially influenced our major institutions and our political behavior. These areas are:

1. Economic policy—which includes the management of the overall economy; taxation, the distribution of income, and welfare matters;
2. Foreign affairs and national security policy—which means the nature of our foreign policy and its military and economic expression;
3. Race policy—which involves governmental action or inaction concerning white-nonwhite relations, including such matters as education, housing, voting, and employment;
4. Civil liberties policy—which encompasses government's relationship to the individual citizen on matters such as freedom of speech, due process of law, public regulation of morality, and church-state relations.

These areas of government decision are self-evidently important, and they provide essential insights into the nature of political power and policy making in America. We find no other areas of government decision making so critically significant nor so useful for purposes of analysis. The point to remember, however, is that we have chosen to emphasize policy because it is a major juncture at which government and citizen meet. It is in the execution of policies that government reaches our daily lives.

But how do most of us understand politics? What is it that impresses us and stays with us over time? It is some combination of early political figures we have strong feelings about, pressing day-to-day issues, and the possibilities of the future. In the next few pages, we present a loose, kaleidoscopic view of American politics, which includes all of these elements. We want to explore the feelings of the 1960s—that decade when most of our readers gained their initial impressions of political life. And then we want to look backward to the 1930s for some comparison with those earlier, also-troubled times. Along the way, we hope to offer a "feel" for the sorts of issues we deal with throughout the book. The intention then is to provide a kind of political home movie from which one can get a sense of the thoughts and passions that make up politics.

. . .

Growing up in the sixties, it wasn't so simple. They say the fifties were easier: Eisenhower's reassuring, paternal manner. But Jack Kennedy's New Frontier promised adventure and excitement. And, before you could turn around, we help invade Cuba in the Bay of Pigs (unofficially, of course) and botch it. Then, jointly with the Soviet Union, we have a "missile crisis," and we almost blow up the world. Again it's Cuba at the center of things. So if you came to consciousness in the sixties, these might be among your earliest political awakenings. Roger, who's nineteen, remembers it this way:

I remember first grade watching Kennedy's Inauguration on television, but it didn't do anything for me. . . . our teacher . . . just put a TV there and told us to look at it. No one understood what was going on really . . . and then the next thing I really remember is—in second or third grade—was practicing for air raids. . . . There was a poster and it says, in case of nuclear attack, take all pens and pencils out of your pockets and stand away from equipment and things like that and get away from anything that is going to explode. Then bend down and put your hands around your head and bend down and say goodbye to the world! Yeah, I was pretty scared because you know it kept coming on the television and all that; people were building bomb shelters around . . . I couldn't understand what was going to happen, but I just had this feeling that something really bad was going to just ruin everything.

". . . this feeling that something really bad was going to just ruin everything." But why? That's the puzzling part. There's more to it: difficult matters like the nature of foreign policy making. There's a history to that. What has the United States been doing in its relations with other countries all these years? Maybe understanding that, one can get a handle on not only Cuba, and missiles, but the draft and even Vietnam, and conceivably even the future. Why do we spend so much (how much) on the military? On account of the Russians or the Chinese? Is that really so? Is it partly on account of us?

But then the sixties took another turn. Roger remembers this too:

Yeah, I remember that cause like my mom cried for five days straight. She loved him. Even my dad, he's a Republican, was pretty shocked by the whole thing. And I remember watching Jack Ruby shoot Oswald on television. And I remember the day Kennedy was shot. It was a Friday and I was in fifth grade . . . I remember looking over to my teacher who was a devout Catholic and I remember she genuflected and then I just saw her start crying.
—How did you feel about it yourself?
—I was pretty shocked, but my immediate reaction was that we got the day of school off.

The first successful assassination attempt on an American President in sixty years. What no one knew then was that assassination was to be one of the trademarks of the sixties. What a way to alter political life—with bullets! Isn't that what democracy is arranged to avoid?

Yet they say some people were glad Kennedy got it. You heard stories of cheering in some schools. But then what did it mean? Five years later, Dale reacted to an act of political violence in this way:

Well, assassination in America had almost become an everyday thing by then. I thought it was horrible; I really felt *sorry* for our country. I thought it was awful that a man of his worth got killed, but I also felt sorry for our country. I really couldn't see how a country as great as we were could allow these things to happen or could come up with this type of thing.

—How do you explain the fact that it did happen, though?

—I can't explain. I still don't have any idea why.

He felt sorry for the country. Is that an odd sentiment? Why bring the country into it? Was there something distinctly American about it? Are we a particularly violent people? But assassinations were not the only violence of the sixties. There were demonstrations, protest, civil disobedience and not-so-civil disobedience, riots. And then the backlash, the National Guard, law and order, tanks, and tear gas and all. Confusing times for some, but others knew pretty well how they felt about it. Nick, who's a bricklayer, for one:

This college protest stuff looks to me like some kind of conspiracy. . . . They say it's the Communists. I don't know. But as for these characters rioting and taking over buildings, I think we ought to start enforcing the law. Right now, they seem to be exempt. . . . These kids are being babied because they're college students. I think the shooting of the students at Kent State . . . was justified. I mean I was in the National Guard and I know if someone was throwing bricks and bottles at me, I would have shot, too. We don't see it much out here in the suburbs, but you read about these revolutionaries. Well, I'm not too worried about them. I mean I always figured that majority rule would take care of things so that if a minority threatened us, the majority would stomp 'em out . . .

Yes, sir, majority rule! But what if the minority is right? A philosopher once said, "Man's capacity for justice makes democracy possible, and man's capacity for injustice makes it necessary." But then, what's democracy? And what's justice and injustice? Who decides? And who acts?

For that matter, what's violence? Say a kid grows up in a ghetto, sees lots of crime around. Gets into dope at age twelve or thirteen. Has trouble in school and turns into an addict or pusher. Has some violence been done to him? Sequoia trees don't prosper in Death Valley. How do people deal with those hassles? Take T. R., for instance; he's about fifteen:

When you live here and you're my age, you've been doing some learning and not in school and you've been doing some figuring out and not with the help of any white teacher or Negro teacher . . . You've discovered that either you stand up and think for yourself and be free, or you're a slave, just like we were before, down there in the South. You're either black or you're nothing at all. . . . I used to sit there in school and the teacher would ignore us and be ready to insult us no matter what we said and I'd take it, man, *I'd take it*. They had me believing I was no good, *no good*. The dealers here, the pushers, they've told me I'm a smart boy. That's what they call me, a boy. They say I'm a natural born leader . . . They say I can be the closest thing to a millionaire I'll ever see . . . I can get pants with pockets that stretch down to my shoes and they can guarantee they'll be filled up with dollar bills those pockets before I'm a year older. I could get the bike I want. I could drive up and down this street on the biggest motorcycle you'll ever see . . . I told my dad and he said he'd kill me first, rather than let me do that. . . . I told him I was fooling him, trying to trick him. I just wanted to get his reaction, that's all . . . I said if I didn't think it was better to be black, to be a black man, than to be a pusher—well, then I'd go and be a pusher . . . But my father is glad I'm no pusher and so is my mother and my grandmother. They don't care whether they're called black or Negro or anything. My father . . . works in a car wash. He hates the white man. Usually he says he doesn't, but once in a while, he'll come home dead tired; and then he admits it—that they bleed us, *they bleed us white* . . . He said white is white and colored is colored and the whites own the world, most of it, and the colored don't and that's the way it is, and no one can go and do anything about it, and maybe the second time around, in the next world, it'll be the opposite, and won't that be good— a relief, a big relief. My poor dad and all the poor Negroes, waiting for the second time around, *the second time around*.

". . . waiting for the second time around." So that's what school integration means: sitting in the classroom with young black men with feelings like that! White reader, what do you think of that? But maybe integration isn't his thing. Is it anybody's thing anymore? What with busing and black power and "neighborhood" schools. Yet, there's been in fact plenty of new school integration here and there. And it's been frightening on occasion, and worse. Bobbie lived through a little something she won't soon forget:

It really had gotten tense in Charlotte with all the busing and the blacks being sent to Marsh Park . . . Eleventh grade nothing really happened . . . It wasn't until my senior year in the fall—up until then I had an open mind, you know, because I had never come in contact with blacks before except for our maid . . . Then, when it's your school and it's your friends getting hit over the head and the bricks come flying through your classroom window . . . It didn't make me hate blacks, but just kind of made me scared of someone because they are black, you know. I know that's wrong, but that's just the reaction that I have from that incident . . . I think it would be better if you could choose what school you wanted to go to . . .

Once it was slavery, then civil war, reconstruction, Jim Crow, back to Africa, integration, civil rights, freedom now . . . the relations of blacks and whites have been a constant theme of American political, social, and one is tempted to say, personal, development. From the start there have been those who fought equality and those who sought it. Those conflicts are not over, but often they take curious forms. They influence American history but are not the exclusive or necessarily the decisive influences. Like everybody, Karen, who is a waitress, has her own slant on these matters: race, politics, Presidents, property, schools, the sixties:

Johnson is the one who signed that Civil Rights Act. . . . I said then, "Well we fought and took this land away from the Indians, we fought, died and everything else and he turned around and give it to the colored people which have been sleeping for over two hundred years! They had no ambition . . . I'd like to see George Wallace make it to the White House. . . . You buy your property for the closeness of your schools, convenience, and then you're gonna find your kids bused ten miles away. That's not right. Wallace is the only one I ever heard say that . . .

Karen has her opinions, like the rest of us, but also like most of the rest of us, she is a viewer of political events, not a participant. We're the audience the drama is enacted before. Then we applaud, nod, hiss, or get up and leave. It's not *our* drama, exactly, though we may care, even care very much about the outcome. Politics does touch us. Don recalls watching this scene:

I remember one march they made through Chicago, no, it was through Cicero. It was like a parade, really. That's what it amounted to. . . . and then all of a sudden—gunshots, the police were all over the place. There were people up in the trees throwing bricks and bottles.

—How come you didn't go out and march?

—I had good sense. Because I wasn't concerned and I didn't know what they were marching for. As for the people opposing it, I didn't know why they were opposing it.

"I didn't know why . . ." But then he was only about fourteen at the time. Why should he know why? Because it's going to affect him whether he knows it or not? Maybe they'll raise his taxes later to pay for more welfare, or more police, or maybe his neighborhood will change complexion. Probably it'll mean money sooner or later; money, and who gets what.

If there's black and white in American history there's also rich and poor, owner and worker. There's money and making a living. For most, that's life. But you've got to figure on fifty years of putting in time— by then, if you make it, you can collect social security.

Well, there's no average man, but then some look a lot closer to it than others. How about Mike, a baker: He's got daily bread on his mind for two reasons:

All the people in my neighborhood are little wage earners, people just like me . . . the middle and the little man has always been manipulated while the big man has been taken care of. That oil-depletion allowance is downright cheating the tax-payers. It's got to be corruption but that's the way government is. Through history, all the way back to Caesar's time, that's the way it's been . . . No matter what we do, power will be abused and money will be stolen and misused. . . . Inflation hasn't hit me hard because when I bought my house fifteen years ago I paid a little less than $9,000. I assume it would cost in the neighborhood of $12,000 today. I still have a long way to go on the mortgage, but what is really helping us is a 4½ percent GI-approved FHA mortgage. . . . Food is our biggest expense item, about $55–$60 a week . . . it gripes me to pay the price they charge now. The government makes deals with the farmers not to grow this, not to grow that . . . I make about $140 to $144 in an average week in the summertime, $107 or $108 clear. . . . more often than not, we manage to stay ahead of our bills. . . . I don't like the idea, but I can see the trend coming to socialism, one step at a time. Prior to 1920, no poor man and very few middle men paid tax. The rich man didn't pay much, but he paid all of it. . . . As soon as Mr. Public had to start paying the tax, everything kept mushrooming . . . There is no way to go back.

Big man, middle man, little man. True, some people have it rough now. But once it was rougher; say, forty years ago. The Depression, the New Deal, Roosevelt saying, "The only thing we have to fear is fear itself." Unemployment increasing. Banks failing. The whole economy running down. Rich men jumping out of buildings. It was a time when something had to happen, and what happened has shaped our lives decisively ever since. Social security, unemployment insurance, recognition of unions, government tinkering and spending and generally fooling around with the economy. What kind of economy do we have now? Creeping socialism, say some; corporate liberalism say others; socialism for the rich; pentagon capitalism; a mixed-economy welfare state. But welfare for whom? How does it look in Appalachia, or Watts, or even Middle America?

In any case, the Depression and its aftermath affect us still. They occupy a major portion of the foreground of the political landscape. The struggles of those times are related to many of our present political conflicts: liberals versus conservatives; national health insurance or no national health insurance; war on poverty or regulating the poor; more profits or more wages; the haves and the have-nots (or not-so-much). The fear of scarcity, the sense of want, the soup lines, and the Grapes of Wrath.

The economic issue is a complex one. It includes growth, the distribution of wealth and opportunity, regulation of various aspects of economic life, environmental considerations, and the tensions of inequalities and desires. Although we are thirty-five or forty years from the Depression (we might exclude those in "depressed areas" such as Appalachia and the ghettos), the issues that it made so intensely felt still persist in one form or another throughout the society. In thinking back to those times, it is easy to see why. Cesar Chavez, organizer of the migrant farm workers into the black eagle United Farm Workers (UFW), grew up then. Like many he has not forgotten those days:

Oh, I remember having to move out of our house. . . . That must have been around 1934. I was about six years old. My dad was being turned out of his small plot of land. He had inherited this from his father, who had homesteaded it. . . . It so happened the president of the bank was a guy who most wanted our land. We were surrounded by him; he owned all the land around us. Of course, he wouldn't pass the loan. We all of us climbed into an old Chevy that my dad had. And then we were in California, and migratory workers. There were five kids—a small family by those standards. . . . When you're small, you can't figure these things out. You know something's not right and you don't like it, but you don't question it and you don't let that get you down. You sort of just continue to move. Labor strikes were everywhere. We were one of the strikingest families, I guess. My dad didn't like the conditions, and he began to agitate . . .

—Did these strikes ever win?

—Never. We were among those families who always honored somebody else's grievance. . . . Even though we were working, we'd honor it. We felt we had to. . . .

—Sometimes when you had to come back, the contractor knew this?

—They knew it and they rubbed it in quite well. Sort of shameful to come back. We were trapped. We'd have to do it for a few days to get enough money to get enough gas. One of the experiences I had. We went through Indio, California. Along the highway there were signs in most of the small restaurants that said "White Trade Only." My dad read English, but he didn't really know the meaning. He went in to get some coffee—a pot that he had, to get some coffee for my mother. He asked us not to come in, but we followed him anyway. And this young waitress said, "We don't serve Mexicans here. Get out of here." I was there and I saw it and heard it. She paid no more attention. I'm sure for the rest of her life she never thought of it again. But every time we thought of it, it hurt us . . . These are sort of unimportant, but they're . . . you remember 'em very well . . .

That is *his* history. But what will the history of the present look like thirty or forty years from now? What will children growing up in the 1960s and 1970s remember as the central personal-political issues of their youth? What will shape their development and their perceptions of politics? Whatever the particulars may be, it seems fairly certain that the issues that will matter will grow out of one or more of the four problems of governance around which we have organized this book: economics, foreign affairs, race, and civil liberties. Our judgment is that these areas include most of the most significant government decisions most of the time. The test will come in your critical appraisal of the arguments in the book, in your own experiences, and in the history to come.

L.L.

UNIT

I

WHAT IS "AMERICAN" POLITICS?

The stars in our symbol (left)— giving shape to the people in the outer circle, initiating the four connecting ribbons, and encompassing the four governmental institutions in the center—represent the context of American policy making. The four connecting ribbons represent government policy decisions—the major juncture at which government and citizen meet. The central star contains the symbols of our nation's four political institutions—they represent the means through which we formalize our political activities. The outer circle represents the people, who affect and are affected by the decisions government makes.

Because this book is about politics and the quality of American political life, we need to raise questions about how power is distributed in America and how democratic a society America is. We want to look at the prospects for American politics in the future: What are the alternatives and how is America changing? In order to do this we must first explore the meanings of some central terms: politics, policies, and power.

POLITICS

Let us begin with politics. It could simply be described as the struggles for control of the main policy-making institutions in a society and as the policies that result from such contests. But how do we know, for example, what the main policy-making institutions in the United States are? The conventional answer leads us (at the national level) to look to Congress, the Presidency, and the courts. But what about other institutions, usually defined as nonpolitical, that seem just as important to the study of policy? Is understanding General Motors, for example, as valuable in explaining American politics as understanding Congress? Although the question will remain open, we can probably say that in all modern societies the study of politics goes beyond the immediately political into other arenas of struggle and power.

Still, this definition fails to tell us how important politics is to us. Does politics matter? A fundamental assumption of this book is that politics does matter; in fact, that for most of us, most of the time, politics is inescapable. A central feature of modern social life is the expanded power of political institutions. They shape or have the potential to shape many features of life previously regarded as "beyond politics." Consider the realm of economics, for example. From the congestion of city streets, to huge dams and electric power, to impressive airports, to unemployment rates, to the price of beef, to the question of who gets higher education—governmental decisions or nondecisions have decisive consequences.

The expansiveness of modern politics is related to the complexities of modern societies. It is quaint to think back 200 years to the day when one of Thomas Jefferson's main expenses as President was for firewood. This growth of governmental powers seems positive when one considers the higher degree of coordination, and thus more accurate planning, that greater size makes possible—how else could the government calculate the resources needed to provide retirement funds for its elderly population twenty or thirty years into the future?

But there is also a negative side. As big government grows bigger, it may serve itself, or serve the most powerful, rather than serving the public good. It may also discourage local and individual initiative, and it may reduce the range of variety and spontaneity. Governments, instead of facilitating life, may constrict it.

There are examples of many sorts of governmental activities in this book. We will leave it to the reader to sort through the evidence and to reach his or her own conclusions regarding the merits of government's expansion.

POLICY

Now for "policy," the term used to describe the patterns of governmental decisions and nondecisions that intentionally or unintentionally affect our lives in significant ways. We must distinguish, however, among the "policies" a government formally proclaims it is executing (but does not intend to carry out); the policies it does in fact intend to carry out; and finally, the results or nonresults of these policies. Each of these three may be significantly different, and in those differences lies much of what politics is all about. For example, governments sometimes issue formal proclamations of intent and then fail to make the necessary funds available (a way of appeasing both supporters and opponents of various programs). Or, government might formally pledge itself to a certain goal, such as full employment; then it provides the funds to create more public service jobs, but lower-level bureaucrats fail to actively implement the program. Yet, unemployment decreases anyway—perhaps and perhaps not the result of planned action. Such is the scramble that politics is made of.

There is yet another dimension to policy making. Government policies are not necessarily coherent. Policy makers may be at odds with one another, and this conflict may result in contradictory strivings; for example, those who wish to stimulate economic growth may be helping to destroy portions of the environment while trying to provide jobs in a poverty-stricken area. Frequently also, there is a trade-off between policies; for example, promoting national security may use up the funds needed for domestic programs. Materials are scarce. Needs are in conflict. One cannot have everything.

Throughout the book we will be elaborating on the idea of policy; hopefully, deepening the reader's sense of its meaning and its attendant complexities. We are committed to the view that to study government, one must understand policy; particularly those policies that matter the most. One more thing might be added: Government policy may deliberately be to have no policy, to delegate policy making to other bodies. For example, government may allow the "market" to determine the unequal wage levels of blue-collar and white-collar workers. The distributions of these powers in a political system— what government chooses to make policy about and the level at which policy decisions are made—are essential elements in the politics of a particular society.

THE CONTEXT

This introductory unit is intended to provide the background needed to understand the specifically American context in which policy making takes place. We have chosen to emphasize three aspects of that context: ideology (what people believe); political institutions (regularized patterns of political behavior and authority); and socioeconomic life (the distribution of economic, status, and power resources—with emphasis on the economic). The conviction is that to understand American politics one must first grasp the kinds of things most Americans believe or have believed in their nation's history; the paths along which political life moves in the United States, involving the relationships among national, state, and local governments; and finally, that one must understand the basic distribution of power, privilege, and deprivation because they both shape and are shaped by a society's politics. These features are universal and would have to be understood in studying any society.

We have employed the term "system" in referring to American politics in order to explain the give-and-take relationships among parts of a whole. Biologists characterize the human body as a system—with its various interacting parts. Or one might think of a particular locale—such as a swamp, with its particular pattern of plant, animal, insect, bacteria, air, and water—as an ecological system. If one part of the system is disrupted, or it grows too important, this may disrupt the *balance* and cause change or even collapse of the total system. We intend to discuss American politics as if a loose system of this sort exists. It involves stable patterns of expectations built up over the years; any disruption of them requires adjustment and creates a sense of disequilibrium or imbalance.

We do not mean to imply that because some sort of loose system exists that it is necessarily a good system, an inevitable system, or the only *sensible* system (it will be clear on many points that we take a critical stance), or that the American system is a coherent one. But we do believe there is a system, that American ideology, economy, and political institutions are intimately related, and that, taken together, they provide the context for comprehending the American policy-making process.

POWER AND THE BASIC ISSUES OF DEMOCRACY

We have used the term "power" without stopping to define it. We mean by power just what is usually meant: the ability to affect someone else's will. But in politics, especially democratic politics, such a simple definition has little meaning. We propose to define power by illustrating its involvement in four theoretical areas.

Twin Issues: The Power Elite and the Pluralist Balance

How is political power actually distributed in America? In an ideal democracy, each individual would hold equal power, with some modification because of interest in politics, talent, and so on. Some specialization would probably be needed, at least from time to time. Some would play leadership roles, and others would specialize in other roles. American society, however, like all modern societies, is far from egalitarian: Wealth and power are distributed in a radically unequal way in America. But how unequally are they distributed and what are the consequences?

The *power elite* argument would answer as follows: The distribution of wealth and political power in America involves a small, rather closely-knit and like-minded group of individuals who have decisive influence over many decisions affecting the lives of all Americans. This power elite would include leading politicians, corporate directors, the military, and other influentials. Such an elite would be able to veto the implementation, if not the initiation, of any serious policies that ran contrary to its desires. The power held by Congress, by the courts, and by other levels of the political system is real, elitists would say, yet not decisive on essential matters.

The *pluralist* argument, in contrast, maintains that political power in America is rather widely diffused among many conflicting and cooperating groups that operate in and around the formal political institutions. Some groups predominate in one area for a time, then others triumph. Instead of some overall cohesive elite, there is the messy give-and-take of interest group politics within the setting of political institutions that are shaped by majority rule.

Even if we assumed the reality of the pluralist image, there would be serious questions: Who gets exactly what from this system and why? Are business interests more successful than labor interests? We would also want to raise the question of balance in this system: Are rewards distributed roughly according to a one-man one-vote principle?

In short, the power elite-pluralist question has two sides: first, is there such an elite; second, if not, how *just* is the pluralism that prevails? In fact, maybe there is a third side: is the system a mixture of elitist and pluralist, with a cohesive dominant group ruling in some areas, while pluralistic conflict of various sorts exists in others?

Democracy and Mass Attitudes

Some claim that a substantial portion of the ordinary citizens in America are not very deeply committed to the norms of democracy, such as freedom of speech and press and the right to a fair trial. These citizens, the argument suggests, would prefer a political system with much less give-and-take and much more authoritarian rule.

In this view—the "undemocratic masses" position—democracy in America is preserved largely by the commitments of political activists rather than by mass sentiment. Therefore, one committed to democratic values must wish that mass political participation not be too extensive or intense, or else the fragile system of liberties we have could easily be jeopardized. Fortunately, mass involvement is infrequent, and it is part of the structure of American politics that many are discouraged from active participation. Those who hold this view see low voter turnout and low interest not as threats to democracy, but as dikes protecting our political life from the flood of destructive antidemocratic activism.

But there are serious difficulties with this picture of democracy. First, there are many un-democrats within the group of political activists, the very leaders who are supposed to support democratic norms. Second, mass movements have often, in American history, been a source of democratically inclined reform: the labor movement and the civil rights movement are examples. Reality is more complicated, therefore, than the argument suggests. But there is another essential point: America is surely not a perfect democracy. So we cannot be interested merely in preserving American democracy, but also in ways of recapturing or extending it. That may mean, in particular cases, that mass activism may be needed to improve democracy, or, of course, it may serve to prevent its improvement.

Freedom, Equality, and Democracy

Freedom and equality: How much of each is desirable to democracy? Must democracy allow all sorts of political and social views to be aired, or is it legitimate to restrict the expression of some? In the matter of equality: How much social and economic equality is needed for democracy, and does more equality mean a better democracy? Of course, democracy can be defined simply as majority rule, with each citizen having a roughly equal vote and various alternative leaders competing for office. This simple definition, however, avoids all the interesting questions.

This book revolves around these questions of democratic political life or, perhaps more accurately, around questions of what a *good* political life truly is. How successfully does the American system provide for this good life? How democratic is our society? How successfully have we dealt with the problems and the possibilities of freedom and equality?

1
THE AMERICAN IDEOLOGY

Figure 1.1 **The Statue of Liberty is a prominent symbol of the American ideology. To successive waves of immigrants it symbolized freedom from the repression of a dominant aristocracy, from Monarchy, and from the Church, and it symbolized freedom to pursue one's beliefs and to achieve according to one's ability, toil, and frugality. But to what extent has America lost that atmosphere of creative ideas and styles that once lured our ancestors to the shores of the New World? Has this proud symbol come to represent conformity and consumption as well as freedom and opportunity?**

Problems that face government—which range from pollution, population growth, and inflation, to war—could probably be dealt with in a number of reasonable ways. But not all reasonable solutions are politically possible. As Chapters 2 and 3 show, America's past political choices, its particular political institutions, and the nature and capacity of its economy rule out the adoption of certain policies. But even if Americans were free of all these restraints, many potential policies would still be rejected. There are many policies Americans would not care to adopt.

What a nation believes, what it honors and desires, what it disdains and rejects, greatly limit its alternatives. Political actions in America must conform to the particular texture and tone of the American outlook, just as policies in Japan or France conform to the beliefs and values of the Japanese and the French. When people say about a particular proposal, "It's a good idea, but the country just wouldn't go for it," they are referring to preferences dictated by the American outlook.

America's reactions to specific political issues and policies are shaped and informed by a cluster of social and political beliefs and preferences commonly called *ideologies* or *belief systems*. The purpose of this chapter is to sketch the most prominent features of the American ideology—that set of beliefs and values that shape America's politics by limiting its alternatives. Where possible, significant instances of dissent from the prevailing American outlook are pointed out. However, the primary concern of this chapter is to outline those beliefs and values that are sufficiently widely held, or are held by groups with sufficient power, so that they operate as major influences on American politics regardless of dissent. Thus, although many ideologies compete within American politics, this chapter is concerned primarily with the American ideology—how Americans as a group view the world differently from the way the British, the Chinese, or the Russians view it.

IDEOLOGY DEFINED

The term ideology is used in a number of ways. Before outlining the American ideology, it is necessary to clarify what is meant by the term.

Frequently, the word ideology implies a set of beliefs that inspire the kind of passion associated with religious faith. Many observers have used the word ideology to identify *secular religions*—political creeds, such as orthodox Marxism, fascism, and Maoism, whose dogmatic character makes them resemble religions rather than other political outlooks (Charles Glock and Rodney Stark, 1965). If the word ideology is used in this way, it is hard to conceive of an American ideology, for the major political currents in America have been characterized by a lack of highly codified political creeds and zealous adherents. Radical politics, on both right and left, has never been of major importance. Instead, mainstream politics has been characterized by compromise and bargaining, by loose coalition and vagueness of political program—all of which are disdained by ideological political creeds. Some observers have therefore concluded that American politics is nonideological (Daniel Bell, 1962).

Other observers prefer to apply the term ideology to all coherent political outlooks. They define ideology as a set of prescriptive positions, more or less logically interrelated, that apply to broad and significant aspects of government and public policy. Thus, ideologies typically include positions on such matters as the structure of government and the distribution of power, society's political objectives and how best to pursue them, and the allocation and distribution of wealth and property.

Defined in this way, an ideology is like a patchwork quilt, with views on particular policy questions making up the patches. Like a quilt, an ideology is more than the sum of its patches, for the connected patches form an overall pattern. A person sees politics ideologically when he applies some overall viewpoint to the multiplicity of particular policy choices (when his political outlook forms a quilt rather than a disorganized pile of patches). A political ideology uses abstract ideas and principles to organize political views into a relatively logical system (Everett Ladd, 1972). As is discussed in Chapter 12, the majority of Americans do not have political ideologies in this sense. Philip Converse has demonstrated that most people's political beliefs and preferences are organized in a relatively incoherent way. Their views are collections of patches; quilts are uncommon (Converse, 1964). Thus, once again it *could* be suggested that American politics is nonideological.

There is yet a third way in which the term ideology is used. The notion that political views must form a

Figure 1.2 Historical Patterns of American Ideologies. Although an individual may not be committed to a particular, clear-cut ideology, speculation suggests that the blend or "patchwork quilt" that an individual possesses is drawn from the various primary ideological movements of his or her era. Although there is much debate over the elements that have gone into the development of America's ideological history, the growth and shrinkage of some selected elements are traced here, through cross-sections of the nation's historical stages.

Communalism is the name given for that ideal and reality of spontaneous brotherhood and equality found exemplified in the tradition of "barn raising," Christian fraternity with the slaves, and the solidarity of early unionism.

Individualism is similar to Liberalism. It connotes the ideas and ideals of self-development and self-expression as well as the winner-take-all aspects of capitalist competition.

Nationalism refers to identification with the welfare, pride, and mores of the nation. It ranges from the national pride of providing help to starving nations to the jingoism of such superpatriots as William Randolph Hearst.

Liberalism is a complex association of values and concepts, detailed in the text, which includes a belief in secular progress and motivation toward material acquisitiveness and competition.

Theocratic elitism may be conceived of as the "rule of saints"; by this is meant the domination of a society by a religious elite, such as the spiritual leaders among the Puritans. In our secular era this is a minor patch in the ideology quilt, but, as in the case of aristocratic elitism, there is a minority that holds such values.

Aristocratic elitism refers to rule by descendants of upperclass families, those born to high status and good education.

Plutocratic elitism is the advocacy of rule by the wealthy; this has had not only de facto support in the United States but also theoretical support associated with the widespread admiration of entrepreneurs such as Carnegie, Ford, and the Rockefellers. To some, especially before the Great Depression and since the rise of the great technological corporations, the "power elite"—translated as the "successful businessman"—has been a term of tribute rather than of fear.

The additional, smaller ideological movements added to the diagram (circled) have evolved out of the basic "patches" upon which they lie or overlap.

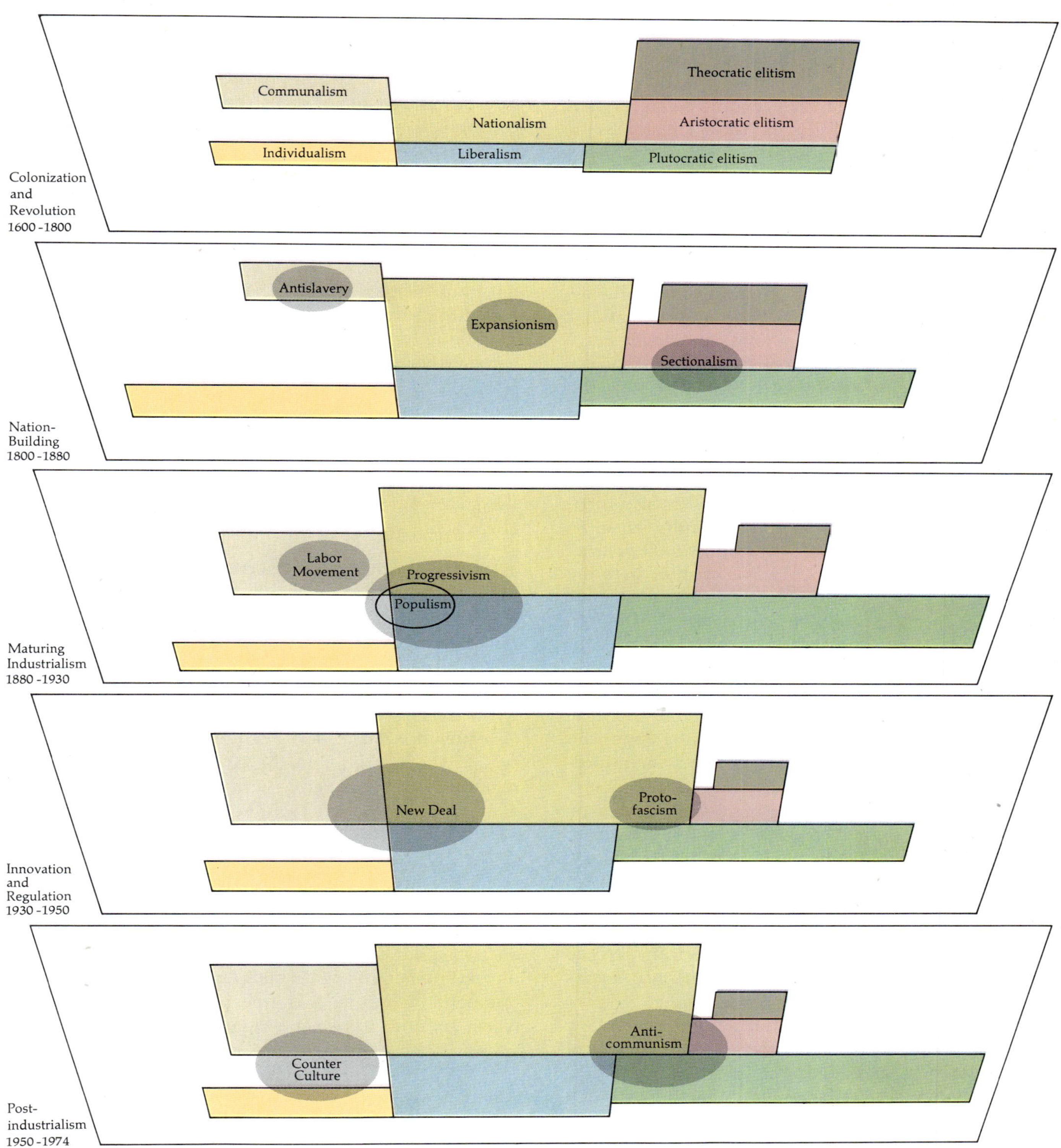

Colonization and Revolution 1600-1800
Communalism
Theocratic elitism
Nationalism
Aristocratic elitism
Individualism
Liberalism
Plutocratic elitism
Nation-Building 1800-1880
Antislavery
Expansionism
Sectionalism
Maturing Industrialism 1880-1930
Labor Movement
Progressivism
Populism
Innovation and Regulation 1930-1950
New Deal
Proto-fascism
Post-industrialism 1950-1974
Counter Culture
Anti-communism

relatively coherent or logical system can be discarded, and the word ideology can be applied to those informal and diffuse collections of political views and values that many people share. When Robert Lane described the political ideologies of "common men," he was referring to the sum total of their opinions and beliefs on political matters (Lane, 1962). For the most part, these ideologies did not constitute well-developed political arguments or viewpoints but instead were characterized as "loosely structured, unreflective statements." In this usage a person's ideology is simply his political-belief system, regardless of how unsystematic it might be. Ideology is the sum total of a person's *cognitive* and *evaluative orientations* toward the society he inhabits, regardless of how logical or illogical, thoughtful or thoughtless, active or passive these orientations may be. In this sense, all politics is ideological; all political outlooks are ideologies.

However, American politics is ideological not only in this third, very loose, sense. It is also ideological in the second, or patchwork quilt, sense. To make the distinction clear, some additional distinctions must be introduced. As this chapter uses the term, nations and groups (such as parties) have ideologies. Individuals have *belief systems.* Although it may seem a big jump from the coherence of an ideology to the disjointed political views of the average citizen, the links are there. Ideologies provide the general landscape for individual political thought—it is within the confines of the American ideology that most Americans develop their individual political-belief systems.

Clearly, then, American politics is not guided by highly specific, dogmatic political creeds with sacred works and zealous followers. The American ideology, as a body of ideas and ideals, is much looser than that. However, most Americans do have some understanding of, and belief in, these ideas and ideals; and, however imperfectly, Americans refer to them when responding to specific political issues and events.

It is important to recognize that a political ideology need not shape the belief systems of a majority of citizens to be regarded as the dominant ideology. Frequently, an ideology does dominate through such a consensus; however, some ideological views may dominate because they are vigorously upheld by powerful social institutions or groups. As is shown in Chapter 7, most Americans have never really understood or adopted the political ideals of such civil liberties as freedom of speech and press. These ideals continue to influence the political life of America because they are protected by the upper classes and by such powerful institutions as the courts and the press.

More than a hundred years ago Karl Marx argued that the ruling ideas of any society are the ideas of its ruling classes. His point was that ideologies do not fall from the sky, nor are they "things" that have a life of their own: Ideologies must be developed and maintained; an ideology must be transmitted to new generations or it will soon perish; and the implications of an ideology for specific issues and events must be determined and communicated. Because powerful groups and institutions are better able to succeed in this process than are less powerful groups, it is often their ideologies that are propagated. Thus, the statement "America believes" is often, but not always, the same as "Most Americans believe."

THEMES IN AMERICAN IDEOLOGY

Many observers have attempted to isolate the main currents in American ideology. Two of the most influential writers came to similar conclusions. In the 1830s a perceptive young Frenchman, Alexis de Tocqueville, traveled across the United States and wrote a classic sociological account of the new nation (Tocqueville, 1835, 1945). Tocqueville concluded that *egalitarianism*—belief in the equality of all persons regardless of social rank—was the central principle of Americanism. In 1955 Louis Hartz expanded Tocqueville's conclusion and argued that *Liberalism,* in the old-fashioned, not the current sense (see □), holds the key to understanding the American outlook. He noted particularly that the United States was settled by an antiaristocratic segment of Europeans and was politically and culturally cut off from Europe during the height of Liberal thought. Thus, a Liberal fragment of Europe was free in the wilderness of North America to become the uncontested whole.

European Liberalism in America

America was born at the juncture of two profound revolutions. First was the *egalitarian* revolution, which attacked the traditional privileges of aristo-

LIBERALISM AND CONSERVATISM

Historically, the terms liberalism and conservatism have had different meanings. What has been described here—classical, or eighteenth-century Liberalism—comprises in its most general sense the world view of the new ("middle") classes that obtained wealth and prestige through the industrial revolution. Liberalism first developed in England as a protest against the prerogatives of the Monarchy. It first took the form of a demand for religious liberties and toleration, constitutionalism, and political rights for the new middle classes. It was essentially negative in character, protecting groups and individuals from government; it sought to minimize government involvement in the social and economic lives of individuals and groups. Conservatism, as the opposite of Liberalism, included the various defenses of aristocratic privileges and institutions.

Beginning with Franklin Roosevelt's New Deal, the terms liberal and conservative assumed new meanings. Those who favored a more expansive role by government in regulating the economy and in guaranteeing the welfare of less-privileged groups became known as liberals, whereas conservatives were those who opposed social welfare initiatives and endorsed relatively unrestricted business enterprise. As Samuel Beer has pointed out, the latter construction of liberalism-conservatism—now so familiar—was not encountered prior to the 1930s. (Beer, 1966)

cratic rank determined by birth. It led to several political developments of great importance: A far larger proportion of the population had to be taken into consideration by decision makers, and popular government, in the form of elected representatives and mass voting, was implemented. The second was the *industrial* revolution, which changed the nature and organization of work and the character of the economy; it undercut the old aristocratic order based on agrarian feudalism and began the rapid exodus of people from the farms into the factory. Perhaps it is most useful to regard these as a single revolution, the ideological and economic aspects of which shattered the old order and fundamentally altered the political institutions of the Western world.

The American ideology owes much of its distinctiveness to the working out of this two-faceted revolution in virgin territory. Tocqueville was thinking of this process when he wrote that it was to America's great advantage that it arrived at "a state of democracy without having to endure a democratic revolution: [having been] born equal, instead of becoming so." Some aristocratic institutions were set up in the colonial period, but they clashed with the wilderness environment in the colonies and were overwhelmed by the antiaristocratic impulses of the population. John Adams described *"this radical change in the principles, opinions, sentiments, and affections of the people"* as the *"real American revolution"* (Adams, 1856). The new aristocratic transplants never really took root and were swept away after 1776.

It is hard to overemphasize the importance of American society's being established anew, cut off from the social, economic, and political institutions of aristocratic societies. Those who rode the crest of the egalitarian and industrial revolution in Europe continued throughout the nineteenth century to confront residues, in varying strength, of the old order. Long-established aristocratic institutions, such as the Church and the Monarchy, were not easily removed. In short, Europeans had to root out what in America never took root.

"Consensus" and "consensual" are terms that have often found their way into descriptions of American ideology in the context suggested above. European societies after the revolution remained battlegrounds for competing positions on such vital political issues as the organization of government, who should rule, the objectives that society should try to achieve, and the proper distribution of economic goods. Ideological conflict on the European continent extended to the core of the political institutions and processes, whereas in the United States conflict has remained largely within a set of accepted processes and institutions. As Louis Hartz stated, "It is only because history had already accomplished the ending of the old European order in America that its 'social revolution,' instead of tearing the soul of the nation apart, integrated it further" (Hartz, 1964).

There has been consensus, then, but only in a limited sense. The American political system has seen much conflict in the nearly two centuries since formation of the Republic in 1789; but it has been conflict within the Liberal tradition, conflict of a different proportion, because Liberalism was without serious ideological rivals.

American Liberalism—capitalistic, achievement-oriented, egalitarian, individualistic, committed to secular progress—did not have to confront established aristocratic institutions and was thus able to dominate the developing nation. In eighteenth-century Europe, Liberalism was known as a "fighting creed," as the ideology of the entrepreneurial (or business-oriented) middle class; once transplanted to the United States Liberalism became *Americanism*, the *American Creed,* or the *American Dream*. An ideology that had arisen at a particular historical moment in Europe in response to the interests and needs of one social class, became more or less permanent and encompassed all classes in America.

These developments are of more than historical interest. Various derivatives of classical Liberalism identify America today; over time they have submitted to less drastic revisions in the United States than in any other nation. The secular flavor of American ideology; the stress on the good life in the here-and-now; the emphasis on property rights and the sanctity of private property; the all-pervasive individualism; the insistence on achievement (heavily economic) as a standard by which men should be judged—all of these aspects of American life testify to the pervasiveness of the Liberal tradition in America.

American Economic Success

Throughout the Western world the experience of industrial-nation-building—moving from agricultural-based to industrial economies, with all the resulting strains and disruptions—has been accompanied by the growth of socialist movements within the working classes (see □). The United States stands as a striking exception, however, for socialism has never been strong in America. No socialist move-

SOCIALISM
There is a wide variety of statements on socialism, all involving a system of social organization that advocates the ownership and control of the means of production, capital, and land by the community as a whole.

Figure 1.3 Although successful in Europe, workers' movements have faced enormous barriers in their attempts to organize support in America. Eugene V. Debs (right) founded the American Railway Union in 1893, then went to jail for his participation in the violent Pullman strike of 1894. He formed the American Socialist Party and ran as its presidential candidate in five elections between 1900 and 1920. In spite of the rapid social changes of those decades, he never received more than 6 percent of the popular vote. A woman labor organizer (far right) speaks out during the important textile strike in Paterson, New Jersey, 1912–1913. In 1912 the mills increased the work load without increasing wages. The Industrial Workers of the World (I.W.W.) organized the Paterson Strike and demanded an eight-hour day and a minimum wage of $12 a week. The violence of the strike was indicative of the atmosphere that surrounded workers' attempts to gain their share of America's relative abundance. Starvation finally forced the textile workers to capitulate.

ment has ever had a serious chance of winning national power. The electoral high-water mark of the American Socialist Party came in 1912. In the presidential election, Eugene V. Debs received 6 percent of the total votes cast, yet received no electoral votes because of the dispersion of the socialist vote. (Had the Debs voters been concentrated in just a few states, as George Wallace's votes were in 1968, he might have carried several states and thus received their electoral votes.) An explanation of the absence of a viable socialist tradition provides interesting insights into American ideology and values.

The demands that citizens make in an egalitarian society are many, but some of the most important and persistent are economic: that the system provide a volume of goods and services and a system of distribution sufficient to meet *perceived* needs. The content of economic demands reflects basic requirements—for food, shelter, and clothing—but also reflects a set of expectations.

Expectations are partially fixed by pictures of what others are doing, and Americans have never, at any point in history, had the example of another nation surpassing their own economically. The importance of this economic success to the development of American ideology is enormous. A number of observers, notably David Potter, have suggested that

relative abundance has distinctively shaped the American character and institutions (Potter, 1954). Even in 1799, the average personal income in the United States was over $400 (in dollars of 1968 purchasing power), higher than the incomes of citizens in many nations today. For example, Brazil, Algeria, China, India, the United Arab Republic, Indonesia, and Nigeria all have average personal incomes today of less than $400 per year. Being ahead economically does not assure basic satisfaction with a nation's institutions, but it does reduce the possibility that expectations far in excess of the system's capacity will generate demands that cannot be met—demands that elsewhere have led to basic dissatisfaction with a nation's social and political institutions.

Not only has the American economy produced more than its rivals, but it has registered impressive gains for well over a century. The valleys have been relatively few and the peaks many as advances in technology and economic organization have pushed productivity ahead. Since 1840 the American economy has grown at a rate of about 1.6 percent per year in real terms, which means that, holding prices constant, average personal income has doubled every forty-three years.

The intention is not to argue that "every day in every way things are getting better and better";

nor do these statistics sustain the view that the American economic system has performed adequately from the standpoint of all groups of citizens or that a rising tide of abundance has washed away all poverty. As Chapter 3 shows in detail, serious problems concerning the distribution of income persist in America. In 1929, to cite just one example of inequality, the 40 percent of American families with the lowest incomes received just 12.5 percent of the total personal income of all families; the highest 20 percent received 54 percent of the total income. Four decades later, in 1970, these disproportions in income distribution had been only slightly modified: The lowest 40 percent of families received 18 percent of the total personal income, whereas the highest 20 percent received 42 percent (United States Bureau of the Census, 1960; 1972).

In spite of such statistics, however, the American economic system has been extraordinarily successful; and it seems clear that the historical weakness of socialism can largely be accounted for by the American economy's having done better than any other, both in total productive capacity and in the amount of income distributed to the average family.

An economic system that exhibits such growth and so high a margin over its competitors has powerful resources for dealing with demands: The type of conflict that results when basic economic demands of a large percentage of society go persistently unmet has largely been avoided in America. Economic success seems to have contributed mightily to a picture of overall success, to a willingness of Americans to work within the boundaries of established social, political, and economic institutions.

Americans as Positional Conservatives

When political institutions are able to persist, they develop a legitimacy based on custom. American political institutions have carried the same names and taken the same basic form for 180 years. They are old friends; they are "natural." It is not surprising, then, that those unhappy with policy developments have been reluctant to "take the institutions on." And because of this reluctance, confidence, in a kind of snowball effect, has grown in the belief that whatever the disagreements, they will be processed within a familiar, stable, and predictable institutional order. Confidence in the system and support

SOCIALIST MAN

To some extent the generational conflict between cooperative and individual-achievement-oriented life styles bears resemblance to the values of individualism stressed in capitalist societies and the ideal of the cooperative "socialist man" of Marxist societies. The central moral vision animating revolutionary socialists, whether they be Marxist-Leninists or Maoists, is the desire to transform human nature. They seek to produce a new human being who lacks competitiveness and acquisitiveness and who functions out of unselfish, cooperative impulses—a person who subordinates his personal desires to the interests of the group or nation.

The ideal of socialist man remains a dream, quite unrealized in any socialist society. And most social scientists doubt that such an ideal could ever be substantially achieved. Nevertheless, the ideal has powerful ideological effects. As Robert Heilbroner stated:

". . . however distant, however vulgarized in practice, however abused as a mere slogan for social manipulation, the conception of Socialist Man provides a spiritual basis for an ideology that is powerfully persuasive. Capitalist nations may be efficient, humane, democratic, permissive, creative, but they do not have a "vision" built on the elements of property ownership and the market—a vision comparable to that which is founded on the ideal of common ownership and sharing." (Heilbroner, 1972, pp. 725–726)

The American ideology is not a tight doctrine, passionately and zealously held, that generates the fervor of an evangelical faith. In this way it differs from the ideologies of revolutionary socialist nations. However, Americans are not totally lacking in evangelical impulses about Americanism; they do sometimes set out with missionary zeal to save the world. But they do so without the degree of certainty and the detailed set of programs typical of Marxists.

for the core political institutions and processes are ingredients of a markedly *conservative* culture. As Robert Lane strikingly stated:

If the Eastport [the name Lane gave to the community in which he was interviewing] common man is a conservative, it is in a special sense. He is not opposed to change, does not take a dim view of human nature (for the most part), has no love of tradition and . . . does not stand for a social hierarchy, either; these are not the ingredients of his conservatism. But he is conservative in the sense that he has no program for structural changes in the society, he is markedly loyal to the prevailing system of government, believes in private property and capitalism, holds that he is living in a moral order where people get pretty much the rewards and punishments they merit, and assumes the general responsibility for his own fate. (Lane, 1962, pp. 250–251)

The American "common man," throughout most of our history, has been a *positional* conservative. He has largely avoided movements calling for drastic alteration of the social and political order, whether socialism in 1912 or the New Left in 1970. Radical movements have been frustrated by this conservatism, which owes more to the relative success of economic institutions than to anything else.

The sources of this economic success, so important to the development of ideology in the United States, should be examined. A number of conditions clearly had to be present: the availability of ample resources; the presence of the necessary technology; political independence (at least to the extent of freedom from constant intrusions by foreign powers); and so on. But along with these prerequisites, there had to be a set of cultural or value orientations, held by most of the citizens, that led to behavior supportive of industrial development.

Americans and the "Protestant Ethic"

In aristocratic societies with subsistence, agricultural economies, most inhabitants could be ignored; they quietly worked the land and were considered happy with their lot. In contrast, an egalitarian society that is embarked on industrial-nation-building requires much of its citizens; the basic industrial plant facilities must be built with the labor of the population. There are several ways of inducing such labor. In the Soviet Union and some of the African nations, the national government has assumed the major role as mobilizer of the population: Using various methods, the government has directed the labor force in ways that industrialism demands. In the United States, however, industrial-nation-building was not primarily state directed. The momentum grew out of a widely held ethic, or set of moral principles, that motivated people to perform, more or less voluntarily, as industrialization required.

The basic tenets of this ethic were self-restraint and self-denial. The good man was one who worked far longer and harder than was necessary to acquire the basic necessities for existence. He saved rather than consumed; he lived frugally in the interest of future consumption.

Not everyone subscribed to this ethic, of course, but a large segment of the American population did. A moral standard stressing work, frugality, and general self-restraint affected a larger population in the United States than it did in perhaps any other country in the world.

One of the founding fathers of social science, the German sociologist Max Weber, attempted to isolate the major elements of this ethic and explore its relationship to the development of industrial capitalism (Weber, 1904, 1930). He found the origins of the work ethic in Protestant theology and argued that the *Protestant ethic* sparked the development of capitalism. Today Weber's analysis seems too restrictive; the motive force underlying the work ethic seems to have little to do with Protestantism or with any other theology. Contemporary Japanese, as well as early European Protestants and Americans in general, seem committed to ethical ideals that support economic development. The *classical Liberal ethic* seems more suitable a term than the Protestant ethic.

Classical Liberalism, as the ideological defense of the interests of the middle class against those of the aristocracy, emerged in Europe in the late seventeenth century. It emphasized economic achievement as the standard by which men should be judged; work as an expression of individual responsibility and discipline; and personal income as the guarantee of the rights of the individual—all highly functional to the business pursuits of the new middle class.

What happened in the United States, as Hartz has so well pointed out, was that a middle-class "fragment" bearing these values set the tone for the whole society. To say that Liberalism became Americanism rather than remaining the ideological defense of the entrepreneurial middle class is to note that ideological orientations associated with the middle class broadly suffused American society. Substantial segments of all classes accepted this ideological tradition of the middle class and came to behave like members of the middle class.

Many have said that farmers in the United States of the eighteenth and early nineteenth centuries did not display the peasant attitudes associated with European feudalism. Rather, they claim, America's "yeoman farmers" held different values; they were agricultural capitalists. They had no landlord, but owned their land and were in business for themselves. The step from agricultural capitalism to industrial capitalism is far shorter than the step from feudalism to industrialism. The values embedded in the Liberal ethic facilitated the processes of industrial-nation-building in the United States.

The ethic of work, frugality, and self-denial, then, is derived from middle-class Liberalism, not from Protestantism. As the most business-oriented and Liberal of all societies, the United States naturally became the most thoroughly capitalistic.

Individualism and the Sense of Community

The work ethic, however congenial it was to capitalist development, has not been completely beneficial. Alexis de Tocqueville stressed the extraordinary American emphasis on private goals and self-gratification rather than on public and spiritual values. He wrote that "in their intense and exclusive anxiety to make a fortune, they lose sight of the close connection which exists between the private fortune of each of them and the prosperity of all" (Tocqueville, 1835). He dwelt on the competitive nature of American life:

It is strange to see with what feverish ardor the Americans pursue their own welfare, and to watch the vague dread that constantly torments them lest they should not have chosen the shortest path which may lead to it. . . . They have swept away the privileges of some of their fellow-creatures which stood in their way; but they have opened the door to *universal competition*; the barrier has changed its shape rather than its position. (Tocqueville, II, 1835, pp. 136–137)

Similarly, Francis J. Grund, a German who lived in the United States in the early nineteenth century, discussed the emphasis on material success in the American value system and the stigma associated with material failure and poverty. Grund explained the addiction of Americans to "business" at the expense of leisure and other pursuits:

Active occupation is not only the principal source of their happiness and the foundation of their national greatness, but they are absolutely wretched without it, and instead of the *dolce far niente* [pleasures of idleness], know but the horrors of idleness . . . the Americans pursue business with unabated vigor till the very hour of death. (Grund, 1837, pp. 202–204)

Charles Dickens was another European observer who commented on the competitiveness and success orientation of Americans. He illustrated this worship of success in an imaginary exchange concerning a scoundrel who had gotten rich by questionable means:

—He is a public nuisance, is he not?
—Yes, sir.
—A convicted liar?
—Yes, sir.
—He has been kicked, cuffed, and caned?
—Yes, sir.
—And he is utterly dishonorable, debased, and profligate?
—Yes, sir.
—In the name of wonder, then, what is his merit?
—Well, sir, he is a smart man. (Dickens, 1934, p. 242ff)

Gabriel Almond has summarized the consistent stream of observations about American value orientations surrounding individual achievement and material success:

The American is primarily concerned with "private" values, as distinguished from social-group, political, or religious-moral values. His concern with private, worldly success is his most absorbing aim. . . . The "attachment" of the American to his private values is characterized by an extreme degree of competitiveness. American culture tends to be atomistic rather than corporate, and the pressure of movement "upward" toward achievement is intense. (Almond, 1960, p. 48)

As the United States has moved from its era of industrialization to its present status as a post-industrial society, the old and deeply entrenched development-ethic is being confronted. The old emphasis on hard work, self-denial, and self-reliance

Figure 1.4 How should the problems of large urban populations be handled? Through the efficient use of resources. But efficient use toward what ends? American coffee shops are efficient places for the ingestion of a short-order meal, but they are hardly as inviting for the pastime of people-watching and people-meeting as the sidewalk cafés of Paris. In the United States we have efficiently used resources to further the isolated, competitive working life of the individual, to foster and support life in that mold. European values, insofar as they retain the influence of the past, attempt to use resources to preserve another style of life, where the rush of production and accumulation of wealth is tempered by habits of communality and leisure time. Although the habits of foreign nations vary from place to place and the regimentation and isolation of modern organization for production creeps into modern life everywhere, the symbol of the Paris café reminds us of alternative goals— "people" goals versus "short-order" goals.

is challenged by new ethical orientations elevating self-expression and freedom to choose one's own style of life. Particularly to many younger Americans, individual competitive achievement represents a distortion of human needs. The emphasis shifts subtly to cooperation over competition, community over individualism. If the standards of the older ethic can be broadly described as restrictive, the newer ethic involves a more permissive posture in all areas of personal activity.

As an older ethic so well suited to industrialism is challenged by newer principles supportive of affluence and post-industrialism, it is almost inevitable that there will be sharp cultural and generational tensions that will be reflected in political life. For millions of Americans the older ethic retains vitality. At the same time, for growing numbers of people, it is seen as narrow, old-fashioned, and hypocritical. Supporters of the competing ethical traditions confront each other, often with little sympathy and understanding. Younger people, with weaker roots in the older society, are naturally more sympathetic to the ethical orientations bred of contemporary change. Any period of rapid social change is accompanied by tensions between the generations; the present age is no exception. The cultural gulf in the contemporary United States inevitably reveals itself in the political struggle: Candidates are judged by both sides, not only on their positions on national issues but also on their perceived postures toward one or the other of the conflicting ethics.

There is in America, in short, a powerful ethical tradition, derived from classical Liberalism, which proved very functional in the enterprise of industrial-nation-building. In the present age of affluence a counter-tradition is arising that challenges important tenets of the older ethic. Proponents of the two traditions face each other uneasily across this vague—but wide and deep—cultural divide.

CONTRADICTIONS IN AMERICAN IDEOLOGY

The American ideology is more a patchwork quilt, a diffuse collection of shared values, than a highly systematized structure with a host of zealous followers. Although there is some consistency among American ideals, there are also some basic value conflicts, some inconsistent impulses at the very core. The contradictions must now be considered: how

Figure 1.5 Once a symbol of progress and wealth, the smokestack has increasingly come to symbolize distorted economic priorities. The idea of "progress," which was inherited from the ideals of the industrial revolution, found fertile soil in America. The villages and towns of nineteenth-century America were hotbeds of "boosterism" and expansion. Industry promised advancement and success to the workingman. Today, however, growth for its own sake is being called into question. The social costs of industrial production can no longer be explained away, and with awareness of these costs comes a reevaluation of economic priorities.

PASTRICK
MAYOR

MORE
MORE
MORE
MORE
MORE
PRODUCTION

Did you risk
a '25 fine today?
DON'T LITTER
PAR

they influence our behavior toward and relationships with other nations; how they operate in relationship to economic and racial inequalities; and how they operate in the American conception of individual freedom and liberty.

Americans and the World Outside

Gabriel Almond has written an insightful commentary on the value orientation of Americans as it affects involvement in world affairs. The American concern with private interests and pursuits has led to a historic attitude of indifference and withdrawal—in times of relative stability—toward the world outside. Such was the case throughout most of the nineteenth century, the period between the World Wars, and immediately following World War II. This historic indifference, Almond observes, has on occasion been broken by "explosions of American energy" (Almond, 1960). Tocqueville also explored this withdrawal-intervention dualism a century and a quarter earlier, detecting periodic evangelical outpourings that he saw as a particular problem in foreign affairs. Such moral outbursts dot American foreign policy. The American entry into World War I, for example, was proudly proclaimed by President Woodrow Wilson as necessary to "make the world safe for democracy."

This moralism is linked to the American sense of mission. Every country occasionally reveals a well-developed self-appreciation, but the United States from 1776 on has displayed an especially lofty sense of its place in the world and of its innocence. America had turned its back on the vices of the Old World and had made a new beginning. It was to act as an example for mankind. George Washington expressed a familiar sentiment when he declared in his first inaugural address that "the preservation of the sacred fire of liberty and the destiny of the republican model of government are justly considered . . . staked on the experiment intrusted to the hands of the American people."

The more skeptical, if not jaded, perspectives of the latter third of the twentieth century should not obscure the realities of this *sense* of mission. Reinhold Niebuhr has noted how "pure our democratic virtue seemed in the eighteenth century, compared with that of the benighted devotees and victims of 'monarchy'" (Niebuhr, 1952). A large part of sub-

Figure 1.6 Nationalism distorts perception of the world. Every nation sees its problems and purposes as the most significant in the world. Here, the artist has represented the chauvinism of many Americans, that well-developed sense of self-appreciation that sees the United States as the "hub of the universe."

Figure 1.7 All nations possess a double image, with one or the other aspect assuming predominance depending on the occasion. America's popular symbols include two very different ones: the generous and protective Statue of Liberty, which represents the current of idealism in American foreign policy. Engraved on her are the words: "a mighty woman with a torch, whose flame/Is the imprisoned lightning, and her name/Mother of exiles. From her beacon-hand/blows world-wide welcome . . ." The other side of the image is the hard-bargaining, self-interested, shrewd Uncle Sam, who represents the current of cynicism in America's foreign involvement. More than that of perhaps any other nation, America's participation in foreign affairs has been characterized by this curious mixture of generosity and idealism on the one hand, and narrow pursuit of self-interest on the other.

sequent American history sustained the initial notions of uniqueness and purity:

We lived for a century not only in the illusion but in the reality of innocency in our foreign relations. We lacked the power in the first instance to become involved in the guilt of its use. As we gradually achieved power . . . we sought for a time to preserve innocency by disavowing the responsibilities of power. (Niebuhr, 1952, p. 35)

Historically, Americans have assumed that their country should expect to gain its ends primarily through moral attraction—by setting an example. But with twentieth-century acceptance of the role of major power, imperialistic tendencies that were always present in the American sense of mission have been revealed.

The success that Americans have enjoyed with political and economic institutions has contributed to an unparalleled optimism concerning the possibilities of decisive action. Margaret Mead has noted this peculiarly American optimism, the confidence that sufficient will and effort can resolve any problem (Mead, 1943). Reinhold Niebuhr has described the United States as a culture that is "confident of the possibilities of resolving all incongruities in life and history." (Niebuhr, 1952, p. 40).

Accompanying the optimism, frequently, is an overly simple view of problems, a failure to appreciate their complexity. This cultural orientation has frequently affected America's foreign affairs, and although its effects are sometimes fortunate, they can also be tragic. The Vietnam War seems a classic illustration of the attitude: "We know what is best for them, and modest applications of 'American know-how' can set things right." But political development in a Southeast Asian nation can be very complicated. It seems evident that the initial acts of military engagement were heavily suffused with a perverse case of American optimism about our capacity to "set things right" (See Chapter 5).

In a fascinating commentary on moral dualism in American culture, Geoffrey Gorer observes that America's popular symbols include two very different ones—the hard-bargaining, self-interested, shrewd Uncle Sam, and the selfless, generous Goddess of Liberty (Gorer, 1964). Almond also noted this dualism in the contrasting currents of idealism and cynicism in American foreign policy. "Americans," he writes, "would appear to be happiest when they can cloak an action motivated by self-interest with an aura of New Testament selflessness, when an action which is 'good business' or 'good security' can be made to 'look good' too." He finds a strong current of generosity and humanitarianism revealing itself in American foreign policy, but alongside it he finds "a deep-seated suspicion that smart people don't act that way, that 'only suckers are a soft touch' "(Almond, 1960).

More than that of perhaps any other country, American foreign involvement has been dotted with a curious mixture of generosity and idealism on the one hand, and narrow pursuit of self-interest on the other. This dualism is pointed up in major international interventions from the Spanish-American War of the 1890s to the Vietnam War of the 1960s and early 1970s. Both strains are genuine—they reflect a tension in values felt by many Americans, including, of course, those charged with the formulation of foreign policy. Any analysis of the Vietnam War that overlooks the hardheaded, ruthless pursuit of big power interests is incomplete. So, too, is any analysis that omits the strong currents of idealism—idealism can serve perverse ends—that also characterize America's military and economic commitment.

The broad sweep of American involvement in the world outside, therefore, is punctuated by a series of recurring dualisms: high-minded idealism versus narrow self-interest; withdrawal to "cultivate our own garden" versus outbursts of evangelism colored by a sense of American "mission"; optimism about our ability to "set things right" (contributing to a willingness to take on large projects, such as the Marshall Plan to rebuild post-World War II Europe) versus our tendency to grossly overestimate our capabilities; and generosity versus a sense of having been betrayed when we feel our actions are insufficiently appreciated.

The Limits of Egalitarianism

Thomas Jefferson's words in the Declaration of Independence are fundamental to the sacred literature of democracy: "We hold these truths to be self-evident: that all men are created equal; that they are endowed by their Creator with certain unalienable rights; that among these are life, liberty, and the pursuit of happiness." American treatment of ethnic minorities, however, has often stood in contradiction to these claims (as is shown in Chapter 6).

America, an egalitarian society that was founded on the premises that men should be judged by their achievement and not by their birth and that political decisions should reflect the views of the citizenry, has permitted gross discrimination against various groups; at times these groups have been systematically excluded from participation. Egalitarianism must be viewed as a limited, and constantly evolving, set of normative assumptions.

The egalitarian revolution was not intended to produce a social situation in which everyone was equal to all others. Rather, it insisted that achievement be substituted for birthright as the determinant of status; that new social groups be involved in the vital decisions affecting social, economic, and political life; that politics cease to be a closed affair played out among members of a hereditary elite. The initial backers of the egalitarian doctrine were the entrepreneurial middle classes so strengthened during the early phases of industrial development. An entrepreneurial class can certainly be found earlier, but during the seventeenth and eighteenth centuries there was a tremendous expansion of this middle class. Having arrived at positions of economic importance in the new order, operating from new centers of power that the economy had generated, confident in their ability to understand the world and to participate in it, and told by the new Liberal ideology that there was no real basis for the continuing privileges of the aristocratic ruling class, these middle classes demanded to participate in the political structure, demands that are called egalitarian.

The link between growing economic resources and egalitarianism is both obvious and important. With the prospect of continuing growth in economic output, it became possible, not a cruel hoax, for Thomas Jefferson to state in the Declaration of Independence that all men have a birthright to the vigorous pursuit of earthly happiness. When the economic and technological developments of the seventeenth and eighteenth centuries began to expand the economic pie, groups of men outside the aristocratic class stepped forward to claim their share of the wealth; they had come to feel that life owed them something other than perpetual wretchedness.

When Jefferson wrote in the Declaration that "all men are created equal," he and the other founding fathers meant all solid, hard-working white men. "All men" to most eighteenth-century Liberals were all *middle- and upper-class* men. Reinhold Niebuhr caught this point nicely when he observed that "equality as a regulative principle of Justice . . . is used by bourgeois man as a weapon against feudal inequality, but it is not taken seriously when the classes below him lay claim to it" (Niebuhr, 1952). Still, the appeals tended to be universalistic, and the economic-technological transformations that nourished them did not stop in 1800. Thus, the egalitarian revolution in the United States (as throughout the world) has gone through a number of stages, each extending the initial processes. Each successive stage has required that new social groups be granted fuller measures of participation and recognition.

The contradiction between creed and practice, then, is not precisely as it first appears. Ideological positions typically are restricted by the historical context that produces them. Egalitarianism has not comprised a static set of value positions. Black Americans simply were not thought of as full and equal participants, or as entitled to full participation, by all whites in 1790, 1870, or even 1935. And today many still deny full equality to blacks and other minorities. Seymour Martin Lipset noted that such incomplete or selective visions of egalitarianism (incomplete in the sense that some groups were simply not included) have generally characterized left-of-center and progressive, as well as conservative, thought: "During the early nineteenth century, when European leftists and liberals were pointing to the United States as a nation which demonstrated the viability of equality and democracy, America was also a land of slavery" (Lipset, 1967).

Egalitarianism has always been in the state of becoming. Each generation has defined its boundaries and put flesh on the basic assumptions. In spite of the sometimes halting progress toward the ideal, egalitarian values have had a powerful impact on American political life. Egalitarianism has provided a framework in which to judge society's performance. Universal in its applications, egalitarianism has become the basis of the appeals of succeeding groups. Although the current quest of black Americans for equal treatment depends on a number of bases, including the demand for political power, their main appeal is that the society live up to its own creed, that it build on rather than run against broadly shared values.

In another sense, however, the ascendancy of Liberal values has retarded equitable treatment for certain minorities. Michael Rogin points to American treatment of the Indians:

Liberalism insisted on the independence of men, each from the other, and from cultural, traditional, and communal attachments. Indians were perceived as connected to their past, their superstitions, and their land. Liberalism insisted upon work, instinctual repression, and acquisitive behavior; men had to conquer and separate themselves from nature. Indians were seen as playful, violent, improvident, wild, and in harmony with nature. Private property underlay liberal societies; Indians held land in common. Liberal relations were based, contractually, on keeping promises and on personal responsibility. Indians, in the liberal view, were anarchic and irresponsible. Americans believed that peaceful competitiveness kept them in touch with one another and provided social cement. They thought that Indians, lacking social order, were devoted to war. (Rogin, 1971, p. 270)

Liberalism became *Americanism*. Groups that did not conform to Liberal principles were unworthy—"un-American." The preeminence of a single value system produces harsh intolerance of groups perceived as not conforming to that system.

Here is yet another of the contradictions that riddle the structure of American ideology and values. The dominance of Liberalism contributed to institutional stability in the United States. It sustained an ethic profoundly supportive of the tasks of industrial-nation-building, on which American economic abundance is based. By becoming equated with Americanism, Liberalism provided a vehicle of entry into the society for people from widely differing ethnic and cultural traditions: If they would only conform to Liberal principles, they would be considered American. But at the same time, Liberalism has a notable blindspot—a gross intolerance of other ethical traditions. As is shown in Chapter 6, American race relations vividly illustrate the effects.

Civil Liberties and Majority Standards

Alexis de Tocqueville was one of the first to deal seriously with the tension between the American commitment to majority rule and civil liberties. "In America," he wrote, "the majority raises formidable barriers around the liberty of opinion." Tocqueville's concern was the potential for a "tyranny of the majority." As a member of the old French nobility, he looked with some suspicion on "majority man," elevated to such a high position in the infant American democracy of the 1830s. But in his book, *Democracy in America,* he largely avoided the wailing of displaced aristocrats. The world, Tocqueville was aware, had had experience aplenty with "tyranny of the minority." Now, he sought to advise his readers, the world would confront challenges to individual freedom resulting from an enthronement of the majority. Majoritarianism in the United States involved not merely procedural standards for decision making (in the 1830s, for example, elections were decided by universal white male suffrage), but it also provided a basis for determining what was right. When the values of a society endow the judgments of the majority with extraordinary authority, the position of those not conforming to the majority's standards may become shaky indeed, a kind of tyranny that is explored in depth in Chapter 7.

Tocqueville was not the only foreign visitor to see the American commitment to majoritarianism as a mixed blessing. In the late nineteenth century an English observer, James Bryce, returned to this theme in "The Fatalism of the Multitude," a chapter of his book entitled *American Commonwealth.* "Out of this dogma [that the majority must prevail]," Bryce argued, "there grows up another which is less distinctly admitted . . . that *the majority is right*" [emphasis added].

The enthronement of majoritarian standards, of which Tocqueville and Bryce wrote in the nineteenth century, is no less a characteristic of twentieth-century America. The basic tension still exists: America's devotion to majoritarianism provides the basis for vastly extended political and social opportunities for common citizens; at the same time, it poses the potential for continuing threats to any minority holding different views.

The American record in civil liberties testifies to the fact that these concerns are not academic. Challenges to the rights of individual expression have often been made in the name of the standards of the majority. In response to this tension, a series of

"In America, the majority raises formidable barriers around the liberty of opinion: within these barriers, an author may write what he pleases; but woe to him if he goes beyond them. Not that he is in danger of an auto-da-fé, but he is exposed to continued obloquy and persecution. His political career is closed forever, since he has offended the only authority which is able to open it. . . . The public therefore, among a democratic people, has a singular power, which aristocratic nations cannot conceive; for it does not persuade others to its beliefs, but it imposes them and makes them permeate the thinking of every one by a sort of enormous pressure of the mind of all upon the individual intelligence. . . . I think that democratic communities have a natural taste for freedom: left to themselves, they will seek it, cherish it, and view any privation of it with regret. But for equality, their passion is ardent, insatiable, incessant, invincible: they call for equality in freedom; and if they cannot obtain that, they still call for equality in slavery." (Tocqueville, 1835, I, pp. 263–264; II, pp. 10, 97)

"In such a country, where complete political equality is strengthened and perfected by complete social equality, where the will of the majority is absolute, unquestioned, always invoked to decide every question, and where the numbers which decide are so vast that one comes to regard them as one regards the largely working forces of nature, we may expect to find certain feelings and beliefs dominant in the minds of men. One of these is that the majority must prevail. All free government rests on this, for there is no other way of working free government. To obey the majority is therefore both a necessity and a duty, a duty because the alternative would be ruin and the breaking-up of laws. Out of this dogma there grows up another which is less distinctly admitted, and indeed held rather implicitly than consciously, that the majority is right. And out of both of these there grows again the feeling, still less consciously held, but not less truly operative, that it is vain to oppose or censure the majority." (James Bryce, 1888, Vol. II, p. 343)

boundaries for majoritarianism have evolved. The boundaries are far from clear, and a large body of court litigation testifies to the lack of consensus about them. But there is widespread agreement that questions of civil liberties comprise an arena of decision making in which majority rule must submit to unusually extensive restrictions.

Responsibility for determining the restrictions rests heavily on the courts, with the Supreme Court the final arbiter. A society that has generally elevated the principle of majoritarianism has had to modify it significantly in civil-liberties policy by erecting what the Italian sociologist Gaetano Mosca called a high level of judicial defense of basic civil liberties (Mosca, 1939). Or, as John Roche has put it, "the individual freedom of contemporary American society is largely a function of . . . a meaningful national legal conception—due process of law" (Roche, 1958, p. 133). With all of its shortcomings, a legal system dedicated to formal and impartial procedures for guaranteeing constitutionally defined rights must be seen as the principal defense of civil liberties.

THE AMERICAN IDEOLOGY

"Can a people 'born equal,'" Louis Hartz asks at the close of his study of the American Liberal tradition, "ever understand people elsewhere that have to become so? . . . Can it ever understand itself?" (Hartz, 1955). The American ideological world, at the outset, was cut off from the conflicts of the European motherlands. Liberalism attained an intellectual stranglehold so complete that its assumptions lost the historical and social limits of its origin.

The preeminence of Liberal values accounts for the pragmatic character of American politics. Basic goals have rarely been questioned. Who was there to question them? There have often been charges that certain actions contradicted the American creed, but where has the creed itself been challenged? Even today, after a decade of searing conflicts, the principal insistence of critics is that America be American and honor its calling. It is striking that, nearly two centuries after the founding of the Republic, no ideological vision seriously challenges that of 1776.

SUMMARY

A nation's ideology—the dominant cluster of social and political beliefs—determines its stands on political questions. The components of the American ideology include: egalitarianism—belief in the equality of all persons; and Liberalism—the non-aristocratic sentiments of Europe that sprouted in the American wilderness to form the nation's dominant ideology.

Ample natural resources, the development of technology, and the work ethic laid the foundations for industrial-nation-building. Americans are positional conservatives—reluctant to change political institutions that have fostered economic success. Yet the undue emphasis on individualism and economic achievement has led to competitiveness, aggressiveness, and often to the disregard of the civil rights and liberties of others.

Thus there are contradictions in the American ideology: strains of generosity alternate with selfishness, naïve optimism with simplistic answers to complex problems, and egalitarian rhetoric with gross discrimination. Yet, egalitarian values have powerfully influenced America, by providing a standard by which to judge society's treatment of those minorities whose values differ from those of the dominant population.

SUGGESTED READINGS

Hartz, Louis. *The Founding of New Societies.* New York: Harcourt, Brace & World, 1964.

Ladd, Everett Carll, Jr. *Ideology in America: Change and Response in a City, a Suburb, and a Small Town.* New York: Norton, 1972.

Lane, Robert E. *Political Ideology.* New York: Free Press, 1962.

Lowi, Theodore, J. *The End of Liberalism.* New York: Norton, 1969.

Rossiter, Clinton. *Conservatism in America.* New York: Knopf, 1955.

Tocqueville, Alexis de. *Democracy in America.* 2 Vols. Phillips Bradley (ed.). New York: Knopf, 1945; first English edition, 1835.

2

INTERESTS AND INSTITUTIONS

The founding of new nations has become commonplace. In Africa alone more than two dozen nations have come into being since 1950. Their first task, after throwing off colonial rule, has been to create a government and its accompanying political institutions—frequently a burdensome task. Many have not succeeded in creating a stable government, and most have initially failed to establish a democratic political system. Frequently, the result has been strongman rule or rule by a religious, ethnic, or political majority that has suppressed and even persecuted minorities.

New nations and their chronic political troubles are today taken for granted. It is easy to forget that the United States was the "first new nation" (Seymour Martin Lipset, 1963). In 1776 the political future of the thirteen colonies was as potentially unstable and undefined as that of new nations today. Even war with a common foe did not unite the colonies. A badly uncoordinated coalition conducted the war, and George Washington could never order the various state militias to duty nor count on their showing up for battle. Once independence had been won from England, the former colonies faced an uncertain political future. Should they become one nation or many? How could they overcome the barriers posed by religious, economic, and legal differences? If they were to unite, how would the new nation be governed? Some preferred a monarchy and proposed George Washington as king. Others proclaimed that a golden opportunity was at hand to attempt a "grand experiment"—democracy.

As the *first* new nation, America was the first to choose its political future. Whether the opportunity would prove to be a blessing or a curse depended on the wisdom of the choices made and whether they would stand the test of time. With admirable hindsight, most of today's textbooks endow the founding fathers with the necessary wisdom and cite the durability of their work as proof. However, as many new nations have since demonstrated, the odds were great that the work of the founding fathers would not survive. In fact, a glance at the beginnings of our government, at the critical decisions won by narrow margins, at all the early crises that were narrowly survived, makes it obvious that an inexhaustible supply of good luck, as well as wisdom, was needed to see the new nation through its travail.

Figure 2.1 Who has power in the United States? The big wheels? But can they turn without the little wheels? Decentralized, broken up, fragmented as the American power scene sometimes seems to be—and as it was intended to be in the theories of at least some of the founding fathers—there are still some gears that are enormously bigger than others. Indeed, the operation of the whole mechanism is so intricate and dependent on power transmission through so many units that no one group can truly be "boss," even though a small group can sometimes have an effective veto when it reacts strongly enough.

This chapter proceeds somewhat differently from most other "founding fathers" chapters in introductory texts. It is not a rehash of what the founding fathers did, but an explanation of *why* they did it; it is not a recital of the formal structures of our government, but an analysis of how the structures operate. These matters form the basis of an understanding of American politics. In fact, the premise of this chapter is that the work of the founding fathers nearly 200 years ago has as much day-to-day relevance as virtually all government decisions made since then. Only during that brief historical moment were so many alternatives open. The choices made at the constitutional convention in Philadelphia during the hot summer of 1787 determined the fundamental structures through which all subsequent American history has been channeled. For good or for ill, the work of the founding fathers substantially defined present political circumstances.

THE FEAR OF MAJORITY TYRANNY

Any attempt to establish and maintain a democratic government faces twin threats. The first threat concerns the tyranny of the *minority*—the ever-present danger that majority interests will be thwarted by a repressive regime serving the interests of a few. The fear of such tendencies led people to advocate democratic forms in the first place. The second inherent danger in democracy is that a *majority* may utilize democratic procedures to usurp the rights and freedom of minorities. As Chapter 1 points out, majoritarian abuses of democratic principles have been a recurring problem in American history.

The founding fathers were aware of both potential threats to democracy. (As Alexander Hamilton stated, "Give all power to the many, they will oppress the few. Give all power to the few, they will oppress the many" [Robert Dahl, 1956].) The desire to create a system resistant to both forms of tyranny molded many of their decisions. James Madison, the principal architect of the Constitution, was particularly sensitive to this problem and therefore attempted to set up a government that would prevent rule by either an "impassioned majority" or a minority opposed to the "permanent and aggregate interests of the community." Such a political system would distinguish between impassioned majorities and sensible ones, between selfish minorities and those

Figure 2.2 The United States of America was called into being with the same kind of interest maneuvering and logrolling that has characterized our politics in succeeding years. The representatives to the constitutional convention (right) had to deal with questions of power, finance, and freedom, while balancing needed votes against regional desires and philosophical commitments. Small states versus large states, strong centralists versus decentralists, loose currency versus tight currency, slave traders versus abolitionists—all these differences were argued vehemently and with great personal commitment.

MAJORITY AND MINORITY

James Madison neatly sidestepped the necessity to define the terms majority and minority, preferring the word "faction" to cover both. Because Madison believed that the "unequal distribution of property" was the major issue that divided people, he tended to see the majority as the unpropertied masses and the minority as the propertied elite. Obviously, in a large, complex society such as the United States today, this definition is much too narrow. Today there are all kinds of majorities—those in favor of consumer protection, those in favor of lower taxes, and so on—as well as all kinds of minorities—ethnic and racial minorities, big businessmen, small farmers, the aged, and so on. Accordingly, the modern meaning of the terms majority and minority is relevant only in terms of particular issues.

Points of Contention, the Constitutional Convention, 1787
Representation of small versus large states   Representation of states' inhabitants
Control of taxation   Organizing and arming militia   Status of slaves
Issuance of currency   Tariffs   Interstate commerce
Payment of Revolutionary War debts
Federation, confederation, monarchy, republic   Control of international commerce

with legitimate interests, and would be able to block the "bad" forces and give full expression to the "good" ones—a neat trick if it could be pulled off.

Madison's Checks-and-Balances Model

James Madison placed his hope in a governmental system built on the principle of fragmented power. Thoroughly imbued with the spell of Isaac Newton's mechanistic theory of the universe, Madison sought a self-regulating system. "First," he said, "you must enable government to control the governed, and in the next place you should oblige it to control itself." He argued forcefully that if the responsibility for decision making could be sufficiently dispersed, minorities would be able to block threats against them by the majority. Similarly, he believed that fragmentation would prevent any particular minority faction from gaining preeminence over the majority. Madison's ideas were implemented in the system of "checks and balances" and "separated powers."

First, Madison divided the governing power between the executive, legislative, and judicial branches (separation of powers). He then fragmented the decision-making process even more by instituting a delicate system of checks and cross-checks. There is thus a multiplicity of operating checks and cross-checks in the American system. The President, through his veto power, is able to intervene in the legislative process; the Senate is granted the power to confirm any appointments made by the President to the Supreme Court and to his Cabinet; the Supreme Court has the power to declare acts of the President and of Congress unconstitutional; and Congress can impeach the President or a Justice of the Supreme Court.

Fragmentation of power remains the primary feature of our governmental institutions. The complex system prescribed by Madison has flourished; decisions do require widespread agreement and compromise. But many argue that fragmentation of power is also the system's chief defect, that it is a wonder that anything ever gets done. James Burns, for one, contends that we are victimized by the diffusion of power Madison arranged:

> We have been captured by that model, which requires us to await a wide consensus before acting . . .
>
> American leaders have had to gain the concurrence not simply of a majority of the voters, but of majorities of different sets of voters organized around leaders in mutually checking and foot-dragging sectors of government. The price of this radical version of checks and balances has been enfeebled policy . . .
>
> Hence as a nation we have lost control of our policies . . . We lack popular control of the policy-making process . . .

IN THE SENATE OF THE UNITED STATES

June 21, 1984

Mr. Zeropop introduced the following bill, which was read twice and referred to the Committee on Interpersonal Affairs.

A BILL

To discourage an increase in population and thus preserve and protect national resources by establishing a tax of $500 for each child born into any family already having two or more children.

IN FAVOR

Persons not intending to have children

Senior citizens

Environmentalists concerned with overuse of resources

Protestants and Jews (usually have small families)

Economic conservatives who resent having to support the welfare system

Politicians representing older-aged constituents

Manufacturers of birth-control devices

OPPOSED

Young couples who want to have more than two children

Civil libertarians who object to government interference in personal decisions

Military strategists desiring a large population for easy mobilization of large army

Catholics

Members of some ethnic minorities (blacks, Indians, Mexican-Americans) who feel that such laws are a form of cultural genocide

Baby-product manufacturers

Toy manufacturers

Many businesses (such as auto, appliance, housing, and clothing companies) that are dependent on a large consumer population

Our government lacks unity and teamwork . . . We oscillate fecklessly between deadlock and a rush of action . . . We cannot define our national purpose and mobilize our strength to move vigorously against a problem. (Burns, 1963, pp. 323–324)

Others have praised Madison's governmental system, suggesting that its inability to move vigorously has spared the country many impulsive plunges into foolish and perhaps dangerous policies prompted by short-lived popular enthusiasms.

However one regards the Madisonian vision of diffused power, the fact remains that the American political system still reflects it and is unlikely to be changed anytime soon. All the original checks and balances laid out in the Constitution remain in force. The *unwritten constitution*—traditions, laws, procedures that have developed around the Constitution—has added countless more.

In any given policy domain there are a great many power points, each relatively autonomous, each responsive to different constituencies and interests, each making and enforcing sometimes contradictory policies. Consider the following power points, each able to make important decisions regarding economic policy:

1. The President, whose broad economic powers include the regulation of wages and prices;
2. The Federal Reserve Board, which regulates the supply of money and credit;
3. Other agencies in the bureaucracy, such as the Pentagon, which influences industry by defense purchases, and the Agriculture Department, which sets farm-support prices and quotas;
4. Congress and its committees, which regulate and subsidize every sector of the economy;
5. The courts, whose power of legislative interpretation affects all economic decisions;
6. The states and cities, whose economic powers and budgets are largely outside federal control;
7. "Private governments," or interest groups, corporations, and unions, which shape the economy;
8. The people, who as consumers, investors, and voters make decisions that regulate the economy.

In any policy area a similar list would show power set against power and group against group in constantly shifting arrangements. The system maximizes the power of minorities to block legislation; in being moved through the elaborate thicket of decision points, programs are subject to dozens of potential ambushes. As Robert Dahl has stated: "The making of government decisions is not a majestic march of great majorities united upon certain matters of basic policy . . . On matters of specific policy, the majority rarely rules" (Dahl, 1956). Many instances of minority rule are discussed in Chapter 12.

Figure 2.3 Analysis of group support for a hypothetical bill (left). As any piece of legislation has its pros and cons, so also it has its supporters and opponents. To study the history of any piece of legislation or indeed of a whole policy area, one must early research which interests will be favored and which hurt by the bill or policy. Sometimes groups announce their positions; sometimes the most effective group actions are taken behind the scenes and therefore made difficult to trace. For this entirely hypothetical piece of population-control legislation we have suggested a possible line-up of pro and con groups to give an example of the results of such an analysis. Do you agree with these line-ups? Would you add or subtract groups?

□

THE FEDERALIST PAPERS

The Federalist Papers are a series of essays written by James Madison, Alexander Hamilton, and John Jay that were originally published in New York newspapers in an attempt to persuade New Yorkers to ratify the United States Constitution. These essays, which have been published under the title The Federalist, are generally regarded as being the best single commentary on the Constitution as well as America's most significant contribution to political theory.

In Federalist Paper No. 10 the authors argued that the best way to ensure liberty was to devise a government in which numerous factions were in a position to struggle with one another. The extension of this argument was that New Yorkers should vote for the Constitution because, by forming a stronger central government, the Constitution would create closer contact between a greater diversity of groups.

The Constitution Reconsidered

The history of the world is strewn with scraps of paper called constitutions. Many are subterfuges for coups, caudillos, and corruption. The American Constitution is rare in its continuing capacity to prescribe rules of governance two centuries after its writing.

The unwritten constitution, by elevating well-proven political practices to the level of constitutional prescription, has helped the Constitution survive. Such practices as nomination of candidates by political parties, the seniority system in Congress, and judicial review of legislative decisions are all parts of the unwritten constitution and are often more important than many parts of the formal document itself.

The Constitution is rare, too, in its semireligious qualities. All constitutions are political documents; they are products of power and result from compromises made between conflicting interests. But a successful constitution develops a symbolic aura as well and even takes on some of the qualities of Holy Writ: written interpretations of it resemble analyses of the scriptures; it comes to prescribe civic virtue and to legitimize good behavior by distinguishing it from bad behavior; and an elaborate code of laws and customs builds up around it, presumably to shape it to the "needs of the times." Often the fact that a constitution was originally a political document is conveniently forgotten.

When the document is criticized, its religious aura becomes most apparent. Charles Beard wrote his controversial *An Economic Interpretation of the Constitution* in 1913; his critics viewed him as not merely wrong but as almost heretical. Beard simply wanted to squeeze some of the mythology out of the Constitution by describing it as a *political* document. To his critics, however, his approach was heresy. It was as though he had created a constitutional version of the "death of God" argument.

The Founding Fathers Considered

For many years the American Constitution was considered an act of divine intervention in the affairs of men. To the historian George Bancroft the ratification of the document represented "the movement of the divine power which gives unity to the universe, and order and connection to events" (Beard, 1913).

Those who doubted (as did the founding fathers

Figure 2.4 The four facets of the American Constitution (reading upward): a legalistic balance of rights and powers; a political, economic balance of regional, ideological, and economic interests after the fashion of James Madison's model; an awesome, quasireligious symbol, which serves to unify the nation; and a combination of the visible, written, time-bound document with the widespread addenda of commentary, usage, and legal decisions that constitute the so-called "unwritten" Constitution.

The Constitution is not a document. It is a many-faceted entity that takes its meaning from the diversity of our national experience, just as it in turn influences the potential of that experience. The endurance of the Constitution is partially the result of the genius of its framers; yet it is the continued flexibility of our political system that has allowed the inclusion of new practices, institutions, and meanings. Our national life continues to embroider and embellish the original document in a living search for a reasoned unity of diverse interests.

Figure 2.5 Many of the delegates to the constitutional convention were either land speculators or holders of public securities, who stood to gain significantly from the ratification of the Constitution. Elbridge Gerry (left) and Edmund Randolph (right) were owed various sums of money by the states and by the continental congress; and even though both men were opposed to ratification, those debts were made good when the document was ratified. Gerry subsequently served in Congress and was elected Vice-President. Randolph became President Washington's Attorney General and, on Thomas Jefferson's resignation in 1793, was named Secretary of State.

themselves) that God troubled himself with the affairs of men accepted a slightly different, although equally benign, view of the framers. According to this view—widely associated with John Fiske's *Critical Period in American History*—the Constitution represented a victory for "straight-thinking" over "narrow-minded" men, for visionaries over parochials, for the public interest over the individual. The framers allegedly saw the weakness of the Articles of Confederation: Under its governance the states were too powerful, Congress had no power to levy taxes or to regulate interstate and foreign commerce, there was no executive power, and the disunited former colonies were military midgets. According to Fiske's view, the founding fathers were thoroughly rational and nonpolitical as they attacked the problems of confederation. It is Fiske's interpretation of the founding of the Constitution that has been propagated in generations of high school civics and history texts.

In 1913 Charles Beard shocked his critics by arguing forcefully that the Constitution was a political document, constructed by men with political interests in mind. He argued that the framers were rich, wellborn, and able; that most of them would have agreed that the preservation of property was the principal object of government; and that several of the framers might have agreed with John Jay, a coauthor (with James Madison and Alexander Hamilton) of the *Federalist* papers, that "the people who own the country ought to govern it." Charles Beard made famous the argument that the men at Philadelphia were scions of wealth, dominated by their self-interest in the preservation of their property, and that they developed the Constitution's checks and balances in order to keep the unpropertied majority from being able to make unwarranted demands on the propertied minority.

Although later historical evidence has tempered the conclusions of Beard, even the fiercest critics concede that the economic interests of the early republic were very much at issue in the framing and ratification of the Constitution. Indeed, one of James Madison's fundamental assumptions was that economic factors were the primary motivating factors in human behavior. He felt that the seeds of political conflict were sown in the economic differences between classes of people.

How, then, should the founding fathers be viewed? The answer depends on the standards applied. From a twentieth-century vantage point they look exceedingly conservative:

John Adams: "If you give more than a share in the sovereignty to the democrats, that is, if you give them the command or preponderance in the legislature, they will vote all property out of the hands of you aristocrats, and if they let you escape with your lives, it will be more humanity, consideration, and generosity than any triumphant democracy ever displayed since the creation."

Alexander Hamilton: "Your people, sir, are a great beast."

William Livingston: "The people have ever been and ever will be unfit to retain the exercize of power in their own hands."

But the founding fathers lived in their times, not ours. To many in their own day, they were considered to be radical revolutionaries who were determined to destroy the individual states by advocating a most questionable form of governance.

However one judges these men, it is clear that the institutional framework they created lives after them. Although the American political system has been gradually made more democratic over the years (through the direct election of senators, the expansion of the right to vote, the emergence of mass-based political parties, and the transformation of the electoral college from a group that chose the President to its current status as a rubber stamp), the constitutional system still reflects the early fears of majority rule and popular control.

WHO RULES AMERICA AND HOW?

The Madisonian system was designed to work against majority control of government. Accordingly, the founding fathers created a structure of government that allowed a proliferation of governmental institutions, or power centers, to develop. When a popular majority today desires a given action, therefore, it must gain control of those power centers in order to be successful. If there were only one power center in the American political system—a democratically elected President, for example—a majority would need to control only the President to work its will. But the diffusion of power requires that the majority capture not one or two but possibly a dozen institutions in order to obtain its goal.

Consider civil rights legislation, for example. To get legislation passed, it is not sufficient to secure a sympathetic President, for he in turn must coax Congress. Even having a majority of congressmen supporting the legislation does not guarantee action, because substantial power is held by committees and committee chairmen. Nor are sympathetic committees able to finalize legislation, for the Supreme Court can overturn legislation. The people who enforce legislation, from the Attorney General to the local sheriff, must also be persuaded to enforce it vigorously. If the majority has to dominate each of these institutions in order to work its will, an opposing minority can stifle or retard action by controlling only one of them. Affirmative action, therefore, depends on the acquiescence of (to paraphrase John C. Calhoun) concurrent minorities. In this way, the fragmentation of power in the Madisonian system facilitates the influence of minorities.

The important question, however, is not whether a majority or a minority rules the system. Rather, the great debate in modern political science concerns minority rule: Are the pluralists correct that government is dominated by many different minorities, or are the elitists correct that it is ruled by a single minority—the power elite?

The Pluralism-Elitism Debate

Pluralists argue that power is shared by contending minorities; each group is able to secure some of its desires, thereby getting a piece of the action. Robert Dahl states the case for "minorities rule":

If there is anything to be said for the processes that actually distinguish democracy from dictatorship, it is not discoverable in the clear-cut distinction between government by a majority and government by a minority. The distinction comes much closer to being one between government by a minority and government by *minorities* . . . A central guiding thread of American constitutional development has been the evolution of a political system in which all the active and legitimate groups in the population can make themselves heard at some crucial stage in the process of decision. (Dahl, 1956, p. 133)

Although the pluralist perspective concedes that majorities do not rule, it denies the existence of a single dominant power clique. Rather, numerous minorities in the guise of interest groups—business,

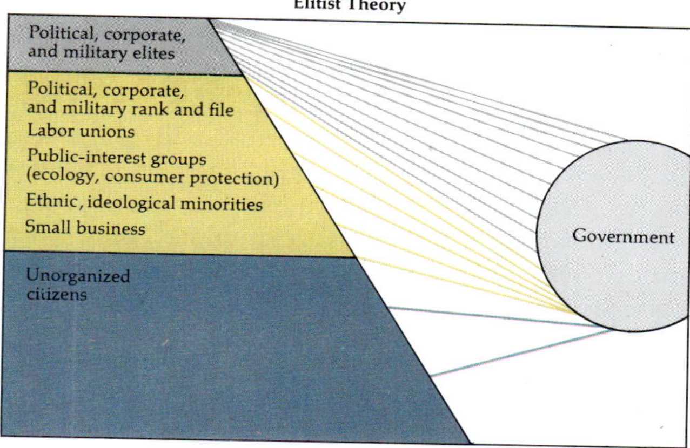

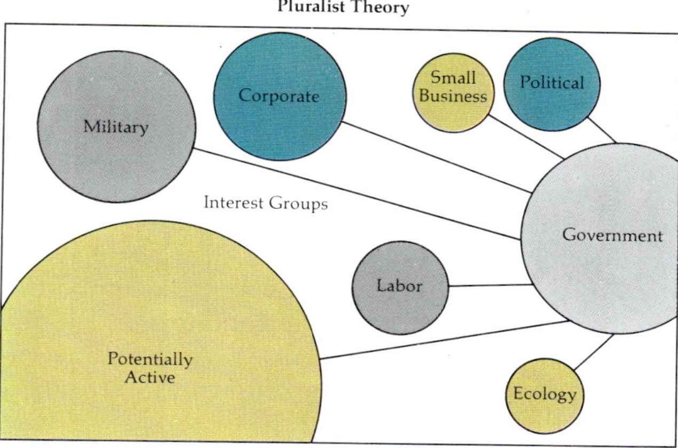

Figure 2.6 In these two diagrams the lines connecting government and the various groups of citizens represent influence or power. In the diagram entitled Elitist Theory, most of the lines emanate from a small stratum of society, called the political, corporate, and military elite. Fewer lines come from the middle group of organized citizens, and only two lines come from the largest group of unorganized citizens. These figures do not pretend to be quantitatively correct; rather, they are intended to give an idea of the relative "clout" attributed to each set of citizens by the theory represented. The lower diagram, entitled Pluralist Theory, shows each group (or potential group) with a single line to the government. This is not to say that all groups exercise the same amount of influence at any one time; it is rather to illustrate the theory's contention that any group motivated strongly enough and consolidating its resources sufficiently can gain access to governmental power—power that is diffused and fragmented and to which there are many routes of access.

labor, ethnic minorities, foreign traders, segregationists—all get a slice of the political pie (see Chapter 15). The size of their slice depends on their motivation and ability to mobilize political resources. Pluralists insist that the diffused structure of power promotes pluralism because no single group can be completely shut out of power and because none can claim enough to ride roughshod over the interests of all others—a kind of modern Madisonian check-and-balance sheet.

The alternate view of power, popularized by the sociologist C. Wright Mills, holds that rule is not by many minorities but by *a* minority—the "power elite." Of course, no one thinks that small farmers, labor leaders, or representatives of the poor constitute a single cadre of the powerful. Rather, Mills argued, power is concentrated in the big three institutions: the corporations, the military, and the governmental bureaucracies (Mills, 1956). The phrase "military-industrial complex" (coined by President Eisenhower) is based on a similar view of power (see the Perspective following Chapter 5).

Another proponent of the power-concentration hypothesis, G. William Domhoff, argues that members of a social and economic elite, composed of a cohesive group of persons from prominent and wealthy families, occupy most major positions of social and economic power. Some of these people represent the old aristocracy (the "eastern establishment"), and others represent the new corporate, technocratic, and intellectual elite. All, however, are in a position to move from one elite role to another, for the skills of governance are the same in the private and the public sectors (Domhoff, 1967). The elitist view echoes Charles Beard's argument that the founding fathers were primarily men of the upper class whose goal was to structure a government in which propertied interests could maintain control.

The fragmentation of political institutions figures prominently in both of these competing views about power in America. To the pluralist the diffusion of power into multiple centers prevents majority rule, but it permits multiple minorities to exercise power. To the elitist the fragmentation of formal power also prevents rule by a majority, but it facilitates control by a single minority. Whatever the accuracy of these two views—and in a sense, this entire book is devoted to the issue—it is necessary to recognize the significance of the political structures of our society, which largely determine how the political game is played.

Private Governments Enter the Power Equation

Private governments—the corporations, the unions, the foundations, the universities, the churches—figure prominently in both the pluralist and the elitist models of the American political system. To the pluralist, the system retains an essentially democratic character because of the competition among private governments. To the elitists, private governments are often more important and powerful than the public government.

As Chapter 15 shows, many vital policy decisions are partly or even entirely determined by private political structures. It is obviously to the advantage of such private structures to capture and control elements of the public government that can benefit or harm their interests. Thus, people who work with real estate like to sit on local planning boards that regulate land use; bankers try to make friends with members of agencies that regulate banking; unions like to see a friendly Secretary of Labor; and transportation interests try to make sure that their people are appointed to the Interstate Commerce Commission.

The United States is unusual in the degree of power it puts in the hands of private governments. People of other nations find it odd that in America many decisions concerning the allocation of resources, the location of factories, and wage and price policies are left so completely to the private sector. Even in foreign relations, some corporations seem to conduct their own foreign policy, often with little regard for the policy of the President or the State Department. The efforts of International Telephone and Telegraph (ITT) to influence the election of Salvador Allende as President of Chile in 1971 are a case in point. Very few nations permit private corporations such latitude.

Institutions and the Interests They Further

The history of American politics can be written in terms of minority interests and the institutions of government that helped or frustrated them. The Supreme Court, for example, has a long history of dominance by one or another set of interests—by the slavocracy before the Civil War and by big business well into the New Deal era. After World War II the Court entered its most activist era in support of the rights of the poor, the ethnic minorities, and the accused (see Chapters 7 and 11). An examination of virtually any other governmental institution

□

THE PUBLIC AND PRIVATE SECTORS

Usually, the term public sector is used to mean the actions of national, state, and local governments. The private sector refers to the myriad decisions made by households and firms. In practice, however, the distinctions are often blurred—sometimes to the point of invisibility. Few actions of the private sector (other than those concerning purely family matters) are free of the influence of governmental rules and policies. When a business calculates its profits or the location of a new factory, it figures in terms of questions of tax advantages, the possibility of government contracts, state corporation regulations, and so on. On the other hand, most crucial decisions made by the public sector depend for their execution on cooperation from the private sector. The defense budget pays the wages of uniformed servicemen, but it also pays the wages and profits of employees and employers working in the private sector under government contract. Virtually all decisions made by the American government involve a mix of private as well as public actions.

Figure 2.7 It is impossible for political institutions to be totally neutral. Even the courts and the clauses of the Constitution wind up identifiably aiding some groups more than others. This matching game (right) shows examples of certain interests or institutions that have become associated with various regional, ideological, or economic groups.

Figure 2.8 Offensive and defensive power of the South (far right). In theory the Civil War determined the primary authority of the central government over the secessionist southern states. Indeed, the power of the United States government has in many instances been applied to the South to halt segregationist activities in such areas as education, transportation, voting, and housing. But the South has been able to fight back, and with powerful weapons—weapons that are inherent in any large political system but that are more profoundly powerful in a federal system. For example, the local power structures and state legislatures have the power to refuse to enforce national laws, and the great weapon of the senatorial filibuster has in years past inhibited Congress from passing integration legislation. Southern dominance over national policy areas such as defense and agriculture has been facilitated by the double barrel of safe electoral districts in single-party states and the seniority rule that gives senior legislators the most powerful voice in committee decision making.

would reveal the same tendency toward domination by one or another of the minority interests.

In politics the cards are always marked, the decks forever stacked. The idea of using institutions to protect or hamper interests is fundamental to the Madisonian system. The Constitution itself was designed to frustrate action by both the selfish minority and the impassioned majority. Figure 2.7 shows some examples of institutions and rules that have advanced certain interests over others. Individuals do not, of course, argue overtly that the cards should be stacked to their advantage. Usually, defenses are couched in terms of positive values supposedly promoted by the rule or institution. Defenders of the filibuster in the Senate do not advocate it because "it frustrates civil rights policy," but because "it lets every senator have his say." Supporters of the oil-depletion allowance do not defend it because "it makes the oil companies richer," but because it allegedly "promotes discovery of new energy sources."

ACTION AND INACTION: THE DIFFUSION OF POWER

Nowhere is the diffusion of power more vividly illustrated than in the decades of action—and inaction—in the cause of racial equality. It was the Supreme Court, the branch of government most immune from popular control, that led the vanguard of civil rights action with its decision in 1954 that legally prescribed segregation in the schools was unconstitutional. Congress and the President seemed to drag reluctantly behind. In 1957 Congress passed a voting rights bill characterized by such timidity that it was an example of symbolic (rather than effective) public policy. President Eisenhower effectively remained in the background. The multiplicity of power centers in the national government and the capacity of an entrenched minority—in this case, segregationists—to thwart majority action were clearly evident in the obstruction of meaningful civil rights legislation (see Chapter 6).

Civil rights policy ran afoul of some crucial structural realities of the American political system:

Even when a majority of Congress has been committed to stronger stands on racial problems . . . the structure, rules, and traditions of the national government favor opponents of innovation. This pro-status quo bias stems from such factors as checks and balances and separation of powers built into the Federal system. (Harrell Rodgers and Charles Bullock, 1972, p. 213)

One particular reality that collided with civil rights action was the seniority system in the United States Congress (see Chapter 8). The diffusion of power to

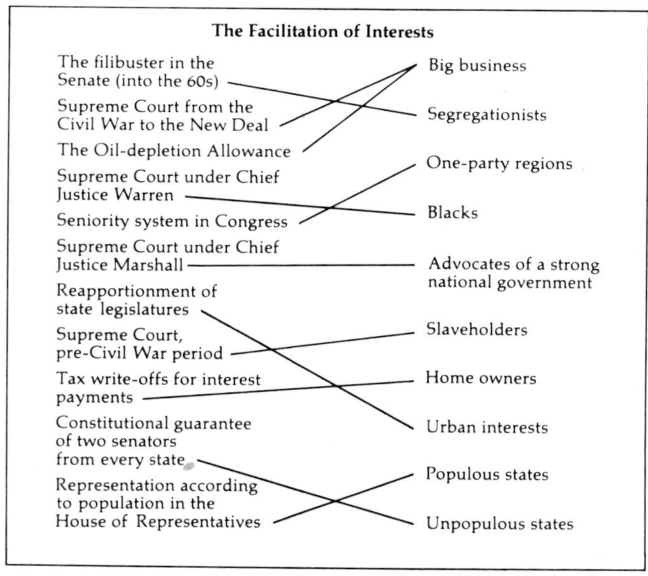

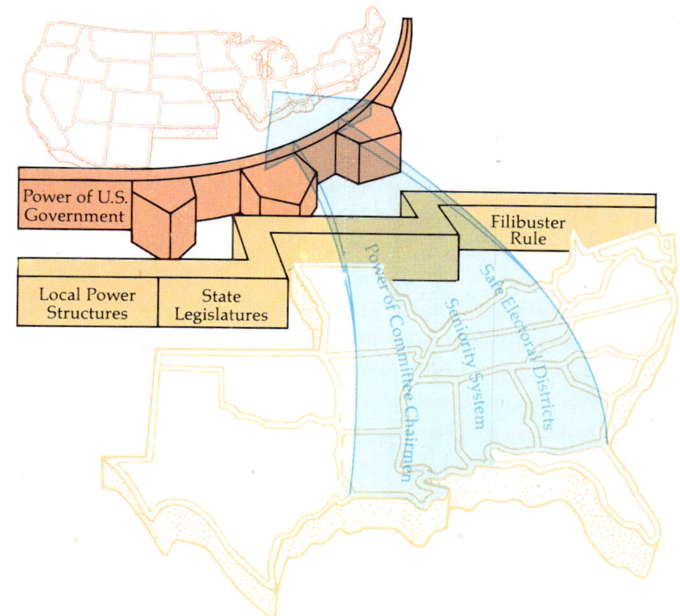

committees and their chairmen (who are chosen according to seniority) has allowed representatives of one-party regions to gain much authority. As an example, the Senate Judiciary Committee, which handles all civil rights legislation, has long been chaired by a Mississippi lawyer and plantation owner, James Eastland, a man who has been bitterly opposed to civil rights legislation for years. In the House, the Rules Committee, which wields great power over all bills, was chaired for many years by southerners whose attitudes toward civil rights legislation mirrored Senator Eastland's.

The use of the filibuster, or "talking a bill to death," also worked against civil rights legislation in the Senate. The United States Senate has long forbidden cutting off debate (cloture) on an issue unless a two-thirds majority could be mustered. The result: Controversial bills, such as those concerning civil rights, are often "debated" until the Senate adjourns (meaning that the issue at hand is not brought to a vote).

Federalism—the system of shared power among the federal (national), state, and local governments—also has empowered forces unsympathetic to racial equality. Governors (who have sometimes literally stood in a schoolhouse door to prevent integration),

state legislatures, local registrars, and school boards have the power to destroy directives from the federal government by refusing to enforce them.

When the implementation of a policy is muted by inaction in competing institutions, a public policy may be transformed from an effective to a symbolic output of the political system (Murray Edelman, 1964). Symbolic outputs, including much of the recent civil rights legislation, may have the effect of raising expectations, perhaps to an intolerable extent, while concealing inaction. Grand pronouncements come from one decision maker (typically the President), while other institutional forces reduce the probability of real change. Such pronouncements raise expectations without producing the promised results. The diffusion of power has made it very difficult for the political system to respond with a single voice.

FEDERALISM AND THE REPRESENTATION OF INTERESTS

In September 1972 a passenger train operating under Amtrak, the federal corporation that runs the nation's passenger rail service, arrived at Oklahoma City's deteriorating railway station. On arrival the local police raided the club car, arrested the bar-

tender, and seized the train's liquor supply. In the opinion of the local law-enforcement authorities, Amtrak was in violation of Oklahoma statutes that prohibit selling liquor by the drink. They seemed unaware of one of the oldest (and most clearly established) principles in the federal system—the fact that federal law overrides state law.

In 1819 Chief Justice John Marshall laid down his famous dictum that the federal government is supreme in its powers. In *McCulloch* v. *Maryland* (see □) the Supreme Court laid down two principles that have remained the cornerstone of federal-state relations: (1) the national government is constitutionally superior to the states, and in the case of conflict the former prevails; and (2) the *implied powers* of the national government give it great leeway in implementing policies that are not specifically authorized by the Constitution.

The doctrine of implied powers comes from the *necessary and proper* clause of the Constitution (Article I, Section 8), which permits Congress to use means that are "necessary and proper" to the execution of its delegated powers. The significance of *McCulloch* is not only that it established the federal government as more powerful than the states but that it paved the constitutional way for countless federal programs to deal with social problems not even dreamed of by the writers of the Constitution.

The Myth of Federalism

Certainly American government—federal, state, and local—has changed considerably from the time the government was moved (literally in the back of two Conestoga wagons) to its new home in Washington, D. C. Federalism, too, has changed, from a state-dominated system in which virtually all government services and policies (such as there were) came from the states, to a system of federal-state collaboration in the making of public policy (true only of domestic affairs, as the Constitution assigned the conduct of foreign affairs to the federal government). The changing nature of the federal bargain has paralleled the massive growth of government involvement in the private sector. Such involvement began in the 1830s when the Massachusetts state government required that local governments provide free public schools, and the city of Boston began to provide a regular police department. Since then, of course, all levels of government have become intimately involved with economic promotion and regulation, social welfare services, and a whole range of domestic policies.

Figure 2.9 There is a big difference between symbolic and effective public policy (left). The promise in the middle, if fulfilled with the real apartments to its right, will satisfy real needs. Promises fulfilled with symbolic "fronts," as on the far left, will hardly keep the rain off anyone.

□

McCULLOCH V. MARYLAND

In 1819, in the important case of <u>McCulloch v. Maryland,</u> the Supreme Court had the opportunity to choose between two different interpretations of the Constitution. The decision that was made set a precedent for the expanding role of the national government.

Maryland had levied a tax against the Baltimore branch of the Bank of the United States. McCulloch, a cashier in the federal bank, refused to pay the tax, arguing that a state could not tax a bank that had been established by Congress. He was defended by Daniel Webster of Massachusetts, an eloquent spokesman for a powerful national government.

John Marshall, the Chief Justice of the Supreme Court, agreed with the proponents of states' rights that the Con-stitution divided sovereignty between the states and the national government. But he also stated that "the government of the Union, though limited in its powers, is supreme within its sphere of action." Although Congress's power to charter a bank was not specifically stated in the Constitution, Marshall said it could be inferred from the "necessary and proper" clause of Article I. Congress had "implied powers" and therefore had the right to legislate with a "vast mass of incidental powers which must be involved in the Constitution, if that instrument be not a splendid bauble."

Marshall agreed with Daniel Webster that the establishment of a bank by Congress was an appropriate use of the implied powers clause. No state could use its reserved powers (the right to tax, for example) to hinder the national government's execution of its duties. "The power to tax," Marshall declared, "involves the power to destroy."

The decision in <u>McCulloch v. Maryland</u> was a momentous victory for the national government. It was based on John Marshall's belief that a narrow interpretation of the Constitution would unwisely restrict the operations of the national government and would make the problems of governing a growing nation even more difficult.

There are few issues more likely to divide Americans than the proper role of the public versus the private sectors in meeting human needs and the proper level of government to accomplish a desired action. Unfortunately, these issues have not always been separated, and sometimes the myth of federalism has blurred the realities.

According to the myth, two things have happened in the twentieth century: (1) government as a whole has grown at the expense of the private sector, and (2) the federal government has grown at the expense of the states.

First, it is true that the size of government *has* grown in the twentieth century. A large proportion of this growth, however (as shown in Chapter 5), comes from the growth of the military establishment, which now accounts, directly or indirectly, for more than half of federal government expenditures. A look at the *domestic* budget as a proportion of the Gross National Product (GNP)—the measure used to count a nation's riches—shows that government expenditures have changed since the time of the New Deal but not so dramatically as the myth suggests. In fact, despite the heavy federal commitments of the 1960s to domestic policies, such as President Johnson's Great Society Programs, the government spends (for nonmilitary needs) only a bit more of the GNP now than it did at the time of the New Deal, when all of the increase in governmental activism began.

The other half of the myth—the belief that the states are near death and that the federal government has swallowed them up—is constructed out of sheer imagination. Mark Twain once remarked when reading his own obituary that "the rumors of my death are greatly exaggerated." The same is true of the widely rumored demise of state and local governments. Whether measured in terms of employment, increases in expenditures, debt expansion, or whatever, the growth of state and local governments outstrips the expansion of the federal government. In fact, the states spend almost two-thirds of all domestic public expenditures in the United States, and they operate the most significant and controversial domestic programs (education, welfare, higher education, transportation, and so on).

Many critics, however, claim that the states are the weak links of the governmental chain and cite

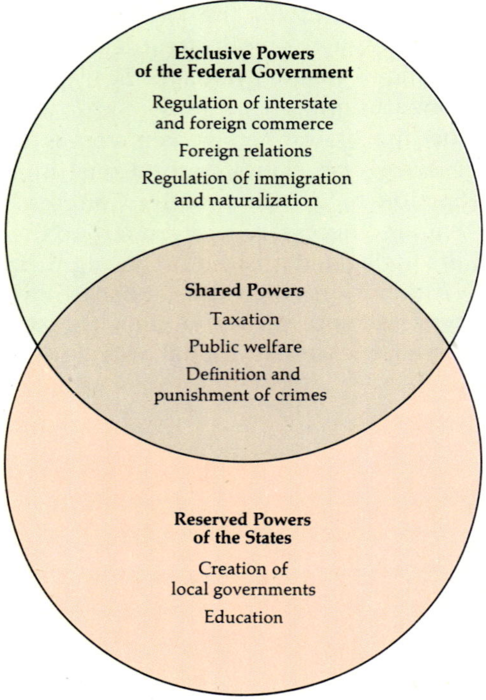

Figure 2.10 The United States Constitution provides for a federal form of government, under which certain powers are the exclusive prerogative of the federal (or national) government, other powers are reserved exclusively for the states, and still others are shared by the two governmental levels. The most obviously national policy area is foreign policy, whereas the most obviously state and local area of jurisdiction is education. Yet this diagrammatic representation tells only a part of the story, for states and local agencies have enormous influence on the actual results of national policies by virtue of their control over the administration of laws and programs at the citizen-consumer level; such implementation is usually in the hands of state or local agencies, whose activities may in effect follow, change, or even reverse the spirit and the letter of the law.

the fact that although the states spend most of the money, the policy initiative in domestic problems has shifted increasingly to the federal government. The states, they note, have long been bastions of rural interests (see ☐) and have left the cities, with all their problems, to fend for themselves. One urban mayor observed that "Everything we've gotten in this city is from the federal government. The state has not done one damned thing for us" (Ira Sharkansky, 1972). Terry Sanford, former governor of North Carolina, concedes in a book about the states that they are often "indecisive . . . antiquated . . . timid and ineffective . . . not willing to face their problems . . . not responsive . . . not interested in cities" (Sanford, 1967).

The states have been limited in their capacities to face twentieth-century problems not only because they have been dominated by rural forces but also because their boundaries encapsulate both their resources and their parochialisms. Economic development in the states has been uneven, and even though these differences have been reduced somewhat over the years, the range in economic well-being—and hence in taxable resources—is enormous. For instance, in Alabama, West Virginia, and Mississippi only one-quarter as many dollars are spent on each child's education as are spent in well-to-do states, such as New York, Connecticut, or Nevada. The federal system, which constitutionally reserves certain powers and therefore responsibilities to the states, thus imposes high social and economic costs on the citizens of the poorer states; because the most significant determinant of state expenditures is the wealth of a state (Thomas Dye, 1966), the poorest states necessarily provide the poorest services (schools, roads, and medical care).

State boundaries also make the enforcement of national policy more difficult. Because state politicians are responsible only to the voters of their state, they can engage in political maneuvers to further their sectional interests. Thus, federalism made it possible for George Wallace and Ross Barnett, governors of Alabama and Mississippi, to delay school integration. In many policy areas the states have the authority to temper, modify, and even negate—by failure to enforce—the impact of federal programs. Similarly, because the states send their representatives to Washington, federal policy mak-

☐

REAPPORTIONMENT

In 1900 three-fifths of the population of the United States lived in rural areas; today, over two-thirds of the people live in urban areas or their surrounding suburbs. But state legislatures have not reflected this increasing urbanization. Legislative districts from which representatives are elected have continued to reflect the rural dominance of 1900. In 1962, for example, the twenty-four inhabitants of the town of Stratton, Vermont enjoyed the same representation in the state's house of representatives as the city of Burlington, with its population of 35,531. Los Angeles County's 6,038,771 people received the same senate representation as 14,196 inhabitants of three Sierra Nevada mountain counties. Such discrepancies left urban dwellers in a far weaker political position than constituents from the countryside.

In 1964, in Reynolds v. Sims, the Supreme Court officially ruled that urban areas must be represented in both houses of the state legislature in direct proportion to their populations. In the words of Chief Justice Earl Warren: "Legislators represent people, not trees or acres." Basic to a representative form of government, the opinion continued, was the right of the citizen to cast his vote and to have it counted in full. Any substantial disparity in the population of legislative districts therefore had the same effect as allotting a different number of votes to different individuals. The Court had laid down the principle of "one man, one vote."

Political scientists have yet to agree on the political consequences of reapportionment. Some, such as Thomas Dye, contend that well-apportioned states are scarcely distinguishable in their policies from malapportioned states. Perhaps reapportionment has simply shifted power from rural, anti-city interests to suburban anti-city interests. The New York State legislature, for example, declined to provide significant help to the New York City subway system, which carries 2 million riders a day. It did, however, underwrite the losses of the Long Island Railroad, which carries 100,000 suburban commuters each day. Perhaps, too, the effects of reapportionment are more subtle and less dramatic than its proponents expected. Whatever the consequences, reapportionment has shifted power in the state legislature away from rural interests.

ing is also a compromise of regional interests (see Chapter 8). Civil rights legislation must therefore pass through Mississippi Senator Eastland's Judiciary Committee. Whether one views this system of regional influence over federal policies as good or bad is a function of one's evaluation of the interests that ought to be furthered or frustrated.

The Changing Nature of the Federal Bargain

There was a time when the states minded their own business (providing such minimal services as there were), and the federal government minded its affairs (which included the formulation and administration of foreign and military policy, operating the post office, and giving aid to favored domestic activities, such as farming and railroads). Cities, from the point of view of constitutional niceties, did not exist; they were legally the "creatures of the state." One early municipal government textbook dismissed the subject of federal-city relations in a single sentence—in that there were no relations, there was no point in investigating the subject. Under the old-style federalism, each level of government stayed out of the other's hair.

The years since the New Deal, however, have seen the explosion of a new-style federalism that has involved the interfacing of various layers of govern-ment. Most domestic programs are now operated jointly by the federal government and the states and/or cities. None of the essential state responsibilities is entirely the province of the state governments—such traditional state functions as education, law enforcement, and highway construction are now partially funded and administered by the federal government. No one has ever counted the exact number of these intergovernmental programs, but they probably exceed 1,000. The *Catalog of Federal Domestic Assistance* contains 180 pages of program descriptions for the Department of Health, Education, and Welfare alone, and most of the programs are intergovernmentally operated.

The Bias of Federalism

Like all political structures, federalism provides advantages to some interests and not to others. William Riker contends that federalism should be evaluated in terms of the interests it serves. A diverse collection of nations, large and small (the Soviet Union, Australia, Switzerland, Canada, Mexico, the United States, and others) are federalisms, and each contains at least one minority interest that is advantaged. As Riker observed:

[F]ederalism is a system of minority decision that imposes high external costs on everybody other than the minor-

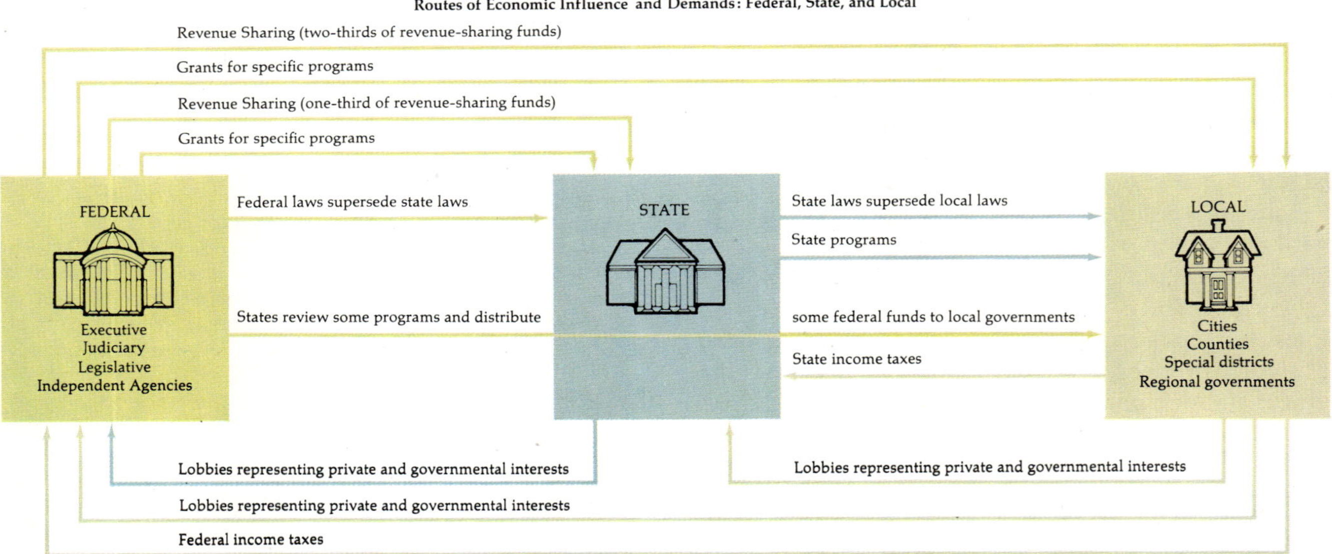

Routes of Economic Influence and Demands: Federal, State, and Local

ity. . . . If one approves the goals and values of the privileged minority, one should approve the federalism. Thus, if in the United States one approves of southern white racists, then one should approve of American federalism. (Riker, 1964, p. 195)

Does federalism promote racism? In an examination of the patterns of decision-making power in the area of civil rights policy it becomes clear that representatives of segregationist interests have enjoyed disproportionate power: They have been able to use governmental structures and institutions to block effective action toward integration. In the implementation process, it is also clear that the decentralization of power in the American federal system has permitted segregationist minorities to inhibit and frustrate the national policy of racial equality. Even though the abolishment of the federal system would hardly end racism in America, it is clear that federalism contributes—like all political institutions—to the furtherance of some interests and the frustration of others.

INTERESTS AND INSTITUTIONS

The institutions, rules, and structures that make up a political system are like a pinball machine in which the high-scoring zones are always controlled by certain interests and not others. Structures are never neutral. The American Constitution itself is an example of the biases inherent in the formal structure of a political system. The constitutional theory of Madison was designed to prevent undesirable interests from securing control of political institutions and running roughshod over other interests. The result, however, has been a system of proliferated institutions that clearly promotes the interests of some privileged minorities over others not so privileged. There are, to be sure, different interpretations of power in the American system. Some hold that power is concentrated in a monolithic elite, whereas others describe a competition of elites in which various interests can secure some of their claims some of the time. Both pluralists and elitists agree, however, that the diffuse nature of the American political structure makes it difficult—perhaps impossible—for a popular majority to work its will.

SUMMARY

The choices made by the founding fathers are as relevant today as the governmental decisions made since then; they provided the fundamental structures through which subsequent American history has been channeled. James Madison, the major philosopher of the Constitution, feared (1) that a minority might thwart the will of the majority, and (2) that an

Figure 2.11 Any federal system of government presents an intricate flow and interplay of influence, authority, and resources among the different levels. Three elements of this interplay are illustrated here: authoritative laws, interest representation (lobbying), and economic distribution. There is no particular beginning or end to this diagram because what is depicted is a continual, dynamic flow. The flow of revenue sharing refers to the enactment of the Nixon Administration's policy of returning to the states and local governments a percentage of the tax money that citizens have paid to the federal government. This program is still in the process of being defined with relation to what stipulations the federal government will attach to the spending of the returned funds and with relation to what authorities—governors, mayors, councilmen, county administrators—should be granted final decision-making power over the use of the money.

PLAYER 1 NATIONAL SECURITY
8 0 9 6
PLAYER 2 POVERTY PROGRAM
1 0 3 2
ACCESS
IDEOLOGY - INSTITUTIONS - ECONOMY
MEDIA ATTENTION
CORPORATIONS
MILITARY LEADERS
SUPREME COURT
PRESIDENT
CONGRESS
BUREAUCRATIC CHANNELS
STATE GOVERNMENT
LOCAL GOVERNMENT
DEMANDS
STATE COURTS
LOCAL COURTS
STATE SCHOOL BOARD
SCHOOL BOARD
HEALTH INSPECTORS
SHERIFF
UNMET DEMANDS
INTEREST
GROUPS
GROUPS
INTEREST

impassioned majority might undermine the freedom of minorities. The framers thus designed a government built on fragmented power—power was separated and was also checked and balanced so that action was only possible when there was widespread cooperation among competing interests.

Majorities thus do not rule; but the great debate in political science is whether contending minorities share the power (pluralism) or whether a single ruling minority dominates the country (elitism).

Federalism—the division of power between the central government, the states, and local governments—magnifies the abilities of minorities to impress their wills on the political process. The Constitution created governmental institutions, rules, and practices that are never neutral. The system was designed to frustrate action by an impassioned majority and to facilitate action by the minority that is able to mobilize sympathetic interests in its behalf.

SUGGESTED READINGS

Brown, Robert E. *Charles Beard and the Constitution.* Princeton, N. J.: Princeton University Press, 1956.

Elazar, Daniel. *American Federalism: A View from the States.* New York: Crowell, 1966.

McConnell, Grant. *Private Power and American Democracy.* New York: Knopf, 1967.

Prewitt, Kenneth and Alan Stone. *The Ruling Elites: Elite Theory, Power, and American Democracy.* New York: Harper & Row, 1973.

Schattschneider, E. E. *The Semisovereign People: A Realist's View of Democracy in America.* New York: Holt, Rinehart and Winston, 1960.

Figure 2.12 The great game of politics. In American politics one interest is played off against another: in reality, against many others. Our pinball machine is involved in the old game of guns versus butter—national security versus aid to the poor through the poverty program. Follow the pinball "demands." The point of access is narrow, and it takes both skill and luck to make it onto the playing board of American politics; once there, the player with the most resource-skills is clearly in a favored position to attain success. Each bounce off the resources of media attention, military leadership, and corporations produces points. Which player is most likely to make the most points here? Of course, hitting the major institutions—President, Court, or Congress—gives a special score. Next in line are the minor point makers at the state and local levels. Using the interest-group flippers with dexterity can smash an ignored demand right back up to the President or Congress. At any time there are a number of unmet demands waiting in the channel to become the concern of some group that has the resources to get into the game in the first place.

BE SOMEBODY

3

WEALTH
AND ITS DISTRIBUTION

Figure 3.1 "Be Somebody." Everyone wants to be somebody—but the question is: How? There used to be easier answers to such a question: Work hard! Be rich! Collectively, Americans are rich. But some are poor or near poor, and many live only on the edge of affluence. The unions help to distribute wealth; but only about a quarter of all workers belong to unions. Shares in corporations are a method of distributing ownership and profits; but although many individuals own stock, most own only a small number of shares and a few individuals and financial institutions own the great majority of shares. Well, people can work their way up; but factory signs that once read, "Irish need not apply," today say to the poor, "unskilled need not apply." How can you be somebody when so many doors seem closed?

Portions of this chapter have been excerpted from *The Economic Problem*, third edition, 1972, by Robert L. Heilbroner, with the permission of Dr. Heilbroner and the publisher, Prentice-Hall, Inc.

Karl Marx believed that economic factors substantially determine the politics, policies, ideologies, governmental structures, and even the histories of nations. Although many political scientists believe that Marx carried economic explanations too far, none would deny that economic factors play a fundamental role in all of these matters. How rich a nation is, where its wealth comes from, and how that wealth is used and distributed are factors that play a determining role in a nation's foreign and domestic affairs. As James Madison recognized, most political conflict is about economic matters: "... the most common cause and the most durable source of faction has been the various and unequal distribution of property. Those who hold and those who are without property have ever formed distinct interests in society" (Madison, 1788).

The three intertwined topics discussed in Unit I —the American ideology, America's political and governmental institutions, and the nature of the economy—are the holes in the IBM card marked "America." They work together to define our political options (see Figure 3.2). This chapter looks at the relationship among these three topics (how they shape and are shaped by one another) after it first considers the broad political implications of the American economy and some of its major internal features. The chapter ends with an examination of the major beneficiaries of government's economic policies and a discussion of the welfare system and the economics of inequality.

AMERICA THE RICH

Most of us have heard so often that the United States is the richest nation in the world that we have grown insensitive to just what "rich" means. Without a concrete understanding of how rich we are, we cannot recognize our position in world affairs nor can we understand how most other nations regard us.

Consider the following facts: Americans make up 5 percent of the people on earth and produce 30 percent of the world's gross national product (GNP), that is, the total value of all goods and services produced in a year. The GNP of the United States is a bit more than $1 trillion a year, an amount equal to the combined GNP of all the nations of Western Europe, Japan, and Canada. Americans use about 40 percent of the world's output of raw materials and produce about an equal amount of the world's waste products and pollution (see Figure 3.3).

To bring such numbers down to the individual level, America's GNP per capita (GNP divided by total population) amounts to $4,300 per year for every man, woman, and child—as compared to $3,700 for the next highest nation, Sweden, and $2,700 for West Germany, the land of the post-World War II "economic miracle." In some Asian and African nations GNP per capita is less than $100 per year—less than some Americans spend annually on cigarettes.

These incredible contrasts powerfully shape America's relations with other nations. Our economic resources make it possible for us to be a military superpower, although we rarely need military might to dominate other nations' affairs. Our domination is primarily economic, through ownership of basic industries in other nations and through the purchase of the raw materials and foodstuffs that are the basis of their economies. Many nations are "client states," whose economic welfare depends on our policies (and the health of our economy). Their internal politics must meet with our approval, because we may punish them economically (or possibly even more directly) if they pursue policies or install a government not to our liking.

Our dominance of other nations' economies and politics is understandably offensive to many of their citizens. They feel that our abundance is at their expense, that they are providing the raw material and the profits that sustain our high standard of living. Whereas Americans annually spend over $250 million (some estimate that the figure is closer to $1 billion) on efforts to lose weight (Robert Sherrill, 1971), many inhabitants of Third World nations (Asia, Africa, Latin America) exist on the borderline of malnutrition, unable to attain even a minimal diet of 2,500 calories a day. Their resentment can easily be understood.

Worse yet, the economic gap between the underdeveloped nations and rich nations such as the United States is getting wider each year. In terms of per capita GNP we are farther ahead of nations such as India and Chile than we were ten years ago.

But what about our foreign aid to these nations and the billions of dollars our banks and industries invest in their economies? Why has the economic gap not been reduced? First, the economies of most Third World nations have expanded considerably in recent years; but their population growth has eaten up all gains and left them worse off than before. Furthermore, much of our economic aid goes into military assistance and is thus unproductive of

economic advances in these countries (see Chapter 5). But most important, our foreign investments are made to earn money, not to give it away. United States corporations, for example, invested $3.8 billion in Latin America from 1957 to 1964 and reaped $11.3 billion in profits—a net gain of $7.5 billion—during the same period. Our foreign investments actually increase the economic gap between us and poorer nations (Howard Sherman, 1972).

To sum up, America is rich beyond the comprehension of most of the rest of the world. But the gargantuan size of our total wealth masks a seamy side of American life.

THE OTHER AMERICA

The wealth is there—but so is an extraordinary indifference in its use. Far from enjoying the highest standard of general well-being of any nation on earth, Americans live with a degree of social neglect comparable to that of some of the poorest nations on earth (Robert Heilbroner, 1971).

Social Neglect

The United States spends a higher proportion of its GNP on health services than any other nation. One might therefore suppose that life expectancy in this country would be the highest in the world. It is not.

In 1968 the United States ranked eighteenth in male life expectancy and tenth in female life expectancy. Perhaps even more shocking, it ranked nineteenth in infant mortality, putting it roughly at the level of Hong Kong.

Or take the quality, rather than the "quantity," of life as an indicator of relative well-being. There exists no official index of the extent of slums or urban decay here or in other nations, but anyone who has traveled abroad knows that to match the lower depths of New York, Detroit, Chicago, or any large American city one must visit not Europe but the underdeveloped world. To put it the other way around, any traveler knows that the general cleanliness and decency to be found in virtually *all* Scandinavian, West German, Swiss, or Dutch cities is simply not to be found in *any* large metropolitan area in the United States.

Nor is it merely a matter of urban blight. The rural slums in America also vie with those of the underdeveloped world in terms of sheer misery and neglect. Nearly a quarter of the (white) population of eastern Kentucky, for example, cannot read or write, and malnutrition to the point of actual starvation has been discovered in some sections of the South and Southwest. If America is the richest nation in the world, it is also one of the more socially neglectful—

Figure 3.2 The IBM card marked "America" (left). Every nation has a special "profile" defined by its ideological, institutional, and economic characteristics. These major facets of a nation's identity work together to define the political options available; they determine what a nation believes, what it honors and desires, and what policies it will disdain or reject.

Figure 3.3 It is obvious from this diagram (right) that Americans constitute an exceedingly small proportion of the world's population, in fact, only 5 percent. It is also clear that Americans both produce and consume much more than their population would suggest, compared to the rest of the world. Other interesting observations may be made from this chart; for example, that Americans import much of their energy resources and many of their automobiles and that they use a high percentage of the world's telephones.

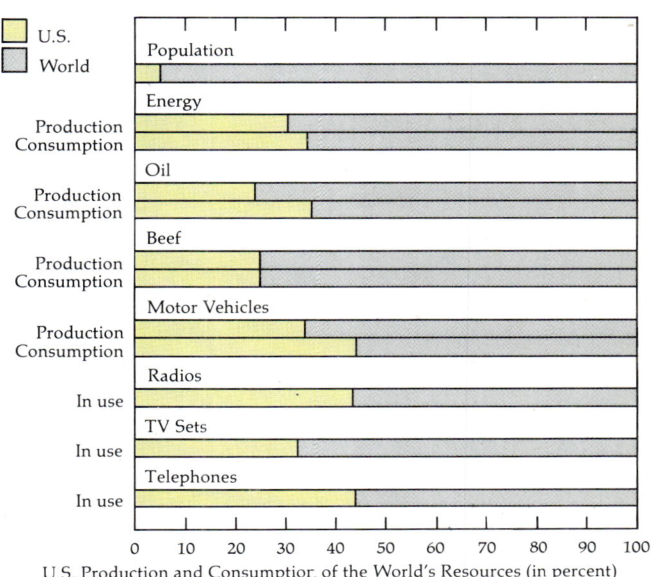

ignorant of, or acquiescent in, conditions that many less wealthy nations no longer tolerate.

Poverty Accepted

Poverty is, of course, a relative concept. A Calcutta family of street dwellers would consider itself unimaginably well-off if it were given rupees equal to welfare payments made to a family in Mississippi (1969: $47 per month).

With all the problems of defining poverty, however, few would call the present United States definition extravagant. The federal government establishes a poverty threshold that ranges from $2,010 for a single person living in a metropolitan area to $6,468 for a city-dwelling family of seven. By this definition, 12.6 percent of Americans in 1970 were poor. For the nation as a whole (with the totals for rural areas added in), roughly one family in seven is officially considered "poor" and perhaps double that number "near-poor" (Anthony Downs, 1970).

But these overall figures dilute what poverty means to those who suffer from it, for the incidence of poverty is not random. Certain groups of Americans—the aged, blacks, broken families—are more likely to regard poverty as a near-normal state of affairs rather than as an unhappy accident. Put differently, whereas 52 percent of all white American families in 1970 enjoyed incomes of more than $10,000 a year, only 28 percent of black (and other racial minority) families had reached this degree of modest affluence; and whereas only 7.5 percent of white families fell below $3,000 a year, 20 percent of minority families were clustered in this lowest range.

Because of this clustering we cannot regard poverty with complacency, secure in the knowledge that the problem will gradually disappear. Although poverty has been slowly shrinking within American society as a whole, it rose 5 percent from 1969 to 1970, reversing a ten-year trend. Furthermore, poverty is not shrinking in certain critical areas. As the racial composition of the cities changes, for example, the concentration of poverty in cities becomes worse, not better. It is estimated that we can expect an *additional* 1.4 million nonwhite poor children in our central cities by 1985 (Downs, 1970). What effect this increased concentration of the desperately poor will have on the crime rate, the drug problem, and the general civility in those cities can only be imagined.

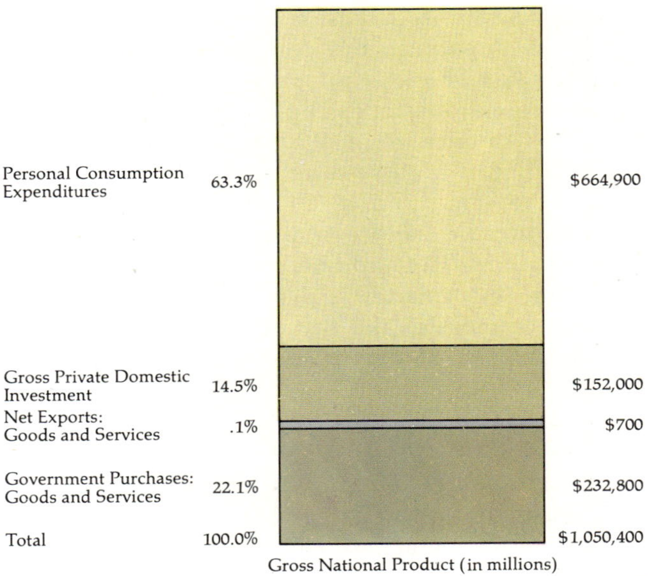

Figure 3.4 The gross national product is the basis for many comparisons of wealth, on a national and international scale (from the Bureau of Economic Analysis).

Figure 3.5 The changes in the total gross national product are seen in relation to the elements that comprised it over the years 1950–1971 (from the U.S. Department of Commerce, 1971).

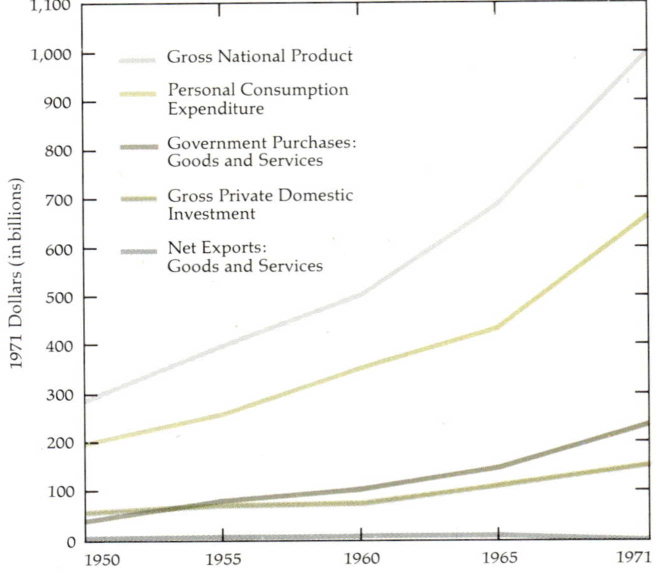

The vast amount of junk that Americans toss away every year includes:

214 million tons of carbon monoxide, sulfur oxides, hydrocarbons, particulates, and nitrous oxides (over a ton per American)

55 billion tin cans (275 for each of us)

20 billion bottles (100 apiece)

65 billion metal and plastic bottle caps (325 each)

7 million cars (our annual output has to go *somewhere* after 100,000 miles or so)

10 million tons of steel and iron scrap (an average of 1,000 pounds each)

150 million tons of garbage and trash (4.1 pounds per person daily)

3 billion tons of tailings, mine debris, and waste (4 tons for each of us each day).

(list from Heilbroner, 1972).

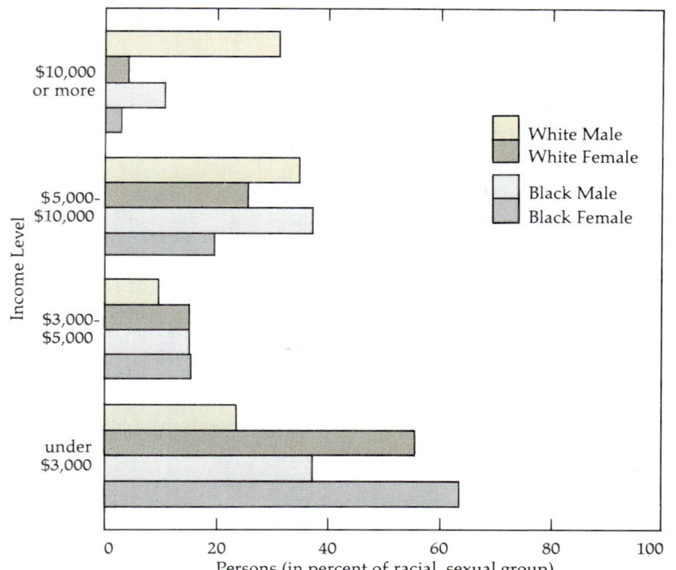

Figure 3.6 **The amount of junk Americans dispense with yearly (above). The discrepancies between the earnings of males and females and between blacks and whites (below). This chart details the amounts of these discrepancies as of March 1972 (from the U.S. Department of Commerce, 1972).**

Poverty must be considered an aspect of social neglect by any nation affluent enough to eliminate it. And for Americans, this aspect is perhaps the most disturbing of all, for the diversion of between 1 and 1.5 percent of the nation's GNP to all officially "poor" families would, within five years, bring them up to minimum levels of decency.

But so far, no such willingness has been visible, either within Congress or elsewhere. As one observer has bitterly commented: "The middle class knows that the economists are right when they say that poverty could be eliminated if only we will it; they simply do not will it."

The fact that America is rich but that many Americans have been bypassed by its riches bears strongly on the political situation. Also important is the fact that the United States operates under a capitalist economic system.

CAPITALISM AND SOCIALISM DEFINED

The most pervasive and enduring political conflict of modern times concerns the relative wonders of capitalism and socialism. Both are praised and damned, both are accused of repression, exploitation, and enslavement, and both are blessed as the road to utopia. Many observers blame all America's flaws on its capitalistic system. They claim that people remain poor in the midst of plenty because of capitalism and that we exploit poor nations because we are capitalistic.

Other observers maintain that we owe our economic success to capitalism and that our flaws stem not from capitalism per se but from peculiar features of our ideology and governmental structure that have little or nothing to do with capitalism. These conflicting claims must be considered. Before they are discussed, however, socialism and capitalism must be defined. Although there are no completely accepted definitions, some general characteristics of each can be outlined.

Capitalism as an economic system permits and protects *legal private ownership of the means of production.* In practice, the capital goods of a society—its factories, machines, land—are owned by individuals who have the right to use this property for their own private gain. In addition, the distribution of resources and wealth is mainly determined by a *competitive market system.* What is produced, what it costs, and who will receive it are determined by competitive operations according to the costs of supply and the demands of consumers. Obviously, all capitalist economies impose some rules and limits on the market system—for example, the United States has outlawed price-fixing and requires that many products must meet quality and safety standards. Nevertheless, most decisions are left to the market. Thus, for example, automobile production and cost are left to the automakers and not set by government economic planners.

Socialism is in many ways the mirror image of capitalism. In principle, socialism denies the right of private ownership of the major means of production; capital equipment is owned in common, either by the government or by other public bodies (for example, communes and cooperatives). Instead of relying on a market system to determine production and distribution, socialism favors a *planned* economy.

To what extent are the accomplishments and the failures of the American economic system a result of capitalism?

It is not at all clear that America's preeminent economic position is the result of capitalism. Many socialist states have vigorous economies, and many capitalist nations do not. Raw materials, geography, and cultural tradition seem to have much more to do with economic power than does the fact that economic power is managed according to socialist or capitalist principles. China has made stunning economic progress since it shifted to socialism. Cuba has not. Russia became a military superpower under socialism, America under capitalism.

Many critics of socialism charge that government planning necessarily destroys freedom. But there seems to be no connection between the two. The most socialistic of the capitalist nations—the Scandinavian block, England, and New Zealand—are among the freest nations on earth. More unregulated capitalist nations such as Greece, Spain, and Brazil are dictatorships.

CAPITALISM AND AMERICAN CAPITALISM

It is not at all clear that the failures of the American economy—poverty and social neglect—are the inevitable consequences of capitalism. The argument that these ills will never be cured "by a government run by and for the rich, as every capitalist govern-

Figure 3.7 We suggest here some of the basic values of certain important ideologies, along with the power and status relationships that seem to arise from the attempted implementation of such values. These forms cannot be applied directly to actual societies and nations, because the complex realities of such nations overlap these models. Thus, the United States lies somewhere in the area between Liberalism II and Democratic Socialism—an area in which the "welfare state" lies—in view of American emphasis on socioeconomic mobility and the rise of a powerful public bureaucracy. Norway is similarly situated although much further along toward Democratic Socialism than is the United States. Soviet leaders assert that their nation is moving from Communism I toward Communism II, although some others perceive a persistent and contradictory elitist factor in Soviet government.

The boldfaced labels for each ideology refer to key goals. For example, in Liberalism I, the ideal type of nineteenth-century (classical) Liberalism, the dominant view of society was modeled after Darwinian competition—it was expected that the most intelligent and industrious would deservedly rise over others to the top.

In Liberalism II (or modern Liberalism), we find competing goals, which create its characteristic ideological fuzziness: the goal of socioeconomic mobility (primarily upward) and the goal of "socially guaranteed security." The economic side of Liberalism is usually referred to as capitalism (free enterprise for Liberalism I and regulated enterprise for Liberalism II). Politically, Liberalism evolved from the ideal of paternalistic elite leadership (Liberalism I) to the ideal of widespread electoral participation and extensive civil rights and liberties (Liberalism II).

The economic goal of Democratic Socialism is scientific integration of production and well-planned distribution of services. This ideology advocates the maintenance of some kinds of incentive systems and private enterprise but a weakening of economic interest-group power. Politically, Democratic Socialism provides for political oppositions, widespread political participation, and attempts to equalize resources for political power.

Communism I provides for collective ownership and control of production, which, it is assumed, will result in greater production once the artificial goals associated with profit motives are removed. Progressive sharing of wealth and economic control is intended to equalize resources for political power: the state operates in the name of and for the mass of workers. To the Communist, this ideological step is a transition toward Communism II, an ideological construct qualitatively different from previous ones. In Communism II there are no more class and power hierarchies as in previous ideologies.

In Communism II, perhaps roughly comparable to commune life in China, economic planning becomes a rationalized, routine chore. With the rationalization of economic life and the abolition of profit motives, all persons become workers in the sense that they contribute according to their gifts and participate in work for its own interest or as a public duty. Individual expression is not abolished, but the problem of individual versus the state dissolves because the state no longer can be influenced by favored minorities. The "state" in the sense of the locus of struggle for power and control "withers away."

The various layers in all of these models are only rough indications of how historical cases that are related to the model actually worked and how values and realities seemed to combine.

LIBERALISM I
Wealthy elite (entrepreneurial wealth)
Aristocracy and political elites
Skilled-worker elite
Low-paid, unskilled, male workers
Upward and downward socioeconomic mobility
Horatio Alger notion
Women and children workers
Marginal poverty class
Impoverished class (unemployed, elderly, sick)

LIBERALISM II
Wealthy elite (inherited and speculative wealth)
Political, social, industrial, and military elites
Worker elites (highly paid, unionized)
Goal of socially guaranteed security
Middle-class clerical and manual workers
Goal of socioeconomic mobility
Women employed in the home
Marginal poverty class
Impoverished class (unemployed, elderly, sick)

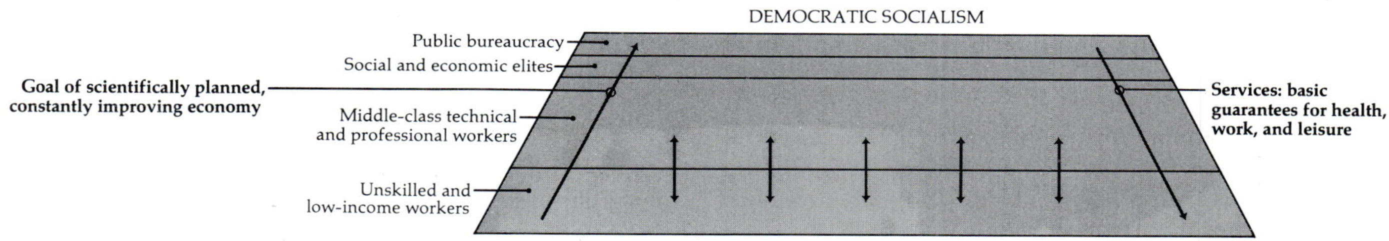

DEMOCRATIC SOCIALISM
Public bureaucracy
Social and economic elites
Goal of scientifically planned, constantly improving economy
Middle-class technical and professional workers
Unskilled and low-income workers
Services: basic guarantees for health, work, and leisure

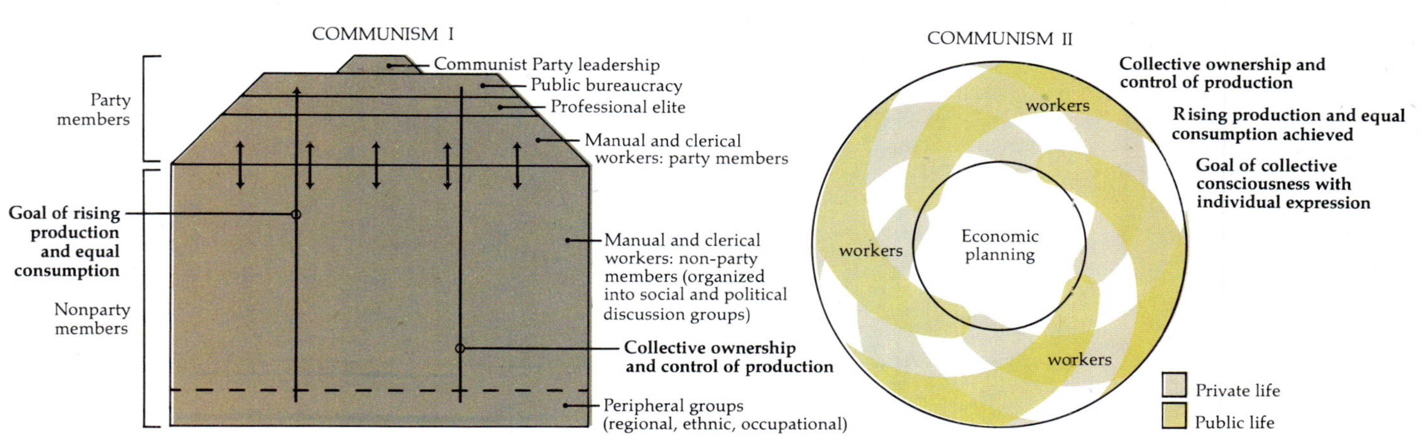

COMMUNISM I
Communist Party leadership
Public bureaucracy
Professional elite
Manual and clerical workers: party members
Party members
Goal of rising production and equal consumption
Nonparty members
Manual and clerical workers: non-party members (organized into social and political discussion groups)
Collective ownership and control of production
Peripheral groups (regional, ethnic, occupational)

COMMUNISM II
Collective ownership and control of production
Rising production and equal consumption achieved
Goal of collective consciousness with individual expression
workers
workers
workers
Economic planning
Private life
Public life

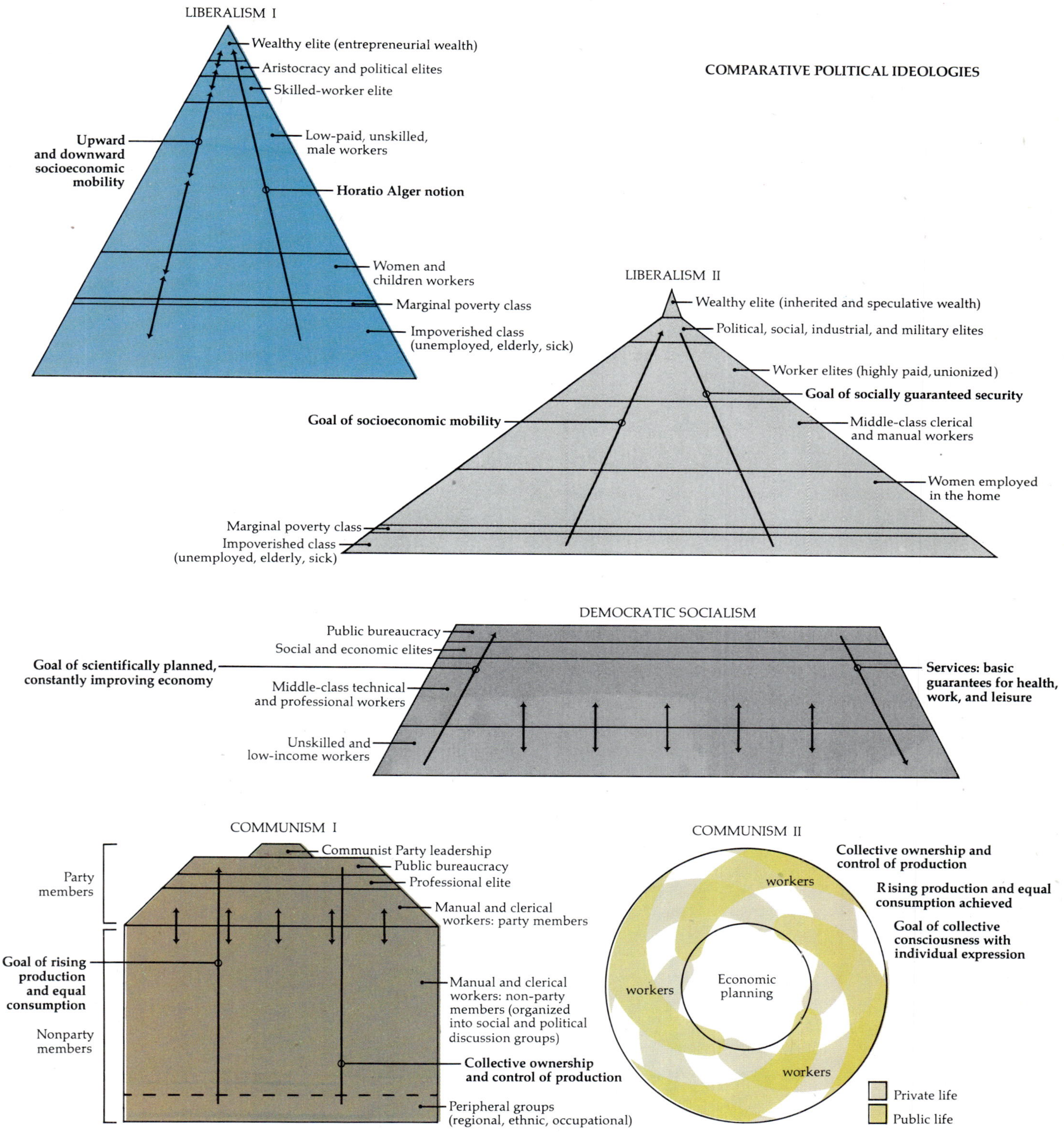

ment is and must be'' (Paul Baran and Paul Sweezy, 1966), breaks down with a glance at other capitalist nations. A comparison between the United States and Norway (both capitalist nations in terms of their private ownership of the means of production) makes the point.

Capitalism Compared: America and Norway

When the United States is compared with Norway in terms of various indicators of social well-being, we show up poorly indeed. Infant mortality in Norway is 50 percent lower than it is in the United States. Norway spends a higher proportion of its GNP on education and on social security than we do; and its cities are essentially free of slums. Although Norwegian citizens have a much lower per capita GNP than American citizens, ''poverty'' as a relative condition—as a human condition of neglect by society—has been virtually eliminated there.

This superior record of social welfare in Norway suggests large differences in the economic structures of the two countries—in their income distributions, for instance. Yet, there are not. The pre-tax distribution of income—that is, the relative income of rich and poor as determined by the market mechanism—is much the same in both nations. The difference lies in a comparison of tax structures. In contrast to the tax structure of the United States, the Norwegian tax structure is one of the most progressive in the world; it includes a system of subsidies to low-income groups, which greatly lightens their net tax burden. The point, of course, is clear: The competition of the marketplace need not leave an irretrievable mark on society, for uneven income distribution can be radically modified through such means as taxes and transfers, as is the case in Norway (Alan Gruchy, 1966).

The implications are sobering as well as encouraging: It seems that much of what troubles America cannot be uniquely attributed to capitalism per se. The low level of social services in America, the enormous role played by the military, the ''rat-race'' tempo of American life, the extent of our slums, the callous treatment of criminals, the obsession with ''communism,'' and many other unlovely aspects of our social system are not predominant in many other capitalist systems.

The problem, in other words, resides more in those elements of our society that are *American* than in those that are capitalist. To put it differently, it is necessary to understand why capitalism here has not achieved the possibilities realized by capitalism elsewhere rather than to compare the deficiencies of life in America with the presumed advantages that so-

cialism might bring. For unless we understand and correct the failures of American capitalism, it is likely that changing our economic system would produce only an American socialism that would manifest many of the failings of American capitalism.

To determine those elements in America that have molded "American" capitalism, it is necessary to reconsider topics taken up in Chapters 2 and 3. There are intimate links between the American economy and the American ideology. Similarly, our political institutions both shape and are shaped by our economy.

Economy and Ideology

The unusual degree of social neglect that exists within the wealthiest nation on earth stems partly from the American ideology—what we believe and value. In turn, the success of our economy reinforces our commitment to those beliefs and values.

Recall from Chapter 1 that the American ideology was free to develop in the virgin territory of the New World, unhampered by the constraints of an aristocratic tradition. However, the very lack of an aristocratic tradition has undercut the development of a sense of social responsibility. The notion of *noblesse oblige*—that it is the duty of nobility to provide for less fortunate subjects—helped the evolu-

tion of welfare-state capitalism in Europe. The lack of such a tradition has presumably hampered a similar development in the United States.

Alexis de Tocqueville, the great nineteenth-century French observer, wrote perceptively about the difference in traditions when he visited America:

Aristocracy [he wrote] links everybody, from peasant to king, in one long chain. Democracy breaks the chain and frees each link. As social equality spreads, there are more and more people who, though neither rich nor powerful enough to have much hold over others, have gained or kept enough wealth and enough understanding to look after their own needs. Such folk owe no man anything and hardly expect anything from anybody. They form the habit of thinking of themselves in isolation and imagining that their whole destiny is in their own hands. Thus, not only does democracy make men forget their ancestors, it also clouds their view of their descendants, and isolates them from their contemporaries. Each man is forever thrown back on himself alone, and there is a danger that he may be shut up in the solitude of his heart. (Tocqueville, 1835, p. 478)

With eloquence and perception, Tocqueville points to a deep difference between democratically based and aristocratically based social systems: an inhibition in the feeling of social responsibility of a democratic society compared with one of more aristocratic

Figure 3.8 Every nation has its temples—stately edifices that convey a sense of respect and reverence. The heavy, solid architecture of banks gives the impression that one's money is safe and secure. But as the banker has been traditionally counted among the pillars of his community, so the pillars he raised in reflection of Greek or Egyptian temples have helped to define the priorities of his community. "The business of America is business," said President Calvin Coolidge, and there have been few who would argue with him. And even though banks have made much effort to erect less formidable structures and to give an appearance of accessibility, questions have begun to arise about the social responsibilities of society's financial institutions. There is increasing concern that the managers of profit and investment must justify their existence not in terms of their architectural facades but instead in terms of fair interest-statements and socially equitable loan policies.

lineage. The suggestion is that Americans have not developed an effective attack on social problems because there is no popular support for the idea that government *should* help the needy. The result has been not only an anesthetizing of the American social conscience but a paralysis of the mechanism by which that conscience might best be expressed.

Thus, social neglect is a direct result of the lack of a sense of community, which stems from the belief that each individual is responsible for his own fate. Many Americans believe that both success and poverty are individual matters. They accept the basic principle of the work ethic (also called the Protestant or Liberal ethic—see Chapter 1) that hard work will be rewarded and that poverty is the result of sinful laziness. It follows that welfare or guaranteed incomes, both provided by taxing hard-working Americans, are unfair rewards for laziness.

From its earliest days America has been considered a land of opportunity. It is true that most immigrants quickly achieved a level of wealth far beyond anything they could have hoped for in their homeland. As a result, their twentieth-century descendants are suspicious of claims that there were others who did not succeed, who became "trapped" in poverty. The incredible level of American success, which is measured in terms of the wealth of the average person, furthers the belief that hard work leads *automatically* to success.

Furthermore, even most Americans who are not very successful tend to blame themselves and not the injustices of the economic situation (Robert Lane, 1962). An important reason is that they do not regard themselves as belonging to a class permanently locked into a low economic position; they recognize that, despite their own lack of success, there is a substantial chance that their children will achieve much greater success.

The proportion of persons rising to economic positions above that of their parents is relatively high in all industrialized nations. What is unusual about upward economic movement in the United States is the proportion of persons from very low economic backgrounds who achieve elite occupational positions. Thus, whereas 1 out of every 10 sons of American fathers with manual occupations rises to an elite professional and managerial position, only 1 out of 30 in Sweden, 1 out of 45 in Great Britain, and only

1 out of 100 in Denmark achieves such a dramatic rise in social standing (Peter Blau and Otis Dudley Duncan, 1967). The Horatio Alger rags-to-riches story is more than a myth in America; the relative frequency with which it actually happens tends to reinforce American faith in individualism.

The widespread and mistaken belief that most poor people are black people also adds to white, middle-class resistance against social programs to help them (see Table 3.1). However, as is shown in

Table 3.1 Poverty in the U.S., 1972

	TOTAL POOR (in millions)	PERCENT OF GROUP'S POPULATION
White	17.5	10
Black	7.5	34

Source: Bureau of the Census, 1972.

the Perspective on poor whites in Appalachia (Chapter 4a), Americans have not been any more responsive to white than to black poverty.

Economy and Political Institutions

Chapter 2 suggests the role that economic interests play in the creation of American political structures. Recall that a major concern of the founding fathers was to block unrestrained majority rule. They designed an elaborate checks-and-balances system within which minorities would have many opportunities to thwart majority intentions. One of the reasons they did so was to protect the propertied class, of which they were a part. The system was designed so that government action would ordinarily require a coalition of minority interests.

Over time, however, the system has been very successfully used for individual interests by those groups that have had the capability of mobilizing political power. To get a larger slice of the action for themselves, these groups have found it necessary to make trade-offs with other groups. Thus, agricultural interests have supported oil-depletion allowances in return for support for farm subsidies, and unions have cooperated with manufacturers to seek trade restrictions in return for higher minimum wage laws.

In many ways the American political system is responsible for the unequal distribution of American wealth. First, the system is ideal for the defense of vested interests. Efforts to remove certain tax benefits given to corporations and the wealthy typically have been ambushed in the thicket of checks and balances (see Chapter 2). Second, groups with little political power tend to get left out of the bargaining process: The system responds to pressure, not to the justice of the plea. Groups that cannot speak for themselves, that are not mobilized, are ignored. Thus, the scattered, unorganized, unsophisticated rural poor have been left out of the American affluence. So too have black people, Mexican-Americans, and Indians. Interests are heard only as they effectively enter the political arena.

WHERE DOES GOVERNMENT GET ITS MONEY?

The United States government and the state and local governments raise most of their money through taxes or by borrowing. The various kinds of taxes collected in the United States are shown in Table 3.2.

Table 3.2   Tax Revenues Collected by Federal, State, and Local Government, 1970–1971

TYPE OF TAX	REVENUE (in billions)
Individual Income Taxes	98.1
Corporate Income Taxes	30.2
Sales Taxes	52.7
Property Taxes	37.9
Social Security and Retirement Taxes	51.3
Other Taxes	13.4

Source: U.S. Bureau of the Census. *Governmental Finances in 1970–71.* Series GF-71, No. 5. (Washington, D.C.: Government Printing Office, 1972), Table 1.

Besides levying taxes, governments resort to borrowing when their tax revenues are not enough for their needs. Borrowing is usually done in the form of selling bonds, on which the government promises to pay a certain amount of interest each year to everyone who holds the bond. Federal government bonds are a very safe investment because they are backed by the United States Treasury. States and localities, however, have sometimes not been able to meet their interest payments. On occasion, such as during the Depression when many cities went bankrupt, cities have been unable to pay back the principal (the amount paid for the bond) that was borrowed. Our national debt, which is the result of federal government borrowing, is very large; it has increased mostly during wars, when the government has been forced to borrow large sums of money to finance its military spending.

If a government cannot collect enough in taxes and cannot raise enough money even by going into debt through bond sales, there is a third way for the government to raise money: It can simply print more money. Of course, this solution can cause problems. When more and more money is put into circulation, rapid *inflation* results—each dollar is worth less in terms of purchasing power. The purchasing power of the dollar can get so low that the cost of the paper on which to print the new money is higher than the value of the new money. In desperation, several nations have printed so much money that it was worth almost nothing—such was the case in Germany in the 1920s.

PUBLIC POLICY: THE ECONOMICS OF POWER

Government is the largest single spender in our economy—about one dollar out of every four of our GNP is a government dollar. Any discussion of the implications that our economy has for public policy must therefore begin with some attention to the economy *as* public policy.

The United States government has always been a big spender, even in peacetime. During the nineteenth century, government at all levels was involved in activities designed to aid the development of industry and commerce. The large sums of money needed for economic development were not available from private sources, so government became heavily involved. Canal builders, bankers, and railroad owners have long been recipients of government aid. Still, by 1929, government spending represented only 9.8 percent of our GNP. The Great Depression of the 1930s pushed government spending to 19 percent in order to fulfill President Roosevelt's promises to keep the country going. During World War II government spending was raised to incredible heights to finance military production—it spent 41 percent of the GNP in both 1943 and 1944. When peace came, spending dropped back to prewar levels. But the Soviet-American confrontation of the post-World

AN ALTERNATIVE SOCIETY

by Arnold Toynbee

Human beings have two problems to deal with: our relations with each other and our relations with the non-human constituents of our habitat—the "biosphere" that coats our planet. Like other living creatures we have to draw on the biosphere's limited resources for winning our material livelihood, and we have far surpassed every other species in compelling the biosphere to yield to us what we want from it.

Human technology is brilliant, and its efficiency is increasing at an accelerating pace. But technology is dependent on sociality. Even the most primitive of our human tools could not ever have been invented and operated by a solitary Robinson Crusoe. The effectiveness of our human technology is limited by the degree of our human society's success; and, unhappily, the brilliance of our technological record presents an ever greater contrast to our dismal social failure.

The social insects' history has been the reverse of ours. The individual bee, ant, or termite has a built-in dedication to the service of its community, and this social instinct has enabled these species to maintain themselves for hundreds of millions of years—in contrast to the couple of million years for which recognizable hominids have been in existence to date.

Mankind needs to achieve a social harmony of the social insects' standard, but this task is harder for us than it has been for them. Our human sociality is not built in to human nature, unlike the social insects'. We have a certain amount of freedom of choice, and we can, and often do, use our freedom to behave antisocially. In the atomic age into which our accelerating technological advance has now carried us, a persistence in antisocial conduct spells, for mankind, the self-extinction of our species. Our present form of human society is morally delinquent. Mankind's most urgent business today is to discover and establish an alter-native form of society that will close our present scandalous and perilous "morality gap" or, short of closing it, will at least reduce it drastically.

The alternatives that we are being offered today are shams. The ideological and religious differences that politicians exploit for arousing mass emotions are superficial. Beneath these specious labels there is today only one single global society. Present-day society is global because present-day technology is. The potency of this global technology requires a society of human beings who are morally fit to handle poisonous tools and lethal weapons. This problem touches the quick, and no current ideology or religion is probing down to it, though there are some private groups of pioneers who are looking for a new way.

The balance sheet of the latest 100 years of human history shows the need for change. On the credit side we have an increase of wealth and health. Even the still indigent two-thirds of mankind are possibly wealthier, and are certainly healthier, than they were 100 years ago. But these gains have been bought at the price of heavy spiritual as well as material losses. The chronic growth of mankind's "gross product" is robbing still unborn generations of their patrimony by polluting the biosphere and using up its material resources. We hold our command of these resources in trust for posterity. We are betraying this trust, and, in committing this and other moral misdemeanors, we are making ourselves profoundly unhappy.

Our increasing material affluence is leaving us unsatisfied, strained, restless, and haunted by a fear of being released by death from a life that we do not enjoy or, for the Hindu and Buddhist majority of mankind, by a more logical fear of being reincarnated. Violence is

mounting (two world wars in one lifetime, genocide, the forcible eviction of
people from their homes, and private
crimes of violence for economic gain,
or out of animosity, or even for fun).
There is an increase in dishonesty and
in the decline of our standard of work-
manship. "Permissiveness" and sexual
promiscuity are undermining family
life—the indispensable psychological
and moral setting for children.

Our children are repudiating the society into which they are growing up.
This society has been made what it
now is partly by the adolescents' pre-
cocious selves, as well as by their
elders and by their predecessors in
previous generations. But the young
perceive only their elders' responsibility, and this has created a generation gap of reciprocal misunderstanding and hostility.

Our present form of society is truly
repulsive. It condemns both individuals
and communities to run a "rat race" in
which success and failure are measured
by the percentage of mankind's gross
product that a community or an individual succeeds in appropriating by
ruthless competition. Human beings
used to be ashamed of the greed in
which they indulged until Adam Smith
suggested that the self-seeking of individuals is beneficial for society. We
have eagerly adopted his doctrine,
without paying attention to his reservations, because in 1776—the year in
which The Wealth of Nations was
published—a great spurt in the advance of technology was giving us the
tools for making our greedy self-seeking
pay unprecedentedly high dividends
to an adroit or lucky minority.

The formidable fundamental question
now is: What is life for? Assuredly
every human being ought to try to
achieve something in his lifetime. But
personal achievement need not, and
ought not, to be found in self-seeking;
it can and should be found in activities
that benefit other human beings, including posterity. This is the professional

objective of doctors—according to the
Hippocratic Oath—and of nurses, probation officers, teachers, and ministers
of religion. Their profession must in-
cidentally win a livelihood for these
dedicated people and for their families,
but this is incidental to their service for
humanity. If and when they make material profit the paramount objective of
their work, they are no longer being
true to their professional ideals. This is
the right standard for all of us.

An alternative society? Here are a
few of the questions that we need to
ask and to answer in exploring alternative social possibilities. Ought we
to love all our fellow human beings
equally, as Mo Ti and Jesus taught? Or
should there be gradations in our affec-
tion and concern, as was held by Con-
fucius and by Mencius? What kind of
family life offers the best start for children? How are we to deal with sex?
Nature has made us sexual animals,
but something has made us also human beings. We need to harmonize the
necessity of sexual procreation with our
human dignity and happiness, which
are not compatible with an unregulated indulgence of our built-in sexual
appetite.

The reduction of the death-rate calls,
in our limited biosphere, for an artificial limitation on the size of the
planet's human population. The op-
timum size of population is the size
that offers the most promising spiritual
and material possibilities for every child
that is born. The estimate is difficult to
calculate, but it is not impossible, and
it must be done; it is indispensable.
Technology has now knit together,
into a single society, all human beings
all around the globe, but the maximum

size of a community whose members
can know each other personally is
small—not more than a few hundreds.
How can we combine the global community, which we need for preventing
war and the pollution and depletion
of resources, with a vast number of
small local communities confined to
neighbors whose relations with each
other can be direct and personal?

How are we to face death? A human
being is unique among living creatures
in knowing in advance that he is going
to die. The Pharaonic Egyptians knew
how, and so did the believers in Ju-
daism, Christianity, and Islam. How
are we to face rebirth, if we believe
(as a majority of human beings do) in
the reality of this? Hindus and Bud-
dhists know how. In order to face either
death or rebirth, we need to be in touch
with, and in harmony with, the ultimate spiritual reality that is in and
behind and beyond the phenomena.
For some people this spiritual presence
is a human-like god; for others it is
a suprapersonal spirit; but, in whatever form we conceive of it, it is a
reality for every human being, including those who fancy that they do not
believe in its existence.

We shall not win an alternative society without winning an alternative
religion; for religion is society's rock
bottom basis. Our present religion is a
consecration of egoism. Our present
ultimate objective is the antisocial pursuit of material gain, both individual
and collective. Because this is an abom-
inable religion, it is not surprising that
we are making ourselves miserable
and are jeopardizing mankind's survival.

War II period—the Cold War—again raised government spending to 23 percent of the GNP, and it has remained between 23 and 27 percent ever since.

When a government disposes of a quarter of a nation's GNP, it is obvious that the priorities of government spending have great social and political ramifications for the society. Table 3.3 gives a breakdown of federal government spending for the fiscal year 1970. Note how much was spent on the military and how little was spent on health, education, and housing. Quite a bit went to social security.

Table 3.3 Federal Government Spending, 1970–1971

EXPENDITURE (by selected categories)	AMOUNT (in billions)
Military and International	$80.9
Postal Service	8.6
Health, Education, and Housing	10.4
Social Security	31.8
Interest on Debt	16.5

Source: U.S. Bureau of the Census. *Governmental Finances in 1970–71.* Series G7–71, No. 5. (Washington, D.C.: Government Printing Office, 1972), Table 2.

It should be remembered, however, that the money for social security comes directly from social security withholdings. "Interest on debt" refers to money paid to individuals (usually in the upper-income brackets) or corporations who hold government bonds.

The Military Economy

If the government is the nation's biggest spender, the military is the biggest government spender. Somewhere between 8 and 11 percent of the trillion dollars of total output of the American economy consists of military goods and services—missiles, bombs, planes, tanks, payrolls of the armed forces, military subsidies to foreign nations, and the like. The "somewhere" refers to the fact that a precise estimate of total military spending cannot be given, because its full extent is only now being revealed. Recently, for example, the Senate Foreign Relations Committee discovered that direct and indirect military assistance to foreign nations for 1971 totaled $6.9 billion, whereas the President's budget message to Congress listed it at only $625 million.

After listening to three days of testimony concerning the hitherto undisclosed flow of military assistance abroad, a senator said:

Most of us in Washington have seen a lot of mismanagement in government programs. But military assistance is the first program I have come across that appears to be characterized by unmanagement.... In some respects, the United States has been transformed from an "arsenal of democracy" to a gigantic discount supermarket with no check-out counters, no store managers—only clerks who blithely deliver to foreign governments of practically any political persuasion whatever they happen to see and like. (Robert Heilbroner, 1972, p. 5)

If there is much that we do not yet know about the extent of our military economy, what we do know is sobering enough. The Department of Defense (DOD) owns property—plants and equipment, land, inventories of war materiel, and other commodities—amounting to $202 billion. It owns 30 million acres of land (roughly the size of Hawaii) and rules a population of 4 million, including civilian employees and soldiers.

The web of DOD expenditures extends to more areas of the economy than one might think. One expects Lockheed Aircraft, with 88 percent of its sales to the government, to be one of the wards of the DOD. One does not expect the DOD to show up as the source of nearly half the revenues of Pan American Airlines or to be, through its Post Exchange (PX) system, the third largest marketing chain in the country, just after Sears Roebuck and A&P.

The very size of the military economy leads to questions regarding its policy implications, both foreign and domestic. The United States needs a strong defense capability; but at what point does a "defense" capability become an instrument for aggressive use in its own right? To what extent does the sheer weight of military power lead to acts of military intervention? On the other hand, what would be the effects on the economy of a major contraction in defense spending? Could the economy continue its upward momentum if substantial cuts in military spending were not counteracted by vigorous expansion of peacetime spending?

Big Business

The DOD is not the only source of our international power nor the only arbiter of our relations with other

Figure 3.9 The American eagle has assumed many shapes since it first appeared as the national insignia. To many it seems to be a consumer-producer eagle, symbolized by spray cans, giant autos, and calorie consumption.

states. Obviously, the White House and the State Department are important, as are a host of other federal agencies. The international operations of American business also have a considerable impact on foreign affairs quite apart from the results of government spending. Many of our largest corporations do substantial amounts of their business, including manufacturing, abroad. In fact, the term "multinational corporation" has been invented to identify these new worldwide corporations.

Consider the example of Standard Oil of New Jersey. By the mid-1960s well over one-third of its assets were foreign based. The reason for such foreign investment is simple: Standard Oil makes better than twice the rate of profit on its foreign investments than it earns on investments in the United States. Standard's example of moving a major portion of its investments abroad has been repeated by most of our largest corporations. Indeed, foreign investment is primarily an activity of big business; very few small businesses invest abroad (and over half of all investments abroad are made by less than fifty giant firms).

The concentration of profits from abroad is even greater than that of investment. In 1966 sixteen firms accounted for 50 percent of the total profit made abroad by United States business—all of these firms were among the top thirty United States firms as listed by *Fortune* magazine (Arthur MacEwan, 1970). Moreover, contrary to the popular impression that America's economy is little affected by foreign investments, from 1950 to 1970 the profits from foreign investments were about 15 percent of the nation's total corporate profits. The 50 percent of this profit taken by the top sixteen firms was a hefty chunk of money for them.

Indeed, the importance of foreign investments for many of our largest corporations often causes them to exert pressure on the government to act on behalf of their interests abroad. In March 1973 an official of International Telephone and Telegraph (ITT) admitted that his company had proposed that the White House and the Central Intelligence Agency (CIA) use economic sanctions against the socialist government of Chile in order to protect ITT investments in that country. Such cases are not uncommon—our economic interests continue to play a major role in our relations with other countries.

Figure 3.10 High rates of profit attract foreign investments into the nations of Africa and Asia. The business and technical expertise of industrialized nations is often welcomed by nations that lack such resources. Yet international trade can also have serious side effects. The consumer at home may find himself a second-class customer for companies that have shifted their production and investment interests to foreign nations, and he may find his tax money being used to safeguard corporate investments abroad. The foreign consumer may find his economic development dictated by corporate profits rather than by national needs and his culture diluted by the promotion of quick snacks and strange architecture.

It is obvious that corporations also play a major role in our domestic economy. Most of the goods and services of America are produced and sold by corporations; most Americans work for corporations. Furthermore, there is obviously an intimate relationship between corporate policies and public policies. Corporations are created in accordance with laws that define their rights and obligations. Many aspects of corporations, especially their financial dealings, are strictly regulated by the government. In turn, as powerful organizations, corporations greatly influence the rules under which they are regulated and indeed are a major power center in the entire political process. The interplay between corporations and government in the operation of our economy is discussed in Chapter 4. The role of corporations in the political process is dealt with in Chapter 15.

The Rich

The American ideology and our highly fragmented government institutions have sustained a pattern in which a minority of Americans live at a level of poverty not experienced by persons in many other industrialized nations, while most of the rest of the population live at a level of affluence available to very few persons elsewhere in the world. It is necessary to examine in greater detail how the economic policies of the government sustain this pattern of inequality.

In theory we have a *progressive* personal income tax in the United States, meaning that people in the upper-income brackets are supposed to be taxed at a much higher rate than are less affluent citizens. In practice, however, the tax law has so many loopholes that the rich pay at about the same rates as the middle class. Of obvious benefit to the richer members of society is the fact that capital gains—the profits derived from selling property (including stocks) after it has been owned for more than six months—are taxed at a much lower rate than other income, such as wages and salaries. Another major loophole is the fact that the interest on many kinds of government bonds is tax-free—upper income people are far more likely to have money available to invest in such bonds and thereby to profit from them.

These matters are of more than minor concern. In 1961 there were seventeen taxpayers who earned over a million dollars but paid no taxes. In 1971 there were 1,300 Americans who earned over $50,000 but paid no taxes. The total loss to the United States government from all loopholes in 1971 was calculated to be about $40 billion. It must be pointed out, however, that the rich, who are the most obvious beneficiaries of tax loopholes, are responsible for only a small portion of the total $40 billion that slips through the loopholes. As is shown in Chapter 4, the middle classes, by virtue of their numbers, are the major beneficiaries of tax loopholes and government subsidies.

State and local taxes also fall more heavily on the poor than on the rich in that they are typically *regressive*. For example, the 5 percent sales tax paid in some states must be paid by the rich and poor alike—the amount of tax on a given object remains constant regardless of the income of the buyer. It is obvious that such a tax eats up a far larger proportion of the poor person's wages than the rich person's. Similarly, in 1968 those families with incomes under $2,000 paid state and local taxes at a rate of 11.3 percent; those with incomes over $15,000, however, paid at a 5.9 percent rate. Thus, the United States system of taxation does little to redistribute income to the poor and in some cases even socks them harder.

GOVERNMENT AND INEQUALITY

Governmental economic policies and programs are hardly limited to the rich, the corporations, or the military. Indeed, economic policies that affect these groups usually affect everyone. For example, sometimes it is true that what is good for General Motors is good for everyone—when this means more and better jobs, a more active economy, lower interest rates, reduced inflation, good roads, and the like. Of course, some things that are good for General Motors, at least in the short run—such as unsafe cars, increased traffic congestion, and pollution—may be bad for the rest of us.

Aside from the fact that policies affecting the privileged have consequences for the underprivileged, there are many governmental economic policies that are meant to affect the underprivileged directly. This chapter has shown that America, in the light of its available resources, is socially neglectful as compared to some other industrialized nations. Nevertheless, we are not totally neglectful. A great many government policies are directly aimed at helping the poor and the disadvantaged. Minimum wage laws, public housing programs, Medicare, and social security are examples of programs meant to redress social inequities. Indeed, our system of public schools, from kindergarten to university, was created to minimize the advantage of family status and to offer more equal occupational and financial opportunity to everyone.

The Welfare System

The welfare system is another government effort to aid the poor. Over the past decade the number of persons on welfare has risen rapidly, causing a considerable financial squeeze on state and local governments. In 1972 more than 3 million families with dependent children—usually families without a father—were on the welfare rolls. In all, a total of nearly 11 million people were on welfare, 8 million of them children. Payments to these families totaled nearly $600 million dollars a *month;* the average monthly payment per family was $196. Welfare payments of all kinds to the poor came to about $15 billion in 1972.

The size of the welfare bill and the rapid increase in the number of persons on welfare have provoked widespread concern and outrage. Many of the complaints and suggestions, although of considerable political significance, are irrelevant to the problem. Demands to remove the "cheaters" erroneously suppose that they are a major source of expense. Efforts to more stringently police the qualifications of recipients result primarily in raising the administrative costs of welfare programs—more supervisors, more clerks, more forms, more red tape. Demands that people on welfare be put to work ignore both the fact that there are not many suitable jobs available and the fact that most persons receiving welfare support are children.

Figure 3.11 The cosmetics industry is a billion-dollar business in America. Some people consider it a social necessity to spend large sums of money on maintaining the correct image—and they would probably argue that they should be free to spend their money as they see fit. But to those who must depend on food stamps and welfare payments for their basic subsistence, it might seem that the priorities represented by make up, wigs, and hair styling are distorted and that the money spent on such luxuries might better be used toward the solution of society's problems.

Figure 3.12 Coupon systems are designed to provide the impoverished person with sufficient purchasing power to cover his or her most pressing needs. Yet such plans are similar to other stopgap measures in that they fail to attack the deep-seated problems behind the poverty cycle.

However, serious critics have identified several fundamental defects in the present system. First, as economist Milton Friedman has pointed out, a major problem is not that government spends too little on welfare but that "most of the money spent on it is not reaching the poor." For various reasons, Friedman argues, present "programs tend to become the preserve of special vested interests and come to serve purposes very different from those that they were initially designed to serve" (Friedman, 1972).

A second way the present welfare system betrays its intended purposes is, according to many critics, by trapping families into permanent welfare dependency. Daniel Moynihan argued in 1973 that welfare dependence can lead to the kind of lifelong stigma that makes many welfare dependents virtually unable to manage their own lives (Moynihan, 1973). If the purpose of welfare is to make life tolerable for those without means and, when possible, to allow them to build a better life, the present system is clearly undercutting its own goals. For example, present rules economically penalize welfare recipients for taking low-paying or temporary jobs; thus, an avenue by which people might eventually escape from welfare is essentially closed. The system seems to be designed to make them passive wards of welfare.

Both Friedman and Moynihan propose direct payments to persons below certain incomes, either through a negative income tax or a guaranteed annual income. Both suggest making it profitable for people to raise their incomes over the minimum. For a period during the first Nixon Administration it seemed likely that a system of guaranteed income (the Family Assistance Plan) would be substituted for welfare. But the bill was stalled in Congress and the Administration eventually renounced it. Nevertheless, although poorly executed, the welfare system does reflect a substantial effort to help the poor.

Whatever the intentions of government programs have been, the results are clear. A substantial number of Americans remain poor in the midst of plenty. They not only fall well below the affluence of the average American, they are much less well-off than are those at the bottom of the economic ladder in many less wealthy industrial nations. The inequities force the conclusion that America's failures to deal effectively with economic inequalities are political. It can hardly be suggested that the nation lacks the economic resources to deal with them.

The Ghetto

Probably the most direct way to show the inseparability of economic and political troubles is to consider the plight of the black urban ghetto. Rather than being an isolated problem, the ghetto reveals the nature of our most fundamental problems.

How many people live in the black ghettos? No one is exactly sure. The census counts may be off by at least 10 percent in neighborhoods where addresses are often impermanent and where citizens avoid interviews by census takers, fearing them to be investigators from the welfare department, bill collectors, or process servers. But a reasonably reliable estimate puts the number of ghetto citizens at about 14 million as of 1970. More important, because blacks continue to immigrate from the depressed rural South, the number can be expected to grow rapidly during the next decade. By 1985 the ghetto population is likely to reach over 20 million and, because of the high birthrate, will reach 17 million even if immigration comes to a halt (W. K. Tabb, 1970).

Life in the ghetto is mean, hard, and poor. Crime rates are higher than elsewhere in the country; housing is scarcer and more expensive. Living is not cheap but expensive: A Federal Trade Commission study has revealed that prices in Washington, D.C. ghetto stores averaged $255 for each $100 of wholesale cost, compared with $159 for stores in nonghetto areas of the city (Robert Heilbroner, 1971).

Typically, unemployment is widespread in the ghetto. In 1970 the unemployment rate in poor urban neighborhoods was 60 percent higher than in the country at large. Among black teenagers it reached a catastrophic level of 42 percent. And even these statistics may understate the problem, for studies of the slum labor market in New York City reveal a subemployment rate that is three times higher than the official unemployment figure. (This rate takes into consideration the special problems of very low-wage employment and the fact that official statistics fail to include those who were so discouraged that they were no longer even looking for work.)

Perhaps worst of all is the outlook for those who grow up in the ghetto and want to work productively in the general economy. The same New York City study revealed how tragically mismatched were the skills (or lack of skills) offered by the ghetto resident and those wanted by the outside world.

Table 3.4 Skills Gap in the New York City Ghetto

SKILL LEVEL	GHETTO UNEMPLOYED 1966	N.Y.C. JOB OPENINGS* 1965–1975
White collar	13.6%	65.7%
Craftsmen	2.8	7.4
Operatives	14.7	7.7
Service	16.6	18.6
Laborers and others	52.3	0.6

* Estimated
Source: "Poverty and Economic Development in New York City." (First National City Bank, December, 1968), p. 12.

As Table 3.4 shows, in only one category—service—was the prospective demand for labor roughly in line with the skills that were available. There was a reasonable employment prospect, therefore, only for maids, restaurant workers, bellhops, and the like—among the lowest-paid occupations in the nation. As for the common laborer, who comprised over half the "skill pool" of the New York ghetto, the outlook for his services was bleak indeed—less than 1 percent of the estimated new jobs would fall in that category. Conversely, for the widest job market in the outside world—the white-collar trades that will offer over two-thirds of the new jobs over the decade ahead—only one-seventh of the ghetto residents were adequately trained. If these figures have any meaning at all, it is that ghetto poverty is here to stay, short of a herculean government-sponsored effort to retrain the trapped ghetto resident.

The Economics of Liberty

It is obvious that in fundamental ways black ghetto-dwellers are not as free as residents of middle-class

Figure 3.13 The slums of East Harlem resemble those of Boston, Chicago, or San Francisco. Those born into a culture of poverty have little chance of escaping the ghetto, for the unskilled jobs of ditchdigger, hod carrier, and iceman are missing in an age when even garbage collection has been mechanized. Between the world of the ghetto dweller and that of the more affluent and successful members of society has emerged a subculture of professionals who substitute in many instances for the social workers and the politicians. But poverty clinics and offices are dependent on volunteers and uncertain government subsidies and can provide only interim solutions to the problems of poverty.

white suburbs. Their freedom is limited not only by racism but also by poverty. Indeed, the extent to which any American—regardless of race, creed, color, or national origin—enjoys individual freedom and liberty is influenced by his or her economic situation. How free can someone be who is hungry, who lives in a rural slum, who lacks the education and sophistication to understand politics, who is too ignorant or frightened to claim his contractual or legal rights, or who has no money to pay for expert advice? What does freedom to travel mean to those who have no money? What does freedom of the press mean to the illiterate?

Perhaps the clearest demonstration of how economic inequality undercuts the American ideal of "liberty and justice for all" can be seen by examining the operation of the legal system. It simply is not true that all persons are equal before the court.

The legal system is separated into criminal and civil jurisdictions. In both legal realms the poor get less justice than do the rich. Much of civil law is designed to benefit the "haves" over the "have-nots." A recent presidential commission on credit reported that sales contracts and legal bill-collection procedures that are in common use victimize the poor because they are designed to mislead and to maximize the advantages of the creditor over the debtor. In addition, most legal defenses against fraud or other damages suffered by the poor at the hands of merchants, employers, or landlords are rarely utilized by the poor; they typically lack the knowledge of their rights or the money to hire lawyers to protect their interests. Thus, they are disadvantaged both in defending themselves against the law and in using the law to protect themselves.

The same inequities exist under criminal law in that many criminal statutes really apply only to acts that are typically performed by poor people. As the nineteenth-century French novelist Anatole France pointed out, "The law, in its majestic equality, forbids all men to sleep under bridges, to beg in the streets, and to steal bread—the rich as well as the poor" (France, 1922).

American history is filled with instances in which "lower class" pastimes and pleasures have been made illegal. Prohibition was one such attempt—drink was seen as the curse of the working classes. The same principle is at work in laws against poker-playing, lotteries, off-track betting, slot machines, cockfighting, streetwalking, and other lower-class "vices." Only those who have the leisure and money to go to the race track or to Nevada can gamble legally, and only those who can afford to invest in the stock market can legally play lotteries.

The poor are also denied equal *protection* under the criminal law. Many commissions and investigations have reported that law enforcement is much less adequate in poor than in wealthy neighborhoods. The police simply do not respond as urgently or give the same quality of patrol in poor as in rich sections of town (Rodney Stark, 1972).

When the poor are accused under criminal law, they once again find themselves treated unequally; they lack the resources to obtain the quality of legal aid available to the middle and upper classes. All criminal defendants are entitled to legal counsel, but court-appointed lawyers and public defenders are not drawn from among the ranks of the most-skilled criminal lawyers. Furthermore, those defending the poor have neither the money for private investigators nor the time to prepare their cases carefully, advantages normally available to high-priced defense attorneys. As a result, the poor are poorly defended and thus more often convicted.

But inequality does not stop there. The poor are apt to receive longer and more severe sentences than are middle- and upper-class people convicted of the same or even more serious offenses. Thus, in May 1972, in the same courthouse, a man who stole $15 from the post office was sentenced to six months in jail, whereas a bank employee who embezzled $150,000 was put on probation (Leslie Oelsner, 1972).

According to United States Attorney Whitney Seymour, Jr., such differences in sentences between rich and poor are relatively common:

There's a traditional difference in sentences for different types of crime, and it tends to discriminate against the uneducated, unloved social reject. . . . The guy who steals packages from the back of the truck is going to get four years, and the guy who steals $45,000 is going to get three months . . . the present system of criminal justice can identify with that kind of defendant (the businessman) but not with that poor black school-dropout. (Oelsner, 1972)

Even when the rich and the poor receive identical sentences, however, inequities frequently result. For example, a $50 fine for speeding simply is not the same penalty for a man earning $50,000 a year as it is for a man earning $3,000 a year. A day at any local traffic court will show many cases in which the offender does not even appear because he could afford to post bond and then to forfeit it as his fine. Meanwhile, many others receive jail sentences to work off fines they are unable to pay—ten days in jail is hardly equivalent to a $100 fine. American justice may in fact be among the fairest in the world —but it is surely not blind to wealth.

Obviously, the courts are only one arena of government in which the poor receive unequal treatment. Another example of the intertwining of government and economics is the expense of political campaigns. As Chapter 14 explores in depth, the rich have a disproportionate capability to wage their own political campaigns, to back the campaigns of others running for elective office, and, indeed, to influence the behavior of officials once elected.

The point seems clear that there are major links between our economy and our politics. James Madison was correct when he concluded that economics is largely what politics is all about.

SUMMARY

The distribution of wealth in America has broad political implications. America is the richest nation in the world and has tended to dominate other nations by virtue of that wealth. America is also among the most socially neglectful nations, a condition that could be eliminated if the political system opted for alternative policies.

The debate over the distribution of American wealth implicitly involves the relative merits of capitalism and socialism. Yet the study of Norway shows that capitalism per se does not lead to social neglect. Rather, the American ideology, with its emphasis on the work ethic, and American institutions, which facilitate certain interests over others, do not emphasize social responsibility.

Because the government spends a quarter of the GNP, its spending priorities have great impact on the economy and on society. The military is the biggest beneficiary of government spending; upper-income individuals are benefited by government's taxing and spending policies; and large corporations are permitted considerable power over the international economy through their international operations.

Certain governmental policies are specifically directed at the poor—welfare and social security, for example—yet the system still disadvantages the poor politically and serves to sustain a pattern of marked inequality of wealth.

SUGGESTED READINGS

Heilbroner, Robert. *The Economic Problem.* 3rd ed. Englewood Cliffs, N. J.: Prentice-Hall, 1972.

Hickel, Walter J. *Who Owns America?* Englewood Cliffs, N. J.: Prentice-Hall, 1971.

Hunt, E. K. and Howard Sherman. *Economics: An Introduction to Traditional and Radical Views.* New York: Harper & Row, 1972.

Reagan, Michael. *The Managed Economy.* New York: Oxford University Press, 1963.

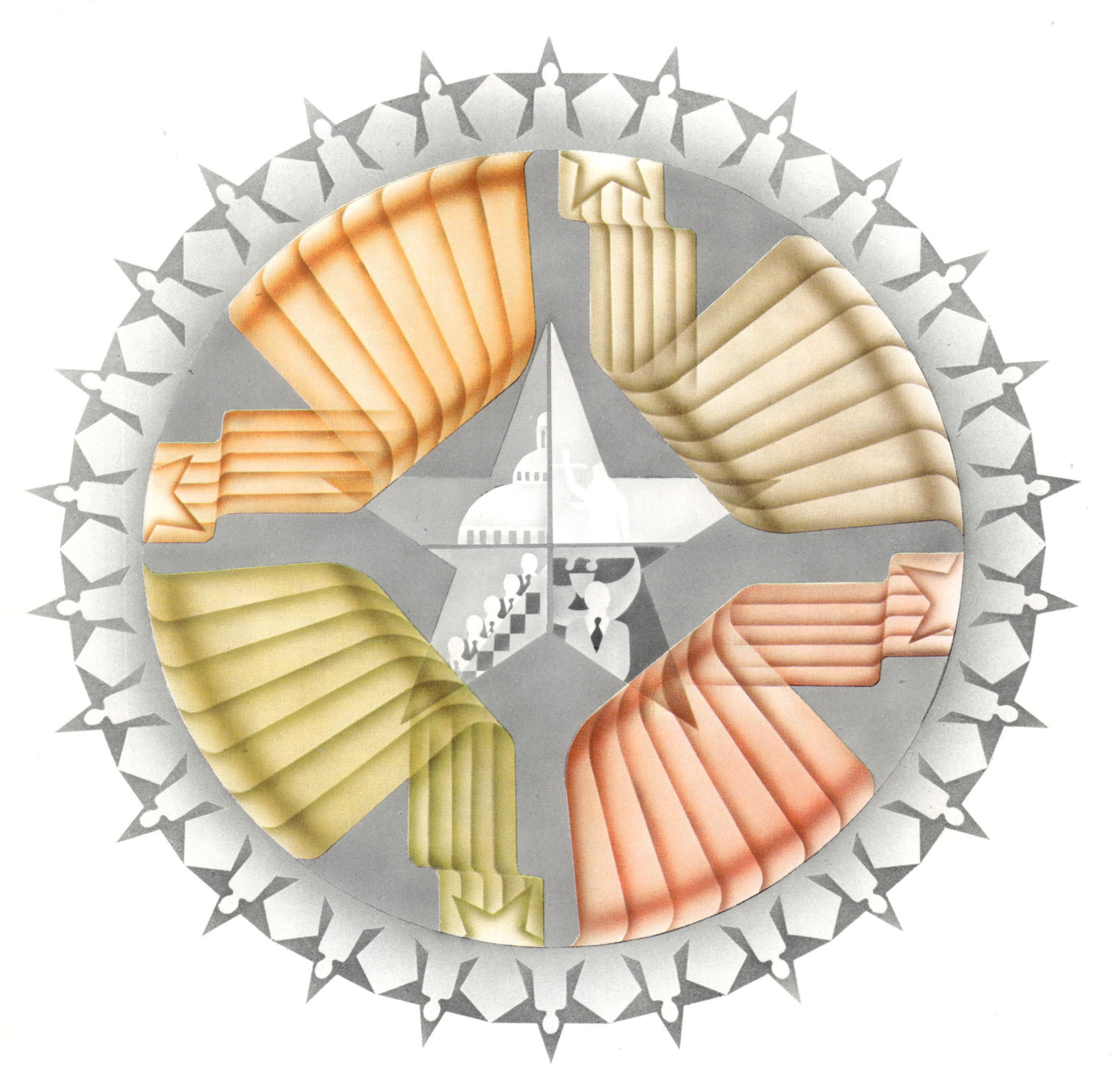

WHAT IS THE GOVERNMENT'S AGENDA?

We begin, in this portion of the book, to examine four broad areas of governance and examples of government's attempts to grapple with them. We have decided to introduce the broad arena of public policy before we discuss political institutions such as the Presidency or Congress, and also before we discuss political processes such as elections and the development of public opinion, for we believe that it is only in the *content* of public policy that we see why politics matters, sometimes so dreadfully much. We see the battlegrounds of public life: the victors, the losers, the survivors, the spectators. And we see also the larger consequences and implications of policy making: what is ignored or neglected; what prospects and is supported; and what it all means for American society.

Beginning with policy is slightly off-beat. It is more traditional to begin with institutions that are, after all, part of the essential backdrop of policy making. But we feel that the discussion of political institutions takes on more meaning when one can understand the *uses* of institutions; as, for example, the wide-ranging consequences of congressional action in a particular area of policy making. Like the shacks, forests, strip mines, and gulleys of Appalachia, or the mood, people, and surroundings of a southern town, this context helps supply the cast of characters, the materials, and much of the plot for the dramas of the present. One can see the ways in which American belief systems, political patterns, and socioeconomic relationships affect and are affected by policy making.

One can note, for example, the pervasive influence of political ideas. The commitment to a capitalist-style economy and the belief in individual success have had a profound effect on economic policy making in America and have shaped the size and style of the programs designed to remedy poverty. Again, the discussion of race policy reveals the contradictions, or perhaps the outright hypocrisy, involved in the American belief system. Equality, but for whom, when, and how completely? The system of ideas characteristic of this country allowed many to be defined as less than human or not deserving of genuine equality. And yet, this very dishonored commitment has occasionally been a spur to change and a banner for the oppressed.

Civil liberties policy and the Perspective on marijuana policy also tell us something more about American ideology. They raise the question, where does a "liberal" society draw the line between law and morality? When is the law being used by a majority against the tastes of a minority rather than as an instrument of just social ordering? This same issue comes up in many areas of liberties policy making.

In relation to liberty it is important to note three other issues. First, civil liberties policy has a great deal to do with the overall culture of a society. The laws may allow people a great deal of freedom, but these people may yet be trained to be quite conformist. Freedom is more than noncoercion. It requires the use of positive ingredients, and these positive ingredients are not always present. People are free not to use their freedom; they may also not be aware of the freedom

The four connecting ribbons in our symbol (left) represent government policy decisions—the major juncture at which government and citizen meet.

that is potentially at their disposal, because of their education, culture, and so on.

Second, in a certain sense civil liberties policy provides a framework within which other battles are fought. The very facts of free speech and press provide a vital arena for political combat over the nature and content of policy making. At the same time, the quality and quantity of liberty are in turn shaped by economic and political realities. This brings us to the third point: It is difficult to fully gauge the overall freedom of a society. In addition to the more usual methods of measuring the openness of a society—such as the state of civil liberties and due process—it is important to pay attention to the freedom of the "least free," those experiencing the most acute deprivation, as a benchmark.

In these chapters we can see the importance of prevailing political patterns and socioeconomic arrangements described in Unit 1. The past does not fix the present, but it does shape it. We can see in a case such as the growth of a very large permanent military establishment, how past patterns can undergo decisive alteration without any sort of revolutionary upheaval.

POLICY AND EVALUATION

We do not pretend in the chapters to follow to take an impartial, above the battle, view of American public policy. Instead, areas of prolonged and intense controversy have been chosen, areas where policy is deeply problematic and also deeply important. This gives the book a rather critical, questioning stance in its attitude toward American public policy, and this is how we wish it to be. The first freedom, as D. H. Lawrence put it, is freedom from lies. At the least, we hope to force the reader to ask himself a few questions; hopefully, some of them will be questions he has not already thought of.

Reading the chapter on economic management and the Perspective on Appalachia that accompanies it, the reader should wonder along these lines: How does economic policy making in the United States affect the distribution of wealth? Why do we continue to have extensive poverty amidst plenty? How does our way of dealing with poverty reflect the political beliefs of the leaders and of the ordinary citizens in America? What does the pattern of economic policy making show us about the ways in which both power and privilege are distributed in America?

The chapter on foreign affairs and national security, supplemented by the Perspective on the military-industrial complex, seems, in some ways, to be telling us a success story: How America coped with the threat of Russian expansion and also prevented nuclear war. But there are also profound and disturbing implications in the growth of a permanent military establishment of such size and influence: Have the Department of Defense and its supporters gained excessive influence over policy making and over the mood of public opinion? Has the weight of American influence had militarizing consequences on the rest of the world? Is it possible to alter the powerful position of the military in federal budgetary allocations as well as the pattern of perceived dependence on military expenditures that extends through Congress and into the factories and voting booths of America? And finally, has the military been dragging down the American economy and thereby threatening future development and progress in other areas that need attention?

The discussions of race policy and school desegregation bring us to some of the most troubling dilemmas of American history. These chapters examine the complexities of policy making in America, the many levels at which decisions can be and are made, the many actors in the drama, and the many methods by which policy can be diverted from its purposes. We see here hatred, hypocrisy, and the highest idealism. We also see crude political dealing, courage, and high-mindedness. We see all of the branches of government and all of the levels—federal, state, and local—enmeshed in policy struggles. As a result, the history of government decisions regarding race can teach us a good deal about the basic nature of American politics.

The reader should also note the catalytic role of nonformal participation—that is, of political participation that occurs outside the formally authorized, constitutional structures of authority by which society is governed. Without the audacity of the civil rights movement, for example, what would race relations in America be like today? In a larger sense, what is the role of civil disobedience, and conceivably even of violence, in a society that also has elections, considerable freedom of speech, and competing political parties? How do these techniques fit with our conceptions of democracy? Is it true that even in a society that theoretically accords each citizen one vote, people must violate the law and the standards of the majority to attain some political influence and stature?

The area of civil liberties policy presents us with a series of issues requiring very careful examination. Some are traditional, the mainstays of political argument for centuries: the uses and limits of free speech, press, assembly, the rights of due process. The Perspective on marijuana exemplifies such classic civil liberties issues as the protections of unpopular minorities and the relationships between law and morality. But there are also some new wrinkles linked to the modern forms of communication and to the more permissive atmosphere in which freedom has acquired new potential meanings.

POLICY MAKING IN PERSPECTIVE

We believe the discussion of these four areas of governance provides a rounded perspective on American policy making and on the dominant issues of public policy. But the need to select means that much has not been selected. In the Perspectives, for example, we could have discussed the Community Action Program instead of Appalachia, or we could have focused on a specific environmental issue related to economic growth, or on an institution like the federal reserve system.

For the military-industrial complex we could have substituted a study of the Vietnam War, or of United States policy in Latin America. Instead of school desegregation, we could have looked at voting rights, or at race and employment. For marijuana, we could have discussed a key Supreme Court decision concerning due process, such as *Miranda,* or the state of women's rights, or the American police or prison system. We have chosen the topics we have because of their intrinsic importance and the way in which they illuminate the enduring patterns of policy making.

POLICY AND POWER

On the basis of our discussion in this unit, what can we say of power in America? First, we can see that some interests have primary influence on policy making while others cry in the wilderness. Second, we can see that the distributions of power change over time, as in the growth of Pentagon power and the intervention of the civil rights movement into the handling of the race question.

From the chapters on economics, we can see that the basic distribution of power in this area has not altered substantially in the last decade. There has been, however, an increased concern for those at the bottom of the social ladder (if it is a ladder). The "rediscovery" of poverty in the early 1960s and the resulting antipoverty programs have somewhat strengthened the position of the least advantaged. And although it does not seem likely that any large redistribution of income or property is on the agenda in America, it does seem that the poorer members of American society will make themselves heard and attempt to consolidate or extend their gains.

On race, it seems safe to say that American blacks have made decisive improvements in their power situation in the last fifteen or twenty years. Nothing ahead seems likely to reverse those gains, accompanied as they are by slow but steady glacial shifts in public acceptance of equality of the races. But, as in the case of school desegregation, the future remains unclear in many areas. Black control of cities may mean little for black power if the cities are bankrupt. We may see a return to separatism, partly as a desire for an intensified sense of identity among certain blacks. Beneath the turbulent alterations of race relations in our time there remain deep-seated problems. Yet power has shifted, and blacks have become full participants in the policy making processes from which they were once almost completely excluded.

The recent past has also been a time for extending the protections of civil liberties in several areas: free speech, the right of dissenters generally, due process. Many have decried these changes and argued that they would bring with them a wave of criminality and anarchy. Perhaps there will be some reversals, made by a more conservative Supreme Court. However, the real issue of the future may not be so much the nature of court decisions as the implementation of them. The Supreme Court may say one thing, but what happens in the local police station may be quite another. It is at this level that the power struggles of the future will be most significant.

With the question of the military-industrial complex we come to truly decisive issues of society-wide power. New forces in American society, especially younger people, are more skeptical of the conduct of our foreign policies in the wake of the Vietnam War. Additionally, the prestige of the military has been rather sharply under attack. A new array of forces will probably emerge in which the military-industrial establishment remains powerful, yet not as unassailable as in recent decades.

What do these reflections tell us about the distribution of power in American society as a whole? Nothing simple. At this point we suggest that the reader reflect on the power elite, pluralist, and undemocratic masses arguments as he or she works through the chapters that follow.

4

MANAGEMENT OF THE ECONOMY

Figure 4.1 Wall Street and the New York Stock Exchange are international symbols for the free market system—the core of capitalism. At the end of the nineteenth century the American economy was truly a free market with unregulated working conditions and cycles of prosperity and depression. Although fortunes were both made and lost on the stock market through luck, wisdom, or manipulation, the demand grew for government action in the economy in ways other than merely providing incentives for business expansion. Today, many aspects of the economy, including the stock market, are regulated to prevent fraud, enrichment through secret knowledge, and conflicts of interest on the part of those decision makers who are closely involved in running the nation's economy.

Government is concerned with the nation's economic health and the general welfare of its population. But what is economic health? What is the general welfare? What promotes them and who is to decide? There is disagreement about the answers to these questions because the American society, like all others, is made up of many economic groups, each with its own interests and conceptions of the common good. For example, the following groups would be expected to answer the questions very differently: producers and consumers, business and labor, lenders and borrowers, farmers and manufacturers, large corporations and small firms, and, of course, the rich and the poor.

It is impossible for government policies to completely satisfy all these segments of society because their interests often conflict, and they compete for society's scarce resources. As a result, the federal government plays a dominant role in deciding what goals to pursue, the priorities among them, the methods to be used, and, therefore, the balance to strike among society's competing interests.

HISTORY OF ECONOMIC MANAGEMENT

Historical perspective makes it easier to understand how the government presently defines the task of managing the economy. Since the colonial period in America there have been three major types of economic policy pursued by the government (William Williams, 1961). A glance at the three policies quickly destroys the myth that governmental management of the economy is a phenomenon of the twentieth century; indeed, in the broadest sense, management of the economy is as old as the nation itself (Louis Hartz, 1948).

Mercantilism

Mercantilism was the dominant policy during the colonial era and well into the nineteenth century. Under mercantilism, the rulers of nation-states such as England and Holland set up government-chartered corporations and gave them subsidies, or financial support, to encourage their growth. The corporations were protected from competition through the grant of monopoly status, and their output, production, and distribution were extensively controlled. Colonies were formed overseas to provide wealth in the form of raw materials and markets for exports. In exchange for protection and subsidization, semi-public corporations had to give the ruler a share of their income, and taxation was extensive. Mercantilism benefited the king and the businessmen, but their profit was often at the expense of the general public, in nation and colony alike.

The American colonies rebelled against the taxation policies and regulations imposed by the British king; in developing their own political system, however, Americans eventually resorted to many of the same mercantilist devices, which aided business growth at the expense of farmers, artisans, and laborers (Richard Hofstadter, 1948). The new government, operating under the Constitution, enacted high protective tariffs, gave subsidies to business, and granted monopoly powers to a national bank. Although the founding fathers disagreed over how extensive government control of economic affairs should be, there was general agreement on one point: The protection and promotion of propertied interests was one of the vital functions of government.

State governments were even more interventionist. They funded canals and built roads. They fostered business growth by establishing state banks, granting charters to corporations, and jointly participating in "mixed" business ventures with private enterprises (James Anderson, 1966).

"Democratic" Capitalism and Laissez Faire

Advocates of the second broad economic policy, often called laissez faire (1840–1900), asserted that national wealth would be increased if government restrictions on economic activity were kept to a minimum. In theory this policy meant the end of mercantilist policies of government-backed corporate monopolies, detailed regulatory laws, and high *tariffs* (taxes on imported goods). In practice, laissez faire was a movement that "democratized" capitalism by allowing any corporation to do business in those areas previously restricted to the government-chartered corporations. President Andrew Jackson endorsed the movement and gave it impetus in his successful fight to terminate the government-chartered National Bank.

The new corporations wanted to be free of competition from government enterprises and from the detailed regulations imposed on the previously chartered companies. As a result, they resisted popular demands for new regulatory legislation (Sidney Fine, 1969). The states, however, bowed to the demands of western farmers and eastern merchants in the 1880s and passed restrictions on the rates charged

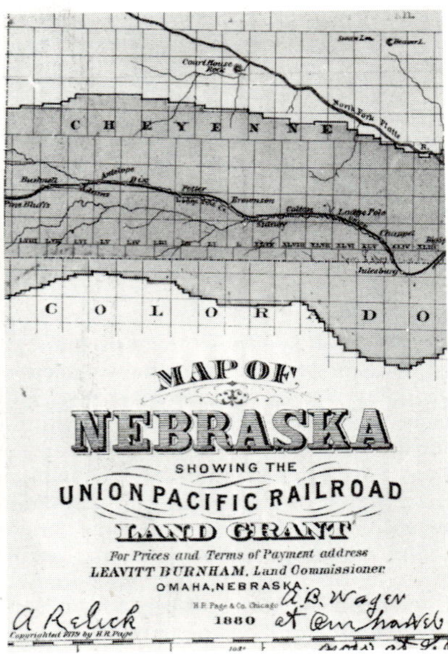

by railroads (Edward Purcell, 1967). New regulatory legislation by the federal government came more slowly because there were doubts raised about its constitutionality; however, the first federal regulatory commission (the Interstate Commerce Commission) appeared in 1887 and others followed (Samuel Hays, 1957; Robert Wiebe, 1962).

In addition to such regulatory legislation, state and federal governments continued to promote business activity. Public lands were often given away to railroads and homesteaders to promote frontier development, and the Department of Agriculture was established to provide services to farmers. In addition, high tariffs were enacted to protect domestic industries. As Sidney Fine has stated:

... the businessman ... was hardly consistent in his application of laissez-faire theories. To be sure, he criticized state action that might circumscribe his activities or that would aid other groups in the community, but he did not oppose such activities of the state as seemed to promote business enterprise or to enhance business profits. (Fine, 1969, pp. 111–112)

The irony of the laissez-faire period was the decline of business competition and the return of monopolies. The more successful corporations expanded and either bought out their competitors or drove them out of business. Threats were often used, and dishonest business practices flourished (Thomas Cochran and William Miller, 1942). The public monopolies of the 1820s had been replaced by the private monopolies of the 1880s. Eventually, public protest, particularly from farmers and small businessmen, led to the passage of the Sherman Antitrust Act of 1890, which was designed to prevent monopolies and *trusts* (the pooling of resources by several companies for the purpose of controlling a market). Only in a few cases, however, was the act enforced with much vigor (Clair Wilcox, 1971).

Policy concerning the availability to the public of money and credit (known as *monetary policy*) was just as controversial as that of trusts. During the first half of the nineteenth century, periods when money and credit were easily available to farmers and new settlers had fluctuated with times when money and credit were hard to get. Frequently, an abrupt change from "easy" to "tough" money policy by government and banks led to business *panics* in which companies were caught short of money and had to declare bankruptcy. The result was often a period in which business growth decreased, prices declined, and more people were unemployed. (This condition is referred to as a *depression* if it is a major economic crisis and a *recession* if it is less severe.)

Figure 4.2 In the age when travel was still an adventure replete with bison and Indians, the government-subsidized Union Pacific Railroad and other railway companies spread their networks west. In the course of providing a convenient mode of transportation, the railroad companies became powerful corporations that manipulated entire legislatures and forced the resettlement of Indian populations along the way. The Union Pacific ticket office (far left) in Kansas City, Missouri, 1892. The driving of the golden spike at Promontory, Utah on May 10, 1869 (center left) marked the completion of the first transcontinental railroad. The locomotives of the Union Pacific and the Central Pacific were drawn together and christened with wine, and the chief engineers of the two railroads shook hands. Just as oil companies and farmers receive government subsidies in modern times, the great railroads received government incentives to expand rail service across the country. This map (left) shows an area in Nebraska in which the government granted land to the Union Pacific Railroad.

In the last few decades of the nineteenth century, farmers had become dependent on large, unstable markets and on monopolistic railroads. They felt that many of their financial problems would be solved if the government would only issue more money. The federal government, backed by businessmen, resisted attempts to create more paper money (greenbacks) or issue large amounts of silver money to supplement that based on gold. They were concerned because if too much money is printed, the value of a dollar is cheapened and prices go up to compensate for the lower value of money. This condition is known as *inflation* and, if uncontrolled, it can ruin a nation's economy. The issue was finally resolved in 1896 when the Democratic candidate for President, William Jennings Bryan, ran on a platform favoring more silver money and was decisively defeated. Preventing "runaway" inflation, which

Bryan's policies might have induced, has been a major goal of the federal government ever since.

Controlled Capitalism

The third era of American economic policy, controlled capitalism, began around the turn of the century and is still evolving today. It is called controlled capitalism because, instead of destroying large corporations, the federal government has created regulatory agencies (see Chapter 10) to oversee and control their activities; one of the chief characteristics of this period has been the transfer to the federal government of many of the regulatory and productive activities formerly handled by the states.

The regulatory agencies increased during the Progressive Era (1900–1917) and reached their height during the New Deal of the 1930s as the nation tried to cope with the Great Depression (William

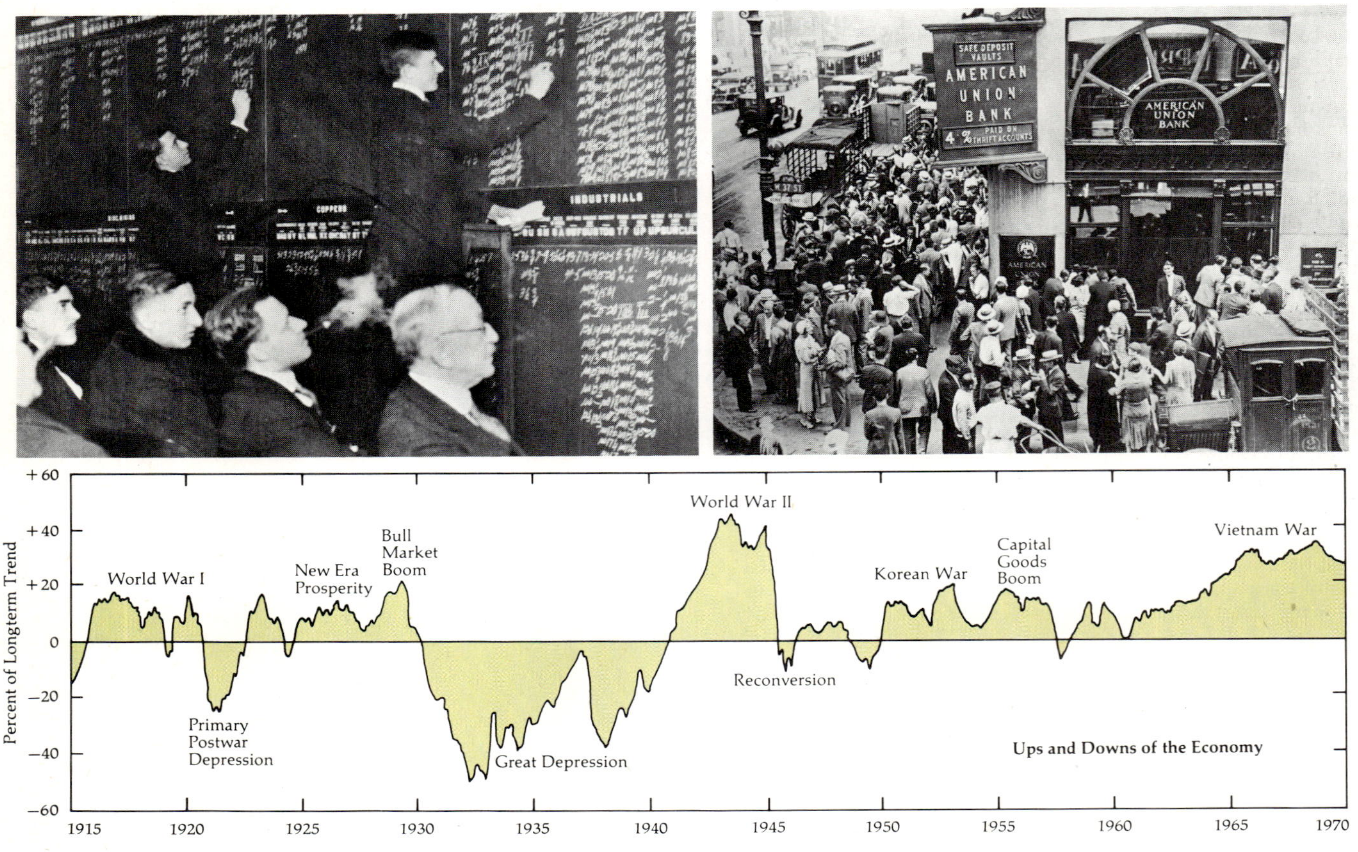

Leuchtenburg, 1963). Public enterprises have also increased in size and number since the New Deal as welfare programs have been created to provide public assistance to the poor and aged. The amount of money spent on public schools and recreational and health facilities has also increased greatly in the last thirty years. Promotional aids to business have continued unabated, and something resembling the old "joint" enterprises of the early 1800s has arisen in the space and defense fields (see the Perspective on the military-industrial complex). Many corporations are either wholly dependent on government contracts for business or are actually owned in part by the government. During the 1930s the federal government, in cooperation with business and labor, even experimented with direct control of the entire economy as it tried to end the Depression; but the approach, embodied in the National Industrial Re-

covery Act of 1935, was struck down by the Supreme Court and has not been tried since.

Contemporary economic policy is most distinctive in its handling of depressions and inflations. The economy goes from periods of "booming" business and high employment to periods of depression and low employment. This cycle of alternating good times and bad times is known as the *business cycle*.

Economists used to feel that nothing could be done to prevent wide swings in the business cycle. Recently, however, a number of techniques have been developed to prevent such swings and to reduce the cycle's harmful effects (Paul Samuelson, 1961). Changing the amount of government spending is one key device: If government spends more money, it will either directly hire more workers or give contracts to businesses that will need to hire more people. Increasing public spending on govern-

Figure 4.3 Ups and downs in the business cycle have characterized the United States economy since its inception. This graph of the American economy since 1915 (left) represents business productivity measured as a percent of long-term growth in the economy. As one can see, recessions and depressions have generally followed wartime economic booms. It is still a question whether government's regulation of the economy will be able to stabilize the ups and downs of the cycle, which economists have identified with the more or less pure capitalist market system. (top left) Brokers follow the stock market at the New York Curb Exchange, 1919. Crowds surround a bank closed during the Great Depression of the 1930s, wondering if they will see any of their savings again—the fear of the reoccurrence of such bank failures led to today's federal insurance of bank deposits. A common sight during the Depression (top right): a bread line for the unemployed. Not all the rich escaped the Depression; many went bankrupt, some committed suicide. As if economic pressures were not enough, farmers also faced drought and dust storms (bottom right) during the Depression years. Here a New Mexico farm is rippled with sand after having been abandoned. Photo was taken by a Federal Resettlement Administration photographer in 1936.

ment construction projects (called *public works*) to aid the economy during downturns can be employed; this device was suggested during the Panic of 1893 by a group of unemployed workers, known as Coxey's Army, that actually marched on Washington, D.C. to demand public works spending. Their pleas were rejected. Another technique government can use to help equalize the business cycle is to issue more money and to ease credit policies as an aid to those in economic distress; as already mentioned, this concept has a long history.

Until the 1930s, however, these "unconventional" ideas were rejected by the government and its economic advisers because they were perceived as dangerous to a sound economy. Businessmen and bankers feared that if the government, by reducing taxes or beginning new programs, spent more money than it received (*deficit spending*), inflation would occur and would wreck the economy. In addition, many Americans had philosophical objections to the notion of government-created jobs. The idea of government manipulation of money and credit policies was also considered a threat by bankers, who correctly perceived that it might not always be in their own short-run interests.

The shift in government attitudes toward efforts to end depressions occurred during the Depression of the 1930s. Although it is conventional wisdom that the work of British economist John Maynard Keynes was responsible for bringing about the change in policy, the Roosevelt Administration was experimenting with deficit spending before Keynes's famous tract on the subject appeared (Herbert Stein, 1969). However, Keynes urged stronger government action to regulate the business cycle, and his ideas had an important impact on policy makers after 1940.

Although it was once thought that there was no way to help cure a depression, the increased spending during World War II pulled America out of the slumps and brought a return to high employment levels by creating more jobs. After the war, government manipulation of spending levels to stabilize the economy became more acceptable. This change was reflected in the passage of the Full Employment Act of 1946, which created the Council of Economic Advisors and authorized the President to deliver an annual economic report to Congress recommending actions to achieve high levels of employment

KEYNESIAN ECONOMICS

The early twentieth century was a patchwork of prosperity and recession. Economists found that they could not understand the reasons for such fluctuations. But when the Great Depression occurred in 1929, it became critical that scholars understand the workings of the economy in greater detail than they had previously.

The central characteristic of an economy is the flow of incomes from person to person. Every cent a person makes comes out of someone else's pocket. And every cent a person spends becomes someone else's income. This process of handing money around is the way in which the economy is revitalized. The level of employment depends on the level of demand for goods and services. People tend to use a certain amount of their income to purchase goods (consumption), and the rest is saved. Most savings are put into banks, or into stocks or bonds rather than put under mattresses. These savings are then lent to businesses by banks and are used to expand business operations.

However, there is nothing automatic about the savings-investment cycle. Business does not usually need savings to carry on its regular operations; it needs money only to expand, because its regular receipts do not provide enough capital to build a new factory or to add new equipment. As long as businesses expand, the savings are circulated to businesses in the form of bank loans, and employment is high. But if business invests less than the community saves, then the demand for goods and services will be insufficient to sustain full employment, and recession results.

Orthodox economic theory held that at this point "natural forces" would bring the economy back into good health. Interest rates were supposed to be the key to economic health. (Money, like anything else, is placed on the market for businesses to buy. The "price" of money is the rate of interest. And the more people want money the more banks can charge.) At the bottom of the economic slump, when there was a flood of savings, orthodox theory said that interest rates should decline. This fall in the rate of interest would become an incentive for businesses to invest because expansion would be more profitable if the price of money were lower, say 3 percent rather than 6 percent. Investment demand would grow; people would buy more and save less, and the level of employment would rise—thus reviving the economy.

The Great Depression demonstrated the fallacy of this self-healing concept. John Maynard Keynes sought to analyze the reasons why economies could become depressed for such long periods of time. Keynes stated that when an economy reaches the point where the willingness to invest is too low relative to the tendency to save, and depression occurs, the depressed state could be permanent because there is absolutely nothing innerent in the system to pull it out. First, Keynes pointed out that interest rates do not fall automatically during a depression. The Great Depression witnessed an equilibrium between savings and investment not by virtue of a fall in interest rates but by a fall in employment, activity, and income. (The economy became stationary during the Depression because businesses continued to operate but did not expand. What occurred was a so-called "economic balance" in which social agony, in the form of mass unemployment, was widespread.) Keynes's cure for this problem was a policy of governmental and central-bank control of interest rates.

But changing the interest rate alone would not solve the huge depression, Keynes said, because savings in banks had dwindled, and people were simply unable to save as they had in prosperous times. So Keynes recommended government spending in the form of extensive public works programs. These programs would provide employment, generate demand for the products of private industry, and thereby set in motion the circular processes of the economy.

THE PRIVATE ECONOMY
HOSPITAL
R R
VETERANS ADMINISTRATION HOSPITAL
THE CONTROLLED ECONOMY
SOCIAL SECURITY
THE PUBLIC ECONOMY

(Stephen Bailey, 1950). In the 1960s a second phase of the shift in economic policy took effect as the Kennedy Administration, acting on the basis of business forecasts, began to adjust taxes and spending levels to stimulate additional growth before a serious recession occurred (rather than acting after its occurrence). Previously, because of the unpopularity of increased spending and deficit budgets, action could be taken only after a crisis existed (Stein, 1969).

The so-called "Keynesian revolution" was resisted on ideological grounds by many businessmen who favored balanced budgets and a minimum of government activity. The economic policies of the Eisenhower Administration reflected these preferences. Today, however, there is general consensus on the need for government manipulation of economic policy. Even though debate continues about *how* the government should act, *whether* it should act is no longer an issue.

THE NATURE OF THE ECONOMY

Today the government actually deals to a greater or lesser extent with three separate economies: the private economy, the controlled economy, and the public economy (Adolf Berle, 1963). The distinctions are important because government has to manage each in a different manner.

1. The private economy—contains those industries in which private enterprise still exists;
2. The controlled economy—includes public utilities (electric, gas, and water power); industries such as transportation and communications, in which federal regulatory commissions control the operation of *privately owned* monopolies or semi-monopolies that provide public services; agriculture, in which a series of laws attempt to control farm production and soil conservation while providing price supports to the farmer;
3. The public economy—includes public enterprises such as schools, the post office, libraries and museums, hospitals, recreational facilities; *publicly owned* power companies, such as the Tennessee Valley Authority (TVA); insurance programs, such as social security, in which local, state, and federal governments provide services that are supported by special taxes, general revenues, or fees.

Although in Chapter 3, for purposes of comparison with Norway, the American economic system was

Figure 4.4 The Tripartite Economy. The American economy is really three economies in one; or, as some would say, it is a mixed economy. The private economy includes those industries in which private enterprise still exists; the government extends loans or subsidies to these industries, passes protective tariffs, and interferes only in terms of taxation and regulation for health and safety. In the controlled economy—where the structure of an industry or service forces a national monopoly or involves a scarce but universally important product or is inoperable without central regulation—the government steps in with full powers of control but not ownership. In the public economy the government is the owner—the provider of goods and services that are not ordinarily supplied by the private economy.

labeled "capitalist," an accurate description is more complex. Notice in this list that the economic system contains large elements of both public and private control of the economy; hence, it is often referred to as a "mixed economy," in contrast to pure socialism, which is totally publicly controlled, or pure capitalism, which is totally privately controlled.

Types of Government Intervention

The government uses various methods to influence the three economies, and the degree of intervention varies accordingly. Generally, government activities can be divided into the three broad categories shown in Table 4.1—promotion, regulation, and production (Lloyd Musolf, 1965; Robert Eyestone, 1972). Promotional activity attempts to stimulate the production of certain goods and services. Regulatory activity seeks to control the conditions under which goods and services are provided, usually through the application of a set of rules that business must follow (or be subjected to a penalty). Through its productive activities, government provides the nation with various goods and services.

In addition to its dealings with the three economies, government also undertakes activities that monitor and manage the economy as a whole. The chief concerns are the achievement of economic prosperity and growth and the maintenance of sufficient income levels for citizens. To achieve these goals, government attempts to moderate the effects of the business cycle, effects that include unemployment during recessions and reduced earning power during inflationary periods when prices are too high. As previously noted, it is in this area of overseeing the total economy (which economists call *macroeconomics*) that government policies have undergone the greatest shift in recent decades.

In the past, government usually reacted to radical shifts in the business cycle after they occurred, if at all. Today, by manipulating its *fiscal policies* (taxes, spending, and borrowing) and *monetary policies* (availability of money and credit), government attempts to achieve economic stability by preventing large swings in the business cycle *before* they occur (Stein, 1969). Macroeconomic policy has become increasingly flexible and broader in scope.

Applying the phrase "management of the economy" to government efforts to influence the business cycle and the three economies should not encourage the thought that government economic policy is always consistent or that various branches and levels of government always pursue the same policies; alternately, it should not encourage the thought that policy is determined in a "scientific" way without any political pressures or value judgments. None of these ideas is true. Rather, there are many managers rather than one management; different parts of the government often pursue conflicting policies; and economic policy is made in a political context and reflects political decisions about how society's resources should be allocated.

The Goals of Economic Policy

Government does indeed intervene in the economic affairs of the nation. But for what reasons? What are its goals? The first broad category of economic policy

Table 4.1 Government Intervention

TYPE OF INTERVENTION	PRIMARY APPLICATION	GOAL	HOW ACHIEVED
Promotional	Private economy	To stimulate production by providing favorable business environment	Through extension of subsidies or loans; lowering taxes; provision of protective tariffs
Regulatory	Controlled economy Private economy	To control conditions under which goods and services are provided; to prevent abuse, fraud, accidents; to protect against too much or too little competition	Through application of rules and standards; provision of penalties for lack of compliance
Productive	Public economy	To provide goods and services not supplied by private enterprise	Through funding of national defense, education, postal service

is macroeconomic health; it includes these goals:

1. "Relative" stability in the business cycle, such as preventing price inflations and depressions;
2. "Maximum" or "full" employment;
3. "Sufficient" economic growth, such as increasing productivity and gross national product (GNP);
4. "Sufficient" income levels, such as the reduction of poverty and provision of public assistance for the poor.

The words in quotation marks represent quantities over which there is much disagreement. How much should each goal be pursued? To the detriment of which others? Which economic groups need the benefits of additional growth, employment, income, and stability? The administration of macroeconomic policy often leads to different impacts on the various elements of society.

The second group of economic goals is concerned with more specific areas of economic welfare; these goals also affect the business cycle and, in turn, are affected by it. They include protection of:

1. The bargaining rights and safety of workers;
2. The health and safety of consumers;
3. The amount and quality of the nation's natural resources (environmental health);
4. The health and vitality of business enterprise, through manipulation of the amount of competition.

Because their impacts are more specialized, these latter policy goals tend to get less attention over the long run from the President and the mass media than does the manipulation of the business cycle. National attention is usually focused on one or more of them when a crisis is perceived to exist (such as a labor strike that cripples part of the economy) or when a sensational event (such as the exposure of the deformities in babies caused by the drug thalidomide) leads to efforts to reform the laws or administrative actions governing them.

Periodically, reform movements are born; advocates of reform urge the government to give more attention to all of these welfare goals and less attention to such macroeconomic goals as economic growth. During the twentieth century there have been three such movements, including the Progressive Era of the first decade, the New Deal of the 1930s, and the current reform movement (symbolized by the activities of Ralph Nader), which began in the 1960s with a focus on environmental, occupational,

and consumer protection (Mark Nadel, 1971).

MANAGING THE BUSINESS CYCLE: A CONFLICT OF GOALS

Which is more desirable: stable prices or full employment? Economists agree it is impossible to achieve both at the same time. Consider the following spiral: As the economy nears full employment, the scarcity of workers increases their bargaining position; wages thus increase faster than productivity (and result in an increase in the labor costs of doing business); companies respond by increasing prices; labor then responds by demanding higher wages. The end result: a "wage-price spiral" and inflation, in which the value of the dollar decreases.

In the years since World War II, policy makers have responded to this dilemma in different ways. Administrations controlled by the Democratic Party, which usually have the support of organized labor, have tended to be more sensitive to the unemployment problem and willing to take the risk of increased inflation. Republican Administrations, with strong backing in the business and banking communities, have been more concerned with inflation, because it adversely affects the confidence necessary to a sound economy and hurts American export business. Export business is affected because inflation causes the price of American goods to be higher than the price of foreign goods.

Of course, both political parties and most Americans are in favor of preventing both high inflation and major depressions. Rising prices accompanying inflation are a particular burden to older persons (who may be Democrats) living on savings, social security benefits, and pensions (or incomes that are fixed in amount); however, higher prices also burden multinational corporations (supporters of Republican Administrations) that sell goods abroad. Mass unemployment, which accompanies depressions and recessions, also hurts all concerned, from the worker who cannot find a job, to businesses, which are hurt by the resulting political instability. For these reasons, any Administration will try to prevent wide swings in the business cycle. But the problem is to find the balance between the economic extremes.

Although Presidents and their advisers have differed over how much unemployment should be tolerated, they generally agree that achieving "full" employment (see □) is undesirable because of its inflationary side effects (Stein, 1969). Believing that creeping inflation is worse than unemployment, mainstream economists point out that poor persons without jobs can be given unemployment compensation or income in the form of public welfare.

Critics suggest that this way of handling the residual unemployment problem may produce less inflation, but it does not always provide enough income or deal with the psychological problems created by unemployment. They argue that the humanitarian goal of providing jobs for everyone is worth a few extra percentage points of inflation; they fuel their argument with statistics showing that the United States, over much of the postwar period, has had one of the lowest rates of inflation of the industrialized nations. According to this argument, the person on a low fixed income who might be hurt by a little more inflation could be compensated by lower taxes or higher social security or welfare benefits. As for the rich and middle-income person, he could afford "to pay 1 percent to 3 percent more a year when he buys a third car" or, for that matter, he could go without it (Robert Sherrill, 1972).

Regardless of the merits of a full-employment policy, Congress made its position clear during the debate over the Employment Act of 1946. Although early drafts of the bill committed the government to a policy of "full" employment, opponents insisted that the wording be changed as the price for their support of the bill. The final draft cited "maximum" employment as the goal of government policy:

. . . there are still people who think that in 1946 Congress enacted something called the "Full Employment Act." It did not. It enacted the Employment Act of 1946. The failure to pass a "Full Employment Act" is as significant as the

□
FULL EMPLOYMENT
The definition of full employment is often obscure. Consider the following observation:
"Economic Council Chairman Paul W. McCracken, who in 1971 defined full employment as 3.8 percent unemployed, [later] redefined it as being in the 4.5 percent zone. The economists juggle such figures very offhandedly; to listen to them, one would hardly realize that each percentage point in an 80-million labor force means 800,000 people [unemployed]." (Robert Sherrill, 1972, p. 217)

Figure 4.5 Wage and Price Interactions Associated with Economic Inflations and Depressions. Beginning at the left of our curve we assume a previous period in which (1) the economy is expanding and employment rising. In an expanding economy, (2) labor may become scarce. If labor becomes scarce, workers are in a better position to negotiate for higher wages. Industry, of course, is aware of this trend. Anticipation that higher wages may stimulate increased consumption as well as costs leads industry to raise prices (3), which, of course, contributes to the demand for those higher wages.

At this point we come to a line: the conventionally acceptable rate of unemployment and inflation, as determined from estimates made by economists and government authorities. This is the rate—for example, it might be around 3 or 4 percent for either unemployment or inflation—beyond which, the authorities believe, the growing productivity of industry can absorb inflation, and unemployment is composed largely of those unable, either permanently or temporarily, to work. There is much controversy as to the data and assumptions that go into the determination of this line.

As wages climb, (4) demand for goods increases. Industry is able to justify rising prices on the basis of greater labor costs, but some industries may take advantage of the situation and raise prices more than what is reasonably justified by costs in order to (5) increase profits. Increasing prices and profits put pressures on labor (6) to bargain for higher wages.

We are now (7) in the stage of rapidly rising inflation where more and more money buys less and less. Such a situation leads to (8) widespread concern over inflation. Hardships are particularly great on persons, such as pensioners, who live on fixed incomes.

(9) Government comes under pressure. In the United States two powerful schools of economic thinking conflict: one school advocates a "hands off" policy to let the free market right itself; the other school, strong since the New Deal programs, advocates intervention by all the legal tools, such as control over interest rates, which are now at the government's disposal.

If the government (10) applies effective wage and price controls, under most situations the inflation cools down slowly to return to an acceptable rate. The drawbacks of such a policy might be the resentment of government interference, the chance that government might make mistakes in timing, extent, and fairness in the application of controls.

If the government (11) does not apply effective controls it is likely that (12) inflation will continue to grow until profits and costs increase so much that demand and buying power are unable to keep up. As this situation occurs (13) workers consume less, industry invests and produces less, (14) the economy stagnates, and unemployment increases—all leading to (15) economic depression.

Again, (16) widespread public concern pressures the government (17) to decide whether to intervene, this time to stimulate the economy by spending or by adjusting tax policies. If the government decides (19) to stimulate the economy, with the attendant drawbacks of intervention, it is likely that the economy will begin to rise rapidly toward an acceptable rate of inflation and unemployment. If the government (18) decides not to stimulate the economy, it is likely that the economy will stagnate for a long period of time (unless an outside event such as war interrupts), with dangers of severe social dislocations and disruptions as were seen in the Great Depression of the 1930s.

decision to pass the Employment Act. . . . [and reveals] the central agreement upon which all postwar economic policy has been based. (Herbert Stein, 1969, p. 197)

The Problem of Forecasting

In regulating the business cycle, government uses a variety of methods. Some of these methods are now built into the government structure and are called "automatic stabilizers" because they operate without the need for specific government directives (Otto Eckstein, 1964). Examples include unemployment insurance, which increases purchasing power during a recession, and corporate and individual income taxes, which help prevent inflation and increase government revenues when the economy is overheated. In addition, there are discretionary controls that include manipulation of the tools of fiscal and monetary policy.

In deciding how to use the discretionary controls, policy makers face a host of problems. The first problem is forecasting. Economists try to predict what the economy will do before they recommend changes in policy (Lawrence Pierce, 1971). Sometimes the beginning of a recession can be discovered and treated before it gets too far along. However, if the prediction of a recession turns out to be wrong, a tax cut, intended as a stabilizing mechanism, can turn out to be inflationary, because it results in people having more money to spend.

Examples from both the Kennedy and Nixon Administrations prove the difficulties of forecasting. Kennedy's economic advisers felt that the economy needed some stimulus and recommended either a tax cut or increased federal spending (Arthur Schlesinger, 1965). Luckily for Kennedy, his forecasters were accurate, and the cuts in taxes in 1962

Wage and Price Interactions Associated with Economic Inflations and Depressions

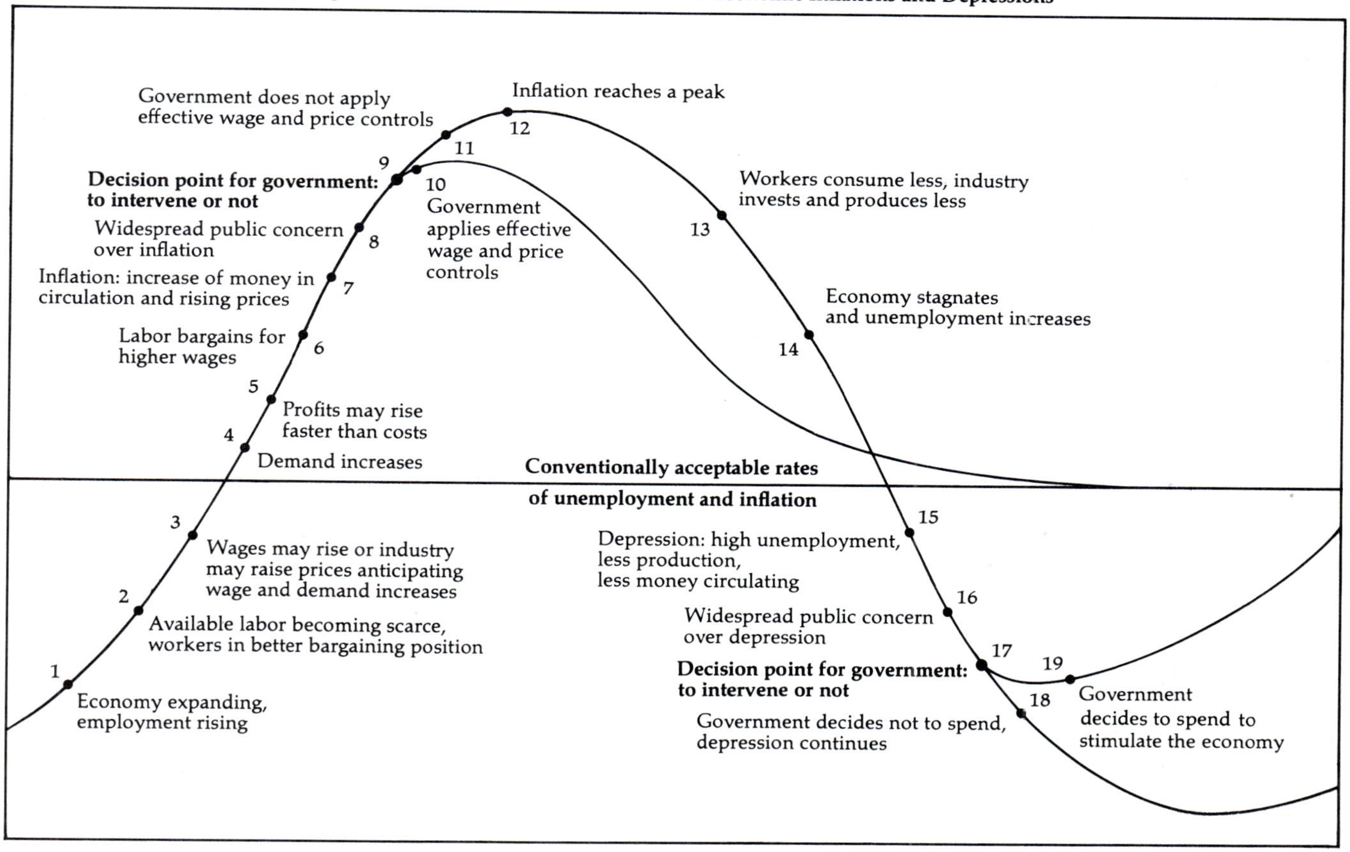

and 1964 were considered successes. President Nixon was not so fortunate. During the recession of 1970–71, President Nixon chose to follow the advice of George Shultz, who predicted a natural economic recovery, which would make further governmental action unnecessary (Rowland Evans and Robert Novak, 1971). Shultz's predictions for 1971 turned out to be incorrect, and the Nixon Administration faced the political problem of a serious recession. The difficulty of making accurate predictions has led some observers to argue that government should keep a "hands off" policy regarding the economy (Stein, 1969). But given the high political stakes, it is unlikely that any Administration will consistently follow such a policy.

Fiscal Policy and the Role of Congress

Once an ensuing economic problem is forecast, the policy makers face the political problem of getting the various branches of the federal government to pursue a common policy. When the President wants to cut or increase taxes or government spending (the tools of fiscal policy), he must get the approval of Congress in the form of legislation authorizing such actions. Getting authorization may be difficult for several reasons. First, tax increases, even though they may be needed, are not popular subjects on Capitol Hill. As President Johnson discovered when he recommended a 10 percent surcharge on income taxes in 1967 to help pay for the war in Vietnam, Congress is reluctant to agree to a tax increase based on projections of future inflation if the economy appears stable at the moment. In addition, tax increases are unpopular with the voters, and some sort of visible crisis is usually needed to get a tax increase through Congress.

Second, power over tax policy in Congress is highly centralized (John Manley, 1970). In the House

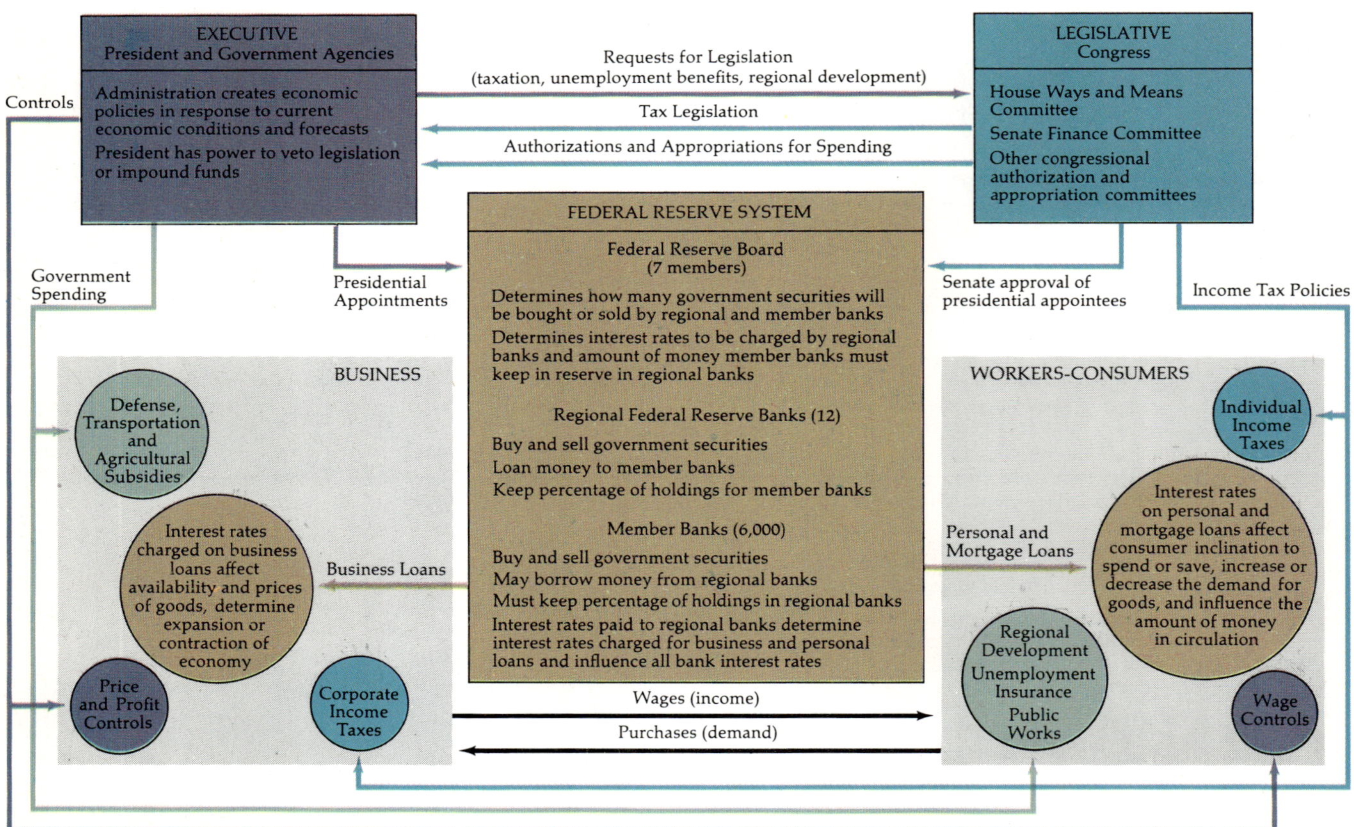

FEDERAL FISCAL AND MONETARY MANAGEMENT SYSTEM

of Representatives, most members defer to the wishes of the Ways and Means Committee and its powerful and knowledgeable chairman, Wilbur Mills. A similar process takes place in the Senate where the Finance Committee writes tax legislation. Because all revenue bills must originate in the House and the current chairman and his staff are more knowledgeable on the subject of taxes than their counterparts in the Senate, Wilbur Mills tends to dominate the legislative process. Any President wishing to cut taxes or to engage in deficit spending usually has to make significant concessions to Chairman Mills, because of the latter's concern about inflation.

An example from the Kennedy Administration reveals the difficulties involved in getting congressional approval of economic policy. In January 1963 President Kennedy submitted legislation to Congress designed to cut individual and corporate income taxes for the specific purpose of stimulating the economy. The House Ways and Means Committee and its Senate counterpart acted very slowly on the bill, in part because they wanted assurances from the President that spending levels would be kept down. After Kennedy's death, President Johnson engaged in some symbolic acts of budget cutting (such as making a point of turning out the White House lights at night) to win the confidence of congressional leaders. The bill was not passed into law until February 1964, eighteen months after it had been submitted. During the interim, economists became concerned that the long delay might cause the tax cut to end up hurting the economy rather than helping it.

The political complexion of Congress also influences the nature and timing of presidential requests. For example, President Johnson delayed asking Congress for a tax increase to fund the war in Vietnam, a decision that had disastrous effects.

Figure 4.6 The Federal Reserve System (left) is central to monetary policy—it determines the availability of money in the economy, that is, its seven-member board determines how willing local banks will be to lend money and how much that money will cost (interest). If high interest rates are charged on business loans, some companies will decide not to borrow money, and business will slacken and prices may recede. The President and his bureaucracy, Congress, the Worker-Consumers, and Businesses are the other elements in the maze of money management. The President may request or demand that controls be placed on prices and wages. In the Congress, the House Ways and Means Committee and the Senate Finance Committee have powerful authority to oversee all tax legislation. Worker-Consumers feel the effects of money management when they find jobs or mortgages hard to get or their pay being eaten up by inflation; their demand for scarce goods helps raise the costs of those goods.

Figure 4.7 Two illustrations of Dr. Arthur F. Burns (right), Chairman of the Federal Reserve Board, suggest the scope of the Board's involvement. Before a secret session of the House Ways and Means Committee to consider tax reform in June 1972 (top), Chairman Wilbur Mills consults with Burns (on the right) to get his views on increasing the national debt. Six months later (bottom), Chairman Burns speaks with Senators Sparkman (D.-Ala.) and Tower (R.-Tex.) before asking the Senate Banking, Housing and Urban Affairs Committee to give the government standby authority to take direct control over wages and prices.

Johnson delayed because he feared that Congress's abhorrence of big budgets and tax increases might result in his getting money for the war but not for domestic programs (David Halberstam, 1972). As a result the government had several years of very large budget deficits that led to a great increase in inflation.

Monetary Policy and the Federal Reserve Board

Complicating the President's job of managing the business cycle is the fact that monetary policy (control of the supply of money and credit) is controlled by an independent regulatory agency, the *Federal Reserve System,* which is the central bank of the United States. The President has no formal control over the "Fed" or its chairman and is limited to the power of persuasion to get monetary policy makers to follow his policies. The Federal Reserve Board oversees the twelve regional Federal Reserve Banks and over 6,000 member banks in the various states. All nationally chartered banks must belong and many state banks voluntarily join. The member banks are required to keep a certain percentage of their assets in reserve in one of the reserve banks. In addition, the member banks may borrow money from the reserve banks to finance their own lending activities.

The Federal Reserve Board can manipulate the economy in several ways. It can change the amount of money in the economy by raising or lowering the percentage of money that each member bank must keep in reserve rather than loan out or invest. More frequently the board manipulates the economy by raising or lowering the interest rate that it charges to member banks; they in turn change the interest rate charged to customers. The lower the interest rate on borrowing money, the more money will be borrowed and the more jobs created through industrial expansion. The board's Open Market Committee also manipulates the economy by dealing in government securities: when it buys them from a member bank, the money that the bank receives for the sale may be used to finance lending operations; when the central bank sells securities, the amount of money available for loans to the general public is reduced, because member banks use up funds in purchasing the securities.

Prior to the implementation of the theories of John Maynard Keynes and the spending policies of World War II, the Federal Reserve Board often contributed to depressions by reducing the amount of money and credit available in the economy, as it did in 1930 and 1938 (Milton Friedman, 1968). In the postwar period the Federal Reserve Board has been criticized for inadvertently contributing to recessions (1953) as well as to inflations (1955 and 1957). It has often failed to forecast the state of the economy correctly, causing it to pursue policies to counter the business cycle (called "countercyclical" or remedial policies) for too long. Because it shares the prevailing philosophy that full employment would cause too much inflation, some economists have called the board "callous" and believe it is overly influenced by the banking industry. A recent chairman of the Federal Reserve Board showed his sensitivity to inflation by remarking: "A 4 percent level of unemployment is very good, though 5 percent would be better" (Sherrill, 1972).

Monetary policy, because its restrictions on money and credit are the same for all borrowers, is often considered less discriminatory in its effects than fiscal policy, in which taxing and spending "victimize" some more than others. But one board member, Andrew Brimmer, points out that when the supply of money is tightened, big business is often unaffected whereas small businesses are wiped out. Brimmer has recommended that two reserve rates for member banks be established: one for lending to high-social-priority areas and one for other lending. The rate for high-social-priority funds would be lower than the regular one, thus funneling more lending money into areas of high social concern (Sherrill, 1972). So far this suggestion has been successfully resisted by the banking industry. Bankers generally feel that the areas of highest priority are already covered by the present system, and they fear that a change might result in fewer loans and less profit for them. The bankers' lobbying influence on Congress has been very powerful.

There has been considerable debate whether the government should rely primarily on fiscal policy or on monetary policy in regulating the business cycle. The proponents of monetary policy argue that it is more direct in application, quicker to take effect, and more effective in stabilizing the economy if used properly (James Anderson, 1966). As long as regulation of monetary policy is outside the control of the

President, however, Presidents will continue to use the fiscal tools more directly under their control; they will refuse to leave the fate of the economy in the hands of an agency that so far has failed to do better than the White House in maintaining a stable business cycle.

Defenders of the current Federal Reserve System argue that bringing it under direct presidential control would mean the intrusion of "politics" into economic policy making. But the current system is also political; it simply serves a different mix of values than does the White House economic staff. Many of the difficulties of the central bank, such as forecasting and goal determination, are shared by policy makers in the presidential sphere—presidential control, therefore, would not solve the key problems of managing the economy. It would, however, give Presidents greater freedom of action in those instances when the makers of monetary policy are reluctant to follow the lead of the White House.

Deficit Spending and Wage-Price Controls

In addition to the problems of coordinating the various branches of government and forecasting the state of the economy, Presidents must decide what methods to use in managing the economy. Reference has already been made to the debate between advocates of fiscal and monetary policy. In fighting recessions the major issue has been whether to cut taxes.

Recessions and Economic Growth

In the three major recessions of the 1950s the government refused to cut taxes for the specific purpose of stimulating the economy. The primary fear of President Eisenhower and his advisers was inflation; they felt that a reduction in taxes would make a later tax increase much harder and thus contribute to unbalanced budgets and inflation.

President Kennedy's decision to seek a tax cut in the hope of stimulating growth and employment in the economy is considered a milestone in economic policy. The move demonstrated that tax cuts and deliberately unbalanced budgets (deficit spending) could be useful in stimulating economic growth; they would ultimately lead to a budget surplus and thus prevent bad inflation. To demonstrate this point to the general public as well as to Congress,

President Kennedy said of his tax cut that "no more important domestic economic legislation has come before the Congress in some 15 years" (E. Roy Canterberry, 1968). Significantly, President Nixon later became the first Republican President to use deliberate deficit spending as a method of managing the economy.

Inflations and Controls

The history of postwar efforts to fight inflations has also involved a gradual evolution in methods. The struggle has been complicated by the fact that the causes of inflation have changed over time. The first two postwar inflations (1947 and 1950) were caused by an excess demand for goods, or too many dollars chasing too few items. The 1947 inflation, in which Americans tried to catch up on purchases of consumer goods unavailable during the war, disappeared after production caught up with demand.

The 1950 inflation, which occurred at the beginning of the Korean War, was caused by consumers' hoarding of goods that they feared would not be available later. The government imposed mandatory controls on the maximum levels that wages and prices could reach, and taxes were increased to reduce the effects of the inflation.

A third inflationary period occurred in the mid-1950s. It differed from the previous two and set the pattern for subsequent inflations. It was not caused by excess demand for goods but by rapid growth in a few sectors of the economy and by certain structural features of our economy. The policies of corporations and unions are among the structural causes of inflation. Because they dominate their markets, large corporations can set prices higher than they would be if there were more competition. In addition, they can give union workers wage increases that are greater than the increase in labor's productivity. The companies can then pass on the cost of the wage increase to the consumer in the form of higher prices. Because the biggest companies have so few competitors, they also resist lowering prices when demand for their products slackens off. The result: Prices tend to go up but never down. Also, the service sector of the American economy, which includes government employees, has grown in size. Because productivity increases are lower in the service sector, the wage boosts that have come with unionization of government employees have been inflationary (William Baumol, 1967; James Kuhn, 1972).

Presidents have reacted to structural inflation in different ways. President Kennedy suggested voluntary wage-price guidelines that would limit wage increases to roughly 3.2 percent, equal to the average annual increase in productivity for the nation as a whole. When segments of the steel industry raised prices in 1962 against the advice of the White House, the Kennedy Administration reacted by imposing economic sanctions on the offending companies and applying both public and private pressure to get the price increases rescinded. The new prices were quickly withdrawn, but the President's actions caused so much nervousness in the business community that he decided not to act when the steel companies increased prices one year later (Grant McConnell, 1962; Jim Heath, 1969).

President Johnson also used economic sanctions against inflationary price increases, but he was more politically successful than was Kennedy because he implemented his policy in quieter ways, causing less nervousness in the business community. However, the voluntary nature of wage-price guidelines led many companies to simply ignore them, and the guidelines were forgotten once the Vietnam War caused rampant inflation.

During the first term of the Nixon Administration the Federal Reserve attempted to cool the economy by tightening the money supply. This action caused a serious increase in unemployment, but price increases did not slow down. The nation was faced with price inflation and unemployment at the same time. Finally, President Nixon imposed the first peacetime wage-price controls to try to stop the inflation while he slowed the increase in federal budgets by refusing to spend money appropriated by Congress (impoundment of funds). There was much discussion whether the wage-price controls favored organized labor or big business, but one thing was certain: As long as the economic situation continued, the biggest losers were the over 4 million unemployed persons and the elderly who were living on the small fixed incomes provided by federal welfare and social security programs. President Nixon's impoundment of funds was also controversial because the impounded money tended to be more in the area of social welfare than in the area of defense spending and because Congress felt impoundment of funds should not be done without its approval.

Structural Unemployment

There are structural causes of unemployment just as there are structural causes of inflation. Structural unemployment refers to those jobless who remain unemployed even when the economy is booming. Often referred to as the hardcore or chronic unemployed, these people may live in a depressed area far away from available jobs, or have inadequate or outdated skills, or be illiterate, or be the victims of discrimination because of race, sex, or age. Structural unemployment was noticed during the Korean War, when the jobless rate remained around 3 percent despite the fact that jobs were available (James Sundquist, 1968).

Regional Development

The Kennedy and Johnson Administrations tried to attack the causes of structural unemployment in a series of measures passed in the 1960s. One of these bills was the Area Redevelopment Act (ARA) of 1961, which provided assistance to businesses and public projects in depressed areas. Because every member of Congress wanted his district represented, eventually one-third of the nation's counties were made eligible for the limited benefits (less than $100 million appropriated) under ARA, thus lessening the effect in given areas.

There were additional administrative and political problems in the implementation of the law: Republicans hinted at partisanship in the awarding of projects, and organized labor worried about business attempts to seek out depressed areas to avoid paying the higher wages prevailing in other areas (Sundquist, 1968).

An additional problem faced the people of eastern Kentucky who found that their region was so underdeveloped economically that no business wanted to seek ARA loans to invest there. The Kentuckians banded together with representatives of other states in the Appalachian Mountain region and requested a special government program to develop the resources necessary for business, such as highways, airports, and water power. In 1965 Congress passed the Appalachian Regional Development Act (ARDA), which authorized up to $1 billion to be spent in that region. When ARA expired in 1965, it was replaced by the Economic Development Act, which applied to other depressed areas an approach similar to that being developed for Appalachia. The experience of the nine-state Appalachian region with these measures is discussed in the Perspective following this chapter.

Manpower Training

In addition to the regional-directed legislation to aid business, Congress passed a job- and manpower-training act for adults and a vocational-training act for students. Basic literacy training was included as one of the categories for which aid could be given, and both state agencies and private institutions were permitted to run programs. The job-training approach proved to be popular with Congress. In 1966 the government claimed it had retrained 370,000 workers with a dropout rate less than that of the nation's high schools (Sundquist, 1968). Unfortunately, many of the retrained workers still could not find jobs.

The Poverty Program

The Economic Opportunity Act of 1964, commonly known as the Poverty Program, was another effort to help alleviate chronic unemployment. The legislation contained numerous approaches to the problems of poverty and joblessness (Donovan, 1967). Some programs, such as the Job Corps and Neighborhood Youth Corps, attempted to provide vocational training and job experience for youths. Other programs provided financial help in the form of aid to small businesses, a work-study program for college students from low-income homes, and direct grants to low-income rural families to help them increase their earning capacity.

The most publicized aspects of the act were the community action programs and the domestic peace corps, known as VISTA. Many of the community action and VISTA projects simply helped communities set up neighborhood health centers, job training facilities, and special educational programs such as Operation Head Start for preschool children. In many communities, however, a key part of these projects was organizing the poor to take political and legal action against local governments or private parties with whom they had grievances. Because the act called for the "maximum feasible participation" of the poor in implementing the community programs, many of the programs were administered by persons who had had no prior experience.

The antipoverty programs encountered many difficulties (Daniel Moynihan, 1969). Local politicians and businessmen resented public financing of political and legal activities directed against them. Middle-class people received aid (particularly in the work-study program) because the definition of poverty had to be stretched to widen political support. Job Corps centers found that surrounding neighborhoods resisted their presence. Also, the community-action programs suffered from inefficiency: In many cases the money originally intended for poor people ended up in the pockets of the administrators of community programs.

Taken as a group, the structural approaches to hardcore unemployment and poverty have so far been a failure. The most commonly cited reason for the failure is lack of sufficient funds to have significant impact (Kenneth Dolbeare and Murray Edelman, 1971). There is much to be said for such reasoning. Once the Vietnam War became a big war, funds for President Johnson's domestic program diminished. However, another reason for the failure of structural approaches to end unemployment and poverty is that most middle-class Americans are ideologically unwilling to give up a significant part of their income to fund programs for the poor regardless of what approach is used (see Chapter 1).

Beneath the problem of money lies yet another issue—whether the problem of the hardcore unemployed has yet been understood sufficiently by economists (Charles Valentine, 1968). There are some who see the problem primarily as one of lower-class culture, which causes the poor to be fatalistic about change in their lives or resistant to the short-term deprivations necessary to holding a job (Oscar Lewis, 1965). Others suggest that persons possessing the personality associated with lower-class behavior, whether they be middle-class "drop outs" or poor people, prefer their present life styles to others and are unlikely to respond to the incentives offered them by society (Edward Banfield, 1968). Two other theories hold that racism is the culprit and that the poor are much too comfortable on welfare to seek work.

It is possible that each of these theories has some validity. But given the complexity of the problem of structural unemployment and the present political resistance to the efforts that try to get at the real causes, it is unlikely that American society will eliminate hardcore joblessness in the near future.

THE TAX STRUCTURE AS ECONOMIC POLICY

It has already been shown that tax rates can be manipulated to help fight inflation or unemployment. Paralleling the conflict between employment and price stability discussed previously is a conflict between two other economic goals—economic growth and an equitable distribution of wealth. An examination of individual and corporate income tax laws reveals the conflict.

Tax Deductions

Many provisions of the tax code were put there for a social purpose. For example, the government wants to encourage the growth of domestic industries. To obtain this growth it sometimes levies taxes on imports (tariffs) or, as it did in 1962, it gives business a special tax credit on new investments. In 1913 Congress decided that it would be fair for companies in natural-resource fields, such as oil, natural gas, and coal, to get a lower tax rate in the form of a special depletion allowance; the justification for this special treatment was that the companies' assets, our natural resources, get used up or depleted over time. Recently, the idea of an oil-depletion allowance has been defended on the grounds that it encourages investment in a high-risk enterprise that is vital to national security and economic growth.

Similarly, corporations are allowed a "tax break" on the depreciation of their machines and other physical capital so that the money saved can be used to acquire new equipment, which, in turn, will expand production. Interest received on loans to municipal governments (municipal bonds) is also exempt from taxation, the justification being that bond sales help finance government projects. A lower tax rate is applied to individually held wealth, such as corporate stock, that has increased in value between the time it was acquired and sold. Known as the *capital gains* tax, this lower tax is justified on the grounds that it encourages individual entrepreneurs and investors. Finally, the individual taxpayer is permitted deductions for such things as the interest he pays on his home mortgage (to encourage homeowning),

charitable contributions (to aid those in need), and medical expenses (in fairness to the ill).

Practically all of these special tax-code provisions were initially designed to serve some social purpose, such as to encourage economic growth or to aid special causes. However, taxes are sometimes applied for other reasons. For example, excise taxes are applied during wartime to the sales of many goods and services, the production of which the government wants to discourage. In addition, individuals often lobby to get special favors written into the law.

Taxes and the Redistribution of Wealth

Of course, special tax provisions that lower tax rates can be termed "loopholes." The problem is that one person's loophole may be another person's "fair treatment," depending on the social purposes one wants the tax code to serve. The chief dispute is between loopholes to encourage economic growth on the one hand and fairness and the need for redistribution of wealth on the other.

Taken as a whole, the exclusions, deductions, and exemptions substantially reduce the areas of income that can be taxed (the *tax base*). The result is that many Americans (those who do not qualify for the exemptions) must pay a higher rate of tax. However, some attempt is made to provide equity and to redistribute income by making the tax rates *progressive*, which means that wealthier persons theoretically pay a higher percentage of their income in taxes than do poor people. The problem is that because there are so many loopholes in the tax structure, the actual average rate that upper-income people pay is not nearly so high as the rate they would pay without all the special provisions. In fact, until the passage of the Tax Reform Act of 1969, there were several millionaires who paid no tax at all. Now, all persons must pay at least a minimum tax of 10 percent on types of income that were previously tax free. In addition, the state and local tax systems, which rely heavily on sales taxes, are *regressive* in the sense that poor people pay a higher percentage of their income to them.

A more fundamental issue than fairness, however, is one of redistribution of wealth. At the moment, the loopholes in the tax laws mostly serve the middle and upper classes. Although poor people do receive governmental aid, it remains true that if a greater

Figure 4.8 Supertax Loophole. Contrary to the myth that it is the holders of great wealth and connections that have cleverly rewritten tax legislation to favor only themselves, in actuality, Supertax Loophole is honored by all those whom he protects—including large corporations and the middle-income home-owner, who are two of his biggest beneficiaries.

amount of money were collected in taxes from the middle and upper classes a greater amount could be given to the poor. The problem is that many of the most popular ideas for tax reform, such as eliminating the oil-depletion allowance and taxing millionaires more, would not raise that much money. To really aid lower-income people in a significant way, the large bulk of middle-income people would have to be taxed at a much higher rate. Many experts on tax policy feel this change would be desirable; however, it would also be difficult politically because, in the words of tax expert Joseph Pechman, "the influence of the groups arrayed against a significant redistribution of the tax burden is enormous, and there is no effective lobby for the poor and the near poor" (Pechman, 1969).

Agricultural Price Supports: Welfare for Farmers

The tax structure is not the only feature of economic policy that gives substantial financial benefits to many who are not really in need. The "farm program," as our nation's policy of agricultural price supports is called, has the same effect. Like tax policies, the idea of price supports originally served a socially useful purpose.

Farmers sought financial aid from the government in the 1920s when there was a decline in the market for agricultural products (James Anderson, 1966). A number of schemes were tried, but none succeeded in raising farm prices, because they did not restrict production. One alternative would have been for the government to do nothing, causing millions of farmers to leave agriculture and find jobs elsewhere, go on welfare, or starve. However, the suffering, the possible violence, and the realization that farmers would vote against politicians advocating such a policy, led the federal government in the 1930s to begin a series of programs to aid farmers.

The legislation that was passed provided price supports to farmers based on the market value they had received during good economic conditions. Government also tried to reduce production so that market prices would be high and expenditures for federal price supports kept to a minimum.

When the farm program first began, price supports were limited to a small number of commodities, and the level of price support given to certain commodities was determined by the Secretary of Agriculture. Over time, however, the agricultural interests have been successful in broadening price-support programs to cover almost all commodities. In addition, production controls have often failed because technological advances sponsored by the Department of Agriculture have helped farmers grow more food per acre. Finally, the logic of farm supports has led to a proliferation of subsidy programs.

The result of these developments has been a cost to the federal government of nearly $4 billion a year since the early 1960s (Anderson, 1966). More importantly, the richest farmers get the lion's share of the farm subsidies. As *Fortune* magazine concluded in March 1973, "price supports have become, in the main, a rich man's welfare program."

Some recent Presidents have tried to reduce price supports but without much success. The agriculture committees of Congress are stocked almost exclusively with representatives of farm areas. The Secretary of Agriculture encounters strong opposition when he tries to radically alter the program, despite the fact that some farm organizations favor elimination of price supports (Anderson, 1966).

A number of reforms have been proposed to redirect the subsidy program. One proposal would put an upper limit on the amount of money any one farm producer could receive from the government; another would replace price supports with greater welfare payments to poorer farmers (who earn little from farm supports). This latter concept is more equitable, but like basic tax reform to aid the poor, it faces the difficult problem of gaining enough political support to be implemented.

THE REGULATION OF COMPETITION

It is frequently noted that despite the presence of antitrust laws, the United States economy is populated with large and powerful corporations whose sales in many industries account for a large percentage of the total business or market. (A corporation's percentage of total industry sales is called *market share*.) Some observers have concluded that the antitrust laws are meaningless or simply serve the symbolic function of reassuring us that we still value the old capitalist ideal of the small, independent businessman (Thurman Arnold, 1937). Others have

Figure 4.9 The American government reacts to many pressures, some of them contradictory. For example, some legislators accept campaign support from tobacco farmers and manufacturers, and the government receives tax receipts from tobacco product sales. At the same time, legislators and bureaucrats are pressured by health authorities and citizen groups to control cigarette advertising and to create antismoking campaigns.

pointed out that without the antitrust laws (and the United States is the only nation that has them), any semblance of competition would disappear because the large corporations would take over the smaller ones (Adolf Berle, 1963).

With such conflicting views among the experts, it is no wonder that public policies toward competition are little understood. However, it must be noted that there are other alternatives open to government besides preserving pure competition or allowing complete monopoly power to develop. At the broadest level, the United States has steered a middle course between the two extremes: In those areas where the economy has most closely resembled pure competition (such as agriculture), it has acted to reduce the harsh effects of the market on business, labor, investors, and the community. In those areas that most closely approximate total monopolies, it has acted in recent times to break up monopolization and introduce some competition (Berle, 1963).

Such has not always been the case. Pure monopolies were often ignored by the government or even encouraged. Early enforcement of the antitrust laws (what enforcement there was) concentrated on the *behavior* of large corporations, penalizing those that cooperated in order to restrain trade or fix prices. In the last few decades there has also been increasing emphasis on the *structure* of companies, with a very large market share being considered sufficient reason to label a company as monopolistic; substantial reduction in competition has provided sufficient reason for government to block mergers between companies (Clair Wilcox, 1971).

Although the owners of small businesses are the first to attack the large corporations and pay lip service to "free enterprise," they have frequently sought protection from too much competition (John Kenneth Galbraith, 1952). And although the government has acted to reduce pure monopolies, it has also acted to restrict competition to help these smaller businesses. In the area of retailing, for example, in which chain stores are able to undersell independents because of their volume buying, the federal and state governments have passed laws prohibiting manufacturers from giving chain stores a special price (price discrimination). Also, *fair trade* laws have prohibited retailers from engaging in certain competitive practices, such as excessive discounting.

Exemptions from antitrust laws and noncompetitive policies have been applied to the shipping industry, to oil production, labor organizing, and to many of the professions. As James Anderson concluded, "the primary intended effect of the various legislative actions . . . has been more to preserve competitors than competition" (Anderson, 1966).

In summary one can characterize current American policies toward competition as the "management" rather than the maintenance of competition. Competition is encouraged where it is almost nonexistent, restricted where it is unwanted, and sometimes moderated where its effects are antisocial.

As noted in Chapter 3, the end result of American policies past and present has been to tolerate an economy with a great deal of concentrated wealth, particularly in the industrial sphere. Most economists agree that within particular industries the degree of concentration of wealth has not increased much in the last fifty years (Wilcox, 1971). In many industries, however, three or four producers account for over 75 percent of production (Richard Barber, 1970). And, in terms of aggregate concentration, the amount of wealth controlled by the 200 largest corporations has increased over the last few decades. The government attitude toward bigness in business has been to regulate it rather than to eliminate it.

The fact that bigness is tolerated at all is a matter of much dispute. Some economists, such as John Kenneth Galbraith, argue that it is the large firms that are most progressive in terms of innovation, efficiency, and the provision of goods at low prices (Galbraith, 1952; 1967). It is true that in many industries a certain size is necessary for efficient operation, but many economists and social critics point out that most of the giant corporations are bigger than this minimum efficient size (William N. Leonard, 1969).

Regardless of whether large corporations are the servants of efficiency, profits, sales, growth, or some other value, most scholars feel they are here to stay. Politicians, like investors, organized labor, corporate managers, and much of the public, do not care for uncertainty and risks. For this reason, they have resisted experimenting with the basic structure of the economy (Berle, 1963).

Large firms have come under attack for possessing too much political power, polluting the air and water, regimenting human behavior, destroying natural resources, producing unsafe products, and a host of other social ills (Mintz and Cohen, 1971). It is not clear, however, that reducing the size of business would cure many of these societal problems. As students of business politics have pointed out, small businesses are often just as guilty of these offenses as are large businesses (Richard Posner, 1971).

Government regulatory agencies charged with protecting the public against social ills have failed to do the job adequately (Louis Kohlmeier, 1969). Their failure has partly resulted from inherent limits to what bureaucracies can accomplish (James Q. Wilson, 1967) and partly from the fact that regulation of business has too often become "self-regulation" by business. This has happened because government agencies are often dependent on industry for technical information, and politicians resist strong enforcement of laws when it might hurt their chances to get campaign funds. In addition, business groups have been better organized for lobbying than consumer groups. In the words of law professor Richard Posner:

The very democratic structure that we so highly—and rightly—prize facilitates the plundering of taxpayers and consumers by interest groups able to use the powers of government for their own ends. The problem is much larger than the 200 largest corporations. (Posner, 1971, p. 121)

Ultimately, the problem is a conflict in goals, as Posner suggests; it is conflict between democracy and authority on one level and quantity and quality on another. Americans can have a better environment, better products, and a better quality of life if they are willing to give up some productivity in the economy and their freedom to share in the corporate spoils. The unresolved issue is whether we are willing to pay the price.

SUMMARY

America has evolved through periods of mercantilism, laissez faire, and corporate capitalism to the current mixed economy—which contains elements of both public and private control. Government regulates the economy to promote economic health and the general welfare and tries to anticipate major shifts in the business cycle in order to prevent depressions or runaway inflations. The major discussion is not over whether government should act but how it should act.

Government intervenes in the economy to promote a favorable business environment for the private economy, to regulate the privately owned monopolies of the controlled economy, and to produce goods and services. Government monitoring of the economy as a whole (macroeconomics) aims at relative stability of the business cycle, full employment, sufficient economic growth, and sufficient income levels. More specific goals include workers' bargaining rights, consumers' health and safety, and the environment.

Is fiscal policy or monetary policy a more effective means of economic regulation? The Federal Reserve Board, which controls monetary policy, is not under direct control of the President, whereas fiscal policy is more directly under his control.

Certain economic problems resist solution through present government policy. Hard-core unemployment persists despite regional development acts, manpower training, and the poverty program. Government struggles to balance economic growth with the need for equitable distribution of wealth. Tax policies such as capital gains, depletion allowances, and agricultural price supports financially benefit many who are not in need.

The American economy is populated with large and powerful corporations that are substantially uncontrolled. Government has tried to encourage competition in certain instances and to restrict it in other instances.

SUGGESTED READINGS

Bell, Daniel and Irving Kristol (eds.). *Capitalism Today.* New York: Basic Books, 1970.

Cotter, Cornelius. *Government and Private Enterprise.* New York: Holt, Rinehart and Winston, 1960.

Monsen, Joseph, Jr. and Mark Cannon. *The Makers of Public Policy: American Power Groups and Their Ideologies.* New York: McGraw-Hill, 1965.

Reagan, Michael D. *The Managed Economy.* New York: Oxford University Press, 1963.

Shonfield, Andrew. *Modern Capitalism: The Changing Balance of Public and Private Power.* New York: Oxford University Press, 1965.

Weidenbaum, Murray. *The Modern Public Sector.* New York: Basic Books, 1969.

Figure 4a.1 What can break through the culturally and psychologically devastating effects of the poverty cycle? Are the Appalachian poor destined always to be only spectators rather than participants in the national prosperity, or can the children of this oppressed region look forward to a brighter future?

In his 1960 presidential campaign John F. Kennedy set out to win the crucial West Virginia primary election by taking an extensive whistle-stop tour of the mountain communities of the state. In the course of that campaign Kennedy glimpsed a way of life that sat like a sore thumb on the clean hand of what John Kenneth Galbraith had termed "the affluent society." The unemployment rate in West Virginia was about 10 percent in 1960, and one-sixth of the state's 2 million residents subsisted on welfare food. Among the coal-mining communities in the southern mountains, the unemployment rate was as high as 15 percent, and over 50 percent of the families in some of these shabby towns had annual incomes below $3,000. The coal mines were models of deadliness with the highest accident rate of any American industry and an accident fatality rate four times that of Great Britain's mines. Neither the United States Bureau of Mines nor the once radical United Mine Workers had attempted to enforce the existing safety regula-

tions. Thousands of crippled ex-coal miners, widows, and middle-aged victims of black lung—a fatal disease caused by coal dust—were living marginally in dilapidated mining camps along with the many unemployed who had not worked since the 1948 recession.

The West Virginia primary is not ordinarily one of the major events along the road to the presidential nomination. It became so for John Kennedy because it was the first test of his ability as a Roman Catholic to carry the votes of an overwhelmingly Protestant and rural state. It was this unusual juncture of events that brought the urbane and wealthy Bostonian face to face with desperate rural poverty. His visible reactions and his promises to push for federal programs to aid such depressed areas not only won him West Virginia's votes but gave sudden impetus to the dawning national awareness of poverty in our midst. Throughout the presidential campaign and during his brief term of office in the White House, John Kennedy attempted to transform

poverty from a stark fact for some into national awareness for all.

Several currents of the 1950s and early 1960s had contributed to the surge of concern over American poverty. The civil rights movement had focused national attention on the prosperity gap between blacks and whites. The idea of structural (or permanent) poverty, based on a poverty mentality that reproduces itself indefinitely, began to be discussed with respect to black Americans. It was only a matter of time before the public became aware that although a majority of blacks are poor, a majority of poor Americans are white. Juvenile delinquency, gang warfare, and crime in general increased throughout the 1950s and ultimately raised concern about the breeding grounds of crime—the ghettos. (The popularity of the movie *West Side Story* testifies to the public awareness, but not to the understanding, of ghetto culture.) Concurrently, the rising unemployment of blue-collar workers, resulting from the industrial automation following World War II, was coming to national attention. The

bitter ideological competition with the Soviet Union during the Cold War years pressed America to solve the domestic problems that marred its selfproclaimed image as a model of liberty and justice.

Within this framework of social, economic, and ideological pressures, Kennedy promised in his presidential platform to give top legislative and administrative priority to aiding depressed areas. As President he received a task-force report on poverty that recommended a multibillion-dollar federal aid program. In May 1961 President Kennedy signed the Area Redevelopment Act (ARA) and sparked a surge of liberal reformist sentiment that resulted in hundreds of books and articles on American poverty. The program came to full bloom in Lyndon Johnson's War on Poverty. It was a bloom with thorns, however, and by 1968 most of Johnson's poverty programs had been impaled on them.

The federal aid program to Appalachia incorporated some of the most innovative ideas about government-sponsored economic development

and was considered to be a show-piece of federal poverty legislation. Yet ten years and billions of dollars later, the Appalachian poor were still as poor as ever. An analysis of the Appalachian program—its hopes and failings—shows the possibilities for success or failure of other regionally focused federal aid programs.

APPALACHIA: THE LAND AND ITS OWNERS

The name *Appalachia* loosely applies to the Appalachian Mountain region, which runs through portions of nine states in the southeastern United States. It includes counties in western Pennsylvania, western Virginia, eastern Kentucky, northeastern Tennessee, most of West Virginia, northern Alabama, and bits of Maryland, North Carolina, and Georgia. The fact that these counties are all considered part of Appalachia is most significant. Because of various geographical, historical, and economic factors, these counties have much more in common with one another than with the other counties in their own states.

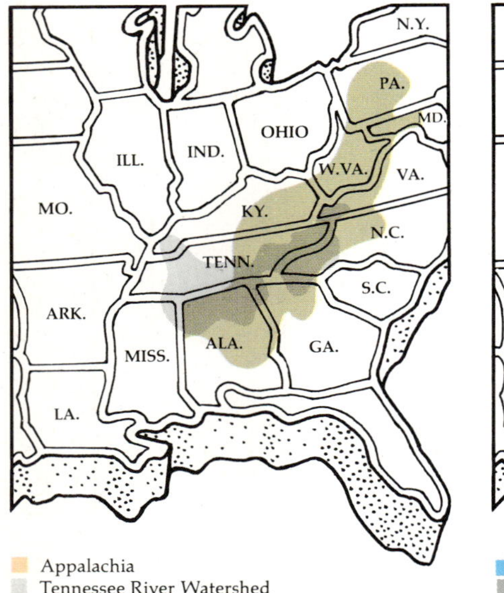

Appalachia
Tennessee River Watershed

★ Beryllium
■ Oil, Natural Gas   ○ Iron Ore
■ Coal Deposits   ◉ Copper

Figure 4a.2 Appalachia and the Tennessee Valley (far left) are areas of great importance to the political economy of much of the nation. To understand the economics, and therefore a great deal of the politics of a region, one must study the region's natural resources—its coal and oil deposits, its minerals, its rivershed. This map (left) shows some of the leading mineral deposits of Appalachia and the Tennessee Valley, resources that either provide the basis for self-development or serve as a lure to outside power.

Figure 4a.3 The miles that separate corporation headquarters from the rich coal deposits of Appalachia serve to insulate corporate decision makers from some of the negative effects their decisions may have on the landscape (right).

The Appalachian Mountain range is quite rugged, and its valleys are fertile and tillable. The heavy rainfall and equable climate will support good crops of potatoes, grains, berries, grapes, and other fruit, and 16 million acres have been judged suitable for pasturage. For the first 150 years of American settlement, the inhabitants of this area lived by farming, as did the rest of the country. The slopes of the Appalachians once were thickly covered by forests of poplar, oak, walnut, chestnut, hickory, maple, and other varieties of deciduous trees. Beneath the now heavily lumbered slopes lies the coal. Even after a century of mining, 250 billion tons of the world's best coal still lies buried in the Appalachian Mountains. Rich oil and natural gas deposits are there, too, along with limestone, talc, cement rock, iron ore, clays, gneiss, gibbsite, and grahamite. In short, the region has vast potential for development. Why, then, are the residents of Appalachia so poor?

The vital clue to this mystery is buried in a thousand records in the tax assessment offices of Appalachian counties and states. An examination of these records shows that most of the mineral and forest resources of Appalachia are owned by the largest corporations in the United States. United States Steel, Bethlehem Steel, International Harvester, Ford Motor Company, Inland Steel, Republic Steel, and Jones & Laughlin are among the names written on deeds of ownership in the county assessment offices. In addition, there are numerous less famous corporations, such as Virginia Coal and Iron, Kentucky River Coal Corporation, and Big Sandy Corporation, that own thousands of acres and lease them to operating companies for the royalties payable on coal, oil, and other minerals extracted. Land-leasing is an extremely profitable business in Appalachia. In 1967 one authority called Virginia Coal and Iron "almost certainly the most profitable investor-owned corporation in the United States." Seventy-six percent of its corporate profits were tax free at the federal level, and after state and county taxes, the company still realized a net profit of 61 percent (Harry Caudill, 1963).

The tax systems of the Appalachian states allow the owners of Appalachia's mineral and forest resources to extract and export millions of dollars worth of these resources every year without paying any significant portion of the profits in local and state taxes. As a result, the counties of Appalachia lack the tax revenues necessary to construct the schools, hospitals, and transportation facilities so desperately needed. It is the tax system, manipulated and controlled by the corporate owners of Appalachia, that has victimized the people of this region while the corporations have grown rich.

The mining and lumbering companies have long controlled the political system of Appalachia and thus have been able to ward off attempts to redress economic inequity. State politicians have until very recently simply ignored the deplorable conditions of their Appalachian communities—undoubtedly because their political careers were largely dependent on the support of such

powerful corporations as United States Steel and International Harvester.

The People of Appalachia

Only very recently have the people of Appalachia involved themselves in electoral politics. Since their arrival in the 1700s the settlers of Appalachia have harbored a suspicion of governmental power that derived from their hatred of the English monarchy. In the fertile and open spaces of the Appalachian Mountains they sought and developed a life style based on self sufficiency and rugged individualism. They worked the land in a primitive and nonconservationist manner— why conserve the soil when there was so much of it? They simply cleared a new patch of land when a field became sterile through the continued planting of a single crop. Until the 1870s there was little need for local government in Appalachia because there were few towns— families preferred to live in isolation. Even the most rudimentary traces of government were slow in appearing. For example, when the new

county of Floyd, Kentucky was organized in 1800, it took sixteen years for the inhabitants to construct a courthouse twenty-two feet square. As soon as the building was finished, it was burned to the ground.

Outsiders Come to Appalachia

Before the Civil War the potential for economic development was limited by Appalachia's subsistence-agriculture base. Appalachian farming methods, like those of the plantation South, were exploitative and inefficient; Appalachian society, however, differing from that of the South, lacked the cohesion necessary to support even a minimum of industrial development. The area was vulnerable to profit-minded outsiders.

With the dominance of the North established firmly by the Civil War, speculators from the industrialized North came to Appalachia and discovered the riches in coal that lay buried beneath the land—riches unperceived by the farmers who worked the fields above. By 1869 the use of coke, a derivative of coal,

had exceeded the use of charcoal in the production of pig iron; by 1880 one million tons of steel were being produced yearly by the Bessemer process of converting pig iron. Northern businessmen correctly assessed the value of Appalachian coal to the industrialization of the North. Furthermore, the valuable stands of timber could be used in constructing the railroads needed to connect the Appalachian coal fields with the markets of the North.

By 1885 large tracts of land had been bought up by northern business interests. The maximum price was about 26 cents per acre. The Appalachian owners—many of whom found they had never gained formal title to the land they claimed—were attracted by the possibility of ready cash. They had no way of knowing the potential value of their property.

The Broad-Form Deed

Most of the land transactions involved the *broad-form deed*, which gave the buyer title to all the coal, oil, gas, mineral, and metallic substances under the land and author-

Figure 4a.4 Poverty is certainly not the prerogative of nonwhites. In fact, there are more whites below the poverty line in the United States than nonwhites. What does poverty mean? It means having many children because birth control information is not distributed or is misunderstood or because birth control devices are too expensive. It means seeing the hope and potential of the children wasted in a lackluster childhood surrounded by parents and neighbors who have lost hope in the future. The lonely stores of Appalachia survive on nickel-and-dime spending and the subsidy of food coupons when they are available to the poor.

ized the buyer to alter the surface of the land in any way "convenient or necessary" for the extraction of the resources. The flexibility of these broad-form deeds, and their liberal interpretation by the courts, enabled mining companies to deforest the countryside to obtain timber for mining props, to divert and pollute the water, and to cover the surface with toxic mining refuse, regardless of the effect of these actions on the inhabitants of the area. Some buyers preferred the short-form deed, which merely gave title to the coal, oil, and minerals beneath the surface without all the immunities and privileges of the broad-form. The short-form also exempted the owner from paying taxes on the surface land, an advantage to early speculators who did not intend to develop their property immediately after purchase.

Coal: The Economic Backbone of Appalachia

By 1910 a major portion of the land, about 75 percent of the saleable timber, and at least 85 percent of the coal and mineral resources were owned by nonresidents of Appalachia. The coal-mining industry was well on its way to becoming the economic backbone of Appalachia. Most Appalachians were pleased at the trend, as worn-out land had made individual subsistence farming increasingly difficult, and the remaining good land was beginning to accumulate in the hands of a few men. Working in a coal mine was better in some ways than sharecropping another man's land. Many of the coal camps offered electricity, medical care, and manufactured goods, all of which represented a degree of affluence to the destitute people of Appalachia.

Such services, however, were not provided by the coal companies out of generosity; the miners had to pay for everything they got, and at prices that assured the companies a profit. The workers had to live in the camps if they wanted to work in the mines. With the widespread adoption of scrip payment to workers—payment in coupons redeemable only at the company store—the coal companies were able to get back most of the wages they had paid out.

In spite of such practices, Appalachians flocked to the mines in the boom years from 1912 to 1927. The dominant emotion was gratitude toward the companies for the work they provided. The bigger coal camps got municipal charters and became incorporated cities whose administrators were hand picked by the company bosses. The bosses controlled the crucial positions of county tax commissioner and county judge by virtue of their ability to intimidate the town citizens (all of whom depended on coal-company employment for their livelihood).

By virtue of their control, the companies were able to keep their tax assessments extremely low, even when population increases made the establishment of schools, roads, and health services a necessity. Individual property owners were forced to bear the brunt of providing the badly needed tax revenues. At one point during the boom years, the tax-assessment value of individually owned land was fifteen or

Figure 4a.5 Americans have ambivalent attitudes toward large corporations and toward the values and attitudes that shape corporate decisions. Executives of large corporations are afforded opportunities, life style, and access to expert assistance and enormous organization that gives them power and responsibilities far beyond the norm. In providing job opportunities in depressed areas, such as Appalachia, they may see themselves as philanthropic. But in addition to jobs, people require self-esteem, responsibility, and the power to make the major decisions affecting their lives. Although the corporate executive wishes to do well, his power still allows him to manage men and industries as he sees fit, which may or may not be in the public interest as the majority would define it.

Robber Baron or Job Provider?

twenty dollars per acre, whereas corporate land and mineral wealth was assessed at only five or six dollars per acre. But the individual land holders of Appalachia simply could not afford to finance the populous communities and, beginning around 1915, various counties began the practice of selling bonds to finance roads and schools. These debts, which the counties were never able to repay, ensured Appalachia's prolonged destitution.

THE NEW DEAL: GOVERNMENT TAKES ACTION

The coal companies' paternalistic employment system, such a boon to the Appalachians during the early years of the coal industry, had also instilled in them a sense of dependence and personal inadequacy. When coal orders began to drop in 1927 and reached an all-time low in 1932, the miners stayed with the companies and went into debt to them, working whenever they could. The Great Depression was, of course, a nightmare for most wage-earning Americans; for millions it was an era of hunger, cold, indignity and, most tragic of all, deepening feelings of uselessness. But whatever its effects on Americans generally, the Depression was nowhere more appalling than in the coal counties of Appalachia. There, destitution came first, stayed longest and, for most, still persists.

In 1933 President Franklin Roosevelt spurred the economic recovery legislation that he had promised would provide a "New Deal" for Americans. The Civilian Conservation Corps (CCC), Works Progress Administration (WPA), and National Youth Administration (NYA) put thousands of mountaineers on their payrolls. An emergency food-dole program was immediately implemented (and in many mining communities the emergency would last ten years), although at the time it was not realized how difficult it was for self-reliant Appalachians to accept food handouts.

The National Industrial Recovery Act of 1933 had a dynamic effect on the coal communities of Appalachia, as it had on many other industries. Both prices and wages slowly rose under the codes of fair competition suggested by the federal government, and the confidence of both miners and operators surged. When the Supreme Court declared the act unconstitutional in 1935, the economy of the coal industry plummeted. In the gloom that followed, trade unionism, which had been held at bay by the hopeful prospects of New Deal legislation, moved in to fill the needs of the desperate miners.

The Unionization Movement

The United Mine Workers (UMW), under the direction of John L. Lewis, had been organizing since 1920. From the beginning, the union had met with brutal resistance from the company operators. The "blacklist" was instituted to intimidate miners from joining the UMW, and armed thugs were imported from Chicago and other nonunion cities to terrorize union men. Such tactics intensified the enmity between miners and the company operators and thus increased the commitment of UMW members to the union's goals.

The National Labor Relations Act of 1935 asserted the workers' right to collective bargaining—which allows union representatives to negotiate wages, hours, and working conditions in behalf of all the company's employees—and thereby gave impetus to the union movement. Within ten years the militant UMW would begin a series of annual strikes to enforce its demands for higher wages and shorter hours. The establishment of a health and welfare fund, based on industry contributions, required the companies to make restitution to the many men it had crippled and to the widows and the orphans of the coal miners who had died. These successes helped assure the dominance of the UMW.

TVA: A Model for Regional Development

One of the most successful New Deal projects was the Tennessee Valley Authority (TVA), established in 1933. It completely revitalized a region similar to Appalachia and has thus come to represent a model for regional economic development.

The Tennessee Valley has a history much like that of the Appalachian Plateau. Its subsistence-farming economy was disturbed by northern speculation after the Civil War; its land was also deforested and its soil ruined. Unlike Appalachia, however, the Tennessee Valley has few coal deposits; the state and local governments, therefore, did not become so intimately bound up with the fate of huge mining and steel corporations. Through legislation approved by state and local authorities, the federal government was able to take control of the region; it authorized TVA to construct and operate dams, electricity-generating plants, and fertilizer plants; and to undertake long-term regional planning, including urbanization, navigation, and conservation of natural resources.

The TVA was extraordinarily successful in developing the economy of the Tennessee Valley. Industry was attracted by the low rates for electricity; the tax base of the area consequently expanded to provide needed schools, hospitals, and public services. Agricultural practices were made more efficient; the hills were reforested; the waterways were made navigable for large freight ships; and lakes were created for public recreation. Congressman John Rankin called TVA "the most profitable investment the American People have made since the Louisiana Purchase."

But there was a hidden price to be paid by the people of Appalachia for the success of TVA—a price to be paid in the form of strip-mined land to provide the low-grade coal needed by TVA's electricity-generating plants. Later in this chapter, that story is told in detail.

THE WAR ON POVERTY

The Area Redevelopment Act (ARA) of 1961 provided for long-term loans at low rates of interest to new businesses planning to locate in depressed areas. It also provided financial aid to depressed communities to enable them to develop the public facilities needed to attract business; it provided for the establishment of training programs to help the unemployed and underemployed get jobs; and it aimed to provide technical assistance

Figure 4a.6 When the poor come into contact with poverty program workers to develop and implement programs, there may well be built-in cultural hurdles to effective agreements. Each side will tend to view the problem from a differing perspective, based on the particular individual's origins, education, and life style. These problems will have an influence whether the particular poverty situation that is being addressed stems from the valleys of Appalachia or exists in the ghetto environments of Chicago or Los Angeles.

to communities for the development of programs designed to stimulate their economic growth. The ARA was administered through the Area Redevelopment Administration, which dispensed federal funds to the poorest one-third of the nation's counties.

The success of the county aid programs was limited. For example, after two years in operation in Perry County, Kentucky—one of the poorest areas of Appalachia—the ARA had created no new jobs and had given job training to only forty-five people, in spite of the county's 14 percent unemployment. The biggest demand for ARA grants and loans came from the recreation and tourism industry. A spokesman for the ARA seemed to approve of the industry's requests, saying, "We really are an affluent society, and if only the affluent people will take their vacations in the depressed areas, things will get spread around" (David Walls and John Stephenson, 1972). It seems unlikely, however, that the growth of this industry alone would significantly raise the standard of living in regions such as Appalachia.

Nevertheless, the Council of Appalachian Governors turned to the ARA for help in 1962. The Council, made up of the governors of all the Appalachian states, had no legal authority or staff to implement any plans it might develop. The ARA shifted the responsibility by recommending to President Kennedy that he establish a joint federal-state committee to study the Appalachian region. The President's Appalachian Regional Committee (PARC) was set up in the spring of 1963, under the chairmanship of Franklin D. Roosevelt, Jr. PARC was responsible for the preparation of an overall plan for the redevelopment of Appalachia.

By autumn 1963 PARC had not developed any concrete—much less creative—plans. *New York Times* articles on Kentucky children so hungry they were eating mud from between chimney rocks, however, apparently roused both President Kennedy and the lethargic PARC to action. In mid-November, Kennedy told his principal economic adviser that antipoverty measures would definitely be part of the 1964 legislative program, and $500 million was tentatively earmarked. That same month Kennedy was assassinated in Dallas.

Lyndon Johnson attempted to follow through on the poverty measures begun by Kennedy. In March 1964 Congress passed the Economic Opportunity Act (EOA), with a proposed budget of $962.5 million. An amorphous piece of legislation, EOA proposed "community action programs" as the vehicle for distributing federal funds, but it failed to define "community." The roles of the various layers of government—federal, state, and local—and of public versus private agencies were all left unspecified.

The director of the Office of Economic Opportunity was expected to define the program. President Johnson chose Sargent Shriver, former head of the Peace Corps and brother-in-law of President Kennedy, as director. Shriver had headed the EOA task force and had pushed for "maximum feasible participation of residents of the areas and the members of the groups served" by the community-action programs (Economic

Opportunity Act, 88th Congress). The implications of this phrase precipitated intense conflict, most dramatically apparent in Appalachia in regard to the VISTA program.

As a domestic version of the Peace Corps, VISTA sent federally recruited, trained, and salaried workers into the Appalachian Mountains to organize community-action programs by working with the people. VISTA workers, who were mostly young and earnest, were responsible to state and local agencies, but in the beginning they had much leeway in carrying out their duties. As a result, VISTA quickly became the core of a grassroots movement that engaged many poor Appalachians in a struggle with their local governments. The run-down roads, the backward schools, and the power of the coal companies all came under attack at P.T.A. and church meetings and in letters to the editors of local newspapers. County officials were confronted and demonstrations were staged. One such demonstration, in Pike County, Kentucky, effectively ended the Appalachian VISTA program.

In August 1967 a retired Pike County miner named Jink Ray, some neighbors, and some VISTA workers physically blocked a bulldozer belonging to the Puritan Coal Company as it was preparing to grade the hillside behind Jink Ray's house. The action climaxed a campaign against strip mining and the broad-form deeds that had allowed coal companies to strip the Appalachian hills with impunity.

The demonstration resulted in an unprecedented show of support from the Kentucky state government. The strip-mining permit was withdrawn from the Puritan Coal Company. The Pike County government, however, took a different line of action. Eleven days later one VISTA worker and two members of another social-action group were arrested in midnight raids. The charge: sedition. The raids were led by Thomas Ratliff, the Pike County prosecuting attorney; he was also a former coal-mine operator and was the Republican candidate for lieutenant governor of Kentucky. Ratliff confiscated what he described as "a communistic library out of this

world" from the room of the VISTA worker. The books included some Russian short stories, *Catch-22*, and an account of the Berkeley student movement (David Walls and John Stephenson, 1972).

The Pike County arrests were obviously a pre-election ploy by Ratliff, but the fear that "communists" were infiltrating Appalachia through the poverty programs was strong enough to be effective against VISTA. The same fear had caused southern congressmen to require a noncommunist oath for Job Corps participants in the amendments to the Economic Opportunity Act in 1965. Apparently under such anticommunist pressure, Shriver cut off all funds to the Kentucky VISTA program one week after the Pike County raids. From that time on VISTA workers organized at their own risk. Local politicians, assured that the federal government would not back up its VISTA workers, jailed them on dubious charges, especially around election time. Since 1968, VISTA operations have been carefully limited. The Appalachian VISTA experience had established the outside

Figure 4a.7   Civilian Conservation Corps (CCC) camp for workers (far left top) building roads through Angel Forest in Lancaster, California in 1937 and (bottom) Work Projects Administration (WPA) water-conservation project near Pierre, South Dakota, which provided work for drought-stricken farmers. The Blue Eagle (left) was the emblem of the National Recovery Administration (NRA), which administered the various regulatory programs authorized by the National Industrial Recovery Act of 1933.

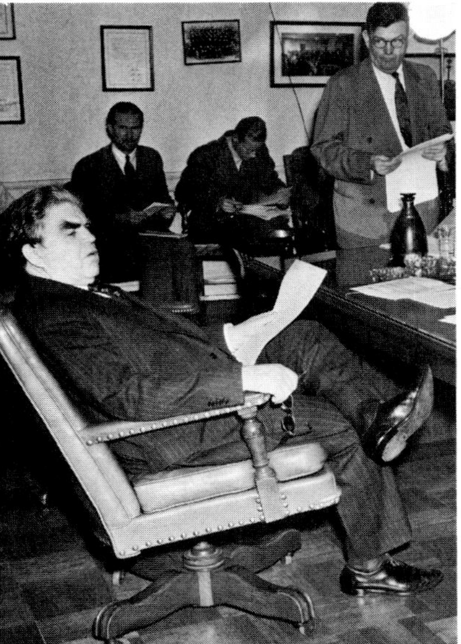

Figure 4a.8   John L. Lewis (1880–1969) worked his way up from the depths of the coal mines to the office of president of the United Mine Workers (1920–1960). During the mining depression of the 1920s, Lewis led a series of strikes to preserve the United Mine Workers. In 1935 he founded the Congress of Industrial Organizations, which later joined with the American Federation of Labor to form the AFL-CIO. The formation of the CIO was Lewis's great achievement: He created a powerful organization of workers in the mass-production industries, even though many had thought that only the skilled-craft industries were adaptable to union organization.

limits implied in the phrase "maximum feasible participation."

The Appalachian Regional Development Act

"Minimum feasible participation" of the poor seemed the motivation behind another Appalachian program passed in 1965. The Appalachian Regional Development Act (ARDA) combined elements of the 1964 report of PARC and the demands of the Council of Appalachian Governors.

In the financial breakdown of ARDA, shown in Table 4a.1, almost 85 percent of the allocated $1.09 billion was earmarked for highway construction, whereas less than 2 percent went for vocational schools and only 4 percent for health facilities. The justification—that roads ensure an adequate foundation for other investments—was possible because the criteria for the distribution of federal funds included both *need,* in terms of per capita income and rates of unemployment, and *location,* an area with "a significant potential for growth." Gaining a return on public investment took priority over clothing and

Table 4a.1   The ARDA of 1965

PROGRAM	FUNDS AUTHORIZED (in millions)
Creation of commission	$ 2.2
Development and access highways	840.0
Construction of regional health centers	41.0
Operation and administration of regional health centers	28.0
Land stabilization, conservation, erosion control	17.0
Timber development organizations	5.0
Mining area restoration	36.5
Water resources survey	5.0
Construction of vocational education facilities	16.0
Construction of sewage treatment facilities	6.0
Supplements to federal grant-in-aid construction and equipment programs	90.0
Financing of local development districts and research	5.5
Total	$ 1.09 billion

Source: Fishman, Leo (ed.). West Virginia University Conference on *Poverty Amidst Affluence.* (New Haven: Yale University Press, 1966)

feeding the poor or building schools to educate them. Roads received top priority because state governors and local industry wanted to ease commercial transport and to attract new industry to the area. The governors received veto power over federal and local proposals for use of ARDA funds.

The 1968 annual report of ARDA stated, "Most measurable improvements in the Appalachian economy since the Act passed in 1965 can be attributed mainly to the sustained growth of the national economy since 1961." These "measurable improvements" included an increase in the Appalachian employment rate of 0.2 percent over the national rate of increase, and an increase in per capita income of 0.36 percent over the national rate. Yet the unemployment rates in Appalachian Kentucky and West Virginia remained respectively almost triple and double the national unemployment rate of 3.8 percent in 1967. The ARDA report concluded that "the people in the Region's most rural areas are still those who feel the impact of economic improvement last" (Annual Report, 1969).

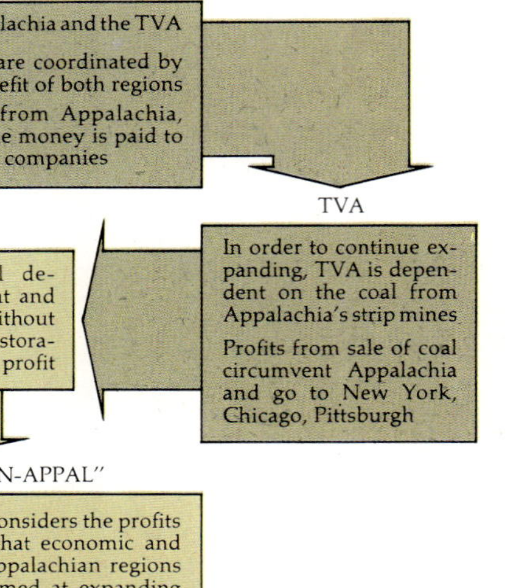

Figure 4a.9 The Tennessee Valley Authority, which is a corporation of the federal government, buys the great amounts of coal necessary for its expansion from the very coal mining companies that are the absentee owners of Appalachia; it thereby contributes to the continuation of strip mining and profit-removal from that region. A possible solution to the problem of rehabilitation of Appalachia might entail the combining of the neighboring TVA and Appalachia projects under an umbrella authority, for which we have coined the word "Tenn-Appal." Such an authority would be responsible for determining the proper overlap of the two projects to maximize the cooperation and mutual aid of both.

If ARDA has had trouble citing its significant contributions to the welfare of Appalachia, the residents themselves have found it nearly impossible. The statistics cited by the 1968 ARDA annual report show only the slightest increase in Appalachian employment and per capita income. Yet in real terms the increases are negligible because a few Appalachian metropolitan areas would naturally have grown without federal help. In addition, the high emigration rate—West Virginia alone lost 6 percent of its population—undoubtedly accounts for lower unemployment.

Why do so many Appalachians leave for other areas? The fact that a major new manufacturing plant in eastern Kentucky had over 6,000 applicants for only forty-five trainee positions suggests the answer. The few vocational schools that ARDA brought to Appalachia are training plumbers and typists for jobs that do not and will not exist in the counties of Appalachia. The lucky graduates of these schools are moving to Chicago and Detroit, as capable young Appalachians have always done.

APPALACHIA AND THE 1970s

The environment of Appalachia is in a shocking state of decay. Ten thousand miles of its waterways are polluted by acid drainage, mostly from strip mines, and mountains of coal waste dot the landscape. The *Wall Street Journal* estimated that water reclamation alone could cost $10 billion. Yet the primary source of Appalachia's environmental pillage continues unabated. Strip mining—an inexpensive method of mining surface coal—was the coal industry's inevitable response to the nation's increasing fuel shortage and rising labor costs.

Strip Mining: The Moonscape of Appalachia

Since World War II a significant proportion (34 percent in 1967) of the United States coal production has been strip-mined coal. Strip mining is cheaper than deep-pit mining because it uses bulldozers and other large machines to scrape the hillsides for coal; output per man-day is roughly double and thus operating costs are far lower. Surface coal is generally of inferior quality, low in heating capacity (or BTU content), but technological advances have facilitated its effective use in electricity-generating plants.

Much of the demand for Appalachia's strip-mined coal comes from the Tennessee Valley. Post-war mechanization and the lure of TVA's cheap power produced increased demands for electricity in the 1950s. TVA's first response was to buy cheap coal from nonunion mines. After 1954, however, government-owned institutions were prohibited from purchasing more than $10,000 worth of materials from companies paying less than union wages. TVA had two options: either limit its production or buy cheap, strip-mined coal. TVA chose the latter. Many Appalachians find it ironic that TVA, a model regional development program, is accelerating Appalachia's devastation.

Attempts at Land Reclamation

Strip mining need not permanently damage the land if conducted under certain conditions and followed by

Figure 4a.10 **The loss of topsoil and the ravages of erosion make strip-mined land resemble the craggy surfaces of the lunar landscape. There is increasing pressure to halt these destructive mining practices and, in some areas, attempts are being made to restore the terrain. Yet the need for inexpensive sources of energy has led to the exploration and development of other, previously untapped deposits of coal and oil—as in Alaska and New Mexico—as well as to expanded research in the areas of solar energy and nuclear fission.**

adequate reclamation procedures. In western Kentucky, for example, two decades of strip mining have not permanently altered the land. The terrain is relatively flat, and pits can be filled once the extractable coal has been exhausted. In mountainous eastern Kentucky and southern West Virginia, however, reclamation is costly, and few coal operators have attempted it. In fact, no successful reclamation has been achieved on slopes greater than twenty-eight degrees. Once the vegetation on these slopes has been destroyed and the land disturbed, erosion becomes uncontrollable. Rainfall becomes a curse, bringing with it the ravages of floods, landslides, and acid-polluted waterways.

Since the passage of Kentucky's reclamation bill in 1966, strip mining has become the work of large companies that can afford to make a show of good reclamation practice. Companies like Beth-Elkhorn, a subsidiary of Bethlehem Steel, recognize the importance of changing the "land-rape" image created by environmentalist exposés. In addition to running full-page ads in local newspapers that list their beautification accomplishments, managers at Beth-Elkhorn gave out jars of blackberry jelly made from berries grown on the site of Beth-Elkhorn's reclaimed mines.

An Alternative: A Public Utility District

On August 28, 1972 *Barron's* financial report characterized the entire Appalachia Poverty Program as a costly failure. A billion dollars had been poured into the Appalachian Mountains, and no significant change in the standard of living had been produced. As an attempt at economic rejuvenation of a region, the federal poverty legislation had failed miserably.

There had been change, however, in the consciousness of the residents of Appalachia. They had been promised that their suffering could and would be alleviated. When real change seemed slow in appearing, they began to organize groups to ask the people in power why it had not appeared. Because of this pressure they began to gain small concessions—a strip-mining company's permit turned down, a compensation bill for victims of black lung. They turned their attention to the UMW. Once militant and bent on reform, the union had declined to the point where a federal jury in Lexington, Kentucky (1969) had found it guilty of conspiring to create a monopoly of the soft-coal industry. This "sweetheart" agreement between the UMW and a large coal company was an indication of the polarity that had developed in the 1950s and 1960s between union leaders and rank-and-file members.

A powerful reform faction, however, began to develop among the rank-and-file miners in the late 1960s. They backed a slate headed by Joseph Yablonski in an election against Tony Boyle and the entrenched union leadership. Boyle won, but the Yablonski group cried "fix" and demanded a federal investigation of the election. Soon thereafter Yablonski, his wife, and his daughter were murdered in their beds. When the paid gunmen were caught, their con-

Figure 4a.11 Tourists and residents alike may marvel at the size of the machines that chew the earth for its coal (top left), but the GEM of Egypt (Giant Earth-Mover) and other strip-mining devices leave much ugliness in their wake. Efforts at land reclamation, here beginning to take hold near Cadiz, Ohio, are successful only in certain geological areas (top right). The mines have been trusted by the area's residents as a constant source of livelihood, but the newer methods of coal mining, which require less manpower, have led to massive unemployment. Without innovative government action, these children have little possibility of breaking the cycle of permanent poverty. United Mine Workers President W. A. "Tony" Boyle (far right), testifying in court regarding attempts to rig a UMW election, efforts that were marked by violence and intimidation.

fessions implicated high union officials as those responsible for the murders. Meanwhile, the union election was declared fraudulent and a new president, Arnold Miller, was elected. He fulfilled his preelection promise to decrease his and other officials' salaries and to auction off the union's Cadillac limousines. It thus seemed likely that the UMW would once again become a significant force on behalf of the interests of miners and of the region generally.

Change is also reflected in the increasing support for the development of a TVA-type public utility district in Appalachia. Many feel that publicly owned energy developments, based on public natural resources, are the only way to generate the revenue needed to bring Appalachia out of its mire.

In 1968 the United States Geological Survey and the Interior Department collaborated in producing a comprehensive catalog of the area's gigantic mineral deposits. "Mineral Resources of the Appalachian Region" points out that power plants situated at the mouths of large mines offer the best hope for lifting Appalachia to economic independence and self-reliance.

To aid the territory rather than to speed its destruction, such plants would necessarily be publicly owned, with the profits flowing into schools, libraries, roads, health facilities, reforestation, reclamation projects, and improvement of agricultural lands. In the state of Washington, publicly owned utility districts have demonstrated that it is possible to generate power without having to ship the profits to corporate headquarters on New York's Wall Street; the lessons learned there should be brought to Appalachia.

For example, the Kentucky Legislature might establish an Eastern Kentucky Development District as a public corporation. The agency would have the power of *eminent domain* (or the power to take private land for public use); the authority to issue self-financing bonds; and the duty to develop and utilize the resources of the mountain counties for the public welfare. Its tax-exempt bonds might be used to build dams and lakes for recreational and industrial purposes. The agency would build coal-fired electricity generators and pay for the coal veins that the district's condemnation suits would restore to the public domain. The massive flows of electricity would help alleviate the predicted energy crisis.

Chelan County, Washington (population 40,000) grosses over $20 million annually from power sales out of a single dam on the Columbia River; by utilizing its vast coal fields and by harnessing the power of its rivers, eastern Kentucky could dwarf this achievement. Conservative estimates indicate that $3 billion could be raised for the territory's revitalization, a process that (after repayment of the initial investment) would clear at least $100 million annually for modernizing facilities and services. Other states could do the same within their respective mountain counties and, through interstate compacts, could establish an Appalachian Mountain Authority to rebuild the entire region.

This look at Appalachia has several implications for the role of govern-

Figure 4a.12 Having grown up in an area of Texas that was hard hit by the Great Depression and the ravages of nature, Lyndon Johnson understood some of the problems of Appalachia. His visit to that destitute area and the legislative program oriented toward it, which formed a significant part of his Great Society program, must have seemed a shot in the arm to the residents of the mountains and hollows. But the temporary morale boost and the legislation that was enacted left many of the area's problems far short of solution.

ment in managing the economy. It demonstrates that for some economic problems there is no alternative to governmental intervention. Only the government possesses the financial resources to deal with problems of such huge scale as Appalachian poverty. Indeed, only the government possesses the power to halt the rape of the mountains and valleys. But this chapter also demonstrates that federal money and the creation of new programs and agencies are no guarantee of significant progress. Government programs may be ill-conceived. Or, they may be deflected away from the real problems. Indeed, it seems likely that government efforts at regional development will always fail unless local citizens become sufficiently organized and involved to give direction to government programs. The mountain folks' traditional pride, rugged independence, and suspicion of outsiders played a major role in creating the poverty trap in which they find themselves.

And these same factors have been exploited to impede government efforts to aid the region. Ultimately, poverty is a human condition, and its solution depends on what people do.

SUGGESTED READINGS

Caudill, Harry M. *Night Comes to the Cumberlands: A Biography of a Depressed Area.* Boston: Little, Brown, 1963.

Coles, Robert. *Migrants, Sharecroppers, Mountaineers.* Boston: Little, Brown, 1967.

Harrington, Michael. *The Other America.* New York: Macmillan, 1962.

Sundquist, James L. (ed.). *On Fighting Poverty.* New York: Basic Books, 1969.

Walls, David S. and John B. Stephenson. *Appalachia in the Sixties.* Lexington: University Press of Kentucky, 1972.

5

FOREIGN AFFAIRS AND NATIONAL SECURITY

In the quarter century between World War I and World War II, concerns at home dominated public affairs. United States participation in World War II and in the Cold War that followed, however, led to a new preoccupation: a worldwide effort to contain the perceived expansion of the Soviet and Chinese nations and to prevent changes in any other nations that might produce governments friendly toward the Soviets or Chinese. These policy objectives displaced all others and led to a widespread public concern with national security and defense that overrode virtually all other questions and pervaded all levels of our foreign policy. In fact, the Cold War philosophy was so pervasive that it noticeably affected America's domestic political scene as well. This chapter will trace the history of the Soviet-American relationship, the domestic sources of and limitations on America's foreign policy, and the effects of America's foreign policy on the process of policy formation itself.

THE ONSET OF THE COLD WAR

Within a few years after World War II, the official American conception of the USSR had shifted from an accent on the heroic Soviet people who had borne the brunt of the war against the Nazis to an accent on the ruthless dictatorship of Stalin. Although the debate continues over which side is responsible for bringing about this transformation, there can be no doubt that in the period immediately following the war the Soviet Union and the United States reached contradictory conclusions concerning each other's intents. Much of this mutual distrust came to focus on the postwar situation of Eastern Europe.

After World War II the Soviets, in an action they believed to be essential to their national security, left their forces in occupation of the nations of Eastern Europe. In thereby extending their *hegemony* over the political and economic systems of the Eastern European nations, the Soviets were reacting in part to a history of German invasions of their homeland. They wanted to erect a barrier against any future German ambitions.

To President Truman and his Administration, however, Stalin's concept of hegemony strongly limited or even precluded Western political or economic access. In Western eyes it seemed that Stalin's actions involved much more than the establishment

Figure 5.1 A high point in recent diplomacy was President Nixon's visit to the People's Republic of China in February 1972, which ended twenty-two years of separation between the two world powers. This diplomatic rapprochement had been preceded by secret talks between presidential adviser Henry Kissinger and Chinese leaders, and it followed by four months the seating of the People's Republic of China in the United Nations General Assembly. The renewal of relations also took place in a period of intense mutual hostility between China and the U.S.S.R. and at a time when the United States was both war-weary and in search of new markets. The new diplomacy marked important changes in the Cold War, a period of tensions that had played a major role in the formulation and implementation of America's foreign as well as domestic policy.

of a buffer against Germany. In fact, the conclusion was drawn that there was a disturbing similarity between Stalin's actions and Hitler's aggressive policies prior to the outbreak of World War II. It was widely believed in the United States that the failure to deal with Hitler vigorously had brought on that war. President Truman did not want to commit the same mistake with the Soviets.

The Truman Doctrine

The shape of America's policy began to emerge in the spring of 1947 when President Harry Truman delivered a special message to Congress that dealt with the civil war then under way in Greece. Truman saw the events of Greece as part of a universal pattern of communist pressure on European nations. The policy implications of the address, which came to be called the "Truman Doctrine," formed the bedrock of American foreign policy up to and even through the Vietnam War.

President Truman asserted that the world was confronted with a choice between two futures. One of the choices was "distinguished by free institutions" (represented by democracy and the West) and the other was "based upon the will of a minority forcibly imposed upon the majority" (represented by communism and the Soviet Union). He added that it was necessary that the United States "support free peoples who are resisting attempted subjugation by armed minorities or by outside pressures." The United States was compelled to resist because "one of the primary objectives of the foreign policy of the United States is the creation of conditions in which we and other nations will be able to work out a way of life free from coercion." Even more important, American initiative and action were required because "totalitarian regimes imposed on free peoples by direct or indirect aggression, undermine the foundations of international peace and hence the security of the United States" (Truman, 1963).

The belief in the confrontation of freedom and totalitarianism as formulated in the Truman Doctrine was to shape the international system within which the United States and all other nations would exist. It was believed that to the extent that "totalitarianism" (as represented by the Soviet Union) came to dominate the international system, the possibility

of peace was undermined and the security of the United States was called into question. The possibility that Soviet policy was basically defensive was rejected. Accordingly, the primary American foreign policy objective became the development of an anticommunist international order.

The Marshall Plan

The common interpretation during the immediate postwar period was that economic instability and low productivity (particularly in Western Europe) constituted a grave threat to the United States. First, economically weak nations could not defend themselves against communist aggression. Second, poor economic conditions provided local communist parties with the opportunity to disrupt political affairs and perhaps even to come to power as the Nazis did in Germany a decade earlier. As Secretary of State George Marshall stated:

It is logical that the United States should do whatever it is able to do to assist in the return of normal economic health in the world, without which there can be no political stability and no assured peace. Our policy should be the revival of a working economy in the world so as to permit the emergence of political and social conditions in which free institutions can exist. (Marshall, 1947)

In line with this perspective, American aid under the Truman Doctrine was to be implemented primarily through a program of economic assistance. Accordingly, under the Marshall Plan of 1947, the United States agreed to fund the economic redevelopment of the Western European nations. Between 1947 and 1952 the United States gave some $15 billion to these countries under conditions that forced them to undertake the initial planning for the economic integration of Europe (essentially accomplished in 1958 in the European Economic Community). The Soviets were invited to join in this plan for European economic redevelopment, but they distrusted the motivations of the United States. They felt the plan involved the imposition of American political and economic control. They thus refused to participate, and a Soviet-American relationship of mutual distrust was firmly established.

THE DOCTRINE OF CONTAINMENT

Within weeks of Marshall's statement, George Kennan, then an official in the Department of State,

Figure 5.2 A post-World War II German poster depicts a truck carrying goods to the European nations (flags) with the initials E.R.P. for European Recovery Plan—the "Marshall Plan." The truck passes through the tollgate between national boundaries, symbolizing the initiation of programs to integrate Western European economic life—one of the stipulations under which American economic aid was extended. In the belief that deteriorating economic conditions threatened countries of the "free world," some $15 billion was spent on the reconstruction of war-ravaged Western Europe.

published an assessment of the threat confronting the United States. Kennan viewed Soviet foreign policy as "a fluid stream which moves constantly, wherever it is permitted to move, toward a given goal. Its main concern is to make sure that it has filled every nook and cranny available to it in the basin of world power" (Kennan, 1947). He asserted that Soviet policies were flexible and, when confronted with obstacles in the path of their expansion, they would accommodate themselves. Kennan reasoned that if the Soviets could be prevented from accomplishing their expansionist goals for a long enough period of time, their internal problems would increase; these problems would in turn force the Soviets to compromise their foreign policy objectives and to negotiate with the West. From this argument Kennan derived his prescription for the future foreign policy:

In these circumstances it is clear that the main element of any United States policy toward the Soviet Union must be that of a long-term, vigilant *containment* of Russian expansive tendencies. . . . the Soviet pressure against the free institutions of the western world is something that can be contained by the adroit and vigilant application of counterforce at a series of constantly shifting geographical and political points, corresponding to the shifts and maneuvers of Soviet policy. (Kennan, 1947) [italics added]

Kennan's thesis of containment thus provided for the application of counterpressure by the United States each time an event, political or military, was interpreted as Soviet "expansion." The concept of containment provided the intellectual framework within which the Truman Doctrine, the Marshall Plan, and subsequent events were viewed. Confrontation was thus firmly established as the dominant motif of the American world view.

Containment in Europe: Berlin

The period between 1947 and 1952 was dominated by a series of near and real crises that led to an increasingly tense Soviet-American relationship. In rapid succession, the Soviets seized power in Czechoslovakia, and the United States announced it would support some form of defensive arrangement embracing Western Europe. The United States also decided to move toward the establishment of an independent West German government. This decision undoubtedly fed Soviet fears of a resurgent

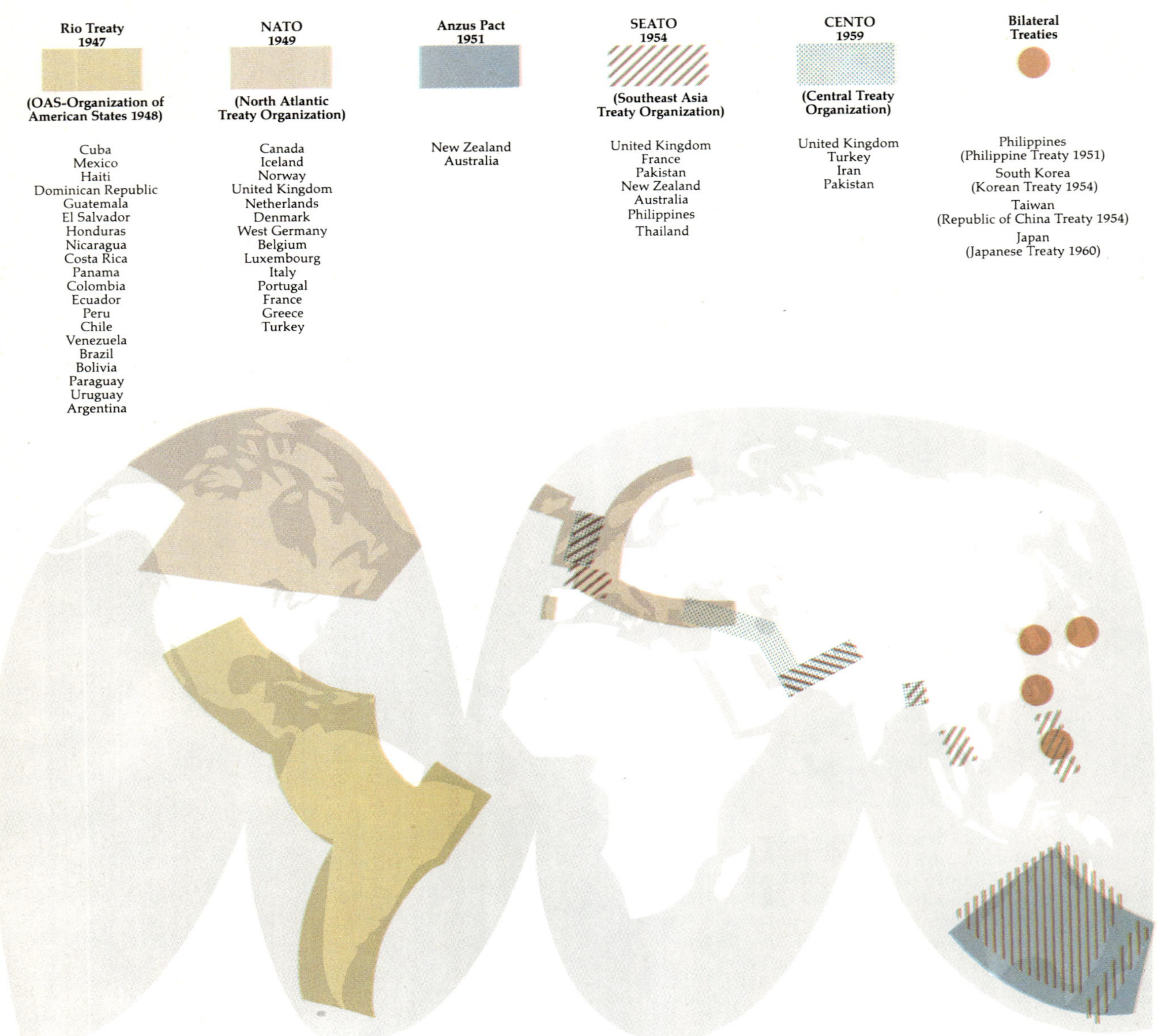

Figure 5.3 American foreign policy in the 1940s, 1950s, and 1960s was founded on the twin concepts of containment and commitment. The development and expansion of these policies can be traced chronologically across the globe from left to right; we see first the securing of relations with our closest neighbors in Central and South America, then with Europe and the eastern Mediterranean, then with Asia and the Pacific. There were many reasons for such treaties: to provide bases for troops, planes, ships, and missiles; to secure shipping routes and access to natural resources and to markets; and to prevent certain nations from considering friendships with those nations defined as Cold War opponents. The lists of signatory nations above refer to the original nations that signed the pacts. Since the inception of these treaties, several nations, such as Cuba, France, and Pakistan, have reduced their participation in meetings and in military and economic programs.

Germany, perhaps their most fundamental security concern. The Soviets reacted by cutting transportation and communication into the Western-occupied sector of Berlin in 1948 (because the divided city of Berlin lies 100 miles inside East Germany, the Soviets felt they could easily make the city "captive"). The resulting *Berlin crisis* stretched through the end of 1948 and into the spring of 1949 and was replete with high levels of tension and the fear of war between the United States and the Soviet Union.

The Soviet blockade of West Berlin failed—largely because of a massive airlift of food and supplies into the city. As the crisis drew to a close, the United States formalized a military alliance with the Western Europeans—the North Atlantic Treaty Organization (NATO). When the Soviets exploded their first atomic weapon in 1949, Congress quickly passed the Mutual Defense Assistance Act, which, in combination with the NATO treaty, provided for a program of military assistance to Western Europe. The policy of containment had become an explicit mix of economic and military assistance.

Containment in Asia: Korea

In late 1949, after decades of Chinese civil war, Mao Tse-tung was successful in establishing a communist regime in Peking. Within months the forces of neighboring North Korea invaded South Korea. Mao's victory and the invasion of South Korea were accepted as evidence of a global extension of the communist threat. In viewing these events, President Truman reasoned that inasmuch as the communist threat seemed to include political and economic subversion (as in Europe), the actual use of force (as in Asia), and ultimately the threat of nuclear war, it seemed necessary that the United States be able to respond at every level. If the policy of containment were to have credibility anywhere, it must have credibility everywhere.

The details of the Korean War need not be discussed in this chapter. It is sufficient to note that President Truman immediately committed American troops to the conflict. Shortly after the war began, Truman, under the urging of General Douglas MacArthur, decided that the original limited objective of repelling the North Korean invasion could be expanded. The decision was made to invade North Korea in an attempt to reunite the two parts of the

Figure 5.4 Two crucial moments in the history of a crucial city. Berlin, 1948 (above): The Americans began a 320-day airlift of food and coal into Tempelhof Airfield to supply 2.2 million blockaded West Berliners. The U.S.S.R., whose occupied German territory surrounded the city of Berlin, had refused to permit the other occupying powers, Great Britain, France, and the United States, to transit across the Soviet zone to supply their portions of the city. Berlin, 1961 (top): The notorious Berlin Wall, here shown in front of the Brandenburg Gate, was erected by the Soviets to stop the flow of East Berliners into the Western-occupied sectors. The second wall was erected several months later and was designed as increased fortification for the first wall.

country. Consequently, MacArthur moved his troops into North Korea despite Chinese warnings that if this action were taken they would intervene.

In November 1950, Chinese troops responded to the threat; they entered the war and pushed American troops south. General MacArthur began calling for a dramatic escalation of the conflict. Truman and the Joint Chiefs of Staff balked, arguing that MacArthur's proposals might bring the Soviets into the war. Instead of accepting Truman's decision, MacArthur pleaded his case before the increasingly war-weary American public. He announced that the President's reluctance was costing American lives and that his proposals would bring an immediate end to the war. Truman regarded MacArthur's action as rank insubordination and fired him in April 1951. The release of General MacArthur unleashed enormous torrents of public and congressional criticism against the President. Meanwhile, the Korean War settled into bloody stalemate.

Domestic Implications: The McCarthy Era

The outpouring of popular frustration that surrounded the Korean War extended beyond the war itself to the entire course of American foreign policy. The war in Korea was requiring an enormous investment of national resources and will and yet seemed to be going nowhere. Furthermore, the President had implied that Korea was but part of a much larger and more dangerous struggle to which the United States was now committed and from which it could not withdraw.

The American public's discomfort was further increased because it did not appear that the policy of the Truman Administration could be carried through to any decisive conclusion. Soviet expansion was only supposed to be contained; there was no provision for total victory. The only thing that appeared certain was more tension, more war, and more domestic dislocation. It was all very confusing, and the American people were quite susceptible to those with explanations.

Conservative members of the Republican Party, such as Senators William Jenner, Richard Nixon, and Joseph McCarthy, seemed to have a simple explanation for American problems. In the words of Senator Jenner, the United States was "in the hands of a secret coterie which is directed by agents of the Soviet Union" (Allen Guttman, 1967). The emergence of Soviet power in Europe, the "loss of China" to communism, Soviet nuclear capability, and of course the prolonged conflict in Korea, could all be traced to "communist agents" infiltrating the government of the United States.

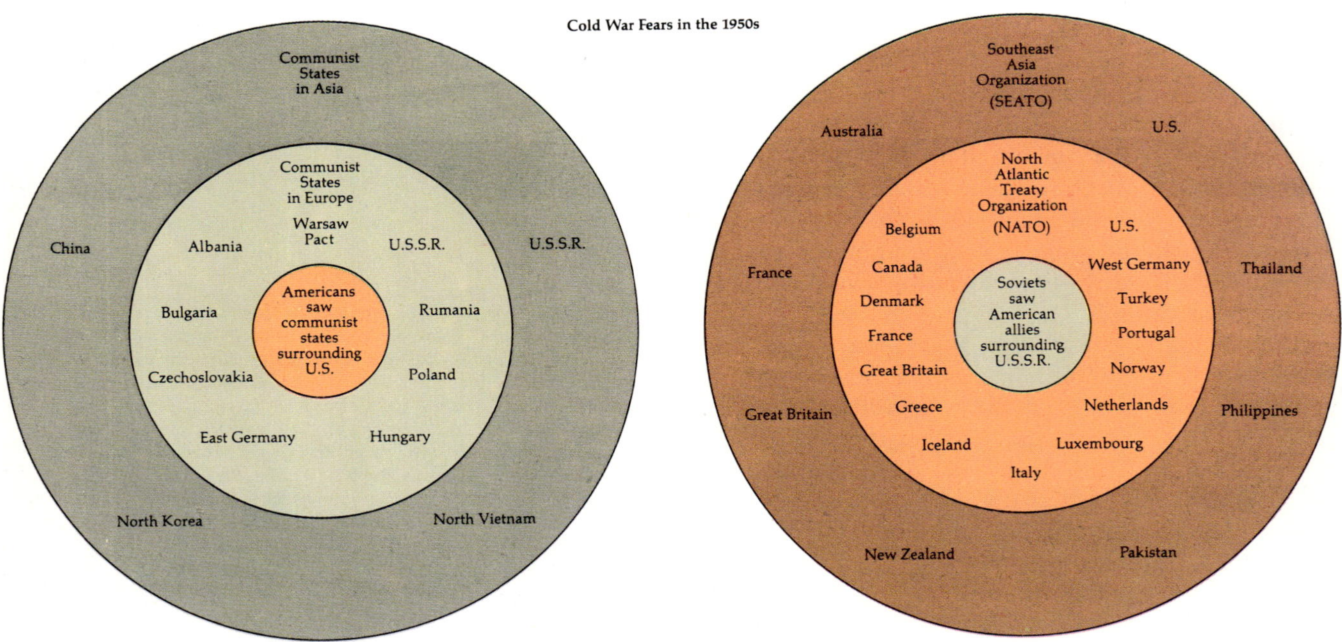

Senator McCarthy launched a public crusade designed to expose and root out those whom he labeled as communists and communist sympathizers throughout the government, particularly in the Department of State. Only a handful of people were ever linked to the Communist Party, and McCarthy himself was subsequently censured by the Senate as his charges became more and more extreme and his demagoguery became apparent. Nevertheless, the attention of the nation was focused on Senator McCarthy. His accusations served to heighten the tension and uncertainty of the early 1950s.

Perhaps even more important, the doubt and suspicion engendered during the McCarthy period found a more or less permanent place in American policy making. Subsequent political leaders have been sensitive to the accusation that they are "soft on communism." They have felt that the belief in communist infiltration of government had thoroughly pervaded public opinion. Many decisions have thus been made in *anticipation* of this perceived public reaction. The fears of a McCarthyite resurgence have been in many instances imagined; nevertheless those fears have colored foreign policy making over the last two decades.

Although millions of Americans never understood or accepted McCarthy's charges, their confusion and disorientation were quite real and to a considerable extent this confusion reflected the uncertainty among America's political leaders concerning the future of the nation's policy.

A "NEW LOOK" FOR CONTAINMENT

When Dwight Eisenhower became President in 1952, American foreign policy had reached an impasse. On the one hand, there was an international situation in Europe and in Asia that seemed to require a decisive response; Republican campaign rhetoric demanded a firm response with calls for a "rollback" of communist power and for the "liberation of captive peoples" in Eastern Europe. On the other hand, the political climate in America was definitely not ready for a decisive response—the public was torn by dissent over Korea and the McCarthy "witch hunt" and was uncertain about the prospects of an increased world role. Eisenhower resolved this broad policy impasse through his handling of the Korean War.

The President felt that the use of American ground troops (the army and the marines) in Asia was bad military strategy, a view that obviously found a strong echo in American public opinion. Eisenhower's solution was to take advantage of United States nuclear superiority. Specifically, he threatened

Figure 5.5 **The tension of the 1950s and 1960s was reflected in the world views of both sides in the Cold War (left). Each saw its own alliance as well intentioned, slow to anger, and hesitant to put resources into military preparations. The opposite side, however, was seen as a monolithic, or coherent, group of nations, united in a ruthless conspiracy, possessed of uncanny wisdom and forethought, and bent on the destruction of its opponents. These views made it difficult to perceive the disparity—reflected in such actions as France's military pullout from NATO or Rumania's economic relations with Western Europe—that actually existed in each bloc.**

Figure 5.6 **General Douglas MacArthur (seated foreground) had a flair for dramatization, for example, in promising "I will return" when retreating from the Philippines in World War II, in developing dramatic military strategies in Korea during the Korean War, and in being dramatically relieved of his post in April 1951 for criticizing President Truman's conduct of the war. On his return to the United States from Korea, MacArthur ended a speech to a joint session of Congress with a line from an old song, "Old soldiers never die, they just fade away," and then subsequently used the "old soldier" slogan as the basis for a presidential campaign.**

Figure 5.7 **The beginning of a long and bloody war, July 3, 1950, when American troops were deployed in South Korea (top). This "exercise in frustration" for the American people was associated with a number of remarkable conditions and events. Because Congress never officially declared war, U.S. participation was essentially a "police action" initiated by President Truman; it brought American troops into direct yet inconclusive battle with Chinese troops; it was a preview of the land war in Asia known as the Vietnam War, which, like that in Korea, never issued in a clear decision; the war pitted President Truman against the hero, General Douglas MacArthur; and it gave birth to the McCarthy period of Communist "witch hunting," which permanently affected Americans' attitudes toward politics. March 20, 1951 American tanks in South Korea pushed northward (bottom) in a cold, hard march that brought them face to face with Chinese troops.**

to extend the war to the Chinese mainland by means of nuclear bombardment unless a truce was negotiated immediately. The message was communicated in May of 1953; by July the stalemate was broken and a truce was underway (David Rees, 1970).

The Korean experience provided what was to be the form and primary tool of American foreign and national security policy for the next decade: *massive retaliation*. The doctrine was summarized by Secretary of State John Foster Dulles in 1954 when he declared that the United States maintained the option to "retaliate instantly, by means and at places of our own choosing" (Dulles, 1954a). The means were left vague, and subsequent statements by Dulles indicated that the new American posture did not necessarily mean that "any local war would automatically be turned into a general war with atomic bombs falling all over the map" (Dulles, 1954b). However, the threat of nuclear attack was implicit in the statement.

The policy of massive retaliation was appealing. It fulfilled domestic political needs because it freed the United States from Korea and promised no further involvements of the sort. It also placed the burden of defending the "free world" on superior American military technology, not on ground troops. Furthermore, the idea of massive retaliation appeared decisive in contrast to the incremental, bit-by-bit nature of Truman's containment policy. Finally, massive retaliation seemed to promise relief from the expensive use of conventional forces in the kinds of military involvements implied by earlier policy. The initial build-up of technology would probably require some short-term increases in defense spending; however, Eisenhower felt that defense budgets would level out in the long run.

The military posture that emerged—the "New Look"—depended on maintaining United States nuclear superiority over the Soviet Union, while general purpose forces—those forces that would be called on to fight conventional wars such as Korea— were curtailed. Accordingly, during the Eisenhower Administration, army divisions were reduced and the total number of active forces declined. At the same time, the strategic forces—those designed to deliver nuclear warheads—and Air Force fighter and attack squadrons were increased. Eleven new tactical missiles and rockets also were developed and deployed along with a number of nuclear projectiles suitable for use in tactical artillery pieces. The Eisenhower Administration also began to develop and to deploy nuclear-armed intermediate, intercontinental, and submarine-launched ballistic missiles (Melvin Laird, 1971).

In sum, communism's advance was to be checked by America's nuclear might, and at lower cost. Campaign rhetoric pushing for complete victory over the "evil" specter of communism was increasingly muted. The Korean War was over, there was a promised drop in defense costs, and most people simply did not care that the Eisenhower national security policy did not aim at conquest.

Extending American Military Presence

The policy of massive retaliation and the New Look defense posture did not involve withdrawal into a nuclear shell. Quite the contrary. The American global presence was dramatically extended, for United States resources were also committed to a large number of allies—the *commitments system.* Thus, during and immediately after the Korean War, the NATO forces were buttressed with large numbers of nuclear weapons (under American control). Another element of this policy was the decision to rearm West Germany and to integrate the new German army into the NATO structure.

It should be noted that the rearmament of Germany and its integration into a strengthened West European-American alliance could only serve to confirm Soviet suspicions and fears. Not only had the Secretary of State implied that America was willing to engage in a nuclear war, but now the forces of NATO had been stiffened with the creation of a new German army—the very forces that had caused millions of Soviet casualties during World War II.

Nor did American commitments abroad stop with buttressing NATO and rearming Germany. The United States also broadened its alliance structure, by use of treaties, executive orders, and congressional resolutions, to include forty-three countries around the world.

The underpinning of these commitments was American nuclear strength. However, the 1950s also saw the rapid expansion of foreign assistance programs. The United States dispensed over $20 billion in military assistance and over $16 billion in economic assistance between 1953 and 1961; additional billions of dollars found their way into the countries falling within the commitments system through the disposal of American agricultural surplus and the loan programs of the Export-Import Bank. Finally, the American presence was evident in the hundreds of military bases scattered around the globe (over 300 major bases in 1969), with especially high concentrations in Germany, Japan, and South Korea (Congressional Quarterly, 1969).

New Look, or Old Wine in New Bottles?

The New Look was meant to provide an alternative to containment. It was to be characterized by a decisiveness and by a dynamism that would set it apart from the lengthy and indecisive global involvement implied in President Truman's policies. There was a certain rhetorical bite to John Foster Dulles's pronouncements concerning rollback, and there was a militancy in his notion that America should assume the psychological and political offensive. In 1954, however, the United States refused to use nuclear weapons to support the French in their effort to hold the Vietnamese portion of their empire, and in 1956 the United States refused to aid the Hungarians in their uprising against Soviet control. These actions demonstrated that, contrary to the rhetoric of the New Look policy, the United States was not prepared to pay the price of rolling back communist power by actually using its nuclear arms or by taking advantage of its alliance arrangements.

The United States was prepared to support, through military and economic assistance, an extended system of commitments. But the objective of this policy was essentially the same as that of the late 1940s: the containment of communist power. The threat of nuclear retaliation had been the crux of the New Look. During the 1950s the Soviets achieved a nuclear arsenal of their own, however, which meant that the threat of nuclear retaliation was sufficient only to provide a check on communist probes, little more. In short, the New Look was nothing more than the old policy of containment in the increasingly dangerous context of nuclear power.

Effects on the Policy Process

It is important to pause for a moment in this chronicle of Cold War events to consider the effects these events were having on the substance of policy—both foreign and domestic—and on the processes by which decisions were made and programs administered. When President Truman assumed the initiative in developing and implementing policies to deal with the crises of the late 1940s, his actions were regarded by many in Congress as extraordinary but probably essential in view of the demands of the role assumed by the United States. Truman consulted Congress on most issues, but it was fairly clear from the outset that the initiative was the President's.

Both the Marshall Plan and NATO met with congressional debate and some resistance. Similarly, the proposed National Security Act of 1947—which provided for the establishment of the Department of Defense, the Central Intelligence Agency, the National Security Council, and in fact provided for the growth of presidential control of policy making in general—was viewed by some conservatives as an excessive concentration of power in the hands of the President. In every instance, however, congressional resistance was overwhelmed by events, and the President got most of what he wanted. The culmination of this sequence was the Korean War, to which President Truman committed American armed forces without asking Congress for a formal declaration of war.

The Eisenhower Administration also confirmed these developments in the policy-making process. Under the authority of the National Security Act, Eisenhower developed a National Security Council system; it was designed to coordinate the foreign policy bureaucracy while further concentrating control of policy in the hands of the President and of the Secretary of State. The emergence of this foreign and national security bureaucracy within the orbit of the White House gave the President an edge in terms of expertise that Congress could never hope to match.

The development in the early 1950s of a defense posture based on the threat of nuclear war and on a widespread system of commitments made presidential control seem even more necessary. It seemed that any element of the East-West confrontation could explode into total war at any time. As a result, flexibility and unity of command certainly seemed in order, and the executive branch seemed the logical focus of this awesome power. It was not surprising, therefore, that in 1955 and 1957, in response to crises in Formosa and the Middle East, Congress granted almost total discretion to the President to use American forces as he deemed necessary (Merlo Pusey, 1969). At every turn during the immediate postwar years, Congress yielded to the real or imagined need for greater presidential prerogatives.

All of this was again to be turned on Congress in 1964 when President Lyndon Johnson used the language and precedent of the Formosan and Middle East resolutions to support his virtually single-handed prosecution of the Vietnam War under the Tonkin Gulf Resolution. In 1957, however, the sweeping confirmation of executive dominance was viewed by Congress as a necessary reaction to the realities of the Cold War.

CONTAINMENT CHALLENGED: THE 1950s

The twin threats of American nuclear superiority and of a NATO alliance strengthened by the addition of Germany seemed to stimulate the Soviets to achieve the capacity to negate those threats. Thus, American policy may have had the paradoxical effect of encouraging the very conditions and behavior it had sought to avoid: a militarily stronger Soviet Union pursuing a more militant and aggressive policy line in Europe and elsewhere.

Soviet Resurgence

After Stalin's death in 1953, Nikita Khrushchev gradually consolidated his position atop the Soviet hierarchy. By 1955 the Soviets were ready to embark on a two-pronged plan of action. First, they attempted to reverse the trend of events in Europe, particularly Germany's new prominence in the NATO alliance. The formation of the Warsaw Pact—a military and economic arrangement that united the nations of Eastern Europe—was a symbolic attempt to counter these events. However, Khrushchev correctly perceived that American nuclear superiority was the basis of the Western position. The second element of Soviet policy was therefore an attempt to modernize Soviet military forces through the development of nuclear capability (Thomas Wolf, 1970).

Between 1955 and 1960 the Soviets developed a modest force of strategic bombers and medium-range ballistic missiles capable of striking Western Europe (enough to give the appearance of nuclear capability). At the same time, they launched Sputnik—the first earth-orbiting satellite—which gave an air of credibility to Khrushchev's self-confident claims that the Soviet Union's development of intercontinental ballistic missiles was surging ahead of America's ICBM program. In retrospect it is apparent that the Soviet Union did not have the broad nuclear capability that many observers inferred from these developments. But the displays of Soviet assertiveness produced much self-doubt within the United States. Khrushchev undoubtedly appreciated the weakness of his hand, but if his opponents were susceptible to a strategic bluff, he was willing to take

Figure 5.8 Evolution of Man the Fighter (left). In every era a significant portion of the human brain pool has been employed in identifying and eradicating human foes. In the most recent stages of this evolution, Man the Fighter has found cleaner ways of delivering more powerful weapons. As the awesomeness of the destructive power has increased, there has been a corresponding centralization of its control. And should the ultimate catastrophe of thermonuclear war occur, it is likely that man's parting shots will have been calculated and fired by those judged the coolest and most rational of mankind.

Figure 5.9 Khrushchev's "gavel" (right). Soviet Premier Nikita Khrushchev's shoe rests on the desk in front of him after he used it in a table-pounding exhibition during a session of the United Nations General Assembly on October 12, 1960. The Soviet leader pounded his shoe on the desk during a speech in which he rebutted a blast by the Philippine delegate against Soviet colonialism in the world.

full advantage of the situation and to assume the policy initiative.

Throughout the middle and late 1950s, therefore, the Soviet leader was alternately friendly and belligerent. The Soviet aim was to undercut the NATO alliance and, in the long run, to make the entire European situation less amenable to American influence. Although Khrushchev succeeded in none of these objectives, the entire tone of Soviet-American relations seemed changed. Whereas the initiative had previously seemed to lie with the United States, Khrushchev's blustering and maneuvering suggested the initiative had passed to the Soviets.

Rise of the Third World

The deteriorating European situation—always the hinge of the Soviet-American relationship—was compounded by developments in Asia, Africa, and Latin America. The emergence of a number of new nations from colonial status during the late 1950s injected a new element into the mix of world politics. The leadership of these new and generally underdeveloped countries—what came to be called the *Third World*—sought rapid economic development, and they showed little desire to use Western methods to pursue their ends. They adopted instead a posture of *nonalignment;* that is, they refused political alliances with both the Soviet Union and the United States. However, they turned to both the big powers for economic assistance.

Political instability seemed to accompany economic development throughout the non-Western Third World. When new governments arrived on the scene, many of them proclaiming anti-American sentiments, many American politicians—conditioned by a decade of intense Cold War—assumed

that the turmoil and the rhetoric were provoked by communist sympathizers and that the Cold War had been extended to the less developed world.

CONTAINMENT ON THE NEW FRONTIER

When John Kennedy took office in 1961 the international environment seemed enmeshed in crisis. The entire postwar policy structure that had been built by Truman and Eisenhower seemed to be on the verge of collapse. Insurgencies in Laos and Vietnam were underway, a communist regime ruled in Cuba in the wake of Fidel Castro's successful revolution, and the tension over Berlin continued—a monumental crisis for the policy of containment.

Containment With Vigor

The closeness of President Kennedy's electoral majority offered no *mandate,* or authorization by the voters, for radical new departures in foreign policy. However, the new President—who had advocated "getting the country going again" during the campaign—did not question the assumptions of postwar policy. The new Administration opened, therefore, with an eloquent and ringing restatement of that policy:

Let every nation know, whether it wishes us well or ill, that we shall pay any price, bear any burden, meet any hardship, support any friend, oppose any foe to assure the survival and the success of liberty.

This much we pledge—and more. (Kennedy, 1961)

Kennedy's inaugural address reaffirmed the American world role that had developed during the preceding fifteen years. He had claimed throughout the campaign that what was lacking was the means to achieve America's postwar policy objectives. The

Figure 5.10 Foreign relations are notoriously unstable—foes in one war are allies in the next. Older generations of Americans remember the images of World War II: Stalin's troops were heroes for their sacrificial resistance to Hitler's power, and the Chinese people were America's allies in resisting the Japanese in Asia. Recent generations vividly remember the postwar hostilities of the Cold War. During this period of missile rattling and fear of Mao's Red Army, the Russian bear and the Chinese dragon (left) took on appearances totally different from their earlier visages as allies. In the seventies, the Russian bear again appears in American politics as a friendly bear—hungry, but this time hungry for American wheat, truck factories, and Pepsi-Cola. The Chinese dragon has similarly reverted to that noble animal it once was—proud and independent but smiling, seeking trade and accommodation.

Figure 5.11 Seven months before the disastrous Bay of Pigs invasion of Cuba, Fidel Castro came to New York to address the United Nations (September 1960). The American embargo of Cuban sugar—the country's main export—was already in effect; Castro's liberal revolution was changing into a socialist revolution, and the Cuban middle classes were deserting him. Soviet Premier Nikita Khrushchev (top right) paid a surprise visit to Castro at his hotel in Harlem during the U.N. session. In October 1962 American delegate Adlai Stevenson (left arm on desk) showed the United Nations Security Council (bottom right) some aerial photographs of Soviet missile bases that were being constructed in Cuba, the trigger that set off the blockade of the island nation and the dangerous face-off between the U.S. and the U.S.S.R.—the Cuban missile crisis.

fault of the Eisenhower Administration, Kennedy said, lay not in the objectives it had pursued but in its reluctance to use the full range of *instrumentalities* necessary to deal with the challenge. In sum, the Kennedy Administration was not concerned with the assumptions and objectives of the policy of containment, but rather with the instruments necessary to implement it. Much of the 1000 days of the Kennedy Administration was devoted to acquiring those means.

Flexible Response and "Nation Building"

Between 1960 and 1964 the United States attempted to build a military force that would enable it to respond to any kind of confrontation that might arise. It therefore dramatically increased the number of ICBMs and submarine-launched missiles in its arsenal in case nuclear response was necessary (Institute for Strategic Studies, 1971). General purpose forces and tactical nuclear capability were also increased to allow greater flexibility in dealing with Soviet and Chinese manpower advantages and to provide a greater war-fighting capacity at the subnuclear level (Laird, 1971).

President Kennedy and Secretary of Defense Robert McNamara felt that there was yet another level of threat with which the United States was ill-prepared to deal: insurgencies and civil wars within the Third World. They felt that the United States needed a specially designed instrument to deal with this kind of conflict. Thus, Kennedy personally supported the expansion of the Army Special Forces, or "Green Berets"—a program actually initiated by Eisenhower. These forces were to be trained in the techniques of insurgency and counterinsurgency so that they might be available and ready for use under all circumstances that required United States intervention.

With respect to the Third World, the Kennedy Administration proposed a new approach, which would not only maintain the system of commitments already established but would also lead to even deeper United States involvement in the internal processes of economic and political development. Consequently, the direction and make-up of American foreign aid programs shifted during the 1960s, with economic and military assistance concentrated almost entirely on the nations of Africa, Asia, and Latin America (United States Agency for International Development, 1971).

Kennedy also established a new foreign military-sales program, which was to provide the new nations with the military hardware necessary to cope with internal and external threats. This program emphasized beyond any doubt that America's nation-building effort was related to the overarching security emphasis of American Cold War policy. Indeed, the use of *non*military instrumentalities of policy before and during the 1960s was always linked to overriding national security objectives.

Nonmilitary Instruments of Foreign Policy

The operation of foreign policy has always involved more than just the threat and the use of force. Nations employ diplomatic representation and persuasion; they maintain propaganda programs; they engage in economic relations with other nations; they offer and administer economic assistance; and they maintain intelligence-gathering operations. Many countries, including the United States, make use of all of these facets of foreign policy.

Throughout the Cold War, the actions of the entire foreign-policy establishment were influenced by the doctrine of containment. The Department of State found itself involved in the tasks of building and maintaining a series of interlocking mutual defense treaties and commitments to supplement the NATO treaty of 1949. Cultural and educational exchange programs were justified before Congress as means of strengthening the linkages of the "free world"; United States participation in numerous international organizations was promoted as a means for achieving world peace. But United States behavior in the United Nations and its specialized agencies was never far removed from the confrontation and struggle with the Soviet Union. Similarly, the United States Information Agency was established at the onset of the Cold War to promote a better understanding of the United States abroad; but the information disseminated was always tied directly or indirectly to the Soviet-American interaction.

As noted previously, the initial foreign assistance program of the United States, the Marshall Plan, was the original United States policy instrumentality during the early years of the Cold War. Subsequent foreign aid programs have also been intimately tied to

Figure 5.12 Uncle Sam as the shrewd Yankee Trader. Foreign aid with no strings attached has always been fantasy, no matter what the country of origin. When nations "give" away money and goods, they expect something in return: favorable trading status, access to natural resources, political and military loyalty —whatever seems most important to the donor nation's global interests at the time. Accepting money from America might require acceptance of more American industrial plants in the country or the purchase of military goods or even food from the United States. The advantages and disadvantages of foreign aid must be carefully weighed by the recipient nation.

the struggle between the United States and the perceived communist threat. For example, a study of American foreign assistance prior to the Vietnam War found that although economic development, or "nation building," was an important element in American aid, the program has always been justified primarily as a means for countering communism (Senate Committee on Foreign Relations, 1966).

Furthermore, the distribution of economic assistance during the 1960s suggests that United States assistance was not spread indiscriminantly around the world with the sole purpose of fostering development. Instead, it was and is targeted on regions and countries that are regarded as most vital to American security interests. The heavy emphasis on military assistance in many aid programs reinforces this thrust. Nowhere are these emphases more in evidence than in the Alliance for Progress—a program developed in the wake of Castro's Cuban revolution that has always been justified as a means for preventing other such revolutions in Latin America.

Inasmuch as the United States regarded "normal economic health in the world" to be the basis of political stability, it seemed logical that the United States—and the dollar—should assume the role of stabilizing international economics. In the 1950s a framework for European economic integration and growth in the European Economic Community was encouraged by the United States, and the next decade saw a rapid expansion of world trade and investment by United States corporations throughout the world. These events were regarded as necessary to the political and military strategy of containment.

THE NEW FRONTIER AT THE BRINK

The Soviet response to the surge of American energy under the Kennedy Administration was a blend of careful calculation and dangerous gamble. It had become increasingly apparent by 1961 that Khrushchev's strategy of wringing psychological advantage from what amounted to a massive strategic bluff was not forcing the United States out of Europe. But Khrushchev decided to play one of the final cards in his hand with yet another crisis in Berlin. Thus, as the world anxiously watched, the Soviet Premier and the new President escalated the crisis through a series of moves and countermoves including call-ups of reserve forces, increases in defense budgets, and the building of the Berlin Wall by the Soviets. In the end, however, it was apparent that the strategy of strategic bluff was nearly bankrupt.

The Cuban Missile Crisis

There was one last dramatic move. Khrushchev at the time was under pressure from many directions: The Chinese were criticizing his leadership of the communist world; his military planners were pressuring him to do something about the widening strategic imbalance; and neither the technological nor the financial resources were available to do very much about the strategic situation in the immediate future. Khrushchev apparently decided on a method whereby the Soviets might regain the initiative: He reasoned that if the Soviets could deploy their existing medium-range ballistic missiles in Cuba—within easy range of the United States—they could significantly increase their strategic capability, strengthen the credibility of their position in Eastern Europe, and simultaneously silence the criticism in their own camp. The entire gamble hinged on Khrushchev's belief that Kennedy's nerve would falter and that he would allow the Soviets to get the missiles into Cuba. Khrushchev's assumption proved to be wrong—Kennedy blockaded Cuba to prevent the missile deployment, and in so doing he forced the Soviets to the brink of war.

The Lessons Learned

Khrushchev backed down, and it seemed that the entire thrust of Soviet policy since 1957 had finally been deflected. However, the Soviets had learned a simple lesson: It was absolutely essential that they achieve real, rather than apparent, military parity with the United States, at least at the strategic level. Between 1962 and the end of the Kennedy-Johnson years, the Soviet policy profile was lower; but during that time they were developing the very thing American policy was oriented against: greater Soviet military strength. Once again, a seemingly decisive Cold War test of will had not led to a more passive Soviet policy response. By the 1970s the Soviets had developed strategic systems that were roughly equivalent to those in the American weapons inventory.

The impact of the Cuban crisis on American policy makers was equally dramatic. Their ability to "face

Figure 5.13 Rise and fall of peace hopes in the Cold War (below). Without making any claim to quantitative exactitude, we offer here a plot of major events in the Cold War, from 1948 to 1958, along with their probable effects on the hopes of those who desired both a resolution of differences and a drawback of the superpowers from the threat of thermonuclear war.

Figure 5.14 There is an interpenetration of private life and public policy—even foreign policy—in every society. What did Elvis Presley, Marilyn Monroe, and fun at a soda fountain have to do with a top-level strategy meeting on the Cuban blockade and a subsequent flirtation with nuclear war? The three pictures in the center hold the key. Underneath the fun and glitter of American "pop" culture of the 1950s and 1960s ran an undercurrent of fear—fear of a world divided between "us" and "them" and the possibility of an ultimate settlement of differences under a mushroom-shaped cloud of nuclear fallout. Escapism was only one of the reactions to this fear. The trial of Alger Hiss was another. Hiss was an intellectual, a civil servant employed by the Department of State, who was accused by Whittaker Chambers of giving away strategic information to the Soviet Union. Senator Joseph McCarthy (far right center) turned the American red scare of the 1950s into a witch hunt, undermining morale in all departments of the government through networks of secret informers. Another response, which colored the political attitudes of millions of Americans, was the fearful fatalism that led to the practice of "drop drills," or air raid drills designed to save a remnant of the society after the carnage of nuclear attack.

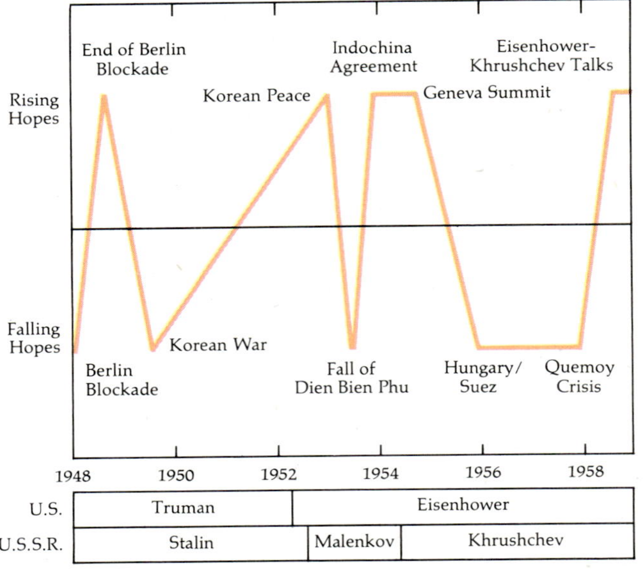

U.S.	Truman	Eisenhower	
U.S.S.R.	Stalin	Malenkov	Khrushchev

down" the Soviets had confirmed the wisdom of the course they had charted. The new Administration had set out to provide America with a broad range of policy instrumentalities, mostly military, that could be used to blunt the thrust of Soviet foreign policy of the late 1950s. Cuba was taken as a decisive test of that policy. The resulting confidence in America's growing military capability and foreign policy objectives established a mental and psychological framework for the middle 1960s, a framework that carried the Kennedy Administration and the subsequent Johnson Administration confidently, perhaps arrogantly, into Vietnam.

VIETNAM LEADS TO REASSESSMENT

All of the Administrations since World War II have followed the policy that the spread of communism must be curtailed and that military force and intervention should play a central role in the implementation of that policy. Thus, Truman sent troops to Korea; Eisenhower intervened in Guatemala (1954) and Lebanon (1956) and began the planning for the Bay of Pigs invasion of Cuba; Kennedy carried out the Bay of Pigs operation (see ☐) and started the build-up of commitments in Vietnam; Johnson sent troops to the Dominican Republic to oust a newly elected "communist" government and expanded the

war in Vietnam; and Nixon began the most intense aerial bombardment in history in order to get the North Vietnamese to the bargaining table.

Seen from this historical perspective, American intervention in Vietnam was part of a seamless web of policy; it was not simply an aberration or an accidental war resulting from human error or fallibility. The United States had been in South Vietnam since the early 1950s; and when the South Vietnamese regime, corrupt and repressive though it may have been, seemed on the verge of collapse in the early and mid-1960s, the situation was perceived as resembling the situation in Greece in 1947, Korea in 1950, and Berlin throughout the 1950s. In short, Vietnam was a part of the system of commitments that made up America's policy of containment and in support of that policy $100 billion was spent and tens of thousands of American lives were lost.

Accustomed to decades of strong presidential leadership, most Americans accepted President Johnson's rationale for American action in Vietnam from 1964 to 1966 (see Chapters 9 and 12). But by early 1968 it was clear that the war was stalemated and that an even larger commitment of men and money would be necessary. Support for President Johnson eroded slowly at first, then more rapidly, as casualties and taxes increased.

☐

BAY OF PIGS

In 1960 President Eisenhower authorized the Central Intelligence Agency (CIA) to train and to arm 1,400 Cuban exiles to infiltrate Cuba. The concept of isolated guerrilla attacks and subterfuge soon evolved into a full-scale plan of attack. When John Kennedy took office in 1961, he was confronted with this plan to invade Cuba and to overthrow Premier Fidel Castro. Kennedy was told that the plan had been drafted under the direction of Eisenhower, a man of obvious military reputation. (Eisenhower, after the invasion, flatly stated that he knew only of the guerrilla training and had never authorized the drafting of further plans.) Kennedy was dubious about the plan but approved it after repeated assurances that the operation would be successful.

However, the operation had been badly planned and the Cuban invaders poorly trained. After the landing in Cuba in April 1961, it soon became apparent that the invaders were being crushed. Simultaneously, world public opinion raged against the obvious involvement of the United States in an attack on neighboring Cuba. These factors led Kennedy to draw back and to cancel a backup air strike—a decision that assured defeat for the invaders.

Figure 5.15 The United States has had a history of direct military intervention in Latin America—extending from the Spanish-American War in 1898 to the landing of troops in the Dominican Republic in 1965 (right). There have been many justifications offered for those interventions; since World War II a common justification for intervention has been "the curtailment of Communism." Beginning with the Monroe Doctrine of 1823, the United States avowed that Latin America is in a special sphere of influence of the United States and that European influences or anti-United States influences would not be tolerated.

But not all Latin Americans are in aggreement with this proclaimed form of international order. The anti-American wall poster displayed here (far right) shows an overpowering Uncle Sam; he is saying "No Peleen" ("Don't hit") while he smashes the "people," who are defending themselves against the military junta that abolished representative institutions in the Dominican Republic (in 1965).

Dissent over the war was not singular in focus. Many, perhaps most, Americans began to reject the war because of its inconclusiveness and cost. Still another group believed in the ends for which the war was being fought but thought that Vietnam was the wrong place to fight for them. A still smaller group questioned not only the costs and the locale of the war but, more importantly, the foreign policy that had given rise to it. These cleavages and uncertainties were painfully apparent in the violent tearing of the American social fabric that occurred in the late 1960s.

The Nixon Doctrine

Richard Nixon's election in 1968 occurred as the twenty-five-year foreign policy consensus seemed to be disintegrating beneath the weight of Vietnam. A part of the public's dissatisfaction centered on the immense costs of Kennedy's and Johnson's policies. The flexible response that had been built into America's military forces had indeed provided a fuller range of military capability; but it had also brought higher defense budgets and a growing military-industrial establishment (see the Perspective that follows this chapter). In the minds of many, the Vietnam War had imposed unacceptable social and economic strains on the domestic system.

By 1968, however, there was a greater tendency to raise more comprehensive questions—questions that had not been raised since 1947—concerning the entire concept of America's world role. The most important of these questions concerned whether the international system of 1968 was not fundamentally different from the international system of 1945 through 1952. Was the United States in fact confronted with an aggressive, expanding communist threat that required a continuation of the foreign and defense policies of the last twenty-five years?

Aware of these questions, President Nixon noted: "The postwar period in international relations has ended." In what is now referred to as the "Nixon Doctrine," he outlined his perception of the new policy posture necessary to deal with the international system of the 1970s: "... the United States will participate in the defense and development of allies and friends, but ... America cannot—and will not—conceive *all* the plans, design *all* the programs, execute *all* the defense of the free nations of the world" (Nixon, 1970). The President's actions regarding China and the Soviet Union, defense policy, and international economic relations suggested that change, continuity, and ambiguity all underlay his statement.

President Nixon had observed that the United States was no longer confronted with a monolithic

communist threat. In the President's view, it had therefore become possible to open negotiations with both major communist powers in an attempt to move away from the Cold War relationships. Accordingly, the President, in a particularly dramatic move, visited China in 1972 and thereby climaxed a three-year effort to improve relations with the Chinese. Similarly, in May 1972, Nixon traveled to Moscow and signed agreements with the Soviets that were designed to expand economic and political relations. These agreements reflected a fundamental and profound new factor in world politics.

The Soviet strategic build-up begun after the Cuban missile crisis had achieved its goals of strategic *parity*—both sides thus had roughly equal nuclear ability. In addition, both the United States and the Soviet Union seemed to believe it was desirable to stabilize their relationship. Thus, while he was in Moscow, President Nixon signed an agreement that placed a five-year limitation on further deployment of certain types of land- and sea-based strategic weapons systems and that banned the deployment of antiballistic missile systems. The Moscow Agreement concluded more than two years of Strategic Arms Limitation Talks (SALT), which had dealt with the issue of limiting the development of new strategic systems. The agreement also gave

impetus to a second round of talks aimed at limiting improvements in existing strategic systems. In addition, the two countries undertook a series of negotiations concerning the possible reduction of troop levels in Europe. After twenty-five years of Cold War, therefore, the great adversaries appeared to be returning to the issues that had given rise to the years of tension and conflict.

The United States had also been forced to confront the economic consequences of its twenty-five year pursuit of national security. Decades of high military expenditures had contributed to an inflated and distorted domestic economy that had undercut America's competitive position with respect to the strong economies of Europe and Japan. The costs of the Cold War had also created a balance of payments problem that had contributed to a decrease of world confidence in American economic leadership. In combination, these forces had caused a series of monetary crises between 1970 and 1973 that had entailed several devaluations of the dollar.

The Nixon Administration had therefore been forced to confront the economically painful reality of an American economy increasingly influenced by the economic activity of other nations. The activities of such large transnational economic actors as multinational corporations, whose individual and

Major recipients of U.S. Foreign Aid, 1962-1971 (in millions)								U.S. Foreign Aid, 1971 (in millions)	
1962		1965		1968		1971		Military	Economic
India	$752	India	$727	S. Vietnam	$1,592	S. Vietnam	$2,433	$2,045	$388
S. Korea	500	S. Vietnam	546	S. Korea	849	S. Korea	875	814	61
Pakistan	476	Pakistan	360	India	677	India	463	257	206
Turkey	450	S. Korea	298	Brazil	368	Cambodia	260	190	70
S. Vietnam	360	Turkey	290	Pakistan	357	Indonesia	213	135	78
Brazil	255	Brazil	288	Turkey	179	Iran	209	209	—
Taiwan	254	Chile	140	Iran	164	Brazil	209	130	79
Chile	188	Iran	123	Australia	156	Turkey	201	147	54
Japan	167	Taiwan	112	Laos	145	Australia	145	145	—
Greece	164	Mexico	98	Taiwan	132	Thailand	137	114	23

collective resources dwarf those of all but the largest national economies, had complicated the picture immeasurably (see Chapters 3 and 15). The interdependence of the international economic system had ruled out the possibility that America could unilaterally solve its economic problems. Consequently, multilateral negotiations were begun in the early 1970s with prospects rather high that future United States economic policy would be closely linked with the policies of others in the industrial world.

The Need for Multilateral Programs

All of these developments pointed to the same general conclusion: The benefits to be gained from unilateral American foreign policies no longer equaled the costs of such action.

After more than two decades of pursuing strategic superiority, the outcome was fragile strategic parity; a decade of unparalleled commitment and cost in Southeast Asia had produced only appalling destruction, human suffering, and a doubtful increase in "national security."

The facts of an economically overextended America had also forced their way onto the public agenda. A foreign policy based on a unilateral pursuit of national and world security no longer seemed appropriate.

By mid-1973, however, it appeared that the break with the postwar international system would not be clean. Even as President Nixon negotiated to stabilize strategic parity, the old policies and reflexes intruded—there were Department of Defense proposals for new strategic bombers, improvements in ICBMs, and a new submarine system. America's withdrawal from Vietnam also had traces of old Cold War policy. For example, even though American troops were being withdrawn from Vietnam, the withdrawal was stretched over four years so that America could extract every bit of military leverage possible from the remaining military presence. Furthermore, once American troops were withdrawn, military pressure was to be maintained through massive aid to the South Vietnamese regime and through a seemingly relentless policy of bombing in neighboring Cambodia in support of a "pro-American" government. It was therefore unclear whether a significantly new foreign policy consensus would emerge.

There was, however, an increasing recognition that the old objectives of the Cold War were no longer relevant. New dimensions of world politics were assuming new prominence in the foreign and defense policy mix. But the apparently new sophistication concerning the demands of the international

Figure 5.16 This chart (left) shows the continuing magnitude of United States military and economic aid in the decade 1962–1971. The changes in aid received by any single country may be determined by drawing a line connecting the figures over the years (as indicated for South Vietnam). Noticeable changes in the amount of aid received are recorded for Indonesia (the result of a coup d'etat) and for Japan. The figures on the shaded portion of the chart reveal both the total aid received by the indicated countries in 1971 and the relative sizes of the military and economic components in that total (after U.S. Department of State, Agency for International Development).

Figure 5.17 The end of active military involvement of the United States in Vietnam (right), Paris, January 23, 1973. Dr. Henry Kissinger (foreground), then Special Assistant to President Nixon, and Le Duc Tho (background), negotiator for North Vietnam, initial the cease-fire agreement.

system had been purchased at great cost. And perhaps the major part of the payment was the consequences of this experience for the American domestic scene. This chapter closes, therefore, with an examination of the impact of American national security policy on American domestic politics and society.

THE COLD WAR AND AMERICAN DEMOCRACY

Assessments of the impact of foreign and defense policy on domestic politics and society commonly point to the magnitude of the resources absorbed by the Department of Defense annually: From one-third to one-half of the outlays of the federal budget since the 1950s have gone to the DOD. Observers also emphasize the pervasiveness of the military in American life, as evidenced by the close relationship between large defense contractors and the DOD (a topic that is discussed in the Perspective on the military-industrial complex). In this concluding portion of the chapter we turn to certain other important relationships that have emerged as the result of America's foreign affairs.

The Rise of Presidential Government

By 1960 the basis for a form of "presidential government" had been laid. We have already noted that the initiative and control of American foreign and defense policy had clearly passed from Congress to the Presidency. The corollary of these developments was the establishment (during the 1950s) of a foreign- and national-security policy bureaucracy whose lines of responsibility and accountability ran to the White House. The foundation was thus prepared for an almost total, and perhaps irretrievable, shift of policy control to the White House.

By expanding the authority of the Special Assistant for National Security Affairs and his staff, Presidents Kennedy and Johnson erected a personalized foreign policy staff within the White House. These men were appointed by, and responsible to, the President; they, along with the personal staff of the Secretary of Defense, emerged as the National Security Managers, or the foreign policy makers, of the 1960s (Richard Barnet, 1972). Their control of information, and thus their capacity to define the options within which foreign policy decisions would be made, was very nearly absolute (see the Perspective on the military-industrial complex).

Given the immense dangers that were supposedly present in the international system, this centralization of authority was believed essential. Consequently, there was no resistance when Richard Nixon institutionalized the national security ap-

Figure 5.18 American foreign policy is the product of many considerations, including the short- and long-range side effects of the policy. If, for example, because of another nation's disapproval of our actions toward a third nation, we made the decision to withdraw diplomatic representatives, reverberations might well be felt in many spheres: there would surely be tenseness felt in the strictly diplomatic aspects of our relations; but effects might also be felt in trade relations, in the popularity of the critic nation's art or literature, or in the credibility of that nation's positions in other areas of politics. One might consider the examples of America's relations with France after its all but complete withdrawal from NATO, and with Sweden following its criticisms of America's Vietnam policy, to determine what side effects may result in actual cases.

paratus that had developed more or less informally during the 1960s. President Nixon placed Henry Kissinger at the top of the structure and invested him with total authority over the foreign and national security policy system; as in the past, the lines of responsibility and accountability ran to the President, not to Congress.

Implications of Presidential Government

Presidential control of America's international affairs raises a number of important questions. The Vietnam War, perhaps more than any other event, was the stimulus for the rising challenge to presidential power. The Presidents of the 1960s, by virtue of their manipulation of the budgetary processes, information, and the other prerogatives of presidential power, had kept the United States in Southeast Asia for nearly a decade despite growing congressional and popular dissent. The result was increasing sentiment that Congress must assert its powers to legislate limitations to presidential power; in June 1973 the two houses of Congress finally agreed to cut budgetary support of the war.

Clearly, there are fundamental constitutional relationships at issue in the debate over presidential power (see Chapters 8 and 9). But the debate entails even more basic questions concerning the relationship of the governed to their government. Just how much power should a President be able to claim in the name of national security? How much should he be allowed to infringe on the civil liberties of American citizens? These questions become relevant when one considers that Presidents have the power to eavesdrop on private conversations, to open mail, or to use other methods of spying on dissenters—all in the cause of protecting national security. Presidents also have the power to silence or discredit journalistic commentary on their foreign and defense policies. Clearly, there are instances in which such actions are justified. Indeed, the civil liberties of American citizens have frequently suffered infringement in time of national crisis (see Chapter 7). There is always the chance, however, that executive prerogatives will be used not for purposes of national security but rather that they will be used to keep controversial policy from public scrutiny and criticism.

To the extent that the misuse of power is possible, one of the most fundamental problems of democracy arises: the accountability of government to the people. The problem is profound. It calls into question the fundamental assertions of the founding fathers that government must be responsive and that it must maintain a separation of powers if the nation is to be

---

Possible Domestic Ramifications of Foreign Policy

If the United States has friendly relations with a nation:

Americans with that national background enjoy a more comfortable status

United States companies can expect stable trade relations with that nation

Culture and ideas from that nation filter into United States culture

If the United States has strained relations with a nation:

Americans with that national background may suffer a loss of status

United States companies can expect less stable trade relations with that nation

Culture and ideas from that nation become less popular

If the United States establishes treaties with many nations that include economic and military aid:

Outflow of money and goods from the United States contributes to an unfavorable balance of trade for the United States (except for those treaties that require aid money to be spent in United States trade)

Military aid creates interest groups in the United States that desire continued foreign military support

If the United States goes to war with a nation:

Certain domestic goods become scarce, as resources are required for war

High wages increase consumer demands for scarce goods and cause inflation

Military service may change or disrupt career plans of young persons

---

Era								
Nixon Era	Surveillance by CIA, Army, and FBI	Vietnam Bombings Pacification Cease-fire Agreement	Nixon Doctrine	Détente with USSR and China	Cambodia Direct Intervention Secret Bombing	Presidential Government	Watergate and Ellsberg Break-ins	
Kennedy-Johnson Era	Alliance for Progress	Vietnam Military Advisers Ground Troops Tonkin Gulf Resolution	McNamara "Flexible Response" Strategies	Military Aid	Support for Chiang Kai-shek	Cuban Invasion (Bay of Pigs)	Cuban Missile Crisis	Middle East Policy
Eisenhower Era	Military Aid	Nuclear Arms Race and Summitry	Dulles's Massive Retaliation Strategy	Department of Defense Expansion	Military-Industrial Complex	SEATO	Economic Aid	McCarthy Red Scare
Truman Era	China Policy and "Police Action" in Korea	Containment	Military Aid	Cold War and NATO	Marshall Plan	National Security Act of 1947 National Security Council	Military-Industrial Complex	Red Scare

Figure 5.19 The Development of "National Security" as a Justification for Foreign and Domestic Policies. During the postwar period, all of the events listed in the building blocks to the left have been justified to the public by political decision makers as being, to varying degrees, necessary to the security of the nation. From the development of the concept of containment to the Marshall Plan, the development of the National Security Council to the McCarthy "red scare," much governmental activity of the late 1940s and 1950s was motivated by Cold War considerations. In more recent years the domino theory was devised to link America's security with the viability of such fragile nations as Laos and South Vietnam, and the pro-Chiang Kai-shek and anti-Mao Tse-tung line of American policy was continued as a means of isolating the Chinese communists from relationships with the western world. The enormous growth of the power of the executive branch of government—deemed necessary to the handling of the complexities of foreign affairs—the overshadowing of Congress, the conduct of an undeclared war, and internal spying by army intelligence and by the FBI were also judged necessary to the security of the nation.

Finally, the culmination of all things dangerous about "presidential government" was the Watergate scandal. Faced with this attempted perversion of representative institutions in the conduct of elections, Americans of a variety of political persuasions began to perceive the dangers inherent in the catchall justification of "national security." The results of this public rethinking—and the possibilities ran the gamut from symbolic attempts at reform to presidential resignation or even impeachment—might become the content of the remaining building block of the Nixon era.

Figure 5.20 In the 1950s national security was the alleged goal of Senator Joseph McCarthy's hunt for "subversives" in the government (far left). McCarthy's allegation concerning subversion at the army's sensitive installations at Fort Monmouth was one of the factors initiating the famous Army-McCarthy Senate Hearings. During the course of these hearings, McCarthy was accused by army officials as well as by Eisenhower Administration officials of attempting to coerce the Army into giving preferential treatment to one of his top assistants, who had been inducted. Although McCarthy was subsequently censured by the Senate, his accusations and actions served to heighten the tension of the 1950s and to engender a fear among policy makers that they might be labeled "soft toward communism." (left) During the thousand days of his Administration, President John Kennedy was involved in several international crises that brought the United States to the brink of war. Crises such as the Berlin blockade in 1961 helped to strengthen the power of the President to the point where the security of the nation became focused on the wisdom and diplomacy of the Chief Executive.

free from tyranny (see Chapters 2 and 15). But to what extent does the fast-moving international situation necessitate the freedom of government institutions from popular and legal limitations to its power?

This chapter has indicated that American foreign policy for the past decade has been formulated around the premise that the government needs to be free of constraints and needs a generous degree of secrecy to achieve its goals. Such a conclusion might not be so disturbing had American foreign and defense policy been conducted with a reasonable degree of sensitivity to the costs and consequences of that policy. Information contained in the *Pentagon Papers,* however, made it clear that American intervention in, and escalation of, the Southeast Asian conflict was undertaken in a manner calculated to hide decisions and their implications from the American people (see Chapter 12). The public was not viewed as something to which policy makers were ultimately responsible, but rather as something to be manipulated in pursuit of the policy maker's, or the expert's, "superior vision." The tragic costs of Vietnam assume added weight in view of this official cynicism.

The antidemocratic implications of the presidential role in foreign policy have affected American domestic politics in yet another way. President Nixon, perhaps more than any previous President, attempted to extend presidential government beyond foreign and security policy. In the creation of a comprehensive staff of advisers accountable only to himself, President Nixon projected the functional equivalent of the foreign and national security policy-making processes into all of public policy. He also, perhaps unwittingly, replicated the mentality that went with it: The needs of the Presidency and the country had seemingly become interchangeable.

The culmination of all things dangerous about "presidential government" was the Watergate scandal. Apart from the sensational aspects of the scandal, one was struck by how many of the old Cold War arguments had been transferred to domestic politics. The bugging, the burglaries, the illegal manipulation of campaign funds, and ultimately the lying to the public were all justified by the need to protect the country from a national security "threat."

Thus, the domestic phenomenon of Watergate had raised a most disturbing question: To what extent had the single-minded pursuit of national security and world order by the United States subverted the nation's domestic system?

SUMMARY

The primary American foreign policy objective since World War II has been the development and maintenance of an anticommunist international order. The policy of containment provided for the application of counterpressure—economic, political, or military—whenever Soviet or Chinese communist expansion was perceived. Confrontation became a dominant motif of America's foreign policy: the Berlin crisis, the Korean War, the Cuban missile crisis, involvement in Third World insurgencies, and the Vietnam War.

The domestic implications of the Cold War were far-reaching: Decision-making power in foreign policy became concentrated in the executive branch, almost to the exclusion of Congress; the influence of the military pervaded many aspects of American economic life; and military superiority was given first priority in the federal budget. Yet the Vietnam War provided the stimulus for challenging the rise of presidential government, a challenge that was given urgency by suggestions that the executive branch, for the sake of national security, had attempted to compromise the nation's domestic political structure and the civil liberties of its citizens.

SUGGESTED READINGS

Gaddis, John Lewis. *The United States and the Origins of the Cold War, 1941–1947.* New York: Columbia University Press, 1972.

LaFeber, Walter. *America, Russia, and the Cold War, 1945–1971.* 2nd ed. New York: Wiley, 1972.

Osgood, Robert, *et al. Retreat from Empire? The First Nixon Administration.* Baltimore, Md.: Johns Hopkins Press, 1973.

Spanier, John W. *American Foreign Policy Since World War II.* 6th ed. New York: Praeger, 1973.

Tucker, Robert W. *Nation or Empire? The Debate Over American Foreign Policy.* Baltimore, Md.: Johns Hopkins Press, 1968.

THE MILITARY-INDUSTRIAL COMPLEX

by Richard Barnet

Figure 5a.1 Messengers use roller skates to get around the seventeen miles of corridors in the Pentagon, the world's largest office building. In the Pentagon are the offices of the Secretary of Defense and the chief officers of the various military services along with the more than 30,000 employees who carry on the daily business of setting and implementing strategies, letting contracts, and pressuring for appropriations. The Pentagon, since its completion in 1943, has come to symbolize the massive power that the military has achieved in our society.

The institutions that support the Military Economy operate by their own inner logic. Each institutional component of the complex has plausible reasons for continuing to exist and expand. Each promotes and protects its own interests and in so doing reinforces the interests of every other. That is what a "complex" is—a set of integrated institutions that act to maximize their collective power. In this chapter we look at the various structures of the military-industrial complex to try to understand how and why the decisions are made to allocate our national resources to the Military Economy.

THE MILITARY ECONOMY: ITS HOLD ON SOCIETY

The defenders of the military establishment like to characterize the growing attacks on the military-industrial complex as conspiracy-mongering. Senator Henry Jackson, one of the staunchest defenders of big military budgets, calls the recent inquiries into military mismanagement and waste the "largest version of the devil theory of history." When George Mahon, Chairman of the House Appropriations Committee and long-time advocate of big defense budgets, was boorish enough to suggest that perhaps the Navy had been a bit careless to let a $50 million nuclear submarine sink in thirty-five feet of water, the late L. Mendel Rivers, the Pentagon's most generous friend in Congress, attacked him on the floor of the House for "playing into the hands of the enemies of the military" (Laurence Barrett, 1969). The enemies he was talking about were not the Russians, but members of the United States Senate.

Nothing suggests the existence of a conspiracy more strongly than concerted efforts like these to protect the military establishment from public inquiry and debate. But conspiracy is not the answer. The truth is that it is not even necessary. To understand the hold of the Military Economy on the country, one needs to look at the behavior of institutions, not individuals.

Men from the services and the

defense contractors are constantly
putting their heads together to in-
vent ways of spending money for
the military. Indeed, that is their job.
As John Moore, President of North
American Rockwell Aerospace and
Systems Group, the nation's ninth-
ranking defense contractor, put it,
"A new system usually starts with a
couple of industry and military people getting together to discuss common problems." Military officers and
weapons-pushers from corporations
are "interacting continuously at the
engineering level," according to
Moore. One of the nation's top military contractors has said that military procurement is a "seamless
web": "Pressures to spend more come
from the industry selling new weapons ideas and in part from the
military (Bernard Nossiter, 1968).

The problem, then, is not that
those who make up the military-
industrial complex act improperly,
but that they do exactly what the
system expects of them. Each part
of the complex acts in accordance
with its own goals and in so doing
reinforces all the others. If we look

at the military-industrial complex
and how it operates, it will become
clear why it has such a firm hold on
American life and why it cannot
be controlled without major institutional changes.

The Rise of the Military Establishment

How did the military establishment
come to acquire such power in a nation that had a political tradition of
condemning large standing armies
and in 1938 ranked eighteenth among
the nations of the world in land
forces? What General Shoup calls the
"new militarism" is an outgrowth of
World War II. As is shown in Chapter 4, the federal government came
to play a major managerial role in the
economy and to help create and to
dispose of a significant share of the
national wealth. Within the federal
bureaucracy the balance of power
shifted decisively to those agencies
that handled military power. In 1939
the federal government had about
800,000 civilian employees, about
10 percent of whom worked for
national security agencies. At the

end of the war the figure approached
4 million, of whom more than 75 percent were in military-related
activities.

Not only did the war radically shift
the balance of power in the federal
bureaucracy, catapulting the military
establishment from a marginal institution without a constituency to a
position of command over many of
the resources of a whole society; it
also redefined the traditional tasks
of the military. The traditional se-
mantic barriers between "political"
and "military" functions were
eroded; in the development and
execution of strategy, the military
were deep in politics.

To maintain and extend their
power in the postwar period, the
military have been able to draw on
a varied and effective arsenal. The
most important weapon has been
organization. As we have seen, the
military bureaucracies came out of the
war with their structures intact. The
institutional relationships of the
Military Economy that had been
created in the war were preserved
and expanded. In this process the

military establishment used two other weapons: secrecy and fear.

In a bureaucracy, knowledge is power (see Chapter 10). The military establishment has made particularly effective use of its jealously guarded monopoly of information on national security matters. Critics have been disarmed by the standard official defense of policy, "If you only knew what I know."

Because of its hold on top-secret information, the Pentagon has been in a position to scare the public into supporting whatever programs the Administration put forward. The Department of Defense has issued regular warnings about a highly exaggerated threat of a Soviet attack in Europe and a nuclear strike against the United States long before the Soviets had the means to carry it out. Joseph McCarthy was a helpful ally in creating this climate of fear (see Chapter 5).

Military officers constantly held up to the public the specters of Hitler and Pearl Harbor. The only security in a dangerous and irrational world was to run it. In 1947 the first Secretary of Defense, James Forrestal, hung a framed card on his office wall, on which was printed the official lesson of World War II: "We will never have peace until the strongest army and the strongest navy are in the hands of the world's most powerful nation." It was now America's turn to be Number One in the world; it did not seem to matter that the age of nuclear weapons had come.

The Militarized Civilians

"The country is looking for a scapegoat. First it was the draft, then recruiters, then Dow Chemical, and now it's the bloody generals," Major General Melvin Zais, Commander of the 101st Airborne Division in Vietnam, complained to an interviewer from *Time* magazine (Barrett, 1969).

Primarily in response to the enormous costs of the Vietnam War, the leaders of the military establishment have recently been challenged to produce facts and rational arguments to justify their claim to the biggest bite of the tax dollar. Credentials alone are no longer enough. Neither, one hopes, are the traditional national security slogans about the Soviet Threat or the Chinese Threat, no matter how blood-curdling the rhetoric. Foolishness and waste in the Pentagon, the inevitable by-products of any institution with too much money to spend, are finally under attack.

Nevertheless, the uniformed military are not the primary target of a serious political effort to shift away from the priorities of the Military Economy. The principal militarists in America wear three-button suits. They are civilians in everything but outlook. Not the generals but the National Security Managers—the politicians, businessmen, and civil servants who rotate through the paneled offices of the Pentagon, the State Department, the Central Intelligence Agency, the Atomic Energy Commission, and the White House—have been in charge of national security policy.

By the end of the Johnson Administration, the uniformed military had acquired considerable independ-

Figure 5a.2 "In Flanders fields the poppies grow, row on row . . ." One recalls the poem consecrating the dead of World War I and then wonders about the new rows of dead, the deadly bombs and wasted material, the uprooted lives, and the men marching off to fight. "When will it ever end?" queried a song of our generation. The power and wealth of military establishments the world over gives one serious pause when estimating the prospects for lasting peace.

ent political power. They had powerful friends in Congress. The Joint Chiefs had their terms of office extended from two to four years, which meant that a new President had to fire the nation's top military if he wanted to appoint his own men. A retired general ran for the Senate in New Hampshire, and General Curtis LeMay campaigned as George Wallace's running mate in the presidential race of 1968. Both argued that the civilian leaders in the Pentagon were selling out the country. These were straws in the wind signifying the increasing frustration and anger of the military against civilian authorities who ordered them into war but would not let them win it.

Thus civilian control of the military has been maintained throughout the long years of the Cold War, but the price has been the militarization of the civilian leadership. Generals and admirals have continued to take orders from the President as Commander-in-Chief, but the President spends much of his time building, or "projecting," America's military power.

The militarized civilians have seemingly surpassed even the military in embracing a "realism" that envisages no alternative to an escalating arms race but annihilation, that perpetuates an aimless war by calling it a commitment, and that measures the nation's greatness in megatons. Far more responsive to the bureaucratic interests of the services than to the wider political interests of the American people, they seem to believe that America's principal role in the world is to acquire more power. Thus it is they, rather than the uniformed military, who must assume responsibility for the distortion of national priorities.

The temptation to try to solve political problems through violence is almost irresistible for the political leaders of a great power because the risk of retaliation seems low and the military man's "solutions" offer the illusion of toughness, practicality, and certitude. Factors that can be fed into computers such as "kill ratios" sound more persuasive than political analysis, which is hard to prepare and hard to comprehend. To understand

the true interests of the American people in a remote area of the world, a diplomat must not only try to understand who the Vietnamese are and what they want, but must continually try to rediscover America's own interests. It is much easier to avoid both processes by treating the outside world as a collection of statistics, nuisances, and threats, ignoring domestic needs and treating international politics as gambling in a good cause. Arthur Schlesinger, Jr.'s account of the deliberations preceding the 1961 Bay of Pigs invasion illustrates the point:

The advocates of the adventure had a rhetorical advantage. They could strike virile poses and talk of tangible things— fire power, air strikes, landing craft, and so on. To oppose the plan, one had to invoke intangibles—the moral position of the United States, the reputation of the President, the response of the United Nations, "world public opinion" and other such odious concepts. These matters were as much the institutional concern of the State Department as military hardware was of Defense. I could not help feeling that the desire to prove to the CIA and the Joint Chiefs that they were not

Canceled Military Projects			
Selected Projects	Year Begun	Year Canceled	Funds Invested (in millions)
Aircraft			
Air Force: ANP (nuclear aircraft)	1951	1961	$511.6
Navy: Seamaster	1951	1959	330.4
Missiles			
Air Force: Navaho	1954	1957	679.8
Ships			
Navy: Type II towed Torpedo Countermeasures	1945	1955	13.0
Ordnance, Combat Vehicles, and Related Equipment			
Air Force: Dyna-Soar	1960	1963	405.0

Source: Adapted from Seymour Melman, *Pentagon Capitalism: The Management of the New Imperialism.* McGraw-Hill, 1970.

Figure 5a.3 Appropriations are often made for defense projects that never reach completion. Like any organization, the Department of Defense can make mistakes or embark on projects that looked good at the beginning but then failed to live up to their promised results. In the case of the Department of Defense, however, mistakes or rejects are ordinarily costly, running into many millions of dollars, as the statistics on these selected projects show.

soft-headed idealists but were really tough guys too influenced State's representatives at the Cabinet table. (Schlesinger, 1965)

THE NATIONAL SECURITY MANAGERS AND THE NATIONAL INTEREST

Who are the key civilian foreign-policy decision-makers? How does one get to be a National Security Manager? Why do they think as they do?

If we take a look at the men who have held the very top positions, the Secretaries and Under Secretaries of State and Defense, the Secretaries of the three services, the Chairman of the Atomic Energy Commission, and the Director of the CIA, we find that out of ninety-one individuals who held these offices during the period 1940–1967, seventy of them were from the ranks of big business or high finance, including eight out of ten Secretaries of Defense, seven out of eight Secretaries of the Air Force, every Secretary of the Navy, eight out of nine Secretaries of the Army, every Deputy Secretary of Defense,

three out of five Directors of the CIA, and three out of five Chairmen of the Atomic Energy Commission. The trend continues in the Nixon Administration. David Packard, head of the important defense contractor, Hewlett-Packard, was the first Deputy Secretary of Defense, and Roy Ash, head of Litton Industries, was made Director of the Office of Management and Budget.

The historian Gabriel Kolko investigated 234 top foreign-policy decision-makers and found that "men who came from big business, investment and law held 59.6 percent of the posts." The Brookings Institution volume *Men Who Govern,* a comprehensive study of the top federal bureaucracy from 1933 to 1965, reveals that before coming to work in the Pentagon, 86 percent of the Secretaries of the Army, Navy, and Air Force were either businessmen or lawyers— usually with a business practice (David Stanley, 1967). In the Kennedy Administration 20 percent of all civilian executives in defense-related agencies came from defense contractors. Defining

the national interest and protecting national security are the proper province of business. Indeed, as President Coolidge used to say, "the business of America is business."

In *Democracy in America,* Alexis de Tocqueville worried that the United States might not be successful in its foreign relations because "foreign politics demand scarcely any of those qualities which a democracy possesses; and they require on the contrary the perfect use of almost all those faculties in which it is deficient." He said that an aristocracy was better for running foreign policy because a government of the few could keep secrets, was invulnerable to the passions of the mob, and knew how to exercise great patience (Tocqueville, 1835). Tocqueville would be greatly reassured by the way the conduct of foreign policy has evolved in America, for the National Security Managers exercise the power to make life-and-death decisions with very little interference from the rest of us.

The National Security Managers, like the uniformed military, have

```
                 DAILY BULLETIN
   Headquarters, United States Army
              Missile Command
        Redstone Arsenal, Alabama
                  35809

                 OFFICIAL

   EFFECTIVE UNTIL 16 FEBRUARY 1970

   NUMBER 11        16 January 1970

   3.  AMBULANCE SERVICE.  Due to a
   critical personnel shortage in the
   Ambulance Section, US Army Hospital,
   it is necessary that all scheduled
   ambulance requirements be received,
   in writing at least 14 days prior
   to the date coverage is required
   so that personnel can be scheduled
   in order to effect coverage.  It
   should be remembered that the pri-
   mary mission of the Ambulance Ser-
   vice is to provide coverage for
   US Army Hospital, and requests
   should be kept to a minimum.
                       (CO, USAH - 2)
```

```
                CHIEF OF STAFF
    Commander Amphibious Force
        U.S. Atlantic Fleet
      Norfolk, Virginia 23520

              01: jrr
          10 September 1971

   MEMORANDUM FOR ALL PHIBLANT
   COMMANDING OFFICERS

   Subj:  Refreshments in
          wardroom

   1.  For your information and
   action as you see fit, I have
   personally overheard Admiral
   Bell say many times that he
   does not like to see kool aid
   served in the wardrooms of
   ships.  Over to you.

          Respectfully,

          J. E. McCauley
          Captain, U.S. Navy
```

Figure 5a.4 The use of bureaucratic jargon and the repeated demonstration of hierarchical authority in even the smallest matters has come to characterize modern bureaucracies, including, as these two memos attest, the armed services.

Reprinted with permission from *The Washington Monthly,* Copyright 1971 by The Washington Monthly Company, 1028 Conn. Ave. N.W., Washington, D.C. 20036

looked at the world through very special lenses, and the result has been a remarkable consensus. As is discussed in Chapter 5, the military policies with respect to NATO, Southeast Asia, and nuclear strategy that were developed during the Truman Administration continue in force into the 1970s despite the Nixon Administration's diplomacy of détente. Most of the men who have set the framework of America's national security policy have come from executive suites and law offices within shouting distance of one another in fifteen city blocks in New York, Washington, Detroit, Chicago, and Boston. It is not surprising that they emerge from homogeneous backgrounds and virtually identical careers with a standard way of looking at the world. They may argue with one another about means but not about ends. Apparently it has not occurred to them to question seriously the basic assumptions of national security policy.

The years of American supremacy have meant wealth, fame, comfort, excitement, and a sense of accomplishment for those who have operated at the top of the society. It is hardly surprising that those who have prospered equate the national interest and the status quo. When the term is ripped of geopolitical metaphor and ideological gloss, national security means nothing more complicated than making sure that the American Way of Life continues undisturbed by foreign challengers. But the American Way of Life means very different things to different people. To a Mississippi tenant farmer trying to eke out a subsistence living it is not a first-priority concern that we scare the Soviets or the Chinese with an extra supply of missiles.

Under the stimulus of defense spending, the American economy has boomed, but its benefits have not been equitably shared. The disparity between rich and poor in America has widened. The National Security Managers have not regarded the redistribution of wealth as a priority concern, for they have had neither the experience nor the incentive to understand the problems of the poor. Their professional and personal interests are with the business and commercial interests that they serve and with which they identify. For a National Security Manager recruited from the world of business, there are no other important constituencies to which he feels a similar need to respond.

When planning a decision on defense policy, he does not solicit the views of civil rights leaders, farmers, laborers, mayors, artists, or small businessmen. Nor do people from these areas of national life become National Security Managers. Indeed, when Martin Luther King expressed opposition to the Vietnam War, a Pentagon official told him that it was "inappropriate" for someone in the civil rights movement to voice his views on foreign policy.

But there is no reason why the National Security Managers should not represent diverse interests, backgrounds, and ways of looking at the national interest. It is almost unbelievable that of the 400 top decision makers who have assumed the responsibility for the survival of the species, only one has been a woman.

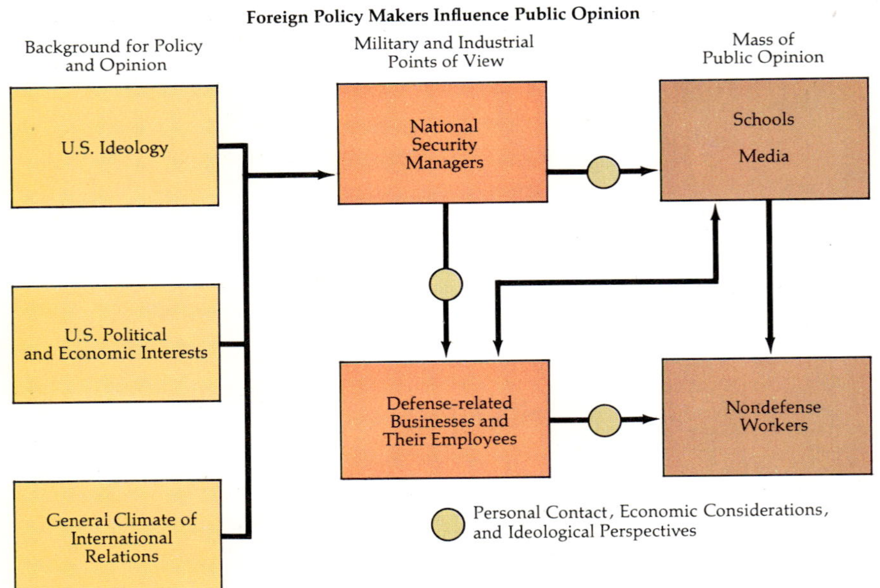

Foreign Policy Makers Influence Public Opinion

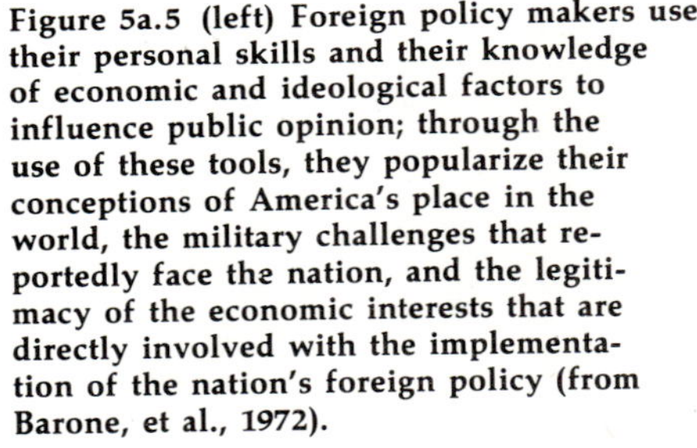

Figure 5a.5 (left) Foreign policy makers use their personal skills and their knowledge of economic and ideological factors to influence public opinion; through the use of these tools, they popularize their conceptions of America's place in the world, the military challenges that reportedly face the nation, and the legitimacy of the economic interests that are directly involved with the implementation of the nation's foreign policy (from Barone, et al., 1972).

Figure 5a.6 Where do the National Security Managers come from? Many have risen to prominence by virtue of their positions in the industrial half of the military-industrial complex (right). The industrial members of this complex are easily identifiable because contract awards are public knowledge. Here are listed the top defense contractors and their subsidiaries, in 1970, producers of military material and contributors to the ranks of the National Security Managers.

CONFLICT OF INTEREST AND THE NATIONAL INTEREST

"One must believe in the long-term threat," James Ling, former president of Ling-Temco-Vought Aerospace Corporation, insisted in an interview with the *Washington Post.* For LTV, which is the eighth-largest defense contractor, the threat is the equivalent of cash.

Much of the pressure for new weapons systems comes from the one hundred largest defense contractors. The weapons-producers are in the business of selling threat-removers, and this requires selling threats as well. Weapons-pushing is an essential activity, and the defense contractors try to foresee the future requirements of the military. Many defense contractors operate "think tanks" that perform contract studies on the "threat environment" for the services to which they also sell hardware.

A number of other defense companies, according to the studies of Professor Alan Westin, have spent money to promote policies that depend on the ever greater use of force.

The American Security Council, according to its brochure, is "an organization through which the private sector of society might utilize its talents and resources in helping meet the Communist challenge to peace and freedom" and to develop "new and original approaches in countering Communism's war to conquer the world."

Men from defense industries also act as consultants to the Department of Defense, lending their judgment on a variety of politico-military questions. Defense contractors play an even more significant role by contributing members to various scientific and advisory boards of the Department of Defense, boards dealing with weapons development and procurement matters. Other members are recruited from the weapons-research laboratories of some of America's major universities. On the Army Scientific Advisory Committee are men from General Electric, Boeing, and Litton, while the Navy has the chief scientist of Ryan Aeronautical Company and the vice-president for engineering of the General Dynamics Corporation on its Research Advisory Committee. The purpose of these committees is to alert the Pentagon to new scientific discoveries that could be turned into weapons and to suggest individuals and firms to work on their research and development.

The National Security Industrial Association, founded by James Forrestal in 1944 to make sure that "American business will stay close to the services," is, according to a Forrestal quote on the masthead of its monthly newsletter, an organization "of plain American citizens who are interested in the security of the United States." To qualify for membership, however, a plain American must also be an executive of a defense contractor. The purpose of the organization is to lobby the Department of Defense to adopt or to continue practices that benefit the member corporations.

For the men who sustain the weapons research, development, and procurement process, service in the Pentagon seems to be an essential element of career-building. Many

---

Top Fifty Prime Military Contract Awards, 1970

Rank	Parent Company	Rank	Parent Company	Rank	Parent Company
21.	American Motors	16.	Honeywell Inc.	22.	R C A Corp.
4.	American Telephone & Telegraph Co.	10.	Hughes Aircraft Co.	25.	Raymond, Morrison, Knudsen
46.	Asiatic Petroleum Corp.	24.	International Business Machines Corp.	18.	Raytheon Co.
20.	Avco Corp.	31.	International Telephone & Telegraph Corp.	50.	R. J. Reynolds Industries, Inc.
35.	Bendix Corp.	11.	Ling-Temco-Vought, Inc.	38.	Singer Co.
12.	Boeing Co.	9.	Litton Industries, Inc.	15.	Sperry Rand Corp.
39.	Collins Radio Co.	1.	Lockheed Aircraft Corp.	42.	Standard Oil Co., of California
37.	E. I. du Pont de Nemours & Co.	26.	Martin Marietta Corp.	30.	Standard Oil Co., of New Jersey
41.	F M C Corp.	5.	McDonnell Douglas Corp.	34.	T R W, Inc.
19.	Ford Motor Corp.	36.	Mobil Oil Corp.	29.	Teledyne, Inc.
2.	General Dynamics Corp.	43.	Morrison-Knudsen Co., Inc.	27.	Tenneco, Inc.
3.	General Electric Co.	44.	National Presto Industries, Inc.	32.	Texas Instruments Inc.
17.	General Motors Corp.	7.	North American Rockwell Corp.	13.	Textron Inc.
49.	General Telephone & Electronic Corp.	33.	Northrop Corp.	48.	Uniroyal, Inc.
23.	General Tire & Rubber Co.	28.	Olin Corp.	6.	United Aircraft Corp.
8.	Grumman Corp.	47.	Pacific Architects & Engrs., Inc.	14.	Westinghouse Electric Corp.
45.	Hercules Inc.	40.	Pan American World Airways, Inc.		

have come to the Pentagon as company vice-presidents and have left to become presidents. There is no proof that any of these men has acted improperly, for, indeed, there are few recognized ethical standards to apply. Moreover, no outsider will ever know the real motive for individual procurement decisions. The important point is that their past careers, future expectations, and professional experience make them tolerant of waste in military spending and seemingly comfortable with the idea of a permanent arms race.

The successful tax lawyer learns the ropes in the Internal Revenue Service. The good broadcasting-industry lawyer may have spent time at the FCC. But the application of this familiar career pattern to the defense business means that virtually the only people making decisions as to whether new weapons systems are needed, whether they cost too much, and who should make them, are men who directly and personally stand to benefit from big defense budgets. Top Pentagon officials exercise especially broad discretion because their actions are subject to very inadequate review both in the White House and in Congress.

Thus, America's leaders have built into the weapons-procurement system a set of incentives for continuing the arms race by recruiting the managers of the Pentagon from the arms industry. The taxpayers have been paying for biased judgment. Professor George Kistiakowsky, former Special Assistant to President Eisenhower for Science and Technology, has pointed out that it is not necessary to recruit the managers of the Pentagon procurement programs from the industries that depend on the defense budget for their survival (Barrett, 1969). The necessary technical knowledge can be found in nondefense industry and in the universities. But profitable patterns developed over a generation are not easily changed. Like other essential links in the military-industrial complex, this one will grow stronger until we recognize that permitting officials to build personal careers by subsidizing defense firms threatens the national security.

THE ORIGINS OF THE MILITARY-INDUSTRIAL COMPLEX

The government defense-industry nexus defies most of the rules of the free-enterprise economy (see Chapter 4). The essence of the free enterprise system is competition, but 57.9 percent of all defense procurement is negotiated with a single contractor and only 11.5 percent through formal advertised competition. Under the capitalist creed, the efficient survive; and those who can neither provide quality nor control their costs fall by the wayside. Defense industry, however, is shielded by the government from the harsher realities of the competitive system. It is relieved of the obligation to be efficient and is protected by the government from most of the normal risks of doing business for profit. Government and a vast dependent industry have struck a bargain under which industry has surrendered a few management prerogatives to the Pentagon in return for substantial subsidies. We shall look more closely at these subsidies, for they go to the heart of the relationship

PATRIOTISM: TWO ORIENTATIONS	
Patriotism I	**Patriotism II**
Objecting to presidential foreign and economic policies by demonstrating and disseminating literature	Objecting to criticisms of the President and of his policies
Objecting to or refusing to pay taxes going toward military and related expenditures	Gladly paying taxes that support a strong military posture
Burning draftcard and refusing to participate in war	Praising military heroes
Wearing the peace symbol	Displaying the flag
Serving in Vista or Peace Corps	Volunteering for military service in peacetime
Displaying bumper sticker: "America: Change It Or Lose It"	Displaying bumper sticker: "America: Love It Or Leave It"

Figure 5a.7 An individual's definition of patriotism depends on his or her own predispositions. Some citizens approve of current conditions, and they have great faith in the political processes that select our decision makers and in the leaders who set policies. These citizens may see patriotism as cooperation with elected leaders and their policies. Others look at the government with skepticism; they put the burden of proof on the government to show the adequacy of its policies in the present and for the future. To these citizens, patriotism is the exercise of the right of critical speech and symbolic action and the right to search for alternatives to policies that they are unable to support.

that we have defined as military socialism.

Military Socialism

It is hardly surprising that leading defense contractors like General Dynamics keep insisting that "we're in [defense] business to stay." According to *The Economics of Military Procurement* (1969), a report of the Joint Economic Committee of the Congress, known as the Proxmire Committee Report, these companies receive a "vast subsidy" in tax dollars. Military socialism offers unique economic advantages to those firms that have come to take the place of the government-owned arsenal. They exercise broad public power and make substantial private profit. How does the system work?

As already mentioned, the defense contractor develops his new products and the market for them simultaneously, often in close, continuous association with the customer, the Department of Defense. Thus he can normally count on selling them. The government does reserve the right to make certain decisions about the internal operations of the firms, operations which, in the private economy, are exclusively the prerogative of management. For example, the Pentagon insists on the right to pass on subcontractors, to decide which products should be purchased in the United States rather than abroad, and what minimum as well as average wage rates will be paid. Such privileges account for much of the waste in defense contracting. The Proxmire Committee Report gives a picture of the dimensions of such waste:

In the past, literally billions of dollars have been wasted on weapons systems that have had to be canceled because they did not work. Other systems have performed far below contract specifications. For example, one study referred to in the hearings shows that of a sample of thirteen major Air Force and Navy aircraft and missile programs initiated since 1955 at a total cost of $40 billion, less than 40 percent produced systems with acceptable electronic performance. Two of the programs were canceled after total program costs of $2 billion were paid. Two programs costing $10 billion were phased out after three years for low reliability. Five programs costing $13 billion give poor performance; that is, their electronics reliability is less than 75 percent of initial specifications. (Joint Economic Committee of Congress, 1969)

The ultimate power to distribute the $45 billion now spent annually on procurement resides in the Pentagon itself. No other unit in government or the private economy comes close to the office of the Secretary of Defense in money to spend, power to decide how to spend it, or respectful attention from every other center of power in the society. However, as Columbia Professor Seymour Melman has noted, it is the Pentagon and not the defense industry whose interests are paramount (Melman, 1970). In the Department of Defense the leading defense contractors are regarded as subsidiaries that must be protected for the benefit of the whole system.

A defense contractor is very little more than an organization of managerial and technical capabilities. The government owns everything else. For example, LTV Aerospace Corporation owns 1 percent of the 6.7 million

Figure 5a.8 American arms sales abroad by the Department of Defense returned almost 13.8 billion dollars to the United States from 1950 to 1972; credit sales during that period added approximately another 3 billion dollars. As can be seen in the table (right), Europe and Canada, the Middle East, and the areas of Asia have been the largest customers. One can add to these sales another 3.5 billion dollars in sales of weapons by private American firms from 1962–1969. The beneficial effects of such immense amounts of cash on the U.S. balance of trade and the fact that France and the Soviet Union are ready to supply the arms that the United States chooses not to provide, creates a continuing economic motivation for such sales (from the U.S. Department of Defense, 1971).

	Cash Sales	Credit Sales
Southeast Asia and Pacific	$1,546	$462
Middle East and South Asia	1,864	2,153
Europe and Canada	9,786	110
Africa	73	53
Latin America	313	377
International Organizations	257	23
Unallocated Credit	—	15
Total	$13,839	$3,193

Military Sales by Region, 1950–1972 (in millions)

square feet of office, plant, and laboratory it uses. The rest is leased from the Department of Defense. To military planners, however, "the team" of managers and engineers is a national asset. The Pentagon is prepared to be lenient with organizations that can innovate in unknown and untried systems. Weapons laboratories that function on the "frontier of technology" are not allowed to fail, for "the team" must stay together and keep the laboratories "hot." If LTV Aerospace did not exist, it would have to be invented. The evidence is persuasive that the Secretary of Defense awarded the TFX plane contract to General Dynamics, against the unanimous recommendation of the Joint Chiefs of Staff that it be given to Boeing, in order to rescue a ranking contractor from probable collapse. General Dynamics, which had lost over $400 million on its Convair division a few years earlier, needed a substantial military contract to survive.

Because there is no catalogue price for a missile and no shortage of money in the Pentagon, procurement officers have had little reason to maintain tight controls over contractors. A military officer whose career rises or falls with a weapons system finds it easy to justify waste in procurement as insurance against technological scarcity.

The concentration of decision making in the office of the Secretary of Defense has given the Pentagon a power that no combination of defense firms can match. The Department of Defense has become the closest thing to a central planning agency in American society. It uses the military budget to stimulate economic growth, to put money into circulation in times of recession, to encourage the development of specific industries, and to assist certain geographical areas.

The Politics of Defense

The alliance of defense contractors and politicians is another cornerstone of the military-industrial complex. Six months after his appointment to the House Naval Affairs Committee in 1937, freshman Representative Lyndon Johnson obtained a major defense contract for his principal financial backers, the Brown & Root construction firm. The same firm thirty years later was called on to turn South Vietnam into a succession of military bases at considerable profit. In the Johnson years, Texas moved ahead to become the third-ranking state in military contracts.

William Phelan, Jr. has studied the political ties of five of the defense companies that experienced the most dynamic economic growth in the 1960s. Each of the following companies increased its revenues by more than 500 percent: Litton Industries, Ling-Temco-Vought, Gulf & Western, Teledyne, and McDonnell Douglas. In 1969 Phelan showed that these large corporations all had powerful political contacts at high levels of government:

The chairman and chief executive of Litton is Charles B. Thornton, a member of the Defense Industrial Advisory Council, long-time associate of McNamara, and close friend of President Johnson. The top man at LTV is James J. Ling, one of Humphrey's leading supporters, a busi-

Figure 5a.9 "They shall beat their swords into plow shares, and their spears into pruninghooks: nation shall not lift up sword against nation, neither shall they learn war anymore" (Isaiah II, 4). The alternatives of guns versus butter are as old as the Bible; but the oldest problems of society seem to be the most insoluble. It is difficult to redirect an economy, especially a sophisticated, technological economy involved to a large extent with the production of war-associated materials, to a primarily peacetime economy. But to change gun production into butter production, or more timely, bomb production into washing machine production, requires a change not only in the temperature of international relations but in the nation's investment priorities.

ness ally of several of Johnson's long-time Dallas backers, and the holder of corporate control over several subsidiaries in whose management Abe Fortas and his law partners have been particularly active. Perhaps the most powerful outside director at Gulf & Western is Edwin L. Weisl, Johnson's most loyal backer in New York. Cyrus Vance went to the Defense Department from Weisl's law firm. The top man at Teledyne, Henry G. Singleton, has long associations with both Thornton and Howard Hughes, an influential man in Johnson's background during much of his career. Teledyne's co-founder and a powerful director is George Kosmetsky, the dean of the business school at the University of Texas.

Finally, McDonnell Douglas is well connected to the Missouri branch of the Democratic Party. In addition to ties to Clark Clifford and Stuart Symington, it at one time included among its directors James E. Webb, until recently head of NASA, and a close adviser of both Johnson and the late and very powerful Senator Kerr of Oklahoma. (Phelan, 1969)

In the 1960 presidential race the Democrats, using erroneous intelligence estimates leaked by the Air Force, cried "missile gap" and called for "an impressive additional ex-penditure of about $4 billion a year on our strategic forces." John Kennedy personally played the preparedness theme to the hilt: "I am convinced that every American who can be fully informed as to the facts today would agree to an additional investment in our national security now rather than risk his survival, and his children's survival, in the years ahead." The Kennedy advisers, who had shrewdly estimated that the number of voters opposed to survival was small, came ten years later to see that such demagogic appeals undermined national security. In 1968 Richard Nixon, speaking a few hundred yards from a General Dynamics plant, charged the Democrats with a "security gap." This time the public was more skeptical, mostly because of the disillusionment with the Vietnam War. Nevertheless, in the same election at least one United States Senator, Joseph Clark of Pennsylvania, was helped to defeat by the efforts of a union upset about his interest in cutting the defense budget and closing down defense installations.

Most congressmen and senators, who have little personal knowledge of defense matters, have generally concluded that the political climate in the country demanded continued support for high-level defense expenditures. Many of them have found it convenient to run against Khrushchev, Brezhnev, or Mao on a "preparedness" platform. Once elected, the safe and easy course was to leave the problem in the experienced hands of the chairman of the Armed Services and Appropriations Committee.

However, the congressional wing of the military-industrial complex has been careful not to hoard everything. "My friends, there is something in this bill for every member," Chairman Carl Vinson of the House Armed Services Committee exclaimed in 1958 as he presented a billion-dollar military construction bill to the whole House. Defense contracts are currently distributed among 363 congressional districts. Congressmen have the incentive to vote right on military appropriations. Many are cultivated with junkets, testimonials,

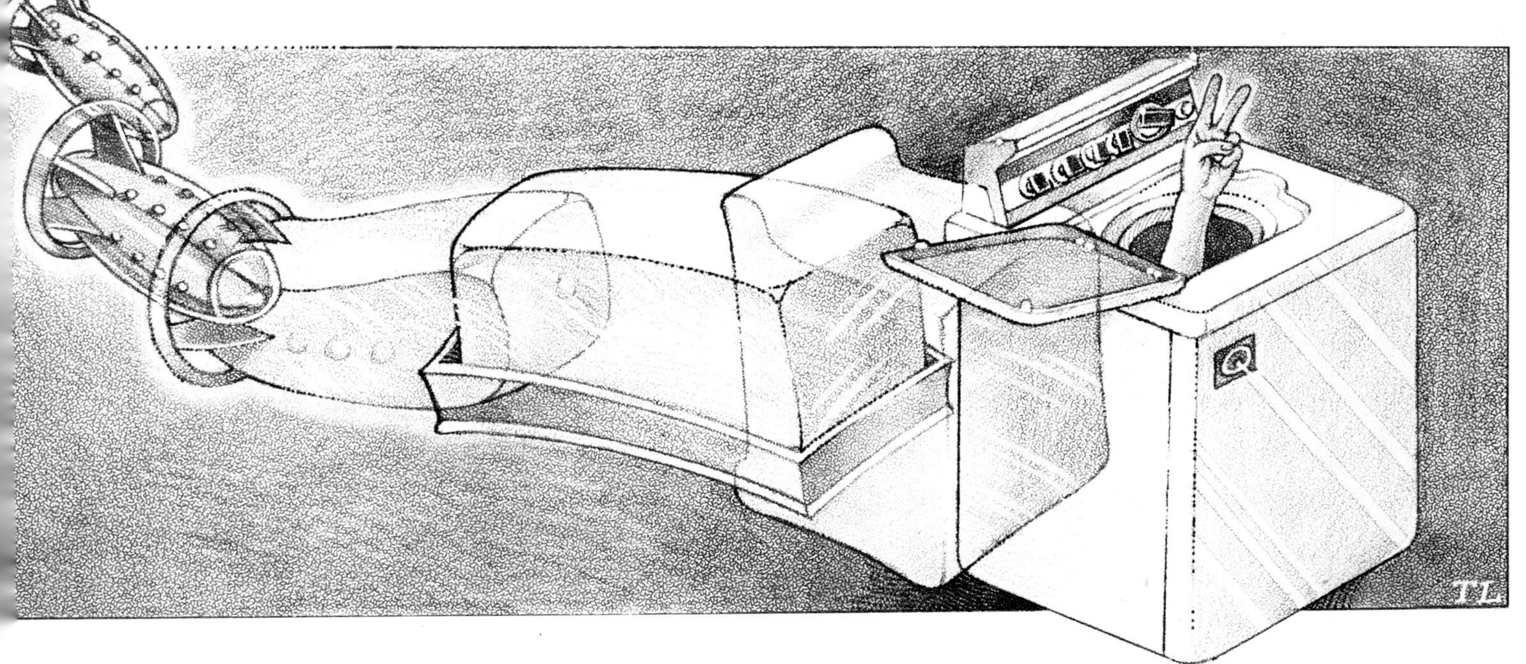

and other similar diversions.

Until late in the Vietnam War, the budget of the Department of Defense was traditionally accepted unanimously in both houses after a few hours of patriotic speeches. "I never voted against a defense appropriation," former Representative and later Secretary of the Interior Steward Udall testified before the Joint Economic Committee. Such appropriations, he said, were "sacrosanct."

Although the critics of excessive military spending have become more vocal in the wake of the Vietnam War, the decisions on whether to give the Pentagon what it wants or more than it wants still rest with a small group of senior representatives and senators. The "age of confrontation" has given way to an "era of negotiation" in which Pepsi-Cola bottling plants and Holiday Inns are becoming part of the Moscow landscape and the head of the Soviet Communist Party publicly applauds the foreign policy of the United States. But even as the rhetoric of the Cold War softens and diplomatic strategies change, the federal budget continues to reflect the nation's military priorities. The institutions of national security developed over a generation of war and preparation for war seem to have developed a life and a logic of their own.

SUGGESTED READINGS

Barnet, Richard J. *The Roots of War*. New York: Atheneum, 1972.

Kolko, Gabriel. *The Politics of War*. New York: Random House, 1968.

McNamara, Robert. *The Essence of Security*. New York: Harper & Row, 1969.

Melman, Seymour. *Pentagon Capitalism: The Political Economy of War*. New York: McGraw-Hill, 1970.

Thayer, George. *The War Business*. New York: Simon and Schuster, 1969.

York, Herbert. *Race to Oblivion*. New York: Simon and Schuster, 1970.

Figure 5a.10 The Cold War has been costly in terms of wealth diverted from nonmilitary sectors of the economy. Immense quantities of manpower, energy resources, production facilities, housing, shipping, transportation, and technology have been invested in our military institutions. It is true that the fear of thermonuclear war has driven the great and middle powers back from the brink of violence; and the fear of great unrest among citizens, whose primary concerns are health, education, and personal goods, has pressured leaders to lower military expenses. But the interests that are primarily benefited by defense expenditures, buttressed by continuing world perspectives of fear and hostility, retain arms development, production, and distribution at very high levels—not only in the United States but around the world.

POLITICAL HISTOGRAPH

The Political Histograph on the following four pages is a visual guideline to selected important events in American political history, categorized according to this book's four major policy areas: Economy, Foreign Affairs and National Security, Race, and Civil Liberties. The advantage of this time-line presentation is that these events can be viewed not only as they progress in time, but also simultaneously across the category columns, to achieve a connected picture of a period of political history. We have chosen eight year periods for our time blocks, which are in phase with presidential terms, as another aid to the recollection of events associated in time.

It is important to realize in studying politics that events never occur in a vacuum, that foreign affairs decisions may be linked to balance of trade considerations, that race problems may be ameliorated or exacerbated by economic ups and downs, or that civil liberties may wax and wane with perceived dangers of warfare and subversion by foreign powers.

No graph in such a small space can aim at complete coverage or great detail, and experts may differ as to what items to include or omit. We have aimed to include sufficient items in each period to provide clues for understanding the general political directions of the period.

Political Histograph

	Economy	Foreign Affairs	Race	Civil Liberties
1772		1775–83 American Revolution 1775 Continental Army is created 1776 Declaration of Independence 1778 Treaty with France, covering commercial, political, military relations	1778 First Indian treaty is signed	1776 Declaration of Independence
1780	1784 Trade with China begins 1785 Federal government grants land to finance schools 1786 First recorded strike by printers of Philadelphia 1787 Shays Rebellion	1783 Treaty of Paris between U.S. and Great Britain officially ends War for Independence	1780–86 Slavery abolished in six northern states 1787 Members of Constitutional Convention agree to count three-fifths of all slaves in apportioning House membership; slave trade not to be banned until 1808.	1787 Northwest Ordinance is adopted, guaranteeing freedom of religion and outlawing slavery in Northwest Territory
1788	1789 First tariff is imposed; Department of the Treasury is established 1791 Bank of the United States is established 1790–91 Funding of national debt on assumption of state debts 1792 New York Stock Exchange established 1793 Cotton gin is invented 1794 Whiskey Rebellion	1794 Jay Treaty with Great Britain is ratified—increases trade but confirms British power on the seas 1795 Pinckney's Treaty with Spain	1790 First census shows black population of 757,181, with 59,557 free blacks; first emancipation petition is sent to Congress 1793 Cotton gin is invented; first federal Fugitive Slave Act is passed	1788 U.S. Constitution is ratified by eleven states and placed in operation 1789 Bill of Rights is adopted by Congress and sent to the states
1796	1803 Louisiana Purchase	1796 Washington gives his Farewell Address, warning against U.S. involvement in foreign disputes 1798 Undeclared naval war with France begins; Alien and Sedition Acts 1803 Louisiana Purchase	1796 First Indian reservation is settled 1800 Free blacks of Philadelphia petition Congress to oppose slavery, the slave trade, and the Fugitive Slave Act of 1793	1798 Alien and Sedition Acts deprive aliens of rights and penalize criticism of government; Kentucky and Virginia resolutions advocate strong states' rights to oppose Alien and Sedition Acts
1804	1804–06 Lewis and Clark explore Louisiana Territory 1806 First industry-wide strike (of shoemakers) takes place 1807 Beginning of the steamboat era	1805–07 Seizures of U.S. ships increase—under British Orders in Council and Napoleon's Decrees 1807 Embargo Act—prohibits U.S. exports to Great Britain and France 1809 Non-intercourse Act against Great Britain and France	1806 Virginia law requires free black men to leave the state 1811 Battle of Tippecanoe frustrates formation of a powerful Indian confederation	1805 First appeal to courts by striking workers
1812	1815 Whaling industry boom 1816 First charter to a railroad company is issued; Tariff of 1816, deliberately protectionist, is imposed 1817 Second Bank of the United States is chartered 1819 Panic of 1819 inaugurates a long and severe economic depression	1812–15 War of 1812 against Great Britain; ends with Treaty of Ghent 1812 First Foreign Aid Act passed by Congress 1817 Rush-Bagot Agreement with Great Britain demilitarizes the Great Lakes 1818 Convention of 1818 settles outstanding differences with Great Britain; transcontinental treaty with Spain acquires Florida for U.S.	1814 Creek Indian War 1815–25 Postwar treaties with tribes north of Ohio River resolve trading areas 1815–60 Underground Railroad in operation 1816 Wars against the Seminole Indians begin, led by General Andrew Jackson	1819 First federal immigration law
1820	1820 Interchangeable machine parts begin to be widely used in industry 1824 Tariff of 1824, highly protectionist, is imposed; *Gibbons* v. *Ogden* establishes supremacy of federal government in areas of interstate commerce 1825 Erie Canal is opened; strike for ten-hour working day by Boston carpenters	1823 Monroe Doctrine 1824 Treaty between U.S. and Russia on Alaskan boundary	1820 Missouri Compromise enacted, prohibiting slavery north of Missouri; first emigration of blacks to Africa is organized 1822 Denmark Vesey's slave rebellion	
1827				

	Economy	Foreign Affairs	Race	Civil Liberties
1828	**1828** Tariff of Abominations is imposed, extracting high protective duties **1830** Beginning of the railroad era **1832–33** Fight over Second Bank of the United States **1833** Compromise Tariff is passed, with plans for a gradual reduction of all duties to 20 percent **1835** Wheat crop failure leads to economic strain		**1830** Indian Removal Act forces resettlement of Indians to land west of Mississippi **1831** Nat Turner leads a black insurrection in Virginia **1832** Black Hawk War **1832–42** Federal government resettles "Five Civilized Tribes" **1834** Proslavery riots in Philadelphia; South Carolina prohibits the teaching of black children	**1833** Oberlin College (Ohio) is first in U.S. to adopt coeducation; *Barron* v. *Baltimore* holds that Bill of Rights applies to federal action only, not to states
1836	**1836** First incorporation law is passed **1837** Panic of 1837 initiates a prolonged economic depression; 618 banks fail **1841** First covered wagon train travels to California **1842** Tariff of 1842 is passed extending protection to American manufactures	**1836** Alamo is captured by Santa Anna; Texas declares independence **1842** Webster-Ashburton Treaty with Great Britain settles Maine boundary	**1836–44** Congress invokes Gag Rule, refusing to discuss slavery **1839–40** Liberty Party (antislavery) is established **1842** *Prigg* v. *Pennsylvania* holds that states are not obliged to enforce Fugitive Slave laws	**1842** *Commonwealth* v. *Hunt* upholds the right of workers to strike and the legality of labor unions
1844	**1845** Texas is annexed **1846** Polk's veto of Rivers and Harbors Bill checks policy of internal improvements **1849** Gold Rush in California; Department of the Interior is established **1850** First large federal land grant for railroad construction **1851** Supreme Court holds that states can legislate in some areas of interstate commerce	**1845** Texas is annexed **1846** Oregon Treaty establishes boundary at 49th parallel **1846–48** Mexican-American War **1848** Treaty of Guadalupe Hidalgo ends the Mexican War **1850** Clayton-Bulwar Treaty—U.S. and Great Britain agree on neutrality in Central America	**1850** Compromise of 1850: (1) California is admitted as a free state; (2) Utah and New Mexico Territories are organized; (3) Texas surrenders claim to an area in New Mexico; (4) slave trade is abolished in the District of Columbia; (5) a more stringent Fugitive Slave Law is enacted	**1848** First Women's Rights Convention **1849** Henry David Thoreau writes *Civil Disobedience* **1850** Flogging is outlawed in the Navy and Merchant Marine
1852	**1853** Territories of southern Arizona and New Mexico are acquired for the Southern Pacific Railroad **1857** Tariffs are lowered to 20 percent; failure of the Ohio Life Insurance Company leads to financial recession **1859** Oil successfully drilled in Pennsylvania	**1853** Canadian Reciprocity Treaty; Gadsden Purchase of portion of Arizona from Mexico	**1852** *Uncle Tom's Cabin* is published and provides fuel for abolitionists **1854** Kansas-Nebraska Act repeals Missouri Compromise **1857** *Dred Scott* v. *Sandford*—Supreme Court declares that Congress cannot bar slavery from the territories **1858** Lincoln-Douglas debates **1859** *Ableman* v. *Booth* declares Fugitive Slave Act unconstitutional; John Brown raids Harper's Ferry and is hanged	**1853** Native American (Know Nothing) Party is formed—prejudiced against immigrants **1857** Literacy tests are instituted as a requirement of suffrage in Massachusetts; *Dred Scott* decision
1860	**1861** Morrill Tariff begins a period of high protection **1862** Homestead Act offers free farms to settlers; Morrill Act grants public land to states for establishment of agricultural colleges **1863–64** National Bank Acts establish uniform paper currency based on federal bonds **1867** U.S. purchases Alaska from Russia	**1860** First Japanese embassy to a Western power arrives in U.S. **1861** Trent Affair—a Union Naval officer seizes Confederate diplomats from a British vessel **1867** Russia sells Alaska to U.S. for $7.2 million	**1860–61** Seven southern states form Confederate States of America **1861** Civil War begins **1863** Lincoln's Emancipation Proclamation **1864** First public-school system for blacks is opened in the District of Columbia **1865** Thirteenth Amendment abolishes slavery; Civil War ends; Lincoln assassinated **1866** Civil Rights Act gives citizenship to all born in U.S. except Indians **1867** Rise of Ku Klux Klan; Reconstruction acts passed	**1861–65** Civil War **1861** Lincoln suspends right of habeas corpus **1863** Antidraft riots protest exemption payment **1866** Supreme Court decision limits suspension of civil liberties even during wartime **1867** Martial law is declared over defeated Confederate states
1868	**1868** Open-hearth steel production introduced; Congress approves eight-hour work day for government workers **1869–73** Moderate prosperity for industry **1869** Transcontinental railroad is completed; farm prices collapse **1873–78** Panic of 1873 begins depression	**1868** Pressure to annex Canada begins **1871** Treaty of Washington settles U.S. claims against Great Britain for aid to Confederacy	**1868** Fourteenth Amendment extends rights of due process and equal protection of the laws to all U.S. citizens **1869–70** First blacks elected to Congress **1870** Fifteenth Amendment extends suffrage to blacks **1870–86** Federal Indian policy, backed by military support, places last of free Indians on reservations	**1868** Fourteenth Amendment is ratified **1869** First women's suffrage law is passed in U.S., in Wyoming Territory **1870** Fifteenth Amendment is ratified
1876	**1876** Telephone is invented **1879** Electric light is perfected; first effective child labor law enacted in Massachusetts **1879–82** Economic recovery **1882** Standard Oil trust is created; Pendleton Act creates U.S. Civil Service	**1880** American foreign trade begins great expansion **1883–90** Development of modern U.S. Navy begins	**1877** Reconstruction ended with withdrawal of Union troops from South; Anti-Chinese riots in California **1882** First Jim Crow law, segregating railroad-car facilities, is passed in Tennessee (beginning of segregation movement) **1883** *Civil Rights* Cases	**1878** *Reynolds* v. *U.S.* decides religious freedom can be restrained in the interest of social or personal welfare
1883				

1884

Economy	Foreign Affairs	Race	Civil Liberties
1884 Panic and depression 1885 Partial economic recovery 1886 Haymarket Massacre takes place; American Federation of Labor (AFL) is organized 1887 Farm prices collapse; Interstate Commerce Act passed 1890 Sherman Antitrust Act is passed; McKinley Tariff Act raises tariffs	1887 U.S. receives exclusive use of the port of Pearl Harbor	1886 Apache Chief Geronimo captured 1890–1910 Jim Crow legislation is enacted throughout South	1882 First law restricting immigration is passed 1888 Secret ballot adopted for local elections

1892

Economy	Foreign Affairs	Race	Civil Liberties
1892 Populist Party begins organization; Homestead Steel strike 1893 Major economic panic 1894 Coxey's army of unemployed marches on Washington; Pullman and general railway strike take place 1895 Westinghouse installs the first generator of hydro-electric power 1896 Depression 1897 Eugene V. Debs forms the Social Democratic Party	1898 American battleship U.S.S. *Maine* is blown up in Havana harbor; Spanish-American War begins and ends (Treaty of Paris); U.S. gains Puerto Rico, Guam, Cuba, and Philippines; Hawaii is annexed 1899 Open Door Policy is imposed on China 1899–1901 Philippine guerrilla war for independence from U.S. rule	1895 Booker T. Washington's "separate fingers" doctrine of racial interaction 1896 *Plessy* v. *Ferguson* establishes separate-but-equal doctrine	1898 *U.S.* v. *Wongkim Ark.* holds that children of aliens born in U.S. acquire citizenship at birth 1900 First direct primary in U.S.

1900

Economy	Foreign Affairs	Race	Civil Liberties
1900–03 Big steel and auto industries incorporate 1902–10 "Muckrakers" stimulate reform 1902 Anthracite coal strike 1903 Wright brothers fly their heavier-than-air machine 1905 Industrial Workers of the World (IWW) is founded 1906 Pure Food and Drug Act is passed	1900 Boxer uprising against foreigners in China begins 1901 Platt Amendment establishes quasiprotectorate over Cuba 1903 Hay-Bunau-Varilla Treaty gives U.S. control of a canal zone, ten miles wide, across Panama	1903 Publication of W.E.B. DuBois's *The Souls of Black Folks* 1906 Antiblack riots in Atlanta, Georgia; the city is placed under martial law 1907 A presidential order excludes Japanese laborers from U.S.	1901 Socialist Party is organized 1904 National Child Labor Committee is organized

1908

Economy	Foreign Affairs	Race	Civil Liberties
1908 *Loewe* v. *Lawler* holds that antitrust definitions apply to labor 1911 Standard Oil and American Tobacco trusts are ordered to dissolve 1913 Federal Reserve System is initiated; income tax adopted 1914 Panama Canal is completed; Clayton Antitrust Act is passed; Federal Trade Commission is established 1915–18 Economic recovery	1911 U.S. intervenes in Nicaraguan revolution 1913 Official recognition by U.S. of new Chinese Republic 1914 Tampico and Vera Cruz incidents 1915 *Lusitania* is sunk without warning; Haiti becomes U.S. protectorate	1909 National Association for the Advancement of Colored People (NAACP) is founded 1911 Urban League is founded 1915 *Guinn* v. *U.S.* declares "grandfather clauses" in the Maryland and Oklahoma constitutions null and void	1910 Mann Act prohibits "white slavery"

1916

Economy	Foreign Affairs	Race	Civil Liberties
1918–23 The Supreme Court hands down decisions that protect private industry from federal regulation 1919 Inflationary boom 1920–21 Deflation and depression leave 5.7 million unemployed 1921 51 percent of the U.S. population lives in cities; labor unions are prosecuted for restraint of trade 1922 Economic recovery	1916 Mexican border warfare 1917–18 U.S. involvement in World War I 1917 Puerto Rico gains territorial status 1918 Announcement of President Wilson's Fourteen Points for armistice 1919 Versailles Treaty rejected by U.S. Senate; the First League of Nations draft is also presented and rejected 1920 *Missouri* v. *Holland* holds that treaties can supersede other legislation 1922 Washington Conference on limitation of armaments limits navies and recognizes integrity of China	1917–18 600 blacks are commissioned officers during World War I; two blacks are the first American soldiers to be decorated for bravery in France 1920 Sudden rapid growth of the Ku Klux Klan 1920–30 Harlem Renaissance	1917 Suffragette pickets are arrested; literacy requirement for immigrants instituted 1919–20 Palmer raids—police round up alleged subversives 1919 Prohibition begins; *Schenck* v. *U.S.* establishes "clear and present danger" test for limiting free speech 1920 Nineteenth Amendment is adopted, granting suffrage to women 1922 *U.S.* v. *Lanza* holds that federal and state trials do not constitute double jeopardy

1924

Economy	Foreign Affairs	Race	Civil Liberties
1925 A land boom takes place in Florida 1926 Taxes are reduced 1927 Construction and auto industries' activities decline 1929 Stock market crash begins the Great Depression 1930 Protective tariff contributes to the economic nationalism of the 1930s; "run" on banks, and 1,301 banks close	1924–25, 1927 Latin American interventions of Coolidge Administration 1928 Kellogg-Briand Peace Pact outlaws war; U.S. renounces right of intervention in Latin America under Roosevelt Corollary (to Monroe Doctrine)	1924 Congress legislates conditional Indian citizenship and suffrage 1927 Deportation of Marcus Garvey 1930 Founding of Black Muslim movement	1924 First woman governor elected (Wyoming) 1925 Scopes trial disallows teaching of evolution in Tennessee public schools 1927 Sacco and Vanzetti are executed 1928 *Olmstead* v. *U.S.* decides that wiretapping is not a search that is subject to the Fourth and Fourteenth Amendments 1931 *Near* v. *Minnesota* holds that the First Amendment freedom of press applies to states

1931

	Economy	Foreign Affairs	Race	Civil Liberties
1932	1932 13 million are unemployed 1932–38 New Deal legislation creates reforms in all areas of the national economy 1934 Trade Agreements Act cuts tariffs 50 percent; first general strike in the U.S. takes place 1934–39 The Supreme Court rules on government regulation of business 1935 Congress of Industrial Organizations (CIO) is established 1938 Stock market declines	1933 Good Neighbor Policy (toward Latin America) announced; U.S. recognizes U.S.S.R. 1936 U.S. volunteers form Lincoln Brigade to fight for Spanish Republic against General Franco; *U.S. v. Curtiss-Wright Export Corp.* decides that the executive branch has primary responsibility in foreign relations	1934 New Indian legislation ends allotment policy, provides for tribal self-government and Indian credit program; the Johnson–O'Malley Act spreads the administration of Indian affairs to many agencies 1935 *Norris v. Alabama* rules that exclusion of blacks from juries is unconstitutional 1937 First black federal judge appointed	1933 Twenty-first Amendment repeals Prohibition 1936 *Brown v. Mississippi* decides that a state cannot use a coerced confession 1937 Minimum wage law for women is upheld; *Calko v. Connecticut* allows two trials for the same crime if there is legal error present 1938 Formation of House Un-American Activities Committee (HUAC)
1940	1941–42 Supreme Court upholds government regulation of business 1942 Price controls on all but farm products 1946 Federal monopoly is established over atomic energy and the Atomic Energy Commission is created; Employment Act is passed and the Council of Economic Advisers is established; price controls end 1947 Taft-Hartley Act is passed	1941 Lend-Lease policy provides Great Britain and France with material for war; Atlantic Charter is formulated; Pearl Harbor is attacked and the United States enters World War II 1943 Italy surrenders 1944 Allies invade France on June 6, D-Day 1945 Atomic bombs are dropped on Hiroshima and Nagasaki, Japan; Germany and Japan surrender, ending World War II; United Nations is established; Potsdam Conference 1946 Philippine independence is granted by U.S. 1947 Truman Doctrine—aid to Greece and Turkey; Marshall Plan is announced; National Security Council is created	1941 Supreme Court rules that separate racial facilities must be *substantially* equal; Fair Employment Practices Commission is established 1942 Formation of Congress of Racial Equality (CORE) 1943 Race riots in Detroit, Harlem 1944 Supreme Court nullifies all-white primaries and party membership restricted by race 1947 First black baseball player is signed in the National League	1940–57 Supreme Court decisions enlarge area of permissible criticism of government 1940 Alien Registration Act forbids subversive conspiracies 1942 Japanese-American "relocation" 1947 National Security Act creates National Security Council; *Everson v. Board of Education* questions states' aid to parochial schools; Supreme Court denies parts of the Bill of Rights to federal workers
1948	1948 Workmen's compensation is legislated 1952 Struck steel mills are seized by Truman; the seizure is declared unconstitutional by the Supreme Court 1953 Department of Health, Education, and Welfare and the Small Business Administration are established 1953–54 Recession 1955 AFL merges with CIO	1948–49 Berlin blockade and U.S.-British airlift 1949 U.S.S.R. explodes an atomic bomb; North Atlantic Treaty is signed 1950 U.S. ends diplomatic and trade relations with the People's Republic of China; North Korea invades South Korea; U.S. agrees to aid South Korea 1952–53 Both the U.S. and U.S.S.R. explode hydrogen bombs; West German peace contract is signed, ending occupation 1953 Korean armistice 1954 SEATO is created; mutual defense agreement is signed with Japan	1948 *Shelly v. Kraemer* declares restrictive housing covenants unenforceable in the courts; the armed forces are desegregated 1953 A joint congressional resolution calls for termination of federal Indian lands policy 1954 *Brown v. Board of Education* outlaws segregated schools, overturning the *Plessy v. Ferguson* separate-but-equal doctrine 1955 Montgomery bus boycott; Interstate Commerce Commission bans racial segregation in interstate carriers	1949 Eleven U.S. Communists are found guilty of advocating violent overthrow of government 1950–54 Senator Joseph McCarthy investigates "subversive activities" 1950 Internal Security Act requires Communist organizations to register; Alger Hiss is convicted of espionage 1952–73 Supreme Court attempts to define "obscene" material 1952 McCarran-Walter Act deports "subversive" immigrants 1953 Rosenbergs are executed
1956	1957–58 Recession; industrial production is lowest since 1953 1960 Recession 1961 Minimum wage is set at $1.25 an hour; Housing Act is passed; Area Redevelopment Act is passed 1962 President Kennedy confronts steel companies on price hike; consumer safety and antipollution movements gain momentum 1963 High unemployment	1956 Suez crisis 1957 First successful Soviet intercontinental missile is tested 1959 Castro assumes power in Cuba 1961 Peace Corps is created; Foreign Aid Bill is increased to over $4 billion; Berlin wall is built; Bay of Pigs invasion of Cuba; U.S. ready to support South Vietnam 1961–63 Build-up of military advisers in Vietnam to 15,000 men 1962 Cuban missile crisis 1963 Atmospheric Nuclear Test Ban Treaty; wheat sale to U.S.S.R.	1957–60 Little Rock, Arkansas integration conflicts require paratroopers to protect pupils 1957 Martin Luther King elected president of Southern Christian Leadership Conference 1960 Student Nonviolent Coordinating Committee (SNCC) is formed 1961 Freedom Riders begin bus trips; closing of integration-ordered schools is unconstitutional 1962 James Meredith admitted to University of Mississippi 1963 Governor George Wallace blocks black enrollment at the University of Alabama; Medgar Evers murdered	1957 Civil Rights Act creates United States Commission on Civil Rights 1960 Growth of John Birch Society 1961 *Mapp v. Ohio* upholds exclusionary rule in search-and-seizure cases 1962 Passports denied to Communist Party members 1963 Equal pay is required for equal work regardless of sex; *Gideon v. Wainwright* requires court-appointed lawyers for indigents in all criminal trials
1964	1965 Appalachian Regional Development Act is passed; Housing and Urban Development Act is passed 1966 Medicare is begun 1967 Supreme Court decisions attack corporate anti competition tactics 1968 Tax surcharge for Vietnam War 1969 Anti-inflation controls, revenue-sharing; malnutrition is widespread; National Environmental Policy Act is passed 1969–72 Inflation and unemployment rise 1970 Anti pollution demonstrations 1971–72 Devaluations of Dollar	1964 Gulf of Tonkin Resolution 1965 U.S. intervenes in the Dominican Republic 1968 President Johnson announces a partial bombing halt in Vietnam 1969–73 Nixon aims to shift war burden to Vietnamese 1970 Nixon Doctrine limits U.S. defense needs of other nations; nonproliferation of Nuclear Weapons Treaty; ground troops sent to Cambodia 1971 China enters U.N.	1964–71 Series of Supreme Court decisions attacking racial discrimination 1964 Mississippi black voter registration drive; Twenty-fourth Amendment bans poll tax in federal elections; Congress passes Civil Rights Act 1965 March for equal rights in Alabama; Voting Rights Act; Watts riot; assassination of Malcolm X 1967 Thurgood Marshall on Supreme Court 1968 Martin Luther King assassinated 1970 Supreme Court orders southern school district integration; Jackson State killings 1971 Indians occupy Alcatraz	1964 Civil Rights Act 1965 *Griswold v. Connecticut* upholds right of privacy in birth-control case 1966 *Miranda v. Arizona* holds that a suspect must be informed of his rights 1967–73 Supreme Court narrows the definition of civil liberties in areas of search and seizure, self-incrimination 1969–71 Supreme Court decisions on rights of juveniles, conscientious objectors 1971 Twenty-sixth Amendment sets voting age at eighteen; courts allow Pentagon Papers to be printed
1972	1972–73 Inflation increases despite continuing wage and price controls 1972 Wage and price controls continue into Phase II; Soviets buy more than $1 billion of U.S. grain; high profits made by U.S. grain firms bring charges of government corruption; Administration-backed filibuster kills the Consumer Agency Bill; increase of $5.3 billion in social security benefits is confirmed 1973 Energy, grain, and meat prices increase; rationing forecast	1972 President Nixon visits China and U.S.S.R.; grain sale to U.S.S.R.; Senate approves Strategic Arms Limitation Treaty (SALT); U.S. pulls all ground combat troops out of Vietnam; Nixon Administration requests $85.4 billion for 1972 military spending 1973 Vietnam Peace Accord; secret bombings of Cambodia revealed	1971–72 Angela Davis is charged with murder and criminal conspiracy and acquitted 1972 Northern senators use filibuster to kill antibusing bill; 20-year relocation policy for Indians is ended; Indians seize control of Bureau of Indian Affairs; President Nixon against busing for racial balance; Court orders busing between Detroit and suburbs to achieve integration 1973 Indian militants occupy Wounded Knee, South Dakota	1972 National Commission recommends less restrictive laws on private use of marijuana; studies reveal computer invasion of privacy by government and business; Watergate affair—burglary and bugging of Democratic national headquarters; Supreme Court decides that capital punishment is unfairly applied under present laws; *Cole v. Richardson* decides that requirement of a loyalty oath is constitutional; *Laird v. Totum* decides that the existence of the Army's intelligence gathering does not inhibit the exercise of First-Amendment rights; women's liberation and gay liberation grow in popularity 1973 Thirteen states vote to restore death penalty

6

RACE AND GOVERNMENT

The American government promises equal opportunity, but the country continues to have chronic problems of racial discrimination and racial inequality. Most like to think that discrimination is merely the expression of popular prejudices and that the power of law is steadily making America a country of equal opportunity for all. In reality, however, governmental power has often been used to increase and intensify segregation and inequality. In fact, many of the major historical figures honored by shrines and statues in Washington favored segregation and assumed that whites were superior to ethnic and racial minorities. These leaders often helped to turn public prejudices into official policy.

This chapter will concentrate on the impact that government action has had on racial discrimination toward blacks and Indians. The suggestion is not that public officials hold the basic responsibility for all of America's racial troubles. Forces ranging from the moral teaching of the churches, to the symbols and stereotypes of the mass media, to the armed terror of groups such as the Ku Klux Klan have all influenced race relations. Any student, however, can well pause to examine the general pattern of governmental action, constantly reminding himself that these actions both occur in a social context and help shape that context. The Perspective following this chapter examines this interrelationship on a single issue—school desegregation—over a more limited period of time.

Periods of racial reform toward blacks and Indians are also discussed, particularly the Reconstruction period (1865–1877) and the 1960s. However, major governmental efforts toward racial equality have been the exception in the American experience. This chapter outlines the very special conditions that produced the reform movements and the conditions that led to their rapid demise.

ALL WHITE MEN ARE CREATED EQUAL

The Declaration of Independence proclaims that "all Men are created equal, that they are endowed by their Creator with certain unalienable Rights, that among these are Life, Liberty, and the Pursuit of Happiness." Thomas Jefferson's immortal statement was revolutionary and is constantly cited as proof of the fundamental American commitment to equal opportunity. The Declaration of Independence, how-

Figure 6.1 The thirteen black members of the House of Representatives comprise one of Congress's several ideological groups; they gather information concerning the general condition of blacks in America and take unified positions on issues and legislation affecting blacks. As a group, members of the Black Caucus represent a national, rather than a regional, constituency, which seems to afford them a degree of freedom from the institutional restraints of Congress that hem in the usual member. The members of the Black Caucus are (left to right): Robert Nix (Pa.), Parren Mitchell (Md.), Charles Rangel (N.Y.), Louis Stokes (Ohio), Ralph Metcalfe (Ill.), John Conyers (Mi.), Ronald Dellums (Ca.), Charles Diggs (Mi.), Walter Fauntroy (Wash., D.C.), George Collins (Ill.), William Clay (Mo.), Shirley Chisholm (N.Y.); Augustus Hawkins (Ca.) is not shown.

ever, was written by a slaveowner and adopted by a Continental Congress that was unwilling to take action against the slave trade.

The Creation of American Slavery

When the Declaration of Independence was written, the law in colonial America had already been used for over a century to create and maintain a harsh form of slavery (in comparison to slavery in Latin America). There had been no recent English tradition of slavery when the Africans first landed at Jamestown. Blacks were initially treated as indentured servants, who could earn their freedom and, when freed, were able to hold their own white indentured servants.

As the years passed, however, racial attitudes deepened. The need for cheap labor and the belief that "heathens" of another race were not entitled to the protection accorded white people were reflected in court decisions that began to condemn blacks to perpetual servitude. Judges began to recognize sales and wills specifying complete servitude. Intermarriage, which was earlier allowed, was now forbidden, in striking contrast to the Spanish and Portuguese colonies in Latin America. Although some of the early moves toward official discrimination were rationalized with arguments claiming that "heathens" need not be accorded the rights of believers, laws began to be passed declaring that Christian baptism did not alter a slave's condition (Winthrop Jordan, 1969).

Although the sketchy records of the time make it difficult to reconstruct the creation of American slavery in detail, the general record is clear. Step by step, debasement and dehumanization of blacks were crystallized in law and then reinforced by the power of law. Discrimination obtained legal sanction, and the law deepened and strengthened prejudice. As the institution of slavery took definite shape, it created powerful economic interests that further reinforced it.

Race and the Constitution

In recent years, judicial interpretations of the Constitution have played a major role in the movement for equal rights. When the Constitution was written, however, the document reflected the racial assumptions of its time. Until the amendments of the Recon-

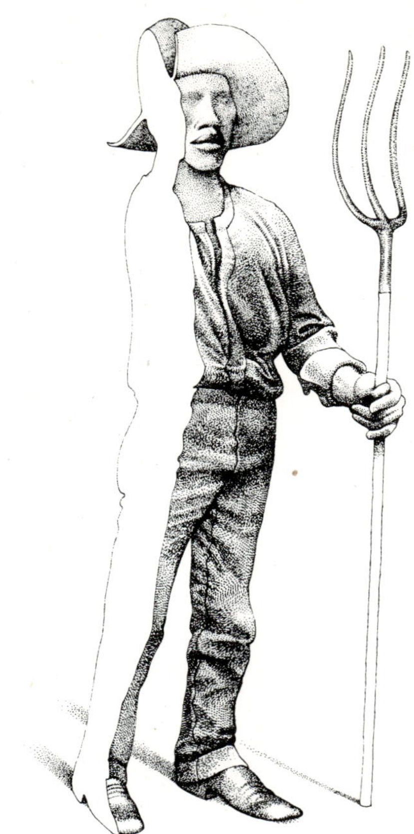

Figure 6.2 Article I, Section 2 of the United States Constitution: "Representatives . . . shall be apportioned among the several States which may be included within this Union, according to their respective Numbers, which shall be determined by adding to the whole Number of free Persons, including those bound to service for a Term of Years, and excluding Indians not taxed, three fifths of all other Persons." The black man was thus considered as three-fifths of a man for purposes of congressional representation—and only whites could vote in congressional elections.

☐
"Then came General Winfield Scott with 7,000 troops. . . . Cherokee men, women and children were seized wherever found and without notice removed to concentration camps. . . . An eyewitness in Kentucky reported: 'Even aged females, apparently nearly ready to drop into the grave, were travelling with heavy burdens attached to their backs, sometimes on frozen ground . . . with no covering for their feet.

Of about 14,000 who were herded onto this 'trail of tears,' . . . 4,000 died on the way. While a hundred Cherokees a day were perishing of exhaustion and cold on that dreadful road, President Van Buren . . . addressed Congress: 'The measures authorized by Congress at its last session have had the happiest effects. . . . The Cherokees have emigrated without any apparent reluctance.'" (John Collier, 1947)

struction period were ratified, the United States had a government of white men for white men.

In deciding on representation in Congress, the founding fathers concluded that neither blacks nor Indians would vote, Indians would not be counted in distributing seats in the House of Representatives, and each black would be counted as three-fifths of a person. The three-fifths rule was a compromise that strengthened the position of the South in Congress by giving southern states credit, in terms of congressional representatives, for a population not permitted to vote. James Madison seriously defended the three-fifths provision on the grounds that slaves were indeed part human and part property and should be counted somewhere in between (Madison, 1788).

Although the violence involved in capturing and transporting slaves repelled even many slave owners, the Constitution ensured decades more of the trade. In fact, worried southerners were reassured with an extraordinary provision (Article V) that denied Congress and the people the right to adopt a constitutional amendment on the subject. Another provision (Article IV) provided that a slave escaping to a free state remained the property of his owner and had to be returned.

INDIANS AND INEQUALITY

Although the position of blacks in American society has always posed a central dilemma, the treatment of another major racial group, American Indians, provides an equally revealing test of governmental performance. Throughout the formative period of the nation, Indian policy was an issue of the first magnitude.

A people who had only recently overthrown British colonialism soon adopted the worst sort of colonial policies in their relationship with Indian nations. Although official policy called for mutual respect and friendly relations, Indians were actually considered to be inferior people without serious legal rights. There was no union of the white and Indian races as there was in Latin America, nor were the Indians allowed to govern themselves. Indians were seen primarily as a military obstacle to white expansion, and Indian lands were considered legally empty until settled by whites. Although the official policy called for educating Indians to par-

ticipate in white society, the practice was to isolate them, take their economic base, destroy their tribal leadership structures, and maintain rigid military control at the least possible cost.

Indians Pushed Westward

There was always division over Indian policy, but the defenders of Indian rights rarely prevailed. The first critical test came in the 1820s and 1830s when a national political battle was fought over the fate of the Cherokee Indians. The Cherokees had amazed the country by rapidly developing an educational system, a well-organized local government, a written constitution, and a newspaper.

In spite of these indications of Cherokee "civilization," white Georgians wanted to force the Indians off their land. President Andrew Jackson, a former Indian fighter, agreed. Jackson maintained that Indians did not own their lands and that their hunting rights should be yielded in the face of white desire for land. Jackson told the Indians to move west of the Mississippi, and Congress passed a law requiring their removal. In clear violation of the treaty, the Georgia legislature passed a law dividing the Cherokee lands, and the federal government cut off education funds. The President warned the tribe that it was "impossible that you can flourish in the midst of a civilized community" (Louis Filler and Allen Guttmann, 1962). Although the President was bitterly criticized by a number of leading politicians and intellectuals, and the case was carried to the Supreme Court, Jackson prevailed. The government fraudulently exacted a treaty from a meeting of a tiny minority of the Cherokees. The Indians were routed from their homes, all their possessions were taken by the whites, and they were forced to walk to Arkansas in the freezing cold of midwinter. Of the approximately 14,000 Cherokee men, women, and children who began the trip, 4,000 died along the way (see ☐).

Tribe after tribe was pushed westward and then was forced to move again when white settlers reached their lands. Large "Indian territories," such as Oklahoma, were replaced by reservations, and early reservations were replaced by newer, poorer, smaller ones. Tribes became dependent on the government, and families could not sustain themselves. Administration was usually in the hands of Indian agents—men who were patronage ap-pointees who often used the job to their own advantage by profiting on the Indian trade or withholding government provisions. The attempt was made to suppress anything that the government felt might produce independence and resistance, including tribal leadership and tribal religions (Dee Brown, 1971).

Problems of Reform

In the 1880s the General Allotment Act was passed in an attempt to turn Indians into small farmers by dividing reservations and distributing parcels of substandard land. Whites were allowed to take whatever was declared excess. The new Indian owners, who understood little of white concepts of property and law, soon lost most of these land holdings. From the 1880s to the 1930s the effort to make Indians small farmers and ranchers cost tribes millions of acres of land. In addition, merchants, doctors, farmers, and businessmen would collect their debts by taking ownership of former reservation lands, thus further decreasing the Indians' holdings. In many reservation areas, virtually all the tribal land of any value passed into white ownership. Today, many areas described on the map as "reservations" actually have little trace of Indian ownership. Only in isolated areas or where there were exceptionally strong and stubborn Indian leaders did the tribes retain their land base. As the Indians lost their last tangible assets, they largely receded from national consciousness.

Historically, American governmental institutions have not dealt very successfully with Indian problems. Leaders of a society that was expansive, individualistic, self-righteous, and built on an agricultural-industrial economy—that is, a society dedicated to the Liberal ethic (see Chapter 1)—could not understand less powerful societies with alien religions and traditions of common ownership of land. As American institutions built a common nationality among immigrants and created a vast continental economic system, there was little sympathy for isolated groups of traditional peoples trying to preserve their cultures. The problems were magnified by the profound conviction of white Americans that they were racially, culturally, and religiously superior to the Indians. The great observer of American charac-

Figure 6.3 Many Indians are bitterly resentful against the United States government, not only for the massacres and relocations of earlier days, but for the relatively recent treatment they have received in the settlement of treaty claims regarding tribal status and lands. In these photos we see manifestations of this resentment against the government. Early in June 1971, approximately fifty Indians occupied an abandoned Nike missile site near Richmond, California (top right), changing the No Trespassing sign from "United States Government property" to "United States Indian property." In November 1972 some 500 Indians took over the Bureau of Indian Affairs offices in Washington, D.C. (bottom right). Indian leaders and government officials negotiated demands, and the affair was settled without bloodshed.

ter and institutions, Alexis de Tocqueville, summarized the record:

The Spaniards were unable to exterminate the Indian race by those unparalleled atrocities which brand them with indelible shame, nor did they even succeed in wholly depriving it of its rights; but the Americans of the United States have accomplished this twofold purpose with singular felicity, tranquilly, legally, philanthropically, without shedding blood, and without violating a single great principle of morality in the eyes of the world. It is impossible to destroy men with more respect for the laws of humanity. (Tocqueville, 1835, p.355)

THE SLAVERY CRISIS

At the time the Constitution was adopted, many hoped that gradual enlightenment of the South would eventually end slavery. The small reform movement in the South soon died, however, and southern officials made the system even more rigid. Terrified by the successful slave rebellion in Haiti, furious at northern abolitionist tactics, and strongly attracted by the rising prices for slaves in cotton-growing areas, southern leaders moved toward an increasingly militant defense of the "peculiar institution" (Robert McColley, 1964).

The compromise embodied in the Constitution was based on a balance of power between the North and the South—a balance that would protect slavery from interference by the national government. As the North grew rapidly and the nation expanded westward, the South attempted to retain its veto power in the Senate by fighting for the extension of slavery to half of the new states admitted to the Union. Political crises that threatened the continuation of the Union in 1820 and 1850 were settled by agreements to maintain equal Senate representation and create new slave states.

The compromises, however, were only temporary solutions. With Congress unable to arrive at any lasting answer, the Supreme Court attempted to solve the dispute through the case of *Dred Scott* v. *Sandford* (1857). Dred Scott was a slave from Missouri who escaped to a free state; his owner tried to get him back, claiming that the Constitution forbade any state to outlaw slavery. In ruling on the case, the Court concluded that the Constitution did not grant Congress the power to forbid slavery, even in the North. The Justices concluded that the Constitution accepted the concept of racial inferiority and denied full citizenship to blacks, even those living in free states. Because the founding fathers had accepted slavery and established a constitutional right to property, the Chief Justice argued, there was a basic right to own slaves. At the time of the constitutional convention, he continued, blacks were regarded as ''beings of an inferior order; and altogether unfit to associate with the white race, either in social or political relations; and so far inferior that they had no rights which the white man was bound to respect'' (*Dred Scott* v. *Sandford,* 1857).

The *Dred Scott* decision only heightened the national struggle and was soon denounced as a perversion of the Constitution that had come from a Court dominated by slaveholders. Abraham Lincoln was one of the rising political leaders who joined in the attacks on the Supreme Court. The spiraling dispute over the decision is often cited as a major factor leading to the Civil War, the nation's ultimate admission of the inability of its political institutions to deal with the issue of slavery.

THE MOVEMENT TOWARD REFORM

Only the calamity of a vicious civil war and the surrender of the South broke the deadlock on the question of slavery. A few years after the Union split, objectives that were held by only a few extremists in 1860—abolition and full equality—became prime goals of the political movement that was able to win dominance in Congress in the late 1860s.

Emancipation and Reconstruction

The war had altered all of the political equations in Washington. Almost all of the southern senators and representatives left Washington, their states thereby abandoning their representation on Capitol Hill. The southern veto was gone. Equally important, because Congress determines the qualifications of its members, the southern states could not regain representation until they had met whatever conditions the remaining members (who were primarily northerners) imposed.

The war itself was the main cause of the drastic change in the goals of northern political leaders. As the awesome costs of the war became apparent, northern opinion moved behind increasingly drastic changes in southern society. The Civil War, one eminent southern historian has remarked, began as a war for union, later became a war to free the slaves, and finally, for many, became a crusade for equality (C. Vann Woodward, 1966).

After the war ended, northern whites were shocked when southern legislatures enacted "black codes" designed to maintain white supremacy. These codes denied blacks the vote, forbade them to bear arms, denied them the right to testify in court, and intimidated them with sweeping vagrancy laws that authorized local officials to seize any unemployed black and sell his labor to the highest bidder. Mississippi blacks were forbidden to own or rent land. In Louisiana, state law required former slaves to be in the regular service of "some white person, or former owner, who shall be held responsible for the conduct of said negro" (William Dunning, 1968).

Northern leaders in Congress, now aware that emancipation would become virtually meaningless without some strong federal action to protect blacks, called for a basic change in federal-state relations on this most sensitive issue. Because the South had no representation in Congress, the regional veto on legislative action was absent for the first time in American history.

The new situation produced a tide of civil rights laws and a fundamental change in the Constitution itself. By 1876, only eleven years after the Civil War, the Constitution had been permanently altered by the addition of the Thirteenth, Fourteenth, and Fifteenth Amendments; they forbade slavery, made "equal protection of the laws" a fundamental principle of law, and guaranteed voting rights. The strong southern resistance to ratification was overcome by the provision that the southern states would have to ratify the amendments as part of the price of readmission to the Union. During this period the broad protections of the new constitutional provisions were supported by eleven major civil rights acts.

On few issues has Congress spoken out more clearly or acted more vigorously, yet the achievement was soon abandoned. Within a generation, most of the laws had been rendered inoperative by court interpretations and the unwillingness of either the Congress or the President to enforce them. Not until the 1950s would the Supreme Court revive the *equal protection* guarantee of the Fourteenth Amendment as a powerful tool for the implementation of racial equality.

Failure of Reconstruction

Reconstruction failed for several reasons. First, the protection of powerless people against strong resistance requires powerful governmental action; when it is local and state governments that are subverting minority rights, the powerful action must come from the national government. However, the traditional American suspicion of a strong central government has often frustrated such action. In addition, reform movements are rarely able to maintain active interest in the details of change once the reform laws have been enacted, except when the interests of powerful groups are clearly benefited.

During Reconstruction these problems were particularly dramatic. There was very little federal administrative machinery because there were few federal domestic programs. National rights could therefore be enforced only through military occupation and takeover of local government functions. Americans had always been opposed to maintaining a large standing army, and the idea of army officials running vital functions of local government was hard to accept. As the passions of war eased and the demand to cut back the army grew, enforcement became increasingly difficult.

Another major barrier to the success of the Reconstruction laws was the artificial and temporary nature of the majority that had enacted them, a majority that existed only as long as the South was excluded from Congress. The restoration of southern political strength and the growing economic disputes between the Northeast and the West soon put the South in a position to exercise decisive power. As public attention turned to new issues and the desire for reconciliation between the regions deepened, northern leaders increasingly concluded that the reforms had been a failure and that control should be returned to southern whites.

In 1876 a great political crisis surrounding the presidential election led to open abandonment of the reform effort. Although the election had ended with an apparent victory for the Democratic candidate, Samuel Tilden, Republican leaders persuaded state election officials in Florida, South Carolina, and Louisiana to report a victory for Rutherford Hayes, which gave him the Presidency by a one-vote margin in the electoral college. This extraordinary move created a deep crisis, and there was even talk of Democratic governors sending their state National Guards to Washington to prevent the inauguration (Woodward, 1956).

The crisis was finally resolved by a deal between the Republicans and southern leaders: Hayes remained President, but the Republicans agreed to remove the last of the federal troops used to enforce the civil rights laws in the South. The troops' departure in 1877 signaled the nation's open acceptance of the restoration of white supremacy. President Hayes formalized the reconciliation with a triumphal tour of the South. "I believe," he told Atlanta blacks, "that your rights and interests would be safer if this great mass of intelligent white men were left alone by the general government" (Rayford Logan, 1965).

As the country turned away from the goals of the civil rights laws, the Supreme Court responded; it began to interpret the constitutional amendments more narrowly and to nullify the controversial laws. In a series of cases between 1873 and 1884 the Justices held that many of the laws protecting blacks were unconstitutional infringements on state powers. Among the laws struck down were measures protecting voting rights and forbidding the terrorist activities of the Ku Klux Klan (Charles Warren, 1922; 1926).

In 1896 the Supreme Court created the *separate but equal* doctrine, which permitted open use of state power to impose segregation as long as a legal fiction of equality was employed (*Plessy* v. *Ferguson,* 1896). In the colleges, many historians denounced Reconstruction as an aberration, and scholars in the new social-science disciplines declared that racial feelings were inborn instincts, that blacks were inherently inferior, and that no real progress was possible (Idus Newby, 1968). Segregation was legal and even respectable. Even the leading black spokesman of the day, Booker T. Washington, accepted racial separation and inequality and urged blacks to work peacefully within the system.

The Return of Official Discrimination

Official discrimination returned with a vengeance. Spurred by the acquiescence of the Supreme Court, southern legislatures poured out legislation that disenfranchised black voters and required the segregation of many public facilities, such as libraries and train stations.

Thus, southern blacks were trapped in an immensely powerful system of social, economic, and political control. At the national level, the worst

The Grades of Intelligence
The Home Library of Useful Knowledge, 1884

Figure 6.4 Nineteenth-century procedures that included filling skulls with sand to establish "brain capacity" and measuring the angle of facial slope (left) provided a basis for twentieth-century racism. Because it was most often northern Europeans who conducted the research, their findings usually endowed their own stock with the greatest intelligence. Only recently have researchers admitted the difficulties in both defining intelligence and in measuring the abilities of different cultures and races. The three-foot pipe (right) that separated these two drinking fountains characterized the racial separation of the 1940s. Do these facilities seem separate but equal, the principle established by the Supreme Court in 1896? Separate yet still equal enough to fight was the order of the day (far right) on the battlefields of Europe in 1942. Black soldiers, who found themselves still discriminated against after loyal participation in the war effort, were motivated to press for change.

came during Woodrow Wilson's Administration. Although leading black spokesmen had joined the reform coalition that elected Wilson in 1913, the President permitted his Cabinet to impose rigid segregation on various federal departments (Arthur Link, 1954). Wilson cut off most of the remaining federal patronage for blacks in the South, and his Administration refused even to investigate the mass murder of blacks that occurred in a race riot in East St. Louis, Illinois. The leading historian of Wilson's Presidency stated:

. . . he and probably all of his Cabinet believed in segregation, social and official. The issue first arose . . . when Burleson suggested segregating all Negroes in the federal services. If there were any defenders of the Negro or any foes of segregation in the Cabinet they did not then or afterward raise their voice. (Link, 1954, p. 64)

As the United States entered World War I as a defender of democracy in Europe, federal officials were segregating restrooms, offices, and restaurants in federal office buildings in Washington and dismissing black civil servants in the South (Link, 1954).

THE COURTS: IMPETUS FOR REFORM

While blacks and their white supporters struggled to organize the black community, and while they carried out endless protests against discrimination in the early decades of the twentieth century, public hostility limited any real progress. Black leaders eventually brought the struggle for civil rights into the courts because they had no other realistic alternative.

NAACP Lawyers

The most important legal struggles were the masterful campaigns conducted by lawyers from the National Association for the Advancement of Colored People (NAACP) against school and housing segregation in the 1940s and 1950s. In both areas, lawyers from the NAACP Legal Defense Fund developed a powerful body of legal precedents that eventually led to Supreme Court decisions outlawing school desegregation and forbidding the enforcement of covenants written into property deeds that made it illegal for many Americans to sell their homes to qualified minority buyers.

The civil rights lawyers developed their arguments step by step, forcing the courts to come to terms with the contradiction between the words of the Constitution and the facts of racial discrimination. The high court had to be persuaded to reexamine the well-established *separate but equal* principle. To accomplish this task, new legal arguments were developed and put into circulation through law

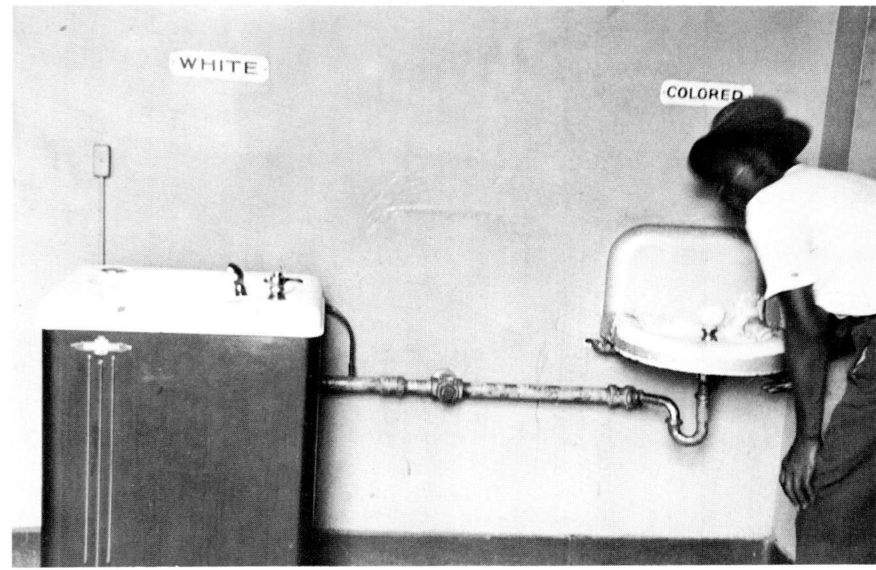

reviews and lower-court cases. (Much of this path-finding legal work was done by a small group of black attorneys associated with Howard University Law School.) Social-science and historical research was done in order to convince the Court of the damage caused by segregation. Indeed, it was this research that laid the groundwork for the 1954 school-desegregation cases.

School Desegregation

The school cases were extremely important in that they called for basic change in the most influential public institutions of the southern and border states. Rather than directly confront the courts with the politically explosive question of remaking southern education, the lawyers first challenged segregation in graduate schools. These cases permitted the judges to consider the issues on a more abstract level and to begin thinking about all the factors that contribute to educational quality.

The first step forward came when the Supreme Court ruled that an institution's refusal to set up graduate programs for black students was a denial of the students' constitutional rights. In 1950 a unanimous Supreme Court took another step, in the case of *McLaurin* v. *Oklahoma,* and forbade the state of Oklahoma to impose classroom, library, and cafeteria segregation on a black professor admitted to a graduate course.

Legal education was the subject of another important case that undermined much of the logic of the *separate but equal* argument. In finding segregated law training unconstitutional in Texas, the Court relied on

   . . . those qualities which are incapable of objective measurement but which make for greatness in a law school. Such qualities, to name a few, include reputation of the faculty, experience of the administration, position and influence of the alumni, standing in the community, traditions and prestige. (*Sweatt* v. *Painter,* 1950)

It was held that these intangible factors made it impossible for a black school to offer equal opportunity in a white-dominated society.

The case law then permitted the NAACP to challenge the whole structure of educational segregation. After the Supreme Court accepted the school cases for review in 1952, both the Truman and the Eisenhower Justice Departments argued that segregated schools were unconstitutional.

In 1954, after a long delay and extremely careful consideration, the Supreme Court announced its unanimous decision against segregated schools in the *Brown* v. *Board of Education* case. The Court's 1955 enforcement decision, which was based on the Justices' assumption that southern leaders would accept gradual school desegregation, called for gradual changes to be worked out in each area by the federal district judge in that jurisdiction. Their assumption that local leaders would comply with the decision proved wrong. For more than a decade, any form of change in southern education would be bitterly contested and very little progress achieved. This struggle is discussed in detail in the Perspective following this chapter.

THE PUBLIC: IMPETUS FOR REFORM

The Supreme Court could create a massive new political issue, but the issue had to be decided by the people. There would be no basic changes in policy until there was a strong majority in the country committed to desegregation and willing to override traditional local powers. The temporary consolidation of that new majority and the transformation of the political role of black Americans were the great achievements of the civil rights movement.

The Rise of the Civil Rights Movement

The struggling civil rights groups were galvanized by the 1954 *Brown* decision. There were powerful new dreams for millions of black Americans, and soon the dreams produced new leaders, new tactics, and a deepening reservoir of public support. People who had hope and who saw themselves as fighting the battle to enforce the Constitution were ready to take serious personal risks to gain rights.

The new mood was first evident in 1955. In Montgomery, Alabama a group of blacks, led by a young preacher, Martin Luther King, Jr., protested the segregation of city buses by boycotting them. Black college students also attracted national attention when they staged sit-in demonstrations and demanded service at segregated southern lunch counters. In community after community, black people risked retaliation to demand change. Local confrontations further dramatized the depth of the

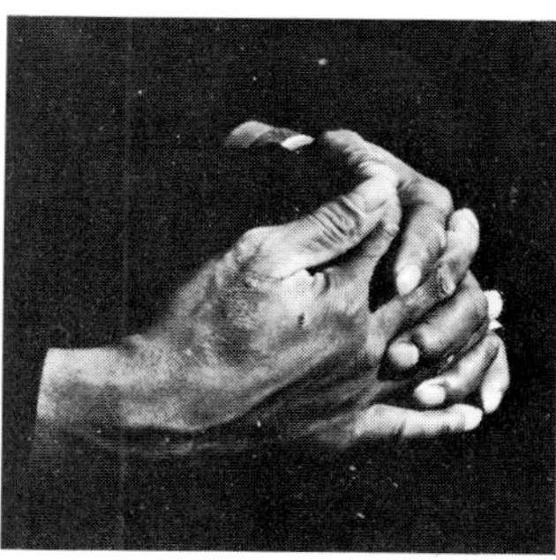

Figure 6.5 "I have a dream." The pursuit of the Reverend Martin Luther King's dream led him and thousands of others (top and center left) out of the courts and churches and into the streets to protest, in nonviolent fashion, some of the indignities suffered by blacks. Yet mass demonstrations were met with police reprisals as in Birmingham, Alabama in 1963 when Eugene ("Bull") Connor (center right), Public Safety Commissioner, chose to express his disapproval of King's tactics with night sticks and police dogs.

problems and forced choices on the nation. Although case-by-case litigation could not hold public attention, community crises produced by mass protests could.

In 1963 the long deadlock in Washington was finally broken by a tidal wave of public concern. There had been growing public support for ending open discrimination in the South, but the political breakthrough came only after the country was outraged by police violence against peaceful demonstrators in Birmingham, Alabama.

Television showed Birmingham policemen beating praying demonstrators—a sense of unambiguous evil confronting unalloyed good was communicated to viewers across the nation. When people saw police dogs and high-pressure fire hoses turned on peaceful demonstrators, they were outraged. People poured into protest meetings and flooded congressional offices with angry mail. Suddenly, the polls showed that issues that had only recently commanded little public attention had become the most visible and crucial issues before the nation.

Civil Rights Legislation

Attention then focused on a momentous struggle taking place on Capitol Hill. President Johnson, who succeeded Kennedy as the House battle over Kennedy's civil rights bill reached its peak, insisted that the far-reaching Kennedy bill—which was to become the 1964 Civil Rights Act—be passed without any compromise. When the bill reached the Senate, southerners staged the longest filibuster in American history. They were confronted, however, by an organized majority responding to the new national mood. The congressional barriers that had stood for almost a century were now assailed by an unprecedented coalition that included labor and religious organizations, black organizations, Democratic party leaders, and the moderate wing of the Republican party. The final step in defeating the filibuster came when a group of Republican conservatives joined the fight.

The 1964 Civil Rights Act reflected the main goals of the civil rights movement: It outlawed segregation in public accommodations, authorized the Justice Department to file civil rights lawsuits, forbade job discrimination, and outlawed discrimination in any program receiving federal money. In one stroke it changed the whole stance of the executive branch from that of a neutral bystander to that of an active supporter of desegregation.

President Johnson's Voting Rights Act was passed the following year. It directly assaulted the political power of the white politicians from the Deep South by automatically suspending voter-qualification tests in the six states where less than half the eligible people had voted in 1964 (Louisiana, Alabama, Mississippi, South Carolina, Georgia, and Virginia). A further provision gave the Attorney General veto power over all changes in these states' election laws—a power needed to prevent the creation of new devices that might be used to prevent blacks from voting.

The United States seemed on the threshold of a remarkable period of peaceful social change in early 1965. There was a broad national consensus for voting rights, the President was fully committed, and national attention had been riveted on the problem. Civil rights reforms that would have been inconceivable a few years earlier were on the lawbooks, and the most liberal Congress since the New Deal had enacted the War on Poverty as well as a large new education program to improve the schools.

CIVIL RIGHTS LEADS TO REDISCOVERY OF THE INDIANS

In the 1960s and 1970s the awakening of black aspirations and white consciousness of the needs of minorities helped generate new aspirations among other forgotten groups in American society. Books and articles were written in great numbers on the poor whites of Appalachia; on the Mexican-Americans and Puerto Ricans in the rural and urban slums of California, the Southwest, and New York; and on the American Indians. Among each group there were new organizations and new demands for full participation in the American economy and society.

The basic Indian policy of the 1880s—which attempted to induce Indians to drop their tribal loyalties and become small farmers (General Allotment Act)—had been suddenly and decisively changed, for a few years, during the New Deal of the 1930s. The national economic disaster of the Depression lessened self-confidence in individual ownership of land and increased receptivity to social experiments in many fields, including Indian affairs. Un-

Figure 6.6 The history of the American Indians since the arrival of the white man has been one of constant struggle to retain their native lands. The maps opposite provide a general overview of the pattern of Indian relocation. In 1750 Indian tribes were scattered throughout the United States. By 1840, however, the Indians east of the Mississippi had been forced to move west of the river; the territory they moved to—Indian Territory—is shown in the detail. By 1900, Indian areas throughout the country were further reduced, a reduction reflected in the decreased size of Indian Territory. The 1973 map represents present locations of Indian reservations. In 1876 an Indian chief went before a commission on Indian affairs and offered the following comments on his people's situation: "I am glad to see you, you are our friends, but I hear that you have come to move us. Tell your people that since the Great Father promised that we should never be removed we have been moved five times. I think you had better put the Indians on wheels and you can run them about wherever you wish" (Virginia Armstrong, 1971).

The following is a chronology of important events and policies in Indian affairs.

1778 The first Indian treaty with the U.S. government, the Treaty of Fort Pitt, provides that friendly Indian tribes may send representatives to Congress and join the U.S. confederation.

1787 The Northwest Treaty Ordinance is passed, which states that Indians' "lands and property shall never be taken from them without their consent."

1802 Congress passes a law forbidding the sale of liquor to Indians. The act is not repealed until 1953.

1809 The Treaty of Fort Wayne is negotiated, by which Indians receive less than one-third of a cent an acre for 3 million acres of Ohio Valley land.

1814 Creeks sign the Treaty of Fort Jackson, which Andrew Jackson uses to demand most Creek lands in Alabama, a strip in Georgia, and 4 million acres of Cherokee territory.

1824 The Bureau of Indian Affairs is established within the War Department.

1830 The Indian Removal Act calls for the relocation of Indians east of the Mississippi in lands west of the river.

1849 The Bureau of Indian Affairs is transferred to the newly formed Department of the Interior.

1866 Congress passes the Civil Rights Act, securing equal rights for everyone in the U.S. except Indians.

1871 Congress ends the practice of making treaties with the Indians. The U.S. has already gained almost a billion acres of land from 371 treaties.

1876 General Custer is defeated at Little Big Horn.

1887 General Allotment Act is passed.

1890 The last major Indian war, the Ghost Dance War, ends with the massacre of Indians at Wounded Knee.

1924 Indians are granted U.S. citizenship and the right to vote. Until 1948, however, Arizona and New Mexico state laws deny Indians the vote.

1934 The Indian Reorganization Act ends allotment and provides legal means for tribal self-government. Reservation land has shrunk from 140 million to 50 million acres.

1950 The Bureau of Indian Affairs begins a program to move Indians into the cities from the reservations.

1953 Congress sets as a goal the termination of federal control over Indians and reservations.

1961 Termination policy is abandoned.

1970 Indians occupy Alcatraz Island for several months.

1973 Indians occupy Wounded Knee, for nine weeks.

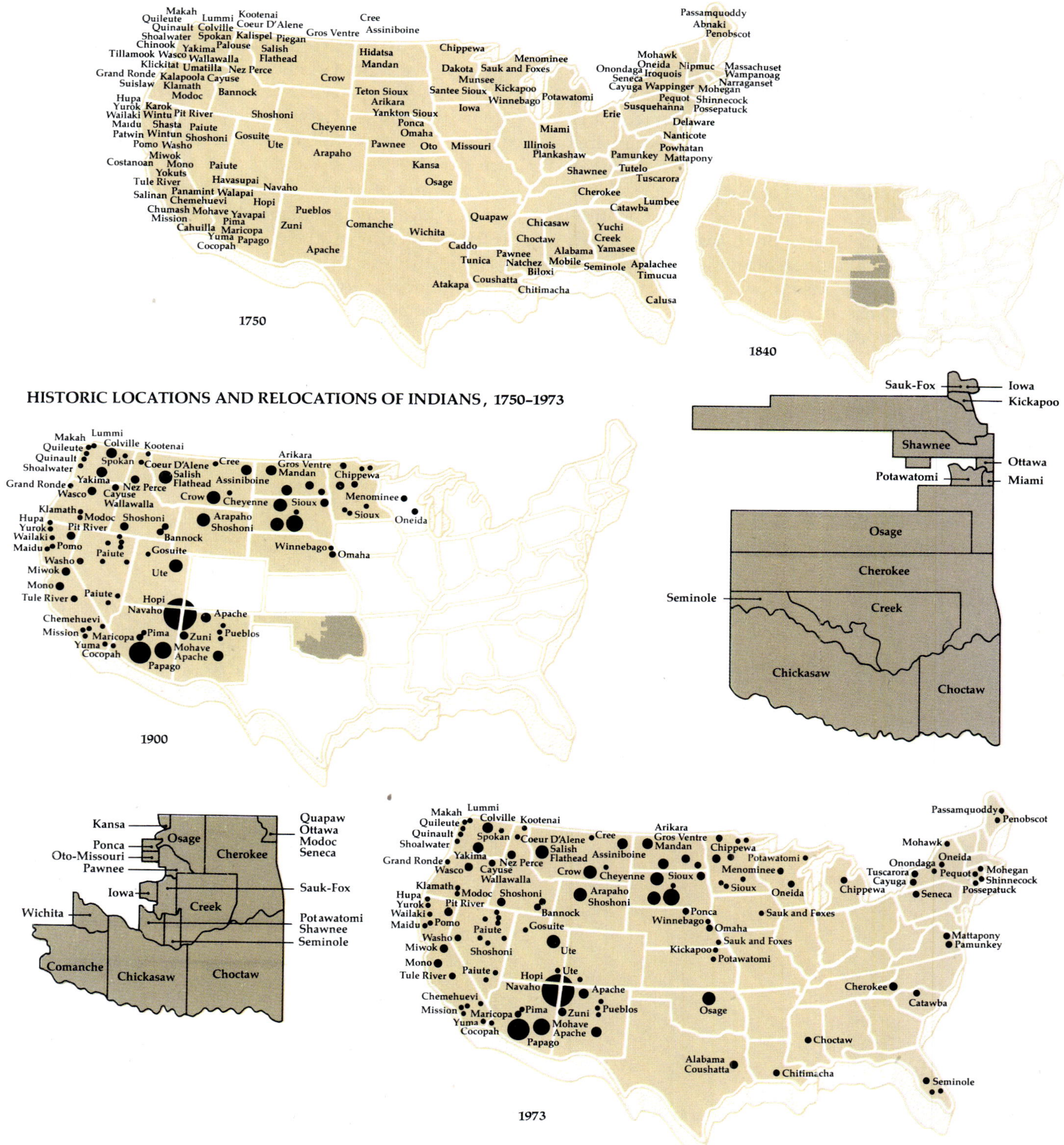

HISTORIC LOCATIONS AND RELOCATIONS OF INDIANS, 1750–1973

1750

1840

1900

1973

usually strong and sympathetic leadership in the Interior Department and the Bureau of Indian Affairs helped launch policies that were intended to preserve tribal culture and land holdings and to grant tribes some measure of self-government. Before the new policies could be systematically implemented, however, World War II caused attention to shift away from domestic concerns.

After the war, policy shifted back to the old pre-New Deal assumptions, and there was a new push for breaking up tribal ownership of land. The drive culminated during the Eisenhower Administration when government assistance to a number of tribes was terminated through legislation that ended tribal ownership of land and cut off the services of the Bureau of Indian Affairs.

The laws were based on the assumption that the only things holding back Indian development and assimilation were governmental bureaucracy and lack of private ownership of land. Conservatives maintained that if the Indians could be freed from existing government services and if common ownership of resources could be replaced by individual ownership, Indians would become similar to white citizens—to the conservatives it was easier to declare people "free" by ending the services provided by government than it was to face up to the economic, educational, and social disaster that existed on the reservations.

The result was disastrous. When the Indians tried to keep their land without federal services or federal tax exemptions, the task was almost impossible. In most cases, tribal lands were sold and the money divided. Soon nothing was left, and the people had no home. Across the country, tribal leaders were terrified by the situation, and the experience made many Indians resist all proposals to change the status quo (Vine Deloria, 1969).

Assimilation through relocation was another major goal in the 1950s and 1960s. The idea was to encourage Indians to find jobs by leaving reservations for distant cities where they might succeed and assimilate. Participants were transported far away, given a temporary relocation allowance, and then forgotten. The jobs were usually menial and sometimes seasonal, and the workers were denied the health care provided on the reservations. Indians were being brought to the cities long after the old urban demand for unskilled labor had given way to a job market requiring education and training. As a result, many Indians ended up in city slums (Stan Steiner, 1968).

Indians began to receive increasing attention in the late 1960s. For the first time in several decades, two Presidents—Johnson and Nixon—sent Congress special messages on Indian affairs. Indians began to organize across tribal lines and develop their own national spokesmen through such organizations as the National Congress of American Indians and the American Indian Movement. Indian authors, including Pulitzer Prize winner Scott Momoday and former National Congress of American Indians leader Vine Deloria, commanded large national audiences. There was a new mood of militance among some Indians. The mood was reflected in fishing-rights demonstrations, the occupation of Alcatraz Island and other public installations, urban demonstrations on cultural issues, the takeover cf the headquarters building of the Bureau of Indian Affairs in 1972, and finally, Indian occupation of Wounded Knee, South Dakota.

Public interest and attention helped Indians win some victories in Congress. After decades of struggle, the federal government returned the sacred Blue Lake to the people of the Taos Pueblo. The 1971 Alaska land-claims legislation dealt far more

Figure 6.7 This image of the Indian family relocated among the brick tenements of Chicago (right) is a far cry from either the negative stereotype of western films or the positive stereotype of a James Fenimore Cooper novel. The American Indian's responses to social and political pressures and coercion have run the gamut from degradation and resignation to appeal to the majority's conscience and demands backed by intimidation.

There is a direct chain of cause and effect between the first European grabs for Indian lands and the Indian stands at Alcatraz, the Columbia River, Washington, D.C., and Wounded Knee. Looking back at an independent past with pride, the American Indian joined with other non-European ethnic minorities in the great protest waves of the 1960s and 1970s (left).

fairly with Alaska natives than had been the case in previous situations, although there were still doubts about the adequacy of the protections of the money settlement. In the courts, young lawyers were fighting to expand the judicial definitions of the rights of Indians.

Terrible problems remained, however. Most reservation Indians continued to live in substandard housing in communities where the majority of the people had no permanent jobs. Funds for economic development were meager even though Indian tribes had excellent repayment records. The 1970 Census showed that most Indians were living off of the reservations and in growing concentrations in such cities as Los Angeles, Oklahoma City, Minneapolis, and Seattle. And even though the federal government had urged the Indians to leave their land, federal officials continued to deny Indian services to those Indians who lived away from the reservations. Change in policy was still at the symbolic level.

THE URBAN CRISIS

The movement for civil rights, which was so strong during the early 1960s, took a sudden turn before the end of 1965. The upheavals that occurred in dozens of ghettos over the next three years suddenly spotlighted the inner cities that were to become so important in the formation of future government policies on race.

The huge demand for labor during World War I had begun the exodus of blacks from the rural South into northern and western cities. When the black migrants reached the North they found themselves forced, by white resistance and by official action, to live in segregated areas and to pay high prices for the limited housing available within ghetto boundaries. Middle-class whites began to move from the central cities into the suburbs, leaving the cities and their massive problems behind. It seemed only a matter of time before some entire cities would become ghettos. The bulk of new jobs—even those requiring semiskilled labor—were being created in the suburbs. Poor people and minority groups, locked into central cities both economically and racially, generally lacked even a public transportation system that could transport them to the scattered job sites outside of the cities.

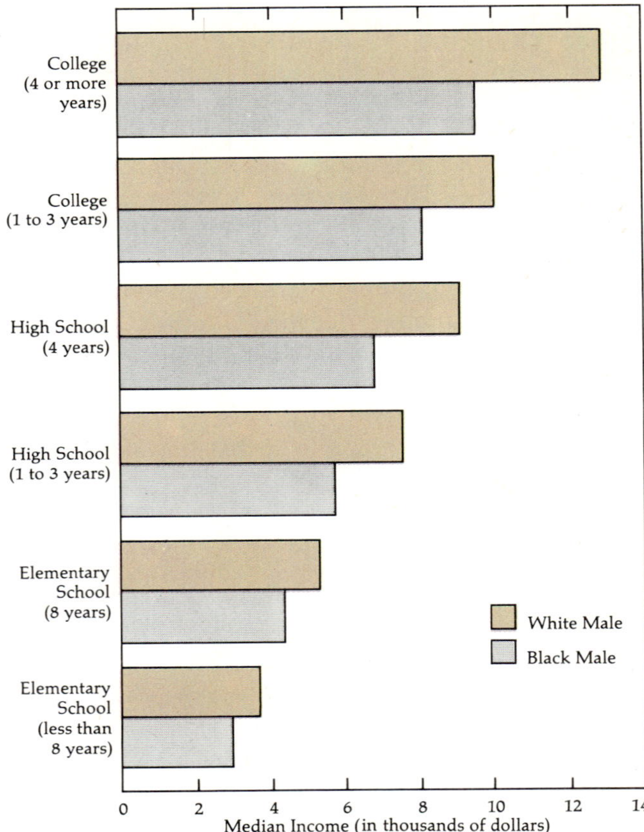

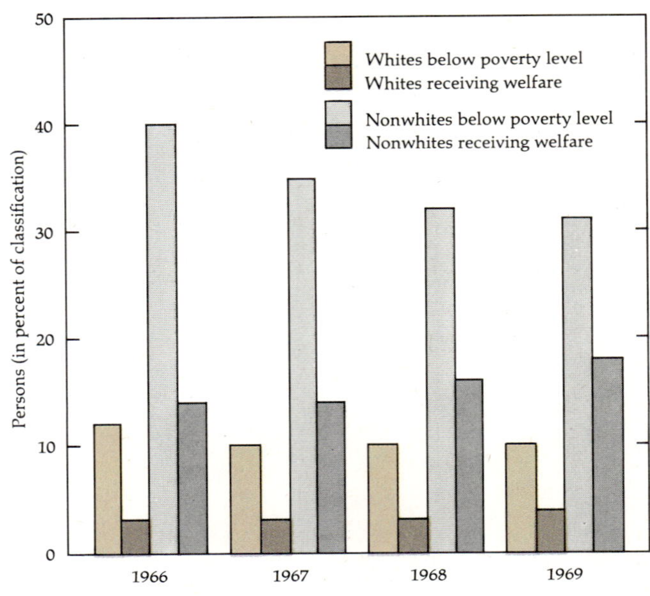

Figure 6.8 The racial upheavals of the 1950s and 1960s led to a proliferation of studies comparing the nation's white and non-white populations. The chart on the left shows that income increases with education. It also shows that the educated black male is not paid at the same rate as his white counterpart (U.S. Bureau of the Census, 1971). Another chart (bottom) compares the percentage of whites and nonwhites whose income places them below the "poverty level"—a determination that is based on government figures for each of the four years shown here. The chart also shows the percentage of the white and non-white populations that received welfare during those years (U.S. Bureau of Labor, 1971). The third chart (below) shows the life expectancy for blacks and whites during the decade of the 1960s. Do black males live as long as white males? as black females? Can trends be mapped for any of the four groups? For example, does black male life expectancy seem to be increasing or decreasing? (U.S. Public Health Service, 1960–1970)

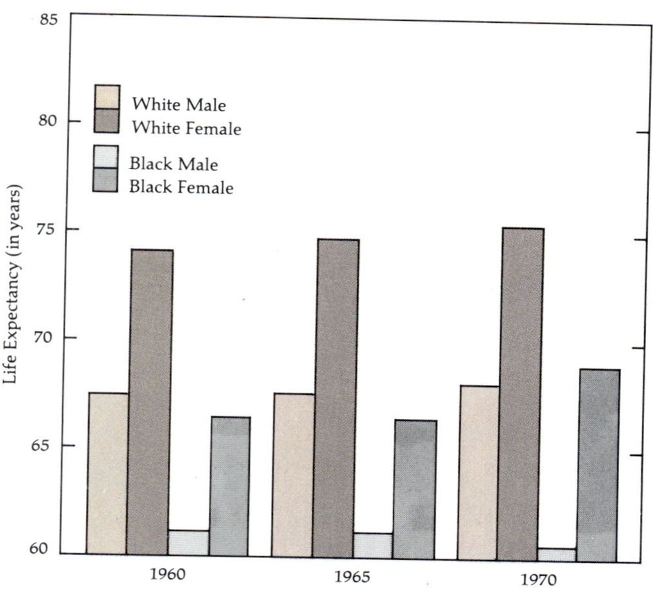

The Rise of "Black Power"

The 1960s found young blacks increasingly unwilling to accept the unequal schools, housing, police service, and jobs that were available in the large cities. A spark was lit in 1965 that crystallized the decades of frustration and led to another change in public sentiment.

Few Americans had ever heard of Watts, the huge black ghetto in Los Angeles, until unprecedented looting and burning erupted along several major streets in August 1965. People were shocked as the police and fire departments temporarily lost control of many square miles of the country's second largest metropolitan complex.

A major ideological shift by some young black leaders away from integrationist goals added another explosive element to the situation. Suddenly the country's racial problem was symbolized to many whites by young black rioters screaming "burn, baby, burn" rather than by the praying marcher in the South.

In 1966, the year after the Watts riot, the Congress of Racial Equality (CORE) and the Student Non-Violent Coordinating Committee (SNCC) were taken over by factions that endorsed "black power" and were unwilling to renounce the use of violence. Although the vague new slogan came to mean everything from black cultural pride, to a desire to expand black businesses, to antiwhite nationalism, it was regarded by many white Americans solely in terms of antiwhite nationalism and therefore was considered a threat. Even within the black community, the unity of the mid-1960s gave way to division and recriminations over the shape that further action should take.

Residential Segregation and the Schools

Although the riots and strident new leaders made the problems of the ghettos far more visible, there was no national effort to reform urban institutions. Instead, Congress rushed to enact anti-riot legislation and poured millions of dollars into arming police forces. The polls showed that whites now felt that blacks were "pushing too fast" and that their demonstrations had become counterproductive (Angus Campbell, 1971).

Lacking national consensus and facing intense political opposition, civil rights groups turned once again to the courts. They alleged that school and housing segregation were largely the result of official actions and that such segregation violated their constitutional guarantee of *equal protection of the laws.*

The urban legal questions were first attacked in the school systems of southern cities. In 1971, in a unanimous decision in the *Swann* v. *Charlotte-Mecklenburg* case, the Supreme Court ruled that cities that had once openly employed the power of law to maintain segregated schools were now obligated to use their authority to provide integrated schools, even if drastic restructuring of the local school system were involved. The Court ordered the school board of Charlotte-Mecklenburg, North Carolina to implement a desegregation plan entailing the busing of thousands of additional students. (The *Swann* case is discussed in detail in the Perspective following this chapter.)

The *Swann* case stirred up a tidal wave of litigation in other cities. The lower courts rapidly ordered similar changes in a number of southern and border-state communities. Outside the South, judges who were confronted with evidence of officially endorsed segregation policies began to impose similar remedies. School boards in many cities, including San Francisco, San Diego, and Pontiac, Michigan, soon came under court orders.

The housing cases were less visible than the explosive busing cases but were of great potential importance. In Chicago a federal appeals court held that the city housing authority and the federal Department of Housing and Urban Development (HUD) were guilty of unconstitutional actions in fostering the construction of public housing in locations that intensified segregation. In *Gautreaux* v. *Chicago* (1969) the city was ordered to reverse this practice. The Court of Appeals in Philadelphia handed down an even farther-reaching decision that required all federal housing programs to be administered in a way that would foster integration. In both cases, however, the impact of the decisions was limited because neither was given national application by the Supreme Court.

THE RISE OF CIVIL RIGHTS OPPOSITION

The litigation and mounting public discussion of the issues raised major policy questions for the first Nixon Administration. The Administration was charged with enforcing school desegregation under the 1964 Civil Rights Act and housing desegregation under a fair-housing law passed in 1968. In each case

the President had to decide whether to adopt the spirit of the new Court decisions or to commit the executive branch to a policy favoring the slowing of urban desegregation.

The Nixon Administration became the first since that of Woodrow Wilson to attempt to weaken existing civil rights protections and to forestall further advances. Within its first year, for example, the Administration urged repeal of a provision of the basic Voting Rights Act that permitted the Attorney General to veto state election laws, opposed a congressional move to give the Equal Employment Opportunity Commission its own enforcement powers, and stopped Health, Education, and Welfare (HEW) enforcement of school desegregation requirements.

After long struggles within the Administration, President Nixon committed the government to oppose what he called "forced busing" and "forced integration of the suburbs." In his major policy statement on the housing issue, the President defended the right of suburbs to exclude people on economic grounds, and he rejected plans of housing officials to withhold federal grants from communities that refused to diversify their housing supply by making low-income housing available.

In 1972 the President called on Congress to declare a moratorium on court-ordered busing and to limit the power of the courts to order desegregation. A modified version of one of the Administration bills passed the House but was filibustered to death in the Senate. Before the 1972 election the President warned that he might support a constitutional amendment to limit desegregation requirements.

The courts are not able to decide the direction of racial policy without public support—they are more effective in preserving the status quo than in fostering change. The unusual thing about the late 1960s and early 1970s was that the status quo included a number of far-reaching civil rights laws and a large body of legal precedents established by the Supreme Court under Chief Justice Earl Warren. In some ways, the position and tactics of the civil rights liberals, especially on the busing issue, came to resemble the defensive strategies of the old southern conservatives who had often used their skills to forestall change. Civil rights supporters found themselves attempting to frustrate the goals of a President and a popular majority by filibustering, by exercising minority vetoes in Congress, and by appealing to the courts to preserve the status quo that was based on their relatively recent civil rights law.

Figure 6.9 For many American citizens these three images evoke intense emotional responses—to some they represent democracy, to others, rebellion, revolution, or violence. This 1970 march to Georgia (far left) was intended to demonstrate that poor southern blacks were capable of organizing and demanding their rights. The bullet holes in a Black Panther headquarters (left) are the result of shooting by police. Although police-Panther confrontations have received much media coverage, the Panthers have also mobilized support in election campaigns, organized community-action programs, and sponsored programs to provide nutritious breakfasts for elementary school children. Angela Davis (right) was fired from her position as an instructor of philosophy at the University of California. Ostensibly she was fired for criticizing the fairness of the American educational system rather than for her membership in the Communist Party (a legally recognized political party). A direct and outspoken intellectual, "Angela" became a rallying call for radicals in the early 1970s.

The Supreme Court became the keystone of this defensive strategy. Thus, after the lower federal courts approved the Nixon Administration's efforts to delay desegregation in 1969 and to win approval of segregated neighborhood schools in 1970, the Supreme Court's position became extremely important. In both cases a unanimous Court rejected the Administration's position and maintained some of the momentum of change, at least for a time.

Urban segregation problems, however, were not solvable through the use of defensive strategies. Neither the political leadership nor the public support required to sustain the process of altering fundamental public and private racial practices in urban areas was in evidence. The President was opposed to most forms of change, and the public was uninterested in some issues and actively hostile to others.

ALTERNATIVES

The faltering strength of the civil rights movement in the late 1960s produced a search for alternative answers to the urban crisis. White reaction and the repudiation of the whole integrationist goal by some black leaders helped generate skepticism about the possibility of desegregation within the foreseeable future. The search for alternative solutions took many directions.

One approach was based on the assumption that deficiencies of public services in the central-city ghettos could best be altered by organizing poor neighborhoods and giving the new organizations some governmental power. This theory was embodied in the requirements for representation of the poor and of neighborhood residents on the governing boards of poverty agencies and organizations such as Model Cities (financed through HUD).

A variation of this approach was developed by some reformers as an alternative to school desegregation. Under the slogan "community control," they fought for neighborhood-level control of school policy and personnel, especially in areas like New York City where desegregation seemed impossible.

Many rising black politicians also appealed for support on the grounds that a black takeover of the machinery of local government would produce great improvements. By the early 1970s there was an unprecedented number of black officeholders, and the seventeen blacks in Congress represented an all-time high. Black mayors had been elected in many cities, such as Cleveland, Newark, Gary, and Los Angeles. Changing population patterns indicated that there might soon be many black mayors.

At a time when there was little disposition to directly confront the problem of racial inequality in the metropolis, the climate seemed right for a return to the traditional set of American answers—racial separation and some new form of the *separate but equal* doctrine. In a 1972 speech, President Nixon called for action to forbid court efforts to desegregate urban schools and proposed a concentrated effort to upgrade ghetto education. His 1973 budget, however, cut the proposed funds for ghetto schools.

Black political leaders who were frustrated with the drive for equality through integration soon found the reality of local political power almost equally frustrating. Kenneth Gibson, the black mayor of Newark, New Jersey, found himself constantly in Washington and Trenton pleading with white politicians and administrators for money to keep the city afloat. The city's tax rates were the highest in the state, but the flight to the suburbs by whites, middle-class blacks, and businesses made necessary an even greater effort just to maintain existing public services. Meanwhile, reapportionment gave the suburban communities more and more strength in the state legislature and in Congress. In Cleveland, black Mayor Carl Stokes refused, out of frustration, to run for office again.

Whites were transferring control of critically ill governmental institutions to blacks while retaining control of the larger governmental structures and the economic institutions whose active support was essential to make the cities viable. Black mayors found there was little opportunity to innovate when they had to worry about the schools closing two months early for lack of funds. Hope and desperation had merged in the rhetoric of black power. In practice, the slogan could not overcome the realities of power distribution in American society. There was no shortcut to equality (Donald Canty, 1969).

SUMMARY

American political institutions have served blacks and American Indians poorly because most Americans have rarely been seriously committed to remedy minority problems and because our structure of

Figure 6.10 Black political power. Inevitably the movement for black rights reached a stage in the late 1960s and early 1970s when black political power flexed its muscles and tried to make electoral use of the urban concentration of black voters (as is shown in the accompanying chart, black populations were becoming concentrated in urban areas, while whites were rapidly populating the suburbs). Black power has had many different expressions and a variety of advocates. In 1972, Gary, Indiana was the site of the Black Political Convention (top left), a black alternative to the Republican and Democratic conventions in Miami. Appointed by the President, Washington, D.C.'s mayor Walter Washington (top center) presides over the nation's capital, a city that is largely black in population. In 1973 Black Panther Bobby Seale (top right) challenged the incumbent mayor of Oakland, the fifth largest city in California, and came close to beating the incumbent mayor in the run-off election. The mayor of Fayette, Mississippi, Charles Evers (above left), brother of murdered civil rights leader Medgar Evers, meets with his constituents to survey their problems and explain his programs. Newark, New Jersey, 1967 (above center): A four-day conference that includes Dick Gregory and others in a large assembly of black power advocates. Inheriting all the problems of a destitute central city populated by the poor, Mayor Kenneth Gibson (above right) of Newark, New Jersey addresses his first mayoral press conference in June 1970.

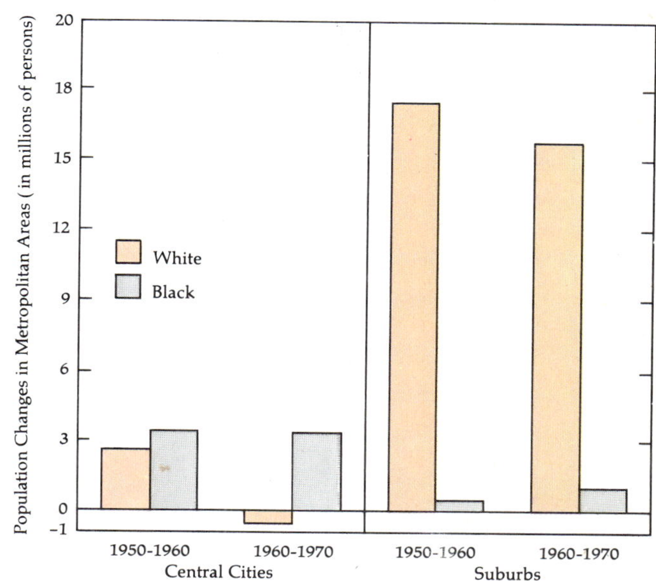

government makes the implementation of any controversial federal action very difficult.

Only very special circumstances have made possible the two brief periods of civil rights reform in American history; there has not yet been a fundamental reform of Indian policy. With the exception of the Reconstruction period, when the entire political system was skewed by the exclusion of the South from Congress, the middle 1960s represents the only sustained national effort to overcome racial inequality. The civil rights movement, however, could retain power only so long as public interest remained intense and public support was sufficiently overwhelming to overcome the powerful tools possessed by local leaders in the American system. These special conditions were gone by the late 1960s.

The 1960s brought a revolution in race relations in the American South. The decade also brought the country face-to-face with an extremely difficult set of new racial questions arising from the intense segregation of the metropolitan areas. It is difficult for any society to sustain rapid social change for long; it is particularly difficult when the apparent solution of one set of historic problems only reveals a more complex, less understood, and equally difficult set of new problems.

As the elemental challenge to the American system spilled out of the South to question the racial practices of major white institutions across the country, resistance intensified. As the early goals were achieved, sometimes with disappointing results, black organizations divided and their allies diverged. As violence, white reaction, and inflammatory racial rhetoric on both sides of the ghetto line built racial polarization, political strategies shifted. The exceptional conditions of the 1960s were gone; deadlock again prevailed, at least for the time. As the 1970s began, the question was whether the nation could consolidate and build on the achievements of the 1960s and eventually face the urban issues or whether it would again return to its normal pattern of "separate but equal."

SUGGESTED READINGS

Canty, Donald. *A Single Society: Alternatives to Urban Apartheid.* New York: Praeger, 1969.

Deloria, Vine. *Custer Died for Your Sins.* New York: Avon, 1970.

Franklin, John Hope. *Reconstruction: After the Civil War.* Chicago: University of Chicago Press, 1961.

Jordan, Winthrop D. *White Over Black.* Baltimore: Penguin, 1969.

Logan, Rayford. *Betrayal of the Negro.* New York: Collier, 1965.

Miller, Loren. *The Petitioners.* Cleveland, Ohio: Meridian, 1966.

DESEGREGATING THE SCHOOLS

by Gary Orfield

Figure 6a.1 On September 13, 1971, in compliance with a court order, San Francisco launched the nation's most massive integration attempt through busing. Obviously, overcrowding on this San Francisco school bus was no problem—parents kept an estimated 44 percent of the city's elementary school pupils away from schools.

Students born after the Supreme Court's 1954 decision against segregated schools are now in college, and the national struggle set off by the Court's action still rages. In the seventeen southern and border states, that decision has revolutionized the schools and has given birth to a great social movement for racial justice. In the North the decision has led to scrutiny of long-established racial practices and has produced a major contest over the make-up of urban schools.

Two decades of intense political struggle over the enforcement of a basic constitutional right to desegregated schools have provided an excellent test of the capacity of American institutions to resolve one of America's deepest social problems. Perhaps no other issue so well illustrates the extent and limits of judicial power in accomplishing social change within the American federal system. The story abounds with examples of the interplay among the President, the Congress, the bureaucracies, state and local officials, and the courts in shaping policy results.

In addition, the history of the school issue shows the interaction between public opinion—the ultimate source of democratic power—and the major institutions of government.

The direction and extent of fundamental social change in America are often posed initially as legal questions. The United States is a society with a strong legalistic tradition and an extraordinary reliance on lawyers for political leadership. Americans, more than most other peoples, tend to view the law as a science of finding, in a nonpolitical way, the true meaning of constitutional words and phrases. Our reliance on a written constitution and our creation of a judicial system that enjoys considerable independence in interpreting the law have in turn intensified the tendency to view political questions as legal disputes.

However, it is easy to overestimate the real power of the courts. Although the courts do have the ability to create new issues, their membership and opinions generally reflect prevailing political forces. In addition, although the courts have some

power of initiative, their enforcement apparatus is weak in the face of noncompliance. The courts are also vulnerable to political retaliation; members of Congress may threaten to restrict judicial powers or may even amend the Constitution if they feel the courts have deeply offended public opinion (see Chapter 11).

The desegregation struggle showed how local politics reaches into the major institutions of national power. Although the President is chosen by a national electorate, for example, he still must build his nomination and election campaign on alliances of local organizations—he does his best to retain and broaden their support. By the same token, Congress actually has very little power to control, discipline, or assure reelection for its members—members of Congress base their reelection support instead on local organizations, local financing, and their own ability to represent local views (see Chapter 13). The result is often strong congressional pressure on federal agencies to bow to local demands. Federal agencies, which must depend on their congressional alliances to protect their legislation and appropriations, often give in to such demands. The entire system makes it difficult to enforce federal rights in the face of determined local resistance.

ACHIEVING SYMBOLIC CHANGE

In a sequence often found in the history of American policy making, the struggle to achieve racial equality in the schools experienced its first successes in symbolic form. These successes were, in large part, embodied in a series of court decisions. Only later were these decisions to be translated into public policy and action.

The Strategy of Litigation

When school-desegregation litigation began in earnest in the 1940s, blacks had very little economic or political power. Most lived in the South, where a variety of state and local discriminatory procedures had been implemented to prevent them from voting. There were no substantial federal school-aid programs, federal enforcement agencies had consistently deferred to local segregationist practices, and Congress had been immobilized on racial issues for generations. With all other avenues apparently blocked, civil rights advocates turned to the courts.

The NAACP Legal Defense Fund began a long and brilliant legal campaign to enforce the Fourteenth Amendment's guarantee of *equal protection of the laws*. By 1950 the civil rights lawyers had won decisions recognizing the fact that separate and obviously inferior programs of graduate and professional education in the South violated this constitutional guarantee. After these decisions the civil rights organizations challenged the constitutionality of segregated public education in a series of lawsuits across the country. The issue was soon before the Supreme Court.

The Brown Decision

In 1954, after consultation with two successive Administrations and lengthy consideration, the Supreme Court handed down a unanimous decision against the principle of

Figure 6a.2 The culmination of more than fifteen years of legal struggle by supporters and lawyers of the National Association for the Advancement of Colored People is crystallized in the headline shown here (left). The 1954 Brown decision overturned the doctrine allowing "separate but equal" facilities for the races.

Figure 6a.3 For two hundred years Americans have believed that education is the ladder of upward socioeconomic mobility. As equal opportunities expand, black parents expect equal education for their children (right).

officially segregated education. The logic of the decision supported a sweeping prohibition of segregation:

We come then to the question presented: Does segregation of children in public schools solely on the basis of race, even though the physical facilities and other "tangible" factors may be equal, deprive the children of the minority group of equal educational opportunities? We believe that it does. . . .

We conclude that in the field of public education the doctrine of "separate but equal" has no place. Separate educational facilities are inherently unequal. (*Brown* v. *Board of Education,* 1954)

When it came time to implement these rights, however, the Court responded to what it perceived as the limits of its enforcement power and delivered a ruling that stressed local authority and gradual change. School officials, the Court held, had "primary responsibility for elucidating, assessing, and solving" the "varied local school problems." Their efforts would be judged not by any clear national standard or timetable, but by the federal district judges in the various areas of the South. School systems that were sued would be expected to "make a prompt and reasonable start," after which the district courts were granted the power to permit delays for a variety of reasons before further steps would be taken. The school systems were told to begin desegregation "with all deliberate speed," but neither the final goal nor the deadline for desegregation was spelled out (*Brown* v. *Board of Education,* 1955).

The enforcement of the *Brown* decision rested on two assumptions. First, the Justices assumed that the southern states would peacefully plan and accept gradual desegregation. Second, the Court assumed that the southern federal judges would, whatever their personal views, be willing to bear the brunt of the burden of forcing a bitterly resented change on the people of their home areas. Both assumptions were incorrect.

Several factors explain the judges' reluctance to enforce the Court's controversial decision. Although in theory the federal judicial system is highly centralized, with judges appointed by the President and insulated from local politics by lifetime appointments, the appointment process is actually dominated by the localistic politics of Congress (see Chapter 8). Political tradition has long since transferred the major role in selecting district court judges to each state's senior senator from the President's party or to ranking state party officials. It is not surprising, therefore, that most district judges and appeals court judges who heard the school cases had grown up in southern states, been educated there, and been deeply involved in state politics. It was hardly a group that could be expected to actively push a social revolution. In the absence of firm direction from the Supreme Court, many of the judges were inclined to permit long delays and to require only token desegregation (Jack Peltason, 1961).

Massive Resistance

Immediately after the Supreme Court decisions, the chances of peaceful, gradual change seemed good. Leaders of the six border states were gener-

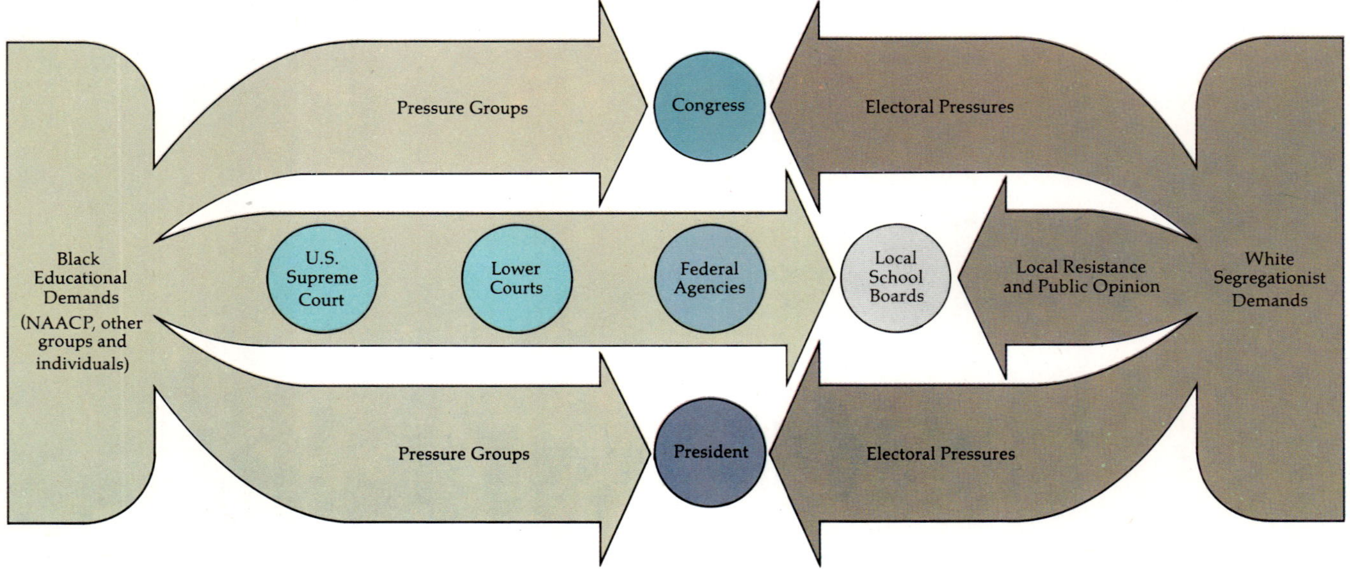

ally willing to begin desegregation, and the first statements of most southern governors were moderate.

The compliant mood was short-lived, however. During 1956, for example, the Virginia legislature enacted a series of laws that enabled the state to use all of its powers to fight desegregation. It even declared that the 1954 *Brown* decision was not valid. Virginia financed litigation against desegregation; harassed the NAACP with investigations and laws to make the filing of civil rights suits very difficult; authorized the governor to close any school that was even slightly integrated; provided tuition grants for segregated private schools; abolished compulsory school-attendance requirements; and set up a state agency to conduct a propaganda campaign against the Supreme Court decision (Benjamin Muse, 1961).

The massive-resistance campaign in Virginia was widely emulated and strongly approved by the 101 southern senators and representatives who signed the Southern Manifesto in 1956. The manifesto claimed that the Supreme Court had substituted "naked power for established law" and that the *Brown* decision violated the Constitution. It argued for every possible form of resistance.

A decisive confrontation came in 1957 in Arkansas when Governor Orval Faubus called out the National Guard to prevent black children from attending a high school in Little Rock. Although President Eisenhower had never endorsed the Supreme Court decision, he recognized his responsibility to uphold the Constitution and to prevent defiance of federal court orders. He took control of the Arkansas National Guard (a power granted him by the Constitution) and ordered in a unit of paratroopers with fixed bayonets to occupy the town and protect the children (Anthony Lewis, 1965).

Southern reaction was intense. The symbolism of armed occupation brought new strength to the region's segregationists. Hysteria impeded the work of the small group of civil rights lawyers, and the courts moved very slowly. Desegregation efforts came to a virtual standstill.

After a year of desegregation in Little Rock, a federal judge granted an order authorizing postponement of desegregation because of disruption and violence in the high school. The Supreme Court angrily rejected this delay:

The constitutional rights of [black children] are not to be sacrificed or yielded to the violence and disorder which have followed upon the actions of the Governor and Legislature . . . law and order are not here to be preserved by depriving the Negro children of their constitutional rights. . . . In short, the constitutional rights of children . . . can neither be nullified openly and directly by State legislators or State executive or judicial officers, nor nullified indirectly by them through evasive schemes for segregation . . . (*Cooper* v. *Aaron,* 1958)

This decision prevented complete collapse of the desegregation effort. Had delay been allowed, the state of white opinion would have become the measuring rod for the constitutional rights of black children, and segregationists would have been encouraged to arouse public hostility to win delays.

Figure 6a.4 The American political system is based on advocacy, conflict, and confrontation. If it were not, there would be no reason for its checks and balances. In this diagram we see the routes taken in the conflict between black groups and segregationists in the area of education. Since the 1930s, blacks have worked through the federal government, beginning especially with the courts and then using the power of federal agencies, to attain equal treatment. Segregationist resistance has been strongest in local districts, pressuring local and national officials to minimize enforcement of the laws passed by coalitions of liberal, black, and labor groups at the national level.

Figure 6a.5 Orval Faubus, Governor of Arkansas in 1957, ordered the Arkansas National Guard to prohibit blacks from enrolling in Central High School in Little Rock. He is shown here announcing his candidacy for the governor's office for the 1970 term. He lost the election.

As the 1960s began, it seemed obvious that the courts could accomplish little more than minor changes. Although the worst of the unconstitutional massive-resistance laws had been overturned and the Supreme Court had belatedly spoken out, even the strongest desegregation orders required only symbolic steps toward desegregation.

Political Deadlock in Washington

From 1954 to 1964 the burden of desegregating southern schools was on the courts. During most of the period, the President and Congress were unable to decide on any effective action. The inaction in Washington, D.C. was not due to lack of public interest—interest was often very high—or to lack of a majority favoring change—the polls generally showed that a substantial national majority supported the *Brown* decision. In Congress there were repeated debates, but the southern veto remained in force. Until 1963, neither Eisenhower nor Kennedy made school desegregation a major presidential priority.

Congress had begun to struggle over school-desegregation legislation in 1955. In that year the NAACP proposed an amendment that would make local compliance with the Constitution's desegregation requirements a precondition for receipt of school-aid funds that would be provided by the President's 1955 school-aid bill. In succeeding years this amendment was often introduced by the country's best-known black congressman, Democrat Adam Clayton Powell. Both President Eisenhower and President Kennedy, as well as many prominent liberal spokesmen, opposed the Powell amendment, arguing that it would kill the school bills. Not until 1963 did the amendment become a serious legislative possibility.

Congress came close to enacting significant legislation in 1957 when the Eisenhower Administration submitted a civil rights bill that would have allowed the Attorney General to sue segregated school systems. If passed, the legislation would have lifted some of the burden from civil rights groups and committed the Jus-

tice Department to a policy of desegregation. When the bill was bitterly attacked by Senate conservatives, however, President Eisenhower said he did not support it; it was subsequently killed in Congress (John Anderson, 1964). In effect, the courts were left for ten years without any tangible support from the executive or legislative branches. The southern congressional veto of civil rights bills, unbroken since Reconstruction, remained intact.

Results of a Decade of Litigation

Only about one in every hundred black children in the South was in a desegregated school when President Kennedy sent his civil rights legislation to Congress in 1963. The few progressive districts were generally operating under "grade-a-year" plans that allowed them twelve years to desegregate, one grade at a time. Even when a grade was officially desegregated under such a plan, the result was minimal—the district merely set up a formal procedure by which a student could apply to a school board to transfer

from an all-black school to an over-whelmingly white school.

Using the appealing rhetorical banner of *freedom of choice,* the courts had developed a legal doctrine that put the full burden of desegregation on black families: After recognizing the right of children to a desegregated education, the courts permitted the right to be ignored except when the black community instituted long and difficult litigation, and black families were ready to challenge the racial status quo by enrolling their children in predominantly white schools. In short, the system did not achieve its goals (United States Commission on Civil Rights, 1964).

ACHIEVING REAL CHANGE

Through the years there has been a moderation of white segregationist attitudes. Although only two-fifths of the white population had favored integrated education in 1942, three-fifths did by 1956, and by 1963 the figure had reached almost three-fourths (Andrew Greeley and P.B. Sheatsley, 1971). There was a grow-ing public belief that the issue was so important that an extraordinary battle must be waged to break the southern veto in Washington. The Birmingham crisis and President Kennedy's dramatic call for federal legislation galvanized a shift in public opinion. An issue that only a few people had thought to be the primary national problem in the early spring of 1963 became the dominant national issue by midsummer.

Presidential and Congressional Leadership

The Birmingham crisis in 1963 began a period of powerful presidential and congressional leadership for civil rights. The change in public attitudes, which occurred at the same time, generated new strength within civil rights forces in Congress.

President Kennedy's 1963 bill (the basis for the Civil Rights Act of 1964) contained two major provisions relating to school desegregation. It proposed giving the Attorney General power to file desegregation lawsuits, and it provided that federal agencies be authorized (but not required) to withhold aid from districts that remained segregated. Congress eventually accepted the first proposal and vitally strengthened the second, turning the authorization to withhold funds into a clear prohibition against federal financing of segregated activities. The power of the Justice Department and HEW could now be implemented on behalf of black children who had been denied their rights.

Enforcing the Law

Once the Civil Rights Act of 1964 became law, the executive branch had the authority to force change. For the first time, the federal bureaucracy would play a major role in the struggle. HEW had the authority to create a single set of national standards and to set up a routinized, centralized process of forcing school districts to comply with the Constitution *before* they received any federal assistance. School districts that refused to comply would not only lose needed funds but would face the threat of litigation by the Justice Department or by civil rights groups.

Figure 6a.6 Landmark events in the effort to integrate the high schools and colleges of the South. September 4, 1957: White students shouted epithets at Elizabeth Beckford (far left) as she tried to pass through lines of obstructing National Guardsmen that had been called out by Governor Orval Faubus. September 25, 1957: President Eisenhower ordered paratroopers flown to Little Rock, Arkansas (left) to ensure the safety of black students entering Central High School. August 18, 1963: James Meredith (right) received his bachelor's degree from the University of Mississippi; his enrollment in the fall of 1962 had been accompanied by violent demonstrations.

On paper these new powers seemed sweeping. But the question remained, would they be used? In the past, federal administrators had had the power to stop aid programs if participants failed to meet program requirements, but they had rarely used it.

As is shown in the discussion of bureaucracies in Chapter 10, federal administrators are normally committed to the value of their programs and are inclined to believe that it is better to have faulty programs than none at all. Furthermore, their primary interest is the success of their particular programs (such as the improvement of reading programs, the construction of needed classrooms, or the establishment of special-education programs for the handicapped) rather than the achievement of a goal such as school integration. To cut off funds for their own programs in order to force local schools into compliance with integration guidelines would require that administrators jeopardize their own projects. Such actions would certainly cause trouble with con-gressmen and local officials who are concerned that the programs be completed. Under such conditions administrators are unlikely to act unless they receive vigorous encouragement from the President and his top officials to do so.

President Johnson and his ranking officials committed their power to enforcing the law. Once the commitment and the will to invoke sanctions became evident, change came rapidly in southern education. During the first year of enforcement, more desegregation occurred than during the entire preceding decade. All but a tiny handful of southern school districts agreed to desegregation plans, most of which required more than the courts had been asking. Across the Deep South, where absolute resistance had been the rule, freedom-of-choice plans with token integration became accepted.

Over the next three years (1965–1968) HEW tightened its standards, causing a number of southern systems to get rid of the last vestiges of the dual school system and exacting promises from most of the other systems to finish the job by September 1969. Two major questions remained, however. First, would Washington show the necessary determination to enforce the plans to desegregate the rural areas of the Deep South? Second, what would be done about desegregating southern cities where *residential* segregation was intense? (Gary Orfield, 1969)

The Response of the Courts

With HEW carrying the administrative burden and taking the political heat, the courts rapidly began to develop school-desegregation laws. Soon, the southern federal courts were adopting HEW's requirements as their own, gladly deferring to the expertise of the educators in HEW on the details of desegregation requirements.

A major breakthrough came in 1966 when HEW and the federal courts began to move beyond the freedom-of-choice system. HEW said that such plans would no longer be accepted unless they actually produced substantial annual progress toward total integration. Later, the

Fifth Circuit Court of Appeals, which had jurisdiction over most of the Deep South, ruled that the real goal of the 1954 *Brown* decision was not just a formal system of choice but was the abolition of racially identifiable schools.

The Supreme Court itself finally spoke out on this central issue in 1968. In the case of *Green* v. *School Board of New Kent County, Virginia* the Court stated that the objective of the process was the abolition of all vestiges of the dual school structure as rapidly as possible. Local authorities, the Court held, must "take whatever steps might be necessary to convert to a unitary system in which racial discrimination would be eliminated root and branch." Unless freedom of choice worked extremely well in a particular community, it was not constitutionally acceptable.

The courts, HEW, and the Justice Department finally worked together toward a common goal, each reinforcing the others. HEW handled most of the massive administrative and political problems, relieving the courts. The courts sustained

HEW standards and moved to settle the unresolved issues in school-desegregation law. The Justice Department, which constituted a threat to those districts that were tempted to defy HEW, provided important support for the courts in the development of new legal principles.

After the 1968 decision against freedom-of-choice, HEW promptly informed the school systems under its jurisdiction that they would have to meet the Court's standard, and the Justice Department rapidly went to court to update desegregation plans in southern districts integrating under judicial supervision. Thus, although the immediate effect of the Court's decision in the *Green* case was on a handful of small rural systems, the new legal principle was rapidly felt across the South.

THE DE FACTO-DE JURE DISTINCTION

The schools of the South had been through a period of drastic racial change by 1968, but the schools of the North and West were more segregated than ever. Although the

Supreme Court had held that segregated education severely hurt black children, the people of the North maintained that their segregation was of a different kind than that of the South and that therefore no changes could be required. The reasoning that prevailed in the early decisions was that southern segregation was different because it had been imposed by state officials. Segregation in northern cities, on the other hand, was portrayed as an accident, an unplanned result of using the neighborhood-school policy in a setting of intense housing segregation. The northern variety was *de facto* (in fact) segregation, whereas the southern variety was *de jure* (under law).

Because the constitutional guarantee of equal protection of the laws prohibited only official segregation, it seemed that nothing much could be done about de facto segregation. For a decade and a half the courts accepted this distinction and required virtually no significant urban desegregation outside the South. Once the rural southern issues

Figure 6a.7 During the 1950s and 1960s the North and West pointed the finger at the South for its continuation of the old institutions of prejudice, whose effects were blatantly visible in schools, political life, and business. During the late 1960s and early 1970s, however, the issue of busing in the North and West to reduce segregation and the evidence of housing and hiring prejudices provided the South with some cause to raise the mirror to the pointing finger. After decades of wrestling with the problem, there was indication that the South had done more toward relieving institutional prejudice than had the rest of the country.

seemed to be largely solved and attention turned to closer examination of urban reality, however, the law changed rapidly.

Actually, the de facto-de jure distinction had been questioned as early as 1954. After the *Brown* decision, civil rights groups in cities across the country had begun to insist that the rights of ghetto children were being denied as surely as were those of black children in the South. What real difference, they asked, was there between the situation of a black child in a segregated southern school and a child in a Chicago ghetto school that had been built for a black neighborhood and was segregated as thoroughly as if law had required it?

The Fall of the Distinction in the South

The de facto-de jure distinction delayed serious litigation in northern cases and prevented HEW action except where official segregation was clearly apparent. In the South, however, the limits of the distinction soon became evident. Obviously,

under the *Brown* decision, state laws requiring school segregation were illegal. But southern federal judges soon had to face the problem of communities in which the unconstitutional laws were no longer in effect but in which segregation remained. Could a district fulfill its constitutional requirements by creating a formal mechanism for desegregation, even if no black children actually entered white schools?

New assumptions began to come into the law. The courts began to assume that some kind of official segregation persisted in those districts in which a freedom-of-choice plan was not working. In so doing, they stretched the meaning of de jure segregation. To meet the requirements of the Constitution, the courts maintained, it was not sufficient simply to have set up the proper procedures—schools actually had to be integrated. Federal judges began to rule that communities with a history of segregation could be forced to go beyond the neighborhood-school-assignment policy to develop real integration.

The Supreme Court finally began to give definite shape to desegregation requirements in a series of major decisions between 1968 and 1971. In 1968 the *Green* case provided the basis for dismissing token desegregation under freedom-of-choice by labeling it "first step." The following year the Court unanimously rejected the Nixon Administration's effort to delay desegregation in Mississippi. The Court discarded the old *deliberate speed* formula and said that after so many years no further postponement could be constitutionally permitted (*Alexander* v. *Holmes*, 1969).

In the case of *Swann* v. *Charlotte-Mecklenburg* (1971) the Court finally faced the important question of urban segregation. The school board of Charlotte, North Carolina attempted to justify segregated schools as innocent by-products of a racially neutral neighborhood-school policy. The Court, however, rejected this argument and said that school authorities must do whatever is necessary, including busing, to achieve integration in southern systems: If there had *once been* official school segregation, the Court said, authorities still had a positive obligation to produce integration.

The Fall of the Distinction in the North

Once the neighborhood-school argument fell in the South, the doctrine was rapidly and successfully attacked in some northern cities. Civil rights lawyers found that the history of segregation in northern districts almost always entailed some official involvement in producing racial separation. Decisions on school sites and attendance-zone boundaries, for instance, maximized rather than minimized segregation. In some cities, school boards had worked with realtors to foster racial separation. In all cities there was considerable evidence of local, state, and federal involvement in practices encouraging residential segregation. Many communities, for example, had been developed during the long period when state and federal courts enforced restrictive residential covenants and the Federal Housing Administration (FHA) required that subdivisions receiving FHA mortgage insurance be segregated (Charles Abrams, 1965). In brief, urban segregation was no accident.

Case by case, the old de facto–de jure distinction was weakened. When one looked closely and defined state action broadly, virtually every district was guilty of some kind of de jure segregation at some time in its history. Some lawyers, including Assistant Attorney General Stephen Pollak, concluded that there was no such thing as de facto school segregation.

Once de jure segregation was proved in any district, the *Brown* decision required desegregation, the *Holmes* decision forbade delay, and the *Swann* decision gave federal judges the authority to order large-scale student busing.

THE CONFLICT OVER LOCAL PREROGATIVES

The civil rights movement began with the goal of equal opportunity, defined largely as the reversal of overt official discrimination. As the issues developed, however, it became apparent that integration would require drastic infringement on traditional local prerogatives. Unless the neighborhood-school system was changed, for example, there was no way of desegregating many of the schools of the urban South and North. Once it became evident that both the freedom-of-choice and the neighborhood-school patterns would be challenged, federal requirements came under fierce political attack.

Beginning in 1966, local protests spurred severe congressional attacks on school-desegregation requirements; as court orders accumulated, the attacks intensified. The House repeatedly passed legislation intended to restrict the enforcement powers of HEW. In 1967 the Senate almost passed an amendment forbidding the use of federal funds for local programs that were meant to remedy racial imbalance.

Busing: A National Issue

Although few busing orders were in effect, Richard Nixon repeatedly addressed the issue in his 1968 cam-

Figure 6a.8 Ever since its formation in 1910 by a coalition of whites and blacks, the National Association for the Advancement of Colored People (NAACP) has worked through legal channels to alter the condition of blacks in the United States. For this reason the association has been criticized by more militant groups that prefer direct action, such as demonstrations and inward cultural development, to create change for the better. Here, Reverend Jesse Jackson, President of Operation P.U.S.H. of Chicago, calls for unity of all black groups as he addresses the 63rd annual convention of the NAACP in Detroit, July 5, 1972.

paign. "I oppose," he said, "any action by the Office of Education which goes beyond a mandate of Congress; a case in point is the busing of students to achieve racial balance in the schools" (Robert Holland, 1968). On another occasion he opposed "withdrawing federal funds to force a local school board to balance its schools racially, by busing children all over a city, for instance" (*New Republic,* 1968).

In place of federal pressure *for* desegregation, there was first indecision and then strong opposition from the new Administration. By mid-1969 HEW had been largely removed from the arena of enforcing desegregation, and the issue turned back to the courts. The role of the Justice Department was also dramatically altered. For the first time since 1954 the Justice Department went to the Supreme Court to plead for a delay in the Administration's policy of desegregation. The Supreme Court rapidly and unanimously rejected the plea.

The school-desegregation movement no longer benefited from the powerful cooperation between the courts and the executive branch. In one year HEW had been removed from the battle and the Justice Department had made common cause with southern school boards. Once again the courts would have to bear the full burden.

The Swann v. Charlotte-Mecklenburg Case

The conflict over desegregation delays was only a faint prelude to the massive battle over urban desegregation. The President was committed to maintaining neighborhood schools, and the Justice Department was intervening in key southern cases in defense of the system. Both the President and the Secretary of HEW publicly criticized the initial district court decision in the *Swann* v. *Charlotte-Mecklenburg* (1971) case, which was to become the critical case for the Supreme Court.

The *Swann* decision gave federal district judges authority to order busing or other remedies wherever there was de jure urban segregation. The law was now clear, at least in the South. In city after city, civil rights lawyers went to court asking for similar orders.

The President, recognizing his obligation to enforce the law, called for compliance, and both the Justice Department and HEW took some initial steps to extend the *Swann* requirements to additional districts. The courts proceeded with a burst of energy. Decisions requiring substantial busing were rapidly handed down in Texas, Virginia, Tennessee, Florida, Mississippi, Georgia, and elsewhere. Large southern cities, which had escaped the brunt of earlier desegregation requirements, suddenly found themselves required to take steps that no sizeable northern community had ever implemented, steps that the President and the Justice Department had repeatedly denounced as unnecessary and extreme (*Race Relations Law Survey,* 1971).

The *Swann* decision was directed specifically at the South, but judges across the country took the Court's strong action as a mandate for rapid, comprehensive desegregation. Judges

soon handed down decisions requiring extensive transportation of pupils in a number of northern cities. The local reaction was intense: The angry protesters filling television screens were as likely to speak in the accents of Michigan or Southern California as of Louisiana or Texas.

As political criticism grew, the Administration responded and again changed its policy. The President announced in August 1971 that HEW and the Justice Department would do everything possible to minimize busing and that officials who disobeyed this directive would be summarily removed. The Administration then took the extraordinary step of formally asking that its own desegregation proposals be disregarded by the courts. Coming just weeks before school opened, the President's new position intensified confusion and resistance.

The final step in crystallizing a hostile majority came when district court decisions threatened that students would be transferred across city-suburban lines. The judges felt impelled toward this remedy because the schools in a number of the nation's largest cities—including New York, Chicago, Detroit, Atlanta, Baltimore, Cleveland, Houston, and Richmond—already had such a large enrollment of minority groups that integration within the cities' schools seemed impossible. Judges and civil rights lawyers were very unhappy with the prospect of desegregation orders that might actually accelerate resegregation and "white flight." When lower-court decisions in Richmond and Detroit suggested the assignment of students across city-suburban lines on a metropolitan-wide basis, suburban resentment was intense. Millions of people who had been unaffected by the southern cases suddenly felt threatened. For the first time since 1954 there was now clear evidence of an overwhelming majority that was actively hostile to the desegregation orders of the federal courts.

THE IMPACT OF A HOSTILE MAJORITY

Although some legislative issues reveal a low correlation between local attitudes and the voting behavior of congressmen, the race issue has been very different. Race is such an emotional issue in American society that when public attitudes are mobilized at the local level, members of Congress often feel that their political survival depends on closely reflecting the dominant mood (Warren Miller and Donald Stokes, 1963).

The primary elections, referenda votes, and opinion polls of the early 1970s all showed a political force that few politicians could ignore. In late 1971, when the Gallup Poll asked about "busing of Negro and white school children from one school district to another," 82 percent of the public opposed it or had no opinion, whereas only 18 percent supported it. Blacks were evenly divided on the question (Gallup, 1972). Surveys taken among educators showed that three-fourths of superintendents and teachers were opposed to busing (*Congressional Record*, 1971).

Public opinion surveys, therefore, showed that opposition to busing had increased drastically during the

Figure 6a.9 Lamar, South Carolina was the scene of destructive rioting by foes of school integration in March 1970. School buses were overturned, patrolmen, rioters, and children were injured, and South Carolina National Guardsmen (left) were summoned to protect black school children. In 1971, by court order, Nashville, Tennessee began a program of massive busing to integrate the area's school system. Students of both races (right) stepped from one of the first buses used in the program.

Nixon Administration and under the influence of stronger court orders and continuing presidential attacks. A national survey conducted at the time of the 1972 election found that the public seriously misunderstood the facts about the busing controversy and that the misinformation was directly related to busing opposition (United States Commission on Civil Rights, 1973).

The public mood was soon felt in the House of Representatives. More than 150 members of the House signed a discharge petition to try to force passage of a constitutional amendment designed to restrict not only busing but all other means of desegregating urban districts. In late 1971 the House suddenly adopted a series of far-reaching amendments designed to restrict the power of the courts and executive agencies to require urban desegregation. Every proposal labeled "antibusing" commanded a two-to-one majority in the House.

The congressional battle intensified in 1972 when the President threw his support behind the drive to restrict the courts either by legislation or by constitutional amendment. Immediately after the Florida primary, President Nixon made a nationally televised speech on the busing issue in which he called on Congress to restrain the courts and to provide money to equalize programs in segregated ghetto schools. The President had earlier given widely publicized attention to the possibility of changing the Constitution itself if necessary.

President Nixon's new antibusing bills set in motion a series of skirmishes and long debates that extended throughout the year. In the end, after months of delaying tactics, the House passed a measure drastically curtailing the power of federal courts to order busing even within a single school district. The bill attempted to repeal the Supreme Court's decision in the *Swann* Case. Joining the huge House majority in this sweeping congressional attack on the independence of the courts were a number of northern congressmen who had once been fervent civil rights supporters.

After House action the President concentrated on the Senate, criticizing its inaction and threatening to propose a constitutional amendment if the Administration's "equal education" bill were blocked. A majority of the Senate was prepared to vote for the bill. Liberals were on the defensive, and the majority was prepared to force a confrontation with the courts. Civil rights supporters, however, resorted to an old southern tactic—they killed the measure by use of a filibuster.

THE LIMITATIONS OF THE COURTS

The urban school cases were some of the few instances in which the federal courts moved far ahead of public opinion on an extremely salient public issue. The ensuing political crisis raised basic questions about the ability of the government system to sustain civil rights law in the face of a hostile majority. Historical evidence strongly suggested that if the hostile majority were to remain actively opposed and the issue continued to dominate politics, the courts would be restrained. Such re-

Figure 6a.10 **The effects of generations of segregation are still with us. Although schools may be officially integrated by redistricting or busing, children may still feel ill-at-ease with others of different races.**

straint could come from within the court system, from new members appointed to the courts, from judicial acceptance of some form of congressional restriction, or from a constitutional amendment.

The first sign of policy change within the Supreme Court came in mid-1972. In considering a case from Virginia, the Supreme Court split for the first time on a school issue since 1954: The long succession of unanimous decisions ended with a close five-to-four division, with the four new Nixon appointees unified against the five senior members of the Court (*Wright* v. *Council of the City of Emporia*, 1972). A divided and weakened Court would thus have to face the pending issues of the northern desegregation cases.

In the early 1970s the United States was making basic decisions about its urban future. In the North, housing and school segregation were still spreading in most metropolitan areas, giving a racial definition to the separation between city and suburbs. Jobs, economic resources, and political power were flowing rapidly outward to the suburbs.

Any change in the deeply ingrained racial patterns of the cities was certain to be difficult and politically explosive. On the other hand, if there were no change, the nation would face the unknown but deeply threatening prospect of a future as a land of two separate and unequal peoples living in proximity, yet with little contact and growing polarization. An elemental decision was before the nation. The issue first came to political focus through legal battles over the segregation of urban education; the courts had done a great deal to make discrimination a public issue. It was very unlikely, however, that the courts could resolve it.

SUGGESTED READINGS

Berman, Daniel M. *It Is So Ordered.* New York: Norton, 1966.

Bullock, Henry Allen. *A History of Negro Education in the South.* New York: Praeger, 1967.

Orfield, Gary. *The Reconstruction of Southern Education: The Schools and the 1964 Civil Rights Act.* New York: Wiley, 1969.

Panetta, Leon, and Peter Gall. *Bring Us Together.* Philadelphia: Lippincott, 1971.

Peltason, Jack W. *Fifty-eight Lonely Men.* New York: Harcourt, Brace & World, 1961.

Sarrett, Reed. *The Ordeal of Desegregation.* New York: Harper & Row, 1966.

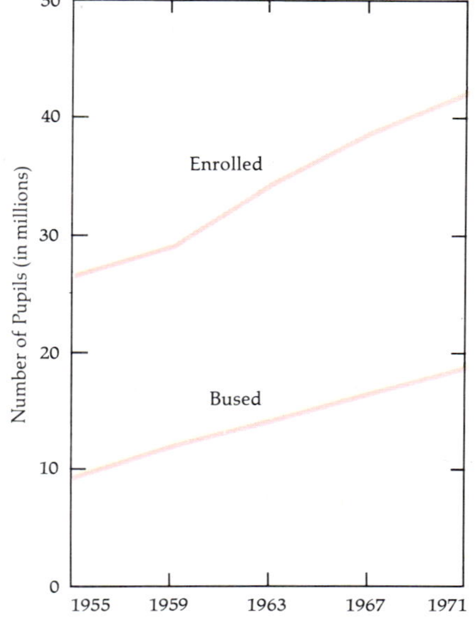

Figure 6a.11 It has long been common practice in rural areas of the nation to bus children to the closest schools. Yet in the late sixties and early seventies, busing became an explosive political issue because it was being used for purposes of integration. Actually, the number of pupils bused between 1955 and 1971 did not increase at the same rate as the number of pupils enrolled, despite emotional claims that the practice had suddenly spread throughout the nation (after David Soule, 1973).

$$7$$

CIVIL LIBERTIES

"The main reason why niggers want integration is because the niggers want our white women." Words out of the 1920s? Guarded comments to friends after a few too many beers? Quite the contrary. A candidate in the 1972 Democratic senatorial primary in Georgia spoke these words in a paid political announcement broadcast over radio and television. Particularly interesting about this racial slur is the fact that the Federal Communications Commission (FCC)—the federal agency that regulates the airwaves—ruled that a political candidate has the right to send these views into the homes of millions of viewers. On what grounds did it make this ruling?

In order to understand why a group of public officials resisted attempts to censor the candidate's message, the development of the American doctrine of civil liberties must be examined. Accordingly, this chapter seeks to identify America's basic civil liberty policies, explore their ultimate justifications, and perhaps most importantly, lead to an understanding of their implications.

Before turning to these matters it will be helpful to have some initial notion of what the term "civil liberty" means. Fundamentally, civil liberties are laws and legal rulings meant to define and maintain freedom, particularly as it pertains to the relationship between the individual and the government.

Although the text of the original Constitution contains a variety of specific references to civil liberties, it is the amendments that are of particular importance in this area. The basis of American civil liberties is formed primarily by the First through the Eighth Amendments; the Ninth Amendment, which holds that the specific stipulations of the first eight amendments do not constitute the entire body of civil liberties; the Thirteenth, Fourteenth, and Fifteenth Amendments (the post-Civil War amendments); and the Nineteenth Amendment, which grants women the right to vote.

For the most part, civil liberty is a *negative* concept—civil liberties entail restricting government's power to interfere with the freedom of the individual. Thus, the United States government may not interfere with religion; it may not impose prior censorship on the press; and it may not require persons to testify against themselves in court.

Beyond this basic definition of civil liberty, it is not possible to understand American civil liberties without viewing them from a historical perspective. Civil liberties in a democracy cannot be set down once and for all—they must constantly be reasserted and redefined as society changes. Consequently, this chapter arrives at no final answers; instead, it outlines fundamental questions about civil liberty and traces how they have been dealt with over time. The intention is to provide sufficient grounds for understanding the ongoing process involved in working out the inherent contradictions between the rights of the individual and the requirements of the state.

THE CONSTITUTION: A HISTORICAL DOCUMENT

When the Constitution was sent to the states for ratification, it aroused considerable public dissatisfaction and suspicion because it did not contain any specific guarantees of individual liberties. Americans had fought the Revolutionary War in order to escape from what they believed was repressive British rule, and they feared that creation of a strong federal government—particularly one that was not bound to respect individual rights—would once again make them vulnerable to government whims. (Recall from Chapter 1 that Liberalism was the dominant political philosophy of the time and that the fundamental concern of Liberalism was to free men from state repression.) In order to gain ratification of the Constitution, the founding fathers pledged to correct the omission of fundamental freedoms by adding amendments. They kept their promise, and by the end of 1791 the first ten Amendments—the Bill of Rights—had been ratified.

It must be remembered that the Bill of Rights—indeed, the entire Constitution—was written at a particular time in a particular place and therefore reflects the concerns and attitudes of that time and place. For example, the Third Amendment prohibits the government from forcing citizens to quarter soldiers in their homes—a common practice of the British Army that was greatly resented by the American colonists, but hardly a concern of citizens in the 1970s. By the same token, the conceptions of the time did not require that the right to vote be extended to women.

The conception of liberty in the Constitution is also an obvious product of the times. It is based on the classic doctrines of Liberalism and resembles the assumptions on which Adam Smith's economic theories were based: Remove the unnecessary impediments, permit the natural outpouring of political activity, and freedom will result. The prime concern is individualism—the best way to ensure equitable relations among people is to permit each person the freedom to pursue his own interests.

Thus, the conception of liberty embodied in the United States Constitution stresses individualism; it is based on the belief that the state is the most likely source of repression. In other times and other places, however, liberty has been defined very differently. Socialist conceptions of freedom, for example, stress the collective welfare and the obligations of the individual to the group; the state is viewed as the source of liberty, not its natural enemy. The difference between the two conceptions is clearly illustrated in the following excerpts of provisions of the Constitution of the Soviet Union:

Chapter X: Fundamental Rights and Duties of Citizens

Article 118. Citizens of the U.S.S.R. have the right to work, that is, the right to guaranteed employment and payment for their work in accordance with its quantity and quality.
Article 119. Citizens of the U.S.S.R. have the right to rest and leisure.
Article 120. Citizens of the U.S.S.R. have the right to maintenance in old age and also in case of sickness or disability.

The subjects that the Soviet Constitution includes in its list of "Fundamental Rights and Duties" are not subjects that Americans commonly discuss as components of their civil liberties. Americans normally consider these subjects as matters of public policy to be decided by the legislature and not as matters of basic liberty to be settled in court.

As mentioned earlier, this difference of emphasis follows from the fact that American liberty policies rest on the eighteenth-century conception of liberty as being essentially negative: If the government would only get out of my way, I would be free. The Soviet Constitution, alternatively, conceives of liberty in positive terms—freedom *to*, rather than freedom *from*—and places the burden of providing these freedoms on the government.

The negative notion of freedom in the American Bill of Rights can be nicely illustrated by comparing our First Amendment with Article 125 of the Soviet Constitution. Article 125 guarantees to the citizens of the Soviet Union (1) freedom of speech,

(2) freedom of the press, (3) freedom of assembly, including the holding of mass meetings, and (4) freedom of street processions and demonstrations. Each of these rights is also protected by America's First Amendment. The Soviet Constitution continues, however, in a manner that would have been totally alien to the framers of the American Bill of Rights: It calls for placing at the peoples' disposal the printing presses, stocks of paper, public buildings, communications facilities, and other materials needed for the exercise of these rights.

The idea that such materials must be provided by government in order to sustain freedom of speech, the press, and assembly is not to be found in the United States Constitution. The founding fathers regarded the government as the main threat to liberty, not as the benevolent provider of liberty. Therefore, American liberty policies take the form not of what the government must do to preserve liberty, but what it must not do in order that individual freedom be sustained.

CLASHES BETWEEN LIBERTY AND POLICY

The rights of the individual versus the needs of the group—the degree to which society should respect the one over the other is one of the oldest and most enduring philosophical dilemmas. Totalitarianists resolve it by granting complete priority to the group. Thus, for example, Hitler demanded that all German citizens be completely obedient to the state. At the other extreme is the anarchists' solution: Smash the state and live a life of wholly unrestricted individualism. Neither of these solutions has proved to be very attractive. Few desire to live a life strictly regimented by the government, and few desire to live in a society in which each person is at the mercy of the behavior of others. The problem that arises, therefore, is how to keep a balance between the rights of the individual and the rights of all others; put another way, the clash is between public policy that provides for the rights of each citizen versus policy that elevates the rights of all citizens considered as a group. A few historical examples illustrate how America has dealt with this problem.

Liberty and Regulation of the Economy

Early attempts by the government to influence economic activities frequently ran up against strict

Figure 7.2 The degree of liberty in a society varies in proportion to the degree of perceived external threat—the graver the external danger, the more power is concentrated in the hands of government. Ex-CIA employee and security officer for the 1972 Committee to Re-elect the President, James McCord, demonstrates for the Senate Select Committee on Campaign Financing (above) some of the electronic equipment used in bugging the telephones at the Democratic national committee headquarters in the Watergate complex (top). During the Senate hearings investigating the Watergate activities, high Administration officials admitted that a complicated plan to spy on the nation's citizens had been approved—a blatant violation of civil liberties that was deemed necessary to national security.

Court interpretations of individual liberty. In 1905, for example, the Supreme Court set aside New York State's attempt to limit the working day of bakers to ten hours (*Lochner* v. *New York,* 1905). Although New York's attempt was intended to ease the working conditions of bakers, the Court held it was an unreasonable intrusion into the rights of mature adults—bakers ought to be free to work longer hours if they choose to do so.

Similarly, the Supreme Court's bitter confrontation with the New Deal in the 1930s stemmed from the inability of the majority of Justices to surrender the notion established in 1905 that the employer-employee relationship was within the sphere of individual freedoms and was none of the government's business. Over time this view of liberty changed. Greater emphasis was given to preserving the freedom of workers from long hours, bad wages, and unsafe conditions than to preserving the liberty of property owners to follow their own dictates in these matters. By 1971 the emphasis had so changed that a Republican Administration's decision to limit both wages and prices was widely perceived as falling within the legitimate scope of governmental power.

Liberty and National Security

Nowhere do individual liberties and national needs more obviously conflict than in the area of national security. After studying many societies, sociologist Gerhard Lenski has concluded that the degree of liberty in a society varies in proportion to the degree of perceived external threat—the graver the external danger, the more power is concentrated in the hands of government (Lenski, 1966). In the United States this trade-off has been reflected in the practice of granting emergency powers to the President in times of war. Censorship of news and personal communications, rationing, restrictions on travel, and the like have all been accepted wartime restrictions on individual liberty.

Military conscription, the draft—perhaps no single feature of national security policy so intrudes on individual freedom. Even during the early days of the

Figure 7.3 Questions of civil liberties, minority rights, and national security became so intertwined as to color the entire decade of the 1960s. The struggle for minority rights and the struggle to stop a war that many judged immoral created a politics of confrontation. Masses of youths seized campuses, demonstrated at political conventions, burned symbolic objects such as the flag or draft cards, and some even immolated themselves, to protest the war. Conservative observers of the movement tried to link it to the old Communist Left or to the Anarchists of the nineteenth century; but the New Left lacked organization and membership, and such comparisons fell short of describing the floating malaise and generational rejection of the established order that had become modern political phenomena. Here (far right), incredulous "long hairs," who have been rounded up at the 1972 Republican presidential convention in Miami, are photographed for police records.

Republic, conscription was considered by many to be an unacceptable government intrusion into the private affairs of citizens. Accordingly, there has been a history of antidraft sentiment, from the riots during the Civil War and World War I to the antidraft demonstrations and draft evasions that marked the period of the Vietnam War.

Civil Liberties and Civil Rights Policies

Until the Civil War, the Supreme Court repeatedly affirmed the property rights of slave owners over the slaves' rights to liberty. Even after emancipation of the slaves during the Civil War, Congress and the courts moved only very slowly to guarantee the rights of citizenship to black Americans. Ironically, liberty policies played a role in impeding the progress toward extension of full civil rights to blacks. Open-housing laws, for instance, were opposed on the grounds that individuals have a right to dispose of their property as they wish. Similarly, the opposition to government intervention into the membership policies of private clubs and organizations, which staunchly maintain their right to choose and thus to exclude various racial and religious groups, has (successfully, thus far) been based on the premise that people *should* be free to pick their associates. Public opinion on this latter issue aptly reflects the underlying dilemma: Although most people think it is unethical for clubs to discriminate on the basis of race or religion, they also think clubs ought to be free to discriminate if they choose to do so (Selznick and Steinberg, 1969).

The Right to Privacy

As has been discussed, liberty policies change over time through interactions with other policy considerations. Sometimes, however, entirely new liberty doctrines arise in response to policy questions. For instance, neither the Constitution itself nor the Amendments explicitly refer to a citizen's right to privacy. This exclusion was a result of the life style and the technology of the time—privacy was taken for granted. At a time when the whole set of government records could be hauled from Philadelphia

to Washington in the back of two wagons, there was little reason to worry about invasion of privacy through bureaucratic record keeping. Furthermore, there were no phones to tap, no listening devices, and no science of fingerprinting. Town gossip was the only real danger to privacy, but it was a subject that was hardly worth constitutional mention.

More recently, privacy has become problematic, and liberty doctrines protecting privacy have been slowly evolving. The government maintains that national security justifies its need to eavesdrop electronically; however, it may do so only when authorized by a court. Similarly, such necessary records as individual tax returns are, by law, supposed to be kept strictly confidential.

Lately, the courts have greatly extended the scope of the doctrine of privacy. In the late 1960s, for example, the Supreme Court struck down Connecticut's laws restricting the use of birth-control devices on the grounds that such laws intruded into the area of personal privacy. On the same grounds the Court in 1973 prohibited the government from preventing abortion during the first three months of pregnancy.

As has been shown, liberty policies influence many aspects of public policy, and such policies change drastically over time. The Nixon Administration's economic policies regulating wages and prices, for instance, would have been inconceivable in 1905—the year the Supreme Court struck down New York's minimum-wage and maximum-hour legislation. Nixon's policies—indeed, all of the policies discussed—were made possible not only by virtue of court decisions but also by changes in social conditions and basic values.

FEDERAL VERSUS STATE CONTROL OF CIVIL LIBERTIES

America operates under a *federal* system—power is divided between the national and state governments. Any discussion of liberty policies must take this division into account, as must the discussion of all aspects of public policy.

Should there be one basic policy on civil liberties, or should each of the states be free to develop its own policies? This question confronted the United States Supreme Court for the first time in 1833. Speaking for the Court in the case of *Barron* v. *Baltimore,* Chief Justice John Marshall held that the Bill of Rights was meant to apply solely to the national government. He argued that it did not place restrictions on the actions of state and local governments. Differing from the national government, therefore, the states were considered free to develop their own policies on civil liberties.

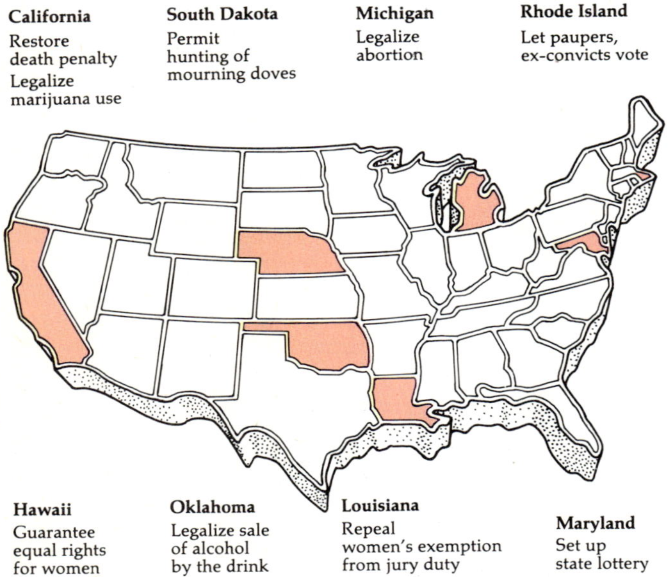

Figure 7.4 The fact that voters on most election days are faced with a large number of civil liberties issues on their statewide ballots is shown in this partial listing of ballot proposals in 1972 state elections (left).

Figure 7.5 Beginning with Gitlow v. New York in 1925, a series of Supreme Court decisions have gradually determined that, through the meaning of the "due process" clause of the Fourteenth Amendment (adopted 1868), the Bill of Rights guarantees (adopted 1791) are applicable to the legislation and to the various actions of the separate states (right). These Supreme Court decisions thus acted like a bridge, carrying to the several states the limitations that the founding fathers thought necessary to apply to the power of the central government.

The consequence of Marshall's decision was that, at least until after the Civil War, there was no systematic national policy in the area of civil liberties. The activities conventionally referred to as civil liberties were subject to control by the states rather than by the federal government.

After the Civil War the Thirteenth, Fourteenth, and Fifteenth Amendments were adopted, which abolished slavery and extended the rights of citizenship (including the vote) to the newly freed Negroes. These amendments had an even broader effect, however, in that they questioned the withdrawal of the federal government from the area of civil liberties. The Fourteenth Amendment was of particular importance to the question of state versus federal control of civil liberties policy.

The Fourteenth Amendment provides in part that "No State shall make or enforce any law which shall abridge the privileges or immunities of citizens of the United States . . ." If one were to argue that the "privileges and immunities" on which the state cannot encroach are those mentioned in the Bill of Rights, then the Fourteenth Amendment could be seen to provide the basis for a unitary national civil liberties policy, applicable to every state.

The interpretation of the *privileges and immunities* clause came before the Supreme Court in the *Slaugh-terhouse Cases* of 1873. The Court took an extremely restrictive view of the clause, ruling that it did not apply the requirements of the Bill of Rights to the states. Thus, the freedoms guaranteed by the Bill of Rights applied only to the federal government in its treatment of the individual—the states were not subject to the limitations and could continue to act independently, just as they had since the *Barron* v. *Baltimore* decision in 1833 (Robert McClosky, 1960).

It was not until 1925 that the Court began to reverse its direction. The device that it employed to apply national standards to state actions in the area of civil liberties was another clause of the Fourteenth Amendment, the *due process* clause, which stipulates that no state may deprive a person of life, liberty, or property without due process of law. In *Gitlow* v. *New York* (1925), the Supreme Court argued that "freedom of speech and of the press which are protected by the First Amendment from abridgement by Congress are among the fundamental personal rights and liberties protected by the due process clause of the Fourteenth Amendment from impairment by the states." Note that the Court did not automatically apply the entire Bill of Rights to the states; rather, it designated certain provisions of the First Amendment as so fundamental as to be *incorporated* in the Fourteenth Amendment.

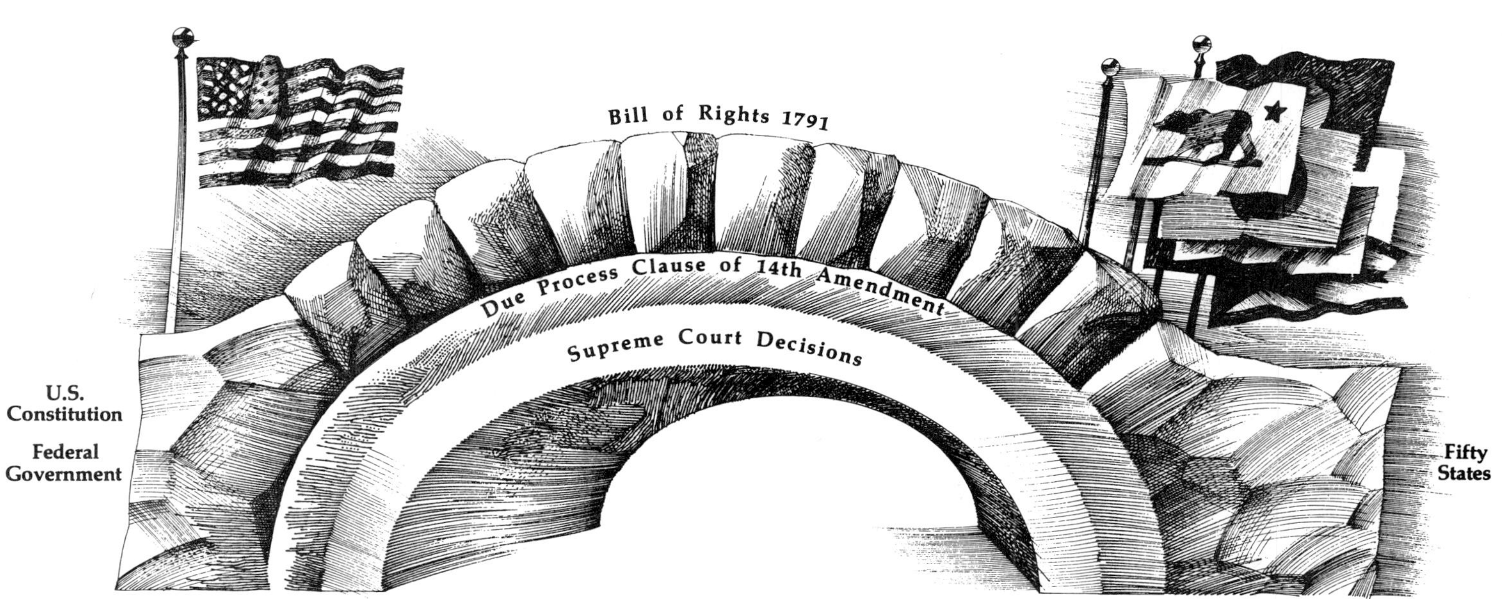

Since 1925 the Supreme Court has been gradually expanding the list of freedoms mentioned in the Bill of Rights that the states may not violate. Some Justices—most notably Hugo Black and William O. Douglas—have advocated the notion that the entire Bill of Rights should pertain to the states—the doctrine that was rejected in the *Slaughterhouse Cases.* Although this view has never been explicitly accepted by a majority of the Justices, over the years they have incorporated almost the entire Bill of Rights into the Fourteenth Amendment. As a result, proponents who favor a uniform, national standard in the area of civil liberties policy have achieved incrementally what they could not achieve all at once.

This excursion into the field of constitutional law is of more than historical importance—a significant policy choice is involved. One might want to argue that certain liberties are so basic, so fundamental, that they must be protected against interference in every corner of the country. Conversely, one might argue—as did the Supreme Court in its 1973 ruling on what constitutes obscenity—that a large, complex nation is best served by permitting the development of standards and policies at the local level. Should the content of the concept "pornography" be identical in New York City and in rural Arkansas, or should it mean one thing in New York, given its norms, mores, and values, and something quite different in a different area? (In the words of one state judge: "I don't care what they do in Las Vegas. We don't have to tolerate topless shoeshine girls in Rutland, Vermont.")

PUBLIC OPINION AND CIVIL LIBERTIES

In principle, the public supports such liberty policies as free speech, freedom of assembly, and freedom of the press. In reality, however, most people support such freedoms only when they are used to express conventional views. Most people, for example, reject the notion of free speech for Communists or atheists (Selznick and Steinberg, 1969), they resent protest meetings and demonstrations for peace or civil rights, and they favor censorship of movies and books in order to remove sexual material (Gallup, 1972). For the most part, it has been the courts, not the public, that have upheld the right of citizens to express unpopular views.

AMERICAN CIVIL LIBERTIES UNION

The ACLU was created in January 1920 in response to the frequent violations and the generally haphazard observation of the Bill of Rights. During and immediately following World War I, government violations of citizens' basic civil liberties reached an all-time high. The government launched prosecutions against the authors of 1,900 speeches and publications, particularly those voicing opposition to the war. Citizens were thrown in jail for expressing unpopular views—even for criticizing the Red Cross. Thousands of suspected aliens were arrested, and one thousand were deported.

In answer to the frightening apathy of Americans toward these gross violations of civil liberties, a group of fifty citizens created the American Civil Liberties Union as a permanent, national, nonpartisan organization with the single purpose of defending the rights of every citizen to the protections of the Bill of Rights. This original group included such famous people as Jane Addams, Clarence Darrow, Eugene Debs, John Dewey, and Felix Frankfurter.

Because the civil liberties of unpopular groups are the first to be violated—for example, labor organizers in the 1920s, Japanese-Americans in the 1940s, Communists in the 1950s, and civil rights and antiwar demonstrators in the 1960s—the ACLU has been identified with liberal causes. Yet the civil rights of all groups of citizens need protection. Thus the ACLU has defended antiunion employers, an anticommunist picketer arrested during Khrushchev's United States visit, as well as many others. The central philosophical position of the ACLU is to defend civil liberties—even for causes that might be considered disagreeable, irresponsible, or hateful— in the belief that everyone's constitutional rights must be upheld.

Figure 7.6 A child waits to be transported to a detention camp for Japanese-Americans during World War II. Following the war, many families returned from the camps only to find that their homes and businesses had been sold. A memorial service, held in 1972 at Manzanar, California before the gravestones of those who had died in the camp, suggested that the disgrace—engendered by prejudice—had not been forgotten. There have been recurring periods in United States history—particularly in times of war or economic dislocation—when the civil liberties of American citizens have been dissolved by the pressures of national security and personal interest.

The courts, however, have not always been willing to uphold liberty policies, especially when public feeling has been intense and another branch of government has been involved. An example of this reluctance occurred in 1942 when one of the most blatant violations of civil liberties in American history occurred—the government rounded up citizens, seized their property, and took them away to detention centers.

On March 27, 1942, General John L. DeWitt issued an order that led to the internment of 112,000 Japanese-Americans in detention centers, which were later called "concentration camps" by one Supreme Court Justice. Who was responsible for this policy? What does the policy indicate about the comparative significance of different institutions with respect to liberty policies?

While the army carried out the internment, it received the active support of the civilian political leadership: The President authorized General DeWitt's order; Congress upheld it by allocating the necessary funds for the relocation centers; and the Supreme Court ratified the entire proceeding. Perhaps most significant of all, however, was the state of public opinion at the time: The internment was possible because of the profound hostility many Americans felt toward the Japanese-Americans. This hostility had been evident in a history of anti-Oriental movements that included lynchings, anti-Chinese mob violence, second-class citizenship for Orientals, and restrictions on Oriental immigration. The Japanese attack on Pearl Harbor in 1941 simply heightened the anti-Japanese feeling that was already widespread.

It would be incorrect to conclude from the case of the Japanese-Americans that political institutions function only to mirror the feelings of the public (see Chapter 6 for a discussion of the role played by the Supreme Court in the area of civil rights). Clearly, however, there are limits to how far out of step with the public mood the political and judicial leadership can be and still hope to be effective.

AN INITIAL ANALYSIS: FREEDOM OF SPEECH

Should an admitted Communist be permitted to make a speech in your community? Presumably many readers would respond affirmatively, quite independently of their views on the merits of communism. Should a television newsman be permitted to call your mother a prostitute, a vicious lie, motivated by personal pique? Perhaps those who answered that a Communist should be allowed to give a speech would have some doubts about whether a newsman should be able to make this verbal attack on someone's mother.

Why are these two cases different? Why should the one kind of speech be protected as a civil liberty and not the other? To answer these questions, one must look beyond the specific implications of free speech to the more basic question: How should one go about discussing a civil liberties issue? The following is a mode of analysis designed to help the reader solve this basic problem. Although the particular illustrations employed in this discussion might already be old hat, the method of analysis will not—the kinds of questions asked here are appropriate questions to be asked about any aspect of civil liberty.

What Is Speech?

A necessary first step in examining any civil liberty is defining the pertinent terms. In an attempt to justify a policy providing freedom of speech, therefore, it must first be clear exactly what the word "speech" means. Does picketing constitute speech? What about silent demonstrations—are they speech acts? What of gestures? Gestures made with the middle finger—are they to be classified as "symbolic" speech acts? Is sound, not in the form of words, speech, or does speech imply the attempt to communicate? (See □)

Clearly, one cannot justify a policy of freedom of speech, or of any other alleged liberty, until the act that is to be free is defined with some degree of precision.

What Is "Freedom" of Speech?

Once one identifies the acts that constitute speech, the next task is to give content to the concept of "freedom" as it pertains to speech. A person is free to say whatever he wants in the middle of the woods when no one can hear him, and he is free to say what his neighbors enjoy hearing. These kinds of situations, however, are not what a person usually has in mind when speaking of freedom of speech.

Figure 7.7 The force of social conformity often militates against the spontaneous expression of our thoughts (right). Although the government has the power to deal with obvious and direct examples of the chilling of free speech, the everyday gag of thinking twice before we make an unpopular statement is beyond the reach of governmental remedy. Parents, friends, and the general milieu of opinion breathe down on us with enormous pressure, as Alexis de Tocqueville observed, to ensure an atmosphere of conformity to community standards.

Figure 7.8 There are times when exposure to public pressure leads persons to confront conformity with their own ideas (below). It helps, of course, to be in the top-winner circle and to have the assured approval of a strong reference group in support—in this case, the black minority of America. This spectacular incident of the giving of the black power salute during the playing of the national anthem at the 1968 Olympic awards raised much controversy. The two black athletes were the object of many "letters to the editor" and criticism directed toward their ideology and the appropriateness of their action.

SYMBOLIC SPEECH

Through the years, the Supreme Court has been reluctant to extend the doctrine of freedom of speech to include gestures and other symbolic acts. In decisions regarding the right to picket, for example, the Court has ruled that the speech aspect of picketing is protected under the First Amendment, but the conduct aspect is much less so. Therefore, the Court held in 1968 that "because of this intermingling of protected and unprotected elements, picketing can be subjected to controls that would not be constitutionally permissible in the case of pure speech." (Amalgamated Food Employees Local 590 v. Logan Valley Plaza, Inc)

Other forms of symbolic conduct are protected even less. For example, four young men were convicted in 1966 for burning their draft cards. They appealed to the Supreme Court on the grounds that burning their cards was "symbolic speech," or "communication of ideas by conduct," and was therefore protected under the First Amendment. With a vote of 7–1 the Justices rejected the plea because they felt they could not accept a principle under which an "apparently limitless variety of conduct can be labelled 'speech' whenever the person engaging in the conduct intends thereby to express an idea." (United States v. O'Brien)

One idea concerning free speech that has considerable historical support is that all speech acts (however defined) should be free from prior restraints. The British common law, for example, stipulated that ideas would not be censored *prior* to their publication; however, after a work was published an author could be punished for expressing "bad sentiments." Although this idea was probably current in America when the Bill of Rights was written (Leonard Levy, 1970), many people would now reject it as being much too narrow a definition, for it is recognized that the fear of subsequent punishment may have what the Supreme Court has called a "chilling effect" on liberty. Is the source of the "chill," however, of significance? If Soviet Jews refrained from speaking openly of their attitudes toward Israel for fear of being imprisoned, most would agree that freedom was being denied. Would freedom of speech still be at issue if they refrained from speaking out because they would be barred from entering the university, or would be denied travel permits, or would lose their jobs?

The concept of freedom is troublesome from still another point of view. Should one speak of free speech in a society in which certain thoughts are never expressed because they are beyond the accepted realm of discussion? It is naïve to assume that the most effective restraint on freedom of speech is the fear of a secret agent under the bed. As Alexis de Tocqueville argued, it is possible that conformity could pose a greater threat to freedom than the censor (see Chapter 1). Perhaps a modern definition of freedom must encompass this case as well.

Free Speech—Why?

It is essential that those who support freedom of speech (or any policy) attempt to identify as explicitly as possible the considerations that led them to advocate the policy. As Justice Holmes wrote: "It is one of the misfortunes of the law that ideas become encysted in phrases and thereafter for a long time cease to provoke further analysis" (*Hyde* v. *United States*, 1912).

One basic justification of freedom of speech (and the press) is derived from the works of John Stuart Mill and John Milton. In their view, freedom of speech is essential if mankind is to advance intellectually—the competition of ideas is a necessary condition of progress. Even if an unpopular view turns out to be entirely incorrect, it should still be tolerated because the challenge of the false view will force the holders of truth to examine their position—to flex their intellectual muscles, as it were.

A different basis for defining policy in this area is provided by Professor Alexander Meiklejohn. Free speech, he argues, is necessary once it is decided that people are to govern themselves; that is, free speech is a derivative right following from the prior commitment to self-government. If the people are to choose their rulers, they need free access to information so that they can make intelligent, informed choices (Meiklejohn, 1965).

The difference between these two positions is easily demonstrated by citing hypothetical cases. Should a Communist be permitted to make a speech? Mill and Milton would say yes, for perhaps the doctrines of communism are true, or at least partially true, in which case human progress requires that they be made known. Meiklejohn would argue that the Communist has an absolute right to speak because communism is a possible form of government, and a free nation must be able to consider its alternatives.

What about the television newsman who wishes to falsely brand your mother as a woman of ill repute? Once again, different justifications for a given civil liberty will lead to different policies. The Mill-Milton position, at least in its extreme form, would tell mother to rely on truth's ability to defeat falsehood. If mother's virtue is besmirched, she can carry a sign saying "I'm not, either." Presumably people will recognize the truth.

Meiklejohn would have no such problem, because he distinguishes between political speech (speech that is related to self-government) and nonpolitical speech. The former is protected absolutely; the latter is also protected, but it is not an absolute right. Thus, Meiklejohn could quite consistently support free speech for the Communist and permit the silencing, or subsequent punishment, of the slanderer, the man who commits fraud, the man who falsely shouts fire in a crowded theater or other public place, and so on.

The Supreme Court has largely supported Meiklejohn's approach, as seen in the fact that it is much more difficult for a person in the political sphere to recover damages for libel or slander than it is for private citizens—if mother's virtue is attacked, she can obtain compensation much more readily than can the President of the United States. If one's basic justification for free speech rests on its contribution to self-government, it is clear that public policy re-

quires greater freedom of discussion concerning the alleged vices of the President than those of mother.

Free Speech—How Much?

Once speech and freedom of speech are defined, and once basic rationales are identified, another difficult question must be confronted: Should there be any limits on the exercises of this right? If so, what should they be, and who is to decide?

Three basic ways of answering these questions can be identified. At one end of the spectrum is the *absolutist* position, held by Justice Black: When the Constitution says "Congress shall make no law . . . abridging the freedom of speech," it literally means *no law* (Black, 1960). This position identifies freedom of speech as being so basic a right as to be without limitation.

An alternative conception is the one most consistently followed by the Supreme Court—the *balancing* approach. According to this position, free speech is important, but in specific cases it must be balanced against other, competing values, such as national defense, stability and order, or privacy. Inherent to this approach, however, is the problem of deciding how one should go about weighing the speech act against the competing claim. The case of *Schenck* v. *United States* (1919) provided one solu-

tion—the "clear and present danger" test. During World War I, Charles Schenck, who was General Secretary of the Socialist Party at the time, had distributed pamphlets urging young men to resist the draft. Justice Holmes, in speaking for the Court about the case, stated:

The character of every act depends upon the circumstances in which it is done. . . . The question in every case is whether the words used are in such circumstances and are of such a nature as to create a clear and present danger that they will bring about the substantive evils that Congress has a right to prevent. . . . When a nation is at war many things that might be said in time of peace are such a hindrance to its effort that their utterance will not be endured. (*Schenck* v. *United States,* 1919)

In the Court's view, Schenck's actions demonstrated a "clear and present danger" of a threat to national security; therefore, Schenck's speech could be silenced.

A third position that has found some favor with Supreme Court Justices is the doctrine of *preferred position.* According to this approach there are occasions when the claims of freedom of speech must yield to competing interests; there is, however, an overwhelming tendency to protect speech. For instance, an act of the legislature is usually presumed to be constitutional until someone who challenges

Figure 7.9 In Schenck v. United States (1919) Justice Oliver Wendell Holmes said, "The most stringent protection of free speech would not protect a man in falsely shouting fire in a theater and causing a panic." Thus freedom of speech was balanced against public safety. But how long should a person keep quiet to make sure there really is a fire? The "shouting fire" criterion is used generally to refer to speech against social ills that may be evident to some but not to all.

Figure 7.10 In their quest to eradicate a perceived Communist "conspiracy" in the early 1950s, Senator Joseph McCarthy (R.-Wis.) and his chief staff aide, Roy Cohn, created a nationwide hysteria that had a chilling effect on free speech in the nation. Persons in and out of government who disagreed with Cold War attitudes and the strategy of containment felt the effects of McCarthy's subcommittee investigations and thought twice before uttering a dissenting note. The fear of "communists" continued well into the 1960s and provoked heated debate over whether a member of the Communist Party should be allowed to speak on college campuses and whether teachers and government employees should be required to sign loyalty oaths to prove their patriotism.

it proves otherwise. Proponents of the doctrine of preferred position, however, assert that an act of the legislature that is said to violate the First Amendment is presumed to be unconstitutional, and the burden of proof rests on those who would support it.

The doctrine of preferred position was asserted by the Supreme Court during the 1940s in cases setting aside attempts by state governments and local police departments to suppress unpopular groups, particularly the Jehovah's Witnesses (a religious group). In recent years the Court has, in effect, employed the doctrine of preferred position in cases involving the civil rights of blacks: Laws that have the effect of limiting the freedom of racial minorities are now inherently suspect—they are presumed invalid until it is shown otherwise (*N.A.A.C.P.* v. *Button*, 1963).

Free Speech: An Analysis

Liberty policies raise questions about which many citizens feel quite strongly. For this reason, discussions about liberty policies frequently suffer from the mixing of *normative* and *empirical* concerns. Perhaps it is only human to assume that things are the way they should be—but it is very poor scholarship. Clearly, discussions of liberty policies (and all other aspects of politics) that confuse the "is" with the "ought to be" will be less than satisfactory.

One of the causes of this confusion is the fascination that courts and things legal hold for many Americans. In a discussion of freedom of speech or other civil liberties issues, people quickly turn to leading decisions of the Supreme Court. To be sure, the Court's rulings are one of the determinants of America's liberty policies. But they are only one among many. To assume that the actual status of freedom of speech in Providence, Rhode Island, Jackson, Mississippi, and Keokuk, Iowa, is equivalent to the Supreme Court's most recent decision is absurd. A person will not discover what the local police chief really says to the local book seller by consulting Supreme Court tomes.

It is also imperative to resist the temptation to generalize from one's own limited experiences. If a student wants to know whether Communists are *in fact* free to make speeches throughout America, he would be extremely ill-advised to ask half-a-dozen college students whether they would permit a Communist to speak—a college campus is in no sense a microcosm of the whole nation. There are systematic, rigorous ways to measure attitudes and behavior that must be used to obtain the answer.

A SECOND ANALYSIS: RELIGION AND CONSCIENCE

As has been stated, liberty policies in general involve the conflict between the claims of the indi-

Figure 7.11 The notion of amnesty for draft evaders or deserters has always been controversial (right). In the period of passions inflamed by war and its aftermath, citizens are likely to be critical of Administrations that are lenient toward those who have chosen not to serve their country in war. Nevertheless, after each war the issue of amnesty necessarily arises, and different Administrations, as can be seen here, have coped with it in different ways. Following the Vietnam War, many American youth remained in Europe and Canada; a small percentage of them chose to give up their American citizenship to become immigrants to new lands. But the large majority preferred to await the declaration of a policy of leniency and understanding of their claims of conscientious objection toward the nation's involvement in Indochina.

vidual and those of the group. One area that has frequently been involved in such conflicts is religion. The question of the rights of the religious was sufficiently important to the authors of the Bill of Rights to be incorporated into the First Amendment in two respects: "Congress shall make no law respecting an *establishment* of religion, or prohibiting the *free exercise* thereof . . ." [italics added].

In that established, institutionalized religions have now lost much of their attraction, one might wonder whether the *establishment* and *free exercise* clauses should be viewed in the same way that the prohibition against the quartering of soldiers is viewed—as products of a particular time and place and therefore no longer relevant. If one reads "conscience" where the Constitution reads "religion," however, the pertinence of these two clauses to contemporary liberty policies becomes apparent.

John Doe receives a draft notice and refuses to go. "A guy could get killed over there," he announces. "I have better ways to spend my time. Who needs it?" Richard Roe receives a draft notice to fight in the same war. He also refuses to go. "I am a Quaker," he announces. "My conscience won't permit me to go."

How should a free society react to these two claims? In America, Richard's claim would probably be respected, and John's would be rejected, because only religious conscientious objectors are excused from military service; persons whose only objection is that they do not want to die are not exempt. Why should this be so?

The answer, of course, is that Americans tend to assume that religious freedom must be respected. However, simply invoking a sacred concept—in this case, freedom of religion and religious conscience—is not an acceptable way of analyzing civil liberties. The questions that must be answered concerning America's policy on religion are similar to those that were asked about freedom of speech. To justify a policy that grants freedom of religion, one must be prepared to: (1) define religion, (2) define freedom of religion, (3) provide reasons for policies based on these definitions, and (4) consider whether limitations can be imposed.

What Is "Religion" (or "Conscience")?

If an individual wants to advocate some form of freedom of religion, he must be prepared to define "religion" and to differentiate "religious beliefs" from other forms of belief. The Quakers are clearly a religion. Is the Communist Party? Can a person have a private religion, or must he join with others in an organization? Does there have to be a "creed"? Clearly, there are many religions that do not require commitment to a creed. Should every belief pattern be considered a religion?

AMNESTY IN U.S. HISTORY

WAR OF 1812

During the war, President Madison gave full pardon on several occasions to deserters who surrendered within four months.

CIVIL WAR

President Lincoln offered full pardons to Union military deserters who returned to their units within sixty days and served out a period equal to the original term of their enlistment.

President Johnson granted full pardon to almost all Confederate soldiers who took an unqualified oath of allegiance to the U. S. Later proclamations broadened the amnesty until, on December 25, 1868, President Johnson granted a full and unconditional amnesty to practically all Confederates.

President Johnson allowed all Union deserters who surrendered by August 15, 1866 to return to military duty, without punishment but with forfeiture of pay.

WORLD WAR I

President Coolidge granted amnesty to about 100 men who had deserted their units after the November 11, 1918 armistice. No amnesty for thousands of wartime deserters or draft evaders.

President Roosevelt, fifteen years after end of the war, pardoned about 1,500 violators of the Espionage Act and draft laws who had completed their sentences. This restored voting and other civil rights usually denied ex-convicts.

WORLD WAR II

President Truman, twenty three months after war's end, pardoned 1,523 out of 15,803 draft evaders in line with recommendations of his Amnesty Board. No amnesty for deserters.

KOREAN WAR

No amnesty of any kind after the Korean War for wartime deserters or draft dodgers. President Truman had given a 1952 Christmas amnesty to those who had deserted their units in peacetime years between the end of World War II and the start of the Korean War in June 1950.

Similarly, what constitutes an act of conscience? Is "conscience" different from "something I really feel like"? When white parents spit at black school children in an attempt to keep them from entering a public school, do the passions motivating these adults fall under the category of conscience? If people wearing clerical collars and waving burning crosses participate, are the actions then motivated by religious beliefs?

What Is "Freedom" of Religion?

The authors of the Constitution were familiar with attempts to punish individuals because of their religious beliefs and affiliations. In the famous Virginia Bill for Religious Liberty, Thomas Jefferson argued against religious discrimination by asserting that religious beliefs should lead to neither the enhancement nor the diminution of one's civil rights; that is, a person's religion should not affect his civil status.

A different, more positive conception of freedom of religion holds that (1) the religious believer is exempt from some obligation that is imposed on all citizens, or (2) he is granted certain benefits or privileges that are not generally available. The exemption from military service granted to religious conscientious objectors is an example of the first condition. The second is illustrated by the Supreme Court's decision that the state of South Carolina could withhold unemployment compensation from persons who refused to accept available employment but that it could not deny such support to a Seventh-Day Adventist who had refused to take a job that would have required her to work on Saturday, her Sabbath (*Sherbert* v. *Verner*, 1963). In other words, if Mrs. Thomas refuses to work on Saturday because she likes a two-day weekend, she has no right to unemployment compensation. However, if Mrs. Smith refuses to work on Saturday because it is against her religion, the state is required to honor her choice and, if no other employment is available, to provide unemployment compensation.

Similarly, if freedom of conscience becomes a distinct concern of liberty policy, respect for an individual's conscience might mean that he would not be punished for his views. Alternatively, he might be entitled to special privileges or exemptions because of his conscientious views.

Freedom of Religion—Why?

Given the times in which they lived, it is not surprising that "religious interests seemed to the Framers to deserve special safeguarding" (Mark Howe, 1965). Religion in the 1780s was felt to be worthy of protection because of its intrinsic merits. A contemporary policy of freedom of religion might be based on similar assumptions—because religions introduce desired elements into the body politic, their status should be constitutionally protected. The same argument might be extended to consciences in general: "Good things" happen when people follow their consciences; therefore, freedom of conscientious belief is desirable. Note that this claim is expressed in empirical rather than normative language—its proponents are therefore obliged to demonstrate that it is in fact the case. They are also obliged to respond to the numerous examples of horrible things that have been done in the name of religion and conscience. Human sacrifice, the Crusades, and the apartheid policy practiced in the Republic of South Africa are examples that come quickly to mind.

A second justification for freedom of religion concerns the intensity of religious beliefs: If religious and conscientious beliefs are those that motivate people very strongly, it is both humane and politic to respect such convictions. According to this approach, if the group adopts a policy to which it only mildly subscribes, but some members dissent vehemently, the group should respect the courage of the dissenters' convictions.

Although this is probably a prudent maxim to be followed in those cases where the majority does not care much one way or the other, it skirts the really difficult questions—it is precisely when the majority cares a great deal that the claim of the religious or conscientious objector becomes significant. For example, the Jehovah's Witnesses' claim that freedom of religion means that they must be excused from saluting the flag is interesting only when someone cares enough to try to compel them to salute (Robert Dahl, 1956).

Freedom of Religion—How Much?

Policy regarding the extent to which minority views should be heeded might rest on an assessment of the impact of coercion on a given individual. For example, seeing-eye dogs are permitted to enter various establishments that are normally closed to pets. This distinction rests on the recognition that the hardship imposed on a blind person if his dog is excluded is qualitatively different from the hardship imposed on a devoted master whose prize pet is barred. Similarly, it might be argued that to force a Seventh-Day Adventist to choose between his Sabbath observance and unemployment compensation is qualitatively different from forcing his neighbor to choose between unemployment compensation and going fishing or taking it easy. In other words, if religious or conscientious beliefs are defined as those that an individual regards as being absolutely central to his way of life, such beliefs should not be tampered with lightly. Just as it is cruel to the blind person to force him to give up his dog unnecessarily, so too is it cruel to force the believer to violate what he views as the ultimate commands of his religion or conscience unless it is absolutely necessary.

In 1802 President Jefferson wrote that the First Amendment's freedom of religion clause was meant to provide "a wall of separation between Church and State." A major focus of the ongoing debate over how wide the "wall of separation" should be is the *establishment* clause of the First Amendment: "Congress shall make no law respecting an establishment of religion . . ." It was on the basis of the *establishment* clause that the Supreme Court banned prayers in public schools, and it is the *establishment* clause that has formed the bulwark of the opposition to various forms of state aid to parochial schools.

Contemporary social scientists have demonstrated empirically what classical political philosophers, such as Plato and Aristotle, asserted centuries ago: Legal order rests on an underlying consensus of basic values. If this proposition is correct, it is important to know whose job it is—if, indeed, it is anyone's job—to provide this consensus. Traditionally, Americans have felt that it is not a legitimate governmental function. Indeed, the "wall of separation" argument rests on precisely this premise: Government should be excluded from the realm of religion—the realm of ethical and normative concerns.

Some claim that it has been possible to leave ethical and normative concerns in the private sphere only because, in fact, there has been widespread agreement on basic moral principles. Events in the 1960s and early 1970s, however, suggest that this consensus is breaking down. Should government passively sit by? Should the state sit on its side of the wall and remain indifferent to the decline of religion and religious values?

Political liberals and, at least to date, the Justices of the Supreme Court have rejected the idea that the government should intervene in religious matters. It might be worthwhile, however, for them to consider the following case. It is widely agreed, and the Kerner Commission has demonstrated, that America is experiencing a severe polarization of blacks and whites. So far, the government has undertaken extensive action in the area of race relations through the legal order (witness civil rights statutes of various types), but it has attempted to steer clear of the *values* involved. Must government remain indifferent to the underlying value choices of whites and blacks, or should it use all the means at its disposal to promote basic agreement on the ethical value of racial harmony and mutual respect? Should the public schools, for example, teach children to love all men regardless of skin color?

Obviously, the government cannot remain indifferent to the disintegration of the political culture that binds black and white Americans together, but it is not at all clear how the government's role should be defined. Although many parents may be happy to have the schools teach their children to love their neighbors regardless of race, the same parents might be much less happy to have the schools teach their children to love Jesus.

Traditionally, political liberals have found it so difficult to define the exact role of government that they have opted for its complete exclusion from the area of morality. This exclusion of government from the field of morality is the basic policy implication of the *establishment* clause; it is an implication far more fundamental than momentary concern with aid to religious schools or any other specific issue—it is a policy choice that requires careful consideration and evaluation.

PROBLEM AREAS: OTHER FIRST AMENDMENT ISSUES

The specific problems that confront the nation in the area of civil liberties are continually changing. The issues of freedom of speech and religion were discussed in considerable depth so as to suggest an approach that is appropriate to the formulation of public policy on any aspect of civil liberty. The following sections are designed to direct attention to a broad spectrum of problem areas. The most difficult task of arriving at possible solutions rests with the reader.

The Right to Privacy

As stated earlier, an idea whose time has arrived is that of the right to individual privacy. One interesting aspect of this concept is the clash between the individual's right to be left alone and the public's right to be informed. To take an absurd case: If the *New York Times* obtained a full-length picture of the President of the United States taking a shower, would it be justified in printing it? What about the First Lady? At what point may a citizen, a businessman, or a public official say to the press: "Go away, I simply don't care to be bothered. I have a right to private actions"?

In a world marked by increasingly sophisticated means of snooping and data collecting, the theory regarding the right to privacy is still at a very primitive stage. Clearly, the development of such a theory requires careful consideration of the conflict between the claims of privacy and those of a free press.

Freedom of the Electronic Media

Whatever the founding fathers thought about a free press, they obviously could not have thought very much one way or the other about radio and television. Are the electronic mass media to be discussed in the same terms as newspapers, books, and handbills? Three important considerations appear to suggest that such analogies are not fully appropriate.

Technological Constraints and Censorship

In a society in which anyone who wants to stand on a street corner and hand out literature is believed to have a right to do so, no one worries very much about not having enough corners to go around. However, it is simply impossible to permit people to send radio signals into the air under any circumstances of their own choosing—if two different broadcasters were to simultaneously occupy the same space on the dial, the resultant signal would be unintelligible. For this reason, the federal government regulates the allocation of space on the airwaves through the FCC. It is technologically impossible to have radio and TV broadcasts without such regulation. This government regulation immediately sets radio and TV apart from the printed media.

If only a limited number of radio and TV stations can operate in a given locality, on what basis should they be allocated? To some extent, the government can employ criteria of technical competence: "Will you build an adequate transmitter?" "Are your engineers certified?" But should the government award TV and radio stations on the basis of the content of the material they broadcast? Should the FCC revoke licenses if it does not approve of the programing?

Imagine a case in which there could be only one additional TV station. One candidate for the position proposes to model his program after *Time* magazine. The other proposes a *Playboy* type of program. In deciding whether the *Time* magazine program or the *Playboy* program is to be broadcast, should the government be indifferent to the contents of the two, or should it decide which one is more "in the public interest"?

One important example of this problem is the case of radio stations in the South, which, it is alleged, systematically discriminate against blacks in their news broadcasts and programing. Should the members of the FCC refuse to renew the licenses of these stations? If so, should they refuse to renew the licenses of stations that play hard rock or other forms of music they do not personally find appealing and license stations that play "good music" instead?

Freedom to Choose

Discussions of the printed page frequently are concerned with the concept of individual choice: "If I, as a mature adult, wish to 'pollute' my mind in the privacy of my own home, that is my personal affair." Even those who advocate total freedom to print and read, however, might well grant the distinction between a magazine and a billboard. If the centerfold of *Playboy* were spread aloft alongside a major highway, those who prefer not to see such things would in fact have little or no choice.

Is it more appropriate to think of television and radio in terms of magazines or in terms of billboards? That is, if network television broadcasts the centerfold of *Playboy* into the living rooms of America, is it reasonable to speak in terms of individual decisions by individual citizens to look at it? The basic policy question appears to be whether the individual's ability to turn the dial is truly comparable to the individual's ability to decide whether he wishes to read books by Communist authors.

The Impact of Electronic Media

Candidates for public office spend a tremendous portion of their advertising budgets on television time and a miniscule portion on the printed word. Why? Because they assume that the impact of the electronic media is considerably greater than that of the printed page. Does this difference in impact affect liberty policy?

The justification of a free press associated with Mill and Milton asserts that open, honest competition between conflicting ideas will result in the emergence of truth. This notion requires that all ideas be able to compete equally. But just as the free market in the realm of economics breaks down when one considers a local merchant "competing" with A & P, I. B. M., or General Motors, so too is the notion of a free marketplace in the realm of ideas grossly distorted by the introduction of the electronic media. How many pamphlets are required to effectively combat half an hour of prime television time? If mother is denounced as a prostitute in the living rooms of 50 million Americans on the network news, is it ever possible to cleanse her good name? In sum, given the tremendous impact of television and radio, should competition from essentially private sources be relied on to preclude abuses? If not, is some form of regulation—censorship—required?

The equal-time doctrine employed by the FCC indicates the problem. If TV networks make time available to one candidate for public office, they are required to make time available to all competing candidates on a comparable basis. Newspapers, however, operate under no such restraints. If a newspaper prints a distorted account of, for example, the behavior of the police during a race riot, it is unlikely that much more than the historical record is at issue. But if a television or radio station sends a distorted interpretation of that same race riot into the homes of millions of citizens, it can have a major impact on the course of the riot. With these considerations in mind, the question can again be asked: Is it useful to conceive of liberty policies relating to the electronic media in terms of the categories developed in relation to pamphlets, manifestoes, or even books?

Government Regulation as a Civil Liberties Issue

Americans now routinely accept the fact that the government is able to require manufacturers to recall defective products; consumer groups advocate federal labeling standards; and a warning from the Surgeon General is placed—as a matter of law—on cigarette packages and advertisements. These examples all illustrate the expanded regulatory role undertaken by the United States government. It is important to note that basic liberty issues are involved in the realm of government regulation.

Ford Motor Company does not wish to recall a car—the government forces it to do so. Have Ford's liberties been infringed? How is this different from forcing an editor to "recall" an article? The Surgeon General forces unwilling cigarette companies to print his warning on their product. Is this different from the censor's attempt to attach his views to literary works?

What about governmental attempts to regulate the "ugly" and the "repulsive"? Ecological controls meant to "clean up" a river are often based on standards of beauty, as are many zoning codes. Communities can prohibit the construction of buildings that would destroy the historic character of a neighborhood, and landlords are often coerced to maintain the exterior of their property, even though it poses no threat to health or safety.

If it is legitimate for a society to control "visual pollution" defined in terms of rivers and buildings, is it equally appropriate for a society to control visual pollution as defined by some people in terms of long hair, interracial couples, and dress styles? If John Q. Citizen is not allowed to throw litter on the highway because dirty roads are unsightly, is society equally entitled to prevent John Q. Citizen from wearing his hair in a pony tail if people find it equally unsightly?

A complex, industrial society requires detailed governmental regulation of entire segments of life that previously went unregulated (television regulation is a case in point). Liberty policies will have to be developed to extend into these areas, areas that were literally inconceivable to the authors of the First Amendment. Surely, pollution is a more significant problem in the twentieth century than is the quartering of soldiers. It is hardly sufficient to speak of the quartering of soldiers as a civil liberties issue because it happens to be included in the Bill of Rights and to exclude pollution simply because it is not.

PROBLEM AREA: DUE PROCESS—CIVIL RIGHTS AND CRIMINAL LAW

Criminal law represents a very special form of encounter between the individual and the group. When an individual is believed to have violated the state's norms, he stands accused by a representative of the collectivity and is judged by a public official who is on the state's payroll. In a sense, a criminal trial is a routinized fight between the individual and organized society.

"Due process of law" refers to procedures that are meant to guarantee that the accused will be treated fairly in his dealings with the court. The notion that the accused is presumed innocent until proven guilty requires that the collectivity, as represented by the court, be unable to win by virtue of sheer weight of numbers or by an imbalance of resources. Due process is meant to ensure that the outcome of *any* given trial is not influenced by the fact that one of the parties is clothed in the mantle of public authority.

Warren Court Decisions

During the tenure of Chief Justice Earl Warren, the Supreme Court devoted considerable attention to the rules under which legal confrontations between the individual and the state should be conducted. Cases that stirred up major public controversy during the Warren Court expanded the right to counsel (*Gideon* v. *Wainwright*, 1963); broadened the protection against self-incrimination (*Miranda* v. *Arizona*, 1966); extended to the states the rule that excludes improperly seized evidence from being admitted in a trial (*Mapp* v. *Ohio*, 1961); ruled that unfair pre-trial publicity could lead to the overturning of a conviction (*Sheppard* v. *Maxwell*, 1966); and, at least to some extent, required that due process standards be applied in juvenile courts (*In re Gault*, 1967).

Rulings in all of these cases marked a basic shift in policy: Areas previously left to the judgment of the individual states were now held to be subject to uniform national standards. Under the Warren Court, "virtually all of the procedural guarantees of the Bill of Rights were incorporated into the Fourteenth Amendment" (Alpheus Mason and William Beaney, 1972).

The Warren Court's detailed rules, which were meant to guarantee a fair trial, were based on the Fifth through Eighth Amendments. These amendments deal with such matters as trial by jury; the right to counsel; the right to confront witnesses; the prohibition of excessive bail, excessive fines, and cruel and unusual punishments; and the general guarantee of "due process of law." Two basic purposes underlie these provisions. First, they guard against the abuse of public power. Judges, policemen, jailers, and other public officials have awesome powers. The procedural restraints imposed on them are meant to limit the extent to which their individual prejudices, predilections, and biases can come into play. Second, these amendments ensure that trials will be effective means of arriving at the truth— only the guilty should be punished. The absence of counsel, a coerced confession, or a prejudiced jury are likely to result in a miscarriage of justice.

Effectiveness of Due Process Rules

The expansion of the rules pertaining to criminal trials led to significant protest from "law and order" circles. The Court was said to be "soft on criminals"; it had "handcuffed the police." Yet at precisely the same time, the court came under the attack of critics from the left. Books with such titles as *Law Against the People* and *With Justice for Some* argued that the courts were in fact part of a repressive social order.

It is important to recognize that the critics of the right and the critics of the left directed their fire at different targets and that they were, in a sense, speaking past each other. The "law and order" critics were concerned that the new rules would give a free rein to criminals. The critics of the left claimed the rules did not adequately describe reality and that in actual practice—in local courts, prisons, jury rooms, and the back rooms of police stations—the poor were still systematically discriminated against.

The critics of the left largely based their arguments on the fact that the overwhelming majority of criminal convictions do not result from trials; the guilty plea is the basic method by which criminal prosecutions are disposed of in this country. *Plea-bargaining*—pleading guilty to a lesser charge in return for a reduced sentence—is the norm; trials are the exception. Thus, in terms of the men and women who are convicted, the Supreme Court's decision regarding the right to trial by jury, for example, is largely irrelevant.

The case of *Gideon* v. *Wainwright* (1963) established the right to counsel. When translated into reality, however, the counsel that one has a right to is more closely approximated by the overworked public defender, who meets his clients in large groups ten minutes before they are scheduled to go to trial, than by Perry Mason (Abraham Blumberg, 1970). A good lawyer knows the intricacies of the *Miranda* rules, but empirical studies indicate that not much has changed as a result of that decision: Police continue to illegally obtain confessions even after reading the *Miranda* warnings (*Yale Law Journal,* July 1967). Clearly, a sophisticated attempt to implement due process standards as the basis of public policy must be concerned with both the details of the rules as established by the Supreme Court and the actual implementation of such rules.

One interesting question that is likely to be of increasing importance in future years is the extent to which due process standards should be applied outside the courtroom. Many institutions—corporations, banks, and schools, for instance—have a far greater impact on most people's lives than do the courts. Should one's employer be bound by due process standards? Should an appellant have the right to be represented by counsel at draft-board proceedings? Should a bank be able to deny an application for a mortgage on the basis of the whims of an official, or does good public policy require that the rights of the applicant be protected by due process standards? As with all issues concerning civil liberties, these are extremely difficult questions that require much thought and careful analysis before they can be adequately answered.

CIVIL LIBERTIES: A MATTER OF PHILOSOPHY

This chapter is built around the basic American conception of civil liberties, which is based on concern for the individual as he confronts society. This orientation is not value free—it explicitly asserts certain values about the worth of individual freedom. A Marxist, for example, would reject this concern with the individual as selfish and would urge that true liberty policy is policy that promotes the ultimate liberties of the working class. In this view, liberty in a bourgeois, or middle-class, society should be conceived of in terms of the revolution that will break the bonds enslaving men's minds and bodies. To speak of the freedom to pass out pamphlets on street corners while a small capitalist class controls the means of production is absurd. In Chairman Mao's view:

Liberalism stems from the selfishness of the petty bourgeois, which puts personal interests foremost and the interests of the revolution in the second place, thus giving rise to ideological, political and organizational liberalism . . .

Liberalism is a manifestation of opportunism and conflicts fundamentally with Marxism . . . [T]here should be no place for it in the revolutionary ranks. (Anne Fremantle, 1954, pp. 198–199)

If the basic unit of analysis for the American civil libertarian is the *individual,* the basic unit of analysis for the Marxist is the *class.* Liberty policies that rest on the attempt to liberate oppressed classes are indeed fundamentally different from those discussed in this chapter.

A second alternative conception of civil liberties rests on the notion of *community.* Proponents of "Black Power," at least in some of its manifestations, reject the individual as the proper focus. They do not ask whether specific blacks have been treated equitably, but whether blacks as a *group* have received their fair share of the goods and services available in society. Freedom and liberty are defined in terms of the black community rather than the individual. For example, the Black Muslims expect their members to submit to rigorous group discipline. The liberty that results is liberty for the black community (Malcolm X and Alex Haley, 1966).

Liberty policy—like all public policy—rests on basic value choices. The Marxist and the Black Muslim challenge the bases on which the American tradition of civil liberties rests. Their critiques are particularly important for being so fundamental. The task of the reader is to attempt to recognize these positions for what they are and to attempt to recognize his or her positions for what they are. If civil liberties are to involve more than mere clichés, it is crucial that all citizens be prepared to undertake the hard work of analysis.

SUMMARY

America's basic civil liberties polices are grounded in the Bill of Rights and the Thirteenth, Fourteenth, Fifteenth, and Nineteenth Amendments. Although the specific meanings of these guarantees have changed over time, it is problematic how much change we accept today.

Our civil liberties policies assume the primacy of the individual; they are defined in terms of freedom *from* governmental restrictions, not freedom *to* act in particular ways. Although initially applied only to the federal government, constitutional guarantees have been incorporated into the Fourteenth Amendment where they determine state policy as well.

Public opinion is a crucial determinant of civil liberties policy, for policy ultimately requires popular acceptance. To analyze a civil liberties issue: define the pertinent terms; relate the question to the concept of "freedom"; identify the reasons for advocating a particular position; and consider the effect of limitations on the exercise of the policy in question.

There are three judicial positions on the constitutional status of civil liberties: *absolutist*—no limits on constitutional guarantees; *balancing*—freedoms must be weighed against competing social values; *preferred*—any law limiting a freedom is treated as inherently suspect and carries the burden of proof.

Debate continues on civil liberties issues to determine appropriate *due process* procedures.

SUGGESTED READINGS

Emerson, Thomas, David Haber, and Norman Dorsen. *Political and Civil Rights in the United States.* 2 vols. 3rd ed. Boston: Little, Brown, 1967.

Howe, Mark DeWolfe. *The Garden and the Wilderness: Religion and Government in American Constitutional History.* Chicago: University of Chicago Press, 1965.

Levy, Leonard W. *Freedom of Speech and Press in Early American History: Legacy of Suppression.* New York: Harper & Row, 1963.

Thoreau, Henry David. *Walden; On the Duty of Civil Disobedience.* New York: Macmillan, 1966. (Many editions available.)

Walzer, Michael. *Obligations: Essays on Disobedience, War, and Citizenship.* Cambridge, Mass.: Harvard University Press, 1970.

Westin, Alan. *Privacy and Freedom.* New York: Atheneum, 1968.

7a

MARIJUANA LAWS AND CIVIL LIBERTIES

by James W. Clarke

Marijuana use is a criminal offense in the United States, punishable by stiff prison sentences in many states. In spite of the severe penalties, however, over 23 million Americans have smoked marijuana—most of them young people. Surveys indicate that approximately 39 percent of all persons between the ages of eighteen and twenty-five have tried marijuana and that its use is common among all young people regardless of background (National Commission, 1972).

Unlike other political issues that are defined in social-class or ethnic terms, the marijuana issue has tended to divide the nation along generational lines. Polls show that many older Americans see a relationship between marijuana use and the rise of new values that they regard as threatening to American society. Accordingly, the marijuana issue has assumed symbolic significance. A person's views on marijuana are thought to reveal much about his or her views on a host of political issues ranging from the Vietnam War and civil rights to appraisals of American capitalism.

Two broad historic questions in American civil liberties policy are involved in the marijuana issue. First, this issue poses questions of majoritarian principles and minority rights: To what extent is the individual free to engage in activities that, although considered deviant by the majority, have no clearly demonstrable consequences beyond the individual? Second, how do legal institutions respond to new ideas and values?

The marijuana issue also raises questions about the relationship between changes in social values and laws that fail to reflect those changes: What are the consequences of such conflicts? In short, what are the political implications of social change?

This chapter attempts to provide some perspective on these questions and some tentative answers by examining the following: the evolution of marijuana laws and some of the assumptions that formed the basis for those laws; a number of court cases illustrating the major constitutional issues involved in legal challenges to existing laws; and the social

PENALTY FOR POSSESSION OF MARIJUANA (FIRST OFFENSE)

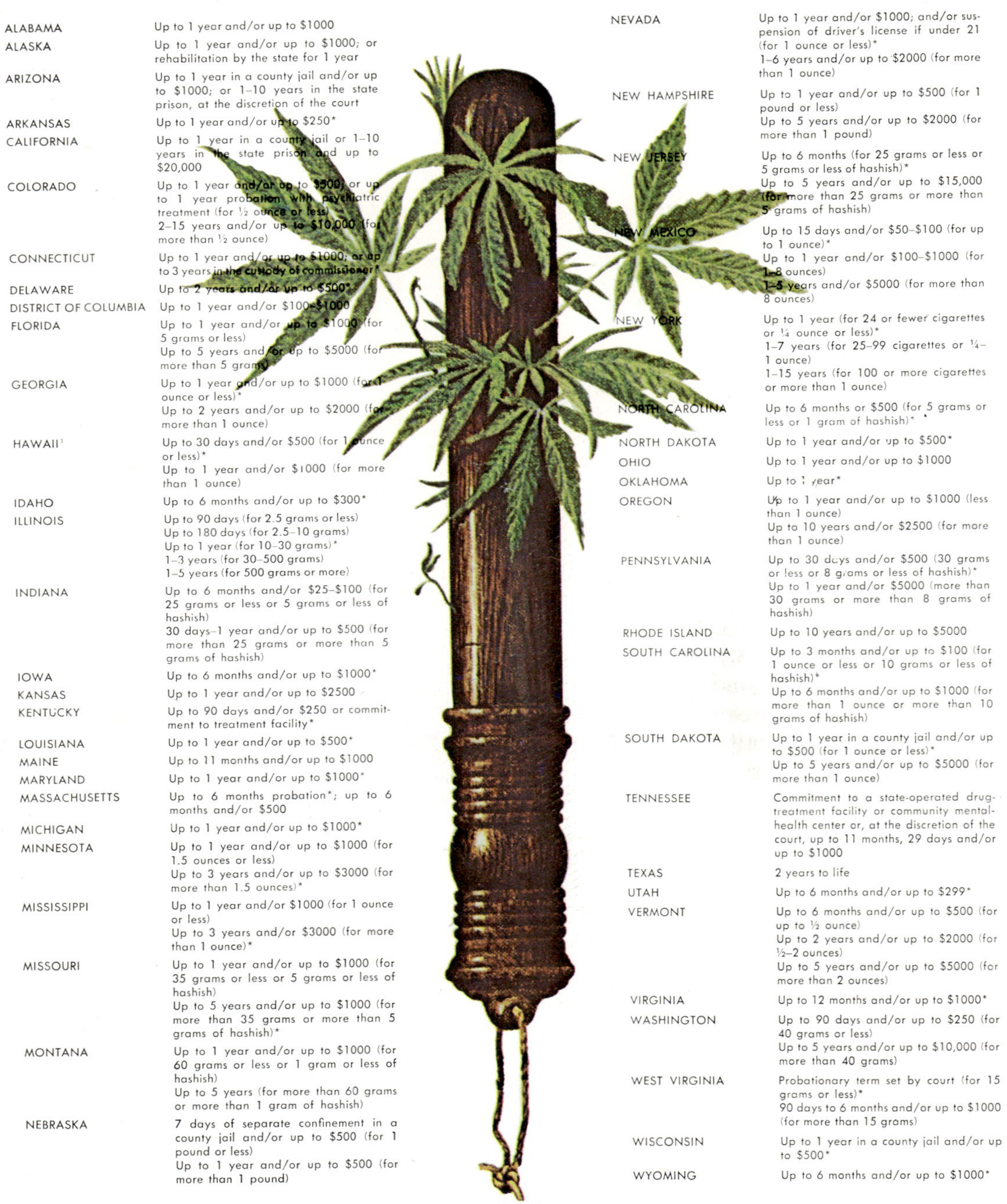

ALABAMA — Up to 1 year and/or up to $1000

ALASKA — Up to 1 year and/or up to $1000; or rehabilitation by the state for 1 year

ARIZONA — Up to 1 year in a county jail and/or up to $1000; or 1–10 years in the state prison, at the discretion of the court

ARKANSAS — Up to 1 year and/or up to $250*

CALIFORNIA — Up to 1 year in a county jail or 1–10 years in the state prison and up to $20,000

COLORADO — Up to 1 year and/or up to $500; or up to 1 year probation plus psychiatric treatment (for ½ ounce or less)
2–15 years and/or up to $10,000 (for more than ½ ounce)

CONNECTICUT — Up to 1 year and/or up to $1000; or up to 3 years in the custody of commissioner*

DELAWARE — Up to 2 years and/or up to $500*

DISTRICT OF COLUMBIA — Up to 1 year and/or $100–$1000

FLORIDA — Up to 1 year and/or up to $1000 (for 5 grams or less)
Up to 5 years and/or up to $5000 (for more than 5 grams)

GEORGIA — Up to 1 year and/or up to $1000 (for 1 ounce or less)*
Up to 2 years and/or up to $2000 (for more than 1 ounce)

HAWAII[1] — Up to 30 days and/or $500 (for 1 ounce or less)*
Up to 1 year and/or $1000 (for more than 1 ounce)

IDAHO — Up to 6 months and/or up to $300*

ILLINOIS — Up to 90 days (for 2.5 grams or less)
Up to 180 days (for 2.5–10 grams)
Up to 1 year (for 10–30 grams)*
1–3 years (for 30–500 grams)
1–5 years (for 500 grams or more)

INDIANA — Up to 6 months and/or $25–$100 (for 25 grams or less or 5 grams or less of hashish)
30 days–1 year and/or up to $500 (for more than 25 grams or more than 5 grams of hashish)

IOWA — Up to 6 months and/or up to $1000*

KANSAS — Up to 1 year and/or up to $2500

KENTUCKY — Up to 90 days and/or $250 or commitment to treatment facility*

LOUISIANA — Up to 1 year and/or up to $500*

MAINE — Up to 11 months and/or up to $1000

MARYLAND — Up to 1 year and/or up to $1000*

MASSACHUSETTS — Up to 6 months probation*; up to 6 months and/or $500

MICHIGAN — Up to 1 year and/or up to $1000*

MINNESOTA — Up to 1 year and/or up to $1000 (for 1.5 ounces or less)
Up to 3 years and/or up to $3000 (for more than 1.5 ounces)*

MISSISSIPPI — Up to 1 year and/or $1000 (for 1 ounce or less)
Up to 3 years and/or $3000 (for more than 1 ounce)*

MISSOURI — Up to 1 year and/or up to $1000 (for 35 grams or less or 5 grams or less of hashish)
Up to 5 years and/or up to $1000 (for more than 35 grams or more than 5 grams of hashish)*

MONTANA — Up to 1 year and/or up to $1000 (for 60 grams or less or 1 gram or less of hashish)
Up to 5 years (for more than 60 grams or more than 1 gram of hashish)

NEBRASKA — 7 days of separate confinement in a county jail and/or up to $500 (for 1 pound or less)
Up to 1 year and/or up to $500 (for more than 1 pound)

NEVADA — Up to 1 year and/or $1000; and/or suspension of driver's license if under 21 (for 1 ounce or less)*
1–6 years and/or up to $2000 (for more than 1 ounce)

NEW HAMPSHIRE — Up to 1 year and/or up to $500 (for 1 pound or less)
Up to 5 years and/or up to $2000 (for more than 1 pound)

NEW JERSEY — Up to 6 months (for 25 grams or less or 5 grams or less of hashish)*
Up to 5 years and/or up to $15,000 (for more than 25 grams or more than 5 grams of hashish)

NEW MEXICO — Up to 15 days and/$50–$100 (for up to 1 ounce)*
Up to 1 year and/or $100–$1000 (for 1–8 ounces)
1–5 years and/or $5000 (for more than 8 ounces)

NEW YORK — Up to 1 year (for 24 or fewer cigarettes or ¼ ounce or less)*
1–7 years (for 25–99 cigarettes or ¼–1 ounce)
1–15 years (for 100 or more cigarettes or more than 1 ounce)

NORTH CAROLINA — Up to 6 months or $500 (for 5 grams or less or 1 gram of hashish)*

NORTH DAKOTA — Up to 1 year and/or up to $500*

OHIO — Up to 1 year and/or up to $1000

OKLAHOMA — Up to 1 year*

OREGON — Up to 1 year and/or up to $1000 (less than 1 ounce)
Up to 10 years and/or $2500 (for more than 1 ounce)

PENNSYLVANIA — Up to 30 days and/or $500 (30 grams or less or 8 grams or less of hashish)*
Up to 1 year and/or $5000 (more than 30 grams or more than 8 grams of hashish)

RHODE ISLAND — Up to 10 years and/or up to $5000

SOUTH CAROLINA — Up to 3 months and/or up to $100 (for 1 ounce or less or 10 grams or less of hashish)*
Up to 6 months and/or up to $1000 (for more than 1 ounce or more than 10 grams of hashish)

SOUTH DAKOTA — Up to 1 year in a county jail and/or up to $500 (for 1 ounce or less)*
Up to 5 years and/or up to $5000 (for more than 1 ounce)

TENNESSEE — Commitment to a state-operated drug-treatment facility or community mental-health center or, at the discretion of the court, up to 11 months, 29 days and/or up to $1000

TEXAS — 2 years to life

UTAH — Up to 6 months and/or up to $299*

VERMONT — Up to 6 months and/or up to $500 (for up to ½ ounce)
Up to 2 years and/or up to $2000 (for ½–2 ounces)
Up to 5 years and/or up to $5000 (for more than 2 ounces)

VIRGINIA — Up to 12 months and/or up to $1000*

WASHINGTON — Up to 90 days and/or up to $250 (for 40 grams or less)
Up to 5 years and/or up to $10,000 (for more than 40 grams)

WEST VIRGINIA — Probationary term set by court (for 15 grams or less)*
90 days to 6 months and/or up to $1000 (for more than 15 grams)

WISCONSIN — Up to 1 year in a county jail and/or up to $500*

WYOMING — Up to 6 months and/or up to $1000*

NORML
National Organization for the Reform of Marijuana Laws
1237 22nd St., N.W., Washington, D. C. 20037
(202) 223-3170

[1]Effective January 1, 1973
*Statute provides for first-offense conditional discharge; record may be expunged
Laws as of November 1, 1972

and political consequences of marijuana regulation. The chapter concludes by offering a possible resolution of the issue.

THE LEGAL STATUS OF MARIJUANA

The legal status of marijuana has evolved in response to the public's perception of the effects of its use, perceptions that have been limited by the scarcity of scientific information on the subject. Because such assumptions have been legitimatized as law, they have in turn reinforced the public's misunderstanding (Barry Wukasch, 1972).

Fundamental Assumptions

The first major piece of legislation designed to deal specifically with marijuana use was the Marijuana Tax Act of 1937. Passage of the act hinged on three basic assumptions put forth by the Bureau of Narcotics: (1) marijuana is a narcotic, that is, a habit-forming or addictive drug, and therefore its use is not substantially different from the use of physiologically addictive narcotics (2) marijuana possesses no medical benefits,

and (3) marijuana use leads to criminal activity—it leads especially to the commission of violent crimes. As Commissioner of Narcotics H. J. Anslinger remarked in 1937:

Perhaps you remember the young desperado in Michigan who, a few months ago, caused a reign of terror by his career of burglaries and holdups, finally sent to prison for life after kidnapping a Michigan State policeman, killing him, then handcuffing him to the post of a rural mailbox. This young bandit was a marijuana fiend. . . . There were 60 [marijuana] cigarettes on hand, enough fodder for 60 murders. (H. J. Anslinger and Courtney Cooper, 1937, p. 151)

A fourth assumption—that marijuana use leads to heroin addiction—came into play more recently. By the early 1950s this "stepping-stone theory" was accepted by the Bureau of Narcotics and became part of its continuous campaign against marijuana (Jerry Mandel, 1968). To a large extent these four assumptions still provide the basis for arguments against marijuana use, despite the fact that the evidence supporting

them is highly questionable, as will be indicated later in this chapter.

State Law Reflects the Assumptions

Federal policy on marijuana from 1937 through the 1950s concentrated on stopping the supply of marijuana at its sources while leaving to the states the enforcement of minor possession violations (National Commission, 1972). Throughout this period the Federal Bureau of Narcotics, consistent with its assumptions about the dangers of the drug, advocated more stringent laws dealing with marijuana use (United States House Hearings, 1951).

In spite of emerging evidence that suggested the dangers of marijuana use were minimal, the punitive views of the Bureau of Narcotics continued to be accepted and implemented in state legislation. In 1962 Rhode Island passed more stringent marijuana laws, which included a twenty- to forty-year penalty for the gift or sale of marijuana and up to life imprisonment for sale to a minor. Second-degree murder, armed robbery, and rape were considered

Figure 7a.1 Varied responses to the drug problem are exemplified by the penalties for marijuana possession in the fifty states (left). If it wished to do so Congress could create national legislation to require that drug laws be uniform in all states; but because of the sensitive nature of the issue and the tremendous conflicts it raises within communities, the federal government has chosen to leave the delicate task of establishing drug penalties to local and state authorities.

Figure 7a.2 In the 1930s Americans were warned of the "evils of the weed" by pharmacists' displays and by films such as the one advertised here (right). Today the same film finds popular success among marijuana smokers as a self-parody of the era of the 1930s and a comment on contemporary American beliefs that brain damage and moral turpitude may be caused by marijuana smoking.

less serious crimes in Rhode Island (at that time) than the sale of marijuana. Georgia and Colorado also maintained severe laws, which included the death penalty for sale to a minor (Erich Goode, 1970).

State marijuana laws were also characterized by their lack of consistency: Until 1969 South Dakota law carried a ninety-day sentence for possession, whereas its sister state of North Dakota imposed a ninety-nine year penalty for the same offense (Goode, 1970).

There were, however, some subtle indications that official views on marijuana control were slowly changing in response to newly emerging facts. Although it dealt principally with narcotics rather than with marijuana, the Narcotic Rehabilitation Act of 1966 revealed some changes in policy perspectives: For example, drug abuse was regarded as a *medical* problem rather than a *criminal* problem. In line with this change in perspective, the rehabilitation program was placed under the jurisdiction of the Department of Health, Education, and Welfare rather than the Bureau of Narcotics. The act also formally recognized the distinction between marijuana and narcotic drugs by eliminating mandatory minimum sentences. The trend has continued toward less severe penalties for possession of small amounts, whereas penalties for cultivation and sale remain quite severe. There is also a trend toward greater consistency in laws among the various states (National Commission, 1972).

CONSTITUTIONAL RIGHTS TESTED

Marijuana laws raise serious questions concerning civil liberties and the constitutionality of laws that restrict the private activities of citizens. How does the government protect the constitutionally guaranteed rights of individuals while maintaining and enforcing the law as it has been formulated and defined by representatives of majoritarian sentiments?

Perhaps the most famous court battle in the history of marijuana control was the case of Dr. Timothy Leary, a former psychology instructor at Harvard, whose academic reputation was established through his research on the use of psychedelic drugs in treating the mentally ill. Leary later became involved in a variety of religious experiences that led him away from his academic interests and into the area of spirituality and psychedelics. As a consequence, he is best known today as one of the early gurus of the drug culture, rather than as a clinical psychologist.

In 1965 Leary, his son and daughter, and two companions were arrested at the Mexican border in Laredo, Texas for possession of marijuana—the evidence consisted of three partially smoked marijuana cigarettes in his daughter's possession and remnants swept from the floor of the car (*Leary* v. *United States,* 1967). Leary was tried in a United States District Court on three counts: smuggling marijuana into the United States; transporting and concealing marijuana that had been illegally imported; and, under the provisions of the Federal Marijuana Tax Act of 1937, concealing

Figure 7a.3 The Department of Justice employs drug-detecting dogs as one of the means of identifying violators of our drug laws. Zorro, a drug-sniffing German shepherd (left), detected the 44 pounds of heroin at San Francisco International Airport in March 1973. The drug had a street value of $14 million, the largest amount of heroin ever confiscated in a single case on the west coast. Does the use of such dogs violate one's privacy? Does a dog's reaction provide reasonable cause for officials to search someone's belongings?

and transporting marijuana without having paid the transfer tax (*Leary* v. *United States,* 1969).

Leary was found guilty on the second and third counts and confronted with a combined sentence of twenty years imprisonment and $40,000 in fines. He appealed the decision. His appeals were based on several constitutional guarantees—his First Amendment rights to the free exercise of religion, his Fifth Amendment rights protecting him from self-incrimination, and the unconstitutionality of certain of the statutory presumptions in the Marijuana Tax Act.

Free Exercise of Religion

The basis for Leary's appeal on the *free exercise* clause was the district court's refusal to instruct the jury to acquit him if it found his religious claims concerning marijuana to be "honest and in good faith." He argued that because the California court had earlier ruled that the Native American Church (*People* v. *Woody,* 1964) could use peyote in its ceremonies, he should also be permitted to use marijuana, especially when there was no evidence that marijuana was any more harmful than peyote. A denial of the right to use marijuana for religious purposes would, Leary contended, represent a violation of his First Amendment rights (Joel Finer, 1968; Barry Wukasch, 1972).

The Court of Appeals rejected Leary's arguments, stating that to permit religion to be used as justification for drug use would preclude the enforcement of existing drug laws. It reasoned further that the analogy between the religious significance of peyote for the Native American Church and Leary's use of marijuana in the practice of Hinduism was fallacious because there was no evidence of marijuana use being an inherent and necessary part of the Hindu religion (*Leary* v. *United States,* 1967).

Self-Incrimination

Leary based a second appeal on the Fifth Amendment's protection against self-incrimination. Leary argued that the third charge brought against him, concealing and transporting marijuana without having paid the transfer tax, denied him protection against self-incrimination. Payment of the marijuana tax would have been an admission of possession and therefore was self-incriminating. The court agreed and reversed the conviction on this count (*Leary* v. *United States,* 1969).

This decision left only the second charge, which was based on the presumption that the marijuana in his possession had been illegally imported. According to the 1937 law, proof of possession constitutes a presumption that the possessor has knowledge that the drug was imported illegally. The court ruled that although the marijuana had been imported, it was not valid to presume that Leary had knowledge of the importation of this marijuana. Thus, the courts accepted Leary's arguments on the second and third counts and reversed his federal conviction.

The Leary case was important because it revealed weaknesses in the federal law regulating marijuana,

Figure 7a.4 Dr. Timothy Leary, former psychology instructor at Harvard. His advocacy of the "consciousness-liberating" use of many kinds of drugs has led to years of difficulties with U.S. authorities and to his exile abroad. Arrested in Afghanistan, Leary steps from an airliner in Los Angeles in January 1973, under heavy escort by federal officers. He faces charges of escape from a California prison in 1970, drug smuggling, conspiracy, and income tax evasion.

but it did not have any dramatic effect, at least in the short run, on federal policy. The court, for example, did not say that the 1937 law was unconstitutional; it merely said that the particular circumstances of Leary's case led to the reversal of his conviction (Wukasch, 1972). Leary's case, however, was the first successful challenge to the law; it also suggested that attitudes about marijuana control might be changing.

But if a change in attitudes concerning the control of marijuana is taking place, this change is uneven, and it is difficult to map its progress, as is shown in the court rulings in the following cases involving the use of marijuana. In these cases other constitutional rights have been tested, such as the right to privacy and to due process and equal protection, as well as the right protecting against cruel and unusual punishments.

The Right to Privacy

The right to privacy is derived from several different sources in the Bill of Rights. The First Amendment right to association implies that a person may or may not associate with others as he so desires. The Third and Fourth Amendments imply the right to privacy in one's home. The Fifth Amendment protection against self-incrimination ensures an area of privacy with respect to testimony concerning one's activities. The Ninth Amendment mentions other nonspecified individual rights that imply the right to personal privacy.

In *Commonwealth* v. *Leis* (1969) the right to privacy was used to defend marijuana use. The defendants in this case had been arrested for possession of marijuana under the provisions of the Massachusetts Narcotics Law.

In an earlier case the Supreme Court had ruled on the issue of birth control and the right to privacy (*Griswold* v. *Connecticut*, 1965). On the basis of the First, Third, Fourth, Fifth, and Ninth Amendments the Court decided in *Griswold* that the right to privacy, or private behavior associated with the mari-

tal relationship, could not be circumscribed by state law.

In *Commonwealth* v. *Leis* the defendants employed a similar argument in contending that marijuana use is a private act. The Supreme Court of Massachusetts rejected the argument, however, stating that "[marijuana use] is not within a 'zone of privacy' formed by 'penumbras' of the First, Third, Fourth and Fifth Amendments and the Ninth Amendment of the Constitution of the United States" and added that "The right to smoke marijuana is not 'fundamental to the American scheme of justice.' " Thus, the Massachusetts court ruled on the particular issue, but it chose to give little or no explanation of the reasoning behind the decision.

Due Process and Equal Protection

The defendants in the *Leis* case also raised the question whether the Massachusetts law, which defined marijuana as a narcotic, was constitutional, when all available scientific evidence indicated that it was not a narcotic. The law, they con-

Figure 7a.5 In its attempts to prevent American access to marijuana and other drugs, the United States government has applied strong pressures to drug-producing countries such as Mexico and Turkey to increase their controls over sources. This 1968 "pot roast" is the result of intensive efforts by the Mexican government to step up its war against narcotics growers. Mexican army troops trucked 38 tons of marijuana, most of it packed and ready for an estimated U.S. sale of $8 million, to this field, doused it with gasoline, and applied the match.

tended, was arbitrary and unreasonable and therefore a violation of the *equal protection* clause of the Fourteenth Amendment. In their view the state legislature's failure to consider scientific evidence in formulating the law represented a violation of their rights under the *due process* clause of the same amendment. The defendants also questioned the constitutionality of dissimilar (that is, unequal) laws controlling alcohol and marijuana consumption. They claimed that evidence overwhelmingly proved the relative hazards—mental, physical, and social—of alcohol consumption over marijuana use.

However, the Massachusetts court denied that unequal punishment for alcohol and marijuana abuse represented a denial of equal protection guarantees of the Fourteenth Amendment. The court reasoned that the effects of alcohol were well known and could therefore be controlled through less punitive legislation; such was not the case with respect to marijuana. Furthermore, the court stated that it was not un-

reasonable or arbitrary to classify marijuana as a narcotic unless the defendant could prove that such a classification was arbitrary and unreasonable; in the court's judgment the defendants had not done so.

The court also rejected the defendants' due process argument that the state legislature had failed to consider scientific evidence in formulating the marijuana statute. The court thereby ruled that the legislature was not obligated to investigate such evidence and so was presumed to have acted responsibly.

The state court of Massachusetts was not the only court to assume a similar stance. The question of arbitrary classification of marijuana as a narcotic was raised in Ohio. The court concluded that the state had the right, under its police power, to define marijuana as a narcotic if it so desired (*Spence* v. *Sacks*, 1962). In a similar decision the Colorado Supreme Court declared that the question of scientific evidence of physical or psychological addiction to marijuana was beside the point. Rather, in the court's view, mari-

juana presented a threat to public safety and welfare, and therefore it was reasonable for the legislature to classify it as a narcotic (*People* v. *Stark*, 1965).

Cruel and Unusual Punishment

Do the severe penalties for marijuana use violate the Eighth Amendment's guarantee of protection against cruel and unusual punishment? The question is based on the claim that crimes with more serious social consequences than marijuana use carry less severe penalties under the law. Consider the resentment expressed by a young man convicted on a marijuana charge:

It's rather discouraging to spend time in jail for the "crime" of possessing a weed. I haven't hurt anybody, I haven't stolen from anybody, I haven't raped anybody's daughter. Why am I in jail? I don't feel like a criminal.

I committed a charitable act . . . I agreed to turn this poor cat on to some grass at his request. He promptly turned me in.

This silly grass law is only one small reflection of the mentality that rules America and dictates what we can read, what we can think and what position we must use when we make love.

My love to all the gentle people. Our day is coming. (Trod Runyon, 1968, p. 66)

The issue of cruel and unusual punishment has been raised at the state level (the United States Supreme Court has yet to rule on the issue). When confronted with the argument that maximum penalties possible under the law were excessive, the Massachusetts Court (in *Commonwealth* v. *Leis*, 1967) ruled that it had confidence in the judge's discretion.

However, one might argue with this ruling on the basis that some judges are totally ignorant of the effects of marijuana. Because its use has been equated with alcoholism, ludicrous "cures" have often been suggested for its users:

. . . a middle-aged Negro defendant appeared before the judge charged with having used and had in his possession one marijuana cigarette during the noon hour at the place where he had worked for a number of years. This man had no previous record and this fact was stated before the court. Nevertheless, a two-year

sentence was imposed to "dry up his habit." (Lindesmith, 1965, p. 239)

In a more recent decision the Michigan Supreme Court granted the appeal of a defendant who had been sentenced to a nine-and-one-half- to ten-year sentence for possession of two marijuana cigarettes. The court so ruled on the grounds that the lower court's sentence amounted to cruel and unusual punishment. In this case, however, the defendant had already served twenty-nine months in prison (*People* v. *Sinclair*, 1972).

Courts Uphold Existing Laws

Two major conclusions emerge from this brief review of marijuana cases. First, with the partial exceptions of the *Leary* and the *Sinclair* cases, the courts—federal and state—have been noticeably unsympathetic toward constitutional challenges to existing marijuana laws. Second, the courts have not felt it necessary to consider available scientific evidence in reaching their decisions in these cases—a fact that contributes to the growing

feeling that marijuana cases are not fairly adjudicated.

The evidence seems to show that the courts have frequently been more concerned with maintaining federal and state marijuana laws than with protecting the rights of individuals on constitutional grounds.

THE RESPONSE TO MARIJUANA LAWS

What are the broader political implications of a disjunction between the social values of a substantial minority and the laws established and enforced by the majority? Among those who feel marijuana is not harmful, there has been a growing feeling that the laws governing its use are unconstitutional and that court opinions are based more on the political and social values of judges than they are on legal principles. When the fairness of laws is in question and appeals to those who have judicial authority to alter such laws are to no avail, government officials are forced to rule through coercion or through the

Figure 7a.6 The ascetic side of the Protestant ethic prohibited the legal sale of "intoxicating liquors" with passage of the Eighteenth Amendment in 1919. But the profit-seeking side of the same ethic encouraged the rise of speakeasies, where a secret knock and a password admitted one to a world of illicit good fellowship and naughty garter flasks. The genial atmosphere of these establishments provided a cover for the suppliers, the world of organized crime—a solid foundation was laid in the 1920s for the Mafia's rise to prominence and the extension of its power into our own era.

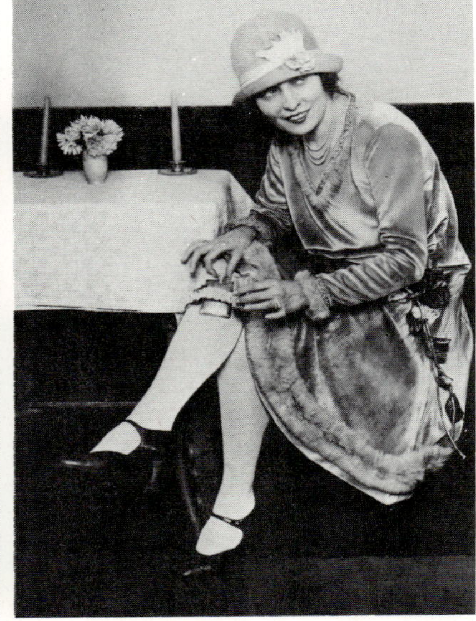

threat of coercion rather than ruling through respect for the authority of the law.

Prohibition of Alcohol: An Analogy

A situation that was similar to that existing with marijuana existed during the period when alcohol was prohibited by the Eighteenth Amendment (1919–1933). Because many people refused to accept the government's policy on alcoholic beverages, drinking went underground; bootlegging operations thrived, and fortunes were made in the illegal traffic of alcoholic beverages simply because many people refused to obey a law they considered unjust.

It was soon realized that it was impossible to enforce the Prohibition Amendment; moreover, organized crime had taken over the liquor industry to supply the demands of ordinary, hard-working, and otherwise law-abiding citizens who saw nothing wrong with drinking. Thus, after fourteen years of unsuccessful enforcement, prohibition was repealed by the Twenty-first Amendment in 1933, and the government decided to control alcoholic consumption rather than try to eliminate it.

A comparable situation exists with respect to marijuana, although there are some important differences. Like alcohol in the past, marijuana is significant as a sociopolitical symbol because its popularity has occurred coincidentally with unprecedented changes in the political and social values and behaviors of American youth—changes that are now referred to as the "youth culture." In Erich Goode's words:

Marijuana can be thought of as a kind of symbol for a complex of other positions, beliefs, and activities which are correlated with and compatible with its use. In other words, those who disapprove of marijuana use often feel that he who smokes must, of necessity, also be a political radical, engage in "loose" (from his point of view) sexual practices, and have a somewhat dim view of patriotism. Marijuana use is seen (whether rightly or wrongly) to sum up innumerable facts about the individual, facts which can clearly place him along the liberal-radical dimension in a number of areas of social and political life. (Goode, 1969, p. 92)

A key distinction in comparing the consequences of the prohibition of alcohol and what has been called the "new prohibition" of marijuana (John Kaplan, 1970) is the characteristics of the offenders. Unlike the alcohol issue, which had urban-rural, Protestant-Catholic, and native-immigrant dimensions, the marijuana issue produces generational differences—the old versus the young and parents versus children—that cut across the more typical social cleavages in the society (National Commission, 1972).

Respect for the Authority of the Law

Within the context of this generation gap, marijuana use has come to symbolize the contempt for authority associated with the young. Many older Americans regard certain youthful attitudes and behaviors as un-American and as indicative of a number of other evil forces at work in society. Kenneth Keniston has de-

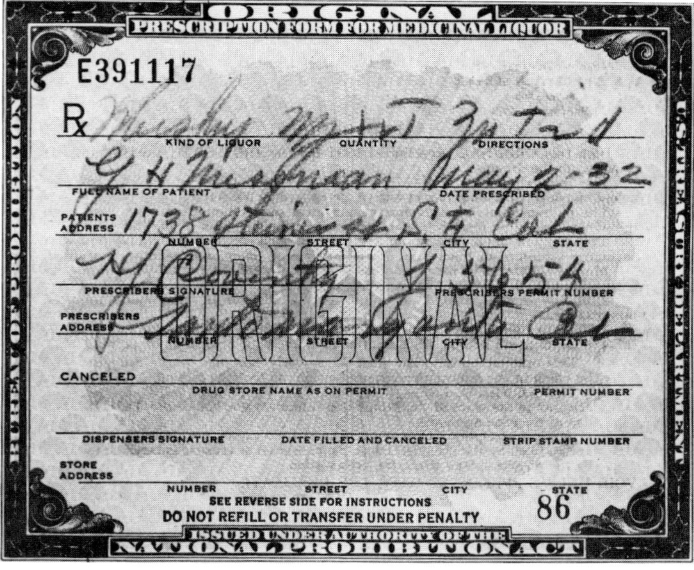

Figure 7a.7 In 1932 it took a doctor's prescription to get a legal swig of whiskey. The passage of the Twenty-first Amendment in 1933 finally ended Prohibition. The experiment had shown the difficulties involved in government's attempts to legislate morality.

scribed this linkage in the public mind between marijuana use and other problems such as "filth pedling," internal subversion, a decline in patriotism, and crime in the streets (Keniston, 1969). In fact, a national survey revealed that 45 percent of the adult respondents thought that marijuana use was promoted by "enemies of the nation." When age groups were compared, generational differences were striking: 58 percent of those persons fifty years and over perceived a conspiracy as compared to 26 percent of those in the eighteen to twenty-five year age group (National Commission, 1972).

The disdain with which older persons view both marijuana use and the youth culture is reciprocated in kind by many young people. They see the older generation as "uptight," neurotic people who possess a variety of hang-ups regarding sex, money, and success and who are using the law in an arbitrary manner in order to force their own distorted value system on society.

Why, such persons ask, must I run the risk of arrest and imprisonment for an act that affects only me and has fewer potentially harmful effects than alcohol, tobacco, and many regularly prescribed drugs? To these people, the state is the enemy, and the police, who enforce the laws of the state, are the criminals. A college student expressed this attitude:

The police don't bust Mafia dealers. The cops are too busy playing games with little people who just, like, go home and smoke a joint. But I guess these people are a threat. They look pretty scary in their long hair and nasty clothes and things like that [laughs]. . . . The cops are a strange phenomenon. They go after the people that *look* weird, because they figure that probably, well, this is my guess, they figure that these are the kids that are into the revolution, they're obviously revolting in some way. (Goode, 1970, p. 268)

Young people view the antimarijuana crusade as a reflection of the inability or unwillingness of older Americans to adjust to new realities. The irony of the older generation's cries of moral outrage on issues of marijuana use and sexual permissiveness and its corresponding support of a morally questionable war in Southeast Asia did not go unobserved among many draft-age young people.

Erich Goode and John Kaplan have both suggested that marijuana has provided a convenient excuse for the arrest of known political radicals whose activities, although offensive, are not illegal. The well-publicized arrests of political radicals on charges of marijuana possession have exaggerated the relationship perceived between marijuana and political radicalism. In Michigan, for example, radical poet John Sinclair was given a nine-and-one-half to ten-year sentence for the possession of two marijuana cigarettes (Agis Salpukas, 1972; *People* v. *Sinclair*, 1972). The act of smoking a joint has become a potent symbol to both the dominant culture and the youth subculture.

When the courts and law enforcement agencies attempt to impose standards of conduct that a substantial minority finds objectionable,

Figure 7a.8 (right)All kinds of information concerning individuals, groups, and businesses—gathered from police records, tax reports, as well as from army records —is available to federal government agents. Without regulation and control, such power could indeed produce a climate of fear and conformity in individual, group, or even local governmental action. But safeguards and barriers do exist. A basic ground rule of the Constitution provides for due process in legal proceedings and the preservation of such civil rights as to assemble and to petition. These basic protections become the basis of congressional legislation and of Supreme Court decisions. But certain powers are left to the states and thus to local initiative and administration. The marijuana issue, for example, is an area that has been left up to the initiative of various states and communities. They are allowed to develop standards applicable to the areas under their jurisdiction, standards that have the potential for coercing citizens to conform to local mores and traditional attitudes.

they do so at the cost of sacrificing their legitimacy in the view of that minority. Although the marijuana user's political ideology (in the conventional liberal-conservative sense) may not be clearly identifiable, there is a definite anti-establishment feeling among users that is measurable (James W. Clark and E. Lester Levine, 1971). After participation in a ''drug bust,'' the chances are that a young person's views toward authority and government will change—law will come to be represented only by the coercive force of the police who act out the sentiments of the dominant culture.

A MELLOWING OF PUBLIC POLICY?

There are indications that attitudes are beginning to change toward the pot-smoking minority. A number of events reflect the beginnings of such changes: congressional passage of the Comprehensive Drug Abuse Prevention and Control Act of 1970, the President's appointment of a national commission to study marijuana and drug abuse, and other governmental activities that seem to augur change.

Comprehensive Drug Abuse Prevention and Control Act of 1970

In 1969 President Nixon sent a drug legislation proposal to Congress that generally reinforced existing federal drug policy with respect to marijuana use (United States Senate Hearings, 1969).

As passed and signed into law, the Drug Abuse Prevention Act of 1970 reflected a modification of the President's proposal. Title I of the act recognized the need for medical research and a public-health approach to drug control and the treatment of narcotic addiction; Title II provided that the production and sale of marijuana would remain felonies carrying penalties of five- to ten-years imprisonment. Relaxation of the old policy position was reflected in the more lenient treatment of first offenders on marijuana possession. Under the provisions of the 1970 act, a judge might grant probation to a person convicted for possessing a small, noncommercial amount of marijuana. If the terms of the probation were successfully met, the judge might remove criminal charges from the violator's record; in the case of minors, all records of the offense could be removed from public record.

The passage of the 1970 act reflected a minor shift in official policy. In response to some of the issues raised during the hearings preceding the act, the President appointed a commission to study and prepare a detailed report on the marijuana and narcotics problem in the United States.

The National Commission on Marijuana and Drug Abuse

In early 1972 the National Commission submitted its report, ''*Marijuana: A Signal of Misunderstanding.*'' The chairman informed the President that the commission had made ''. . . an all-inclusive effort to present facts as they are known today, to demythologize the controversy surrounding marijuana, and to place in proper perspective one of the most emotional and explosive issues of

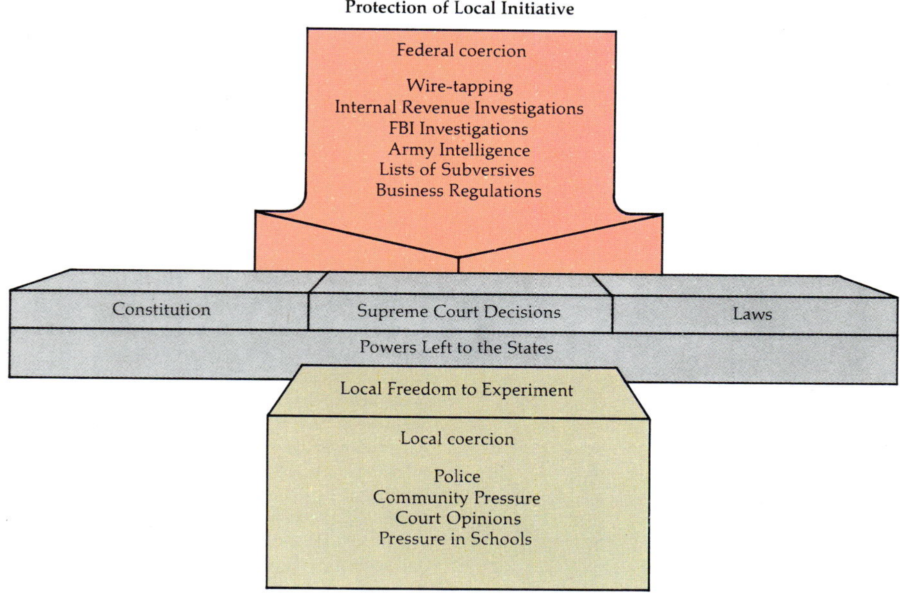

our times" (National Commission, 1972). The commission listed the following among its conclusions:

1. *Lethality:* "A careful study of the literature and testimony of the nation's health officials has not revealed a single human fatality in the United States proven to have resulted solely from ingestion of marijuana."
2. *Genetic Damage:* "Although a number of studies have been performed, at present no reliable evidence exists indicating marijuana causes genetic defects in man."
3. *Effects on the Body:* "No objective evidence of specific pathology of brain tissue has been documented. This fact contrasts sharply with well-established brain damage of chronic alcoholism."
4. *Addiction Potential:* ". . . cannabis does not lead to physical dependence. . . . Although evidence indicates that heavy, long-term cannabis users may develop psychological dependence, even then the level of psychological dependence is no different from the syndrome of anxiety and restlessness seen when an American stops smoking tobacco cigarettes."
5. *Progression to Other Drugs:* "Marijuana use *per se* does not dictate whether other drugs will be used; nor does it determine the rate of progression, if and when it occurs, or which drugs might be used . . . the user's social group seems to have the strongest influence on whether other drugs will be used; and if so, which drugs will be used."
6. *Crime and Violence:* ". . . neither informed current professional opinion nor empirical research, ranging from the 1930s to the present, has produced systematic evidence to support the thesis that marijuana use, by itself, either invariably or generally leads to or causes crime, including acts of violence, juvenile delinquency or aggressive behavior. Instead, the evidence suggests that sociological and cultural variables account for the apparent statistical correlation between marijuana use and crime or delinquency."
7. *Automobile Driving:* ". . . the acute effects of marijuana intoxication, spatial and time distortion and slowed reflexes, may impair driving performance. That the risk of injury may be greater for alcohol than marijuana matters little."

Although the commission was able to conclude that "[marijuana use] at the present level does not constitute a major threat to public health,"

some concern was expressed about two potential effects dealing with psychological functions:

8. *Effects on the Mind:* "No outstanding abnormalities in psychological tests, psychiatric interviews or coping patterns have been conclusively documented in studies of cannabis users in other countries of the world."

On this point some qualification was required. There is some evidence that marijuana in sufficiently large doses can cause transient psychotic effects. Some researchers feel that such psychotic episodes occur only in predisposed individuals, whereas others feel the effects are most closely linked to the amount of the dosage (National Commission, 1972, pp. 71–72). Further research is required before the issue can be resolved.

9. *Effects on Motivation:* ". . . the chronic heavy use of marijuana may jeopardize social and economic adjustments of the adolescent."

This impairment in adjustment patterns has been called an "amotiva-

Figure 7a.9 As all important social issues, marijuana use has complex antecedents and internal dynamics. Visualized here as cavities of molten material and channels under pressure, these factors contribute to the explosive potential of the issue; others, leading away from the central mouth of the volcano, serve to leak away the pressures and to allow them to escape slowly through side vents, that is, to issue in such a form as to help society adjust to and work with the problem. The changes listed at the bottom of the diagram are here depicted as the "heat" responsible for the rise of the issue to public concern. In the body of the volcano are to be found a diversity of elements—including the structure of American institutions, the effects of international crime, government research findings, political opportunism, and others—all arrayed and contributing to the potential explosion or to the successful accommodation of society's pressures.

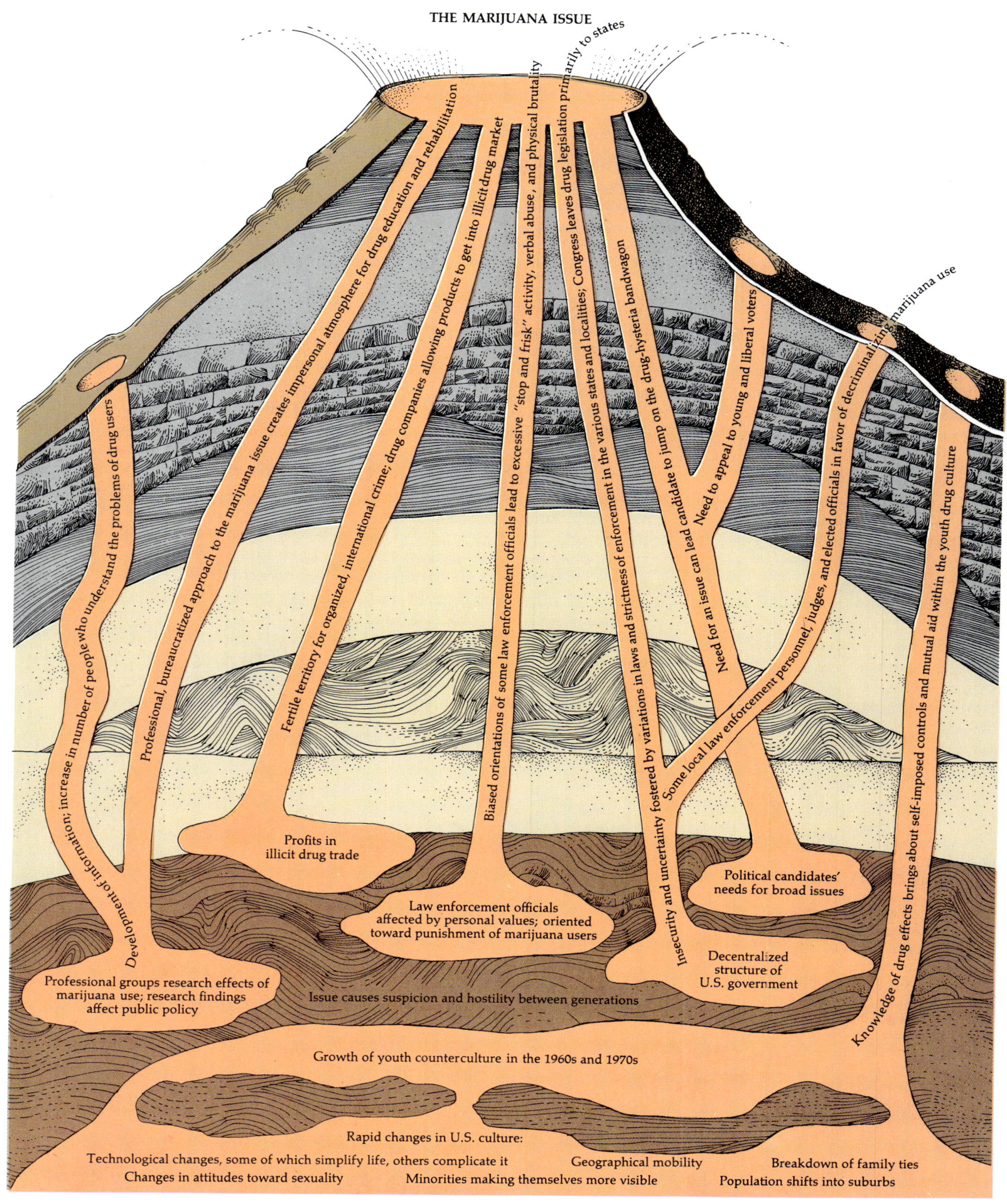
legislation primarily to states
Drug education and rehabilitation
Professional, bureaucratized approach to the marijuana issue creates impersonal atmosphere for drug education and rehabilitation
Fertile territory for organized, international crime; drug companies allowing products to get into illicit drug market
Biased orientations of some law enforcement officials lead to excessive "stop and frisk" activity, verbal abuse, and physical brutality
Congress leaves drug legislation primarily to states
Strictness of enforcement in the various states and localities; Congress leaves drug-hysteria bandwagon
Insecurity and uncertainty fostered by variations in laws and strictness of enforcement
Some local law enforcement personnel, judges, and elected officials in favor of decriminalizing marijuana use
Need for an issue can lead candidate to jump on the drug-hysteria bandwagon
Need to appeal to young and liberal voters
Knowledge of drug effects brings about self-imposed controls and mutual aid within the youth drug culture
Development of information; increase in number of people who understand the problems of drug users
Profits in illicit drug trade
Professional groups research effects of marijuana use; research findings affect public policy
Law enforcement officials affected by personal values; oriented toward punishment of marijuana users
Issue causes suspicion and hostility between generations
Political candidates' needs for broad issues
Decentralized structure of U.S. government
Growth of youth counterculture in the 1960s and 1970s
Rapid changes in U.S. culture:
Technological changes, some of which simplify life, others complicate it
Geographical mobility
Breakdown of family ties
Changes in attitudes toward sexuality
Minorities making themselves more visible
Population shifts into suburbs

tional syndrome," which has as its behavioral components lethargy, present-orientedness, and a loss of interest in activities other than marijuana use. The primary concern of such "amotivated" persons is staying "high"—an escape mechanism that allows the individual to withdraw, or "drop out" into self-oriented concerns to the exclusion of all else. Clinicians disagree on the reasons for this phenomenon. Some believe it is caused by excessive marijuana use; others believe that marijuana is merely the escape chosen by some predisposed individuals, whereas other individuals may withdraw, for example, into alcohol, sleep, TV viewing, or even political science.

Thus, according to the commission's findings, there has been a great deal of misunderstanding involved in the marijuana issue. In its attempt to clarify the situation two important facts emerged: First, marijuana is not a narcotic, that is, it is not addictive in a physiological sense. Second, it *can* be abused through excessive use, and it can result in psychological dependence—

just as alcohol, tobacco, coffee, and candy can be abused. As one observer stated, "Whatever an individual is, in all his cultural, social and psychological complexity, is not going to vanish in a puff of marijuana smoke" (National Commission, 1972).

The commission further stated that public misunderstanding had been reflected in the formulation and administration of unreasonable state marijuana laws; arbitrary legislation had in turn undermined the confidence in adult authority held by many young people (National Commission, 1972). The commission reiterated the recommendation of the Comprehensive Drug Abuse Prevention and Control Act of 1970 that marijuana should not be classified as a narcotic by uninformed state legislatures.

In its policy recommendations the commission attempted to straddle the issue by suggesting that the system of total prohibition be discarded and replaced with a system of partial prohibition: such as, possession and nonprofit sales of marijuana should no longer be punishable under the

law as long as these activities occurred in private; penalties for commercial distribution and sales should remain felonies as defined under the 1970 act.

Because of the legal and logical ambiguities in these recommendations, they are important in a symbolic sense rather than on a pragmatic level of policy implementation. The commission attempted to eliminate much of the misunderstanding concerning marijuana by systematically documenting its conclusions. The official reaction to the commission's findings, however, illustrates a theme of this chapter: Views on an emotionally laden issue such as marijuana are not easily changed by facts. President Nixon's rejection of the findings of the commission, which he appointed, bears out this contention. The President undoubtedly recognized that a majority of Americans would not agree with the commission's report regardless of the facts presented; and, it being an election year, he simply dismissed it.

More recently, however, President Nixon accepted the advice of the

Figure 7a.10 **The findings of presidential commissions are only advisory, and the President can accept or dismiss the commissioners' advice as he chooses; however, at times his outright dismissal of findings may be embarrassing to the commission or to the President. In 1972 President Nixon rejected the report of the President's Commission on Marijuana and Drug Abuse insofar as it traced marijuana dependence to a predisposition toward drugs, advocated reduced punishments for infractions, and advised the reclassification of marijuana out of the narcotic category. Whether or not the President accepts the recommendations of a report such as this, the facts and expert judgments contained in such a study become public knowledge.**

National Commission on Marijuana and Drug Abuse when it called for the establishment of an independent "superagency" to take over all drug programs—education, law enforcement, research, and treatment. (The commission advised that to avoid the creation of a permanent establishment this agency should be dissolved after five years.) The commission stated that response in the United States has tended to perpetuate the drug problem rather than solve it. The long-run solution, it contends, "lies in a far-reaching change in American attitudes toward drug use," attitudes that are at present "'inconsistent and founded on many misconceptions.'" Thus, according to the commission, "the use of alcohol ('without question . . . the most serious drug problem in the country today') and barbiturates ('America's hidden drug problem') is condoned, but the use of marijuana and heroin is condemned" (Stuart Auerbach, 1973).

The commission repeated its recommendation to eliminate criminal penalties for the private use of marijuana. On the commission's advice, in March 1973, Nixon called for the creation of a new agency—the Controlled Substances Commission. Thus, even at the executive level of government, attitudes toward marijuana, and drug use in general, are changing. In fact, in recent years authorities and interest groups at all levels of government have begun to act on the basis of these changes.

Changes in Attitudes Reflected

Although the public most commonly associates marijuana with radical politics, events at all three levels of government indicate increased effort of a conventional political nature to legalize marijuana or, at least, to reduce the penalties for violators.

On the national level such groups as the National Organization for Reform of Marijuana Laws (NORML) are attempting to legalize marijuana through state referenda and lobbying activities. The members of such organizations depart from the stereotype of marijuana users in that they are, as often as not, "straight" in appearance. They are also nonradical in their attempts to change the law through initiative and referenda movements that are within the tradition of American political reform. Further evidence of NORML's respectability as a middle-class reform effort is that it can claim the membership of former deputy director of the United States Narcotics and Dangerous Drugs Bureau, John Finlator, who feels that marijuana is less harmful than smoking cigarettes or drinking alcohol (Dana Schmidt, February 12, 1972). A number of other prominent persons, including former presidential candidate Eugene McCarthy and conservative political commentator William Buckley, have gone on record favoring legalization of marijuana.

In California a group called the California Marijuana Initiative succeeded in placing the legalization question on the ballot in the November 1972 general election. The passage of Proposition 19 on the California ballot would have made it legal to cultivate, process, transport, possess—but not to sell—marijuana.

Although preelection polls indicated that a majority of the newly enfranchised eighteen to twenty-one age group and close to a majority of the twenty-one to thirty-four age group favored legalization, support for the proposition was not restricted to younger voters. Proposition 19 had the backing of two prominent state legislators, San Francisco's sheriff, a general counsel for the Bank of America, and the San Francisco Bar Association. In spite of this support, however, Proposition 19 was defeated by a two-thirds majority of California voters.

On the local level, the city council of Ann Arbor, Michigan decided to issue a five-dollar fine to marijuana violators and thus, in the words of the city attorney, made the penalty "sort of like a parking ticket" (*Arizona Daily Star,* 1972). The passage of such an ordinance by a city council (despite the fact that it was later ruled unconstitutional by a district court) indicates a more relaxed view of marijuana use.

Other local authorities, who have not yet relaxed officially, are recognizing the futility of attempts to prohibit marijuana use. In the Southwest, for example, local officials in San Diego, Tucson, Albuquerque, and El Paso complain that antimarijuana laws are unenforceable at rock concerts because of the thousands of young people who smoke during the performances. After a "Rolling Stones" concert in Tucson, in which the community center was blue with the sweet-smelling haze of *cannabis sativa,* one of the youthful lawbreakers observed that "the cops were pretty good-natured about it—probably because there was so much grass in there everyone was wrecked—even the cops." About all the police can do in these cases, where perhaps three- to four-thousand persons are breaking the law—short of risking a riot by attempting to make mass arrests—is to ignore the violations and step outside for some fresh air; or remain inside, relax, breathe deeply, and enjoy the music.

THE COSTS OF ENFORCEMENT

The coincidence of events at the national, state, and local levels of government within a relatively short period of time can be interpreted as a trend toward a liberalization of marijuana laws, and perhaps, in the not-too-distant future, legalization. After a similar political gestation period some forty years ago, Prohibition was finally reversed and alcohol was legalized.

If marijuana is legalized, however, it will not be the result of legal interpretations alleging the unconstitutionality of present laws, even though such cases are important in the overall political process. It will be because authorities will decide that the costs of enforcing antimarijuana laws simply outweigh any benefits.

The "law" in America has frequently been honored in the breach: Americans and their political representatives have at times been staunch supporters of the letter of the law; but they have just as often considered the law to be symbolic, to be a statement of ideology rather than of commitment. Accordingly, the legal guarantees of the Thirteenth, Fourteenth, and Fifteenth Amendments were not extended to black citizens until authorities, after nearly a decade of conflict in the 1960s, realized that the social and political costs of ignoring the laws were greater than the costs of enforcement.

Less dramatically, the trends observed with respect to the marijuana issue reveal a similar reassessment. Given that marijuana has not been proven a harmful, physiologically addicting drug, the question that must be addressed is: What are the gains and what are the losses under present laws? The gains are hard to document because the laws appear to be unenforceable and largely ineffectual in prohibiting the use of marijuana. But the losses are undeniable when the decline in confidence and respect for the authority of the law is assessed.

SUGGESTED READINGS

Blum, Richard H., *et al. Society and Drugs: Social and Cultural Observations* (Vol. I), and *Students and Drugs: College and High School Observations* (Vol. II). San Francisco: Jossey-Bass, 1969.

Clarke, James W., and E. Lester Levine. "Marijuana Use, Social Discontent and Political Alienation: A Study of High School Youth," *American Political Science Review*, 65 (March 1971), 120-130.

Goode, Erich. *The Marijuana Smokers.* New York: Basic Books, 1970.

Kaplan, John. *Marijuana: The New Prohibition.* New York: (Pocket Books) Simon and Schuster, 1971.

Mason, Alpheus T., and William Beaney. *American Constitutional Law.* 5th ed. Englewood Cliffs, N.J.: Prentice-Hall, 1972, chapters 9 and 11.

Meiklejohn, Alexander. *Political Freedom: The Constitutional Powers of the People.* New York: Oxford University Press, 1965.

National Commission on Marijuana and Drug Abuse. *Marijuana: A Signal of Misunderstanding.* New York: New American Library, 1972.

The historical and legal discussions presented in this chapter are drawn primarily from Barry C. Wukasch, *Marijuana and the Law: An Analysis of Evolving Drug Policy* (unpublished dissertation: University of Arizona, 1972).

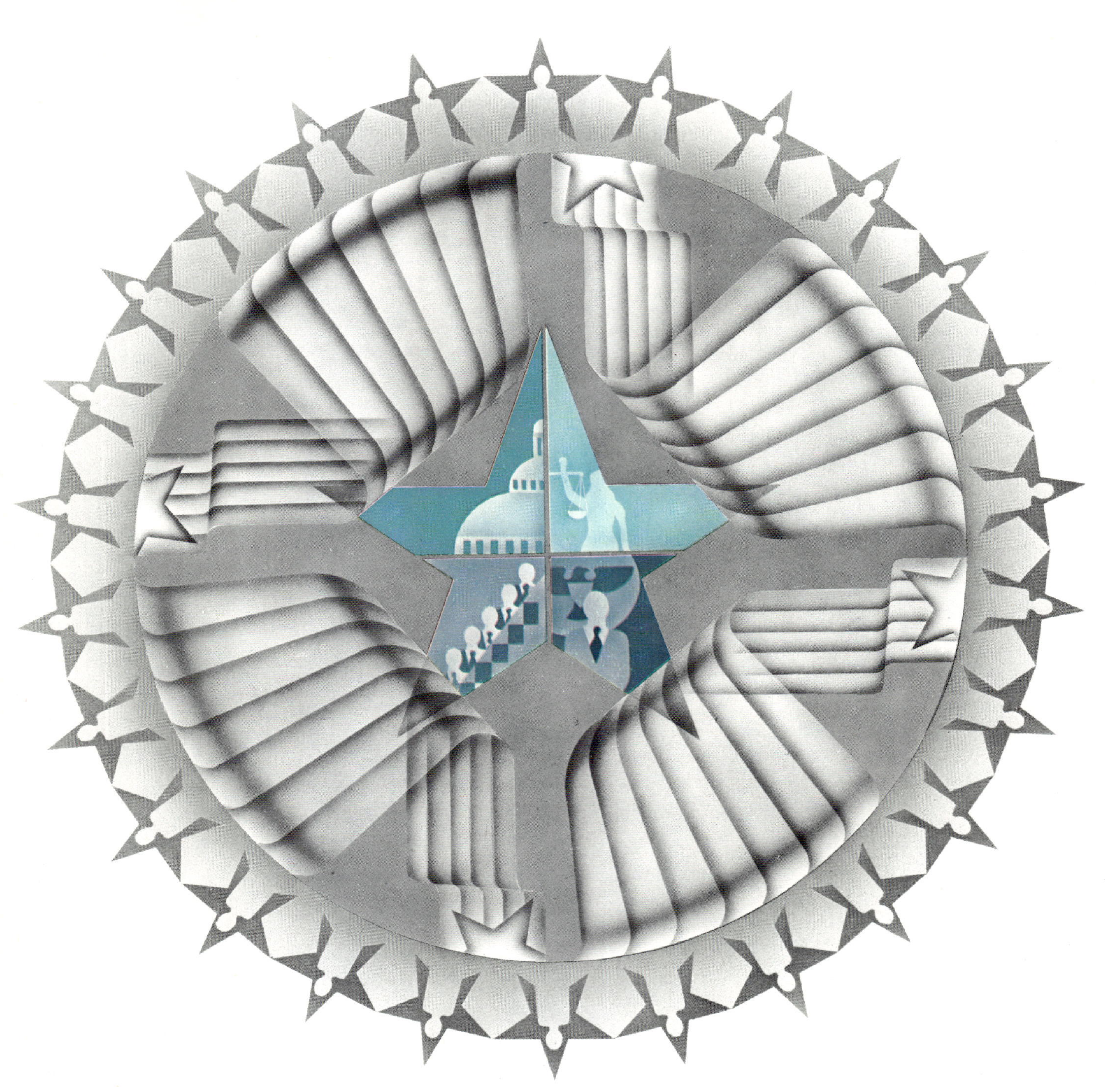

UNIT III

WHO RUNS THE GOVERNMENT?

Political institutions are the means through which we formalize our political activities. They are the channels into which conflicts and cooperative efforts flow. They are the rituals that we share in the process of regulating ourselves in our day-to-day efforts at political creation.

The four institutions discussed in this unit—the legislative, executive, bureaucratic, and judicial—are elements common to most modern societies. Yet the particular form these institutions take and the ways in which they relate to each other vary according to the nation's culture and its past political struggles.

Yet political institutions not only reflect, they also shape the culture of which they are a part. The fact that America has a President who is independently elected, rather than a Prime Minister chosen by Parliament as in the British system, provides us with some special problems and opportunities. Similarly, the existence of a Supreme Court with the power to declare acts of Congress unconstitutional is a rather unique and profoundly influential fact of our political life. Many issues in American political history might have worked out differently if our particular institutional arrangements had been different. Had it not been for the Supreme Court's powers, for example, the process of school desegregation might have occurred in a radically different fashion. Had the President not acquired overwhelming powers in foreign policy, the nature of our Vietnam involvement might also have been considerably different. In any case, the particular forms that political institutions take have important influence on the nature of policy. In the chapters that follow, we will be exploring the ways the American institutional arrangement affects policy making and thereby affects the quality of our public life.

POLITICAL LEGITIMACY AND POLITICAL INSTITUTIONS

In the 1960s many Americans began to raise serious questions regarding the legitimacy, or the trustworthiness, of their political institutions. The statistics are rather startling:

Public Trust in Political Institutions

QUESTION	RESPONSE	PERCENT RESPONDING	
		1964	1970
How much attention do congressmen pay to the people who elected them?	Good deal	44	31
	Some	40	46
	Not much	16	23
Do you trust the government in Washington to do what's right?	Always	15	7
	Most of the time	63	48
	Some of the time	22	45
Is the government run mostly for the big interests or mostly in the interests of all?	For all	69	45
	For big interests	31	55

Source: Survey Research Center, University of Michigan, Ann Arbor, Michigan.

The central star of our symbol (left) contains our nation's four political institutions—they represent the means through which we formalize our political activities.

What do these trends mean and what accounts for them? How *do* they or how *will* they affect the functioning of our political institutions? These are not simple questions. Yet we can say for certain that the decline in trust of political institutions is related to the sorts of issues that American politics dealt with in the 1960s and to the ways those issues were handled. The many faces of the race issue, Vietnam, civil liberties questions, urban problems, poverty—all of these issues combined to provide a bitter testing of America's political institutions. Many paradoxical things emerged from the 1960s, one of which was a considerable transformation in the ways different groups regarded the main political institutions.

Congress

Congress entered the 1960s as one of the world's strongholds of gerontocracy, or rule by the elderly, and it was predominantly rule by the southern elderly at that. The seniority system, the filibuster, and the conservative Democrat-Republican coalition meant that all serious liberal legislation had to surmount a series of obstacles on the way toward passage.

These structural traits of Congress were defended by many moderates and conservatives as a necessary counterweight to the liberal, innovative tendencies of the executive branch. Congress generally, and the House of Representatives in particular, was said to be "closer" to the people—and, although the assertion enraged the liberals, it was probably true as long as one thought of the "people" as those who opposed significant change (which meant some Americans all of the time and all Americans some of the time).

Firmly established as these patterns seemed to be, the acids of the sixties ate away at them and reshaped important aspects of congressional power. The southern gerontocracy gave ground. The filibuster ceased to be so formidable a weapon. The conservative Democrat-Republican coalition lost some of its zap. Some senators even had the audacity to argue that the Vietnam involvement was immoral and that the President of the United States had lied about our participation.

Overall, the seventies began with Congress seeking to limit presidential prerogatives and the White House reasserting the need for wide latitude in its executive initiatives.

The Presidency

As the sixties began, the Presidency was the chief hope of liberals and the chief fear of conservatives. Liberals, observing a virtual stand-off in Congress and having little faith that the Democratic Party could truly get itself together, looked to a progressive President as the main source of policy innovation and as the leader in efforts at social justice. Both John Kennedy and Lyndon Johnson fulfilled these liberal hopes to a considerable degree. Both were activist Presidents. The very title of Kennedy's Administration—The New Frontier—implied his activist style. And yet, his crash program of missile building and his belligerent stance in several international crises, particularly Berlin in 1961 and Cuba in 1962, led many of his earlier backers to doubt the wisdom of his policies. Although there is some indication that Kennedy was revising his view of the international scene, his assassination in 1963 made it impossible to know what sort of President he would have become if elected a second time.

Lyndon Johnson's landslide over Barry Goldwater in 1964 provided liberals with the congressional majority they had been seeking for years. There followed a flood of liberal legislation—the Civil Rights Act of 1964, antipoverty legislation, and Medicare—but the domestic tranquility many liberals expected would coincide with these increased governmental efforts did not occur. Beginning in the Watts section of Los Angeles in 1965 and continuing for four successive summers, black riots erupted in most American cities. These shocks to the expectations of many liberals were doubled when Johnson dramatically expanded the American military involvement in Vietnam and sent the marines to invade the Dominican Republic on the pretext that the Communists were taking over the government there.

These developments, all part of a highly activist Presidency, left many liberal supporters of that institution in a dilemma. The disillusionment went deep. If the Presidency, which since Roosevelt and the New Deal had stood for liberalism and reform, could also be turned to malign purposes, then liberal trust in the Presidency would have to be reassessed.

The first Nixon Administration was also notable for extensive executive initiatives in both domestic and international affairs. Yet certain factors concerning the extent of the Presidency's expanded power produced a permanent set of doubts. Liberals and conservatives alike had begun to reconsider the importance of Congress, the political parties, and grass-roots politics in terms of creating a healthier, more balanced polity.

The Bureaucracy

Bureaucracies are one of the distinguishing features of modern governments. They are not a new invention, but in the twentieth century their use has been perfected, or perhaps overperfected. Modern governments engage in complex and extensive forms of planning, delivery of services, and regulation. They also govern very large populations. Bureaucracies have grown in order to cope with these matters. That is, they deliver services, they plan, and they regulate. They have obvious virtues and in many cases it is difficult to imagine how problems can be dealt with except bureaucratically, as, for example, in planning and carrying through a pension system, tax collection, and fielding an army. But bureaucracies have some not so obvious defects: They seek power for themselves, resist change, and impede local initiative.

In American mythology, conservatives have often pictured the federal bureaucrat as a Satanic figure. The federal government is said to be too powerful, with its bureaucrats trying to run people's lives. For liberals, the bureaucrat has often been seen as a kind of citizens' helper, who is trying to create a fairer, more just society. Of course, neither stereotype conveys the complexities of bureaucratic life. In the last decade several significant themes have emerged concerning government bureaucracy, themes that touch on, yet go beyond the images of both liberals and conservatives.

There has been a reawakened interest in decentralization. Black power advocates called for "local control" as a way to gain power. The resentment of what was regarded as insensitive and sometimes malicious bureaucratic interference, however, went beyond racial politics. Many social theorists argued that excessive centralization— of government as well as of corporations—was one of the plagues of modern life because of its inhibition of local initiative. There was a call for the "humanization" of bureaucracies, which might include decentralization, the creation of mechanisms like the Swedish "ombudsman" to air citizen grievances, and the creation of more interesting forms of work.

In the meantime, bureaucracies remain subject to serious inefficiencies and weaknesses. Many regulatory agencies are captives of the very interests they are supposed to regulate. Bureaucracies have become laws unto themselves and go about their business with little criticism and external direction. Bureaucrats can establish alliances with Congress, or with outside interests, and thereby become strong enough to resist effective regulation. The Perspective on the military-industrial complex shows this process in an extreme form.

The Supreme Court

Perhaps even more than the Presidency, the Supreme Court has been a center of controversy in the post-World War II period. During the 1950s and 1960s the Court created a series of startling new precedents. In doing so it sought to remedy many long-standing injustices in the society—ones that the other two branches were generally too stalemated or lacking in principle to deal with effectively. The Court's capacity to act in areas such as school desegregation, reapportionment, school prayers, civil liberties, and the rights of accused persons showed the advantages of its relative insulation from the rough and tumble of political life.

The sweep of the Warren Court decisions was truly epic although not all-encompassing. (There were areas, such as foreign policy and economic regulation, that the court generally steered away from.) It took on much of the most difficult public business of the day and steered conflicts into new channels. Of course, many of its actions disturbed the domestic tranquility, and the Court's opponents had considerable success in blunting the effects of the new decisions. However, the Court had broken through the political and moral logjams of generations and had set free much new energy.

The new Burger Court, with four Nixon appointees, has taken on a more moderate cast than the Warren Court. Liberals and conservatives, who had tended to take rather strong sides concerning the Warren Court, have switched places. Yet the significance of the Warren Court went beyond the particular decisions it had handed down. The Supreme Court had shown it could be a decisive and even adventurous instrument of progressive change—a strikingly new role for an institution with such a conservative past. The Court's ideological significance appeared to be in transition.

INSTITUTIONS: AN OVERVIEW AND SOME ISSUES

The developments of the 1960s led to some important alterations in the American political landscape. Public attitudes shifted toward skepticism or outright hostility toward political institutions. Liberals and conservatives were forced to rethink their assessments of the roles of Presidents, Congress, and the courts. The political scene became more complex in that the old remedies no longer worked so well (or, in some cases, they did not work at all).

Given the changes in attitude, it is not easy to predict the future relationships between national political institutions and policy making. Although it is clear, for example, that the Supreme Court will no longer play its intensely activist controversy-courting role, one cannot yet guess if the Court will try to turn back the clock and actually reverse earlier precedents. Similarly, although Congress is no longer the bastion of delay and veto that it once was, its activist potential remains questionable. The role of the Presidency is also uncertain, in that indications of scandal and corruption in high places threaten to weaken its activist role.

Probably the most significant issue for the future is whether the political institutions we have can cope effectively with the sorts of problems we will confront in the rest of this century. These include environmental matters, social and economic justice, coping with technological change, planning for an expanding population, providing people with meaningful opportunities for creative work, restructuring priorities to provide more adequate social services and better planned communities, fashioning a more humane foreign policy. These things cannot be accomplished without considerable social and political creativity. It is an open question whether the present functioning of our national political institutions provides the context in which enough of such creativity can emerge.

Questions of power are also at stake. Blacks have made a significant impact on national and local politics in the last decade, but will this development continue or grow? A similar question relates to other of society's relatively powerless groups, such as women and various minorities: Will the rules of the American political game prove flexible enough to allow for a more varied and contentious pluralism in the future? We take up these issues again in the Epilogue.

8
CONGRESS

Historically, Congress has played a major role in policy making. Viewing the legislature as the keystone of democracy, the authors of the Constitution listed the powers of Congress in Article I. Except in times of crisis, it was the men of Congress who refined the few great issues of the day; as late as the end of the nineteenth century, Woodrow Wilson announced that "Congress is the dominant, nay, the irresistible power of the federal system" (Woodrow Wilson, 1885).

Few observers today would describe Congress in such expansive terms. "The decline of Congress" has been universally commented on, by friends as well as foes, by liberals as well as conservatives, and by congressmen as well as outside observers. Gloomy phrases, such as those found in Ralph Nader's report on Congress, are frequently used to describe Congress's fallen estate: "the great American default"; "a continuous underachiever."

On the other hand, few observers today would deny the rapid growth of the power of the Presidency vis-à-vis Congress. The shaping experiences of the twentieth century—two world wars, the Depression, and the extended Cold War—have greatly increased the policy-making power of the President. In the area of foreign policy Congress has yielded much of its constitutional power to "advise and consent" by deferring to the President's ability to handle the fast-moving international situation. On the domestic side as well, the complexity of governmental transactions and the need for flexibility have led to increased executive involvement at the expense of Congress. And yet the disillusionment that has followed in the wake of the nation's involvement in Vietnam has led to fundamental questions regarding the desirability of this concentration of power, its effects on the content of public policy, and the possible alternatives.

In view of these considerations, this chapter singles out several factors that strongly shape Congress's policy-making role: the President's influence over the legislative process; the burdens of work load and constituent demands that influence the decisions the congressman makes; and the organizational traits of Congress that have developed in response to the volume of work and the general political environment. The chapter ends with an analysis of Congress's role in the four areas of decision making

Figure 8.1 O, Congress! Object of awe, derision, love, distrust, and hope. The 1970s have found Congress locked in fierce battle with the White House. Hidden beneath the smooth courtesies of platform oratory and invitations to White House dinners lies an earnest struggle for control of the legislative process.

around which this book is developed—the economy, foreign affairs, race, and civil liberties—and a discussion of the implications of the ongoing debate between Congress and the Presidency.

THE POLICY PROCESS: A PRECARIOUS BALANCE

Consider the dispute between the President and Congress over a policy matter of great domestic importance—the control of federal spending. In January 1973 the Nixon Administration announced that it was *impounding,* or refusing to spend, the funds that had been appropriated for federally subsidized housing programs—programs that had been enacted by Congress and signed into law. Furthermore, the President announced he was abolishing other congressionally enacted programs by refusing to provide for them in his proposed budget (some $12 billion worth, according to some estimates). Many of the programs he chose to cut, as critics were quick to point out, were parts of President Johnson's liberal domestic program, known as the "Great Society." Nixon's justification for the cuts was that the responsibility for the programs, as well as the previously allocated funds, was being shifted away from the federal government and back to the states.

Many Presidents have impounded funds in order to control the federal spending authorized by Congress. Congressmen have understandably been irked by this method of accounting imposed on them by Democratic as well as by Republican Presidents. But the issue involves much more than the image of a congressman standing with hat in hand pleading with the White House to spend funds that have been allocated for a pet project. Impoundment involves the *power of the purse,* the power to appropriate funds that is constitutionally granted to Congress and that is fundamental to Congress's participation in the policy process. In the words of Senator Edward Brooke (Rep.-Mass.) the impoundment issue involves "the right of the executive to refuse to carry out programs which have been enacted into law."

But the President's influence over legislation begins long before a bill is enacted into law. What are the sources and the forms of this influence?

The President as Chief Legislator

The Constitution is vague in its delineation of power. It vests Congress with "all legislative powers" (Article I, Section 1); however, the President "shall from time to time give to the Congress information on the state of the Union, and recommend to their consideration such measures as he shall judge necessary and expedient" (Article II, Section 3). From these constitutional provisions has grown the President's power to participate in setting the legislative agenda of Congress—a vital first step in the policy-making process.

However, the President *influences* rather than *dominates* the legislative process for the following reasons. First, many presidential proposals are reactions to issues that are already being considered in Congress—proposals to protect consumers and the environment are examples. Second, many of the President's proposals represent long-standing positions of his political party, which are echoed by members of that party in Congress. Third, interest groups and other policy makers in and out of government help to determine the priorities of both the President and Congress. Finally, presidential initiatives are conditioned by *anticipated reactions;* that is, the President's proposals are shaped and modified by his assessment of what Congress will accept. In sum, the President is forced to react to congressional initiatives just as Congress must react to his. The President's influence in setting legislative priorities is great, but it is not the only influence nor is it always the most important.

Setting the legislative agenda is only the beginning of policy making. Legislation must be enacted, and the President has many resources to facilitate or to stop passage of a bill. He has the benefit of the Constitution; he can *veto,* or refuse to sign into law, a measure with which he disagrees. Although it is a powerful device, the use of the veto has been compared to using a machine gun to shoot a rabbit; that is, if the President objects to only one feature of a bill, he has the choice of vetoing the entire measure or accepting the objectionable provision. He has no "item veto," a device long urged by those who favor increased presidential power.

The veto power does not have to be used to be effective, for even the threat of its use has considerable impact. Executive disapproval of a pending bill (similar to the "Change-It-or-Lose-It" sentiment of automobile bumpersticker fame) is subtly transmitted to Congress. Congressmen who favor the

Figure 8.2 The President "shall from time to time give to the Congress Information of the State of the Union, and recommend to their Consideration such Measures as he shall judge necessary and expedient . . ." (Article II, Section 3). This constitutional directive to the President has been translated into the annual ceremony known as the State of the Union address. Appearing before both houses of Congress, the President reports on Administration achievements and reveals his legislative priorities. This occasion dramatically emphasizes the President's influence on the legislative process.

legislation in question must then either remove the objectionable provision to avoid presidential veto; override the veto by garnering the necessary two-thirds vote of both House and Senate; or include a pet provision of the President's in order to induce him to sign a bill he might otherwise veto.

The President has many other methods of influencing Congress. The power of presidential favor is most persuasive. By accepting the advice of congressmen in making political appointments, the President can create good will, forge alliances, and build a store of political IOUs that he can call in at a later time.

A more frequent source of presidential sanctions and rewards is the President's discretion over federal spending. The placement of army bases and federal office buildings and the granting of Small Business Administration loans are important to congressmen. Receipt of such favors is visible evidence of their ability to deliver greater prosperity to their districts, and those who are successful stress the fact during their reelection campaigns. Conversely, the closing of federal installations is a weapon of presidential reprisal.

The White House also dispenses symbolic rewards. The President or Vice-President may personally campaign for favored incumbents, for new candidates, or even for allies who belong to the opposition party. For example, President Nixon informally endorsed the reelection of Mississippi's Democratic Senator James Eastland, Chairman of the Judiciary Committee, after Eastland supported the President's Supreme Court nominees.

Congress: A Rubber Stamp?

In spite of his unique advantages in the legislative process, the President is far from supreme in his relations with Congress. Congress has never served as a "rubber stamp" for the Chief Executive; on the average, Presidents from Eisenhower to Nixon have had slightly more than 50 percent of their proposals enacted. However, as is shown in Figure 8.3, the congressional vote generally supports the position the President has taken on given issues before the Congress.

All in all, Congress has been uniquely successful in preserving its prerogatives. Many nations, faced with accelerating social and political change, have either relegated representative bodies to secondary status or have dispensed with them. Dictators, military *juntas*, party councils, and, in industrialized nations, massive bureaucracies have taken over functions that historically have been reserved for representatives of the nation's citizenry. Compared with legislatures elsewhere in the world, Congress's grip on policy making is impressive. An outline of Congress's legislative functions makes the point.

Of the numerous legislative functions, the one most frequently associated with Congress is *law making*—deliberation, often at a highly technical level, over the content of policies. Other functions, however, are no less important. Probably uppermost in voters' minds is *representation*—a legislator must serve the needs of his constituents, or the people he serves. Congress promotes *policy clarification* by providing a public platform where issues can be identified and policies can be explored. *Consensus-building* is the traditional bargaining process through which various constituency demands are combined into winning coalitions for policies. Congress provides *legitimization* when policies of the various interests are combined in an appropriate manner. Once policies have been enacted, Congress may provide *oversight,* or review, to ensure that programs and policies are being implemented.

The struggle over the proper role of Congress is, in reality, disagreement over the relative emphasis given to these various functions. Defenders of Congress assert that it should retain a tight grasp on all of these functions, especially law making, consensus-building, and representation. Advocates of presidential authority tend to emphasize instead such functions as legitimization and oversight. The debate over congressional powers, which would hardly surprise the founding fathers, continues unabated. Only the faces change, with shifts in the policies being fought over. In reality, the conflict is a struggle over policy making for the nation's future. To understand Congress's role in the process, it is necessary to look at the average congressman and his job.

THE CONGRESSMAN AND THE FOLKS AT HOME

Who becomes a congressman? Who does he represent? How does he spend his time? An examination of an average senator's morning suggests some of the answers:

The senator starts his typical day tired. He returned very late last night from a speech back home, and he had to get up early this morning to present himself at a breakfast sponsored by utility executives. ("These guys come here mostly for a good time, but to make it look official, they nail me for an hour when I can't claim a conflicting engagement.") In the gray light of the cab, he gives his *New York Times* a 10-minute reading, hoping that his aides will let him know if anything important happened yesterday. . . .

He arrives at his office at 9:30 A.M., already thirty minutes late, grousing to himself about the three hurried minutes it takes to get down the long corridor. . . . He goes in through his private door, so visitors won't see him. He has the usual committee meeting scheduled at ten o'clock . . . but a check confirms his suspicion: his waiting room is crowded with people he can't ignore. He apologizes to his assistant and tells his secretary to "run them in." One of them helped him in an election back in the dim past. ("He just wants to say hello and show his wife that he has entrée to a senator's office.")

. . . By now, the committee hearing has already started. But there are more constituents, or self-proclaimed representatives of constituents, to be seen. He greets them, one after another, listens, nodding agreeably for a few minutes, and turns them over to his executive aides. But he worries. He gets a lot of votes by helping constituents, and this service is one of his major assets during campaigns. He knows it takes up half the time of his staff, time that he needs for help on the issues. And . . . even though he helps these people, he knows that most of the things they ask are wrong or antithetical to the public interest. (James Boyd, 1970, pp. 104–106)

Who Is the Average Congressman?

Before examining the average congressman's relationship to his constituency, it is necessary to take a look at the congressman himself. Who is he, and what background does he bring with him to office?

To begin with, Congress is by no means *demographically* representative; that is, it does not mirror the nation's population. The average congressman is in his mid-fifties, a decade older than the average voter. The formal qualifications of office—age (25 years for the House, 30 for the Senate); citizenship (7 years for the House, 9 for the Senate); and residency in the state—are fairly permissive, although in the wake of the Twenty-sixth Amendment, which lowered the voting age to eighteen, there have been moves to lower the minimum age requirement. However, not all Americans enjoy an equal statisti-

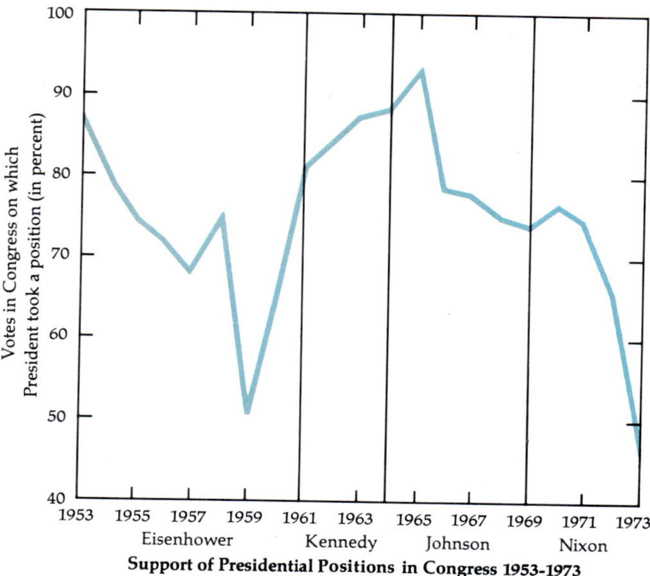

Figure 8.3 A multitude of variables operate on congressmen to determine whether or not they will support the positions the President takes on legislation being considered by Congress. One of the most important variables is party orientation; another is ideological orientation (for instance, southern Democrats often find themselves able to support the positions of Republican Presidents). A President who faces an opposition-dominated Congress and economic difficulties can expect his chart of success with Congress to take a nose dive. For example, President Nixon, who during his second term was faced with an opposition Congress, economic crisis, and a scandal of major proportion, found his success with Congress reduced significantly. At the time this chart was drawn, there was much major Nixon legislation still in the works, and the President had been cultivating congressional support with greater intensity than in previous years. Nevertheless, the crises of his Administration had made it unlikely that Nixon would be able to better his legislative track record for 1973 with a Congress that was determined to reinstate some of its prerogatives (from the Congressional Quarterly, 1973).

cal chance of serving in Congress (Roger Davidson, 1969). Among members, educational achievement is high. The professions predominate—especially law (the background of almost two-thirds of all members), business, agriculture, education, and journalism. The "log-cabin-to-Capitol Hill" myth does not apply to contemporary legislators: An examination of senatorial careers shows that future senators tend to grow up in middle- and upper-class families (Donald Matthews, 1960). Only a handful of blacks serve in Congress, although their number is growing. Congress is also a predominantly male institution; in the 93rd Congress there were only fourteen females.

This demographic imbalance means that congressional policy making is dominated by individuals who are unrepresentative of the population in terms of age, education, wealth, color, and sex; the same is true of the courts and the executive branch of the government. However, it is by no means self-evident that Congress must be demographically representative in order to be a representative institution. For example, a legislator from a coal-mining district may be an effective spokesman even though he has never worked in the mines himself.

Furthermore, the demographic imbalance of Congress is softened by the fact that its members must solicit public support. Virtually all senators and representatives have served a lengthy apprenticeship in state and local politics, especially the state legislatures, before being elected to Congress. Occasionally, aspirants have bypassed this convention by virtue of nonpolitical achievement—military service or some form of celebrityship; but in general, Congress is a body of political professionals.

The significance of political accountability may be seen by contrasting the congressman's political professionalism with that of other important policy makers on the President's staff. For example, in the early days of the Kennedy Administration, Vice-President Lyndon Johnson met, and was mightily impressed by, the top Cabinet officers and bright young assistants to the President. He later enthused about them to House Speaker Sam Rayburn. Rayburn listened and then perceptively commented, "Yes, but I'd feel better if just one of them had run for county sheriff" (David Halberstam, 1972). The subsequent covert engineering of the Vietnam War by

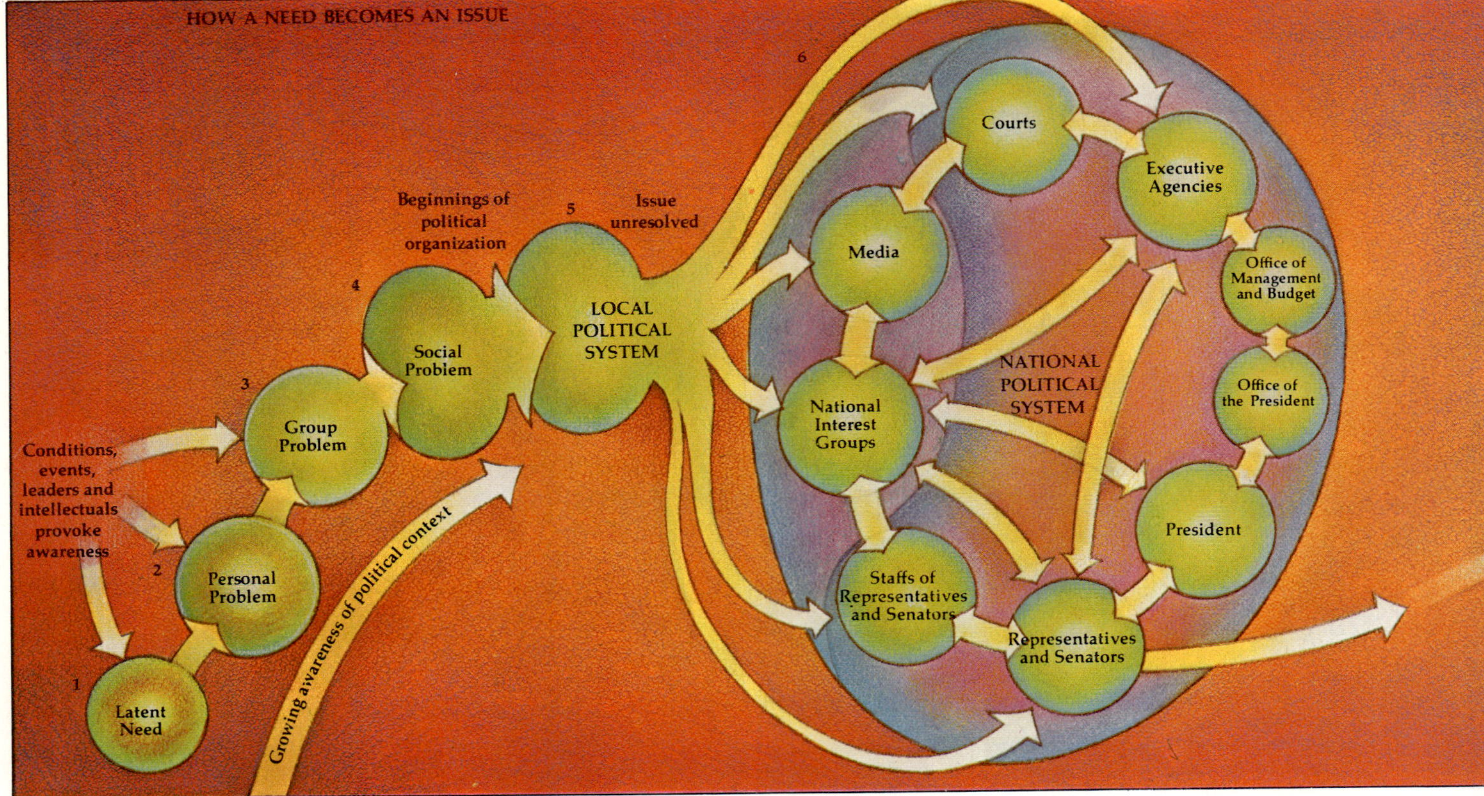

Figure 8.4
How a Need Becomes an Issue:

1. Latent needs are needs that one is either not conscious of or unable to verbalize. For example, a poor person may be suffering from malnutrition, and he may attribute his symptoms to "bad blood" or to aging. Conditions, events, leaders, or intellectuals can begin the process of growing self-consciousness or awareness, the process of better relating one's problems to their correct origins. For example, a poverty program community organizer may explain to the afflicted person that his symptoms are those of malnutrition, and he might explain the components of a sound diet.

2. After identifying a need, it reaches the status of a personal problem to be solved; at this stage, it is still a problem limited to the individual.

3. With the help of an event—for example, the hospitalization or death of several children from diseases made severe by malnutrition, or the advice and instruction of a respected community leader or outside expert—individuals with a similar problem may become aware that they share a group problem and that they must look for a solution together.

4. The big breakthrough in this process of growing awareness of political context is the recognition of the role the social, economic, and political environments have in causing or in curing the group's problems.

5. Recognition of social influences can motivate a group to seek remedies of assistance from the political system of the society, for example, public funds or expertise. At this point it is most likely that the group would attempt to find assistance from the local political system. If the problem, which has been made a local issue, now remains unresolved, new steps may be taken to contact other groups and to find ways to go beyond the local political system.

6. All arrows in the National Political System denote the most likely pathways by which an issue may enter into the national political system and, once within it, the ways the issue may be passed from one section of the system to another. All the components of this system are parts of the government, except for the media and national interest groups. The ultimate goal of our political group is to guide its issue through as many of the pathways as necessary to get it finally to a representative or to a senator who will sponsor it in Congress. (Note: Many pieces of technical legislation actually originate in federal executive agencies or in the national interest groups, but ultimately they find their origins in the needs and desires of particular people.)

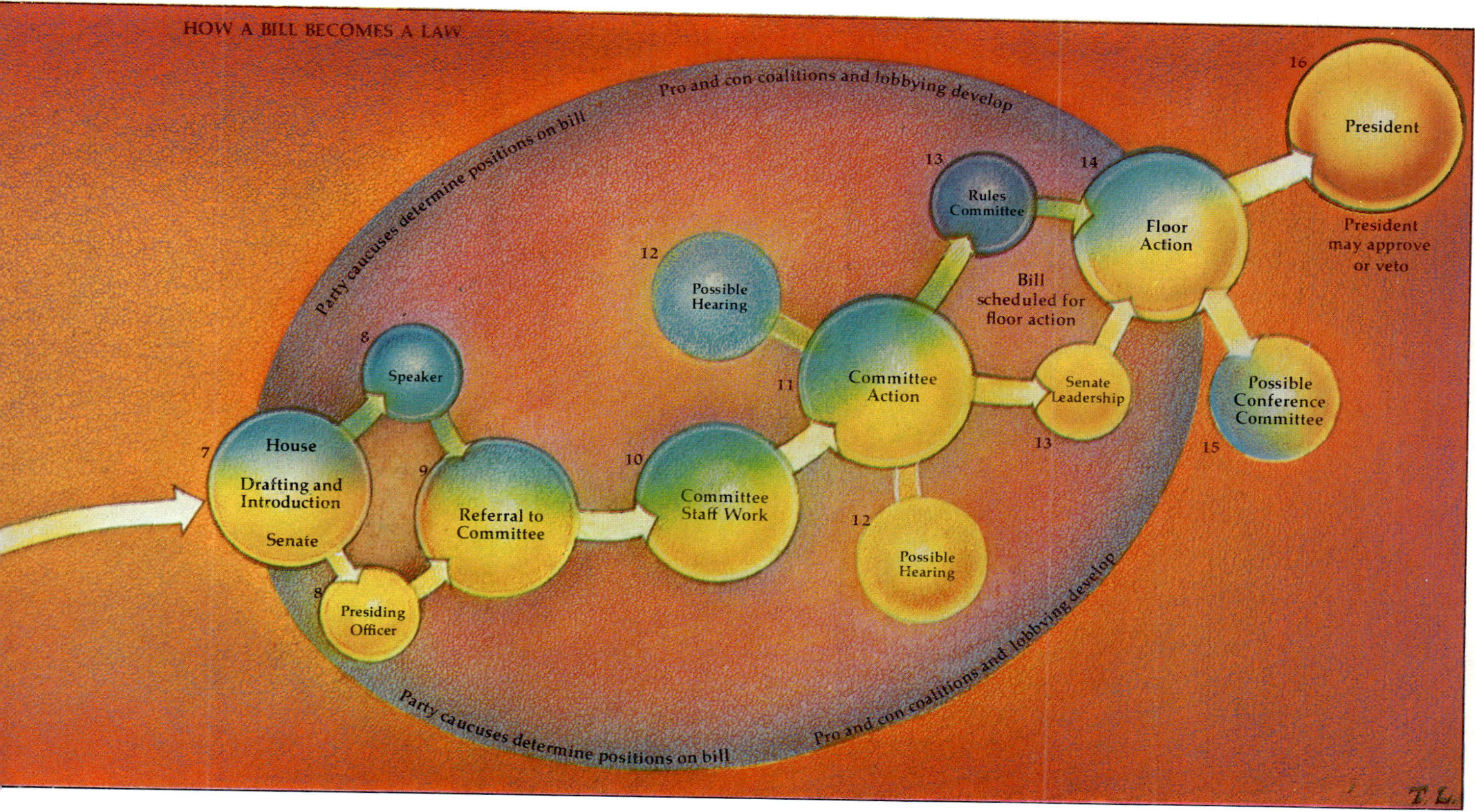

How a Bill Becomes a Law: (unless specified, these steps are essentially the same in both the House and the Senate)

7. The intended remedy to the group's problem must now be technically written (drafted) into a piece of legislation. This work may be done by the original group in association with other groups, by experts in a government agency, by a congressman's staff, or by all three working together. It then must be formally introduced into the work of the House or Senate by members of those bodies.

8, 9. In the House, the Speaker officially determines to which committee the bill will be referred; in the Senate, the presiding officer performs this function. Usually the decision where to refer a significant bill is influenced by the desires of congressional leaders, by the position taken by the parties, or by lobbyist actions. Such influences may have begun even earlier in the drafting stage and usually will continue until final presidential action has been taken.

10. Committee staff work is one of the most important elements of the legislative process; it includes research and rewriting of legislation in consultation with others.

11, 12. Committee action is dominated by the chairman; it may include rewriting, deferring action until later, pigeon-holing (stopping the bill completely), or holding private or public hearings on the bill. Usually a subcommittee of the entire standing committee works on the bill and reports to the full committee. The committee may also write an entirely new bill on the subject.

13. The bill is scheduled for appearance for a vote. In the House, the Rules Committee is responsible for scheduling; in the Senate, a bill is scheduled by consultation among leaders. The schedulers also determine under what rules of debate the bill will appear.

14. Floor action in the House and the Senate essentially consists of debate and vote (passage requires majority vote), but the amount and the informality of debate may vary.

15. If the bills finally reported out of the House and the Senate on the same topic are different, it is necessary to appoint a conference committee, made up of concerned members of both houses, to iron out differences. If successful, the now-identical bills return to their respective houses for a final attempt at concurrent passage.

16. If approved by both houses, the bill is sent to the President for his signature or veto. If the President vetoes the bill, it may still become law if passed by a two-thirds vote of both houses. The results of the law—what the bill in its final form does or does not accomplish in terms of satisfying the need that was its origin—may lead to new latent needs, and the process may be begun again.

these same bright young men suggests the virtue of policy making by those who must look to the people for support.

Who Does He Represent?

Many legislators are by nature transplanted locals, who reflect the values and attitudes of their home communities; out of necessity, they remain attuned to their constituents' demands (Roger Davidson, 1970). Thus, to understand the roots of legislators' behavior, it is necessary to look to the constituencies that elect them.

The States Represented: The Senate

Each state is represented equally in the Senate (two senators per state). Because states vary widely in population, the Senate is the one legislative body in the nation where the "one man, one vote" rule decidedly does not apply. The founding fathers decided that senators would be chosen by their respective state legislatures (rather than by the voters, who chose members of the House) in order that the Senate might function as a counterweight to the more popular interests represented by the much larger House of Representatives. Although this distinction was destroyed in 1913 by the Seventeenth Amendment, which provided for direct popular election of senators, Article V of the Constitution assured each state its equal representation, regardless of the size of its population.

As long as states were relatively small and senators selected indirectly, the Senate tended to be a collection of spokesmen for dominant state or regional interests—cotton, oil, tobacco, banking, and so forth. Today, however, a majority of states boast highly developed and varied economies, and statewide electorates are often *microcosms* (or representative miniatures) of the whole nation. States are increasingly dominated by metropolitan areas, with all their ethnic, racial, and social issues. As a result, the Senate, during the past generation, has become more representative of the national majority and has begun to support more liberal policies (Lewis Froman, 1963).

Although the six-year senatorial terms are relatively long (in comparison to the two-year House terms), reelection is somewhat more difficult than in the House of Representatives. With their wide variety of interests, statewide constituencies tend to be more competitive than the smaller House districts, with the result that senatorial elections tend to be closer and incumbents more often defeated (Barbara Hinckley, 1970). In 1970, for example, seven, or 20 percent, of the thirty-five incumbents up for

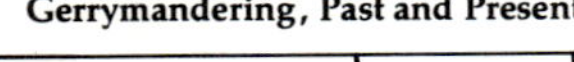

Gerrymandering, Past and Present

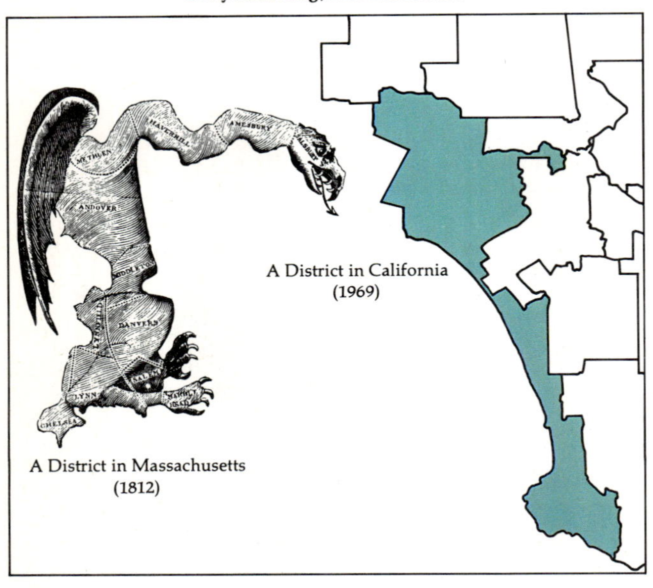

Figure 8.5 Few political practices in the United States have remained essentially the same from 1812 to the present, but the fine art of gerrymandering seems to be one of the few. In the notoriously misshapen 28th congressional district of Los Angeles county (left), one can recognize the same fierce winged creature that united the towns of Massachusetts under Governor Gerry.

Figure 8.6 (right) By luck, pluck, and sometimes even by a wise marriage, a congressman ascends the rungs of influence in Washington, D.C. Some rise faster than others: perhaps they bring to Congress a name that is already well known or perhaps they are preceded by good words from notables in their state, in the party, or even from the President himself. Whom you know, what you know, and how fast you learn the rules and the subtleties—all make for influence in Congress.

reelection were defeated either in the primaries or in the general elections.

The People Represented: The House

The 435 House seats are apportioned among the states by population, although even the smallest state is guaranteed at least one representative by the Constitution. On the theory that the House was intended to be popularly representative, the Supreme Court directed (*Wesberry* v. *Sanders,* 1964) that districts be substantially equal in population within each state. Districting is the responsibility of state legislatures and governors. If they fail to agree on an acceptable plan—as frequently happens, considering the high political stakes—courts may be called in to draw the lines (see Chapter 2).

The requirement that districts be equal in population (the average district now approaches a population of half a million) has given new impetus to the time-honored practice of *gerrymandering*—the art of drawing district lines cunningly in order to maximize partisan advantage (see Figure 8.5). There are two gerrymandering techniques, jokingly referred to as *packing* and *cracking*. To pack a district is to draw its lines to include as many of one party's voters as possible in order to make the district safe for the incumbent. In cracking, an area of one party's strength is divided among two or more districts to minimize that party's voting leverage.

The technique of gerrymandering has tended to increase the homogeneous nature of the average representative's district; as a result, House seats are among the least competitive offices in the American political system (Joseph Schlesinger, 1966). However, House districts have not been drawn to parallel other political or natural dividing lines; the candidate who purchases TV time may be speaking to many viewers who live outside the district he represents. This reinforces the natural advantages enjoyed by incumbents: staff help, knowledge of national problems, and free mailing privileges.

How Does He Spend His Time?

As members' backgrounds and constituencies vary, so do their job performances. From the individual legislator's perspective, the job is composed of two major tasks: *legislation* and *constituent service.* In his daily activities these tasks are closely interwoven; a look at a typical senator's afternoon shows how the tasks are combined:

It is past eleven o'clock when [the senator] gets to the committee hearing. During the walk over, his legislative assistant gives him a hurried, capsule briefing, just enough to confuse him. In the hearing, he asks the wrong ques-

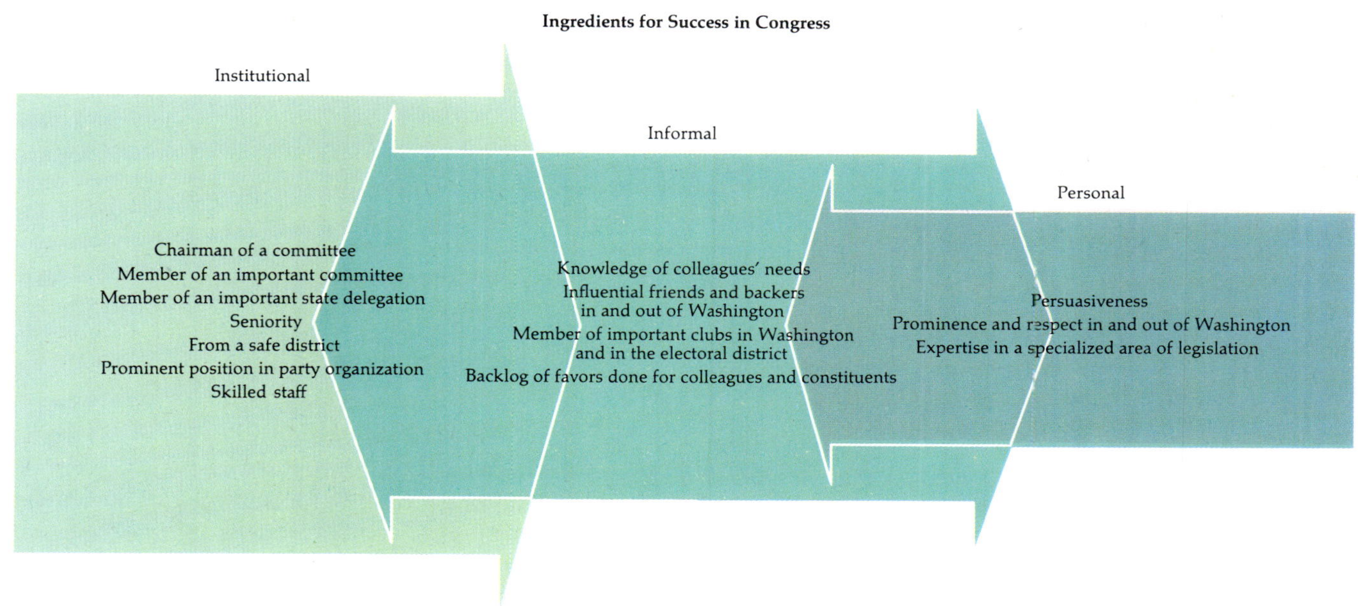

tions. So do other senators who come and go every few minutes . . . By ten minutes of twelve, he has picked up the thread, but now it's time to get to the Senate floor to insert into the *Congressional Record* a number of press releases just handed him by his head speechwriter. ("If I get there late, I'll have to wait my turn, behind all the windbags, and then I'll be late for lunch with my campaign finance chairman. *He* can't be kept waiting.")

. . . It's now two o'clock. The Senator is back in his office, and the afternoon schedule shapes up like a nightmare. But somehow, alternately helped and hindered by his staff, he gets through it. He signs a week's accumulation of letters—the 1 percent of the outgoing mail that commits him to things too important to be signed on the autograph machine. ("I wish I had time to read them carefully.")

. . . Throughout the afternoon, the bell in his office calls him to the floor to vote. He misses one vote because he has gone downtown briefly to tape a discussion program, but he does make three votes. Each time, however, it takes twenty minutes to get over to the floor and back, so there goes an hour.

There are two afternoon committee sessions on his schedule. He goes to the one that's being televised. . . . He has his picture taken on the steps of the Capitol with a high school class from back home. . . . ("They'll all be voters in three or four years, and their parents are voters now.")

He is late for his 4:30 appointment at the National Aeronautics and Space Administration (NASA), but he knows that the top men there will wait for a senator. . . . He is accompanied by businessmen from his state who are bidding for a new government contract. The meeting is mercifully short. ("I loused up my presentation, but I think I pulled it out. I gave them that I'll-remember-at-appropriation-time look and I don't think they'll give me the run-around again.") Lobbying for businessmen eats up his time in great chunks. He sometimes feels that he is forever cajoling a government contracting agency, or appearing before a regulatory commission, or testifying before the Senate Appropriations Committee at the behest of some business or other.

He is back in his office in the evening, but by now, his aides can tell from his gray countenance that he is bushed, so they don't press him for decisions. Tonight, he has dinner scheduled with a columnist who has seven outlets in the Senator's state. ("I'd better not have that third drink.") And, after that, he has promised to take his wife to an embassy party. . . . Maybe, when he gets home, around midnight, he'll take an hour to dig into his briefcase, to read that material on the population explosion, on starvation in Mississippi, on a new idea for housing in the ghetto, on the missile defense system, on the currency crisis, on the nuclear nonproliferation treaty. Yes, he's been trying to get to that briefcase for days, and maybe he will tonight. But he knows he won't. (Boyd, 1970, pp. 106–109)

The Congressman Legislates

As can easily be seen, the sheer volume of business taxes the congressman's finite resources of time, energy, and intellect. Legislators must therefore rely heavily on the views of others, including outside experts, lobbyists, and especially colleagues. However, it remains true that senators and representatives, almost alone among legislators in today's world, actually do fulfill the classic lawmaking role.

Legislators differ widely in their approach to lawmaking tasks. Because of the size of their work load, legislators cannot possibly be authorities on all matters; accordingly, they receive cues on how to vote from a variety of sources (Matthews and Stimson, 1970). Some rely on their own knowledge or conscience in making choices. Others follow "instructions," either actual or implied, from their voters. Skillful legislators anticipate voter reactions even in the absence of formal communications, and they soon learn to identify the issues that matter most to their constituents. Their freedom of action is expanded because, on most issues, a large majority of citizens are uninformed or unconcerned. Most elected officials would agree with the legislator who explained that everything he did had a relationship to the district, but it was not the only basis for his choice.

Legislators differ as to *which* constituency they are attuned to. Some claim to use the entire nation's welfare as a guidepost; others act as spokesmen for local interests. Usually, legislators find it impossible to relate to the entire electorate in all its complexity; rather, they rely on their conception of their district and on associates with whom they communicate to transmit cues about voter needs or desires (Warren Miller and Donald Stokes, 1963).

The Congressman Serves His Constituents

Constituency service embraces a variety of activities of the legislator and his staff: answering mail, aiding in constituents' problems, making speeches in the state or district, disseminating information by

Casework (services to individuals). Arises usually out of a constituent's personal request. Examples: Citizenship problems, questions about social security and veterans' benefits.	
Interest Group Representation (services to interest groups). May arise from contact with group representatives in Washington or in the district (lobbying). Examples: introducing legislation, providing economic or technical data, speaking to groups.	
Whole District Representation. Originates in legislator's general knowledge of the district gained from media, polls, or government agency sources. Examples: efforts to stimulate government investments, such as defense contracts or park and highway construction, in the district.	
Nondistrict Representation (in areas of little interest or importance to most of legislator's constituents). Originates in his own interests, knowledge, conscience, or the influence of bureaucrats, scholars, or other legislators. Examples: foreign relations or government operations.	

Figure 8.7 Legislators relate to their districts in a variety of ways. Presented here are the four major characterizations of congressional-district relations. Any real congressman, of course, represents a combination of these approaches, with one or the other usually predominating. But one generalization tends to be constant in its power to evoke a congressman's concern: the narrower the issue and the more directly it involves the district, the more the congressman is concerned over the attitudes of his affected constituents. On issues of little district-wide concern, constituents tend to "turn their backs" and allow the congressman a freer rein in his legislative determination.

newsletter or press release, and meeting with constituents. Many of these are "errand-boy" or "casework" tasks, which help citizens to cope with an ever more complicated government bureaucracy. Besides serving as *ombudsmen* in handling constituents' problems (for example, investigating errors in social security or veterans' payments), legislators use casework as a way of garnering support for reelection.

Legislators' work loads have reached staggering proportions. "It was a pretty nice job that a member of Congress had in those days," recalled Representative Robert Ramspeck (Dem.-Georgia), who arrived in Washington in 1911 as a staff aide. A congressman's mail was then confined mainly to the problems of rural mail routes, Spanish War pensions, free seed, and very occasionally a legislative matter. A single clerk was sufficient to take care of the correspondence (George Galloway, 1962). Larger and more sophisticated constituencies, not to mention the enlarged role of government in citizens' lives, have ended all that. Expert staffs, in Washington and in district offices, are required to handle the work load. As a consequence, legislators have found themselves to be the heads of small but growing bureaucracies, in which congressional staff members have assumed greater importance and a larger role in policy making.

Localism and Policy

The localism of representatives, and to a lesser extent of senators, has important policy implications. On issues with special impact for their districts, congressmen naturally tend to place their districts first and to play down larger interests.

The problem of localism is especially apparent in the issue of international trade. A congressman from a district with a dominant industry that is threatened by foreign competition, such as textiles, is likely to support high tariffs on textiles imported from abroad. He approaches the question from the *protectionist* perspective of his district rather than from considerations of international economics or the national interest. Free, unrestricted trade may actually be better for all citizens in the United States, but some congressmen cannot permit themselves the luxury of that long-range view if they want to be reelected. Similarly, many congressmen would like to see superfluous military bases cut back except when it affects their own locality. Such perspectives naturally translate into less free trade and more military waste than anyone would theoretically like. Nonetheless, in a system designed to accommodate the competition of interests, the protection of local interests is an integral part of the political system.

Localism also affects policy when it is combined with *seniority;* that is, when a congressman serves enough consecutive terms that he attains the chairmanship of a powerful committee, he may succeed in translating his policy preferences (and/or those of powerful local interests) into national policy. Thus, a chairman of the Agriculture Subcommittee of the House Appropriations Committee, whose constituency may be the dominant wealthy agricultural interests of a southern district, may succeed in blocking effective hunger-relief programs for poor people all over the nation. As a result of certain structural aspects of Congress, policy-making power is sometimes delegated to firmly entrenched and locally oriented committee chairmen who are totally unaccountable to the vast majority of citizens.

THE STRUCTURE OF THE TWO HOUSES

If one mainspring of congressional policy making is the individual legislator and his constituency, another is the structure of Congress itself. Policy making is influenced by the unique structure of the Senate and the House of Representatives. As noted in Chapter 2, the structure of an institution is never neutral; it resembles a pinball machine in which the high-scoring zones are always controlled by certain interests to the detriment of others. Congress has developed certain structural or organizational traits, such as *hierarchy* of leadership, *specialization* of function, and *routinization* of procedure, in response to the demands of size, work load, and political environment. Various interests represented in the two houses of Congress have been able to make use of these organizational traits to advantage certain policies over others.

Hierarchy: The Leadership

In view of the diffusion of congressional power, it may seem odd to use the term "hierarchy" to describe the leadership structure. But certain legislators are decidedly more equal than others; and although power may not be centralized in the manner of a bureaucratic agency, inequalities of influence are very real.

Leadership in the House

The House of Representatives has a sporadic history of strong leadership. The few powerful leaders of the

Formal Hierarchy of Congress

President Pro Tem of the Senate — Speaker of the House

Majority Leader

Minority Leader

Chairmen of Major Committees

Majority and Minority Whips

Other Committee Chairmen

Senior Minority Members of Committees

Figure 8.8 This pyramid (left) depicts the formal hierarchy of influence and power in the houses of Congress. In many ways it conforms to reality; in other ways it is like any static job description in that it is misleading as to the location of actual power. For example, the Speaker of the House is truly one of the most powerful men in Congress, indeed, in the entire country; but the President Pro Tem of the Senate is merely a position of honor. A chairman of a major committee may be more powerful than a minority leader, although certain subcommittee chairmen, such as Senator Joseph McCarthy in the early 1950s, may wield more actual power, by virtue of personality, than do the party Whips. Formal prerogatives and statutes may well be the source of real power; but informal relationships with colleagues, specialized knowledge, forceful personality, and executive relationships also add up as important power resources.

nineteenth century included Henry Clay, who first demonstrated the potential power of the Speaker (the presiding officer in the House), Thomas ("Czar") Reed, and Joseph ("Uncle Joe") Cannon. When Cannon pushed the Speaker's powers beyond the limits acceptable to the membership, the office was stripped of some of its powers, especially selection of committee members and control of the influential Rules Committee. Even after the revolt against Cannon in 1910–1911, the office remained potentially powerful—although the Speaker's resources were more personal and informal than before.

The Speaker of the House is the most influential person on Capitol Hill. He manages the business of the House and thereby controls an array of formal powers that permit him to regulate the flow of legislation—including the power of recognizing members on the floor (that is, granting them the right to speak), voting to break tie votes, and referring bills to committees. The Speaker's unwritten powers depend on his personality and skills. He may influence the assignment of members to committees, influence the activities of the various committee chairmen, and take the lead in scheduling legislation for floor consideration.

The Speaker is aided by the Majority Leader, who traditionally succeeds him when he retires or dies.

The Majority Leader is chief floor spokesman for his party, scheduling bills and maximizing his party's voting strength. He is assisted by the Majority Whip, who notifies members of pending business, polls them on their voting intentions, and endeavors to bring them to the floor at the right moment to vote on key issues. The Minority Leader (who is the opposition party's candidate for Speaker) and Minority Whip perform similar tasks, although with fewer rewards to dispense among their colleagues.

Leadership in the Senate

In the smaller Senate, strong leadership has been the exception rather than the rule. Not until the end of the nineteenth century did coherent leadership patterns appear, and they were no match for the powerful Speakers then functioning on the other side of the Capitol building (David Rothman, 1966).

The presiding officer of the Senate is relatively unimportant. (The Vice-President is the constitutional presiding officer, and the President *Pro Tem* is an honorific title bestowed on the senior majority-party senator; usually, freshman senators take turns presiding over the Senate.) Floor leaders and Whips operate much as they do in the House, although with noticeably looser reins on their troops.

In the twentieth century, floor leaders have varied

Figure 8.9 Patterns of informal congressional interactions (right). The work of Congress and the behavior of congressmen can only be truly understood against a background of complex social and professional relationships among the members of the two houses. Serving in the same state delegation or belonging to the same partisan club in Washington are extremely important ways in which congressmen gain help for advancement or cooperation on particular projects. Providing technical knowledge to a colleague or doing favors such as speaking in behalf of a colleague's proposed bill, creates a backlog of credits, which, when needed, may be "cashed in" for assistance.

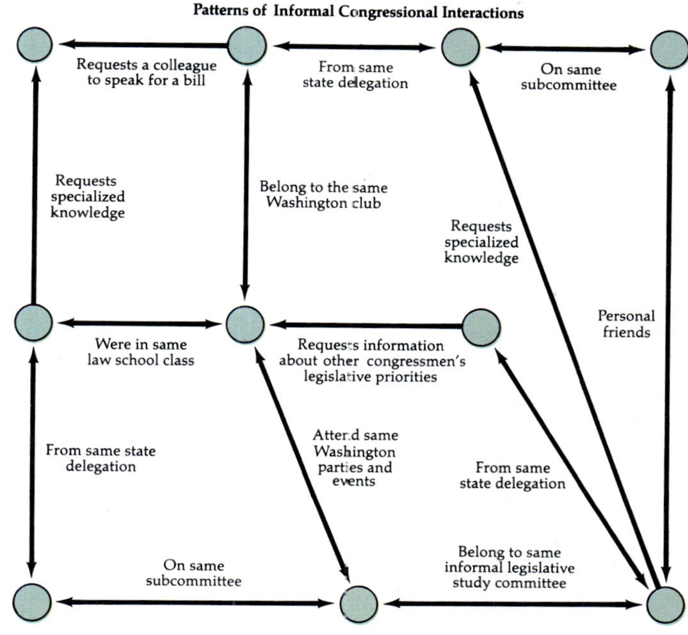

in effectiveness. Lyndon Johnson's success as Senate Majority Leader (1955–1961) was largely a result of his unique persuasive skills. He helped to foster a consensus atmosphere that encouraged senatorial courtesy, specialization of activities, and deference to members who had attained seniority. The unique character of the 1950s also contributed to Johnson's success: Party and seniority leaders were mostly conservative, and President Dwight Eisenhower did not press for much new legislation. Liberals, who were obsessed with such control by a tight ruling clique, or "inner club," undertook the lonely task of appealing over the heads of the conservative Senate elders to public opinion (Ralph Huitt, 1961).

The so-called "Johnson rule" helped to change the situation. An informal policy of assuring each new Democratic senator at least one major committee assignment brought broader distribution of desirable committee seats. Successive elections swelled the liberals' ranks, and as they gained greater seniority, they began to wield more influence. "We had a dispersal of responsibility," explained Johnson's successor, Mike Mansfield (Dem.-Mon.).

Party Leadership in Congress

Congressional leadership is determined by party status in the House and Senate, with the titles Majority Leader and Majority Whip belonging to leaders designated by the controlling party. In addition to determining congressional leadership, parties play a crucial organizational role in Congress.

Party leaders bring together the scattered work groups of Congress and orchestrate their efforts to produce coherent legislative results. In attempting to influence the legislative course of events, party leaders can draw on four types of resources. First, they are in an advantageous spot to use the rules of the House for partisan ends. One frequent tactic, especially for the majority party, is to delay the scheduling of a controversial bill until the leaders gather enough votes for passage. A second leadership resource is control of influence over many of the tangible rewards for individual members. For example, leaders usually have a strong voice in assigning members to committees. Third, they control many psychological rewards; leaders are often able to influence the attitude of House colleagues toward a member, with isolation the possible fate of the maverick. Finally, by dominating the legislature's internal communications process, party leaders monopolize vital information: knowledge of the upcoming schedule, the substance of bills, and the intentions of other congressmen or of the President (Randall Ripley, 1967).

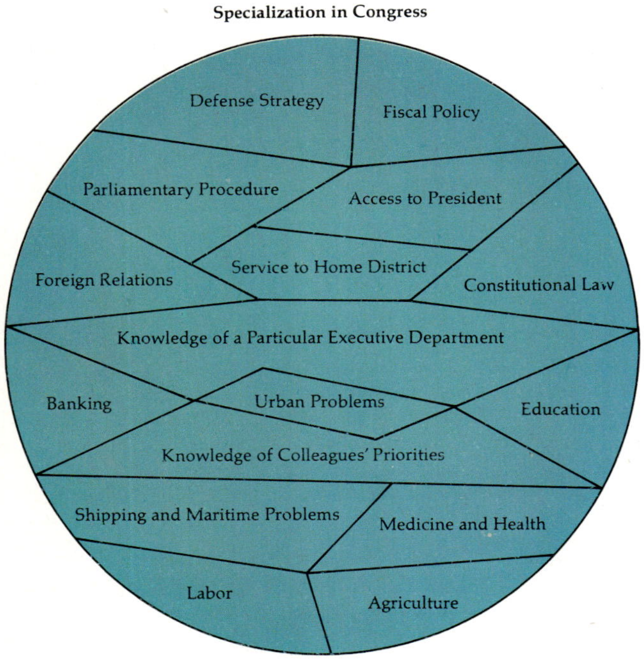

Specialization in Congress

Figure 8.10 Specialization in Congress (left). Because of the work load in Congress, members have found it necessary to specialize—in a few or even in one policy area. Members thus must depend on each others' expertise, and the work of both houses is expedited by the intermeshing of so many special functions and areas of knowledge.

Figure 8.11 Rules and realities in Congress (right). Congress-watching is as demanding a pursuit as following any complex sport, such as football or baseball. A superficial acquaintance with Congress usually stops with the learning of a simple structure and its set of particular rules. Longer acquaintance and closer watching will reveal the amazing intricacies of formal and informal procedures, which are not secret but which are learned by the relative few who have sufficient interest. The same might be said for any sport—it offers most to those who go beyond the score card to the subtleties of strategy and the intricacies of the professional's rulebook.

Like American political parties generally, congressional parties are the despair of friends and critics alike. They attempt to serve as unifying forces, and in that task they must strive mightily to counteract the pull of constituency interests and the semiautonomy of the committee structure. Looking with horror at the seeming chaos of congressional parties, many observers have urged that steps be taken to achieve a modicum of "party government," or party solidarity, within the halls of Congress.

Nonetheless, the parties are the most stable and significant groupings in Congress. Although party discipline is loose, party loyalty is firm and is the strongest determinant of voting in the two houses. Republicans tend to vote together because they represent similar constituencies (which tend to be of higher socioeconomic status, more suburban, and composed of fewer nonwhites and foreign-born); the same is true for Democrats (they are of lower socioeconomic status, they are more urban, and there are more nonwhites and foreign born). Congressional mavericks, whose votes in Congress usually diverge from those of other party members, tend to represent districts whose characteristics resemble those of the opposition party.

During the 1921–1964 period, the issues on which the parties most consistently split were foreign trade (tariffs), the degree of governmental activism, fiscal and monetary policy, conservation, and health and welfare. "Only on issues which failed to ignite significant ideological controversies, which promised little reward to the party faithful, or which did not mobilize significant economic interest groups did the parties fail to present clearly differentiated records to the voter" (Julius Turner and Edward Schneier, 1971).

However, partisan differences in voting have exhibited a long-term decline, and many forces chip away at party lines. Regional differences are especially conspicuous. Southern Democrats are markedly less loyal to the party than are nonsoutherners; and the North-South split within the Democratic party has widened in recent decades. Often such factions have produced a so-called "conservative coalition" composed of southern Democrats and Republican conservatives. Less frequently, liberal northeastern Republicans may deviate from the conservative mainstream of their party. Other sources of influence on legislators include interest groups (see Chapter 15), state and regional delegations, committees, and various informal voting blocs. In sum, party loyalty remains important, but it is challenged on every side and its overall impact seems to be on the wane.

Rules and Realities in Congress

Rules	Realities
Committee assignments are open to all interested members.	By tradition, certain states have a given number of seats on a committee (for example, representatives from midwestern farm states will sit on agricultural committees); such state delegations fill vacancies when their members retire.
Committee hearings are held to find facts to aid in writing laws.	Committee hearings are held to find facts, publicize social problems, or to provide committee members with public exposure; often the general conclusions of the hearings are established before the hearings are held.
A "discharge petition" signed by a majority of the House can remove a bill from a hostile committee to the floor for a vote.	Discharge petitions are used only as a last resort because they call into question the committee system and can be construed as an attack on the integrity of the members of a committee.
The agenda of business of the House of Representatives is set by calendars on a first-come, first-served basis.	Most bills are given a special order of business by the House Rules Committee at the request of the substantive committee chairmen and thus are brought up outside the regular calendar of business.
Each bill is to be fairly heard in committee.	Bills are heard by committees according to the wishes and scheduling of the committee chairmen. Delaying a bill (especially towards the end of a session when the schedule is crowded) can force supporters to compromise in order to get the bill out of committee.
Committee members may call a committee to order even in the absence of its chairman.	The challenge to the chairman is so great and his powers of retaliation so strong that this difficult process is rarely attempted.
Congressional deliberations are recorded for public inspection.	When a bill arrives from a committee for debate and vote, the House dissolves itself into a "committee of the whole," which is the same House of Representatives, but sitting under special rules that are more lax than usual and under which there are no recorded votes.

Specialization: The Committees

If hierarchy in Congress is fitful, another organizational trait—specialization—has reached an advanced stage. Specialization is usually associated with the committee system; as Woodrow Wilson observed long ago, congressional government is committee government. "Congress in session is Congress on display, but Congress in committee is Congress at work" (Woodrow Wilson, 1885).

Committees are the key policy-making bodies in Congress. Aside from the leadership, the effective influence of members of Congress is based primarily on their committees and their position on them. Thus, the individual majority-party senator is usually more influential than the individual House member because even relatively junior senators chair their own subcommittees. Thousands of bills are introduced into Congress each year, but only a few are seriously considered by the committees, and it is only those few that can be enacted into law.

Specialization arises mainly from the rising volume and diversity of the congressional work load. Committees have been formed as new public problems have been identified or new governmental responsibilities assumed. The Legislative Reorganization Act of 1946 consolidated and reduced the number of standing committees but did nothing to halt the proliferation of work groups. Whereas the number of standing committees has remained fairly constant (seventeen in the Senate, twenty-one in the House), the number of subcommittees—not to mention single-purpose, temporary, and joint committees—has reached enormous proportions. No less than 338 formal subgroups were in operation during the 92nd Congress, not counting state and regional caucuses, voting-bloc organizations such as the Democratic Study Group, and other associations.

Most commentators cite specialization as a dominant characteristic of Congress. Complex measures cannot be worked out by a large body of people meeting together; a frequently expressed sentiment on Capitol Hill is that "you can't write a bill on the floor." Specialized work groups permit simultaneous consideration of a variety of matters, and enable individual legislators to concentrate on a manageable range of problems.

Committee Assignments

Committee assignments are the responsibility of the party caucuses (which include all members of the party in each house). Their decisions hinge on the prestige of the committee assignment, the goals of the legislator, his seniority, and whether the committee has in the past maintained a particular state

Figure 8.12 Coalition building in Congress (right). A hypothetical aid-to-education bill and a simplified four-member coalition, formed by vote trading, illustrates how votes can be gathered to further a bill in Congress. The left side of the diagram identifies an abbreviated ranking of the four congressmen's legislative interests. On the right (facing page) the arrows trace the vote trades, negotiated by those strongly in favor of the bill, to secure the votes of the others that are less interested. A similar process of negotiation—oriented toward those legislators who, to varying degrees, oppose the bill—would be engaged in by the opposition. Below is indicated one particular congressional coalition of long-standing nature. The coalition of conservative Republicans and conservative southern Democrats has been based both on legislative preferences and on vote trading in areas of civil rights and economic issues.

Conservative Republican–Southern Democrat Coalition

Liberal Democrats	Moderate Democrats	Conservative Democrats (usually from the South)	Conservative Republicans	Moderate Republicans	Liberal Republicans

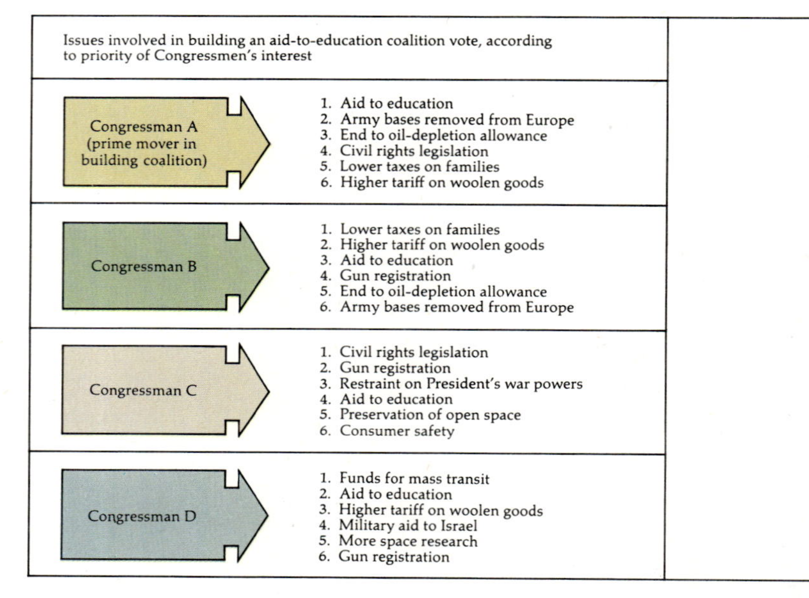

or regional representation pattern. Although party leaders exercise some influence, they generally concentrate on the most prestigious committees—Rules, Appropriations, and Ways and Means in the House; Appropriations, Finance, and Foreign Relations in the Senate. To be appointed to such committees, members must usually demonstrate "responsibility," or the ability to cooperate and accommodate different viewpoints. The most important single factor in committee assignments, however, is the member's own desires and whether the assignment will help his reelection (Nicholas Masters, 1961). One result of this practice is to place like-minded legislators on the same committees; committees in turn tend to embody a homogeneous view.

Once given their assignments, legislators have a right to the assignment for the duration of their tenure in Congress. (Sometimes a junior member may be "bumped" from a committee if his party loses enough seats to justify changing the ratio of partisans on the committee. Even rarer are the cases of members who change party affiliation, placing themselves at the mercy of their new party for their assignment.) Equally by convention, committee members advance by *seniority* (defined by continuous terms of committee service), with the senior majority-party member being named chairman.

The Seniority System

Although the seniority "rule" is rarely circumvented, it is not a formal requirement, and the appointment of committee chairmen must be approved by the party caucus. Several recent precedents exist for caucus modification of seniority privileges: In 1970–1971 both parties in the House adopted guidelines for caucus review of such assignments. However, tampering with seniority hardly happens everyday.

No feature of congressional practices has drawn as much criticism as seniority, which the Ralph Nader study derided as a Darwinian parody of "survival of the survivors." Certainly the practice fosters congressional careerism and discourages committee-hopping, but it also wastes the talents and energies of middle-seniority legislators. It enhances the independence of Congress in dealing with the President; however, it helps to scatter power within the houses, making party government virtually impossible. It reduces conflict by providing for automatic selection, but critics counter that the public interest should place the clash of issues over the convenience and good feelings of a few legislators.

The most serious charge against seniority is perhaps that it fosters unrepresentative policy making. By rewarding long service, critics contend, seniority awards chairmanships (and ranking minority posts)

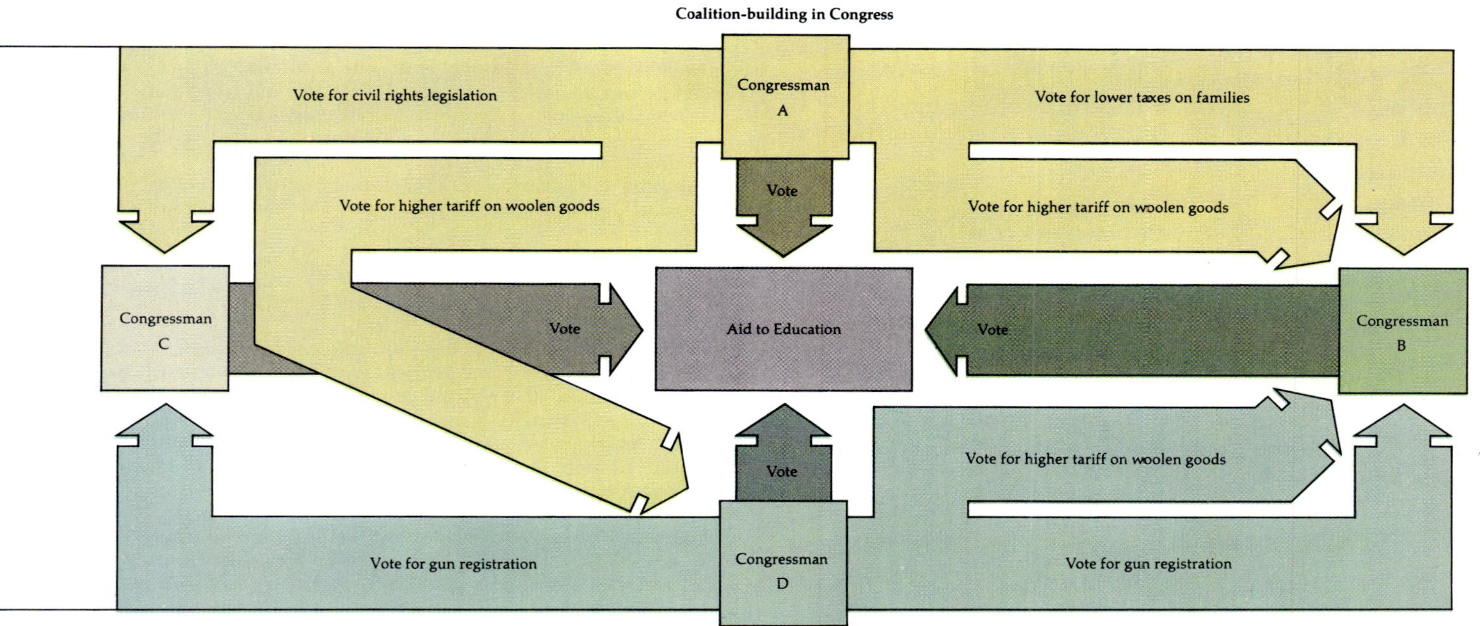

disproportionately to legislators from the safest seats, especially southerners in the Democratic Party and midwesterners in the Republican Party. Because "safe" seats are alleged to be rural and conservative, the system underscores the rural-conservative bias of policy making.

There is some truth to these allegations. Clearly, traditional areas of party strength are overrepresented in the leadership posts of both parties; members from marginal areas are less likely to gain the longevity necessary for committee leadership. (It is fair to remember, however, that *most* representatives and many senators come from relatively safe constituencies.) Moreover, there results a time lag in committee leadership: Shifting centers of a party's strength may not be reflected in the leadership structure for a number of years. For example, the relative decline of the South in the Democratic membership, which dates from the early 1960s, was not reflected in the senior ranks for about a decade. As a result of such lags, congressional committee leaders are often at loggerheads with the policies of their national parties. "On many of the crucial votes," concluded a Democratic Study Group survey of 114 House committee or subcommittee chairmen in the 90th Congress, "one-third of Democratic committee chairmen voted against the Democratic Administration, Democratic party principles, and the majority of their Democratic colleagues—and were responsible for the defeat of many Democratic programs" (Democratic Study Group, 1969). Political scientists concede that such biases exist, but careful study has indicated that critics of the system may have overstated their case (Hinckley, 1971).

Indeed, a majority of the members of Congress seem satisfied with most decisions reached by the seniority system. In 1973, for example, all the committee chairmen in the House had to be ratified by the Democratic Party caucus. All those who either would have continued as chairmen or who would have become chairmen on the basis of seniority alone were duly elected—all by wide margins.

Committee Leadership

"The power of the chairman is a more fundamental issue in sound committee preparations than is his method of selection" (Joint Committee on the Organization of the Congress, 1966). Chairmen range

Figure 8.13 Background sketches of selected representatives, whose committee assignments lie in the four issue areas of this book: the Economy, Foreign Policy, Race, and Civil Liberties.

Louis C. Wyman (R.-N.H.) is a low-ranking minority member on the Defense Subcommittee of the House Committee on Appropriations. Wyman, a strong conservative, was a leader in the move to impeach Supreme Court Justice William O. Douglas; he is known as a staunch anticommunist. In 1970 his district received over $123 million in Department of Defense contracts, $12.9 million of which went to Simplex Cable Co. for ocean cable for an antimissile system. There are 138,000 voters in the district, 59 percent of whom were Republicans in 1970. In 1970 Wyman won 67 percent of the vote. With the support of the conservative Manchester Union Leader newspaper, Wyman's popularity seems to indicate a very safe district.

John M. Ashbrook (R.-Ohio) is one of Congress's young conservative ideologues appointed to the Education and Labor Committee, the scene of intense fighting on issues of race, unemployment, and educational philosophy. Ashbrook became well known in 1972 when he challenged President Nixon for the Republican presidential nomination, arguing against the nonconservative nature of Nixon's economic policies of regulation and his foreign policy of détente with the Soviet Union and China. At age 45, Ashbrook is the second-ranked minority member of Education and Labor. He is a practicing attorney and newspaper publisher. He is also the senior minority member of the House Internal Security Committee, formerly the House Un-American Activities Committee.

Ogden R. Reid (R.-N.Y.) was the president and editor of the New York Herald Tribune and has inherited the fortune connected with that newspaper. He was ambassador to Israel, 1959–61. His district is a center of very wealthy liberal Republicans. He was first elected in 1962, and his voting record has always received high ratings from liberal interest groups. He receives high majorities in general elections, but in primaries, where only registered Republicans can vote, his victories are much closer. He is the top-ranked minority member on the Subcommittee on Foreign Operations and Government Information of the Government Operations Committee. He is also the fourth-ranked minority member on the Education and Labor Committee.

Wilbur D. Mills (D.-Ark.) has been the sole candidate for Congress from Arkansas's 2nd district for the last decade. He entered the House in 1938 and not long after was favored by Speaker Sam Rayburn with a seat on the Ways and Means Committee. As present chairman of that committee, Mills is one of the most powerful men in the U.S. Although Mills is willing to seek compromise, he can be a formidable check on the President's legislative agenda. Mills's power derives in part from his authoritative knowledge of our intricate tax laws and of other economic matters. His power also derives from the fact that the Democratic members of Ways and Means are in charge of assigning other Democratic representatives to committees.

George H. Mahon (D.-Texas) One of the most powerful men in Congress, 73-year-old Mahon was first elected to the House in 1934. The defense budget is Mahon's specialty, and he is chairman of the Defense Subcommittee of the Appropriations Committee. Mahon is a moderate conservative, considered knowledgeable and responsible. He trims defense budgets, but liberals charge he trims domestic programs more. He was unopposed in his Texas district in the 1970 primary and general elections. There has been no Republican opposition since 1964. The district's economy is based on oil and ranching and received a $51 million Department of Defense outlay in 1970— mostly for Reese Air Force Base.

Shirley A. Chisholm (D.-N.Y.) was appointed to the Committee on Veterans' Affairs when she first arrived in the House in 1968. Such a post was peripheral to the problems of her district. Using her position as the first black woman in Congress, her direct speaking style, her national visibility as a speaker, and perhaps her support for Hale Boggs as Majority Leader, she achieved a position on the House Education and Labor Committee. Congresswoman Chisholm's district was 66 percent black in 1970. In 1968 her opponent, James Farmer, former director of CORE, based his appeal for votes on black male pride, not realizing that perhaps 60 percent of black voters are women. In 1970 Chisholm won by 82 percent.

John E. Moss (D.-Calif.) was first elected to the House in 1952 and has built up considerable seniority in his twenty-year incumbency. He was chairman of the Foreign Operations and Government Information Subcommittee and as such earned a high reputation for his studies of foreign aid programs and land-reform programs in Vietnam. Moss, a liberal Democrat from the liberal Sacramento area of California, is best known for his fight for the Freedom of Information Act, which, with certain qualifications, has opened up the bureaucracy's files to the public and has thereby contributed to the success of some of Ralph Nader's investigations. In 1970 Moss won 62 percent of the vote and was unopposed in the primary.

Joel R. Broyhill (R.-Va.) is a conservative member of the Ways and Means Committee (5th-ranked Republican). Because his district, adjoining Washington, D.C., is the home of many federal government employees, he spends much time aiding constituents, especially in his capacity as a member of the District of Columbia Committee. A real estate developer who first won office by 322 votes in the Eisenhower landslide of 1952, when the district was created, Broyhill has often found himself faced with stiff liberal opposition. Broyhill supports tough anticrime legislation and advocates crackdowns on alleged welfare chiselers.

from the ineffectual to the dictatorial, but they wield impressive formal and informal powers. "The committee member who has served 20 years is not just 5 percent more powerful than the member who has served 19 years," Representative Morris Udall (Dem.-Ariz.) observed. "If he is chairman he is 1,000 percent more powerful." There are enough detours in the legislative process so that a stubborn chairman can tie up important items of legislation for extended periods of time. As a result, many committees have struggled to adopt rules of procedure to protect the views of committee majorities against such chairmen.

The Committee as Policy Maker

Specialization is a necessary legislative response to a complex and growing work load, but it imposes serious costs on policy making. "The role of the House," one of its historians has written, "is now largely limited to ratifying decisions made by its committees" (George Galloway, 1962). This judgment is somewhat exaggerated, but it conveys a genuine problem. Specialization has helped preserve legislative influence over policy, but it has done so for legislative subgroups rather than for the legislature as a whole. Like the congressional hierarchy, functional specialization heightens inequalities of influence among legislators. Serious problems of coordination occur as committees struggle to retain their jurisdiction over matters that are broad or interrelated. Hardly a problem arises today that is not impaled between two or more congressional committees, each jealously guarding its prerogatives. Specialization encourages the piecemeal, incremental resolution of public problems; and it underscores the widespread tendency for those closest to a given policy problem to wield virtually unchecked influence in resolving it. This bit-by-bit approach is another example of the strategy of *anticipated reaction*—make a move, see how the President and bureaucrats respond, make another move, and so on.

Routinization: The Power of the Rules

Procedural routinization characterizes mature institutions that are struggling with demanding work loads. In order to increase efficiency, institutions develop methods of circumscribing those tasks that are subject to controversy. The seniority "rule" for selecting committee leaders is one such routine, as is the emergence of a ladder for promotion of party leaders among House Democrats. Routinization also helps Congress dispose of a large number of relatively minor matters, such as approving executive appointments of officials in the Senate and other minor matters that clutter up the daily agenda.

Committee Rules

Rules of procedure have been developed by both houses to govern committee behavior (found in the Legislative Reorganization Acts of 1946 and 1970), although neither house closely regulates the activity of its committees.

Committees are also empowered to frame their own procedures, and most have done so. For example, whether a whole committee considers a bill, or whether it divides itself into subcommittees, is left up to the committees themselves to decide. Procedures for removing a bill from an uncooperative committee are available, but they are cumbersome and, most importantly, there is a strong tradition that argues against overruling committee decisions. Thus, in most cases the committees exercise life and death control over measures—between 80 and 90 percent of all bills introduced in Congress die in committees. Committees are also empowered to add amendments, delete provisions, or rewrite a bill entirely before sending it to the House or Senate floor for a vote. Committees are often accused of abusing these powers, but in all probability the bills that fail to survive committee scrutiny would not pass on the floor.

Rules in House and Senate

The House and Senate have evolved their own distinctive sets of rules to govern their own activities, in accord with the constitutional provision that "each House may determine the rules of its proceedings" (Article I, Section 5).

The larger House of Representatives has evolved a tight system of procedures, leaving little room for delaying-tactics on the floor. The House has granted extensive scheduling powers to its Rules Committee, which stands as a gatekeeper between the legislative committees and the House floor. An examination of the power of the House Rules Committee shows its power over the content of legislation.

The Rules Committee must grant a "rule" under

which a bill is to be considered on the House floor. When a rule is requested by a legislative committee, the Rules Committee must first decide whether or not to hold hearings; if it does, it may then vote on whether or not to grant a rule. The committee may specify the time for debate and whether amendments will be in order—"open" versus "closed" rules (James Robinson, 1963). Because of its power to withhold bills from floor action and to bargain for inclusion or deletion of given provisions, the Rules Committee often moves beyond its traffic-cop role to that of final arbiter on the content of bills.

In the smaller and more leisurely Senate the rules are simpler and more lenient. Debate is typically fixed by unanimous consent; as in the House, standard practice is to divide and control time between proponents and opponents of the bill by prior agreement. The Senate cherishes its privilege of free and unrestricted debate. A cloture rule is available to shut off debate on the vote of two-thirds of the senators, but it is rarely invoked. Senatorial courtesy demands that members be accorded ample time to pursue the subject at hand; repeated efforts to tighten the cloture rule have met with little success.

Rules as Policy Makers

In legislative bodies the rules and procedures are intimately related to the ongoing political conflicts over policy issues. Far from being neutral, the rules themselves encourage certain types of strategies and discourage others. Rules are resources, and mastery of them is a form of power in Congress. There is very little that the houses cannot do under the rules, so long as the action is backed up by votes and support. If the members are of one mind on an issue, for example, they can suspend the rules and accomplish in a few minutes what otherwise might take months to do. Yet such consensus is not easily obtained, and the rules persistently challenge the proponents of legislation to demonstrate that they have both resources at their command. By the same token, there is little to prevent obstruction at every turn, except the tacit agreement that the business of the houses must go on.

Congressional Structures Make Policy

Newspapers and magazines frequently analyze the organization of Congress to determine why certain kinds of policies are advanced and others frustrated. Thus, throughout the 1960s it was commonly accepted that such features as the filibuster and the great power of committee chairmen, when combined with the seniority system (which elevated conservative southerners to those chairmanships) were responsible for the long delay in passing civil rights legislation. The theory had much evidence in its favor. Congressional procedures were so closely tied to policy that the first order of legislative business in the Kennedy Administration was to enlarge the House Rules Committee (giving it a liberal majority) in order to forestall its obstruction of liberal legislation. Clearly, congressional procedures have crucial policy consequences.

The question, however, is whether those procedures always favor one side and not the other; the answer is less than clear. The filibuster was the hope of southern conservatives and the despair of liberals when it was used to block civil rights legislation. By the early 1970s, however, some northern Democrats and Republican liberals expressed their reluctance to support changes in the rules that would have made it easier to shut off debate; they expressed fear that the Nixon Administration would sponsor legislative proposals that they considered repressive or reactionary. The senators felt their vital interests might be threatened by an opposing majority in the Senate. Increasingly, liberals have used the filibuster as a tactic to gain time, concessions, and, occasionally, victory against such issues as government funding of a supersonic jet transport. Indeed, a recent study demonstrated that a majority of senators of both parties have repeatedly declined to support changes in the rules that would have made it easier for a majority to invoke the cloture rule (Raymond Wolfinger, 1971).

Seniority is also viewed in a different light in the 1970s. Whereas southern Democrats held the chairs of nine out of seventeen Senate standing committees in 1973, liberal northerners were next in line in four of those, including Armed Services, Banking, and Housing and Urban Affairs. With liberals moving up the seniority ladder in these and other important committees in the House as well, ideological positions on seniority are beginning to shift. Liberals have noted, for example, that Senator J. William Fulbright, an outspoken and effective opponent of the war in Vietnam, would probably have lost his chairmanship of the Senate Foreign Relations Committee if not for the seniority rule.

In general, then, the structural traits of Congress influence policy outcomes; however, the relative advantage accruing to different ideological, economic, and sectional interests changes with time, and people's attitudes toward those procedures likewise shift depending on whether they are advantaged or disadvantaged by them.

Although the effects of congressional procedures on substantive policy vary, their impact on policy making *as a process* is more predictable and has three main effects. First, as noted already, the American policy-making system is characterized by its incrementalism (that is, the bit-by-bit nature of its decisions). The congressional policy-making process reinforces that incrementalism. Specialization assures that congressmen approach policy from a narrow and a particular viewpoint; farm policies, for example, are pursued by the Agriculture Committees without much reference to how those policies affect areas other than agriculture. Furthermore, specialization goes hand in hand with seniority to produce a system in which those congressmen having primary responsibility for an area of policy have been involved in that area for many years; having partici-

pated in formulating existing policies in the first place, they are unlikely to pursue sweeping changes. The result: Innovation is slow and comes only in small increments.

Second, the structure of Congress has important implications for the balance of policy-making power between the branches of government. Power that is concentrated in committees and in high seniority congressmen with independent local bases of support is insulated from the President. The President's ability to push his policy preferences through Congress is reduced by a system of congressional power, the sources of which are beyond his control. For example, without the seniority system a President whose party controlled Congress would be much more likely to intervene in the choice of committee chairmen. Under certain circumstances, such intervention may have beneficial results. But what would be the effects of such a decrease in congressional independence when Chairman Sam Ervin of the Senate Constitutional Rights Subcommittee stands up for continued protection of basic civil liberties? The norms of Congress may indeed make that body more rigid and ponderous, but certain of those norms provide a powerful shield against the enlargement of presidential power.

Finally, the system of congressional committees

Figure 8.14 Incremental decision-making. The step-by-step method of decision making and legislating provides ample time and opportunity for careful review and calculation. But it may also compromise the final results by frustrating initial expectations. The process is symbolized here by the goal of the ideal male physique (above) and the male figures below, which are being stripped, step-by-step, of the covering of promises that were initially made. Political decision makers may thus be left with outcomes that are only slightly more satisfying than previous policy decisions, or indeed with outcomes that may prove politically embarrassing to the decision makers or to the political actors involved.

may stifle innovation in some ways, but it promotes new policy initiatives as well. Particularly in the Senate, where relatively junior members of the majority party are able to chair their own subcommittees, new issues are frequently explored—such issues as the protection of the consumer and the environment were advanced by members who were using the committee system and the norm of specialization to their advantage.

PATTERNS OF POLICY MAKING

As we have noted, the structural traits of Congress strongly affect the decisions congressmen make. It is now necessary to look at the four areas of decision around which this book revolves—the economy, foreign affairs, race, and civil liberties—to see how these traits make their marks on congressional decision making.

Economic Issues

Economics lies at the heart of many, perhaps most, congressional issues. Nearly every congressional committee and subcommittee finds itself embroiled in economic issues—some occasionally, many others nearly all of the time. Indeed, economic power is equated with political power in the ranking of committees. Thus, many observers count the Appropria-

tions Committee (which has primary jurisdiction over spending) and the Ways and Means Committee (which has primary jurisdiction over all tax matters) as the most powerful committees in the House of Representatives. Rather than consider economic policy making as a whole, three major areas of congressional economic policy making will be described.

First, Congress participates in the *distribution* of economic benefits. As the elected caretakers of their communities' well-being, legislators are inevitably drawn into efforts to secure new facilities and projects for their states or districts. The voters back home expect them to work for the district's economic prosperity by helping to secure government contracts, public-works projects, and industries that will bring new wealth to the area.

To "bring home the economic bacon" and thus to ensure reelection, legislators must participate in the practice of mutual accommodation (known by the more contemptuous term "pork barreling"). However, an entire legislature composed of politicians supporting one another's pet programs creates a demand for the broad distribution of public expenditures, a practice that often negates the economic impact of a program. For example, when Congress had finished writing the eligibility requirements for the 1961 Area Redevelopment Act, a measure de-

signed to provide federal aid for economically de-pressed communities throughout the nation, almost one-third of the nation's counties were qualified for aid (see the Perspective on Appalachia). As a result, the appropriated funds were spread so thinly that the law had little effect.

However, when Congress considers questions of economic distribution, decisions are made with the guidance of various "subgovernments," composed of congressional committees, the relevant executive bureaucrats, and outside interest groups. Typically, the economic interests of the producer are overrep-resented while those of the consumer are neglected. Agriculture is a particularly striking case in point. The House and Senate Agriculture Committees are divided into commodity subcommittees, most of whose members are from areas that produce those commodities. Millions of consumers who are affected by agricultural policies are virtually unrepresented on these committees. A similar pattern is found in numerous other policy areas.

Second, Congress participates in the *regulation* of economic activity. This regulatory function involves issues such as labor-management relations and protection of the consumer and the environment. Heated battles ensue between those who support and those who question the increasing extent to which the government participates in economic regulation. Conflict of this nature often focuses attention on real and important needs. Congress's influence on economic regulatory policy is minor, however, compared to the bureaucratic regulatory agencies that are chiefly responsible for implement-ing those policies. Congressional supervision and review of these agencies have always been rather lax and sporadic (see Chapter 10). As a result, Congress's role in regulatory policy is often preliminary rather than final.

A third area of congressional involvement in eco-nomic policy is the *redistribution* of government benefits in the form of taxes and subsidies. The pro-gressive system of taxation (see Chapter 4) should, in theory, adjust inequalities of income by collect-ing far more tax revenue from upper-income individ-uals than from other members of society and then redistributing that revenue in a fair way. However, such tax loopholes as the oil-depletion allowance, tax-free income on certain investments, and a va-riety of so-called tax shelters obviously benefit the rich far more than the poor. Congress has generally deferred to the demands of its moneyed constituents and refused to restructure the tax system along more socially equitable lines. As a result, lower- and middle-income wage earners who do not qualify for such deductions often pay a disproportionate amount of their salaries to the government.

Civil Rights and Civil Liberties

As is described in Chapter 6, Congress has been delinquent in passing civil rights legislation that would translate the promises of the Constitution into concrete guarantees. Congress has a history of in-sensitivity to the issues of civil rights. After the end of the Reconstruction era (1865–1877), blacks and certain other minorities were more or less systemati-cally discouraged or excluded from voting and were rarely elected to Congress. From antilynching laws to school busing, congressional proposals for equal-izing rights have met with stubborn opposition.

Certain structural attributes of the twentieth-century Congress aided the opponents of civil rights legislation. For generations southern voters elected Democratic legislators who were dedicated to main-taining racial separation; continued reelection, abetted by the seniority system, placed these incum-bents in key posts on Capitol Hill. For many years southerners composed the largest single bloc within the party, and when the party controlled Congress, these southerners held a disproportionate influence in Congress. Between 1953 and 1968, in seven of the nine conservative filibusters, the issue was civil rights (Wolfinger, 1971).

Spurred on by Supreme Court rulings and led by a rising tide of black activism, Congress cautiously made a gesture of concern with the 1957 and 1960 Civil Rights Acts. Then, in the wake of acute racial tensions and with strong leadership from President Lyndon Johnson, the landmark Civil Rights Act of 1964 was enacted. It provided for equal use of public accommodations, guaranteed fair employment prac-tices, and empowered federal officials to enforce civil rights law. The Voting Rights Act of 1965 strength-ened the Justice Department's powers in enforcing equal access to the polls.

The record of Congress in the civil liberties area is even less distinguished than is its record in civil

Figure 8.15 Congress claims broad powers to investigate all manner of public problems. The year 1973 was marked by Senate investigation into the activities of government and corporation executives. Senator Sam Ervin (D.-N.C.)—an authority on constitutional law and an ardent defender of civil liberties— and his Senate Select Committee (above) investigate the break-in and bugging of Democratic Party headquarters in the Watergate complex. The Senate Foreign Relations Subcommittee on Multinational Corporations (right) investigates the efforts made by International Telephone and Telegraph Corporation (ITT) to prevent Salvador Allende from becoming president of Chile and the alleged special favors granted ITT by high officials of the Nixon Administration.

rights. Because they are elected politicians, members of Congress are necessarily responsive to their constituents' prejudices against many civil liberties issues—for example, the rights of criminal defendants, prisoners, dissenters, protesters, and religious or political minorities. However precious the rights of such people may be in the abstract, they run counter to the middle-of-the-road patriotism that pervades the rhetoric and behavior of the average legislator. For this reason (and because of the lack of presidential initiative), Congress has produced over its history a series of restrictive and sometimes constitutionally dubious laws—from the Alien and Sedition Acts of the 1790s designed to counteract "subversion," to the Internal Security Act of 1950.

In one respect, the activities of certain congressional investigating committees have occasionally threatened civil liberties. Legislatures claim broad powers to investigate all manner of public problems—claims that have in general been upheld by the courts. Investigative powers are not unlimited, however, as "exposure for exposure's sake" is presumably ruled out. Legislative investigations in the past have sometimes turned into "witch hunts," as aggressive legislators and their staffs run roughshod over hapless witnesses.

In the post-World War II period, anticommunist sentiment was translated into spectacular investigative forays conducted by the House Un-American Activities Committee and Senator Joseph McCarthy's (Rep.-Wis.) Permanent Investigations Subcommittee, in which abuse of witnesses abounded. Because committee hearings are not courts of law, procedures are not designed to protect the rights of witnesses. As in civil liberties cases generally, the victims of irregular procedures are frequently those whose political views are unpopular.

Foreign Affairs

Defense and foreign policy issues have always dominated the congressional agenda, although the work load in that area has necessarily increased as the nation has attained the status of military superpower. Because of its constitutional role in advising and consenting to treaties and diplomatic appointments, the Senate has historically been a forum for momentous foreign policy debates. Traditionally, the House of Representatives played a subsidiary role; however, with the advent of programs requiring large budgetary appropriations, the House has become a major partner (Holbert Carroll, 1966).

Defense and foreign policy issues fall conveniently into two categories: distributive and strategic. In the former category are matters pertaining to the allocation of resources. They resemble the *distributive* economic questions previously described, and legislators vie with one another for home-district benefits. Military installations, which are scattered across the geographic and political landscape, are the mainstays of the economies of countless congressional districts. Legislators, especially those on the Armed Services Committees, bargain actively for a share of defense activities. Military decision makers are, on the whole, eager to accommodate friendly legislators in return for protection for their pet programs.

Strategic issues, by contrast, are not easily handled by the legislative machinery of the Congress, and decision making in this area has increasingly passed to the Presidency. In the absence of war or other crisis, foreign policy usually takes a back seat to domestic issues in the public consciousness. Few legislators (except presidential aspirants) specialize in broad foreign policy matters out of concern for their constituents; fewer still have been elected on this issue. Moreover, the President, as Commander-in-Chief and Chief Diplomat, can claim historical and constitutional preeminence in matters of foreign policy. Indeed, it is widely conceded that the executive branch possesses overwhelming advantages in conducting the nation's relations with foreign powers.

Presidential leadership in foreign policy was severely challenged during the Vietnam War. At first, Congress eagerly provided moral and financial support for the undeclared war, but as the war dragged on and public support dissipated, Congress became a forum for dissent. The Vietnam War became the occasion for renewing the classic debate over presidential and congressional prerogatives. Can Congress meaningfully assert its power to declare—or refuse to declare—war? Can Congress act as a partner in foreign policy making, where the virtues of speed, coherence, and expert advice seem so important? And, ultimately, can the checks-and-balances system devised by the founding fathers work in the executive-centered environment of contemporary policy making?

CONGRESS AS POLICY MAKER

With these questions regarding congressional powers over foreign policy making, we have come full circle in posing the question of the relative functions of Congress. Although commentators are in basic agreement over present trends, they are hopelessly divided on the *desirability* of these trends. Those who find themselves in accord with the dominant role of Presidents tend to advocate executive latitude as the only way of dealing effectively with delicate and fast-moving international developments. Others, less sanguine about the quality of recent policies, advocate limitations of presidential powers along with a vigorous congressional partnership in decision making. Thus, the political and constitutional debate rages on.

The issue is not simply one of legal or academic interpretation. In a very real sense, the struggle between Congress and President is a war over the future shape of public policy and the kinds of constituencies that will dominate the policy-making process.

SUMMARY

Recent conflicts between the President and Congress underscore the ascendance of presidential power. The President can both veto congressional legislation and participate in setting the legislative agenda. Yet Congress has impressive strength: its functions include lawmaking; appropriation of funds; representation of constituents; and policy clarification, legitimization, and review.

The performance of congressional functions is influenced by the dispositions of the legislator and his constituency and by the following structural traits: (1) leadership—congressional leadership, which is based on party strength, influences legislation; (2) specialization—committees (with their powerful chairmen) are the key policy-making bodies of Congress; (3) routinization—accepted procedures allow Congress to handle the work load and to avoid distracting controversies. These structural traits of Congress are not neutral; they tend to encourage certain interests and to discourage others.

Economic policy—Congress distributes economic benefits, regulates a variety of economic activities, and acts to redistribute government benefits with taxes and subsidies. Civil rights—Congress has stubbornly opposed equal-rights legislation until it enacted the 1964 Civil Rights Act. Civil liberties—Congress has often bowed to constituency demands and passed laws that restrict civil liberties. Foreign affairs—distributive questions have always dominated the congressional agenda; strategic issues have proven difficult to accommodate to the legislative machinery and, in the past, they have largely been left to the executive branch.

SUGGESTED READINGS

Cummings, Milton C., Jr. *Congressmen and the Electorate.* New York: Free Press, 1966.

Davidson, Roger H. *The Role of the Congressman.* Indianapolis: (Pegasus Books) Bobbs-Merrill, 1969.

Davidson, Roger H., David M. Kovenock, and Michael K. O'Leary. *Congress in Crisis: Politics and Congressional Reform.* Belmont, Calif.: Wadsworth, 1966.

Goodwin, George. *The Little Legislatures.* Boston: University of Massachusetts Press, 1969.

Matthews, Donald R. *The United States Senators and Their World.* Chapel Hill: University of North Carolina Press, 1960.

O'Keefe, William J., and Morris S. Ogul. *The American Legislative Process: Congress and the States.* 3rd ed. Englewood Cliffs, N.J.: Prentice-Hall, 1972.

WELCOME TO
THE
WHITE HOUSE

PUSH BUTTON

9

THE PRESIDENCY

The year 1972 could be called the year of the school bus. During the Florida and Michigan presidential primaries, the busing issue was so prominent in the speeches of the Democratic presidential candidates that it sometimes seemed as though they were candidates for the local board of education. Although the other Democratic contenders tried to shy away from the issue, candidate George Wallace, the governor of Alabama, focused on the busing issue. He vigorously denounced busing, placed his opponents on the defensive, and scored clear majorities in the Florida, Michigan, and Maryland primary elections.

Although a single issue rarely dominates an election, it can happen when the issue is sufficiently important to a large number of people and when the people perceive differences between the candidates on the issue (Angus Campbell *et al*, 1960). Busing and the broader question of civil rights provide a good illustration of the role of policy in the 1968 and 1972 presidential elections.

THE PRESIDENT AND POLICY: AN ILLUSTRATION

In 1968 the front runner for the Republican presidential nomination was Richard Nixon, but he faced Governor Ronald Reagan of California as a rival for the votes of conservative convention delegates, particularly from the South. Nixon, however, secured the South with the help of a new ally, ex-Democrat Senator Strom Thurmond of South Carolina. Thurmond helped secure southern support by assuring white southerners that Nixon was sympathetic to their position on civil rights. An implicit bargain was struck—southern support in exchange for Nixon's pledge that he would slow down or reverse some of the civil rights policies that so outraged conservative southerners.

Using this strategy, Nixon sought to outflank Reagan for the nomination and to erode Democratic strength in the South. The strategy was successful. Although Republican leaders denied the existence of the "southern strategy," they were somewhat embarrassed when a former Nixon campaign worker wrote a book proudly proclaiming the strategy as the key to a new Republican national majority (Kevin Phillips, 1969).

That the strategy existed is not in doubt, but a question still remains: What were the consequences for presidential policy making?

Figure 9.1 The White House is an international symbol of the power and responsibility of the United States. As the country has grown and its relations with other nations have become an overriding political concern, the decision-making power of the Chief Executive has begun to outweigh that of other governmental institutions. Along with power and responsibility has come both metaphoric and physical removal from the people who have elected him. Watched over by zealous aides, wrapped in a blanket of national security considerations, and surrounded by secret service and military protection, the President does indeed appear at times as a lonely, far-off character— as much an object of curiosity as a figure of power.

President Nixon kept his campaign promises and considerably changed the tenor of White House involvement in civil rights. He proposed no new civil rights legislation, unsuccessfully proposed that Congress eliminate the provisions of the Voting Rights Act of 1965 that applied specifically to the South, and in many cases sought to modify or delay the applications of the school desegregation guidelines established by the Department of Health, Education, and Welfare. The President publicly announced his opposition to busing as a tool of desegregation, and he kept his promise to nominate southerners to the Supreme Court. Although his first two southern nominees were rejected by the Senate amid allegations of conflict of interest, racism, and incompetence, the President scored a symbolic victory in the South by claiming that the Senate rejection was an act of "regional discrimination."

Although these actions did not substantially change the course of school desegregation in the South, President Nixon was able to shift the onus to the courts and thus appear to the South as the first sympathetic President in a generation.

Thus, vote-getting strategy became White House policy, and it is reasonable to assume that the actions taken during his first term contributed significantly to the Nixon landslide victory in 1972. The President carried the South with unprecedented majorities—72 percent of the southern popular vote, as compared to 61 percent nationwide.

But civil rights was only one campaign issue in 1972. An end to the war in Vietnam topped the policy priorities of George McGovern, Nixon's Democratic opponent. However, the relationship between foreign policy issues and presidential elections is far weaker than is the case with domestic policy.

NOTABLE PARTY PLATFORM FIGHTS

DEMOCRATIC (1924)   A minority plank was presented that condemned the activities of the Ku Klux Klan. The plank was defeated, 542 to 543, the closest in Democratic convention history.

REPUBLICAN (1928)   Sen. Robert M. LaFollette, Jr. (R.-Wis.) presented a radical minority platform calling for the stabilization of farm prices above the costs of production and government development and operation of electric power systems at Muscle Shoals, Boulder Dam, and other strategic points. No formal action was taken on the proposals by the convention.

REPUBLICAN (1932)   A minority plank favoring repeal of the Eighteenth Amendment (Prohibition) in favor of a state-option arrangement was defeated, 460 to 690.

DEMOCRATIC (1948)   An amendment to the platform, strengthening the civil rights plank by guaranteeing full and equal political participation, equal employment opportunity, personal security, and equal treatment in the military service, was accepted, 651 to 582.

DEMOCRATIC (1956)   A minority report to strengthen the civil rights plank was rejected by voice vote.

DEMOCRATIC (1960)   A motion to strike the civil rights plank from the platform was rejected by voice vote.

REPUBLICAN (1964)   An amendment offered by Senator Hugh Scott (R.-Pa.) to strengthen the civil rights plank by including voting guarantees in state as well as in federal elections and by eliminating job bias was defeated, 409 to 897.

DEMOCRATIC (1968)   A minority report on Vietnam called for cessation of the bombing of North Vietnam, halting of offensive and search-and-destroy missions by American combat units, a negotiated withdrawal of American troops, and establishment of a coalition government in South Vietnam. It was defeated, 1,041 to 1,567.

Figure 9.2 The party platform is a list of party positions, adopted at the presidential convention, that the party expects will characterize the Administration of its nominee, once he is elected. Party platforms are thus notoriously general, although there have been exceptions. This list (left) contains some of the most notable controversies over platform contents, instances when the insertion or the omission of controversial issues in the platform has led to convention fights that were indicative of serious rifts in the party.

Figure 9.3 (right) What sort of person makes the best President? An authoritative elder statesman? An astute politician? A with-it intellectual? It is useful to try to imagine the particular mixture of styles that would characterize the best leader. Indeed, this is the problem that faces the presidential candidate who seeks the support of a varied population: how to be folksy but prestigious, expert but understandable, authoritative but approachable. Obviously, it is a tough job.

Political scientist Stephen Hess has observed that foreign policy issues have not been decisive in presidential campaigns (Hess, 1972). Voters have less knowledge and interest about foreign policy; consequently, the issues are presented in highly simplified and sometimes grotesquely exaggerated form. Indeed, foreign policy discussion in elections is somewhat muted by the traditional American belief that "politics stops at the water's edge." Discussion centers largely on which candidate is most likely to bring or maintain peace.

Given the limited effect of foreign policy on elections, it is not surprising that elections have little specific effect on the conduct of the nation's foreign affairs and national security policy. As will be elaborated later in the chapter, Presidents influence the attitudes of citizens toward foreign policy rather than vice versa.

So far the relationship between campaigns, elections, and public policy has been briefly discussed. But before the relationship between the Presidency and policy is further explored, it is necessary to take a look at the President in office.

THE PRESIDENT IN OFFICE

With the election behind him, the victorious candidate is transformed from campaigner to President-elect. Changes occur in his relationship with his friends—he is no longer Jack, or Lyndon, or Dick, but "Mr. President." The power that will soon be formally bestowed on him in the inauguration ceremony is now universally acknowledged, and he is met with great deference. Indeed, something mystical is assumed to have happened to him. He has become "presidential." The imagery of this change is striking in Theodore H. White's account of the

change he noticed in Richard Nixon when he first saw him as President:

What was different was the movement of the body, the sound of the voice, the manner of speaking—for he was calm as I had never seen him before, as if peace had settled on him. . . . Now he was in repose; and the repose was in his speech also—more slow, studied, with none of the gear-slippages of name or reference which used to come when he was weary; his hands still moved as he spoke, but the fingers spread gracefully, not punchily or sharply as they used to. (White, 1969)

Presidential Transition

To appear to be presidential, however, is not enough. The President-elect must prepare himself to assume the responsibilities of the office. The process of preparation and change in anticipation of a new President is called *presidential transition.*

The transition consists of two intertwined processes. First, the President-elect must put together his own team—the new Administration (see Figure 9.4). Second, the members must learn their new jobs. Officials (including the President) must learn how to discharge their new responsibilities and how to use the machinery of government to facilitate the policy goals of the Administration; both of these processes can be greatly facilitated by cooperation between outgoing and incoming Administrations. Increasingly, both sides recognize that a smooth transition is in the best interest of the country and also of the incoming Administration.

The Job of President

The process of assuming the responsibilities of office is in itself a major task. But this assessment does not answer the question: What does the President do?

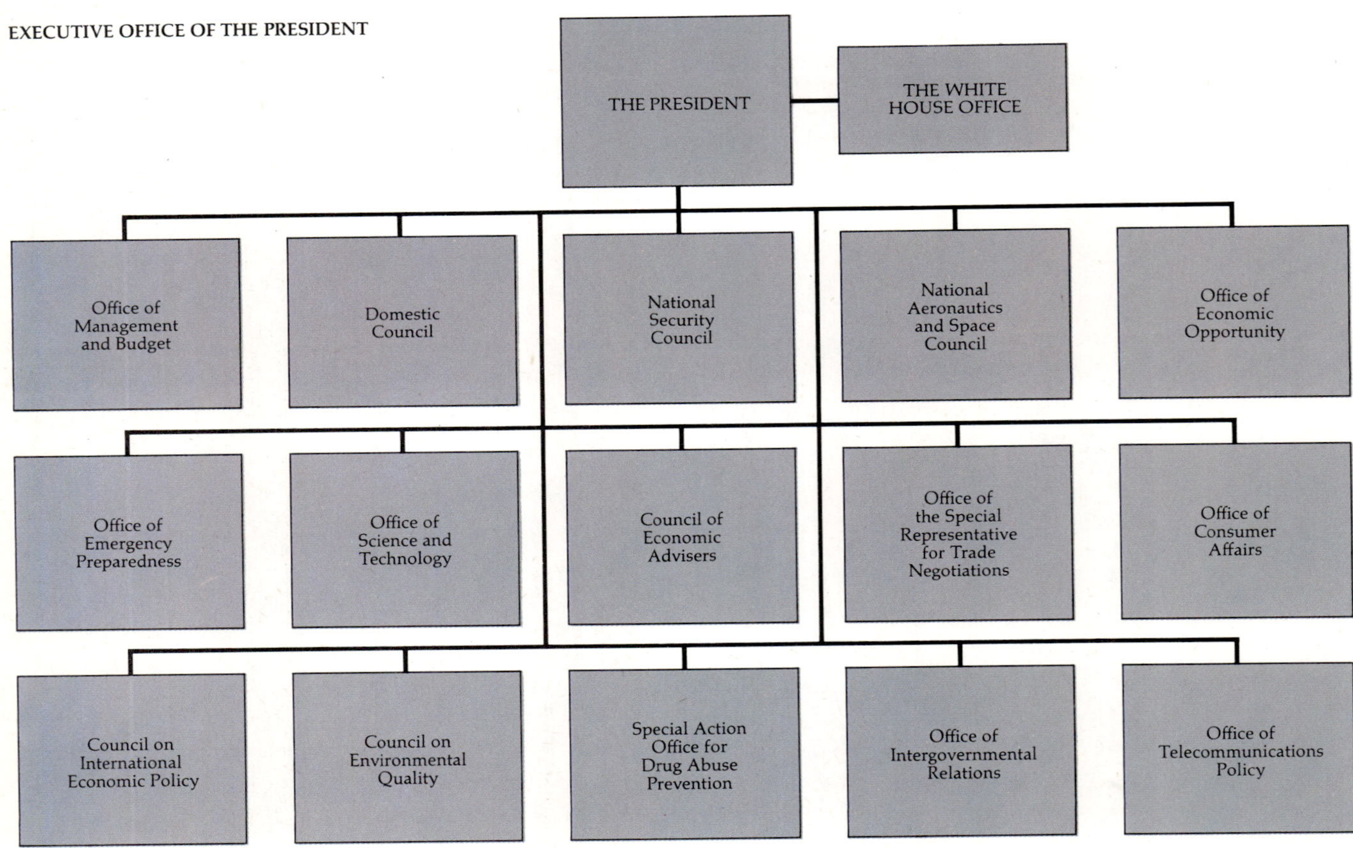

In his celebrated account of the Presidency, Clinton Rossiter delineates the roles of the President:

1. Chief of State. He represents the American people as a nation.
2. Chief Executive. He manages the government's executive branch.
3. Commander-in-Chief. He is first in command of the nation's armed forces.
4. Chief Diplomat. His primacy in foreign affairs has been recognized since the time of President Washington in spite of the Senate's power to advise and consent on treaties.
5. Chief Legislator. He plays an important role in determining the legislative agenda of Congress.

As Rossiter notes, the roles of the President have their roots in specific constitutional grants of responsibility. Additionally, Rossiter cites five presidential functions that have evolved:

1. Chief of Party. The President is elected in the first place through the efforts of his political party, and he seeks to advance the fortunes of that party in order to enhance his own power and success.
2. Voice of the People. He influences public opinion and the agenda of the nation's public discourse.
3. Protector of the Peace. The public instinctively turns to the President in times of crisis.
4. Manager of Prosperity. The President is held accountable for stable economic conditions.
5. World Leader. Given the power and influence of the United States, the election and subsequent actions of an American President are of genuine concern to other countries—the world-wide expression of grief at the assassination of President Kennedy attests to the world position of the American President. (Rossiter, 1960)

These roles and functions suggest the vast scope of the modern Presidency. But once all the pomp and

Figure 9.4 The scope of presidential duties has led to the growth of the President's Executive Office. The councils and offices on this diagram (left) represent a variety of advisory, administrative, and cross-agency units that are under the direct authority of the President.

Figure 9.5 An irony of American politics is at times demonstrated in the rites of transition from one President to another. In the cases illustrated here, each outgoing President is turning over the reins of office to an opposing party: sometimes the smiles seem a bit forced.

ceremony of the office have been stripped away, the primary job of the President is to participate actively in the initiation and implementation of public policy. The size of the work load and the fact that most of the work must be delegated points up one of the most important aspects of the modern Presidency— the growth of the *institutionalized* Presidency. The President is one man, but the Presidency is many men. The institution of the Presidency has expanded to keep pace with the President's importance in the policy-making process.

THE PRESIDENT AND THE PRESIDENCY

Presidential campaigns are full of promises of all things to all men, but once in the White House, the President must attempt to transform some of these promises into workable policies or programs. To accomplish this task, the President needs help from the institutionalized Presidency. His needs can be broadly defined into two functions—the need for advice and the need for action.

The President needs several types of advice. One type might be labeled "political": Is there enough support in Congress to pass a revenue-sharing bill? Will Congress and the public accept a tax increase? A second type of advice is "technical": How can the Administration reduce inflation? What will the Soviet Union do if the United States accelerates the air war in Indochina?

Both types of advice call for the uncertain art of prediction, and there are frequently no right answers. To confound matters even more, the two types of advice are rarely independent. An example from Chapter 4 concerning the Johnson Administration makes the point. Several of President Johnson's economic advisers had urged him to ask Congress for a tax increase as the Vietnam War became a major conflict. He resisted this and other normal wartime economic measures in an effort to downplay the short-run domestic impact of the war. The political considerations, which included the possible loss of congressional and public support, outweighed the technical advice of his economists. The resulting inflation was the price paid by Johnson's heeding the military advice that the war would soon be won (and that a tax increase was therefore unnecessary).

The second need of the President is the need for action. The operational needs of the Presidency are

Figure 9.6 The President is a person and also an institution. The President as a man can attract loyalties and stimulate fears and animosities. The Presidency as an institution is a number of offices and roles that compete in the Washington arena for authority and power. Who are the competitors of the President? Who seek to whittle down and bind the power of the man and the office? Who are the yes men of the President? Who are the men who sometimes distort the truth in search of favors? Indeed, the President holds the weapon of the veto in his hand; but given a damaged presidential image and division in the Administrative ranks, other sectors of government, such as Congress and the bureaucracy, begin to take over unused powers, and individuals who have been previously overshadowed begin to rise in the public's eye. Who is loyal? Who disloyal? Who are the innocent bystanders, and who are the waverers who will not act until the outcome of the battle is known? The struggles among the giant repositories of power and among the myriad power seekers in Washington are dramatic.

obvious: Speeches must be written, trips must be planned, strategy must be outlined with congressional allies, and so on. On a more substantial policy-making level, the President's needs are more subtle and complex. A basic task confronting the President is to plant the stamp of his Administration on the operations of the federal government because the various agencies and departments do not automatically respond to presidential dictates and desires. Once an order has been given, there must be someone to follow up on presidential instructions, someone to continually impress the presidential will on the bureaucracy (see Chapter 10). For example, during the Cuban Missile Crisis in 1962, President Kennedy was astonished to discover that the United States still had missile bases in Turkey even though he had ordered the State Department to arrange their removal more than a year before. Presidential instructions must be enforced by a coterie of assistants whose primary loyalty is to the President.

The Executive Office

The needs for action and advice became particularly acute during the Administration of Franklin Roosevelt. The scope of governmental activity had expanded drastically and with it the preeminence of the President as policy maker. In 1937 Roosevelt appointed the Committee on Administrative Management, called the Brownlow Committee after its chairman, Louis Brownlow. The committee's recommendations were tersely summed up in one sentence, "The President needs help." In response, the Executive Office of the President was established, marking an important departure from the tradition when Presidents existed with a personal secretary and a handful of clerks. The components of the Executive Office operate under the direct control of the President.

The White House Office

Closest to the President is the White House Office, which consists of the President's top personal aides. The titles and corresponding duties change from President to President, but whatever the titles, these assistants are the President's closest and most trusted associates. The members of this staff are responsible only to the President; they do not need senatorial approval and can be compelled to testify before Con-

Figure 9.7 The President is the focus of many pressures and demands. Obviously, his own personal experiences and moral values will influence his decisions. Most importantly, it is the President himself who must decide to whom he will or will not listen, who will share his closest confidence, and who will be left knocking on the White House door. Every President must make the effort not to be swamped by petitioners desirous of an audience. Presidents thus have staffs and specialized agencies that serve both to buffer the President from pressures that do not warrant his time and to synthesize the material for decisions that do demand his attention. Unfortunately, buffering and synthesizing can lead to isolation and special influence. The President must save himself and his time, but he must also be open to ideas and information from many sources. Striking this dynamic balance is one of the greatest challenges to the man in the White House.

INFLUENCES ON PRESIDENTIAL DECISION MAKING

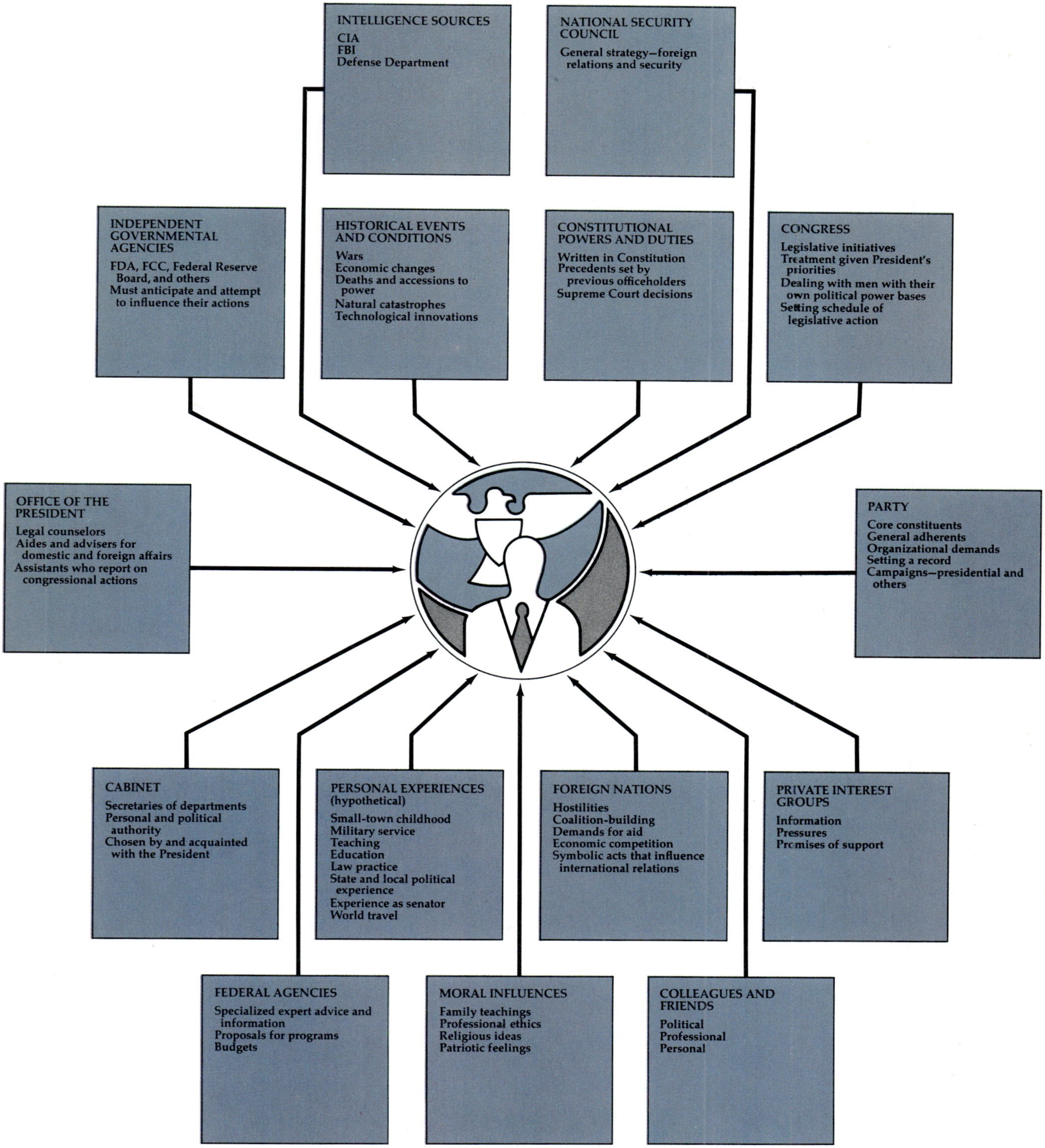

INTELLIGENCE SOURCES
CIA
FBI
Defense Department

NATIONAL SECURITY COUNCIL
General strategy—foreign relations and security

INDEPENDENT GOVERNMENTAL AGENCIES
FDA, FCC, Federal Reserve Board, and others
Must anticipate and attempt to influence their actions

HISTORICAL EVENTS AND CONDITIONS
Wars
Economic changes
Deaths and accessions to power
Natural catastrophes
Technological innovations

CONSTITUTIONAL POWERS AND DUTIES
Written in Constitution
Precedents set by previous officeholders
Supreme Court decisions

CONGRESS
Legislative initiatives
Treatment given President's priorities
Dealing with men with their own political power bases
Setting schedule of legislative action

OFFICE OF THE PRESIDENT
Legal counselors
Aides and advisers for domestic and foreign affairs
Assistants who report on congressional actions

PARTY
Core constituents
General adherents
Organizational demands
Setting a record
Campaigns—presidential and others

CABINET
Secretaries of departments
Personal and political authority
Chosen by and acquainted with the President

PERSONAL EXPERIENCES (hypothetical)
Small-town childhood
Military service
Teaching
Education
Law practice
State and local political experience
Experience as senator
World travel

FOREIGN NATIONS
Hostilities
Coalition-building
Demands for aid
Economic competition
Symbolic acts that influence international relations

PRIVATE INTEREST GROUPS
Information
Pressures
Promises of support

FEDERAL AGENCIES
Specialized expert advice and information
Proposals for programs
Budgets

MORAL INFLUENCES
Family teachings
Professional ethics
Religious ideas
Patriotic feelings

COLLEAGUES AND FRIENDS
Political
Professional
Personal

gress only with the President's approval, an immunity called "executive privilege." The President hires and fires them at will, and there is a complete turnover in the White House Office when a new President is inaugurated.

The White House Office both advises and acts for the President. It includes those aides who are the President's closest advisers on national security, the economy, urban affairs, and other policy areas. Other assistants provide liaison with Congress and lobby for the President's legislative program. Others write speeches, handle press relations, plan trips, and work with state and local political leaders. Included also are those who provide for the ceremonial and social aspects of the office, aides such as the chief usher.

The power of a presidential aide is exemplified by H. R. (Bob) Haldeman, who was President Nixon's chief of staff from 1969 to 1973. This former advertising executive became one of Washington's most powerful men: It was he who decided who would see the President and who would not. Like all other presidential aides, Bob Haldeman served at the discretion of the President. He was forced to resign when he was implicated in the Watergate scandal in May 1973—only a few weeks after a *Newsweek* magazine cover story touted him as the most powerful member of the President's staff.

The Office of Management and Budget

The largest of the Executive Office components is the Office of Management and Budget (OMB), formerly the Bureau of the Budget. Although this little-known office with the somber title may convey the image of wizened old men with account books who work in an atmosphere of unbearable dullness, OMB is actually a dynamic and vitally important tool in running the government, and it greatly increases the power of the President.

The OMB has two main functions, the first of which is the preparation of the budget of the United States. Every year, OMB solicits the appropriations requests of all the various departments and agencies in the federal government. It then determines a budget request for each department—based on department needs and the Administration's financial constraints—and sends its recommendations to the appropriations committees of Congress for approval.

Thus, when department heads appear before Congress, they are formally requesting the appropriation amount set by the President through OMB; they cannot request appropriations without this procedure. In the case of a few politically popular departments, however, a friendly appropriations subcommittee chairman may acknowledge that "yes, the department could use more funds than OMB has allocated." One such agency is the Federal Bureau of Investigation (FBI), which frequently receives more money from Congress than it officially requests.

The second OMB function is legislative clearance. Before an executive agency can submit new legislation to Congress, it must be cleared by OMB to ensure that it is consistent with the goals and policies of the Administration. OMB also provides the President with summaries and analyses of the budgetary implications of legislation enacted by Congress. When the Executive Office was reorganized by President Nixon in 1970, OMB was given additional responsibilities. It was charged with the coordination of governmental programs between various agencies and became increasingly active in evaluating the efficiency and effectiveness of executive branch programs.

The Council of Economic Advisers

A third component of the Executive Office is the Council of Economic Advisers (CEA), which interprets economic developments for the President and advises him on economic policy. Although council members are usually chosen from among the country's leading economists, they have at times been accused of tempering their public economic pronouncements with political expediency. For example, during the inflation that beset the Nixon Administration, CEA spokesmen regularly predicted that prices would level off. The passage of time proved them wrong.

The National Security Council

The National Security Council (NSC), the fourth major component of the Executive Office, is a good illustration of the institutional response to the President's policy-making needs. It was created by the National Security Act of 1947 (which also created the Central Intelligence Agency, the CIA, as another part of the Executive Office) in response to the need to coordinate domestic, foreign, and military policies in planning overall national security policy. NSC consists of the President, Vice-President, Secretary of State, and the Secretary of Defense. The President may also include other officials whose knowledge he considers relevant to defense planning or in whom he has particular confidence. Thus, President Kennedy included his brother Robert, then Attorney General, in NSC meetings, although the Justice Department is not normally involved in defense planning. The NSC is served by its own staff, which prepares detailed analyses and policy options. Once small, this staff has grown to over 200 under President Nixon's Special Assistant for National Security, Henry Kissinger.

The foreign and military policy-making apparatus of the NSC has attained new preeminence under Kissinger's direction. To a much greater extent than previous National Security Assistants, Kissinger has drawn national security policy making more firmly into the White House and has supplanted the advisory roles of the Secretaries of State and Defense, particularly the former. Thus, he has neatly side-stepped the obstacles presented by vested interests in the traditional agencies of foreign and military policy making, the Pentagon (the Department of Defense) and the State Department.

Certainly, circumventing bureaucratic channels speeds up and simplifies the decision-making process, but the process also tends to undermine the morale and authority of the by-passed departments. Congressional leaders have complained that this centralization of power removes them, and the constituents they represent, even further from the foreign policy-making process. And because of the custom of executive privilege, personal advisers such as Dr. Kissinger cannot be compelled to testify before Congress, nor does approval of his position require Senate confirmation.

The Domestic Council

The newest addition to the Executive Office is the Domestic Council. Created by President Nixon in 1970, the council was set up to formulate and coordinate the President's domestic policy recommendations. It is primarily an advisory arm of the President; that is, it recommends on matters of policy formulation. It differs in this respect from the Office of Management and Budget, which helps determine how policy should be carried out. The council was originally envisioned as the domestic policy equivalent of the National Security Council, but it has yet to achieve that preeminence.

The Cabinet

Every President, from Washington to Nixon, has had a Cabinet; yet there is no constitutional basis for this advisory body (or for any specific executive department). Although custom created the Cabinet, it certainly did not dictate how it would function. Franklin Roosevelt's Cabinet meetings were unstructured, chatty affairs held with little regularity, whereas Eisenhower's were regularly scheduled meetings with fixed agendas.

Cabinet meetings with the President fulfill a "sounding board" function, insofar as the heads of the eleven executive departments represent the views of their important constituencies, such as labor unions (Secretary of Labor), big business (Secretary of Commerce), and agriculture (Secretary of Agriculture). The Cabinet, however, has not been able to coordinate the activities of the various departments or to collectively advise the President on useful policy alternatives (Richard Fenno, 1959).

The failure of the Cabinet to adequately provide coordination and advice points up the dual nature of the Cabinet member's job. Although he is appointed by the President and politically allied with him, he is also head of an executive department and usually develops loyalty to that department.

The Cabinet member is the man caught in the middle, with a delicate balance to maintain. If he begins to view policy largely from his department's perspective, he can hinder the coherence of the administration and the policy of the President. If he is entirely the President's man, he may find himself in conflict with the career bureaucrats in his department, many of whom have been there longer than he has, and he will have difficulty in managing his department (see Chapter 10).

For these reasons, coordination within the government's executive branch is difficult. Recent administrations have responded by granting the task of coordination to such interdepartmental bodies as the National Security Council and the Domestic Council. Indeed, these groups, rather than the Cabinet, have emerged as the essential advisory and policy-making bodies for the President.

The Advisory System

In concluding this discussion of the advisory system, one point should remain clear—the Cabinet and the Executive Office bear the personal imprint of the Chief Executive. Presidents differ in personality, experience, and politics, and all of these factors shape their Administrations.

Compare, for example, the contrasting administrative styles of Franklin Roosevelt and Dwight Eisenhower. Roosevelt, confronted with the crisis of the Great Depression, had a constant need for policy innovation. He used rivalry between his aides to his own advantage. He would have two or three groups work feverishly on a problem, each unaware of the work of the other groups. Lines of authority were unclear, jurisdictions overlapped, and the President had complete control. Although on the surface the system looked like a shambles, it worked for Roosevelt. Differences of opinion were not muffled, and power was firmly in his hands—he had the ability to choose between the options.

President Eisenhower, on the other hand, believed in a more rigid staff system of the type that had served him so well in the army. He wanted dif-

ferences of opinion resolved before they were brought to him. As a result, he requested that advisory memos that included the policy recommendations of his staff be boiled down to just one page. Although the procedure simplified the President's administrative burden, it also removed from him some of the power of decision making by removing or compromising the options before they reached his desk.

THE PRESIDENT AS POLICY MAKER

In discussing the President's role in the policy-making process we come to the most important aspect of the modern American Presidency. Whether he seeks the power or not—and Eisenhower was the only President since 1932 who has tried to shy away from the role—the President is central to the policy-making process.

Presidential power has greatly increased in the twentieth century, an expansion that has resulted largely from a changed conception of the proper role of government and from changes in America's world position. President Roosevelt's New Deal Administration in the 1930s sparked the growth of *positive* government—policies and programs that directly affected the lives of all Americans. The executive branch, which administers these policies and pro-

Figure 9.8 President Nixon's advisers demonstrate why "the President needs help." Here, top economic and domestic advisers sift through more than one hundred bills passed by Congress; they review the bills' spending ramifications and help determine the Administration's policy orientations.

grams, has expanded in response. Presidential power has also increased as a result of the vital importance of foreign policy since World War II. As foreign affairs came to occupy a dominant position in national political life, so too did the President, who has clear supremacy in the area of foreign affairs and national security policy. To execute his duties the President has become intimately involved in both the initiation of policy and its implementation.

The President Initiates

The President's most important function in initiating policy is his influence in *setting the agenda* of issues, that is, determining which subjects receive political action. Indeed, nothing happens until a subject somehow becomes viewed as a political issue. What constitutes an "issue" has not been precisely defined by political scientists; however, when a topic is investigated in congressional hearings, when it receives extensive coverage in the press, or when it is the object of substantial presidential attention and comment, it has passed the major tests. The political scientist David Easton has visualized the issue-making process as one that begins with various "wants" in society. These wants are translated into "demands" by various "gatekeepers" who translate diffuse wants into more specific political issues

(Easton, 1965). And the President is one of the most prominent of those gatekeepers.

But issues do not arise solely because the President (or other gatekeepers) create them. People were poor and the welfare system was inadequate long before these became issues. Racial inequality was the subject of public awareness, if not concern, long before it received presidential attention. The President is only one among many who may raise issues to public consciousness; but he has preeminent power in defining the issues—particularly foreign and military matters.

Thus, the Vietnam War was seen by many Americans as resistance against communist aggression, in line with the views of Presidents Kennedy, Johnson, and Nixon. Although critics increasingly characterized the conflict otherwise, President Johnson was able for a long period to shape the public's perceptions of the war. Several factors enable the President to define issues and initiate policy through his influence on public opinion.

First, the President is the single most visible participant in the political process. Scarcely a day goes by when he is not before the public eye, either on the front page of newspapers or on the televised news. Such exposure does not guarantee influence, but it does give the President the opportunity to

□

THE PRESIDENT MUST HAVE HELP

"I am sure you . . . realize the Presidency has been dramatically changed in recent years by the increasing complexity of the nation's foreign and domestic problems.

"A domestic issue which simply could be considered and resolved by one agency head in 1935 or 1940 without involving the White House today probably involves the conflicting interests of two or three major departments of the federal government and frequently results in dispute which only the White House can resolve . . . Our concept of government's role has changed, and with it, the Presidency has changed qualitatively and in terms of the work load.

"As this dimension and complexity has compounded, the demands and claims for the President's personal time and attention and his personal decision has steadily escalated . . .

"And so the President must have help. He has a staff and he must have some system for delegating and for determining which of all of these claims deserve and require his time . . .

"For example, there has been some surprise expressed that Mr. Dean, his counsel, did not have easy entry to the President's office . . ." (John Ehrlichman before Senate Select Committee on Campaign Financing, July 24, 1973)

present his views to the public and thereby to define national concern. Second, the status of the presidential office is accorded great respect and lends credence to the President's policy choices. By making use of the greater visibility accorded the President over other politicians, he can convince many people that his policies are in the national interest.

As a measure of the respect accorded the President, Gallup poll ratings show that only rarely do less than 50 percent of the public think the President is doing a good job. The President is also usually first on the annual Gallup poll list of most admired men. In short, people are generally predisposed favorably toward a President, acknowledge his importance and even his supremacy in national politics, and usually approve of his conduct in office (see Chapter 12). The President's words have great weight, a fact that increases his ability to inspire public acceptance of White House policy.

Setting the agenda by influencing public opinion is a precursor to policy initiation. The more formal means of presidential policy initiation is found in the President's constitutional power to deliver to Congress an annual *State of the Union* message; the President uses this power to participate actively in the determination of legislative priorities. Although the constitutional powers of Congress are many, the President does have formidable powers in influencing Congress. By virtue of his use (or threat) of the veto power, his control of federal spending, and his power to dispense favors of immense importance to congressmen, the President has unique advantage in the legislative process (see Chapter 8).

Policy Implementation

In the traditional formal model of American government, Congress legislates (initiates policy) and the President executes the laws (implements policy).

Figure 9.9 The President has plenty of power—but using it effectively can be difficult. Standing with the presidential seal, the President can easily appeal to the loyalties of the people. But unwieldy, disloyal, or incompetent governmental agencies can frustrate even this great power.

Figure 9.10 Presidents have programs and priorities and a set of powers and resources with which to advance them (right). However, each President is confronted by a wide array of hurdles, which have the power to obstruct the successful implementation of his desired programs. Some of these hurdles are formal, legal, and institutional—for instance, the briefness of the presidential term or the fixed spending levels for given programs. Some of the hurdles are informal—such as the pressures from the news media or from political conflicts with an opposition Congress. At first glance the President's powers seem numerically fewer than the hurdles he faces, even though several of these powers, especially his prestige and his national and international leadership roles, seem to be able to outweigh numerous challenges to them. However, many recent observers of the Presidency agree that the number of hurdles to the exercise of presidential power seem to be expanding, whereas the powers and resources of the President are being sorely tested.

Just as the matter is not so simple in regard to passing legislation, the execution of the laws is not *entirely* in the hands of the President. Indeed, the President may encounter as many difficulties in implementing policy as in getting it through Congress. Contemplating the Eisenhower Presidency in 1952, Harry Truman said of Eisenhower, "He'll sit here and he'll say, 'Do this! Do that!' *And nothing will happen. Poor Ike—it won't be a bit like the Army. He'll find it very frustrating*" (Richard Neustadt, 1960). Truman was right: Eisenhower was continually surprised that his policies were not being implemented.

Eisenhower's problem (as well as every other President's) is that it is the bureaucracy and not the President that directly implements the laws. As already noted, the bureaucracy has interests and preferences of its own. Although Cabinet members or bureaucrats are rarely insubordinate to the President in the face of a direct command, such direct commands are rare. The President is too busy to confront every situation in which his preferences are being frustrated.

To overcome these obstacles, Presidents have turned to institutions closer to the White House—particularly the Office of Management and Budget—for aid in policy implementation. By virtue of OMB's power over agency budgets and its continuing surveillance of agency programs, the President is better able to keep agencies within the presidential orbit.

Congress is a second obstacle to presidential domination of the policy-implementation process. Congress possesses the formidable power of the purse; that is, Congress has the power to authorize a set amount of funds for governmental programs and can thereby cripple government programs by funding them at impossibly low levels.

Congress can also check the executive branch by its power of investigation. It can call Cabinet mem-

Possible Hurdles to Presidential Power

Possible Hurdles				Presidential Powers over Hurdles
Congressional Conflicts with opposition party Power of senior congressmen Government Accounting Office investigations Need for congressional consent for appointments and treaties Congressional power over appropriations Congressional investigations and hearings **Legal** Constitutional limitations Statutory limitations	**Within the Federal Executive Branch** Agency and personal rivalries Reinterpretations, slowdowns, and noncompliance with Administration policies Spending priorities that prevent or deflate achievement of Administration policy goals Predetermined increases in expenditures for certain programs Leaks of information to opposition or to the public	**The Presidency** Briefness of the four-year term Policies and precedents set by previous Presidents Personal limitations of the man in the White House President ill-informed or unaware of certain events and information due to insulation by staff **State and Local Governments** Reinterpretations, slowdowns, and noncompliance with Administration policies Pressures from states competing for federal grants and contracts Power and attitudes of governors and legislators	**Nongovernmental** Economic and political power of private industry Opposition of nongovernmental opinion leaders Ingrained prejudices and habits of thinking Pressures from the news media **Other** Power of independent regulatory agencies Domestic and world events beyond the President's control	Appointment of loyal personnel Constitutional and statutory power Executive orders Executive agreements with foreign countries Great prestige of the Presidency Favor-trading with congressmen Importance of national security and role of Commander-in-Chief Information from privileged sources Symbolic leadership, setting an example Lawsuits challenging acts of noncompliance Presidential veto Control of federal spending

bers and other agency heads to account for their actions, and such investigations may be given full media exposure. One of the most effective forums used by critics of the Vietnam War was the Senate Foreign Relations Committee, whose hearings received wide publicity. More recently, the Senate investigation into the Watergate affair was given extensive live television coverage to the continual embarrassment of the Nixon Administration.

Congressional investigations have been limited somewhat by the use of *executive privilege,* a doctrine that, it is claimed, allows presidential aides to refuse to testify before Congress. Executive privilege exists by custom rather than by law, and the extent to which it may be invoked has been a continual source of conflict between Presidents and Congress.

The Supreme Court is another check on presidential policy making—although it has exhibited an increasing reluctance to use its powers, especially in regard to the President's war powers. Clinton Rossiter expressed the view of most scholars in observing, "For most practical purposes, the President may act as if the Supreme Court did not exist" (Rossiter, 1960). In spite of numerous challenges, presidential policies involving curtailment of civil liberties in wartime have never been struck down by the Supreme Court while those policies were still in effect. The Court has also positively upheld the President's discretion and supremacy in foreign affairs.

However, the Supreme Court has more actively intervened in the President's domestic policy goals. The most conflict-ridden episode of this kind was the Court's invalidation of several important pieces of New Deal legislation. The Court held in 1935 that the President does not have the authority to remove a member of an independent regulatory commission (*Humphrey's Executor* v. *United States*). The Court also invalidated President Truman's seizure of the steel mills during the Korean War (*Youngstown Sheet & Tube Co.* v. *Sawyer,* 1952). More recently, the federal courts have frustrated President Nixon's attempts to slow the pace of racial desegregation in the nation's schools (see Chapter 6).

On the whole, however, such curtailments have been infrequent and short-lived (Glendon Schubert, 1957). In fact, Presidents have attempted to use the courts to implement their policies. When several of

Franklin Roosevelt's New Deal programs were blocked by the Supreme Court, he retaliated with his ill-fated attempt to "pack" the Court; by increasing the membership from nine to fifteen, Roosevelt could have appointed six judges on whom he could have depended for support. Although his plan failed, his strategy worked—the Court thereafter chose to uphold the constitutionality of the New Deal programs.

Reciprocity of the Policy Process

The most dominant theme that emerges from a consideration of the President as a policy maker is that of *reciprocity;* that is, for every resource of power there is a corresponding constraint. He has the power to influence the congressional agenda, but he cannot be assured that his policies will be either initiated or implemented. He has definite advantages in obtaining favorable public opinion, but this influence does not automatically translate into support for his pet programs. In short, the President is powerful, but he is not omnipotent, and the view of presidential power from the White House can be considerably more limited than it appears to Congress or to the public (Thomas Cronin, 1970).

In addition to specific resources and constraints there are more general factors that affect the President as policy maker. First, the political environment: A Congress controlled by the opposition party serves as a substantial constraint on a President's policy-making ability. Second, some policy choices prevent others. The amounts of money spent to maintain President Johnson's Vietnam policy made the continued growth of his Great Society domestic policies impossible. Third, domestic and world events beyond presidential control make some policy choices inevitable and others impossible. International crises abroad or riots at home compel the choice of certain policy initiatives over others.

PATTERNS OF POLICY MAKING

So far in this chapter we have used the term "policy" in its most general sense. It should be noted, however, that the power and politics of the President allow him to make different kinds of decisions in each of the four areas of policy making around which this book is organized. To examine these differences and also to provide a more concrete discussion of

Figure 9.11 The Presidency of the United States has been called the most powerful office in the world. But the power of that office is not unlimited. In the case of the steelmakers' price increases in 1962, President Kennedy sought first to persuade and then to coerce the price raisers to rescind the announced increases. Here, Kennedy holds a news conference to rally public opinion to his side in the dispute.

the President as policy maker we turn now to a discussion of the President's decision-making role in economic policy, civil rights and civil liberties, and foreign affairs.

Economic Policy

Certain aspects of economic policy are determined independently of the President; that is, they are beyond his direct control. The Federal Reserve Board, by its financial power over the nation's banks, affects the flow of credit. The independent regulatory agencies are more responsive to Congress than to the President. The President must get the consent of Congress to raise or lower taxes. And many special tax provisions are so firmly embedded in the relationship between powerful interest groups and the congressional committee system that they are beyond the President's ability to affect tax policy.

However, the President is ultimately held responsible for the overall management of the economy (see Chapter 4). It is the area in which the public is most concerned: The President (and his political party) incurs the public wrath if during his tenure the country drifts into a recession or experiences any period of economic instability. Economic slumps are associated with small but significant declines in the popularity of the President (John Mueller, 1973).

Particularly high on every recent President's list of economic problems is inflation. Since 1961 every President has sought to use his authority to encourage both prosperity and stable prices. In an effort to prevent inflation President Kennedy established a wage and price guidepost policy in 1962. He relied on the prestige of his office to influence businesses and unions to exercise restraint in prices and wage demands. When problems in the steel industry led United States Steel to announce that it was raising prices by six dollars a ton—and the other major companies immediately followed suit—Kennedy felt betrayed. The Administration's response illustrates the full range of techniques available to the President in situations of this nature.

The fight was waged on two fronts. First, the President directed the Justice Department to investigate the situation for a possible violation of antitrust laws; he appealed to the Defense Department to study the use of alternative materials and to buy steel from the smaller companies that had not yet raised prices. Second, the President relied on the prestige of his office to mobilize public opinion. The day after the price increase was announced, Kennedy held a press conference in which he denounced the price hike, calling it a "wholly unjustifiable and irresponsible defiance of the public interest." Tapping the full emotional potential of the situation, he concluded by saying, "Some time ago I asked each American to consider what he could do for his country and I asked the steel companies. In the last twenty-four hours we had their answer" (Theodore Sorenson, 1965).

Within a few days United States Steel followed the lead of the other steel companies and announced that it was rescinding its price rise. Although there is controversy as to whether it was the power of the Presidency or the power of the free market that prevailed (Grant McConnell, 1963), it was widely thought that the President's intervention was, indeed, successful and that public opinion had supported his actions.

In a head-on collision between the President and industry, the resources of the Executive Office are considerable. The President had no specific legal mandate for his actions. He relied entirely on the prestige of his office, his ability to mobilize public opinion, and his ability to apply tangential pressure through the Departments of Justice and Defense—all in the name of economic stabilization.

The economic obligations of the Presidency tend to override ideological distinctions. Compare, for example, the economic policy considerations of Richard Nixon, a conservative, to those expressed by a liberal President, John Kennedy. Approximately ten years after Kennedy confronted the steel industry, Nixon came into office in the midst of a rising surge of inflation and a worsening American position in the international economy. Unlike President Kennedy, Nixon initially declined to manipulate the economy via presidential prestige. Instead he relied on the tools of fiscal policy to bolster the country's economy.

But as the problems of inflation and unemployment increased, the Nixon approach began to change. In a vigorous exercise of presidential power, President Nixon asked Congress for legislation allowing him to control wages and prices for a limited period. In 1971 Congress extended this authority. By so doing, it made public the fact that the economy was not improving—contrary to the continuing claims of Administration spokesmen—and acknowledged the responsibility of the Presidency for managing the economy (or passed the buck to the President, depending on the point of view).

Finally, in August 1971 President Nixon made an unexpected and dramatic announcement that wages and prices would be "frozen" for ninety days. At the end of that period, the Administration announced "Phase II," which set up the mechanism to control most wages and prices over a longer period. Subsequently, price controls were lifted even though inflation continued.

Two significant features emerged from Nixon's economic policy. First, the President demonstrated his ability to take bold action—even action that suddenly contradicted and reversed previous policy. Second, the President received wide public support for his actions. These two factors are not independent of one another. To implement the authority given him by Congress, the President needed public support, and with the important exception of some labor leaders, he received that support.

Foreign Policy: Vietnam

Aaron Wildavsky has suggested that there are two Presidencies—one for domestic and one for foreign policy (Wildavsky, 1966). In domestic policy the President's main problem is obtaining congressional support; in foreign policy his problem is to formulate a viable policy. Although the President is not without opposition in foreign and military policy, he can almost always gather sufficient support to implement his national security policies. By its power of appropriations, Congress can affect foreign policy at the margins—particularly in regard to foreign aid. But in the major issues of war making and relations with other countries, the President is preeminent, and public opinion supports his position. Congress, although it has debated the subject, has until very recently been unwilling to trim the President's power—even in the wake of the Vietnam War.

An analysis of the decision making that led to United States involvement in Vietnam illustrates the President's domination of foreign policy. Presidents Johnson and Nixon usually spoke about Vietnam in terms of "American commitment" and "national

Figure 9.12 Although the President and his advisers are usually able to wield public opinion on foreign-policy matters, the Vietnam War ended with much dissension over the Administration's conduct of it. Many felt the President's conduct of foreign policy should not be beyond the realm of public criticism. This advertisement was intended to take the President and his retinue down a notch or two—to make the foreign-policy President as naked to criticism as the domestic President. It is instructive that this advertisement was sponsored by senatorial candidates; given the Senate's national visibility and its history as a forum for debate, it was the natural locus of challenge to the President's foreign policy.

security," which made American involvement appear inevitable—an automatic response to external events. But the commitment that did exist was a function of presidential interpretation of the situation. To act on the "commitment" through military intervention was a decision of the President and those close to him (David Halberstam, 1972).

The President and his advisers authoritatively interpreted the situation—a situation that was highly ambiguous and subject to alternate interpretations. For example, each of the following interpretations was made by both Johnson and Nixon, and each was increasingly challenged by a substantial body of expert opinion: First, the initial conflict in Vietnam was an example of armed aggression from another nation rather than a civil war; second, the United States was required under treaty obligations to come to the defense of South Vietnam; third, North Vietnam was acting primarily as a surrogate for a monolithic communist bloc, and therefore it was prudent to stop communist aggression in Vietnam rather than somewhere closer to home (the *domino theory*). This interpretation of events guided not only Administration action, but also largely structured public opinion (which changed only near the end of the conflict). By and large, the public agreed that it was necessary to "stand up to the communists."

The most striking observation in regard to Vietnam is that the decisions leading to eight years of full-scale war were, for all practical purposes, made entirely by the President and by advisers who were responsible only to him. These decisions included: increasing a token force of military advisers to a fighting force of more than 500,000 men; bombing North Vietnam, invading Cambodia, mining and blockading North Vietnamese harbors; and finally ending American involvement in the war.

Yet in spite of this usurpation of power, the other branches of government refused to take any meaningful steps to end the Vietnam conflict. Congress continued to appropriate the funds needed to continue the war, and the Supreme Court continued to sidestep the issue of the war's constitutionality.

Perhaps the most striking phenomenon of all was the President's power to shape public opinion regarding the war. Even after 1968, by which time a clear majority of Americans thought that the United States should never have intervened in Vietnam, most Americans continued to support every dramatic move made by the President, be it a bombing halt or the invasion of Cambodia.

But the best proof of the President's ability to influence (if not mold) public opinion is illustrated in Table 9.1. Questions were asked immediately before and after three policy decisions were announced: the bombing halt of March 1968, the American invasion of Cambodia in 1970, and the plan for American troop withdrawal announced by the President in 1969. Thus, decisive presidential action appears to be able to build its own support. Rather than being controlled by public opinion, a President is able to count on the acquiescence of a new majority to his policy decisions (see Chapter 12).

Table 9.1 Public Approval of Vietnam Actions

ACTION	FAVORING PROPOSED ACTION	FAVORING ACTION ALREADY TAKEN
Invade Cambodia	28%	50%
Bombing Halt	40	64
Rate of Troop Withdrawal	31*	56†

* Favored withdrawal at the then current rate
† Favored rate after President's speech on November 2, 1969
Source: After Mark V. Nadel, "Public Policy and Public Opinion," in Robert Weissberg and Mark V. Nadel (eds.), *American Democracy: Theory and Reality* (New York: Wiley, 1972), p. 539.

The President's ability to mobilize public support in questions of national security policy is not, however, confined to actual wartime situations. Decisive actions in foreign affairs almost always increase the popularity of the President—even if the action is unsuccessful. For example, President Kennedy's popularity increased by 10 percent after the disastrous Bay of Pigs fiasco in 1961.

The great reversal of American policy toward the People's Republic of China during the first Nixon Administration is a more recent example of the President's ability to make bold foreign-policy decisions and carry public opinion with him. From 1948 onward American policy toward China was characterized by hostile isolation—a hard-line policy heartily endorsed by Mr. Nixon.

In 1971, however, it was suddenly announced that the President's Special Assistant for National Security Affairs, Dr. Henry Kissinger, had secretly visited China and that the President himself would

Figure 9.13 "Summitry" is a word coined for meetings at the summit, that is, meetings between representatives at the highest levels of government. Although officials at lower governmental levels often do much of the work of hammering out international agreements, the effects on public opinion are far stronger when national leaders personally cement their nations' agreement by handshake, state dinner, and official ceremony.

soon make a state visit. At the same time, the United States dropped its opposition to Chinese membership in the United Nations, and China was admitted. Thus, the closed door between the United States and China was opened, and in 1973 the two countries exchanged diplomatic representatives.

Civil Rights and Civil Liberties

Although a President, merely by his words, cannot change long-engrained habits of thought and action, his attitudes can contribute toward making racism either respectable or not respectable; the degree of his own personal commitment to civil rights can therefore have important policy consequences. Such symbolic leadership is only a part of a President's civil rights approach, but it is a part that can signal what is to come and provide inspiration to others involved in civil rights policy making. Thus, it was a strikingly significant moment when President Lyndon Johnson, a southerner, presented his voting rights bill to a joint session of Congress in a nationwide televised address. In concluding his message the President said, "Their cause must be our cause too, because it is not just Negroes, but it is all of us, who must overcome the crippling legacy of bigotry and injustice. And we shall overcome." Similarly, it was an equally significant moment when President Nixon went on television to oppose involuntary busing of children to achieve equal opportunity in public education.

Words, of course, are not enough; substantive policy must be initiated. In an all-out effort to pass legislation, the President's participation in the legislative process is extensive. The efforts of Presidents Kennedy and Johnson that led to the eventual passage of the Civil Rights Act of 1964 demonstrate a President's formidable array of legislative powers. The following list describes the major actions begun in 1963 by President Kennedy and completed after Kennedy's death by President Johnson:

1. Legislation was drafted and sent to Congress.
2. President Kennedy worked closely with the Leadership Conference on Civil Rights, the coordinating body of civil rights organizations. Competing positions were argued, and a strategy was planned.
3. Meetings were held with thousands of concerned individuals, including religious leaders, businessmen, and representatives of specifically affected groups.

4. President Kennedy entered negotiations to guide a bill through the House Judiciary Committee. Aides from the Justice Department were also utilized at this and later stages to take part in congressional negotiations.

5. By threatening his full support for a discharge petition, President Johnson cajoled the chairman of the House Rules Committee to hold hearings on the civil rights bill.

6. As part of the strategy to win a cloture vote against an inevitable southern filibuster, the President made it clear to the Senate that this was top-priority legislation and that other presidential programs could wait.

7. The President worked closely with the Senate Democratic leadership, but also kept constant pressure on Republican Minority Leader Everett Dirksen. The President won the support of Dirksen and previously uncommitted Republicans. The southern filibuster was thus beaten, and the bill was enacted. (James Sundquist, 1968)

Legislative leadership is one of several ways in which a President can initiate and implement policy; another is the executive order. President Truman helped further the cause of racial equality by desegregating the armed forces by executive order in 1948. Presidents Kennedy and Johnson used executive orders to compel nondiscrimination in hiring by federally contracted firms—a practice made unnecessary by equal-employment legislation in 1964.

Given the continuing controversy and intense political pressures surrounding civil rights policy, executive policy implementation is particularly important. In two areas in particular the President is given considerable discretion. First, the Voting Rights Act of 1965 requires that either the United States Attorney General or the federal courts approve all changes in state election laws in those states in which voting rights were previously infringed upon. This key provision, designed to prevent state legislatures from circumventing federal law, allows the President, via his Attorney General, to act as guardian of minority rights if he chooses to do so. The second area involves school desegregation. Title VI of the Civil Rights Act of 1964 prohibits discrimination in any program receiving federal assistance and requires fund-granting agencies to issue rules that must be approved by the President in order for the provision to be implemented.

Under this law, the Department of Health, Education, and Welfare (HEW) has issued a series of guidelines for school desegregation; it has the power to cut off federal funds for school districts that do not comply. The guidelines are formally enforced by the Office of Civil Rights in HEW, but the office must remain carefully attuned to presidential desires. A striking demonstration of the relationship occurred in 1970 when President Nixon fired Leon Panetta, the Director of the Office of Civil Rights, who had refused to allow continued delays in compliance by southern school districts.

Additionally, the President can affect the implementation of desegregation plans by requiring that the Attorney General bring suit to order compliance or by asking the courts to delay previously court-ordered compliance. And he can implement policy over the broad spectrum of civil rights issues by appointing his own personnel to lead the bureaucracy, particularly in HEW; by making appointments to the federal courts; and by directing orders to the executive departments under his control.

There are, however, limitations on the President's ability to initiate and implement civil rights policy. Whether his aims are to quicken or to retard the pace of civil rights, every President inevitably faces opposition—in Congress, in the public, and even in his own bureaucratic agencies. For example, the FBI ignored President Kennedy's request that it take a vigorous role in protecting civil rights workers in the South. The federal courts can also constrain the President's freedom of action; indeed, the ultimate responsibility for the approval of specific desegregation plans lies with the courts.

In the area of civil liberties the President has usually been the citizen's antagonist; that is, the exercise of presidential power has more often threatened than protected civil liberties, because civil liberties represent a citizen's refuge from governmental powers.

During the Civil War, with the threat of subversion in the Union by southern sympathizers, President Lincoln suspended the constitutional privilege of *habeas corpus* (protection from illegal imprisonment) on his own authority. In 1863 Congress passed the Habeas Corpus Act, which legitimized the President's action. During World War II President Roosevelt ordered the removal and internment of over 100,000 Americans of Japanese descent—of whom

Figure 9.14 The circle of presidential confidants. Woodrow Wilson's sounding board and trusted adviser was Colonel Edward M. House; Franklin Roosevelt's influential friend was Harry Hopkins. In more recent days there has been a succession of famous advisers: Dwight Eisenhower's close adviser, Sherman Adams, once governor of New Hampshire and Ike's successful campaign manager, eventually brought discredit on the Administration through his involvement in far-reaching scandals. Probably the closest relationship ever to occur in the White House existed between John Kennedy and his brother the Attorney General, Robert Kennedy; both victims of tragedy, the two men worked closely on day-to-day matters as well as on crises such as the Cuban missile confrontation. President Nixon confers in his airplane (bottom right) with Secretary of State William Rogers and his far-ranging aide and adviser Henry Kissinger. After setting up various trips to Peking and to Moscow and negotiating the Vietnam cease-fire, Kissinger formally assumed the title of Secretary of State on Rogers's resignation. Below, Nixon confers with his old friend and supporter, campaign manager and Attorney General, John Mitchell. Similarly to Sherman Adams, Mitchell left the President's circle under the cloud of scandal arising from accusations about his involvement in the Watergate burglary and cover-up.

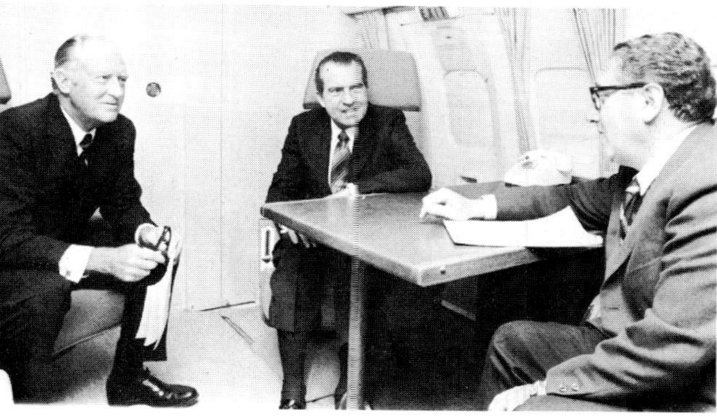

70,000 were American citizens. In spite of constitutional challenges, the Supreme Court side-stepped the issue. More recently President Nixon sought and received from Congress the power to use electronic surveillance equipment (wiretapping) in cases involving national security. Permission to use such equipment is granted not by court order but by a presidential appointee, the Attorney General. Subsequently, this power was limited by the Supreme Court to cases involving foreign countries.

However, executive restriction of civil liberties has never been a primary policy goal. Rather, those infringements that have occurred have been incidental to the exercise of presidential power for other purposes. The President, therefore, plays an indirect policy-making role in civil liberties, with the courts acting as mediator between the policies of the executive and the protected areas of individual freedom.

THE PRESIDENT: IMAGE AND INSULATION

Until recently the consensus of most historians and political scientists was that the President was and should be the center of American political life. He was seen as being uniquely equipped and situated to carry out wise policies in the public interest. However, the war in Vietnam and the revelations of the abuse of power in the Watergate scandal substantially chipped away at such faith in the beneficence of presidential power. Many scholars now think that presidential power is more of a problem for the public than a sure route to representation. At the heart of the problem is the vast growth of the Presidency and its increasing insulation from popular control. Both of these phenomena become apparent as they relate to public opinion and the press.

The Press "Checks" the President

Clinton Rossiter argued that the President *anticipates* public reaction and can act only within broad guidelines established by the public (Rossiter, 1960); however, the President has considerable resources with which to shape public reaction. Traditionally, the press has been considered an essential "check" on governmental power. Ideally, it should subject governmental actions to scrutiny and provide alternative views and assessments of governmental policy. Presidential press conferences are useful in that the President is asked to account for his actions. For all

Figure 9.15 Presidents are people. In fact, it is not a bad idea for a President to have the press catch him in a relaxed mood every so often in order to promote popular identification. Dick and Ike enjoy foot-long hot dogs at a ball game despite Secret Service watchdogs. In common with his close contemporary Winston Churchill, Ike had the hobby of painting. Harry Truman was an enthusiastic pianist, but he played even better with inspiration from movie star Lauren Bacall. Part of the New Frontier Kennedy image was the look of active, affluent youthfulness. Although hampered by a bad back, JFK swam and sailed with his handsome wife Jacqueline, leaving the nation a wistful image of Camelot. Ever anxious to maintain ties with Americans of middle-class suburbia, whence he sprang and source of his political power, President Nixon relishes press coverage of his participation in such diversions as watching football on TV and bowling. Even the towering Texan leader Lyndon Johnson demonstrates his style of herding "dogies" down on the Pedernales River where his ranch spread for 400 acres.

of these reasons there has always been a tension between reporters and the White House.

In recent years, however, the importance of the
press as an overseer or critic of the Presidency has
diminished for several reasons. First, Presidents
have shied away from direct contact with the press
and have relied instead on spokesmen whose comments are frequently "off the record." Press conferences that are attended by the President have been
sporadic and of limited usefulness because there is
scarcely ever an opportunity for sustained dialogue
on any one topic (see □). Second, recent Presidents
have side-stepped the press and gone directly to the
people via television. Third, during the Nixon Administration there has been a continuing attack on
the credibility of the press. Rather than responding
to specific stories reported by the press, Administration spokesmen have frequently denounced the
newspaper, television network, or magazine that
presented the story.

However, as is discussed in Chapter 14, there is
no evidence that Administration attacks have actually undermined public confidence in the news
media. The attacks have instead aroused considerable apprehension among newsmen about freedom
of the press—especially among TV newsmen whose
medium is subject to federal licensing and thus is
vulnerable to retaliation by the executive branch of
government.

The Watergate scandal, however, altered the conflict between the Nixon Administration and the
press—from an embattled press to an embattled Administration. The tough investigative reporting of
the *Washington Post* was one of the key factors in
bringing forth many of the details of the affair. But
it should not be forgotten that for months the *Post*

□

THE PRESS CONFERENCE
*Some hundreds of people are packed into a room, only a
fraction of whom will be recognized for a question. Some of
the ablest men, the ones who know, are passed over in favor
of administration shills. And, when rarely a sharp and hostile critic is allowed to pose a question, the answer can be
evasive, misleading, or dishonest because you are not allowed
a second question. It is one to the favored customer, and
even if you get lucky and are called on and you get one of
those double-talky answers, you cannot get the floor again
and say, "Mr. President, you didn't answer the question."*
(Nicholas von Hoffman, Washington Post, May 11, 1970)

was almost the only news organization that consistently dug into the story. The bulk of the American news media passively reported Administration denials and attacks on the *Washington Post* in the nine months until the newspaper was vindicated.

There is an inherent and beneficial conflict in the relationship between the Presidency and the press. And it is the business of the press to report bad news as well as good.

Advisers As Yes-Men

In *The Twilight of the Presidency,* George Reedy, former press secretary to President Johnson, focused on the problem of the insulation of the Presidency (Reedy, 1970). He charged that Presidents were shielded from the realities of America and the world by a staff that too often told them what they wanted to hear—as was exemplified by the eight years of glowing reports of American "success" in Vietnam.

In a television interview two years after he left office, Lyndon Johnson vigorously disputed this insulation theme; he somewhat ruefully pointed out that the President had numerous critics whose views he could not help hearing. Certainly no President is deaf to the criticism around him; however, the fact that he regards arguments contrary to his policies as carping criticism rather than as serious options simply indicates the degree to which the President is isolated. Because presidential advisers have their own interests in mind, as well as those of the President, it is difficult for the President to maintain a situation whereby aides vigorously present arguments contrary to the President's initial preferences. And once the President is committed to a course of action, he will find few within the White House who will tell him he is wrong.

Figure 9.16 (left) Presidents are careful to set the correct stage and atmosphere for press conferences and special announcements. Lyndon Johnson conducts the first color televised press conference—for which the East Room of the White House was rearranged and some of the more attractive women members of the press corps seated at the front. President Nixon and New York Governor Rockefeller hold an informal conference at Key Biscayne, Florida.

Figure 9.17 (right) A classic example of a conflicted relationship between a President and his adviser is the case of John W. Dean III and President Nixon. Dean, as White House Counsel (that is, one of the President's close legal aides) was said by the President to have been assigned the task of investigating complicity of members of the President's staff in the Watergate burglary or cover-up. According to the President, Dean never gave him the unwelcome information that the huge cover-up project touched on many personalities in the White House. According to Dean, however, speaking in his own defense, the President knew of the cover-up, and the President's assistants had chosen Dean as a scapegoat. Rarely does the conflict of interest between the President and his assistants and among his assistants come so dramatically to light as in the Watergate dissection of White House relationships.

The personal insulation of the President is compounded by the growing importance and power of the institutionalized Presidency. In order to make the federal bureaucracy responsive to the Chief Executive, policy-making power must be concentrated within the Executive Office. But those who make up the Executive Office are presidential aides, responsible only to the President and beyond the control of Congress or the public. This situation puts a serious strain on the constitutional system of checks and balances.

Constituents View the President

The ultimate check on a President—at least a first-term President—is the electoral process. However, it is especially difficult to unseat an incumbent President; only one President in this century, Herbert Hoover, has been defeated for reelection (although President Johnson probably avoided a similar fate by choosing not to run for a second term).

The Incumbent Remains Seated

The President has an impressive array of resources to facilitate his reelection. First, the President has some control over the timing and appearance of world events, and although he lacks complete control, his opponent has none. Especially, history indicates, when the country is in the midst of war, voters are reluctant to unseat an incumbent President. Their reasoning seems to be that "it is no time to change horses in the middle of the stream."

Second, the incumbent has definite publicity advantages over his opponent. He is not only a candidate, but he is President and inherently more newsworthy than his opponent who must buy most of his own publicity. For example, in 1972 when candidate George McGovern's task force on national security released its report on McGovern's defense position, it got little media coverage. It was buried in the inside pages of the *New York Times* and the other newspapers as well. NBC and ABC television

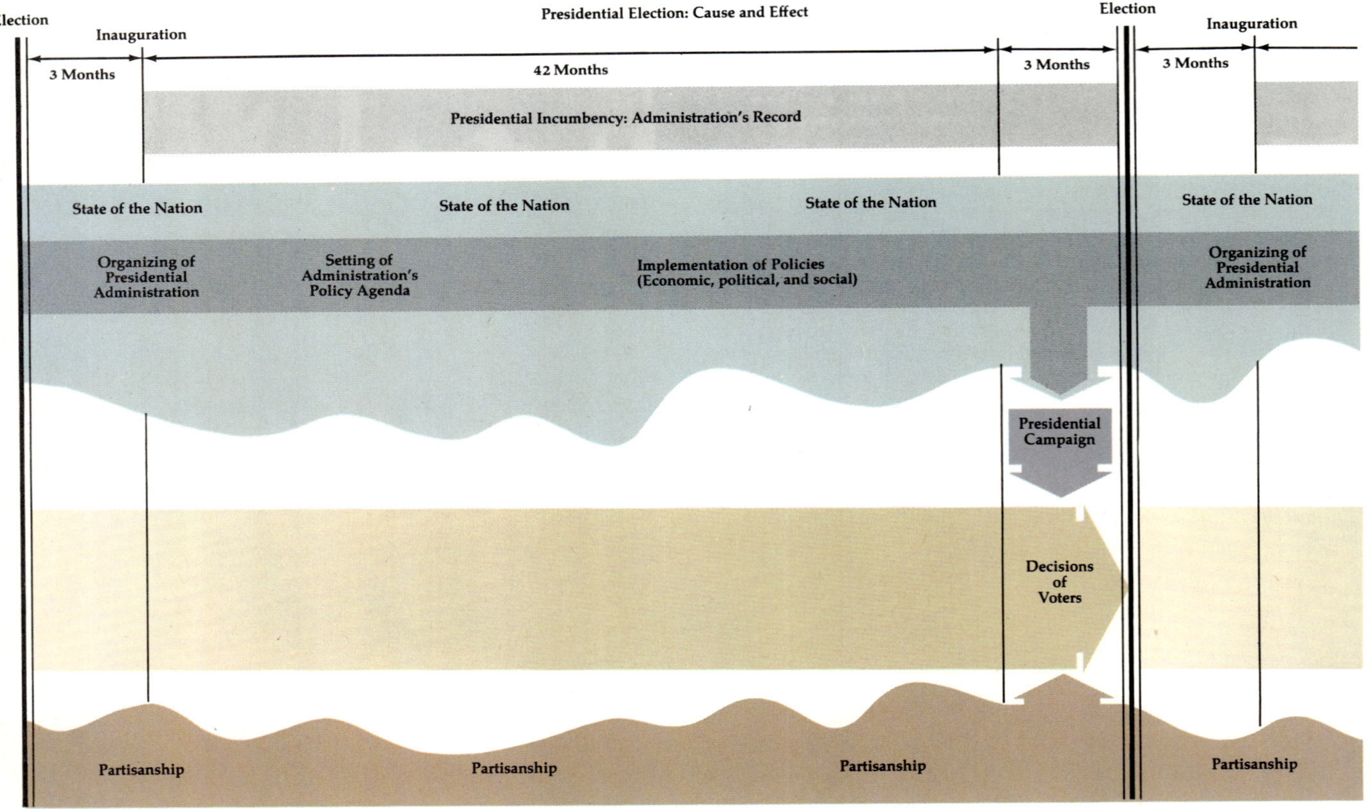

news programs devoted more time to a story about the collision between a man on a bicycle and the President's limousine—and the President wasn't even in the car at the time.

A third factor that favors an incumbent is his ability to use federal funds to his Administration's advantage. For example, in a bid for the votes of Mexican-Americans, the Nixon Administration in 1972 channeled $47 million into federal projects specifically designed to benefit Mexican-Americans in the Southwest. This tactic is not unique to Republicans; farm subsidies and other federal booty are normally manipulated to maximum advantage when incumbents run for reelection. The President can also increase his popularity by claiming credit for widespread federal benefits such as increases in social security payments.

Finally, the incumbent President can tap the vast resources of the federal bureaucracy. Incumbent Presidents normally use part of the White House staff, whose salary is paid by the taxpayers, as their personal campaign staff. Indeed, in 1972 the President's Special Counsel, Charles Colson, sent a memo exhorting his subordinates to devote all their energies to the reelection of the President and to work twenty-four hours a day for that goal. In 1972, and in preceding elections, Cabinet members traveled throughout the country, often at government expense, making thinly veiled campaign speeches. Local officials were enlisted to draft memoranda showing the enormous benefits of their particular programs for whatever group the President was courting—older people, farmers, blacks, and so on. Indeed, as came to light during the Senate investigations of the Watergate scandal, it appeared that presidential aides and former Cabinet members had quite surpassed themselves in their zeal to reelect President Nixon.

Despite all of his formidable advantages, the President is ultimately accountable to the people—or is

Figure 9.18 Is it possible to map, in a general way, the voter's decision-making process? This summary diagram (left) attempts to chart some of the elements. The focus is on the arrowheaded decisions of voters, which develop from left to right during the forty-eight months between presidential elections. By "state of the nation" is meant the total picture of economic, social, and political stability, including such elements as international security and confidence in political authority. The bottom layer of "partisanship" refers to the wavering of the public's identification with the political parties, as the fortunes and reputations of the parties wax and wane (although such shifts of identification do not usually affect the basic core of party identifiers). At election time, a complex blend of the presidential Administration's record, the current state of the nation, and the memories of the public provide a background to the presidential campaign, affecting and being affected by the simultaneous trend in public partisanship.

Figure 9.19 Four children aged eight to ten draw their interpretations of President Nixon. Children usually look up to the President as an awesome source of authority and protection, without understanding much about the complexities of government. They also tend to follow their parents' political attitudes.

he? Clearly, if the national situation, particularly the economy, suffers disastrous reverses and shows no sign of improvement, as in 1932, the incumbent is held accountable and is not returned to office. Indeed, the incumbent is held responsible for a variety of things over which he has little control, such as urban riots or certain economic dislocations. Nonetheless, recent experience demonstrates that elections are a weak means of popular control of the Presidency and are useless in binding the President to the specific commitments that he has made during his campaign.

Campaign Promises and Constituents

Consider President Johnson's solemn pledge to the nation in 1964 that "we are not about to send American boys nine to ten thousand miles away from home to do what Asian boys ought to be doing to protect themselves." There is no evidence, however, that the citizenry felt betrayed when shipload after shipload of American GIs were sent to Vietnam. It was not until 1968 that many Americans thought the country had made a mistake in getting involved in the war, and opposition did not hinge on the issue of a broken campaign pledge.

Even more striking was President Nixon's 1968 pledge to end the war in Vietnam. In an attempt to discredit his 1968 opponent, Hubert Humphrey (who had served as Vice-President under President Johnson), Nixon stated that the Johnson Administration's failure to end the war indicated that they did not deserve another chance. Nixon was elected in 1968 and failed to end the war within his own four-year term of office. However, he was reelected in 1972 by a landslide vote. And in spite of his inability to end the war during his first Administration, a preelection poll found that 48 percent of the public thought that President Nixon would be "more likely to end United States involvement in Vietnam sooner" than his Democratic opponent (Harris Poll, October 23, 1972).

Nor does the matter end with broken campaign promises. In spite of a flurry of preelection leaks that hinted at the involvement of high-level Republicans in the Watergate scandal, Harris poll respondents replied that President Nixon was better able than Senator McGovern to "keep corruption out of the federal government" (by a margin of 40 percent to 29 percent). Given the Nixon landslide, the figures might indicate that the voters perceive the issues in favor of the man they have already chosen rather than vice versa. In any case, the President's freedom of action is little diminished by previous campaign pledges nor by voter behavior in his next election.

Platform vs. Performance, 1968

Most of Nixon's major programs and initiatives, both domestic and foreign, which he has undertaken since assuming office were foreshadowed in the 1968 Republican platform. A comparison between some of his policies and his party's platform reveals the following:

Vietnam
Republicans promised "a strategy permitting a progressive de-Americanization of the war, both military and civilian . . . that will enable and induce the South Vietnamese to assume increasing responsibility." The result was the President's "Vietnamization" policy announced early in his Administration and the signing of the cease-fire agreement in 1973.

Government
The President's revenue-sharing proposals were explicitly outlined in the Republican platform: " . . . we propose the sharing of federal revenues with state governments. We are . . . determined to revise the grant-in-aid system and substitute block grants whenever possible."

Crime
The Republican platform asserted that "lawlessness is crumbling the foundations of American society." It proposed a series of measures to combat crime. Many of them were enacted into legislation. Among them: a new grant program to improve correctional facilities, authorization of $3.5 billion for the Law Enforcement Assistance Administration (LEAA) for three years, and a series of provisions to make it easier to combat organized crime.

Welfare
"Welfare and poverty programs will be drastically revised to liberate the poor from the debilitating dependence which erodes self-respect and discourages family unity and responsibility," said the platform. On August 8, 1969 President Nixon proposed a major reform of the welfare system to provide a federal minimum guaranteed income and include the working poor among those eligible for assistance.

But there are also features of the Nixon Administration that were not outlined in the 1968 Republican platform. In fact, in a few areas, pledges have been directly contravened by events. For example:

The Economy
The platform declared, "New Republican leadership can and will . . . avoid such economic distortions as wage and price controls." Yet on August 15, 1971 Nixon announced the imposition of a wage, price, and rent freeze, followed later by a system of controls.

Foreign Policy
"Under existing conditions, we cannot favor recognition of Communist China or its admission to the United Nations," the platform stated. On July 15, 1971 the President announced he would go to Peking in early 1972 for discussions with Communist Chinese leaders; on August 2, 1971 Secretary of State William P. Rogers said the United States would abandon its opposition to seating Communist China in the United Nations.

To that extent, popular control of the Presidency is made increasingly tenuous.

SUMMARY

The shaping experiences of the twentieth century have greatly increased the powers of the Presidency. The President's many roles and functions attest to his vast power and to his need to delegate authority. Presidential authority has become institutionalized—the advisory system includes the various components of the Executive Office, the Cabinet, and the interdepartmental bodies of the National Security Council and the Domestic Council.

The modern President plays a major role in policy initiation. Because of his ability to influence public opinion, the President largely determines what issues receive political attention. Yet his powers are checked by the powers of the bureaucracy, by Congress's powers of appropriation and of investigation, and by the Supreme Court's powers of intervention.

Economic policy—the President is ultimately held responsible for the overall management of the economy; his tools include forecasting, persuasion, and use of fiscal tools. Foreign affairs—in the major issues of warmaking and foreign relations, the President is preeminent. Civil rights—Presidents have generally followed rather than led the fight for civil rights legislation. Civil liberties—the exercise of presidential power has more often threatened than protected civil liberties.

The beneficence of presidential power—of its scope and insulation—has come under question in the wake of Vietnam and Watergate.

SUGGESTED READINGS

Binkley, Wilfred E. *President and Congress.* New York: Random House, 1962.

Cronin, Thomas E., and Sanford D. Greenberg (eds.). *The Presidential Advisory System.* New York: Harper & Row, 1969.

Davis, James W., Jr. *The National Executive Branch.* New York: Free Press, 1970.

Mueller, John E. *War, Presidents and Public Opinion.* New York: Wiley, 1973.

Neustadt, Richard. *Presidential Power: The Politics of Leadership.* New York: Wiley, 1960.

Wildavsky, Aaron (ed.). *The Presidency.* Boston: Little, Brown, 1969.

Figure 9.20 Although party platforms are full of generalities and the winning presidential candidate is not usually expected to be tied down by party promises made in the heat of a presidential convention, party platforms are nonetheless of considerable interest as possible foreshadowings of an Administration's policy preferences and legislative goals. As can be seen here (left), it was possible from the 1968 Republican Party platform to make general predictions of some of the actions the Nixon Administration would take in certain issue areas. In certain other areas of foreign policy and the economy, however, the pressure of economic conditions and world opinion redirected President Nixon from the stated Republican preferences.

10
THE BUREAUCRACY

There are certain names, places, and words with established reputations or connotations that are hard to undo. Bureaucracy is one of them, with its aura of endless red tape, inefficiency, and unresponsiveness. Most people have probably developed their feelings about bureaucracy while filling out a tax form or standing in line in a post office. But there are many other ways that the workings of bureaucrats touch people's lives Consider the following hypothetical account of a week in the life of a "typical" college student.

He gets out of bed in his room in a dormitory built with the assistance of federal funds. He goes to his first class in the new science building, built largely with federal funds. Later in the day he takes a drive in his new car. He forgets to put on his seat belt and the warning buzzer goes on, a device required by federal regulations. As he steps on the accelerator he notices that his new car does not perform as well as his old one because of the new emissions-control device, required by federal regulations. Several days later, he feels sick, goes to the student health center, and gets a prescription—the drug's ingredients must meet federal standards. At the end of the week he gets on a plane and flies home. The airfare must be approved by the federal government, and the aircraft as well as the plane's maintenance and operations crew must be federally certified.

Clearly, the lives of all citizens are affected by the federal government in a variety of important ways. And yet it is not the President, the Congress, or the courts that most directly affect people's lives. Rather it is the men and women (the bureaucrats) who work for the government's various agencies (the bureaucracies) who are generally responsible for delivering government programs to citizens.

The term bureaucracy is loosely applied to the millions of full-time career employees who do the day-to-day work of the government. Their impact on government policy is immense. Regardless of what laws Congress enacts or what directives are issued by the President, in the most fundamental sense government policy is no more and no less than what the bureaucracy does. When the bureaucracy cooperates, policy decisions often become realities. On the other hand, the bureaucracy often thwarts, redirects, and even works in opposition to decisions laid down by Congress or by the Administration.

Figure 10.1 Bureaucracy links people's activities in routine, specified ways. One image of bureaucracy is that of impersonal yet efficient action directed toward specific purposes—the computer image. The other image is that of a crazy maze of meaningless rules that are followed for their own sake or out of habit with an end result of zero productivity and maximum frustration. Yet the realities of bureaucracy are complex when examined under the microscope of political analysis. Meaningless rituals become more understandable when they are analyzed in terms of political power and the enormity of society's needs.

The Constitution is silent on the structure and on the role of the bureaucracy. It merely recognizes the right of the President to demand periodic reports from the head officials in the executive departments. The founding fathers recognized that the details of administrative organization would need to remain flexible to change with the times. But it is probably also true that the founders failed to anticipate how the government would grow. To them, executive departments represented only small operations aiding the President, hardly a major matter in 1792, when the federal government had only 780 employees.

Today 3 million Americans (not counting the armed forces) are employed by the federal government—1 out of every 27 employed persons is a federal government worker. And even though omitted from the Constitution, the bureaucracy must be included in any effort to understand government decision making.

This chapter examines the nature and the role of the federal bureaucracy. It is addressed to a series of questions: Is bureaucracy really a bad thing? Who works for the government? How do they get their jobs? What kinds of things do they do? Why are they so powerful? Why doesn't the bureaucracy function more effectively?

LARGE-SCALE GOVERNMENT

Those parts of government having the greatest day-to-day impact on the lives of citizens are parts of the bureaucracy. Most of us experience government by paying our taxes or by dealing with the various government agencies that regulate our actions. No one much likes to be regulated. Indeed, there has probably never been a time when such officials as tax collectors, inspectors, or other government servants were popular.

A major objection Americans seem to have about bureaucrats is that there are so many of them. This objection is another manifestation of general dissatisfaction with the sheer size of modern societies. Many people long for the "good old days" when there were many fewer people and when organizations—both governmental and private—were much smaller and therefore more personal. George Washington probably knew nearly everyone employed by the government during his Administration. In the 1790s there were so few government employees that they could easily have been invited to a single party. Indeed, when the British burned the capital during the War of 1812, Washington, D.C. was still just a village.

But today few of us live in villages, and life is no longer simple. In a nation of more than 200 million (instead of the 2 million of 1775), it is impossible to have small-scale government organizations. The many responsibilities of government, from providing for national defense to inspecting food purity, require large numbers of governmental organizations and employees. Although nearly everyone thinks the government is too big, it is difficult to find support for substantially reducing any specific part of government.

The Extent of Federal Service

Some idea of the extent of the federal bureaucracies can be gleaned from the following facts:

1. Excluding the armed forces, there are approximately 3 million employees of the federal government. Of these only 10 percent are in the Washington, D.C. area, and the rest are spread around the country in regional or local offices.
2. The Department of Defense employs more than 1.3 million *civilian* workers (apart from its uniformed personnel), a figure that represents approximately 40 percent of the total government employees. The DOD is not only the biggest government employer, but it is also the largest single employer in America. (The largest private employer is General Motors with nearly 800,000 employees in 1970.) The next largest government employer is the Post Office with over 700,000 workers.
3. Despite the great size of the federal bureaucracy, it is relatively small when compared with the number of employees who work for state and local governments. Only 22 percent of all government employees work for the federal government. In 1970 more than 7 million persons were employed by local governments, and 2.7 million worked for the states.
4. About 85 of every 100 federal employees are career civil service employees, and their salaries are set by the General Schedule as appropriated by the Congress. Government salaries are relatively comparable to those paid by industry. The lowest salary goes to those in Government Service grade 1 (GS-1), primarily clerks with less than one year of seniority—$4,798 a year in 1973. The highest paid civil service employees (GS-18) received $41,734 in 1973.

Figure 10.2 The spoils system reached its peak during the Presidency of Andrew Jackson and continued unabated until well after the Civil War. When President James Garfield was assassinated by a disappointed office seeker in 1881, the popular dissatisfaction against the spoils system became clear. President Chester Arthur responded by supporting a bill calling for a Civil Service Commission to administer competitive examinations and to make appointments to office based on merit. Above, a poster used in the 1887 presidential campaign of Grover Cleveland, who, as governor of New York, had built up a record of reform and personal honesty against the corrupt political practices of Tammany Hall.

5. Only about a half million government employees have characteristically bureaucratic jobs, such as clerk or general administrator. The government also employs 147,000 engineers and architects, 84,000 scientists, and 2,400 veterinarians.

6. Most government employees are white males. In the lower levels of government service, blacks are represented well above their proportion in the population; whereas 12 percent of the population is black, 20.5 percent of federal employees in Grades GS-1 through GS-14 are black. However, only 1.8 percent of employees in grades GS-12 through GS-18 are black. The same pattern occurs for females. Nearly one-third of all federal employees are women. About two-thirds of the lower-level white-collar workers are women (mainly secretaries and typists). But in the upper salary ranges the proportion of women dwindles rapidly. In 1973 only 148 of the 8,856 federal employees with the rank of GS-16 or above (who earned more than $36,000) were women.

7. In a sense all of these figures are misleading because much of the work of governments at all levels is done by what are called *contract bureaucracies*. The government hires much of its work done by private firms. As is discussed in the Perspective on the military-industrial complex, the Department of Defense hires firms such as the Rand Corporation to "think" about defense strategies and military tactics—hence the nickname "think tank." The DOD hires firms such as Boeing and Lockheed to design and to build military hardware. The Army Corps of Engineers hires private firms to design and to construct dams and hydro-electric projects. Most of the personnel involved in the Space Program are also contract bureaucrats. In this way a great many Americans work indirectly for the government by being employees of firms with government contracts. However, they do not show up in the budget under the federal payroll but only under various procurement budget items. Furthermore, they are not protected in their jobs by civil service regulations.

The Civil Service System

The first federal job appointments were made by George Washington, who declared his choices were based entirely on "fitness of character." But it soon became apparent that those he found fit were mostly associated with the emerging Federalist Party, the party that he and Alexander Hamilton essentially led (see Chapter 13). When Thomas Jefferson became President in 1801, he set a precedent by dismissing hundreds of Federalists from their government jobs and by installing his supporters in their places.

This practice became known as the *spoils system*—the right of elected officials to reward their friends and supporters with government jobs. The system reached its peak under President Andrew Jackson. After his election in 1828, he dismissed more than one-third of the 600 upper-level officeholders and from 10 to 20 percent of the 10,000 government officials who occupied lower-level positions.

To some extent the spoils system made sense. Some degree of *patronage,* or the power of appointment to government jobs, is needed by political parties in order that they may reward party workers for their dedication. Furthermore, any President is entitled to place people who share his political philosophy in certain key positions; obviously, a President must have Cabinet officers who support his aims. Furthermore, during the nineteenth century the government had little need for trained specialists so that a high turnover in personnel probably did not endanger operating efficiency.

Nevertheless, by the 1870s the obvious abuses of the spoils system had produced demands for reform. The demands led to the passage of the first civil service law in 1882—the Pendleton Act. The act—also known as the Civil Service Reform Act—established the bipartisan Civil Service Commission to choose the federal employees from lists of those who had passed competitive examinations (the so-called *merit* system). By 1971, 85 percent of the federal bureaucracy was appointed under the merit system; therefore it is not only "who you know" but also "what you know" that counts. The most recent extension

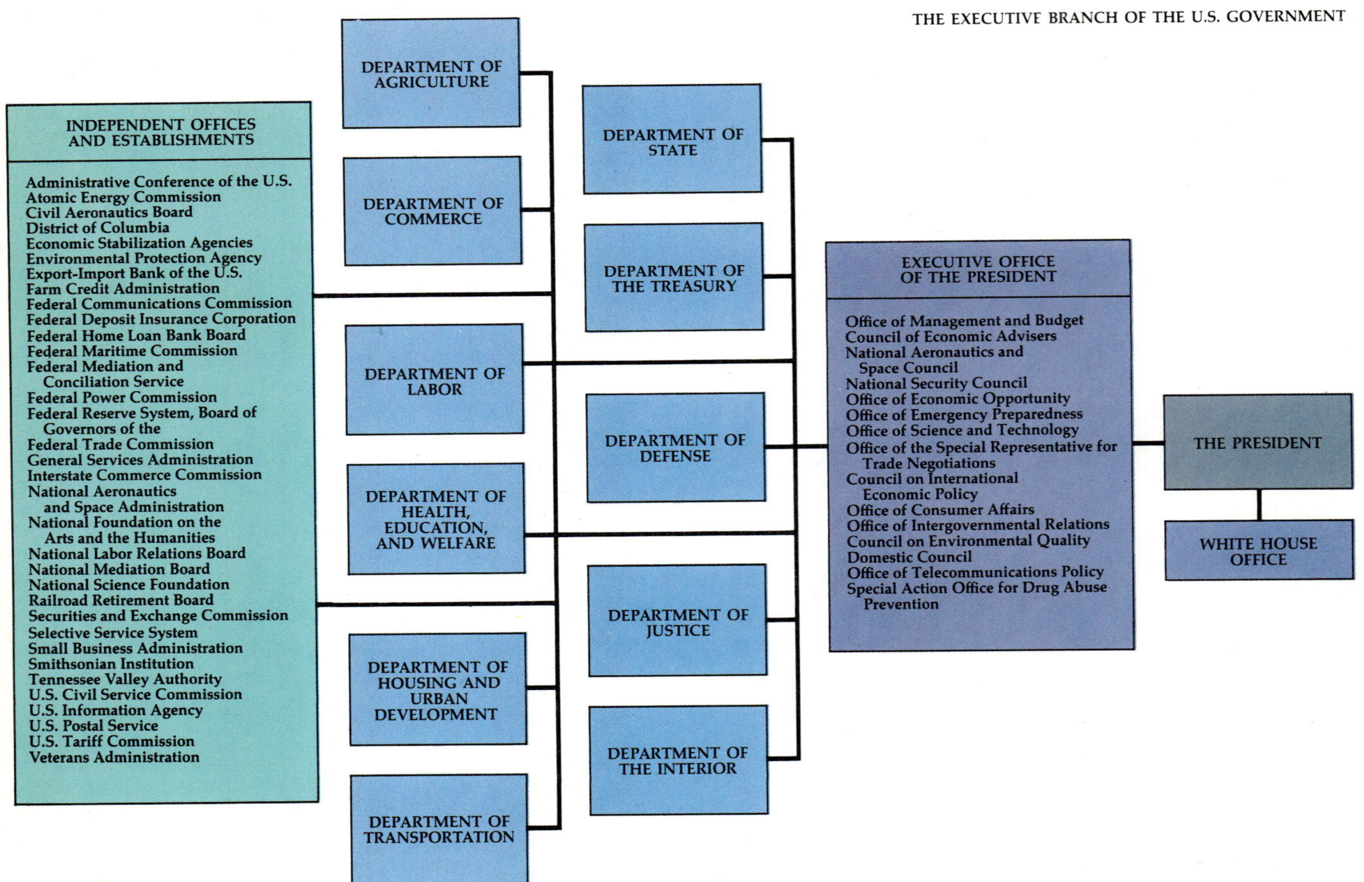

THE EXECUTIVE BRANCH OF THE U.S. GOVERNMENT

of the national civil service system came in 1969
when President Nixon issued an executive order
placing under merit procedures the jobs of some
70,000 postmasters and rural mailmen—the "last
great pool of patronage in the federal service" (Felix
Nigro, 1970).

Thirty-three of the fifty states have also adopted
comprehensive merit systems, and there appears to
be considerable momentum in the direction of civil
service reform in most of the other seventeen states.
At the local level about 75 percent of the employees
are hired on a merit system.

Civil service systems involve the formal description of job requirements and the classification of
persons according to job description. Once the describing and classifying process is established, examinations are developed that are used to determine
those candidates that are best suited for the available
positions. After taking examinations, candidates
are placed on lists from which agencies can select
their employees from the top three to five candidates.
In many merit systems there are further job requirements, such as height and weight requirements for
policemen, high school or college graduation for
particular occupations, and certifications or licenses
for many civil service positions, such as those for the
position of attorney or physician.

Civil service systems are so well developed that
it is commonplace, particularly in the federal bureaucracy, to find most bureaus filled with college
graduates. It is also common to find very high levels
of educational specialization in the bureaucracy.
Chemists employed by the Department of Agriculture, biologists employed by the National Institutes

Figure 10.3 (left) One response to the evils of the spoils system,
under which jobs were handed out to friends and political
supporters, was the evolution of the traits of specialization and
professionalization in the executive branch. An organizational
chart does not do justice to the resultant complexities and
tremendous size of the agencies involved, but it does give a
generalized map of most of the major groupings of the bureaucracy in question. The Executive Office is of direct aid to the
President with relation to special issues and areas of operation
that need to cross over departmental jurisdictions. The eleven
executive departments (the Cabinet) are themselves slightly
more removed from direct presidential control, and each of the
departments is as organizationally complex and elaborate as the
present chart. The Independent Offices and Establishments are
even more independent of presidential control, although the
President maintains a degree of influence by virtue of his
power to appoint their governing officials.

Figure 10.4 (right) A simple organization chart of a bureaucracy
does not do justice to the important political aspects of the
institution. Bureaucracies are political in the sense that they
(or their sub-units) can and do develop policy preferences, and
they nourish power resources that they use on other agencies
or branches of the government to achieve their ends. This chart
lists three main roles of bureaucracies, of which the neutral
administration role is the one most commonly referred to by
persons unfamiliar with the other two important roles of bureaucracies. The resources and strategies listed here are commonly
resorted to by agencies within the bureaucracies in pursuit
either of their policy goals, as decided by professional or political criteria, or of their self-interested goals, defined by the
welfare and power of the organization itself.

Bureaucratic Roles, Resources, and Strategies

Roles

Self-interested Organization
Neutral Administration
Part of the Policy-making Process

Resources

Sheer number of government employees creates powerful
interest group

Diffusion of power and authority in departments gives
independence to bureaucrats

Number of agencies and degree of specialization hides them
from the public eye

Bureaucratic discretion because laws rarely apply specifically
to particular cases

Bureaucratic expertise provides advice and defines alternatives

Abundance of time and people available to work on a problem

Extent of information collected on subjects and persons

Support from business or other clientele

Support from congressional committees or powerful legislators

Abundance of technical and personal information

Control of flow of information

Strategies

Building an image of service in the public interest

Granting special favors to legislators and private interests

Classifying of information and operations as "top secret"

Isolating work under separate jurisdiction and budget

Earmarking of sources of revenue for particular purposes

Asking for larger appropriations than finally expected

DEPARTMENT OF HEALTH, EDUCATION, AND WELFARE

SECRETARY

Undersecretary

Deputy Undersecretary

OFFICE for CIVIL RIGHTS

AMERICAN PRINTING HOUSE FOR THE BLIND (at Galludet College Howard University)

ASSISTANT SECRETARY (Community and Field Services)

ASSISTANT SECRETARY (Legislation)

ASSISTANT SECRETARY (Health)

ASSISTANT SECRETARY (Planning and Evaluation)

GENERAL COUNSEL

ASSISTANT SECRETARY (Administration and Management)

ASSISTANT SECRETARY (Comptroller)

ASSISTANT SECRETARY (Public Affairs)

Public Health Service

FOOD and DRUG ADMINISTRATION

Office of the Commissioner

Bureau of Drugs

Bureau of Product Safety

Bureau of Veterinary Medicine

Bureau of Foods

Bureau of Radiological Health

HEALTH SERVICES and MENTAL HEALTH ADMINISTRATION

Office of the Administrator

National Center for Family Planning Services

National Center for Health Services Research and Development

National Center for Health Statistics

Center for Disease Control

National Institute of Mental Health

Health Care Facilities Service

Community Health Service

Regional Medical Programs Service

Indian Health Service

Federal Health Programs Service

Maternal and Child Health Service

Bureau of Community Environmental Management

National Institute of Occupational Safety and Health

Health Maintenance Organization Service

Comprehensive Health Planning Service

National Health Service Corps

NATIONAL INSTITUTES of HEALTH

Office of the Director

Bureau of Health Manpower Education

National Cancer Institute

National Heart and Lung Institute

National Institute of Allergy and Infectious Diseases

National Institute of Arthritis and Metabolic Diseases

National Institute of Child Health and Human Development

National Institute of Dental Research

National Institute of General Medical Sciences

National Institute of Neurological Diseases and Stroke

National Eye Institute

National Institute of Environmental Health Sciences

National Library of Medicine

Fogarty International Center

Clinical Center

Division of Biologics Standards

Division of Computer Research and Technology

Division of Research Resources

SOCIAL and REHABILITATION SERVICE

Office of the Administrator

Rehabilitation Services Administration

Community Services Administration

Administration on Aging

Medical Services Administration

Assistance Payments Administration

Youth Development and Delinquency Prevention Administration

SOCIAL SECURITY ADMINISTRATION

Office of the Commissioner

Bureau of Data Processing

Bureau of Disability Insurance

Bureau of District Office Operations

Bureau of Health Insurance

Bureau of Hearings and Appeals

Bureau of Retirement and Survivors Insurance

OFFICE OF EDUCATION

Office of the Commissioner

Office of Special Concerns

Deputy Commissioners for: Planning, Evaluation, and Management
External Relations

Deputy Commissioner for School Systems
Bureau of Adult, Vocational and Technical Education
Bureau of Education for the Handicapped
Bureau of Elementary and Secondary Education

Deputy Commissioner for Renewal
National Center for Educational Research and Development
Experimental Schools
National Center for Educational Statistics
National Center for Educational Communications
National Center for Educational Technology
National Center for the Improvement of Educational Systems

Deputy Commissioner for Higher Education
Bureau of Higher Education
Bureau of Libraries and Learning Resources
Institute of International Studies

REGIONAL OFFICES

Regional Directors

Regional Food and Drug Directors

Regional Health Directors

Regional Social and Rehabilitation Commissioners

Regional Social Security Commissioners

Regional Education Commissioners

Figure 10.5 This organization chart of the Department of Health, Education, and Welfare is certainly not an exciting pin-up for a dormitory wall. But it does point out rather clearly that government bureaucracy is based on specialization—and sub-specialization and sub-sub-specialization. Each one of the myriad of bureaus, administrations, centers, services, corps, divisions, and institutes noted here on the chart represents the locus of jobs, prestige, and political pushing and sharing for dozens or hundreds of persons. And the decisions that are made in these offices—from the Youth Development and Delinquency Prevention Bureau to the Bureau of Radiological Health—affect the lives of real persons.

of Health, safety engineers employed by the Federal Aviation Agency—all typify the high degree of specialization and education found in the modern public service.

ORGANIZATION: THE COMPONENTS OF BUREAUCRACY

Bureaucracies tend to be structured by specialization; that is, there are agencies that handle only law enforcement, others that handle only medical care, and so on. It is this specialized competence that is the basis of bureaucracy. The principle of organization by specialization can be seen in the organization of the federal executive branch outlined in Figure 10.4. But before we take up the difficulties engendered by bureaucratic specialization, let us look at the primary components of the bureaucracy—the Cabinet departments, the independent executive agencies, and the regulatory commissions.

Cabinet Departments

In 1789 only three Cabinet departments were created—State, War, and Treasury. Today there are eleven such departments. As new needs have arisen, new departments have been created. In 1849 the Department of the Interior was created to deal with the vast government land holdings and with the problems of the expanding frontier. The Department of Agriculture was created in 1862 and the Justice Department in 1870; the Departments of Commerce and of Labor were added in 1913. The War and the Navy Departments were merged into the Defense Department in 1947; Health, Education, and Welfare was created in 1953; Housing and Urban Development in 1965; and Transportation in 1966.

Cabinet departments are the major parts of the federal bureaucracy. They employ the majority of federal workers (although the Veterans' Administration—which is an executive agency—is larger than many departments). Figure 10.5 is an organization chart of the Department of Health, Education, and Welfare. The number and diversity of the agencies and bureaus included in HEW gives some indication of the administrative burdens placed on Cabinet Secretaries. It also gives some idea of the diffusion of power and policy-making authority within any department. It would be simply impossible for a Cabinet Secretary—the head official in the depart-

APOLOGIES FOR DELAYS IN CONGRESSIONAL RESPONSES

MEMORANDUM

DEPARTMENT OF HEALTH, EDUCATION, AND WELFARE   OFFICE OF THE SECRETARY

TO   : Assistant Secretaries and
           Agency Heads

FROM   : The Secretary

SUBJECT : Apologies for Delays in
           Congressional Responses

Since overdue letters to Members of Congress undermine our efforts to work effectively with the legislative branch, I am requesting your particiaption in a new effort to repair the badly damaged relationships which result from HEW's negligence in failing to acknowledge or respond promptly to Congressional inquiries.

Hereafter, when your office is responsible for a long overdue letter either because you have failed to prepare the response accurately by the due date or because you have held it up during the clearance process, I will be asking you to call the offended Congressman personally and apologize to him for the wanton disrespect for the legislative branch which occurred in your office.

The following talking points are suggested for such a telephone conversation:

1. Secretary Richardson has reminded me of the fact that I have been negligent in failing to acknowledge your inquiry of (date) about (subject) and, I am calling at the Secretary's request to personally apologize to you for my failure to respond in a timely and comprehensive manner.

2. I know how important your work in Congress is to the effectiveness of this Department. Your work determines what we can do, what resources we have for achieving our objectives, and, to the large extent, how we do it. Therefore, I know that your inquiries should receive our highest priority attention. My failure to see that this attention was given to your letter of (date) is inexcusable, and I want you to know that I will make every effort to see that it does not happen again.

3. The reason why we have not been able to respond completely so far is as follows (here insert the reasons such as (a) although the letter was sent forward to the Secretary, I had misspelled your name, (b) although the letter I sent forward was quite long, it did not respond to your questions, etc.).

4. I have told Secretary Richardson that we will reply to your inquiry by (date) . At that time, we will provide you with a complete and responsive report on (subject) .

   When I request you to make a telephone call of apology, please be sure to call within 48 hours since I have instructed the Congressional Liaison Office to call the Congressman 48 hours after my request to you to make sure that (1) the Congressman has talked to you personally and (2) he is satisfied with your response.

You can avoid the need for these calls if you prepare an interim acknowledgement which tells the Congressman when a complete response will be prepared. Of course, it is important that you follow through to make sure that the due date is met. When the delay is a result of failure of an OS office to clear a letter expeditiously, I will ask the appropriate Assistant Secretary to make the apology. In those few cases where an Assistant Secretary cannot clear a letter because of the need for OMB approval or other circumstances beyond his control, the Assistant Secretary should prepare an immediate interim acknowledgement even though the action was not originally assigned to his office.

ment—to review the hundreds of decisions on programs and policies being made in these many agencies under his supervision, let alone bring such matters to the attention of the President.

The Cabinet Secretary is appointed by the President, and he is the department's representative in the President's Cabinet. The other top officials in departments are also appointed by the President. They usually have no prior experience in the department, and they are rarely in office for more than a few years. But just below them are career civil servants who have risen through the ranks and whose experience and skill is vital to the running of the departments. It is hardly surprising that these senior civil servants have powers that must be reckoned with when policies are being formulated.

Independent Executive Agencies

The heads of the independent agencies also serve at the pleasure of the President. With several exceptions, these agencies tend to be smaller than Cabinet departments, and they have a considerably more focused mission. Most came into being to serve some very specific function; for various reasons they were not placed under a Cabinet department. An example of such an agency is the Selective Service System. It was created hastily during World War II, was kept out of the War Department (now the Department of Defense) to reassure citizens that the draft was a civilian operation, and was expected to be in existence for only several years. The Central Intelligence Agency is another example. It was created to centralize the many competing governmental intelligence agencies; it was not placed under a Cabinet department because its creation was intended to resolve interdepartmental power struggles.

Many of the executive agencies are obscure—for example, the American Battle Monuments Commission. But also included on the organization chart with the independent agencies are the government corporations—the Tennessee Valley Authority (TVA) and the Federal Deposit Insurance Corporation, which guarantees bank accounts up to $20,000.

Regulatory Commissions

The regulatory commissions are quite different from the other two major components of the federal bureaucracy. Their purpose is to regulate certain kinds of activities, particularly in the economic sphere. They perform a quasi-judicial function in that they can bring charges, hold hearings, and impose penalties for violations of rules. For example, the Federal Communications Commission may revoke the licenses of television and radio stations for a number of reasons, including a station's failure to provide sufficient community-service broadcasting. In that these commissions not only interpret rules but also make them, they are quasi-legislative bodies. For example, the Federal Trade Commission has recently imposed a wide variety of new regulations on manufacturing and on advertising in order to protect consumers from unsafe or misrepresented merchandise.

Originally, the independent regulatory agencies were set up outside the normal executive branch chain of command (that is, they were not made directly responsible to the President) in an effort to keep them free of "politics." As a result, commission members are appointed by the President for relatively long terms, and their appointments are subject to Senate confirmation. Once in office they are not required to report to the President and may not be removed until the end of their term except through impeachment. Unlike Cabinet officers and heads of other executive agencies, they do not resign when a new President is elected; they serve until their terms expire. Thus a new President can only name new members to commissions as terms expire or as vacancies occur because of death or retirement. Furthermore, by law members of these agencies must be drawn from both major political parties.

In spite of these precautions, the regulatory commissions are not completely free of partisan politics. A two-term President can expect to place most regulatory agencies under the control of his own appointees because few commission terms run for more than seven years and many run only for five. As a result, the commissions are not nearly so insulated from the White House as are the courts, which have lifetime appointments.

A more difficult problem has been to insulate the commissions from the influence of those they are supposed to regulate. Commissions, it has turned out, are just as subject to the pressures of interest groups as are all other policy makers (see Chapter 15). Although many of the independent regulatory agencies were originally established in the early 1900s in response to protests by consumer groups against predatory or dangerous practices by various industries, their orientation has changed over the years. The agencies gradually shifted their orientation and became the "captives" of the groups they were supposed to regulate. Often appointees were (and still are) selected from the very industries that the commissions were created to regulate. Commissioners often take high-level jobs in such industries after finishing their government service. There have also been frequent revelations of commissioners fraternizing with representatives of regulated industries, of their willingness to accept favors such as industry-paid vacations. For all of these reasons, critics have pointed out that some commission members seem more interested in protecting the interests of airlines, drug companies, trucking firms, stock brokers, and other industries that they are supposed to regulate rather than in directing their energies toward the protection of the interests of the public (Bernard Schwartz, 1959).

The activities of the Interstate Commerce Commission (ICC) illustrate this tendency. Originally set up in 1887 to protect consumers against predatory practices of the railroad monopolies, by 1920 the agency was almost solely responsive to the railroads against the interests of consumers and against other forms of interstate transportation. In case after case, the ICC's rulings benefited the railroads. More recently, the ICC has struck a balance between the interests of railroads and trucking companies, but the interests of consumers are still virtually ignored.

An additional barrier to effective regulation stems from the fact that federal commissions typically have insufficient staff members to cope with the staff resources of the industries they are supposed to regulate. Hearings to fix new rates on such activities as air travel or rail freight often reveal a handful of civil service accountants and lawyers opposing battalions of highly paid industry lawyers and accountants (Schwartz, 1959).

BUREAUCRACIES AS POLITICAL PARTICIPANTS

Writing in 1885, Woodrow Wilson drew a sharp distinction between *politics* and *administration*. Politics, he declared, was concerned with basic decisions of what public policies ought to be. Administration entered after those basic decisions had been made

Figure 10.6 Bureaucracies are firmly within the political process. To illustrate this fact, consider the politics of automobile safety and the role played by the Department of Transportation. The department conducts many tests, including the impact tests shown at right; it decides the relative merits of various devices and orders the adoption of the best device. But the politics of an issue are much more complex than indicated by analyses and recommendations. When Ralph Nader first began investigating car safety in the mid-1960s, he was shadowed by agents of General Motors in an attempt to discredit his investigations; although the head of GM later apologized for the incident, Nader's findings clearly stood to set in motion a political process that it was in the corporation's best interests to suppress, if possible. The Department of Transportation expert also receives much resistance against the new air bag safety device—both from drivers who are scared and from auto companies that are cost-minded. But the political ramifications of the issue do not stop here. For example, who pays for the new safety devices put into autos? Can the government require companies not to pass on their costs to the consumer? And there is another political question: will the Administration, which forces producer and public to pay for the safety devices, lose support among consumer/voters and among campaign financers? After all, even safety is political.

☐

THE ENERGY CRISIS—PLAN OF ATTACK
In 1973 President Nixon proposed the formation of a radically new energy establishment. If passed by Congress, the plan would coordinate the overlapping maze of government agencies that have had a stake in energy matters.

The reorganization of energy agencies has two main parts. One is the redesign of the Cabinet-level Department of the Interior as the Department of Energy and Natural Resources. DENR would absorb functions from the Departments of Agriculture and Commerce as well as from the Army Corps of Engineers. The other element of the reorganization would separate the research and regulatory functions of the Atomic Energy Commission. AEC would be renamed the Nuclear Energy Commission and would deal solely with the environmental and safety aspects of licensing nuclear facilities. AEC's nonregulatory programs, including its defense projects, would be spun off as the core of a new Energy Research and Development Administration (ERDA), similar in structure to the National Aeronautics and Space Administration.

The DENR and ERDA proposals, which both need congressional approval, fit in with a widely held view that more centralized management of federal energy agencies is drastically needed. Nixon's proposal to split up the AEC pleased environmentalists who have complained that the agency has promoted as well as regulated nuclear power.

To orchestrate the new set-up, Colorado Governor John Love was asked to serve as White House energy policy coordinator (as the so-called "Energy Czar"). He would monitor research programs as well as coordinate policy on crucial economic issues, such as natural gas regulation, and complex energy-environmental problems, such as the Alaska pipeline and strip-mining controls (Business Week, June 30, 1973).

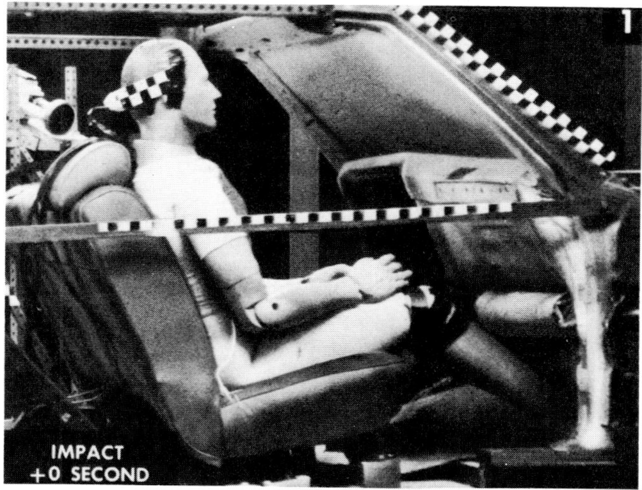

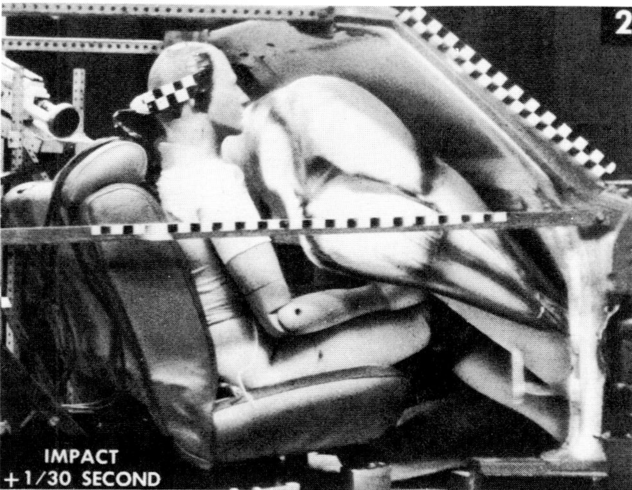

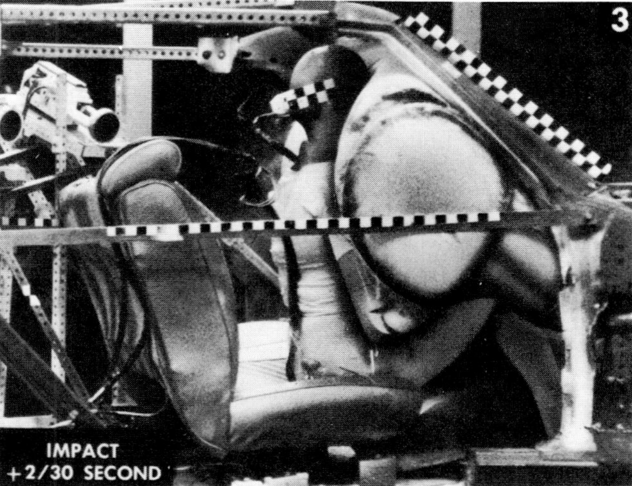

and was concerned with implementing policies. Civil servants (bureaucrats) therefore did not make policy—they simply implemented it in the most efficient manner possible. This neat and tidy distinction between politics and administration prevailed for many years through several early textbooks on public administration. The problem is, however, that that distinction is no longer valid—if indeed it ever was. Bureaucracies are firmly within the political process; they have as much influence over the formation of public policy as do certain interest groups, Congress, the President. and the courts—even greater influence than these policy makers, some observers would contend.

Bureaucratic Discretion

An inherent aspect of the bureaucratic function—*discretion*—provides the basis for bureaucratic political participation. Legislation is never so specific that bureaucracies do not have considerable latitude when they apply it to particular cases. For example, the Food and Drug Amendments of 1962 required that new drugs had to be effective as well as safe in order to receive approval from the Food and Drug Administration (FDA). But it was up to the FDA to determine specific standards of drug efficacy. Similarly, when and whether to prosecute an antitrust case has vital consequences for national policy on economic concentration and is a policy-making procedure in the hands of the Justice Department—yet another bureaucracy. In these and hundreds of other cases, government bureaucrats make policy by applying the broad powers that have been given to them by Congress and by the President.

There are several aspects of the legislative decision-making process that lead to bureaucratic discretion. First, it would be impossible for a legislature to establish clear rules to cover all contingencies. It has neither the time nor the expertise for such an exercise, and therefore this function must be delegated. Second, the lack of clear rules or guidelines is often intentional and represents a compromise within Congress. Those conflicts that cannot be resolved in Congress are simply handed over to the bureaucracy. Thus it has been noted that bureaucratic administration is simply the extension of the legislative process. Affected parties then seek to advance their interests by lobbying in the offices of the bureaucracy—indeed, administrative lobbying is as important in Washington as is legislative lobbying.

In the exercise of their policy-making functions, bureaucracies are not merely neutral battlegrounds that reflect only the political power of other contending forces. Rather, they have interests of their own that they push in the political process. Like most participants in the political system, bureaucrats claim that programs they administer are in the public interest and that expanding those programs (and their power) would likewise be greatly beneficial to the nation. Sometimes these claims are cynical, but usually they are entirely sincere. Believing in the value and efficacy of their programs, bureaucrats naturally seek to expand or at least to protect those programs (and their agency) by pushing for favorable legislation and appropriations.

In addition to bureaucratic discretion, the agencies of the bureaucracy have a variety of political resources at their disposal. As Francis Rourke has noted, the power of government bureaucrats stems from two types of political resources: (1) the mobilization of political support, and (2) the utilization of bureaucratic expertise (Rourke, 1969).

The Mobilization of Support

The mobilization of political support is a strategy aimed at two closely related groups—the general public and Congress. The most basic and simple requirement in dealing with the general public is the building of a favorable image—demonstrating to the public that the agency is doing something useful and beneficial for the public. This demonstration can take the form of public-service television messages, such as those of the FDA on the proper use and storage of hazardous household products. The Agriculture Department has an extensive series of pamphlets available to the public on such topics as cooking, canning, and gardening. Probably the most extensive public relations operation, however, is that of the Defense Department. Dubbed the "Pentagon Propaganda Machine" by Senator J. William Fulbright, the Defense Department tries to promote a favorable image by aiding the production of war movies by friendly television and movie producers, by providing impressive tours of military installations to influential citizens, by providing military speakers for civic groups, and by producing recruiting advertisements that present a positive image of life in the armed services (see the Perspective on the military-industrial complex).

Yet public relations is only one way the bureaucracy builds support. For even though there are inevitable conflicts of interest, bureaucratic agencies are dependent on maintaining good relationships with those interest groups that are directly affected by the agency. The groups are frequently referred to as *clientele* groups because they are the most immediate recipients of the agency's bestowal of benefits and controls. Thus the railroads and trucking companies are clientele groups of the Interstate Commerce Commission, labor unions are the clientele groups of the Labor Department, and so on. As long as these groups benefit from agency programs, they will direct their lobbying efforts toward defending the agency from adverse action by Congress or by the President.

The importance of politically powerful clientele groups can be seen in the case of the Office of Economic Opportunity (OEO), which President Nixon attempted to dismantle by executive order in 1973. Having only loosely organized and politically powerless poor people as its clientele, the OEO was particularly vulnerable, and its congressional allies were unable to marshall the overall political support that would have been needed to save it from extinction (see Chapter 16). Contrast this situation to President Johnson's 1967 proposal to merge the Labor and Commerce Departments into one department. Both labor and business groups were unwilling to give up their own departments; their political strength was such that President Johnson abandoned the idea after the howl of protest from the clientele groups.

An important part of the strength of the clientele group is its position of influence in Congress. Indeed, the most common pattern is for the bureaucratic agency to be linked with a clientele group and with a congressional subcommittee in a kind of three-part alliance. This pattern is also found in the oft-discussed military-industrial complex. The Pentagon is very closely linked with large defense contractors who in turn have a great deal of influence in Congress—particularly with congressmen in whose districts defense spending is an important source of employment. Although the military-

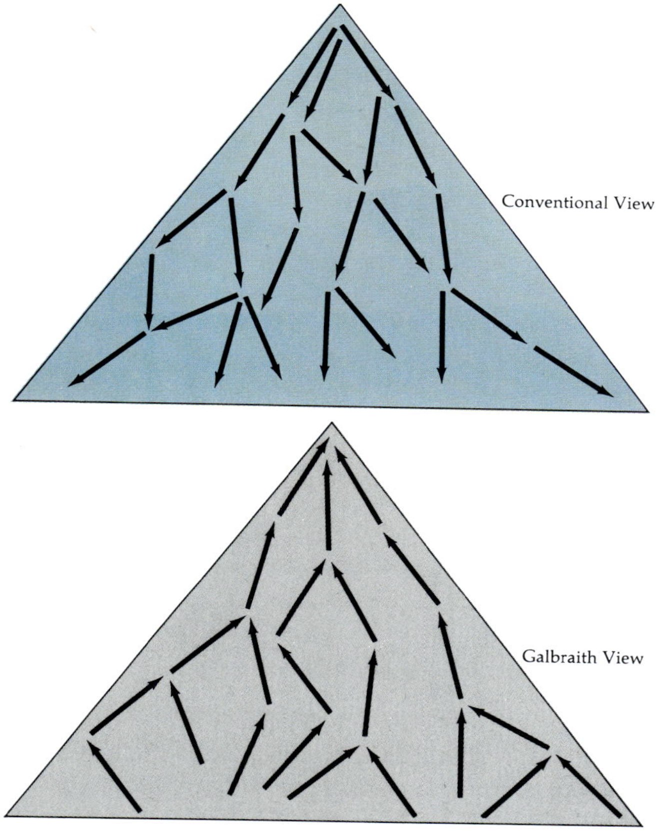

Figure 10.7 The conventional view of the flow of decision-making power in bureaucracies—both private and public—is that the central authority lies in some top group, such as an executive committee, a board of directors, or a President and his Cabinet; power is then transmitted downward through various levels of authority and responsibility (top).

In the view of John Kenneth Galbraith (above), especially as set forth in his book, The New Industrial State, decision-making power appears to flow, surprisingly, from the bottom up. This reversal is true in spite of organization charts, bylaws, or constitutions that vest formal authority at the top of the pyramid and specify that authority flows downward from there.

Galbraith argues that, because of technical expertise and the complexity of modern organization, task groups and managerial groups that are closest to the specific details of a project are the only ones who know enough to state the options for decisions; by the time questions for decision have found their way to the managerial levels, the options have been so narrowed and set that, in effect, the people "below" have essentially made the decisions.

industrial complex is a mammoth example, the same phenomenon is common with successful bureaucracies.

Bureaucratic Expertise

Expertise is another source of bureaucratic power. The basic function of a bureaucracy is to apply specialized competence to an area of policy. Bureaucrats frequently have a near monopoly of expertise in certain policy areas. Who, for example, knows more about sending a man to the moon than the National Aeronautics and Space Administration? Even more frequently, bureaucracies claim that they know more about an area than any competing group. Thus, educators usually claim that they are the most competent judges of "what is best" in education. As long as other policy makers accept those claims of expertise, the bureaucracy will have an important power resource.

This bureaucratic expertise provided a fundamental focus for a study by the noted Harvard economist John Kenneth Galbraith. He pointed out that technology has become so complex that it would take a formidable genius to command all of the knowledge and skill required to deal with even a few of the ordinary decisions confronting business or government organizations. Responsibility has therefore passed to groups composed of various specialists—indeed, as he put it, one could do worse than to think of modern organizations as composed of a "hierarchy of committees." Decisions tend to flow upward from these committees, and the man at the top lacks the special knowledge and skills to challenge those decisions. Galbraith recalled that during his days in charge of the Office of Price Administration during World War II he was nearly helpless to alter decisions fixing particular prices when these decisions came to him "after an extensive exercise in group decision-making in which lawyers, economists, accountants, men knowledgeable of the product and industry, and specialists in public righteousness had all participated." To challenge such a decision he would have needed a similar committee to guide him. He concluded that "To have responsibility for all of the prices in the United States was awesome; to discover how slight was one's power in the face of group decision-making was sobering" (John Kenneth Galbraith, 1967).

Galbraith correctly saw that under present conditions of technical and organizational complexity, power inevitably passes into the hands of a great many subordinate specialists in business or governmental agencies; he labeled this powerful set of specialists the *technostructure*. The alternatives that they favor are ultimately reflected in public policy because other political participants accept the presumption that the particular bureaucracy must know what the best alternative is.

The utilization of expertise as a political resource is seen largely in two forms. First, some bureaucracies have an important advisory role—particularly in relation to the President. Bureaucracies are not only able to recommend a course of action, but equally important, they frequently define what the alternatives are to be. As Galbraith noted, the President would have to convene an alternate group of specialists in order to come up with alternatives that were as well reasoned. Second, in dealing with Congress in the areas of legislation and appropriations, bureaucracies are usually able to approach issues with far greater competence than Congress can muster. This facility does not mean that bureaucracies always get their way; but they are far better off than would be the case if Congress always had an equally competent alternative source of knowledge.

In light of these factors, it is easy to understand what President John Kennedy meant when in response to proposals for government action of one kind or another he would say, "I agree but I don't know whether the government will agree."

PATTERNS OF POLICY MAKING

It has already been noted that government policy is no more and no less than what the bureaucracy does. But let us look at some of the ways that bureaucracy most fundamentally determines the shape of government programs that reach the citizen.

The Economy and the Bureaucracy

As is discussed in Chapter 4, many aspects of the American economy are regulated by the government; the federal bureaucracy plays a very important role in this regulation. One of the fundamental means by which bureaucrats exercise control over policy is through the executive budgeting process. In many local governments, in almost all states, and in the federal government, a special staff agency exists for the purpose of the annual preparation of the budget. This staff agency—in the case of the federal government it is the Office of Management and Budget—is an arm of the elected executive; it attempts to control the programs and the policies of government by controlling the flow of money to those programs.

Aaron Wildavsky, in his study of the politics of the budgetary process, suggested that the budgetary process is highly routinized and predictable; it involves an annual calling for estimates, an annual comparison of the previous year's appropriation, and an additional asking amount or increment to the present appropriation in order to provide for the growth and expansion of programs (Wildavsky, 1964). Bureaucrats routinely assume that their requests are going to be cut. As a result, they ask for a larger appropriation than they can realistically expect to receive. Whereas this tactic may appear to be simply a matter of strategy, it also represents the conviction of most bureaucrats that their particular program is important to the government. Therefore, in their annual budget request, they represent their specialized preferences. The budgetary process thus becomes a process of comparing the demands of competing specialized agencies and bureaus, and it usually results in slight increments from year to year in the amounts that are appropriated to the individual agency.

These increments often go up; seldom do they go down. Consequently, the size of the budget grows, and the size of the bureaucracy grows with it. It was for this reason that President Nixon's attempts to slow the rate of inflation were fundamentally tied to an attempt to control the size of both the federal budget and the federal bureaucracy. The relationship between the size of a bureaucracy and the level of government expenditures is very close: It is estimated that between 80 and 90 percent of state and local government expenditures are ultimately made up of salaries and wages. Thus, the size of the government work force is directly linked to the state of the economy. If there is dramatic growth in the size of the government work force and it is coupled with salary increases for government employees, the effect on the economy is generally inflationary.

Another form of bureaucratic behavior is illustrated in the fiscal processes of government. James

Thompson argues that bureaucracies will attempt to isolate their specializations and to ensure the resources for those specializations (Thompson, 1967). An example of this process can be seen in the separation of public education from the other functions of local government. There is no particular logic that leads to schools being operated under a jurisdiction that is separate from that which controls the police, the fire department, and the public works department. Nonetheless, educators have been successful in isolating their specializations and in gaining a separate and guaranteed pattern of access to government revenues.

The key to understanding the success of educators as bureaucrats is an understanding that school bureaucracies (which range from the Office of Education in the Department of Health, Education, and Welfare, to the local school superintendent and his bureaucracy) are also political interest groups. They not only carry out policy, but they almost completely dominate it.

At all levels of government, bureaucrats attempt to achieve the same objectives by "earmarking" sources of revenue to be used for particular purposes. In some states the revenues gathered by taxes on cigarettes and alcohol are earmarked for higher education. In many states taxes on gasoline can only be used for road building and for maintenance of the highways.

The ultimate earmarking system, and one of the most politically controversial, is the National Highway Trust Fund. This fund is another illustration of the tendency to isolate a specialization or at least a special interest and then to guarantee resources to support it; in this case, federal taxes on gasoline sales are set aside for building the huge Interstate highway system. Battles have frequently been fought to alter the trust fund statute so as to rechannel some of the revenues toward the building of rapid transit systems—particularly transit systems in the inner cities of the nation. In these battles, however, the bureaucracy that administers the trust fund and the construction firms that build the highway systems work in close cooperation with the House and Senate appropriations committees in order to maintain the status quo. The bureaucracy is a potent political force in the "network of mutual support" for the highway trust fund.

Defense and the Bureaucracy

The largest bureaucracy in American government is the United States Department of Defense. The size and power of the defense establishment illustrates two basic characteristics of both American government and bureaucratic behavior. First, the dramatic growth of the power of the government's executive branch traces directly to the special powers of the President in times of war (see Chapter 5). But the second characteristic of bureaucratic behavior exhibited by the defense bureaucracy greatly inhibits the ability of the President to curb either the power of defense or the size of the defense bureaucracy and budget. The defense bureaucracy is part of an elaborate network of mutual support—labeled the military-industrial complex (see the Perspective on this subject)—which includes the following basic interrelationships:

1. The military services have developed an intimate relationship with the legislature and particularly with the House Armed Services Committee. Through the National Guard and Reserve systems, through the power to appoint cadets to military academies, and through a variety of other devices, the defense bureaucracy and the legislature have developed a mutually beneficial relationship.
2. The interrelationship between the legislature and the defense bureaucracy is associated with the geographic location of military facilities, which include military bases and posts as well as contract firms. The geographic spread of these military facilities and the economic stimulation they provide for their constituents cause many legislators to be most reluctant to resist DOD plans and programs (see Chapter 8).
3. Specialized industries that rely almost entirely on contracts from the Department of Defense constitute an important interest group that supports the extension of defense programs. These industries often have close relationships with the specialized parts of the military establishment and with specific members of the House or Senate.

This network of mutual support represents the ultimate in bureaucratic achievements—that is, the defense bureaucracy maintains support in the legislature where the purse is held; it has a clientele or a set of interest groups that provide geographically widespread support; and the build-up of many years of expertise in the defense bureaucracy has left Congress dependent on that expertise.

Civil Rights, Civil Liberties, and the Bureaucracy

The behavior of bureaucratic organizations and the preservation of the basic civil rights and liberties of citizens have always been in tension. As a reflection of their tendency to insulate themselves from political buffeting, bureaucratic organizations engage in secrecy, they invade the privacy of citizens through their use of "security checks," and they generally constrain the rights of individual bureaucrats to stand in public opposition to either the stated policies or the covert policies of bureaucracies.

The *Pentagon Papers* case is an example of a bureaucracy's ability—in this instance, the Department of Defense—to infringe on the rights of the public to be informed. The DOD can legally indicate which of its policies and positions are secret because they involve what the DOD or the President has labeled "national security." As a consequence, public knowledge of a particular policy may thereby be greatly restricted. The celebrated trial of Daniel Ellsberg and Anthony Russo is a contemporary example of the DOD's labeling as "secret" a study of the history and the policies of the federal government with respect to the Vietnam War. The study had been done by a combination of RAND Corporation officials (contract bureaucrats) and officials of the DOD. Ellsberg and Russo made the papers public and then were taken to trial on the grounds that they had breached the security of the nation. In their overzealous attempts to gather information for the prosecution, however, government officials wound up destroying the government's case against the two men (see Chapter 12). Although the *Pentagon Papers* case is a well-known example of the tension between civil liberties and bureaucratic behavior, bureaucratic organizations routinely make public only those activities that tend to portray a generally favorable impression of the organization.

Perhaps the most critical issue in the tension between bureaucratic organizations and civil liberties centers on those bureaucracies that are charged with enforcing the law—the local police, the county sheriff, the state police, and the FBI. In their drive to be effective, law enforcement agencies seek to gather information on citizens who violate the law; this information is gathered in a variety of ways, from the collection of fingerprints and their filing in a huge fingerprint data bank at FBI headquarters in Washington, to the development of "background information," or files on persons who have ever been arrested. Even organizations that are not primarily law enforcement bureaucracies, particularly the DOD, maintain files on persons suspected of being in opposition to government policy. The Vietnam War brought into critical focus the ability of the DOD to label those who publicly opposed the war as potential "subversives."

A similar example of the invasion of privacy was seen in the FBI investigation of Martin Luther King, Jr. After his assassination, it became publicly known that the FBI had tapped the telephones, bugged the rooms, and generally spied on the civil rights leader, evidently thinking him to be a potential threat to the nation.

Although bureaucratic organizations have a distinct capacity to infringe on basic rights and freedoms, it is those same organizations that are established to protect civil rights and liberties. The safety of the citizen in the streets, his right to the privacy of his home and of his property, is a bureaucratic responsibility. In an era that has been characterized as "lawless," law enforcement bureaucracies are perhaps faced with an impossible task. But the entire criminal justice system—the loosely interlocking set of bureaucracies that include the police, the courts, the probation, parole, and prison officials—is a stark example of the failure of legislative bodies to devise a workable approach to the problem of lawlessness and the failure of the bureaucracies involved to cooperate in working toward an integrated approach to the problem (see Chapter 11).

GOVERNMENT ACCOUNTABILITY

Everything John Kenneth Galbraith said about the power of the technostructure applies equally to organized groups such as corporations. Yet when we think of bureaucrats we tend not to think of the design department at Ford Motor Company or the Economic Forecasting Committee at Bank of America. We invariably think of government workers when we use the term bureaucrat. Why is this so? Probably it is because Ford and Bank of America function reasonably well—technostructure and all—whereas in some ways the government hardly seems to function at all.

Public Versus Private Bureaucracies

What is it about government that prevents it from operating effectively? The answers to this question share a common theme: We make demands on government and impose constraints on it that private bureaucracies do not have to cope with (and probably could not cope with any better).

First of all, it is somehow expected that government services should be free. Repeated public opinion polls have found that nearly all Americans think taxes are too high and that they want cutbacks in government spending. But when specific government programs are mentioned, the majority of Americans do not favor cutting them (Gallup, 1972). This peculiarity is not limited to Americans. Peter Drucker has pointed out that when the British adopted "free health service," most of them believed that health care would be free. But doctors, nurses, and hospitals cost money, and somebody has to pay. In contrast to these expectations that government benefits are free, everyone expects to pay for services received from Ford or from Bank of America.

The analogy brings us to a second difference between public and private bureaucracies. Private bureaucracies have the capacity to go bankrupt, to cease to exist. Whereas this capacity may be worrisome to stockholders, it is a fundamental strength of private bureaucracies. It forces them to continually demonstrate their right to exist and thus their ability both to achieve intended goals and to adapt to change. In contrast it has been well put—if a bit cynically—that if the government had designed the Ford Edsel, it would still be building Edsels by the millions. Consider that over the past thirty years federal subsidies to the big cities have increased by almost a hundred times. There are ten times as many federal agencies concerned with city problems as there were in 1939. There is even now a Cabinet department devoted to city problems. But the cities are obviously in worse shape than ever.

Once a government program is launched it takes on a life of its own. A great many people build careers on running these projects, and vested interests continue to demand the program. Indeed, as Drucker has noted, "the typical response of government to failure of an activity is to double its budget and staff" (Drucker, 1969).

A major reason why government cannot tell when it is building Edsels (although Ford caught on very quickly) is its failure to develop reasonable measures of performance. Business is blessed by the fact that money in the form of profits is easily registered on the account books. Government is not a profit-making enterprise; therefore, it has lacked a ready-made gauge of the success of its programs.

This deficiency does not mean, however, that government cannot develop such gauges for most programs. Indeed, there has been considerable enthusiasm in some management circles about implementing the "planning-programing-budgeting-system" (PPBS) as a method for gauging government effectiveness. In general this system has three aims: (1) to fix the goals of the organization; (2) to establish criteria for determining the extent to which they are accomplishing these goals; and (3) to use the data to determine the relative costs and benefits of different methods of achieving such goals.

An example may clarify this approach to making government programs accountable. Suppose one day a welfare agency sat down and tried to determine what its goals were. Most likely it would decide on the following goal: to minimize the time people spend on welfare by returning the maximum number of persons to self-sufficiency in the minimum amount of time. If that goal were adopted it would be relatively easy to create numerical measures of success or failure. For example, one could keep track of changes in the rate at which people leave welfare for self-sufficiency (having defined what it means to be self-sufficient) and of the average time people are on welfare. Armed with such data it would be possible to tell which programs are more or less successful and which administrators are doing a better or a worse job. It is needless to say, however, that suggestions for the implementation of programs such as PPBS meet with considerable hostility from federal employees, who have vested interests in not having their success or the lack of it established.

This discussion leads to another problem of federal bureaucracies. Not only is it not ordinarily possible for programs or agencies to be declared failures, it is also very difficult for individuals to fail in their jobs. Nearly all government employees are under the civil service system. They cannot be removed from their jobs except for gross misconduct. A considerable amount of promotion is on the basis of seniority, not on merit. The purpose of such a system is to insulate the bureaucracy from unwarranted political interference. But it also protects bureaucrats from demands for high performance. As Peter Drucker pointed out, it is probably the case that "mediocrity in the civil service is a lesser evil than politics . . . [but] a good many people today have come to believe that we need some way of rewarding performance and of penalizing nonperformance, even within the civil service"(Drucker, 1969).

Nevertheless, even the most talented and dedicated civil servants cannot be nearly so efficient nor so creative as their counterparts in business organizations because of the extent of government red tape. Government workers must spend immense amounts of their time filling out forms and detailing how they spend their time. They also must account for every penny spent and every penny's worth of material used. The reason for this rigid accounting is the pervasive fears of government graft and corruption. In contrast, such strict accounting is regarded as prohibitively costly by private business, which typically selects random samples of items to audit in the same way that public opinion pollsters select samples of people to interview. These methods are just as accurate (some argue even more accurate) as total audits, and they cost much less. In our fear that someone is putting some public money in his pocket we waste prodigal amounts of time and money.

An additional problem faced by most government agencies is lack of competition. One need not be a reckless admirer of competition as the cure-all for society's problems to admit that some competition is probably beneficial for all organizations. If one is running the only game in town it is natural to be-

Figure 10.8 There are numerous influences and pressures on the bureaucrat's day-to-day decision making, which might be categorized according to their source: There are personal influences that stem from the bureaucrat's background or from his or her profession, and there are influences that originate in requests made by representatives of other agencies or branches of government or by the bureaucrat's individual clients. Far from the usual notion that the bureaucratic role is neutral and rule-restrained, in actuality the bureaucrat faces a complex set of often-contradictory pressures in making his or her day-to-day decisions.

come complacent. Citizens cannot shop around for welfare or for farm price supports. When people can choose alternatives to government it seems to make a difference. The recent success of private mail systems has caused considerable reorganization of the Post Office and it may even lead to better postal service.

A final point on monopoly is that government seems to operate most efficiently when it leaves the "doing" up to contract bureaucrats—employees of private firms who are contracted to work for the government. Such firms escape many of the problems that beset government. This fact has led many to suggest that the government should contract out many of the operations it presently carries on.

Bureaucracy and Democracy

Much of our antagonistic response to government relates to the liberal heritage of the American ideology. For the overriding issue in the study of bureaucracy is the question of the balance between the need for administrative excellence and the need for popular control. The issue is illustrated by the dilemma posed in the question: Whom should the bureaucrat obey? The bureaucrat finds himself operating within a maze of forces: Should he be primarily responsible to his administrative superior? to the Chief Executive? to the legislation that authorizes the programs of his bureaucracy? to the courts and their interpretation of that legislation? to his own conception of the public good or of the public interest? to his professional norms or codes of ethics? All of these answers are right under particular conditions, but it is sometimes difficult for the bureaucrat to know when to shift his loyalty.

As Frederick Mosher has noted, bureaucracy has evolved to the point where it is a series of highly specialized, often unionized, highly insulated (from

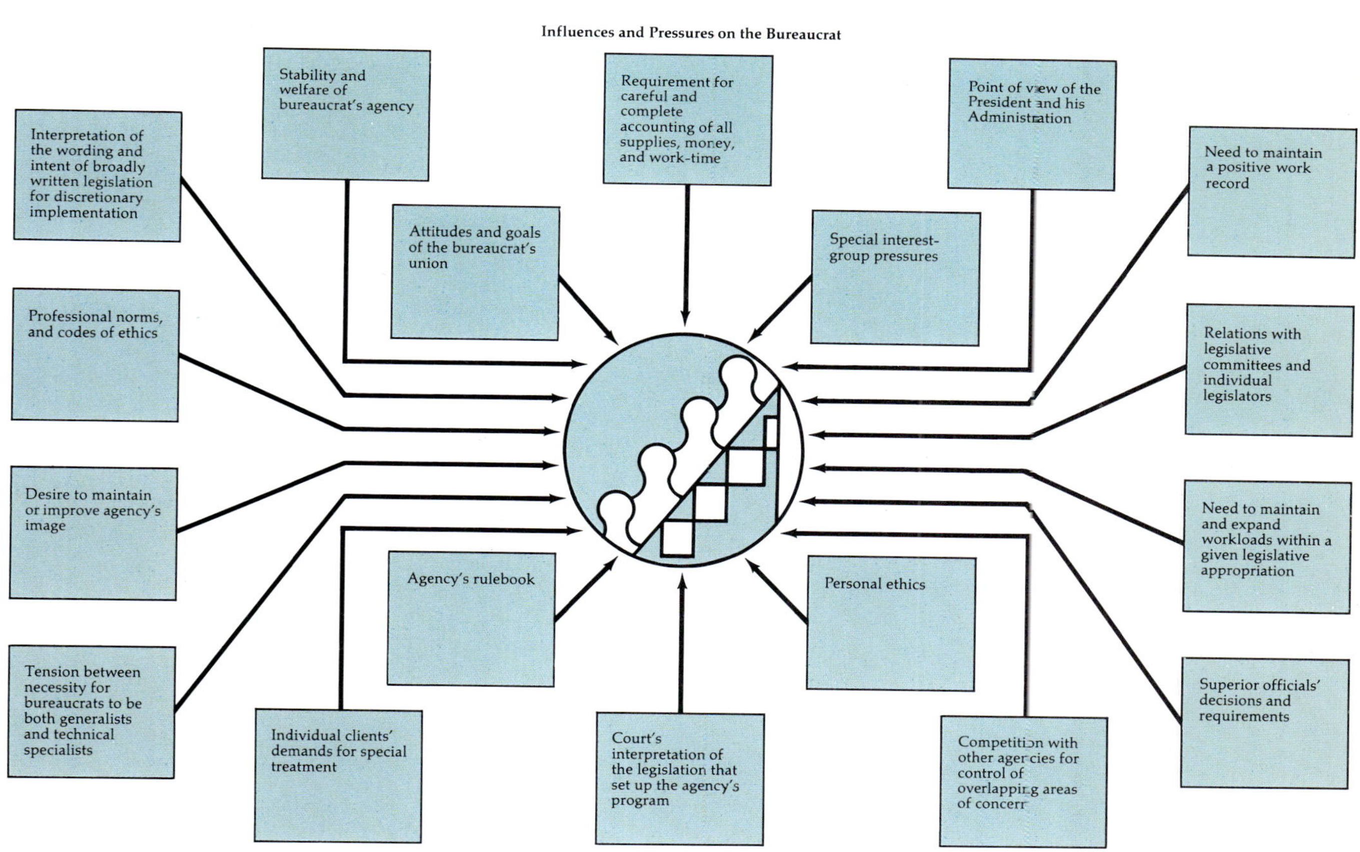

THE TOWNSEND HERESY

To: All Government Employees
From: The Head Bureaucrat
Subject: The Townsend Heresy

1. In a recent best seller called Up The Organization, Robert Townsend (1970), who rose to fame as the man who got Avis to "try harder," made a shocking proposal. He said that his first act if he were again to take charge of a company would be to draft a memo reading: "This is the last memo."

2. It has come to my attention that this dreadful idea has gained a certain sympathy among the ranks of those employed in government positions. Nothing could do so much harm to the position, purposes, and yes, the traditions of government service than to yield to this pernicious temptation to do away with memos.

3. It has been said that memos are the footprints of government-- indeed, they are the footprints of all organizations. Quite true. It is through memos that we keep track of what we have done, are doing, and hope to do. Our memos are the fundamental source material for future historians.

4. What are the uses of memos? Why write them? Quite simply a bureaucrat without memos will soon be a bureaucrat without influence: a bureaucrat who will be blamed for the failures of others, and a bureaucrat without a job. Memos are written to preserve in writing all business transacted within government. They guard against misunderstandings that might arise if oral exchanges were relied on. A complete memo file of all instructions received or issued, of all arrangements entered into or rejected, is the only insurance policy a bureaucrat has.

5. As a practical example let me offer the following hypothetical case. Suppose sometime that top officials in the Department of Justice decided to make daily intelligence material gathered in the Internal Security Division available to persons employed by a political campaign organization devoted to the reelection of the President. Such a decision is, of course, contrary to wise and ethical standards. A department subordinate directed to participate in this arrangement would be well advised to submit the following memo to his chief:

"I shall, of course, energetically carry out your verbal instructions concerning the sharing of secret information of my division with representatives of the Reelect Committee. However, out of loyalty to you I feel I must suggest that this arrangement could be subject to various unfriendly interpretations should it become public. I realize you have considered many aspects of this decision of which I am probably unaware. Nevertheless, I feel bound to share with you my unease about this arrangement because it appears to depart from the rules of access as laid down in previous memos and directives to this office."

This memo is an excellent example of the "safety play." The subordinate is protected against his superior because he reaffirms his obedience and also because he possesses knowledge his superior would hardly want to provoke him into revealing. On the other hand, should a day of reckoning come, the subordinate can pull this memo from his files and thus demonstrate that he acted only under orders and after having lodged his objections to those orders with his superior.

6. Political administrations come and go; but, armed with memos, the bureaucracy shall endure.

To: The Head Bureaucrat
From: The Head Paper-Shredder
Subject: Overload

It is all well and good for you to remind our colleagues of the utility of writing and keeping memos, but I feel it is urgent to bring to your attention that few show any tendencies to fail to do so. On the contrary, the problem of paperwork is getting out of control. At present the written records of the federal government considerably surpass more than 25 million cubic feet. If I were to shred these at the rate of one sheet per second, working 'round the clock it would take me 2,000 years to finish. Enough is enough. Do you realize that more than 360,000 different forms are in use by the government? And what about computers? One computer all by itself can turn out a stack of paper more than a mile high each year. The government has thousands of computers. It is urgent that I receive many new shredders and a great increase in manpower.

the public), and essentially self-governing fiefdoms backed by subdivisions of the Congress and by powerful interest groups (Mosher, 1968). Yet these conditions are increasingly being challenged by citizens demanding their right to participate in government decisions that affect their lives. Accordingly, neighborhood control and decentralization are on the upswing in bureaucracy. Programs now call for higher levels of citizen involvement and the willingness of bureaucrats to be directly responsive to locally defined needs. And yet it is no wonder that public servants have difficulty accommodating to these new circumstances. Under neighborhood control it is not always clear who "represents" the neighborhood and in which directions responsiveness should flow—the complex politics of the community may be a mystery to the bureaucrat. As a result, neighborhood control holds some promise of democratizing the bureaucracy; however, because of the problems it entails, administrative decentralization does not necessarily imply much relaxation of administrative domination of policy.

It is impossible to imagine a functioning government in our modern and complex society without a fully staffed and qualified bureaucracy. Yet it is a critical test for any democracy to nurture the development of its governmental services and hence its bureaucracy without losing popular control. At this point in the relationship between bureaucratic power and democratic control the tilt is clearly in the direction of powerful bureaucracies, although there are signs pointing to the development of new means of public control over bureaucracy in order to bring the system back into balance.

SUMMARY

Bureaucracy is the branch of federal government that most directly affects people's lives, for it delivers government programs to citizens. The major components of the bureaucracy are the eleven Cabinet departments; the independent executive agencies, which have a considerably more focused mission than the Cabinet departments; and the regulatory commissions, which, in regulating certain economic activities, perform a quasi-judicial function.

Bureaucracies are participants in the political process by virtue of their expertise and because of the ambiguity of much legislation. Bureaucracies carefully maintain their public image and work to maintain congressional as well as clientele-group support.

Economic policy—the bureaucracy regulates many aspects of the economy and exercises control through the budgeting process. Foreign affairs—the military-industrial complex illustrates the network of mutual support between the military bureaucracy and the economy. Civil rights and liberties—bureaucracy and the rights and liberties of citizens have always been in tension.

Private bureaucracies, because of established methods of measuring performance, are often more successful than government operations. The overriding issue in the study of bureaucracy is the proper balance between administrative performance and popular control.

SUGGESTED READINGS

Drucker, Peter. *The Age of Discontinuity; Guidelines to Our Changing Society.* New York: Harper & Row, 1969.

Galbraith, John Kenneth. *The New Industrial State.* Boston: Houghton-Mifflin, 1967.

Jacob, Charles. *Policy and Bureaucracy.* Princeton, N.J.: Van Nostrand, 1966.

Rourke, Francis. *Bureaucracy, Politics, and Public Policy.* Boston: Little, Brown, 1969.

EQUAL JUSTICE UNDER LAW

11
THE COURTS

In June 1971 several newspapers (most notably the *New York Times* and the *Washington Post*) began to publish articles based on a previously secret government study of the decision-making process that led to United States involvement in Vietnam. After asking the newspapers to stop the publication of these documents, Attorney General John Mitchell sent Justice Department lawyers into federal courts to seek injunctions requiring the newspapers to cease publication of the *Pentagon Papers* articles. The government claimed that the publication of the materials endangered national security. The newspapers countered with the claim that their publication was protected under the provision of the First Amendment protecting freedom of the press.

During the 1940s and early 1950s attorneys for the National Association for the Advancement of Colored People (NAACP) worked in conjunction with parents of black children attending segregated schools in various southern and border states to map out a strategy to outlaw segregation. In a series of suits they asked state and federal courts to declare that the practice of legally required segregation of the races violated the right to *equal protection of the laws* guaranteed to all citizens under the Constitution's Fourteenth Amendment.

In 1970 the Massachusetts legislature passed an act calling on its state attorney general to file a suit seeking to settle the question of the constitutionality of the commitment of troops to Vietnam. Massachusetts filed a suit requesting that United States participation in Vietnam be declared "unconstitutional in that it was not initially authorized or subsequently ratified by Congressional declaration."

All of these issues dealt with important divisions in American society about public policy concerns. In all of these cases the interested parties—individuals, groups, and governmental institutions—sought to get their way by going to court and arguing that the fundamental issue was one of constitutional interpretation.

In the *Pentagon Papers* case the Supreme Court acted with almost unprecedented speed. Only fifteen days after the federal government had initially gone into lower federal courts, the Supreme Court announced its opinion. By a 5–3 vote, the Court upheld the right of the newspapers to continue to publish their stories based on the *Pentagon Papers*. Although

Figure 11.1 "Equal justice under the law"—a concept easier in the saying than in the doing. The American court system is an intricately layered system in which ideals, mundane facts of business and social relations, and the passions and intrigues of politics are intermingled. "Equal," "justice," and "law" are three concepts that have been interpreted and reinterpreted through the ages. Does equal mean being able to seek a decision through the courts, or does it mean access to legal aid of equal quality whatever one's income? Does justice mean referring questions strictly to the letter of the Constitution and statutes, or does it allow for wide interpretation by judges? Is law a set of statutes and legal precedents, or is it the claims of individual conscience and inalienable rights? The American court system seeks the answers to these questions in a competitive, "adversary" situation, forcing the definition and redefinition of statements in our Constitution and law books.

the case against Daniel Ellsberg and Anthony Russo —the men who had originally copied and distributed the documents to the press—was tried in a federal district court, it was subsequently dismissed when it was found that the government had used improper wiretaps to gather evidence.

In the school desegregation cases, the Supreme Court held in 1954 that legally imposed segregation of the races violated the Fourteenth Amendment, and in 1955 the Court ordered the lower courts to desegregate schools "with all deliberate speed." These landmark cases not only initiated the process of school desegregation throughout the South, but they also placed the mark of legitimacy on the cause of civil rights generally. The Court decision contributed to the development of civil rights activity in the legislature and in the streets as well, ultimately resulting in gradual desegregation of most public places in the South. Yet, as is shown in the Perspective on school desegregation, the process was a slow one; ten years after the *Brown* decision, only about 2 percent of black children in the South were attending schools with whites. Even though the Court had announced a new public policy, it had by no means settled the matter (see Chapter 6). Rather, the decision of the Court interacted with the behavior of other governmental officials—federal, state, and local—and with public opinion to produce gradual change. Success in Court did not signify immediate success in changing public policy.

The Supreme Court of the United States refused to hear the Massachusetts suit challenging the validity of the war. The members of the Supreme Court have almost total control to decide the cases they will consider, and they refused—without explanation— to hear the Massachusetts suit. In a variety of other suits as well, most involving the drafting of men for service in Vietnam, opponents of the war attempted to get the Supreme Court to consider the question whether the Vietnam involvement violated the Constitution. Yet the Court simply refused to get involved. On this important issue the Supreme Court's contribution to public policy was one of *nondecision;* the issue was thus left to other governmental institutions.

These three examples reveal several aspects of the American legal system. In our society many people turn to the courts when they wish to get their way

in matters of public policy. Sometimes they succeed in getting courts to hear their cases, and sometimes they succeed in getting the courts to declare that their desired policy is the correct one. Sometimes a court decision effectively ends the matter: The court is obeyed and the issue is settled, at least for a time. Sometimes, however, a court decision is but the first step in the development of public policy. Events occurring in other arenas (in the state and federal legislatures, police departments, executive offices, bureaucracies, the public at large) interact with the court's contribution to provide for the gradual development of public policy.

This chapter explores the role that courts play in public policy formation. The chapter begins with an examination of the general structure and function of the American court system and provides a look at the path the typical case follows in the legal system and at the factors that affect judicial decision making. Next the chapter looks at the source of the courts' powers in making public policy and some of the limitations on these powers. Finally, there is an examination of some of the areas in which the courts have recently played a role in policy making.

THE AMERICAN LEGAL SYSTEM: AN OVERVIEW

All court cases begin with a dispute: It may be a dispute between two private citizens, between two government institutions, or between a citizen and a government agency. Jones may sue Smith to recover damages caused by a traffic accident; acting under the provisions of a civil rights statute, the United States government may sue the state of Mississippi to force its officials to stop discriminating against blacks in the electoral process; the state of Nebraska may charge Adams with burglary and bring him to court to answer the charge; a group of women may be dissatisfied with the abortion law in their state and may attempt to have it declared unconstitutional. Thus, court cases begin with dissatisfactions and disputes. Unlike legislatures or bureaucracies, courts do not place issues on their own agendas. Judges do not decide that they wish to make policy about abortions, voting rights, or racial discrimination and then announce their "decisions." Rather, courts are passive; they must wait for others to bring matters to them for resolution. In the course of resolving the disputes that are

Figure 11.2 The disputes that begin a court case may occur between persons, groups, or agencies, public or private, as illustrated by this series of collisions (right). At the top are shown two private citizens in an unfortunate accident, which would result in Citizen Doe and Citizen Roe (or their insurance agents) meeting in court. A collision between the state, in the person of a patrol car, and a private citizen's auto may be the fault of either; in any case it might lead to a suit of Citizen Roe versus the state of "X" for damages done to car and to person. States and the federal government are often at issue over distribution of funds or applications of rules—in our illustration the case is more direct: the state's patrol car has collided with a federal truck, and the result will be a federal case. Finally, in our series of collisions, Citizen Roe smashes headlong into the power of the federal government in the form of a mail truck. Can the ordinary citizen sue the United States government? The anser is yes, as the suit, Roe v. the United States, will soon attest. And if Roe is not satisfied with the outcome and if he can show the court's failure to apply his constitutional rights of due process in the proceedings of his case, he may appeal his case all the way to the Supreme Court.

CRIMINAL AND CIVIL COURTS

Many of the criminal courts in this country are run like production lines because they are burdened with many more cases than they can adequately handle. They not only deal with serious crimes, such as robbery and murder, but with victimless crimes, such as drunkenness, prostitution, and drug addiction, which hardly seem to belong in a court.

The typical criminal court in this country is characterized by bargaining over charges and sentencing and not by the excitement of a Perry Mason drama in which the brilliant lawyer ferrets out the truth in a tension-filled trial. The need to get things over with rather than concern with the rights and needs of defendants characterizes most of the criminal courts (Leonard Downey, 1971; Jonathan Casper, 1972).

The civil courts are not much different. Their calendar is crammed with cases involving collection agencies and recalcitrant bill-payers, repossessions, and angry landlords and frustrated tenants. They are also burdened with large numbers of automobile injury cases. In some of the larger metropolitan areas, the lag between an automobile accident and the trial concerning it is more than four years. Imagine the difficulty of tracking down witnesses, not to mention trying to prove to a jury that a defendant whose accident-related injuries are healed actually suffered great pain and aggravation. All in all, the activity of the lower courts paints a bleak picture. In terms of the everyday life of the average citizen, much important litigation takes place in the lower courts. However, because of the volume of the case load, justice in the lower courts is not always characterized by either lofty ideals or dignified behavior.

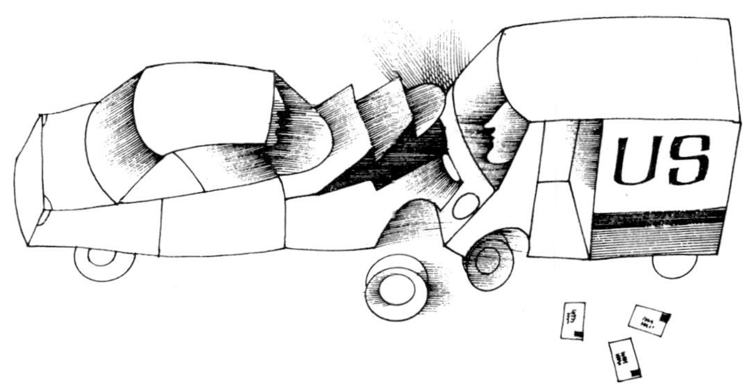

brought to them, legal institutions may simply affect the interests of the formal parties to the dispute, as in the case of the typical civil suit or criminal prosecution. But they may also use the *occasion for decision* provided by a particular dispute to develop policies affecting broad classes of the society.

Recall from Chapter 7 the major decisions of the Supreme Court of the 1960s (the so-called Warren Court): Court rulings dealt with such issues as criminal justice, racial discrimination, prayers in the schools, reapportionment, and freedom of expression. In all of these cases the occasion for decision was used to establish rather broad policy rather than simply to settle the particular dispute that led the parties into court in the first place.

A look at the formal structure of the American legal system and at the path a court case follows as it moves up the appeals ladder on its way to the Supreme Court of the United States will reveal the policy-making potential that the courts possess.

Courts: The Dual Hierarchy

The American court system, as part of the federal system of government, is characterized by dual hierarchies: There are both state and federal courts. Each state has its own system of courts, composed of civil and criminal trial courts, sometimes intermediate courts of appeal, and a state supreme court. The federal court system consists of a series of trial courts (called District Courts) serving relatively small geographic regions (there is at least one for every state); a tier of Circuit Courts of Appeal that hear appeals from many District Courts in a particular geographic region, and the Supreme Court of the United States. The two court systems are to some extent overlapping, in that certain kinds of disputes (such as a claim that a state law is in violation of the Constitution) may be initiated in either system. They are also to some extent hierarchical, for the federal system stands above the state system in that *litigants* (persons engaged in lawsuits) who lose their cases in the state supreme court may appeal their cases to the Supreme Court of the United States (see Figure 11.3).

Thus, the typical court case begins in a trial court—a court of general jurisdiction—in the state or federal system. Most cases go no further than the trial court: for example, the criminal defendant is convicted (by

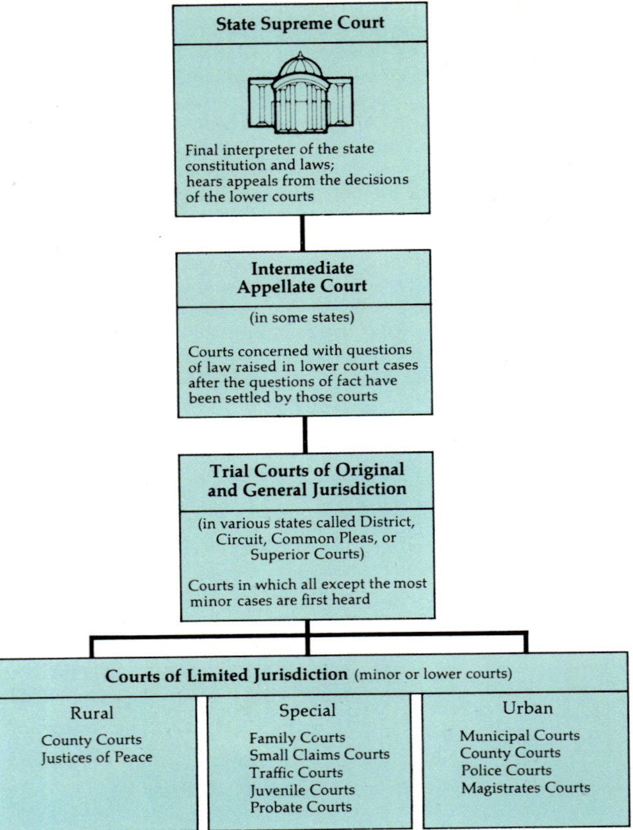

Figure 11.3 The state and federal components of the American court system. In the state system (above), we begin at the bottom with the most specialized courts, the county or municipal courts. All cases originate either in these special courts or at the next higher level, the trial courts. The two topmost levels deal only with cases appealed from the lower courts.

The federal court system (right) contains one element entirely different from the state system, that is, the quasijudicial agencies. These governmental agencies decide on specific questions, such as those regarding business-labor relations or agricultural allotments; their decisions can be appealed. The federal system also has a number of courts of special jurisdiction, similar to the lower rung of the state system. These courts, the Customs Court and the Tax Court, have well-defined areas of competence, and appeals from these courts are heard in special appeals courts, as are appeals from courts martial (which operate under military law) and certain public contract cases.

The main body of federal cases originate in the federal district courts, which spread throughout the states and territories. Appeals from these courts are usually heard in federal courts of appeals, according to areas, or circuits, or jurisdiction.

The United States Supreme Court hears selected cases from the federal courts of appeals or the state courts of last resort (state supreme courts)—cases that, according to the Supreme Court Justices, involve questions of federal consequence.

U.S. Supreme Court

Original jurisdiction:

Cases involving ambassadors, ministers, and consuls

Cases in which a state is a party

Appellate jurisdiction:

From the lower federal courts

From state courts of last resort if a federal question is involved "under such regulations as the Congress shall make"

Appellate Courts

Court of Customs and Patent Appeals

Review of decisions of Customs Court and Patent Office

Review of certain findings of the Tariff Commission on matters of law only

Court of Claims

Claims against the U.S. other than tort actions (many cases involving claims arising out of public contracts)

Limited appellate review of tort actions against the U.S.

Court of Appeals for D.C.

Appeals from district court for District of Columbia

Review and enforcement of actions of certain quasi-judicial agencies

Courts of Appeals in Numbered Judicial Circuits

Appellate jurisdiction from district courts

Review and enforcement of actions of certain quasi-judicial agencies

Court of Military Appeals

Review of courtsmartial

Highest State Courts

Jurisdiction over many cases that involve federal questions, as well as matters of state law

From State Court System

Customs Court

Jurisdiction over disputes involving tariff duties

District Court for D.C.

Jurisdiction similar to that of other district courts

Tax Court

Jurisdiction over disputes involving overpayments or underpayments of taxes

88 District Courts in 50 States

General original jurisdiction over:

Federal crimes

Federal-question cases where the amount in controversy exceeds $10,000 (jurisdictional amount waived in cases brought by the U.S. or involving admiralty, bankruptcy, commerce, patent, copyright, postal, internal revenue, civil rights law)

Suits between citizens of different states, where amount in controversy exceeds $10,000

Suits between citizens of one of the 50 states and foreign states, or their citizens or subjects, or the District of Columbia, where amount in controversy exceeds $10,000

Review and/or enforcement of actions of certain quasi-judicial agencies

Tort claims against the U.S.

Concurrent jurisdiction with Court of Claims to hear claims up to $10,000 against the U.S. other than tort actions, such as those to recover for overpayment of taxes or for breach of contract on the part of the U.S.

4 District Courts in Territories

Mixed federal and local jurisdiction

Quasi-judicial Agencies

Certain orders of:

Atomic Energy Commission
Civil Aeronautics Board
Federal Aviation Administration
FCC (other than broadcasting)
Federal Power Commission
Federal Reserve System
Federal Trade Commission
Interstate Commerce Commission
Federal Maritime Commission
National Labor Relations Board
Railroad Retirement Board

Securities and Exchange Commission
Secretary of Agriculture (packers, commodity exchange)
Secretary of the Army (navigable waters)
Secretary of Health, Education, and Welfare (food and drug)
Commissioner of Education
Secretary of Labor (wages and hours)
Secretary of the Treasury (alcohol administration)
Surgeon General (certification for hospital grants-in-aid)

Quasi-judicial Agencies

Federal Communications Commission (broadcasting)

Secretary of Agriculture (sugar-allotment orders)

Secretary of Commerce (ship-registry orders)

U.S. Postal Service

a trial or a guilty plea) and sentenced by the court and his case ends; the personal injury suit results in a judgment by a trial court (or an out-of-court settlement by the parties while the court suit is pending) and the parties leave the court system. But sometimes the losing party at the trial court cares enough about his cause that he does not let the matter end there. Some criminal defendants believe that their convictions were based on errors by the trial judge (such as the admission of evidence that ought to have been excluded); a litigant who asks the trial court to declare the malapportionment of his state legislature unconstitutional may be dissatisfied with the refusal of the trial court to issue the injunction he requests. In these and other cases, the "loser" at the trial court may appeal to the next higher court. If the case is in a state court system, the appeal will go to the intermediate court of appeals, if the state has one, or to the state supreme court. If the case began in the federal District Court, the appeal goes to the Circuit Court of Appeals for that geographic area. If the appeals court agrees to hear the case and renders a decision, the losing party may still care enough about the issue to be willing to spend the time and money necessary to ask the Supreme Court of the United States to review the ruling of the state supreme court or the Circuit Court of Appeals.

The Supreme Court has almost complete control over its own docket. Each year, 3000–3500 "losers" in lower appeals courts ask the Court to review their cases. The typical request is the filing of a petition for *certiorari*—a legal document that sets forth the facts of the case, the decision of the lower court, and an argument as to why the Supreme Court ought to agree to hear the case. Some of these petitions are very complex and polished legal documents. In recent years nearly half of them have been documents, of varying legal sophistication, filed by prisoners in state and federal prisons asking that the Court review their convictions. Of the 3000–3500 cases presented to the Court in the typical year, about 250 are actually decided by the Court. The remainder are simply not heard: Without giving a reason, the Court simply decides not to consider the case. The Court follows what is called the *rule of four* in deciding which cases to hear: If four of the nine Justices on the Supreme Court vote to hear a case, the case is placed on the Court's docket, briefs are subse-

quently filed, oral arguments heard, and a decision in the case is rendered.

The Flow of Litigation

Several characteristics of the flow of litigation are significant. First, the process is characterized by a great deal of *winnowing*. Most cases that get into court end at the level at which they begin—the winner and loser are either satisfied with the outcome or have exhausted their resources to the extent that they cannot appeal the outcome. For every case that is appealed to the next higher level, hundreds of cases die. This fact suggests a second point: The process of appeals is a costly one, both in time and in resources. The typical case that gets to the Supreme Court has been in the court system for two or three years. In addition to time, litigation costs money—money to hire attorneys, to do legal research, to prepare briefs, to deliver oral arguments. The time and expense explains in part why so many lower court cases are not appealed. It also suggests that cases that do go on through multiple appeals survive because the parties have the resources to pursue them and because they care enough to mobilize and invest these resources in litigation.

In addition to the litigants' intensity of interest, cases survive because appellate courts choose to hear them. Winnowing occurs not only because litigants give up or run out of resources but because appellate courts refuse to hear their cases. Cases that reach higher appellate levels, especially the Supreme Court of the United States, typically involve important issues—issues that are of sufficient importance that the litigants choose to spend the time and money required to pursue them and the Justices of the Supreme Court agree to deal with the matter.

This description is not intended to suggest that the work of appellate courts deals with important issues and that the work of lower courts is simply technical and unimportant. Indeed, in terms of defining the quality of the lives of most citizens, the posture and decisions of lower courts have a much more direct impact on their lives. Lower-court decisions that deal with the enforcement of criminal statutes, traffic laws, and the application of legal norms involving credit or landlord-tenant relations probably have more direct impact on the daily lives of individual citizens than do decisions of the Supreme Court. By the same token, however, the participation of the legal system in important areas of social change—of the development and modification of legal norms—is more often the province of appellate courts.

In sum, the following points are important. The legal system is characterized by a large number of courts, arranged in a roughly hierarchical pattern. The appellate process—the pursuing of cases from lower courts to higher courts—takes time and money, and it is characterized by a great deal of winnowing and broadening of issues. Although most associate the "important" decisions in recent years with the Supreme Court of the United States, a great deal of important activity also takes place in lower courts, part of whose function is to translate the decisions of the Supreme Court into the day-to-day world of litigation.

THE JUDICIAL DECISION-MAKING PROCESS

The course the typical case takes is an arduous one, and the issues that arrive at the Supreme Court for resolution are often ones involving issues that are not only of importance to the litigants but also to the society at large: what kinds of investigative techniques are permissible in producing evidence against a criminal defendant; what shall be the norms governing the legal status of black citizens; what are the obligations and limitations on the authority of government in dealing with environmental pollution? The disputes that come to court often reflect basic disagreements in the society at large about public policy. As courts participate in the development of public policy, they must make choices. How does a judge decide a case?

The appellate judge often decides cases dealing with *constitutional* issues—with allegations that certain policies being pursued by government do not conform to the requirements of the Constitution—or with matters of "statutory construction"—the interpretation of what legislatures meant when they passed statutes (such as the operational meaning of the phrase that forbids "combinations in restraint of trade"). There is persistent belief that what judges do in either of these cases is to apply "the law" to the specific situation that is involved in the dispute before them. This mechanical view of the judicial decision-making process was described by a Supreme Court Justice as follows:

The Constitution is the supreme law of the land ordained and established by the people. All legislation must conform to the principles it lays down. When an act of Congress is appropriately challenged in the courts as not conforming to the constitutional mandate, the judicial branch of the government has only one duty—to lay the article of the Constitution which is invoked beside the statute which is challenged and to decide whether the latter squares with the former. (*United States* v. *Butler,* 1936)

This view has sometimes been referred to as the "slot-machine" theory of judicial decision making, for it involves simply feeding in the statute and the Constitution and by a mechanical process arriving at the correct answer.

The difficulty with such a view of the judicial decision-making process is that it is too simple, that it assumes certain characteristics of the judge's job that are unrealistic. Reflection on some of the provisions of the Constitution makes this point evident. The Constitution says, for example, that police may not engage in *unreasonable searches and seizures;* that no citizen should be deprived of *equal protection of the laws* or of *due process* in the implementation of laws. What might it mean, as Justice Roberts' remark suggests, for the judge to compare a statute or the behavior of a governmental official with these provisions of the Constitution? Does a police officer's stopping and frisking a suspicious-looking individual constitute an unreasonable search and seizure, or is it constitutionally reasonable? Does the racial segregation of school children deny blacks equal protection of the laws or does it not? Does a law regulating the wages and hours of employees deprive them of their right to contract with employers for their services without due process of the law, or is it a valid regulation of behavior?

Clearly, past decisions provide a *gloss,* or an interpretation, of the words of the Constitution that makes its provisions less ambiguous than the plain words of the document. Yet the fact that judges have long disagreed with one another over the answers to the above questions suggests that the decision-making process is somewhat more complicated than simply applying the law to the facts or the Constitution to the statute. Judges, like other policy makers in the society, are faced with choices in which they have a great deal of latitude; moreover, the choices they make can have an important impact on the development of public policy. The personal values and characteristics of the judge, his interactions with his fellow judges, and the limitations placed on a person by virtue of his role as judge (see □) all work together to produce the votes and opinions of judges. Although at this time there is no complete and verified theory that explains the judicial decision-making process (nor is there one for legislators, executives, or members of bureaucracies), it is reasonable to say that judges are like other political officeholders—their decisions contribute to the development of public policy and are made on the basis of many of the same criteria that determine the choices of other political decision makers.

In this section, we have provided a brief overview of the American legal system and suggested the course that the typical case must follow through the appellate process. We have pointed out that cases go through a great deal of winnowing and that issues are broadened as they are considered at higher levels of the judicial system. We have suggested that the decision-making behavior of judges is best understood not as some kind of peculiarly legal phenomenon, but as another aspect of the exercise of choice by political officeholders. In some respects judges *are* different, but in other important respects—in the breadth of issues they are confronted with and in the kinds of factors that affect their judicial decisions—they are best understood as persons who occupy a significant role in the American political system.

THE AMERICAN COURTS AND JUDICIAL REVIEW

In comparative terms, the court system in the United States has enormous power. Many matters that other nations regard as being outside the realm of legal institutions become legal issues in the United States. A glance at the nature of judicial power, at its development, and at its limitations is necessary to an understanding of the significant policy role played by the courts.

The Concept of Judicial Review

The great power of the legal system in this country stems from the exercise of the function of *judicial*

Figure 11.4 The judge's lot is not an easy one. The difficulty of the role arises in the idealism associated with it. Justice is supposed to be blind—but blind to what? As an intelligent individual, the judge is aware of his or her surroundings. And to be aware means to be aware of pressures and conflicting social demands; it means to have hopes for the progress of the nation and to have personal desires that are both selfish and unselfish. The ideal of fairness requires restraint and balance: the balancing of the facts of a particular case with the procedural and substantive requirements of the law and with the realities of society.

□

ROLE OF THE JUDGE
Justice Frankfurter—one of the most influential men to sit on the Supreme Court in this century—referred often to his very strong notions of the role of the judge. Asserting that he often voted to uphold governmental activities that he personally might not endorse in his role of private citizen, he asserted: "It cannot be emphasized too much that one's own opinion about the wisdom or evil of a law should be excluded altogether when one is doing one's duty on the bench." Although there is, of course, no single judicial role, this view suggests that in deciding cases the judge must often subordinate his own preferences to the need to remain within the constraints of the role of judge. Thus, for all judges, and perhaps more for some than for others, the variable of role is an important influence on their decision-making behavior. (Alexander Bickel, 1962; Charles Black, 1960)

Facts of the Case
Political Climate
Precedent
Constitution
Judge's Background and Conscience
Economic Conditions
Interest Group Pressure
Social Conditions

review, in which the courts review the acts of legislatures and of members of executive agencies to determine whether they conform to the provisions of the Constitution. Thus, for example, state laws dealing with abortion or the apportionment of legislatures, congressional legislation dealing with subversive activities, and police activities in investigating criminal suspects have all come under the scrutiny of legal institutions.

Judicial review seems an extraordinary power, for it vests in courts—constrained only by the rather vague provisions of the Constitution—the power to overturn the activities of other branches of government. Some have argued that judicial review is highly undemocratic because judges serve for long terms or for life and are not responsible to the public in the way that elected officials are thought to be. Others have argued that democracy consists of more than simple responsiveness, that the protection of the rights of the minority by means of judicial review is a vital function in a free society; they feel that courts have the necessary detachment to restrain the volatile and sometimes repressive will of the majority.

The power of judicial review in this country is not explicitly spelled out in the Constitution. Indeed, much discussion centers on the question of whether courts should properly enjoy this power. During the drafting and ratification of the Constitution, the framers were ambiguous about the constitutional function that courts were to serve. Some of the *Federalist* papers (especially Hamilton's *Federalist* No. 78) indicate clear support for judicial review; yet much of the rhetoric concerning the practice was in response to suggestions that the Constitution provided too much power to the President and Con-

□

MARBURY v. MADISON

Thomas Jefferson was elected to the Presidency in the fall of 1800. Between his election and inauguration, the "lame duck" President, John Adams, made a series of appointments to federal judgeships designed to ensure continued Federalist control of the judiciary. When Jefferson was inaugurated as President, he refused to allow his Secretary of State, James Madison, to deliver to William Marbury—a newly appointed Justice of the Peace—the documents necessary for him to assume his judicial office.

Chief Justice Marshall, a Federalist, wrote the majority opinion for the Supreme Court in the case of Marbury v. Madison. *In the potentially explosive decision, Marshall both side-stepped the central issue of the case and at the same time established the principle of judicial review. Marshall held that Marbury was legally entitled to the commission that Madison was withholding. But, Marshall concluded, the Supreme Court lacked the authority to issue the writ. The Judiciary Act of 1789, which had set up the lower federal court system and established its jurisdiction, had also conferred on the Supreme Court original jurisdiction to issue writs of mandamus to federal officials. But, Marshall pointed out, the Constitution itself specified those areas in which the Court was to exercise original jurisdiction and left to Congress only the power to specify its appellate jurisdiction. Therefore, this section of the Judiciary Act was unconstitutional, for Congress had sought to do what the Constitution said it could not—fix the original jurisdiction of the Court. Marshall asserted that the Constitution was the supreme law of the land, binding on judges and all other government officials. Therefore, Congress could not pass a law that contradicted the Constitution: "a law repugnant to the Constitution is void; . . . courts as well as other departments are bound by that instrument."*

Thus, Marshall scolded Madison and Jefferson for their failure to deliver the commission to Marbury, but he did not require them to issue it.

gress in their relations with the states. The rhetoric in support of judicial review may thus have been aimed at quieting those fears rather than truly supporting the power of courts to declare legislation unconstitutional.

Thus, the framers' intent concerning the power of judicial review is unclear. Certainly they were aware that it was an issue, but they did not expressly indicate whether the Constitution was meant to provide for it or to forbid it. Instead, judicial review simply evolved. The courts asserted that they had the power of review, and although specific instances of the exercise of it have been highly controversial, by now judicial review is simply part of the American system.

The first case in which the courts asserted the power to declare federal legislation unconstitutional occurred in 1803. In the case of *Marbury* v. *Madison*

Chief Justice John Marshall declared a provision of the Judiciary Act of 1789 to be in violation of the Constitution and thus null and void (see ☐). He reasoned that the Constitution was the supreme law of the land and that the legislation in question contradicted it. Hence, the statute must be void; if it were not, then the Constitution would not, by definition, be "supreme law." Clearly the implications of the cases were enormous, for the ruling gave legal institutions the power to declare the activities of other branches of government unconstitutional. Because many of the provisions of the Constitution are rather vague, application of them in the context of judicial review gives enormous power to the courts.

Over the following fifty years, the Court built slowly on the provisions of the *Marbury* case. In 1819 Marshall invoked the *supremacy of national law* clause

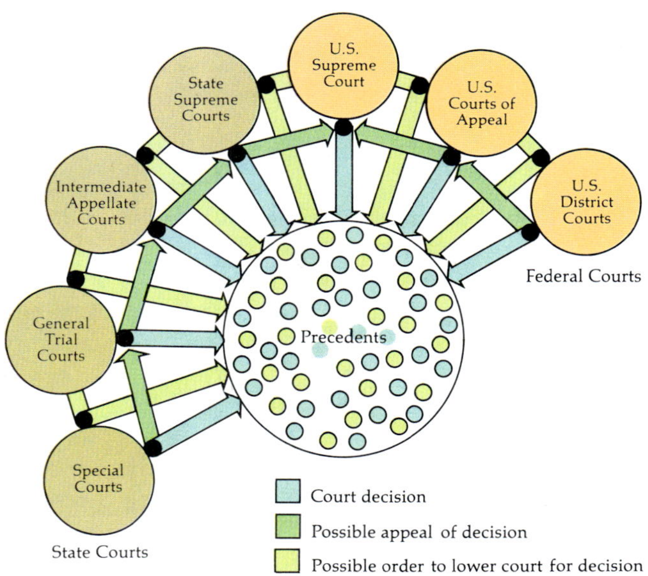

Figure 11.5   Precedents are court decisions that, because of their similarity, are referred to when later cases are being decided. Physically, precedents are recorded in the massive volumes one sees in lawyers' offices or in law libraries. These books are intricately cross-indexed; they provide lawyers, judges, and their legal assistants and clerks with well-marked trails of similar cases, extending from the most recent, most trivial, and most peripheral cases, to the earliest, most significant, and most directly related cases. Precedents may arise from legal decisions made by courts at any level; they may arise from a single appeal, from the last decision in a long chain of appeals, or may emanate from the Supreme Court itself.

of Article I in ruling that Maryland's attempt to tax national banks was unconstitutional—the case of *McCulloch* v. *Maryland* (see Chapter 2). In the same year, in the *Dartmouth College* case, Marshall held that states might not pass legislation impairing contracts. Then, in 1857, the Court again struck down an act of Congress, in the famous *Dred Scott* decision (see Chapter 6).

These famous cases established the power of the Supreme Court to sit in review of the other branches of government. The history of judicial review has been somewhat checkered; there have been periods of judicial activism and of judicial passivity. There is still much debate over whether the Court ought to be active in protecting the constitutional rights of citizens against infringement by government or whether it ought to defer to the activities of other more responsive democratic institutions. But few would question that the Court does possess the power of judicial review (Charles Black, 1960; Alexander Bickel, 1962).

Judicial Review and the Economy

It is useful to look briefly at some of the areas in which the Supreme Court has used its powers of review. In the area of economic legislation the Court utilized its power to promote a *laissez-faire* economic policy from the last third of the nineteenth century until the mid-1930s. The Justices of the Supreme Court interpreted the due process clauses of the Fifth and Fourteenth Amendments to mean that government could not interfere with the "freedom" of employers and employees to deal with one another in any way they wished—thus, for example, laws dealing with child labor, with regulation of wages and hours, and with working conditions for employees were declared unconstitutional. Moreover, the use of lower-court injunctions to oppose labor union organizing and activity was encouraged by the Supreme Court. This period marked the growth of corporate capitalism (see Chapter 4), and the courts were an important force in protecting the rights of employers to deal with their employees free of the constraints of either government regulation or employee organizations.

As the society gradually became convinced that the free-market economy produced neither the stability nor the types of working conditions that were acceptable to most employees, more and more legislation was passed attempting to regulate the economy and promote the activities of labor unions. This movement reached its peak during the early years of Franklin Roosevelt's Presidency with the passage of the New Deal legislation designed to promote recovery from the Depression via governmental regulation of the economy. Still pursuing its *laissez-faire* interpretation of the Constitution, which held that such legislation violated due process, the Supreme Court struck down much New Deal legislation. President Roosevelt then attempted to enlarge the court from nine to fifteen Justices in an effort to mold a court that was more favorable to his economic programs. The Court eventually yielded—in the "switch in time that saved nine"—and suddenly began to uphold the types of legislation that a few years before it had held unconstitutional. Thus, for a period of fifty years, the Court had stood as a bulwark for the free-market economy and a major impediment to governmental regulation of the economy; it yielded only grudgingly to a national consensus that called for different policies.

Judicial Review and Civil Rights

As is shown in Chapter 6, the Court exercised its power of judicial review in promoting the policy of segregation developed after the Civil War in the southern states. In the *Civil Rights Cases* of 1883, the Court overturned an act of Congress designed to outlaw segregation in such public places as restaurants and railway cars. The Court ruled that the Fourteenth Amendment prohibition against any state's denying its citizens equal protection of the laws applied only to activities of *state governments;* hence Congress could not base legislation outlawing discrimination by private parties such as railroad companies and restauranteurs on the Fourteenth Amendment. Similarly, in 1896 the Court upheld the principle of *separate but equal,* holding that a state did not deny its citizens equal protection if it segregated them by race as long as the facilities (such as schools and railway cars) were reasonably equal (*Plessy* v. *Ferguson*). Thus, the Court played an important role in legitimizing the system of Jim Crow laws in the South and in erecting barriers to the passage of legislation designed to aid integration.

Not until the 1930s did the Court begin to cast a

SUPREME COURT DECISIONS AFFECTING GOVERNMENT REGULATION OF BUSINESS, 1903–1942

PRO-GOVERNMENT DECISIONS

Champion v. *Ames* (1903)—The "Lottery Case"—Decided Congress may validly bar from interstate commerce those commodities that are dangerous or otherwise objectionable.

Muller v. *Oregon* (1908)—Validated Oregon ten-hour-day law for women as satisfying "due process" (Brandeis brief)

Clark Distilling Co. v. *Western Maryland Railway Co.* (1917)

United States v. *Hill* (1919)—Upheld legislation forbidding shipment of intoxicating liquors into dry states or territories.

Texas & N.O.R. Co. v. *Brotherhood of R. & S. S. Clerks* (1930)

Virginian Ry. Co. v. *System Federation No. 40* (1934)—Upheld legislation forbidding railroad interference with the integrity of labor union organization. (Broadened interpretation of interstate commerce.)

Nebbia v. *New York* (1934)—Abandoned the concept of a business affected with a public interest as the constitutional criterion of price control.

Whitfield v. *Ohio* (1936)

Kentucky Whip and Collar Co. v. *Illinois Central Railway Company* (1937)—Upheld legislation prohibiting shipment of convict-made goods into states prohibiting their sale.

National Labor Relations Board v. *Jones and Laughlin Steel Corp.* (1937)

N. L. R. B. v. *Fruehauf Trailer Co.* (1937)

N. L. R. B. v. *Friedman-Harry Marks Clothing Co.* (1937)—Upheld Wagner Act protecting union organizations operating in manufacturing concerns. Based on broad interpretations of interstate commerce.

Charles C. Steward Machine Co. v. *Davis* (1937)—Declared provisions of Social Security Act of 1935 constitutional on grounds that its purposes fell within the scope of providing for the general national welfare. Ignored "dual federalism."

West Coast Hotel v. *Parrish* (1937)—Overruled Adkins to uphold Washington state minimum wage statute.

Mulford v. *Smith* (1939)—Upheld Agricultural Adjustment Act of 1938

United States v. *Rock Royal Co-operative* (1939)

Hood & Sons v. *United States* (1939)—Upheld Agricultural Marketing Agreement Act of 1937 against the charge that it invalidly delegated legislative powers of control of interstate commerce to the Secretary of Agriculture.

United States v. *Darby* (1941)—Overthrew *Hammer* v. *Dagenhart*; allowed Congress to regulate wages and hours in industries related to interstate commerce.

Wickard v. *Filburn* (1942)—Upheld Agricultural Adjustment Act of 1938 (different application of this act from that found in *Mulford* v. *Smith*)

PRO-BUSINESS DECISIONS

Lochner v. *New York* (1905)—Held unconstitutional New York statute regulating length of working day in the baking industry. Relied on concept of "liberty of contract."

Adair v. *United States* (1908)—Voided legislation penalizing a business for firing a workman because he belonged to a labor union (narrow interpretation of interstate commerce).

Hammer v. *Dagenhart* (1918)—Congress may not forbid interstate commerce of products of mines or factories in which children are employed.

Bailey v. *Drexel Furniture Co.* (1922)—Invalidated tax placed on products of child labor.

Adkins v. *Children's Hospital* (1923)—Invalidated as a denial of due process the minimum wage law passed by Congress in 1918 for the District of Columbia.

Wolff Packing Co. v. *Industrial Court* (1923)—Narrowly defined businesses "affected with a public interest" thus limiting Congress's ability to regulate services and prices.

Schechter Poultry Corp. v. *United States* (1935)—Declared unconstitutional Congress's delegation of power to the President to regulate manufacturing as part of the National Industrial Recovery Act.

United States v. *Butler* (1936)—Declared Agricultural Adjustment Act unconstitutional because power to regulate agriculture was said to be reserved to the states ("dual federalism" doctrine).

Figure 11.6 The Supreme Court is involved in balancing conflicting interests according to basic rules set up in the Constitution and particular rulings found in precedent-setting cases. As the United States economy grew and enterprises no longer confined their impact to a local area or to a small number of employees, governments at both state and federal levels found it necessary to attempt large-scale regulation of the economy. Certainly, the Great Depression of the 1930s and the controversy surrounding much of President Roosevelt's New Deal legislation spurred the Supreme Court to take up many cases dealing with governmental regulation of the economy; but much judicial ground had already been laid in previous decades. The Supreme Court responsible for many of the decisions named above is shown at the right in a photograph taken in 1937.

critical eye at discrimination of various forms—especially in voting, housing, and schools—and in the *Brown* decision of 1954 the Court finally discarded the principle of separate but equal and came to the forefront of the struggle for racial equality. Thus, the power of judicial review was exercised for a long period of time in favor of racial discrimination; only in the last forty years has it been exercised in behalf of the elimination of racial discrimination.

Judicial Review and Civil Liberties

Similarly, in the area of civil liberties, judicial review has facilitated certain policies over others. Until the 1960s most states were not bound by the provisions of the Bill of Rights dealing with the administration of justice. The Supreme Court had held in 1833 that these provisions applied only to activities of the federal government, not to those of the states (*Barron* v. *Baltimore*). The passage of the Fourteenth Amendment in 1868 opened the door to the applications of the Bill of Rights to state as well as federal criminal proceedings (see Chapter 7). The protection of the Bill of Rights now extends to such issues as unreasonable search and seizure, the right to counsel and to trial by jury, the privilege against self-incrimination, and the prohibition of cruel and unusual punishments. Until the past thirty years, however, the Court refused to make most of these provisions applicable to states.

Under the leadership of Chief Justice Earl Warren, the Supreme Court in the 1960s effected the so-called "due process revolution," in which the Court ruled that nearly all the procedural protections of the Bill of Rights were applicable to states via the due process clause of the Fourteenth Amendment. The activities of state police officers and court officials—including the arrest of a suspect, procedures of interrogation and of introduction of evidence to the trial, as well as the rights of appeal by the defendant—were made the subject of court-developed rules dealing with the rights of criminal defendants. Again, the power of judicial review was invoked by the Supreme Court to attempt to shape an important aspect of public policy.

Judicial Review and Policy

In sum, judicial review has somewhat uncertain historical roots but has long been characteristic of the American political system. It has been used by courts both to oppose progressive legislation and to defend the rights of minorities in their attempts to enter the political system and to protect themselves from majority tyranny. Whether acting as forces of reaction or of progressivism, courts have used this power to become important participants in the process of public policy making. But such powers are not unlimited, and the role played by courts is shaped by and subject to a series of constraints imposed by their position vis-à-vis other political institutions.

The Limitations of Judicial Review

As already mentioned, the appellate process provides appellate courts with occasions for decision: Large numbers of disputes get into court, but only a few are pursued up the appellate ladder. Judges exercise a good deal of discretion about what cases they wish to hear, and the combination of the relative generality of many of the provisions of the Constitution and the power of judicial review gives them an opportunity to participate in public policy making in our society. But the power of the judiciary is far from unlimited. Several factors operate to constrain it: (1) the relative passivity of legal institutions and the requirement that cases be brought to court before the legal system can become involved; (2) the constraints that the role of judge places on members of the judiciary; (3) the potential reactions by other branches of government to judicial decisions, and (4) the relative "play" in the system, which permits a good deal of activity to intervene between judicial decisions and actual changes in behavior. All of these factors interact with the power of judicial review not only to limit the power of the legal system, but also to integrate judicial policies with those policies preferred by groups in the society at large and by other governmental institutions. Of course, there is not always a neat congruence between public opinion, the activities of executive and legislative institutions, and the decisions of the courts. Rather, the policy areas chosen for discussion in this book—those recurring areas of dispute and concern that define American politics—are never finally "decided." Instead, they continually evolve as a variety of answers are suggested by various institutions and segments of society. The court system is one source of answers, but the courts no more finally "decide" disputes over economic management, foreign affairs, civil rights, or civil liberties than do the laws passed by legislatures or the pronouncements of Presidents. Rather, they all interact to provide approximations of answers to current disputes in the society that suffice until they are modified by futher consideration.

Recruitment

An important factor influencing the decisions of legal institutions is the recruitment process. As already suggested, one influence on judicial decision making is the backgrounds of the persons appointed to the court bench. (Although we are dealing here with the recruitment of federal judges, many of the same characteristics affecting their recruitment are also relevant to the selection—either by appointment or election—of state and municipal judges.)

In the federal judicial system, judges are nominated by the President and must be confirmed by the Senate. The recruitment process is quite complex and involves a variety of participants: the President and his staff; the Attorney General and his assistants; the Senate and its Judiciary Committee; the American Bar Association's Committee on the Federal Judiciary; the senators from the state in which the proposed nominee resides; interest groups such as the NAACP, labor unions, the National Association of Manufacturers, the Chamber of Commerce; the potential nominees and their friends and political allies (Joel Grossman, 1965; David Danelski, 1964). A great deal of "politics" surrounds the choice of federal and state judges: lobbying in favor of various candidates; judgments about the kinds of decisions a person might make if appointed to the bench; campaign or other partisan debts owed or receivable; and considerations of the symbolic effects of judicial appointment (the notion of a Catholic, Jewish, black, or, soon, a woman's "seat" on the Supreme Court indicates the kind of symbolic patronage that exists in Supreme Court appointments).

Traditionally, nominees to federal judgeships (including Supreme Court nominees) come from backgrounds that involve prior political activity: The typical nominee has participated in public affairs before he ascends to the bench. Political activity is important for several reasons. First, an individual ordinarily comes to the attention of decision makers who choose judges by virtue of some form of political activity. Second, it is through such activities that individuals develop the personal relationships and dependencies that lead to appointment to the bench. The conclusion should not be made that most judicial appointments are "payoffs" to otherwise unqualified political hacks; rather, judicial offices are desirable positions in American society and are not given out cavalierly. They are typically given to men or women who have participated to some extent in the process of public life.

Such participation is important for another reason: It is by virtue of such activity that a person makes his or her posture toward public policy known. Because those involved in the appointment process—especially the President—are likely to want to appoint men or women whose philosophy of government is not radically different from their own, they tend to pick people who have made a record in some aspect of public affairs and hence whose behavior on the bench is in some measure predictable. President Nixon wanted to appoint judicial conservatives; he therefore nominated men whose records of public service indicated adherence to the kinds of values he desired. Clearly, such predictions are not 100 percent precise: Three of his four nominees voted to strike down state abortion laws, a policy Nixon did not support. However, participation in public life does provide a forum in which a person's philosophy of public affairs is likely to develop and be articulated, and hence such participation is useful to those who must select nominees.

A final aspect of the recruitment process—and of the importance of political activity by most nominees—is the link that recruitment provides between the bench and other institutions of government. Selection of men and women for the bench, because it involves the participation of other political institutions, serves as a means of integrating the judiciary with currents in the society at large.

Historically, the typical President has been able to appoint a Justice to the Supreme Court every two years; as a result, the President who serves two terms can typically appoint nearly half the Justices. The ongoing recruitment process not only ties the Supreme Court into the same broad currents of thought that are at work in the political system, but it also produces more direct ties. When shifting alliances produce a change in the party that controls the White House, those shifts are also likely to have an impact on the Court.

A recent example from the Nixon Administration makes the point. President Nixon was elected, in part, on a party platform that urged a shift in the course to be followed by the Supreme Court. Nixon had argued that the Warren Court had been extravagant in its interference with other branches of government and with the affairs of the states in its zeal to protect the rights of minority groups such as blacks, poor people, and criminal defendants. By 1973 the President had appointed four Justices to the Court. Although it is too soon to be certain about the directions the Court will take, there are strong indications that it is moving toward a more passive posture, toward more deference to other government institutions; it has already exhibited less willingness to intervene in the policy process than was characteristic of the Warren Court. Those who were sympathetic with the decisions of the Warren Court may be disappointed by this apparent shift in the course followed by the Supreme Court. But it is a prime example of the way in which the recruitment process ties the court to the broader political process and affects the kinds of decisions that emerge from the Court. As Robert Dahl has argued:

. . . the Supreme Court is inevitably part of the dominant national coalition. . . . [it] is not, however, simply an *agent* of the alliance. It is an essential part of the political leadership and possesses some bases of power on its own, the most important of which is the unique legitimacy attributed to its interpretations of the Constitution. (Dahl, 1958, p. 293)

In the short run there have been notable differences between the kinds of policies pursued by the Court

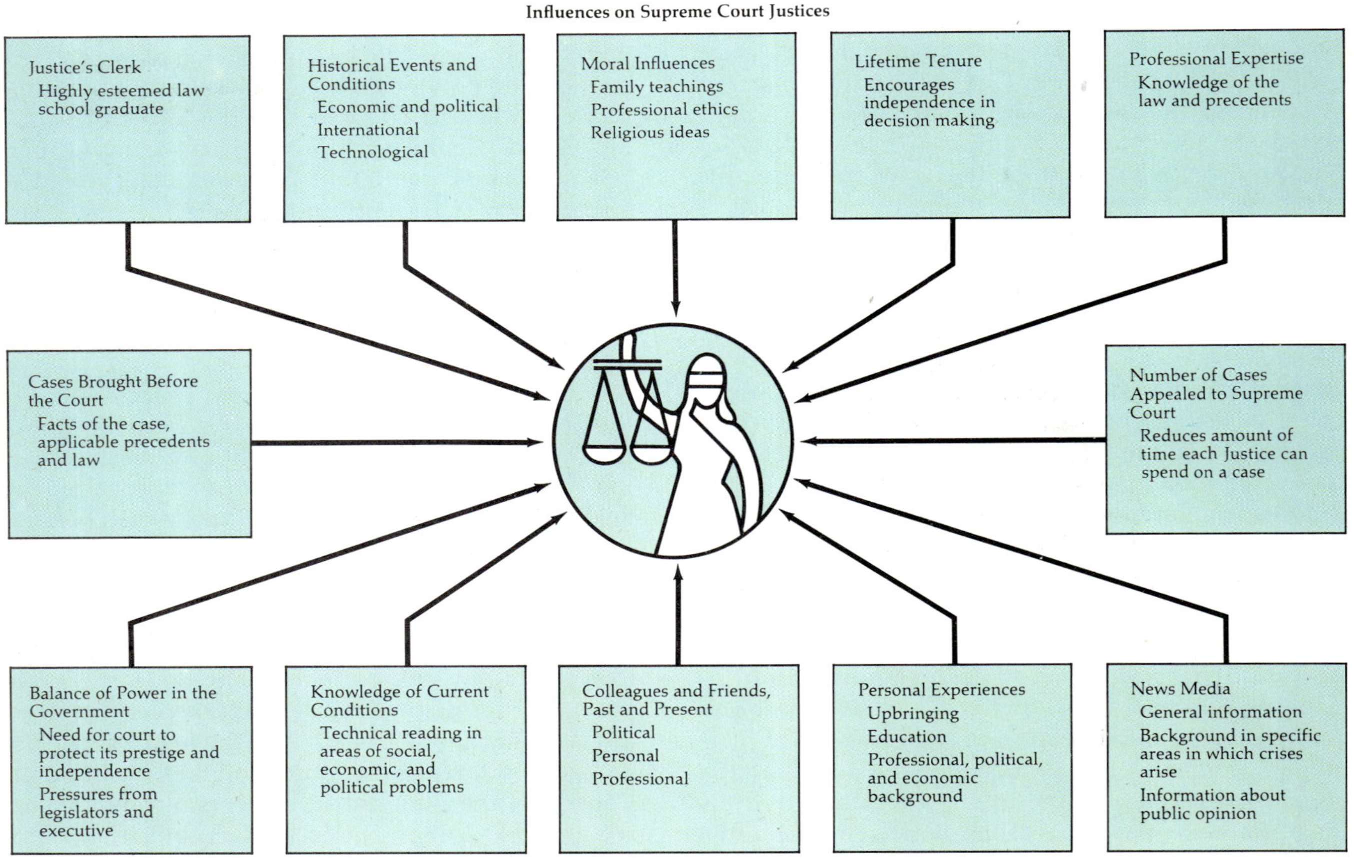

Influences on Supreme Court Justices

and those pursued by other branches of government—the laissez-faire Court of the 1930s and the Warren Court in the late 1960s are examples of such divergences. However, there are concurrent forces at work that tend to integrate the policies pursued by the various institutions of government.

Rules for Self-Restraint

Another factor that influences and restricts the exercise of judicial authority is a series of self-imposed rules for restraint. Our constitutional courts have developed a set of norms that are designed to restrict their entry into public policy making. For example, courts will consider only those cases in which the parties have *standing to sue;* that is, a party complaining about some government activity must demonstrate that he or she is actually being injured—losing money, property, or freedom—by the

activity. For a long period of time, the Court utilized the standing rule to avoid suits by taxpayers alleging that activities of government were unconstitutional. Accordingly, an individual could not sue to stop the federal government from engaging in an activity simply because tax dollars were being used in the effort—he had to show a more direct interest in the matter. The Warren Court relaxed the standing rule to some extent, permitting taxpayers' suits against certain government activities, including federal aid to education.

Another rule for self-restraint has involved the doctrine of *political questions*. The courts have held that certain types of issues were political rather than legal questions. For example, for a long period of time, the courts refused to hear suits dealing with malapportionment of state legislative and congressional districts, holding that the issue (whether a

Figure 11.7 (left) Because the Supreme Court is part of the political leadership of the country, it stands to reason that its members cannot divorce themselves from the political present or from the traditions of the nation. Like all other individuals, Supreme Court Justices are influenced by their personal backgrounds and by their moral and professional schooling. Like other political figures, they are conscious of the shifting sands of political power and of the currents of national and international events. What is special to judges is that there are very strong influences on their behavior that are structured by their professional role: namely, the expectations of fairness, the pressures of maintaining job tenure, the rules of procedure, and, most strongly, the impact of legal precedents laid down in previous court decisions.

Figure 11.8 The laissez-faire Court of the 1930s challenged the New Deal's regulation of industries by hitting the National Recovery Act (NRA) codes of fair competition. The action was one of several that led President Roosevelt to embark on his much-publicized court-packing scheme.

CRIMES WITHOUT VICTIMS

by Alexander Smith and Harriet Pollack

Few people would dispute that crime probably heads today's list of troubles besetting our urban population. City-dwellers are afraid of being mugged, robbed, raped, or murdered. In addition, they are disgusted: by the blatant soliciting from prostitutes; by gay bars; by seedy pornography shops; by openly sold heroin and marijuana; and by crooked cops. The response on the part of our law enforcement agencies has been to attempt better surveillance of high crime areas in order to protect people against assault and robbery, and to mount campaigns to clean up the downtown neighborhoods where pimps, female and male prostitutes, bookies, and pornographers all assemble.

Whatever the merits and feasibility of increased police patrols to handle street crime, there is at least no doubt that citizens need to be protected against thieves and murderers. There is a real question, however, whether campaigns against gamblers, prostitutes, and dope pushers are not actually counterproductive in terms of producing a decent, stable society.

Is there some relationship between the use of the criminal justice system to police our morals and its failure to protect our persons? Is how to handle prostitutes and pornographers the problem, or is it the larger question of whether morals offenses should be considered as crimes?

Conceptually, our penal code prohibits two kinds of acts: those that are malum in se *(evil in themselves) and those that are* malum prohibitum *(evil because prohibited). Malum in se acts (murder, rape, arson, assault) are true crimes in the sense that no society can tolerate such conduct and survive. But a large part of our penal code is concerned with acts that are not universally considered evil, but that we, for a variety of reasons, have labeled as sufficiently undesirable to be punished by the criminal justice system. In New York State, for example, gambling is prohibited by law, and the*

police, courts, and jails are expected to deal with numbers runners, bookies, and the like. At the same time, the state permits gambling at the race tracks and derives revenue from offtrack betting.

Our attitudes toward drug use are equally inconsistent: We forbid the use of marijuana and heroin; yet we tolerate the limited use of amphetamines and barbiturates, and we encourage, through ubiquitous advertising, the indiscriminate sale of pills for every conceivable purpose.

Hundreds of sections of the criminal law are concerned with acts that are criminal mainly because society at large says they are: homosexual activity between consenting adults, prostitution, gambling, possession of obscene and pornographic materials, to name a few. The enforcement of these laws takes a lion's share of our criminal justice resources. For every murderer arrested and prosecuted, literally dozens of gamblers, prostitutes, dope pushers, and derelicts crowd our courts' dockets. If we permitted the sale of heroin on a controlled prescription basis (as the British do, and as we do with other dangerous drugs), we would probably eliminate well over half of the cases going through our criminal courts. Myths to the contrary, there is no scientific evidence that the use of heroin, in or of itself, causes criminal conduct. By cutting off all legal access to heroin, however, we have driven the price so high that experienced observers estimate that more than half the crimes in New York City are committed by addicts seeking drugs or the money for drugs.

In short, the net effect of our drug laws is highly counterproductive in that they create more antisocial conduct than they prevent.

Morals laws that do not reflect contemporary mores or that cannot be enforced should be removed from the penal code through legislative action, because, at best, they undermine re-

spect for the law, and, at worst, as in the case of our drug laws, they make a tragic situation worse. Admittedly, such a deliberate legislative policy would fly in the face of all historical American experience.

The reasons are obvious: Any such attempt would lead to an outcry by small but militant minority groups who would convert a simple act of legislative housekeeping into a debate over morality. No legislator wants to be cast in the role of the defender of immorality, even in the case of a custom widely accepted and practiced by a good part of his constituency. It is much easier to ignore the issue.

Unfortunately, we can no longer afford the luxury of waiting for administrative action (or inaction) to catch up with public morality. Possibly because we live in an era that has seen great changes in public mores in a relatively short time, we have too many laws that the police are attempting to enforce and the courts to handle that large segments of the public simply will not obey.

There is something very frightening to most people in advocating repeal of morals laws. It is as though, by advocating repeal, the conduct that heretofore has been forbidden is being endorsed. Nothing could be further from the truth. In repealing morals laws, the legislature is not proposing that people become immoral; it is simply declaring that the criminal sanction will no longer be used to enforce a particular mode of conduct. Most human conduct, after all, is regulated by nonlegal institutions: the home, the school, the church, the family, the peer group. The unpalatable truth is that passing a law does not mean that it will be obeyed or that it can be enforced. Conversely, the repeal of a law does not necessarily mean an increase in undesirable conduct.

Not only are morals laws frequently counterproductive in terms of their causing more crime than they prevent, but their enforcement is particularly dangerous to civil liberties because crimes resulting from their violation have no victims. The prostitute's client has not been forcibly seduced; the housewife who bets a quarter on the numbers has not been robbed; the dope user has harmed only himself. Because there are no victims available to testify for the state, the burden of producing enough evidence for the prosecution rests entirely on the police. It is this need for evidence to make morals offense violations "stick" that traditionally has produced the greatest number of civil liberties violations by the police. Prostitutes, for example, are frequently victims of entrapment by plainclothesmen. If their customers will not testify, who besides the plainclothesmen can? And what better way of establishing a case than by offering an obviously willing girl a little "encouragement"?

Such violations of civil liberties occur not because the police prefer to act illegally, but because it is difficult to build a legitimate case where there is no real victim. In dealing with pimps, numbers runners, and dope pushers, police must make a case the best way they can, and frequently this involves illegal searching and arrests.

The enforcement of morals laws not only involves the police in violations of civil liberties but is the source of most of the corruption within police departments. The most common type of police corruption is the pay-offs policemen receive (and pass along to their superior officers) from criminals involved with drugs, gambling, or prostitution. This sort of graft is almost impossible to eradicate, partly because the illegal activities involved are so profitable and the pay-offs so lucrative, and partly because the activities themselves do not seem terribly immoral to the police, possibly because the crimes have no real victims.

Perhaps the most important benefit that would result from the elimination of morals offenses from the penal code would be the relief of the criminal justice system. No one knows how much time is spent by police, prosecutors, and courts in processing morals defendants, but it has been estimated that as little as 10 percent of the courtroom hours available in our criminal courts are now devoted to the processing of serious crimes. If we were free to devote the remaining 90 percent of our courtroom hours to the handling of dangerous offenders or serious crimes of property, we might be able to overcome most of the shortcomings of our present criminal justice system.

At the moment, proposals to repeal morals legislation are neither popular nor acceptable. Such proposals are attacked from both ends of the morality spectrum. On the one hand, guardians of public order are outraged at the prospect of "legalizing" gambling, drug sales, and sexual soliciting. On the other hand, many people are making a very good living out of dope peddling and gambling, and they are not likely to give up their livelihood without a struggle. What the ties of the underworld to elected and appointed officials are, no one really knows, but they exist, and organized crime is certainly capable of exerting pressure behind the scenes to discourage unfavorable legislation.

One can only hope that the uncommitted majority will come to realize the price we pay in corruption, the denial of civil liberties, and the overburdening of our criminal justice system for the luxury of using our penal code to enforce our behavior preferences. We need courage enough to admit that certain kinds of behavior cannot be controlled through the punitive sanction, and faith enough to believe that cultural pressure (or innate decency) will suffice to keep us from mass dissipation and self-destruction. And we need political leaders with guts enough to get up and say so.

particular legislator or congressman should be seated) was properly the function of the legislature rather than the courts (see the note on reapportionment in Chapter 2). The same political-questions doctrine has been used by the courts to avoid becoming involved in issues of foreign policy. As in the case of the rules dealing with *standing to sue,* these principles of self-restraint are flexible and have sometimes been used to avoid issues.

Similarly, when the Court desires to avoid a particular issue, it can simply refuse to hear cases. Although the Warren Court often made the decision to become actively involved in the political process, it did refuse to consider such "hot" political issues as the Vietnam War and school busing in the North. These self-imposed constraints serve to temper the intervention of the judiciary system—especially the Supreme Court—into certain policy areas. They are highly flexible and are invoked when members of the Court wish to avoid an issue; they are ignored when the Justices wish to get involved.

Legislative Reaction

In addition to changes in personnel via the appointment process and the use of self-imposed rules for self-restraint, more direct forms of resistance act as a brake on the power of the court to participate decisively in public policy making. One of these is the reaction of Congress—in the form of legislation or proposed constitutional amendment—to unpopular court decisions. Even when such attempts at overruling court decisions do not succeed in passing, they can provide important cues to the courts that they have gone too far and that they ought to reconsider carefully the policy they are pursuing.

Recall from Chapter 5, for example, that during the 1950s the anticommunist impulse in this country became very strong. As our erstwhile ally in World War II—the Soviet Union—became our enemy in the Cold War, many people in America became afraid of the possibility of "internal subversion," the destruction of our democratic institutions by the activities of highly ideological and clandestine Communist Party members and their "fellow travelers." Although the perspective of a later generation tends to make these fears seem highly exaggerated, there can be no doubt that they had real meaning for many Americans. Such fears produced a great deal of gov-

Figure 11.9 Justices are chosen for the Supreme Court because of their superior qualifications as well as for their social and political outlooks. Although some Justices may use the freedom afforded them by lifetime appointments to the high bench to make decisions that previously would not have been thought characteristic of them, it remains true that Presidents attempt to use their power of appointment to impose their stamp on the Court. The Supreme Court in 1973 reflects a series of presidential Administrations and points of view, going back to Roosevelt's New Deal: as this list shows (below), Republican Administrations have appointed the majority of the present Court's Justices.

SUPREME COURT, 1973

	Age	Appointed by	Date
Chief Justice:			
Warren E. Burger	65	Nixon	1969
Associate Justices:			
William O. Douglas	74	Roosevelt	1939
William J. Brennan, Jr.	67	Eisenhower	1956
Potter Stewart	58	Eisenhower	1958
Byron R. White	55	Kennedy	1962
Thurgood Marshall	65	Johnson	1967
Harry A. Blackmun	64	Nixon	1970
Lewis F. Powell, Jr.	65	Nixon	1972
William H. Rehnquist	48	Nixon	1972

ernmental activity designed to ward off the perceived communist "menace." Many of these activities—such as, prosecutions under laws that made it a crime to advocate the violent overthrow of the government; extensive activities by legislative investigating committees seeking out information about the associations of various individuals; extensive screening programs for government employees and those in "sensitive" industries designed to exclude those whose loyalty was suspect—involved very serious restrictions on the rights of speech and association protected by the First Amendment. The Supreme Court chose to uphold most of the governmental activity in the 1948–55 period. As some members of the Court pointed out, the extent of majority fear and the probable inability of Court decisions to stop the flood of repression played a role in the Court's rather deferential course of action. Justice Black said in 1951, dissenting from a Court decision that upheld the conviction of several Communist Party leaders for *conspiring to advocate* the violent overthrow of the government:

Public opinion being what it now is, few will protest the conviction of these Communist petitioners. There is hope, however, that in calmer times, when present pressures, passions and fears subside, this or some later Court will restore the First Amendment liberties to the high preferred place where they belong in a free society. (*Dennis* v. *United States*)

In 1957 and 1958, members of the Court (some of whom were new and somewhat more liberal than those they replaced) apparently came to feel that the "calmer times" longed for by Black had come. In a series of decisions, the Court imposed severe restraints on a variety of the loyalty-security programs. The legal issues involved in the cases were not greatly different from those that had come before, so that it seems plausible to assert that what had changed was both the personnel of the Court and their judgments about the political climate. Senator Joseph McCarthy, the most powerful leader of the anticommunist hysteria, had gone too far with his allegations—attacking even the United States Army— and had been censured by his Senate colleagues in 1954 for his intemperate remarks. The public at large seemed to have become weary of the constant search for communists and to have turned its atten-

tion to other matters. These factors seemed to indicate to the Court that the political climate had changed. However, the decisions of 1957–58 in fact produced a storm of controversy, especially in the Senate, indicating that the Court had probably misjudged the direction of the political winds.

The Court's decisions had introduced limits on the power of congressional committees to investigate communists, on the use of criminal sanctions against members of the Communist Party, and on the ability of government agencies to dismiss employees whose loyalty was suspect. In Congress and in the newspapers, opposition to these decisions (several of which came on a single day, referred to by opponents as "Red Monday") grew, and legislation was introduced to change them. In addition, there was talk of legislation designed to change the appellate jurisdiction of the Court. The Constitution specifies what kinds of cases are properly *begun* in the Supreme Court (called "original jurisdiction," and involving such things as suits between states) but leaves to Congress the power to determine what kinds of appeals the Court shall hear. Thus, potentially at least, Congress could pass legislation restricting the Court's ability to hear appeals of lower-court decisions dealing with such matters as loyalty and security. This power is a potent one indeed, and although the legislation did not pass Congress the message to the Court was unmistakable.

During the 1959–61 period, the Court returned to the area of loyalty and security and rendered a series of decisions that seemed to take back many of the restraints imposed in 1957 and 1958. Again, it is difficult to avoid the argument that what had changed was not the Constitution or the factual issues of the cases, but rather the willingness of the Court to intervene in this area. Thus, the congressional and public response provided a cue to some members of the Court that if they were to avoid a serious constitutional crisis, they might do well to ease up a bit in their rulings that dealt with the powers of the government to restrict liberty in the name of national security (Walter Murphy, 1962).

The Implementation Process
Noncompliance is the most powerful limitation on the power of the federal government to decisively make public policy. Local officials, school boards,

and bureaucracies in both the public and private spheres constantly assert their braking power on policy emanating from the courts as well as from Congress and the Presidency. In deciding cases, courts issue orders, some of which have widespread applicability; refusal to obey such orders is therefore an important check on the courts' ability to make effective policy. It has already been noted that local school districts, in the wake of the 1954–1955 *Brown* decisions regarding school desegregation, used a series of evasive schemes to thwart the Court's goal rather than comply with it (Jack Peltason, 1961).

Many other cases of noncompliance might also be cited. For example, in 1963 the Supreme Court held (in *School of Abington Township* v. *Schempp*) that the reading of the Bible as part of devotional services in public schools violated the First Amendment. Yet teachers continued to read the *Bible* as part of services held in the morning. Similarly, in 1966 the Court held (in the *Miranda* decision) that all police officers were required to give criminal suspects a series of warnings about their rights before engaging in interrogation and that statements obtained from suspects in the absence of the warnings would not be admissible in court. Nearly ten years later, however, some officers continue to interrogate suspects without giving the warnings, or to give the warnings in tones that imply they are meaningless (Michael Wald *et al.,* 1967).

Court decisions are not self-executing. In order for them to have meaning, they depend on the behavior of others. Some decisions are very narrow and require relatively simple changes in behavior: Let John Smith out of prison or give him a new trial. Other decisions such as those discussed previously in this section, require changes of behavior on the part of large numbers of people if they are to be translated into changes in public policy.

There is a tendency to react to the instances of non-compliance to Court decisions as though they were manifestations of something wrong in the system— if the school boards, teachers, and police officers were doing what they ought to do, they would obey the orders from their superiors. But it is also possible to view noncompliance as a defining characteristic of the American political system. As already suggested, the kinds of broad policy areas that define politics in this country are recurring issues, ones in which various individuals, groups, and institutions continue to be involved. The court system participates in the process by deciding cases, and in so doing it sometimes announces broad policies. These policies then reenter the arena of public affairs and are reacted to by other institutions and groups and by society at large. If the issue is one about which people in the society both care and have strong preferences—as is often the case in foreign affairs, economic policy, race relations, and civil liberties—then it is unreasonable to suppose that any policy-making institution can finally resolve the matter.

Noncompliance is thus a kind of safety valve that permits society to react to court decisions, to modify them, and to integrate them into the continuing process of decision making about public policy.

PATTERNS OF POLICY MAKING

In understanding the roots of the legal system's participation in policy making, it is useful to glance at the role the courts have played in two of the decision-making areas with which this book is concerned: the area of foreign affairs, in which the courts have largely chosen not to become involved, and the area of the courts and criminal justice, an aspect of civil liberties with which the courts have dealt frequently.

Foreign Affairs

Throughout our history, the courts have deferred to the President in the area of foreign affairs. Citing such factors as the necessity for a unified policy in dealings with other nations, the President's constitutional responsibility for diplomatic relationships, and his powers as Commander-in-Chief, the courts have given the President great latitude. As the Supreme Court held in a case in the 1930s:

Not only . . . is the Federal power over external affairs in origin and essential character different from that over internal affairs, but participation in the exercise of the power is significantly limited. In this vast external realm, with its important, complicated, delicate and manifold problems, the President alone has the power to speak or listen as representative of the nation. (*United States* v. *Curtiss-Wright*, 1936)

Although experience with the Vietnam War may make many wonder about the wisdom of the philosophy expressed by the Court, the remarks do underscore the traditional deference given the President in the field of foreign affairs.

As noted at the beginning of this chapter, the courts had several opportunities to intervene in the course of policy making that dealt with the Vietnam War. The suits questioned the constitutionality of the war in Vietnam and thereby raised an issue of "hot" political controversy. The President was obviously committed to his Vietnam policy, and judicial intervention would have provoked a dangerous power struggle between the executive and judicial branches. Given the limited power that the Court possesses, a decision against the war might have been practically impossible to enforce. Thus, Vietnam was an archetypal example of the policy pursued by the Court system in most areas of foreign affairs: The courts simply chose not to get involved.

Civil Liberties: A Due Process Revolution?

In no area has the judiciary system—especially the Supreme Court—attempted to play a more significant role in the development of public policy than in the administration of justice. In a series of decisions in the 1960s, the Court moved to introduce radical changes into the process by which criminal suspects are apprehended and guilt or innocence is determined. The Warren Court was responsible for what has been called the "due process revolution"— the introduction of a series of procedural protections into the process by which criminal justice is administered.

As noted in Chapter 7, the provisions of the Bill of Rights were long held by the Court to apply only to the activities of the federal government. Gradually, however, during the twentieth century, the Court began to hold that the protections of the Bill of Rights were incorporated into the *due process* clause of the Fourteenth Amendment and hence were applicable to the activities of state as well as federal officers. The bulk of this incorporation took place in the 1960s.

Due Process: The Philosophy

These procedural protections are representative of a particular philosophy of the criminal justice process: They stress the *adversary* nature of the system (the "contest" between the state and the defendant) and the restrictive rules for the contest (certain types of activities are not allowed, even though they might be useful in apprehending criminals). As a result, the American criminal justice system stresses the distinction between "factual" and "legal" guilt. Factual guilt deals with the question: Did the defendant commit the criminal act with which he is charged? Legal guilt asks the question: Can the state prove that the defendant committed the crime, given a series of constraints about the kinds of evidence that can be used against him and the kinds of procedures police officers and courts must follow? Thus, if the state cannot bear its burden of proof, the person who is factually guilty may not be legally guilty.

A brief example makes the point. John Smith may be stopped on the street by a police officer, searched, and found to possess some heroin. He is factually guilty of the crime of possession of heroin. Yet if the police officer's search is not permissible under the Fourth Amendment's prohibition of unreasonable search and seizure, the evidence against Smith may not be admitted in court. He may thus be found innocent of the charge.

In the criminal justice decisions of the 1960s, the Warren Court attempted to tighten up the requirements of legal guilt, placing constraints on the kinds of evidence that could be introduced and on the types of procedures followed in criminal courts. The Court was attempting to "judicialize" the system; that is, it sought to strengthen elements of the adversary system. Two basic concepts formed the touchstone of this trend. First, the Court held that defendants were entitled to *counsel*. They may be represented by attorneys when being interrogated by police; at line-ups; during preliminary hearings; at trial; and during the appeals process. Moreover, the Court held that at all of these stages of the judicial process a person who could not afford to hire an attorney was entitled to have one paid for or provided by the state. The Court reasoned that representation by an attorney was the best way to ensure that defendants were aware of and able to protect their rights.

The second basic principle of the due process decisions was the concept of *exclusion:* If the state's officers obtained evidence against a defendant by activities that violated his constitutional rights (such as evidence gained via a search of his person, his car, or his premises; or by questioning him), that evidence was to be excluded from the courts and could not be introduced against him. Exclusion has two purposes. First, it is designed to make sure that no defendant is convicted on the basis of evidence that has been illegally obtained. Second, it is a means of affecting the behavior of police in general; that is, if officers cannot *use* evidence obtained in illegal searches and seizures or interrogations, they will presumably be less likely to engage in such practices. Thus, exclusion is a means of inducing police officers to follow legal and constitutional principles, for they will not be "rewarded" (by a conviction) if they behave illegally.

There are a variety of justifications for the Warren Court's decisions beefing up due process rights. One deals with the very heart of the civil liberties doctrine—the need to protect the dignity and humanity of citizens. The Court argued that certain types of procedures simply did violence to the basic human rights that citizens ought to enjoy. Another justification deals with the need to reach the truth: In order to avoid mistakes, such as convicting an innocent man, certain procedures should be followed. Finally, some of the procedural protections—and the principle of exclusion—have been justified by the need to protect against too much intrusion by police in the lives of citizens. Random searches, dragnet arrests, and interrogations of suspects may be very useful tools in catching lawbreakers, but they are not justified in a society of limited government.

Thus, the Warren Court attempted to impose a large number of constraints on the activities of agents of the state in apprehending and convicting those accused of crime. The decisions, however, were not received sympathetically by either the legal actors involved or the public at large. This hostile reception reflects a basic ambivalence in our society. The substance of the criminal law and the establishment of institutions such as police departments, prosecutors, judges, and jails reflects a desire for *law enforcement,* for the efficient apprehension and punishment of those who break legal norms. Competing against the need for law enforcement, however, is the desire for due process, for restrictions on the powers of the state when it is engaged in law enforcement activities. To put it another way, the concern for law enforcement stresses the importance of factual guilt, whereas the concern for due process stresses the importance of legal guilt (Herbert Packer, 1968).

Many of the due process protections operate in a

counterfactual fashion; that is, they operate most obviously to the advantage of the guilty. Invocation of the exclusionary rule by throwing out an illegally obtained confession, for example, may result in a suspect's acquittal. There is no doubt that due process concerns do interfere—as police and prosecutors have complained—with efficient law enforcement. Many would argue that such interference is a price well worth paying for by a society in which the human rights and dignities of the citizen—guilty and innocent alike—are protected. But it is this dispute that underlies the tension between due process and law enforcement values.

Due Process and the 1960s

The criminal justice decisions of the Warren Court occurred during a decade of increasing social, racial, and generational polarization, a decade in which white, middle-class citizens were fleeing the cities, in part as a result of an allegedly dramatic increase in crime. Thus, the due process decisions emerged in a social and political climate in which large segments of the public were fearful of their safety and defensive about their values—in short, a period of deep public concern with effective law enforcement. Predictably, many people were not especially sympathetic to court decisions that seemed to make it more difficult to catch and convict criminals. Moreover, the Court's decisions were met with great hostility by police officers and prosecutors, hostility occasioned by a stronger attachment to the value of law enforcement than to due process.

Policemen are, by the nature of their job and the values that they learn as members of the police force, basically concerned with factual guilt. They not unnaturally see themselves as craftsmen, who desire to use the tools of their craft to catch criminals. The due process protections, therefore, are, for the policeman, not simply rules designed to protect the rights of *all* citizens; they are a set of working conditions that make the cop's job harder. Thus, in addition to an inclination to view law enforcement as more important than due process, police officers have been hostile to the due process decisions because they act as constraints on their job (Jerome Skolnick, 1967).

The Supreme Court pursued a policy of beefing up due process protections in a society in which the public was not very sympathetic and in which the individuals whose behavior was to be modified—police officers—were not inclined to obey unless forced to do so.

For a variety of reasons, the due process revolution did not by any means revolutionize the administration of justice. First, the effectiveness of the due process decisions was influenced by the attitude of many police officers. Many were not inclined to obey the decisions; as a result, compliance was far from complete. Second, the ambiguities in the rules themselves made enforcement difficult. For example, many of the procedural protections—such as those concerning search and seizure or interrogations—were somewhat uncertain. What constitutes a "reasonable" and hence legal search was not always clear.

A third factor that greatly influenced the effectiveness of the due process decisions was the sheer volume of the work load before the courts. Given the number of cases and the relatively limited number of judges, prosecutors, and defense lawyers, the courts would literally have collapsed under the weight of their own work if many more defendants had gone to trial instead of taking the much less time-consuming option of the guilty plea. (Called *plea-bargaining,* the practice enables the defendant to receive concessions from the prosecutor, such as a reduced sentence or probation, in return for his guilty plea. In making this trade, however, the defendant actually suppresses legal issues by failing to assert his legal rights.)

The final factor that served to limit the effects of the due process revolution was the general political environment. The 1960s were years of growing social and political fear, and the *law and order* issue was fertile ground for political debate. The notion that the Warren Court had gone too far in protecting criminals at the expense of the law-abiding had powerful popular appeal. In short, the policies pursued by the Court had interacted with the attitudes and beliefs of the population to make public policy toward criminal defendants an important issue in American politics.

The law and order theme was taken up in the 1968 presidential election. Richard Nixon was elected on a platform that in part called for changes in Supreme Court personnel. In his subsequent appointments to the Court Nixon selected Justices who were more sympathetic toward efficient law enforcement. By mid-1973 it had become evident that the Burger Court was going to be much less active in pursuing due process rights than the Warren Court had been and would be more deferent in permitting activities designed to promote efficient law enforcement. The filtering of decisions through the various prisms of politics had not only produced significant changes in the actions of police, prosecutors, defense lawyers, and judges, it had also produced a reaction in the society at large that had affected the composition, and thus the work, of the Court itself.

This discussion of the due process decisions points up the theme of this chapter as a whole: The legal system does make important contributions to the development of public policy. Surely the Warren Court decisions in the area of criminal justice had important impacts on the treatment of suspects and defendants. Yet court decisions are by no means decisive. Because they must be obeyed if they are to make a difference in the society, because the policies pursued by courts are the subject of consideration of others in the society who can influence the appointment of new judges, because decisions deal often with issues that members of the society care about deeply—for all of these reasons the courts can only *contribute* to the development of public policy. The American political system is one in which courts are called upon to decide issues that affect broad segments of the society. Yet the issues are ones that are of recurring interest—indeed, ones that define American politics. Thus, courts do not decide these issues, any more than do legislatures, bureaucracies, or Presidents. Rather, they contribute approximations of answers that enter into the broader political system, are tested out in the other arenas of politics, and are often modified. In this way courts, like other institutions, continually confront problems of public policy, problems that previous generations have "solved," but problems that are in constant need of readjustment.

SUMMARY

The courts play a distinct role in the formation of government policy. A dispute between members of society provides courts with the opportunity to make judgments that may broadly affect society. The appellate process results in much winnowing and broadening of the issues. Although the Supreme

Figure 11.10 Thurgood Marshall (left), the first black man on the Supreme Court, was appointed in 1967 by President Johnson. Having been active in much civil rights litigation as chief lawyer for the NAACP, Justice Marshall found it necessary to excuse himself in the determination of certain Court cases. Justice William O. Douglas (right), was elevated to the Court in 1939 by President Roosevelt. As one of the most liberal members of the high bench, Justice Douglas has been acclaimed for his outspoken position in defense of free speech and in criticism of executive branch interference with personal liberties. Although he has an electronic heart pacer, Justice Douglas travels throughout the world and is a strong advocate of strenuous outdoor living.

Court makes the resulting "important" decisions, lower courts translate these decisions into day-to-day litigation.

Judges' personal backgrounds and values affect their decisions, which in turn are the basis for their recruitment to the higher bench. Recruitment thus ties courts to the broader political process.

Judicial review is the source of the Supreme Court's participation in the policy process. This broad power is limited by: the requirement that the Court await the "occasion for decision"; constraints of the role of judge; potential reactions of other branches of government; the "play" in the system—court decisions are not self-executing—which permits modification and integration of decisions into the continuing process of decision making. There are self-imposed rules of judicial restraint that are used when members of the court wish to avoid a particular issue.

Economy policy—the Court enforced a laissez-faire economy until public opinion forced its reversal in the 1930s. Foreign affairs—the Court has tradi-tionally deferred to the President. Civil rights—the Court has promoted both racial segregation (*Plessy* v. *Ferguson*) and integration (the *Brown* decision). Civil liberties—the Warren Court's work in the area of criminal justice effected the "due process revolution."

SUGGESTED READINGS

Casper, Jonathan. *American Criminal Justice: The Defendant's Perspective*. Englewood Cliffs, N.J.: Prentice-Hall, 1972.

———— *The Politics of Civil Liberties.* New York: Harper & Row, 1972.

Dahl, Robert. "The Supreme Court as a National Policy-Maker," *Journal of Public Law*, 6 (1958), 279–295.

Lewis, Anthony. *Gideon's Trumpet*. New York: Random House, 1964.

McCloskey, Robert. *The American Supreme Court*. Chicago: University of Chicago Press, 1960.

Skolnick, Jerome. *Justice Without Trial*. New York: Wiley, 1967.

UNIT

IV

WHERE DO WE COME IN?

This unit involves the "democraticness" of the American political process: the nature of public opinion, the significance of elections, the organization and responsibleness of political parties, interest-group influence, the political roles of mass media and money, and the importance of political participation that occurs outside the formal political process. We cannot exactly assess the quality of American democracy, but we hope to provide the beginnings of an evaluation.

DEMOCRACY IN PERSPECTIVE

Supporters of democracy have traditionally emphasized that it was a form of government in which all could participate in ruling. Democracy presented itself as a method of governance that could avoid the excesses and the potential for abuse that are common to political orders ruled by a more restricted group.

In modern times, democrats have fought to widen the circle of those permitted to influence the political process. Throughout the seventeenth and eighteenth centuries, arguments had raged about the capacity and right of the "masses" to have a say in their governance. The American and French Revolutions changed the complexion of things by striking out decisively in the direction of popular government, yet matters remained essentially unresolved. The nineteenth and early twentieth centuries were filled with battles over the suffrage. In America, white male suffrage came rather early, but women waited until 1920 to gain the right to vote, and only in 1965 were many American blacks effectively provided with that right.

During the struggle over the suffrage, various religious, racial, property, and educational requirements were used to limit the vote of certain minorities, and frequently of the majority. In practice, fear of the majority meant fear of the decisions that might be made by the many who were relatively poor and uneducated.

The arguments against universal suffrage now appear more like defenses of privilege than genuine efforts to deal with the matter. Yet some of those same criticisms of democracy now haunt those concerned with the quality of the political process. For example, are the issues of modern politics too complicated for the ordinary person? Are leaders interested in informing rather than in manipulating the electorate? Can political parties act responsibly? Are the issues of war and peace ones that electorates of tens of millions can decide? Can the roles of money and media be constructively channeled in contemporary politics? What about the influences of private groups on the political process? How do they fit with democracy, and what about those groups that are not effectively represented? These are the sorts of issues we need to grapple with if we are to understand the problems of making democracy meaningful today.

THE PUBLIC AND DEMOCRATIC POLITICS

Does the ordinary person know or care enough about politics to make reasonably intelligent choices, to make democratic procedures mean-

The outer ring of our symbol (left) represents the people, who affect and are affected by the decisions government makes.

ingful? The answers are unclear. To begin, many Americans care little about politics, and they participate even less. Even in presidential elections, turnout is often 60 percent or less of the eligible citizens. As Chapter 12 points out, most Americans think first of other matters when asked about their deepest personal concerns. Most speak of their health or of their financial situation and see little connection between these matters and political issues.

Next, most Americans are socialized rather early to a trusting view of their political leaders. The image of a benevolent President is likely to produce an attitude of deference to elite decision-making. Most Americans also know little about the great issues of public policy; they frequently change their minds and spell out their political views with little depth or subtlety.

Yet the confusion, lack of depth, and disinterest of the electorate has its parallels at the elite level. Perhaps it is not just a reflection of citizen knowledge and sophistication about politics that many Americans know few of the details of policy. Perhaps more deeply, it reflects the forms of competition among political leaders. For example, do leaders genuinely attempt to educate the electorate through campaigns or are the attempts directed toward creating an "image"? The use of money and media (see Chapter 14) is bound to lead to cynicism about the "good intentions" of the American political elites. In the struggle for office, frequently some form of sloganeering triumphs over more honest and thorough discussions.

Even more basic, however, is the difficulty of comprehending the intricacies of the American party system. Our parties are not well-disciplined, mass-membership organizations. Rather, they are collections of state and local party organizations that may or may not hold common views on many matters. With such an arrangement, it is no wonder that many Americans are confused about where political responsibility lies.

But it remains clear that American parties do not attempt comprehensive political education and that most citizens find it difficult to tell the parties apart on many issues. This is not to deny, of course, that the parties are actually different in some important respects. They are, and most Americans know it. But the dividing lines are often hard to discover, even for a sophisticated observer.

PUBLIC AND PRIVATE POWER

The question of the relations between public policy and private organizations is also complicated. As Chapter 15 explores it, the public and private spheres overlap considerably. By virtue of their licensing functions, many private interests are deeply involved in the day-to-day processes of government. They lobby and otherwise represent their interests. They are a permanent part of government. But is this important? The answer seems to be "yes," for there is danger that a few policy makers (perhaps bureaucrats), together with private interests, could hold excessive influence over the shape of policy.

It would be neither possible nor desirable, of course, to rid public
life of the private influences of organizations such as unions, oil companies, major corporations, and religious groups. Yet the public significance of these organizations involves questions of the openness of
decision making, the diversity of political influences, the clarity of
public responsibility, as well as the fascinating question of the structures of rule within these organizations. Though we seek democratic
rule in our politics, we rarely insist on democratic procedures in
private organizations. After all, corporations are not run by the votes
of workers. Traditionally, democracy has meant political democracy,
but some have called for a broadened conception: democracy as social
democracy and as economic democracy, meaning democratization of
private organizations and some greater equality of living conditions
in society at large. Such possibilities raise considerable problems,
but they are an interesting area for potential democratic experimentation. Certainly the inner government of private organizations is of
public concern, for it is generally at work that most people spend
most of their lives.

POLITICS OUTSIDE THE FORMAL POWER STRUCTURES

In the early days of the civil rights movement, critics spoke of how
the unrest and agitation it stirred up were antithetical to that "domestic tranquility" essential to proper government. After all, wasn't
constant disruption a rather high price for a society to pay in order
to allow people to express grievances, when there were "normal"
political channels to employ? Howard Zinn responded to such critics
by arguing that although he too was concerned with domestic tranquility, the fact was that the "domestics" were not "tranquil" (in
specific reference to Rosa Parks, the "domestic" whose refusal to sit
at the back of the bus ignited the Montgomery bus boycott of 1956).
But he was referring more generally to the seething sense of oppression
among American blacks. Order on the surface does not necessarily
mean genuine tranquility in society, especially if some are afraid
to voice their discontent.

The experiences of the civil rights movement and of the later antiwar movement raised serious questions about the appropriateness
of protest. As Chapter 16 explores more fully, civil disobedience and
protest are usually weapons of the weak, and they are not adequate
substitutes for more stable, institutionalized forms of power. And
yet, what are the reasonable limits of disobedience? What about violent protest? Is disobedience catching and therefore especially dangerous? Is disobedience more justified on some matters than on others?

The use of civil disobedience made clear certain unpleasant realities
about the nature of power in American politics. Perhaps most essential, it showed that certain groups of citizens had been excluded from
full participation in the political process despite traditional American
principles of political equality. The *principles* were ones that most
Americans could readily accept. But integrated housing, greater

equality of incomes, and open admissions to universities were something else again.

With these kinds of goals, the civil rights movement ran into problems of strategy and tactics. Sitting-in at a lunch counter might be an effective way to combat segregated practices: the act of civil disobedience is closely connected to the object of the protest. But when demonstrators sat down on the Triborough Bridge in New York City to stop suburban commuters and force them to look at the ugliness of East Harlem, the protest seemed more an annoyance than a vivid method of confronting unacceptable realities. Likewise, whenever the grievances involved wide-ranging social problems, traditional sorts of civil disobedience were less effective. These grievances required well-organized and persistent political action.

The antiwar protests arose in part from a desire to "educate" the American public about what the protesters considered the realities of the Vietnam War and of the democraticness of the policy process—protest was thus a method of communication rather than an effort at coercion. The early teach-ins in 1965 were designed as educational devices, places where the war could be debated, as it had not been in Congress. These protesters pictured themselves as partly performing the tasks the political system should have, but had not, performed: debate, public education, the clarification of responsibility.

These issues are still with us in the 1970s, and they seem perpetual ones for modern democratic politics. Throughout the Vietnam debate, government representatives argued that the President was better informed than anyone else, and therefore the public, and even the Congress, simply had to defer to presidential judgment. For most people, most of the time, such an argument carried the day. But the sequence of obvious failures in Vietnam, plus the independent moral and political perspectives of a few protesters, finally led to some significant changes in public opinion about how good the judgments of the "experts" were. Vietnam demonstrated that the supposedly "best informed" could actually be insulated from unpleasant truths and thereby deceived about reality, that electoral promises are rather easily broken, and that governments often mislead their citizens and even their citizens' representatives. It thereby raised afresh the question of the right of the public to know about even the most delicate foreign policy matters: How are citizens to inform themselves? Does democracy mean much if it cannot extend to the crucial issues of war and peace? The case of the *Pentagon Papers,* discussed in Chapter 12, demonstrates these issues in an intriguing way.

One conclusion emerges rather forcefully from the protest movements: The role of the mass media is crucial in providing public information, and at its best, in educating on controversial issues. The significance of the media makes the issues of freedom of information and generally of the regulation and of the use of media, all the more important. Who should own them? What should they be required to do, if anything? The issue involves questions of civil liberties, of property, and of the way to make democratic discussion more meaningful in modern mass societies.

Civil disobedience presses us toward a clarification of the meaning and of the limits of contemporary democracy—difficult issues. Even if there is a legitimate place for civil disobedience, what about protests that go beyond it, to evasion or coercion. for example. What about the destroying of draft files to oppose the war, or the ghetto riots? Can such activities find some legitimacy, perhaps as outcries of those intense commitments or troubles that have no other channel, as gestures of the impotent? The conflict here is between law and justice, between a man's or a woman's personal conviction about what is right and his or her society's verdict. We cannot expect law to excuse riots or the destruction of government property. It is another question, however, what we the citizens decide is reasonable for us to do in a particular circumstance. The protests of the sixties reawakened many to these difficult questions.

OBSERVATIONS ON DEMOCRACY

American democracy, like all contemporary democracies, has serious flaws. Some are common to modern western societies: sheer bigness, problems of citizen education and communication, the irresponsibility of political leaders, excessive influence of money and prestige. Some flaws are rather uniquely American, especially the fragmentation of the party system, which makes voter decision making rather difficult, and the wide-open quality of political campaigning, which makes money and the media more important in the electoral process. The American political process, however, also has the virtues of these defects. Party fragmentation probably makes Congress more important and thereby preserves an important place for the legislature. The wide-open quality of campaigns means there is more room for individual enterprise and flair and for the influence of political movements. Although Americans have had much to protest and much to commit civil disobedience about recently, it is also notable that the seeds of republican virtue and courage are still there and ready to sprout.

To make democracy more meaningful in our day, we will have to pay special attention to the issues of political socialization, public education, and the powers of private governments. In a mass democracy with a huge electorate and complex public issues, the requirements for a decent political life involve more public enlightenment, freer individuals who can look more open-mindedly at political life, more intelligent limitations on the role of money in campaigns, and more effective public control of private power. Whether such issues emerge on the political agenda of the next decade or not, they are the issues most closely related to the nature of democratic life in American society.

end hunger in America.
I Have A Dream...
UAW SUPPORTS
AMERICA
Why Not NOW?
ABOLISH SLUMS & GHETTOS
I Have A DREAM OF AMERICA
UAW SUPPORTS COLLECTIVE BARGAINING RIGHTS
Jobs Or Income For ALL Americans

12
PUBLIC OPINION

Until the development of public opinion polls in the 1930s, American political leaders had no way of accurately gauging where the general public stood on any given issue or candidate. Elections offered some systematic insight into the minds of voters, but it still was usually impossible to sort out the effect any given issue had on the vote. Had most voters voted for candidate Smith because of his stand on issue A or on issue B, or had they voted for him despite his stands on these two issues?

Through public opinion polls, reliable data are now reported frequently on virtually all questions of current political interest—from public attitudes about Vietnam or Watergate to voter preferences among potential political candidates. But how much should the public's opinion count? To what extent should public officials be responsive to the wishes of the people?

DEMOCRATIC THEORY

Many observers have been skeptical of the intelligence and competence of the people to govern. Machiavelli, for instance, warned in his classic *The Prince* that "the masses of the people resemble a wild beast," and General William T. Sherman, hero of the Civil War, wrote his wife that "the voice of the people is the voice of humbug." Others, the democratic theorists, have argued that in a true democracy the will of the people should be paramount, that officeholders ought to base their decisions on what the people indicate they want. Thomas Jefferson, for instance, wrote, "I am not among those who fear the people," and many contemporary spokesmen reaffirm their faith in the wisdom and virtue of the people and demand "Power to the people."

How well is democratic theory borne out in America? The fundamental premise on which democratic theories have been based is twofold: First, the mass of citizens have both the capacity to participate wisely in politics and the will to do so; second, mass participation is necessary to preserve individual liberty. As will be shown, the first part of the premise does not seem to be evidenced in the United States— the majority of citizens neither care very much about politics, nor are they very well informed. As for the need for mass participation to preserve individual liberty, it is interesting to note that in the United States, liberty has best been preserved by the

Figure 12.1 Those who hold consistent political opinions or are active and informed about politics in the United States represent only a small percentage of the total population. Those who are active—those who march, speak, or who contribute campaign funds—are able, if well organized, to exert significant influence on officeholders. The rest of the population, although relatively inactive, tends to set the channels and boundaries beyond which public action becomes exceedingly difficult.

courts—the branch of government that is supposedly the least influenced by the popular will (see Chapter 11).

Some observers have claimed that the basic assumptions of democratic theory are not only unrealistic, they are undesirable. Suppose, they argue, that instead of the present apathetic and rather uninformed majority, American society was composed entirely of people who were highly and continuously interested in politics. Would such a society be tolerable? Bernard Berelson, for one, doubts it would be, because "the possibilities of compromise and of a gradual solution of problems might well be lessened to the point of danger" (Berelson, 1966). In order not to break down in endless bickering and political maneuvers, societies seem to require a fair amount of political disinterest.

An additional objection raised against traditional democratic theory is that modern society is so complex that it is impossible for the public to play a major role in policy making. There are so many significant policy issues to be dealt with at any given moment that few, if any, persons can be informed about them all. Furthermore, many of these issues are extremely complex and require special knowledge and training to be understood. The problem of deferring to experts, to people who are supposedly better informed than the average man and who are therefore better equipped to make decisions concerning public policy, is brought up in greater detail at the close of the chapter.

The dispute over how much public opinion should count can in large part be clarified by answering quite concrete questions about the nature of public opinion. To what extent is there public opinion on various political questions? What is the basis of that opinion? How do most Americans form their political outlooks? How do most Americans relate their political outlooks to current issues and events? Only after assessing these questions is it possible to discuss the appropriate role of public opinion in democratic politics.

IS THERE A PUBLIC OPINION?

Each week the press reports the results of public opinion polls. The polls state that 82 percent of Americans oppose busing, that 29 percent would not vote for a qualified woman running for President, and so on (Gallup, 1972). Although statistics are generally arrived at through highly sophisticated and accurate measuring techniques, they do not necessarily reflect public opinion. Why not?

The word "opinion" implies that a judgment has been made, that some thought has been given to a

Figure 12.2 Television Referendum (left). Why not let the people vote on everything? Let Congress propose and debate legislation and at the conclusion of publicized hearings and floor debates, let the people (those identified as eighteen years and older) ballot in a national referendum. Do the people not know enough? Perhaps the impact of actual decision-participation will stimulate a desire to learn. Are the problems too complex? Let Congress narrow the questions and each person be free to decide whether to participate or not. A crackpot suggestion or a possibility of direct democracy using new electronic media? What should be the role of public opinion in the legislative process?

Figure 12.3 Most Americans are not interested in politics, seeing little connection between politics and the details of their daily lives. As in the artist's interpretation, Americans tend to view politics through the wrong end of the telescope (right). They view government as if it were at a great distance from them, when, in fact, acts of government influence almost every detail of their lives, from their right to privacy to the sales tax they pay on cigarettes and beer.

question and an answer arrived at. It is possible, however, that many people will respond to a political question even though they may know nothing or next-to-nothing about it. It is therefore necessary to find evidence that the responses the majority of people give to a poll question reflect both understanding and interest before the pollsters claim that the results reflect public *opinion.*

Public Political Awareness

Do the average voter's stated preferences on political questions reflect opinions based on some understanding, or are they based on ignorance? Just what does the public know? Consider the following brief quiz on American government. Each of the questions has been asked of a nationwide sample of voting-age Americans (Gallup, 1972). Below each question is the percentage of the population able to answer correctly. The year the question was asked is in parentheses.

1. What are the three branches of the federal government called?
   19% correct (1954)
2. What is meant by the term "electoral college"?
   32% correct (1960)
3. Can you recall the names of your state's senators?
   28% correct (1967)
4. Can you tell me the name of your congressman?
   53% correct (1970)
5. Do you happen to know when he [your congressman] comes up for election next?
   30% correct (1965)
6. Is he [your congressman] a Democrat or a Republican?
   59% correct (1965)
7. Do you know how he [your congressman] voted on any major bills this year?
   19% said yes, but there was no check on correctness (1965)

People who do not know the names of their senators and representatives, when they come up for reelection, or where they stand on any current legislation cannot be called politically informed. Indeed, as is discussed later in this chapter and again in Chapter 14, great masses of voters do not even know the names of presidential candidates or the current Vice-President and have never heard of political issues that are major news stories. It cannot be denied: Only a minority of American voters know even elementary facts about their government.

Public Political Interest

A major reason why people are so uninformed on political matters is that they are so uninterested.

When asked in a 1968 study how interested they were in politics, campaigns, or government, less than a third of voting-age Americans polled expressed any substantial amount of interest (John Robinson, Jerrold Rusk, and Kendra Head, 1968). Interestingly, American political disinterest closely parallels political disinterest in other democratic nations—the overwhelming majority of citizens in Great Britain, West Germany, Mexico, and Italy also say they do not regularly follow the accounts of their government's political activities and governmental affairs (Gabriel Almond and Sidney Verba, 1963).

This low interest in politics seems to result from the fact that the majority of people see little connection between politics and the things that immediately concern them—their families, their health, their jobs, and their personal property (Albert Cantril and Charles Roll, 1971). But when Americans do perceive politics as relevant to their personal lives, they take considerable interest.

Numerous examples of the inattentiveness of the public could be cited. The 1969 Senate fight against the proposed antiballistic missile, for instance, characterizes typical public opinion. Despite daily speeches and extensive press coverage of the matter, just one week prior to the Senate vote only 69 percent of the polled voters claimed to have heard or read anything about the issue, and 28 percent of these "informed" voters were "undecided" on the issue. Only 41 percent of the people asked were both informed and had an opinion (Gallup, 1972). In such instances, what does it mean to listen to the voice of the people? Should one listen only to those with opinions, or should one listen to the mass of expressed views, including all those based on impulse and ignorance? Or should elected representatives try to determine what is in the best interest of the nation and ignore all public sentiments?

The views of the electorate cannot be entirely ignored. For one thing, the minority of voters who are informed and concerned must seriously be taken into account, if for no other reason than the fact that such people are much more likely to vote in the next election than are uninformed voters (Angus Campbell, Philip Converse, Warren Miller, and Donald Stokes, 1960). As will be seen, informed and concerned voters are also more likely to contribute time and money to election campaigns. Furthermore, even the general public does not remain uninterested and uninformed on all issues. When political actions exceed the broad limits the majority imposes on policy, the usually apathetic majority can be stirred to considerable concern. Busing proved to be such an issue, the Watergate affair, another. (Within days of the

Figure 12.4 Frequently, the only symbolic link that children have to public power is the figure of the President. Party labels and emotions related to the personality of the President are communicated to children by their parents; these communicated attitudes continue to provide the basis for children's predominant political perceptions throughout grade school.

first major disclosures that White House staff members might have been involved in the Watergate scandal, for instance, nearly all Americans had heard of the affair, and most expressed considerable concern [Gallup, 1973]).

In sum, the role that public opinion plays in politics takes two primary forms: A concerned minority tends to exert influence on officeholders on most major issues, and the majority creates something akin to a system of dikes within which political actions must be channelled (V. O. Key, 1961). To further understand public opinion and how it affects the political process, it is helpful to understand how public opinion is formed. How do most people develop their political consciousness? How does an individual become a Democrat or a Republican, interested or apathetic?

POLITICAL SOCIALIZATION

Social scientists use the word *socialization* to refer to the process by which infants are transformed into competent members of society. The term literally means "to make social," and it reflects the fact that human offspring must learn how to be humans through interaction with other people. It is only through socialization that people learn the myriad things they need to know to operate in society. (Obviously when people say they were born Republicans, they really mean they were raised as Republicans.) How early and how much do children learn about politics, how lasting is what they learn, and from whom do they learn it?

Children's Politics

"Young Democrats" and "Young Republicans" are often very young indeed. According to a study by Robert Hess and Judith Torney, 66 percent of second graders know the meaning of Republican and Democrat, and 36 percent of them have chosen one of the labels as their own. By the fifth grade 91 percent of school children know the meaning of these party labels, and 55 percent have adopted a party identification. Furthermore, 80 percent know what party the President belongs to and typically are happy to see their party win elections (Hess and Torney, 1967). The political awareness of grade-school children seems to be limited mainly to party labels and the office of the President, however. Only later do children begin to develop a conception of government that extends beyond the Presidency and allows for conflicts and complexities.

For the young child, government is what David Sears calls a "benevolent monolith"—trustworthy and above criticism (Sears, 1969). According to a 1968

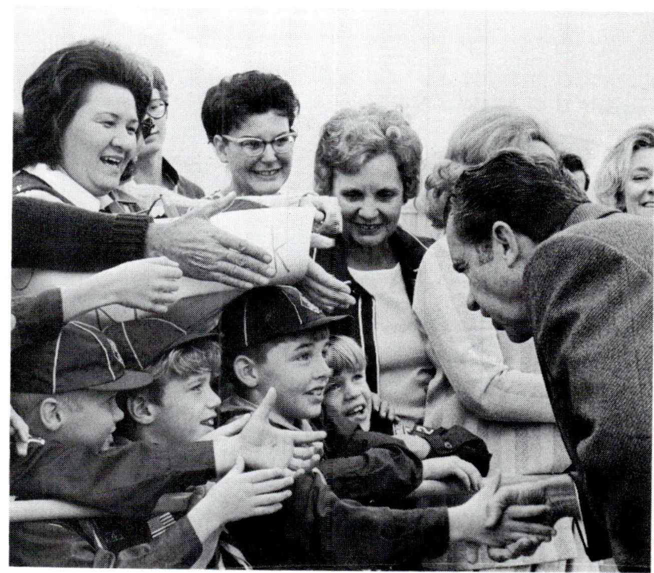

Figure 12.5 A group of impressed Scouts meet President Nixon. Surely the memories of this meeting will stay with these boys into adulthood, even though their perceptions of him and his role will change appreciably.

study, 80 percent of grade-school students agree that "government usually knows what is best for the people." Similarly, 72 percent of fourth graders believe the President rarely or almost never makes mistakes. With greater age comes greater realism: Only 51 percent of the eighth graders that were tested agreed the President rarely makes mistakes (David Easton and Jack Dennis, 1968).

Studies have identified the years from seventh to ninth grade as the critical period when children's political perceptions become adultlike. This maturation of political views represents a shift from conceiving of government simply as some "good people" to understanding the role of government in society—indeed, it represents a growing ability to grasp abstractions, such as government, community, and society. Such abstract concepts are beyond the grasp of most fifth graders; instead, they understand such things in purely personal, not social terms. For example, 70 percent of fifth graders who were asked about vaccinations revealed that they thought of them only as a way to avoid personal illness. Virtually all students in the ninth grade, however, were familiar with the community-health aspect of vaccinations (Joseph Adelson and Robert O'Neil, 1966).

By the end of the eighth grade, students' attitudes on political issues closely approximate those of their parents. The average American eighth grader is equipped with a party identification (usually inherited from his parents), some sense of civic duty, and a fair portion of positive feelings about government. He is, in short, little different from the average American adult.

The claim that young people are very much like adults politically was aptly demonstrated in the 1972 presidential election. Many Nixon supporters feared that because the voting age had been lowered to include eighteen-year-olds, the larger number of young voters would adversely affect their candidate's chances—they automatically assumed that all young people are more liberal than older people. Their fears turned out to have been groundless—young people were not very different in their party choices than were older people. Although Nixon did not run quite as strong a race among eighteen- to twenty-year-olds as he did among older persons, he nevertheless was the majority choice of voters from all age levels.

Family Politics

A major reason young people resemble older people politically is that the family plays a major role in establishing an individual's political choices. Although many people do shift away from their par-

ents' party preferences, most do not. M. Kent Jennings and Richard Niemi found that 60 percent of the high-school seniors they questioned claimed the same party affiliation as their parents. Furthermore, only 7 percent claimed to be affiliated with the party opposite to that of their parents. The rest claimed to be independents (Jennings and Niemi, 1968).

When it comes to positions on specific political issues, however, the correspondence between the views of parents and children is much smaller. One possible reason for this decrease in correspondence is that, as mentioned in Chapter 1, the majority of adult Americans are quite inconsistent in their political views. Such inconsistency would necessarily reduce the degree of correspondence that could be found at any given moment between parents and their children.

It is also highly probable that the differences found between the politics of parents and children are more a reflection of the parents' disinterest in politics than they are of anything else. Only 71 percent of the seniors in Jennings and Niemi's study could correctly name or guess the actual party affiliation of their parents, a percentage that is only slightly higher than the proportion who shared their parents' party affiliation. (In contrast, virtually all young people know their parent's religious affiliation, and

74 percent of those in Jennings and Niemi's study claimed the same religious membership as their parents.) The three out of ten students who did not know what party their parents supported clearly must have come from homes in which political discussion was virtually nonexistent. Considering the extent of political disinterest and ignorance, it should hardly be surprising that this is the case. Much of the apparent slippage in political attitudes between parents and children, therefore, probably reflects a lack of parental political attitudes as much as it reflects disagreement between parents and their children.

Schools and Politics

Many parents and various political interest groups have expressed considerable concern about what the schools might be doing to the political outlooks of students. Are the children being inculcated with "alien ideologies"? Are they being taught to be antipatriotic? If the answers to these questions were yes, one would expect young people as a whole to be quite different politically from older generations—which is not the case. Furthermore, students do not perceive schools and teachers as having much impact on their politics. In fact, only 2 percent of students tested even mentioned their teachers as a

Figure 12.6 Changing Images of the President. As the child matures, the naïve, worshipful image he or she has of authority figures, especially of such a figure as the President of the United States, tends to become more realistic. Criticisms of the President by friends and adults engender adolescent doubts, while taxes, the experience of political campaigns in which incumbents are criticized, and the growing firmness of personal attitudes whittle the presidential image down to size for the adult.

Figure 12.7 Although politics is not a topic of primary interest to most people, government does indeed influence the life of every citizen. As you go through the coming week, consider the number of activities in which you engage that are assisted, limited, permitted, or regulated by some law, agency, government fund, or government policy. Begin by working on this test (right), then relate it to your own surroundings by adding specifics or new categories.

<table>
<tr><td>Government on the College Campus Test*</td></tr>
<tr><td>

To what extent does the government participate in and influence the following:

1. The general financial support of your college

2. Individual financial resources needed for education

3. Interpersonal relations
    a. Sororities and fraternities
    b. Sexual relations

4. Availability of courses and selection of reading materials

5. On-campus speakers

6. On-campus politics

7. Off-campus politics

8. Collegiate sports

9. Health facilities

*See next page for answers

</td></tr>
</table>

source of influence on their choice of political candidates (Jennings and Niemi, 1968).

What the schools teach is not politics, but civics and citizenship. Students are taught the names of the three branches of government, how long senators serve, and how old a person must be to become President. They are only rarely exposed to arguments about political values or policies. Teachers claim to give considerable attention to citizenship—65 percent of second-grade teachers say they give as much coverage to citizenship as to reading and arithmetic. Because the subject of citizenship is treated in quite nonpartisan terms, however, it is unlikely to influence the partisan political views of students, which is undoubtedly as most parents would wish (Harmon Zeigler and Wayne Peak, 1970).

Unfortunately, the information most children learn about government does not stay with them. Although young people did somewhat better than average on the Gallup questions on government reported earlier in this chapter, there were no significant differences among the performances of people twenty-five years old and up—they all did poorly. Thus, only a few years after leaving school, most people have forgotten what the electoral college is ("Isn't that a school over in Kansas," one person guessed) and how often congressional elections are held. As for the duties of the good citizen, nearly half of the adult population does not bother to vote in presidential elections, and in state and local elections the turnout is much lower.

College and Politics

More than half of high-school graduates now enter college. Thus, if college has a significant impact on political socialization, its effects are potentially

---

Government on the College Campus Answers

1. The government supplies grants for academic research (some percentage of which goes for school administration); grants for educational experimentation; grants for new buildings, library and laboratory supplies; and total government support for state colleges and universities.

2. The government provides scholarships, guaranteed loans, subsidized housing, benefits to veterans and the handicapped, and work-study programs.

3. a. Sororities and fraternities must abide by laws concerning discrimination and hazing; their residences must also conform to the health and building codes of the local government.
   b. Supreme Court, state, and local government decisions determine availability of birth control devices, abortions, and sexual and marriage counseling.

4. Constitutionally determined civil liberties (as interpreted by the courts) protect the rights of the educational institutions to allow the presentation of all sides of controversial issues.

5. Constitutional rights balanced against powers of college administrators and governing boards (appointed by political officials or elected) determine breadth of institution's policy on campus speakers.

6. Constitutionally protected civil rights require equal treatment and protection for all nonviolent campus groups.

7. The Constitution protects students and faculty from school punishment because of political beliefs or off-campus legal activities.

8. Financing and conduct of collegiate sports are regulated by legal codes, which protect amateur status and delineate the standards of financing of collegiate sports.

9. Governmental health regulations govern food and housing quality; government financing provides medical clinics in state institutions.

widespread. Throughout the 1960s it was commonplace to hear charges that colleges were hotbeds of radicalism, and, indeed, young radicals were quick to agree with this assessment. But the question remains: Were the radicals in college during the late 1960s actually few in number but very visible and active, or were many young people actually being radicalized by the college experience?

Comparing the political outlook of lower- and upper-division college students gives the misleading impression that students do become more liberal the longer they are on campus. In a 1971 Gallup survey, for instance, only 28 percent of freshmen identified themselves as being politically on the left, whereas 40 percent of seniors did so (Gallup, 1972). It is inappropriate to conclude from these statistics, however, that the differences result from the amount of time that has been spent in college—there are many other factors that must be taken into account. For instance, the majority of freshmen and sophomores in America are in junior colleges, and the majority of upper classmen are in universities. In that university students tend to be more liberal than junior-college students, some of the difference found between classes is not the result of students changing their political outlook (Peter Rose, 1963). Furthermore, a great many students who begin college do not finish, and those who drop out are typically less liberal than those who stay in. This factor also would cause an increase in the proportion of liberal students in the upper classes (Travis Hirschi and Joseph Zelan, 1973).

When it comes to specific political issues, it is even harder to find signs that college has a liberalizing effect. For one thing, on virtually no issues, except the legalization of marijuana, are college-age people

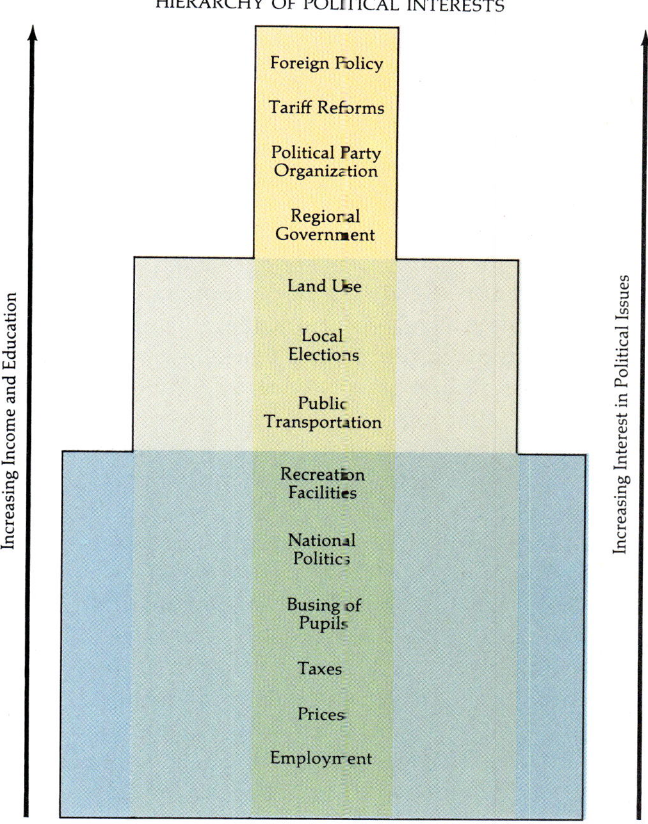

Figure 12.8 As income and level of education increase, so do political interest, knowledge, and involvement. Although it is difficult to predict precisely what the concerns of a person in any particular socioeconomic stratum may be, it can safely be predicted that the higher a person's education and income level, the greater the chance he or she will be concerned with foreign policy. It is also true that far more people are aware of and interested in presidential elections than in local elections, probably because the former achieve much more intense media coverage. These differences are illustrated in the above chart. People of the highest income and education brackets (the tall, narrow box) tend to be interested in the entire spectrum of political issues, from employment concerns to tariff reforms and foreign policy. As one moves down the income and education scale, however, the range of interests and involvement tends to decrease, as is illustrated by the two shorter boxes.

more liberal than older people. Indeed, despite all the mass protests on campuses, studies repeatedly found that younger people were *more hawkish* on Vietnam than were older people (see Table 12.1).

Table 12.1 Attitudes Regarding Vietnam War According to Age, 1968

AGE	SUPPORT FOR STRONGER STAND	SUPPORT FOR IMMEDIATE WITHDRAWAL
28 and younger	43%	16%
29–38	31	18
39–48	36	16
49–58	35	19
59–68	29	30
69 and older	21	21

Source: Adapted from William H. Flanigan, *Political Behavior of the American Electorate.* 2nd ed. (Boston: Allyn & Bacon, 1972), page 92.

As it turns out, the largest political gap among Americans exists not between the old and the young, but between young people in college and those not in college. A study by CBS in 1969 found that only 48 percent of college students were political moderates or conservatives on a variety of issues, whereas 71 percent of their peers who had gone to work instead of college were moderates or conservatives (Seymour Lipset, 1971). Similarly, a survey by *Fortune* magazine in January 1969 found that college students were in much closer agreement with leading corporation executives in their opposition to the war than they were with noncollege young people. The study showed that young workers tend to retain simple conceptions of "my country right or wrong," and college students and the chief executives of the largest corporations do not.

The difference between college students and non-students is aptly reflected in the differences between the young people who supported Senator Eugene McCarthy and those who supported Governor George Wallace during the 1968 presidential campaign. Both the liberal McCarthy and conservative Wallace attracted considerable support from young people in the North. McCarthy's support came largely from college students. Wallace's strongest northern support, however, came from noncollege young people who were "appalled by the collapse of patriotism and respect for the law" they perceived

in the nation (Philip Converse, Warren Miller, Jerrold Rusk, Arthur Wolfe, 1969).

But is it college that makes students different from their working peers? To date, there is no clear evidence that it is. In a study published in 1973, Peter Rose reported that he found no meaningful patterns of political attitude changes among college students over time. But he did find that differences between students at different colleges stemmed from differences already present among entering freshmen (Rose, 1963). For complex and barely understood reasons, the majority of persons who attend college tend to be more liberal than those who do not. In short, like grade school and high school, college seems to be a place to which young people *bring* political views, not a place where they find them.

Media and Politics

So far, the relative effects that family and school have on an individual's political outlook have been discussed. The mass media—television, radio, newspapers, and magazines—are a third potentially important factor in political socialization.

Obviously, politicians and parties use the mass media—especially television—to attract public support and to influence public opinion. Because of various limitations, however, such attempts at swaying the public are not as easy as politicians might wish. First, the doctrine of equal time—if one candidate gets free time on TV his opponents must receive equal free time—and the attempts of newscasters to be nonpartisan mean that viewers are about equally exposed to competing messages. Another limitation to any partisan influence the mass media might have on the political commitments of viewers is the general public's widespread lack of interest in politics and government. It is a rare occasion, for instance, when the nightly network news specials and interview shows, such as "Meet The Press," are watched by even a small proportion of the public.

Another barrier to mass media impact on voters is selective perception—the partisan loyalties of a great many Americans seem to cause them to misperceive where candidates stand on issues. Large numbers of voters consistently report erroneously that candidates they support hold views similar to their own, and they exaggerate their disagreement with candidates they oppose (Bernard Berelson,

OFFICIAL SOURCES OF GOVERNMENT DECISIONS

To find out what the federal government is doing it is first necessary to get exact information. One can read newspapers or watch television, but these sources do not usually give in-depth or precise information. What follows is a list of publications devoted to the activities of the various branches of the federal government.

The text of any statute enacted by Congress is published in the United States Statutes at Large. Statutes are grouped under the headings of public and private law. The text of legislation currently in force on a given topic is more readily found in the United States Code, which is officially revised every six years. There are also commercial publications, the United States Code Annotated and the Federal Code Annotated, which provide additional information, such as notes on court interpretation of statutes.

The Federal Register, issued five days per week, contains the executive orders, rules, proclamations, and regulations issued by the President or by any other executive department, agency, or independent regulatory commission. These are published together in the Code of Federal Regulations and the Public Papers of the President.

Decisions of the Supreme Court are published in volumes known as the United States Reports. Cases are referred to by volume and page number, such as Ginzburg v. United States, 383 U.S. (1966). Lower federal court decisions are available in the Federal Supplement and in the Federal Reporter.

The activities of Congress include more than the enaction of statutes; committee hearings and reports are often of great significance, as are the reports of administrative agencies. These are all indexed in the Monthly Catalog of United States Government Publications. This source book is generally available in reference libraries (Robert Salisbury, 1973).

Paul Lazarsfeld, and William McPhee, 1954). Thus, researchers have found dedicated union members who speak glowingly of the pro-labor record of their party's candidate for governor despite the fact that the candidate has made hostile statements about unions.

Pointing out these limitations is not to argue that the mass media have no impact on political commitments; it is simply to say that the effect of the media is not known to be dramatic. As is taken up in Chapter 14, perhaps the primary impact the media have on public opinion is that they increase the proportion of voters who know who is running for office, and they give voters a chance to observe candidates close up. Although such exposure may greatly influence people's reactions to particular candidates, it is not clear that it has any significant influence on people's party affiliations or their general political outlook. Conceivably, the mass media could be used to greatly influence political choices; to date, however, no one seems to have any clear idea of how to go about doing it.

IDEOLOGY AND PUBLIC OPINION

Chapter 1 outlines the major elements in the American ideology. It argues that the American ideology is not highly codified and consistent but is best compared to a patchwork quilt of very general political ideals that do not easily lend themselves to resolving concrete political questions. The chapter further points out that although it is useful to speak of an American ideology in general, the majority of Americans do not necessarily have an organized political ideology; instead, the political views of many—perhaps most—Americans consist of a hodgepodge of attitudes. To what extent, then, *do* Americans possess reasonably coherent and consistent political views?

In Search of Liberals and Conservatives

Virtually all informed discussions of politics utilize the concept of a left-to-right political spectrum. Ideas, parties, candidates, and philosophies are ordered on a scale ranging from liberal and radical on the left, to moderate in the center, to conservative and reactionary on the right. Although this conception of political positions can serve as a useful tool in analyzing politics, it rests on two basic assumptions: First, political opinions, parties, and candidates form some coherent unity (Republicans will tend toward conservative programs, and Democrats toward liberal programs); and second, there is a common element in political views that remains consistent across a wide selection of issues and proposals. Few political scientists seriously doubt these

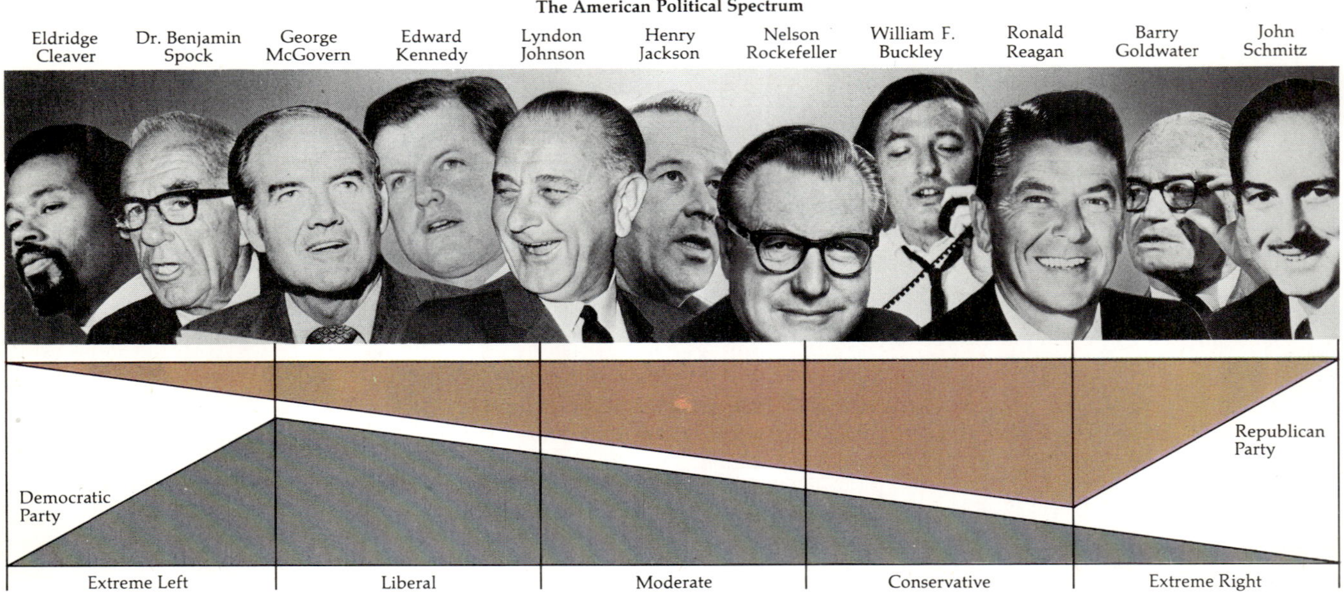

assumptions—such common elements are easy to observe. The question is, however, to what extent does this left-to-right spectrum operate in the perceptions of the average voter? More importantly, are the political opinions of the average voter sufficiently coherent to be assigned a place on the spectrum?

Although about two-thirds of American adults who were polled in 1968 were willing to describe themselves as liberals or conservatives (John Robinson, Jerrold Rusk, and Kendra Head, 1968), only rarely can a majority of voters actually distinguish between liberal and conservative positions on specific political issues. In a 1971 poll, for instance, 51 percent of the respondents correctly replied that "increasing federal programs to help the poor" was a liberal position, 19 percent identified it as a conservative position, and the rest said they did not know. On less obvious items, the proportion of errors and "don't knows" increased: 44 percent correctly identified the "abolition of welfare and making people who collect it go to work" as a conservative position, whereas 20 percent thought it was a liberal position (Louis Harris, 1971).

Similar failures by the majority to correctly identify liberal and conservative positions were found on items concerning student protest, law and order, Vietnam, tax breaks for corporations, and unions.

Persistently, one-fifth or more guessed incorrectly (and how many were correct by guessing?), and nearly a third simply admitted they did not know the answers (Harris, 1971). These data make it clear that for the majority of voting-age Americans, the terms liberal and conservative are just words. Even if a person is willing to adopt one of the labels when asked by an interviewer, chances are he has virtually no understanding of the political views implied by the term he chooses.

Does it make any sense, then, to apply the terms liberal, moderate, and conservative to the American electorate? Obviously the terms have meaning when applied to the minority who correctly use and understand them and who hold reasonably consistent liberal, moderate, or conservative political views. But for the majority of Americans, the political labels of left and right have little meaning or applicability. As William Flanigan has stated, "As with other political ideas in the minds of Americans, political ideologies are vague, superficial labels applied rather indifferently in their environments" (Flanigan, 1972).

Random Politics?

One still might argue that whether or not Americans can correctly identify liberal and conservative positions on major issues, it remains possible that

Figure 12.9 This political spectrum approximates the positions of some of our best-known public figures and also gives a rough indication of the numbers of party adherents (voters plus activists) who fall into each of the common categories of political ideology. Of necessity, our categorization of an individual's position must be based on a general summary of his record, because his decisions over time may not follow a completely predictable pattern. Note that the largest categories of the Democratic Party are liberals and moderates; the Republican Party finds its majority among conservatives and moderates. It is interesting to note that for reasons of location, personal history, or confusion, the two parties contain extremes that are usually associated with the other party; but these exceptions are so minor as to be of little importance. Those on the extreme left (sometimes called radicals) are interested in rapid and basic change toward new goals and institutions, primarily in favor of greater equality of power and participation. Those on the extreme right (sometimes called reactionaries) are interested in basic changes that entail a return to values, institutions, and purposes that, in their opinion, once existed but then were lost. Liberals, moderates, and conservatives fall in between these extremes as to their goals and the degree of change they favor.

most Americans hold relatively consistent sets of political opinions. If it were true that Americans are consistent in the way they respond to political issues, knowing how people stand on one issue would make it relatively easy to predict where they will stand on some others. For example, on logical and philosophical grounds, one would predict that a person who favored increased Medicare benefits would be likely to favor increased social security payments. The extent to which such predictions are accurate, however, is limited. Only a minority of Americans hold positions that are reasonably consistent across a number of political issues. Furthermore, on most major issues there is only a small difference in the proportion of Republicans and Democrats taking a given position—any notion that Democrats and Republicans will consistently agree with their parties and disagree with one another is usually unwarranted (Robert Erickson and Norman Luttbeg, 1973).

One of the reasons why poll results show such inconsistency is that some portion of opinions expressed by people being polled are apparently based purely on impulse. As mentioned in Chapter 1, Philip Converse attempted to find the structure of public political attitudes by interviewing a random sample of American adults on several different occasions and comparing the consistency of individual answers from one time to the next. From one interview to the next, he found great inconsistency in the average person's expressed political views. His conclusion was that the responses of the majority could best be compared to guessing the answers on a true-false test (Converse, 1966).

One major exception must be made to this image of fluctuating, capricious public opinion: Party identification is a very stable phenomenon in American society. Recall that party labels are one of the first things children understand about politics, and most children affiliate themselves quite early with one of the two parties. These early choices seem to last a long time. Studies have shown that few persons change their party identification—only 5 percent did so between 1956, a Republican year, and 1960, a year the Democrats recaptured the White House. As Table 12.2 shows, the proportion of Americans calling themselves Democrats changed little between the years 1940 and 1970. Republicans have gradually lost supporters over the same period, with the gain going to the group who identify themselves as independents. Overall, however, the picture of party affiliation is one of considerable stability.

Thus, the primary features of political identity for most American adults seem to be the same as those for schoolchildren: They know what party they be-

<table>
<tr><td colspan="3">Interpretations of a Campaign Promise</td></tr>
<tr><td>The Campaign Promise:</td><td colspan="2">How it might be interpreted by a:</td></tr>
<tr><td rowspan="4">"I promise to work for increased freedom for all and a better standard of living for everyone."</td><td>Competing politician
"increased freedom" and "a better standard of living" mean that the candidate is skirting the real issues and does not want to make any definite commitments.</td><td>Militant anticommunist
"better standard of living for everyone" means creeping socialism and loss of profit incentive.</td></tr>
<tr><td>"Law and order" advocate
"increased freedom" means moral and political permissiveness.</td><td>Small businessman
"increased freedom" means reduction in number of government forms to be filled out, lower taxes for middle class, and greater restraints on big corporations.</td></tr>
<tr><td>Welfare rights advocate
"better standard of living" means increased welfare payments.</td><td>Civil libertarian
"increased freedom" means more restraints on police searches and provision of better lawyers for indigents.</td></tr>
</table>

long to, and they know who is President. Beyond this rudimentary knowledge, however, things rapidly begin to get hazy. Public opinion is normally a

Table 12.2 Party Identification of the Electorate for Selected Years

PARTY PREFERENCE	1940	1944	1954	1958	1962	1966	1970
Democrats	41%	41%	47%	47%	47%	45%	43%
Republicans	38	39	27	29	27	25	24
Independents	20	20	22	19	23	28	31
No preference	1	—	4	5	3	2	1
Size of sample	—	—	1139	1269	1317	1291	1507

Source: 1940–1962 figures from William H. Flanigan, *Political Behavior of the American Electorate* (Boston: Allyn and Bacon, 1968); 1966, 1970 figures from Inter-University Consortium for Political Research.

minority phenomenon in America—the majority of Americans have no real opinions most of the time.

MINORITY POWER

As is shown in Chapter 13, a minority of Americans are responsible for the outcome of most elections. Even in presidential elections, only a bare majority of Americans actually vote; in most state and local elections, less than a majority do so. Earlier chapters have suggested many other ways in which minorities dominate majorities in the political process. This chapter has illustrated one important reason why this is so: For the most part, only a minority of Americans know and care about politics. Unless aroused by truly major events—such as economic collapse or war—or events that strike dangerously close to home, such as "forced" busing, the average American is not a very political animal.

Because of the complacency of most Americans, their opinions tend to be counted for little in the decision-making process. It has already been shown that most citizens do not know how their congressman has voted on any given bill; furthermore, on most matters, the average voter has no firm or informed view about how he *should* have voted. Thus, a public official usually does not need to be unduly worried about how his stance on legislation will affect the mass of voters. Understandably, politicians pay most attention to those citizens who pay the most attention to them. Thus, if 20 percent of the public *actively* oppose some program while 80 percent *passively* support it, it is highly probable that the minority is going to have more influence than the majority on the outcome of the issue.

A good example of how an active minority can be more influential than an apathetic majority is the

Figure 12.10 By making very general campaign statements and promises, candidates try to avoid alienating voters. This tactic is used especially with large and ideologically diverse constituencies. In the absence of specific information, citizens tend to view such promises through the filters of their party's biases, of the general image they have of the candidate, or of their own preferred sentiments. The accompanying chart (left) provides an example of the numerous, contradictory ways a single statement can be interpreted according to an individual's predilections.

present state of gun control legislation. For decades the overwhelming majority of Americans have favored strict gun control laws. Back in 1938, Gallup reported that over four-fifths of the public believed all handguns should be registered. In 1959 three-quarters of Americans believed no one should be permitted to buy a gun without a police permit, and in the aftermath of the political assassinations of the 1960s, public support for gun regulation continued to be overwhelming (Gallup, 1972). Congress has so far failed to act, however, because the majority has remained passive while the gun lobby, led by the American Rifle Association, has very vigorously campaigned against gun legislation. Many congressmen have explained in private that voting to control guns would earn them very few votes but would very definitely lose them a substantial number of votes from the anticontrol minority.

In sum, majority opinion usually serves as a latent limit on government action. Officials avoid actions they believe would arouse the majority—a kind of "let sleeping dogs lie" strategy. Outside of these limits, however, the opinion of the apathetic majority has little real impact.

MOBILIZING THE APATHETIC MAJORITY

The views of the American majority cannot have much impact on policy decisions unless they become mobilized—unless the majority becomes concerned about some issue, forms opinions about it, and is willing to take some action to make its opinions count. When such mobilization occurs, the majority can indeed affect public policy. As the Perspective on school desegregation makes clear, public opinion was highly mobilized against early efforts to end racial segregation of the schools. Similarly, recently aroused public opposition to the busing of school children has stymied efforts to achieve racial balance in northern school systems.

In some instances, politicians cite poll findings on majority opinions to justify their course of action in the face of vigorous minority opposition. The Johnson Administration's conduct of the war in Vietnam is a case in point. As President Johnson was to learn, however, such a strategy can turn out to be a double-edged sword: Over time, majority support for the war turned into majority opposition. Because Johnson had justified continuing the war on the basis of mass support, it then became embarrassing to ignore majority opposition.

Public Opinion and Policy

Did the shift in public opinion away from support of the war have any impact on policy making? There is no easy yes or no answer. It is clear, however, that as the public turned against the war, they also lost confidence in President Johnson, and he chose not to seek reelection. It seems plausible that Richard Nixon's pledge to end the war quickly played a part in his winning the Presidency in 1968. But beyond this point it is difficult to gauge the influence of public opinion in policy formation

Once in office in 1968, President Nixon correctly recognized that, although he had promised to get the troops out of Vietnam, the public would allow him considerable freedom of action. He probably was not free to significantly increase the number of troops or long continue operations resulting in high American casualties. On the other hand, he could expect the public to grant him a reasonable period of time in which to resolve the conflict.

The course Nixon chose to follow greatly confused the public and further increased his freedom of action. While he resumed the bombing in North Vietnam and launched incursions into Laos and Cambodia, he continued each month to ship more troops home. The public no longer confronted a question of seeking victory *or* peace—American forces were both fighting and leaving. The most prominent question became whether the President was using the best means for getting out of the war. Thus, although the majority against the war continued to grow during Nixon's first term, approval of his Presidency remained relatively high. Such mixed opinions tend to be self-canceling and to leave leaders with much leeway within which to determine policies. Indeed, for many Americans who opposed the war, getting the boys back home was the whole basis of their concern, and Nixon had mainly accomplished this before the 1972 election. The election returns of that year indicated that most of the people were satisfied.

Policy by Experts

The Vietnam War illustrates yet another aspect of public opinion and policy making—the tendency

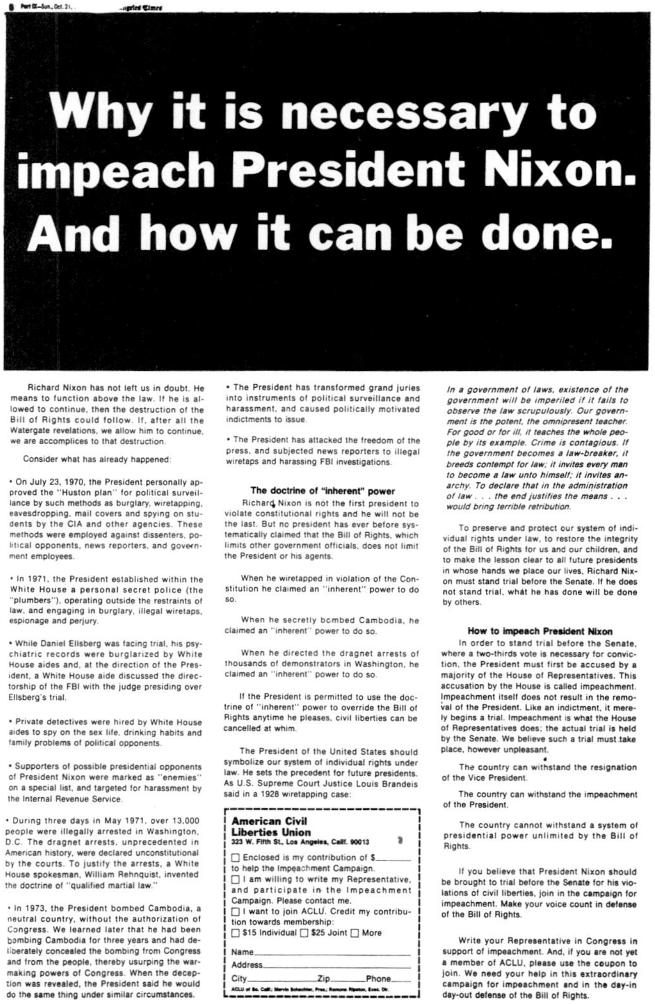

Why it is necessary to impeach President Nixon. And how it can be done.

Richard Nixon has not left us in doubt. He means to function above the law. If he is allowed to continue, then the destruction of the Bill of Rights could follow. If, after all the Watergate revelations, we allow him to continue, we are accomplices to that destruction.

Consider what has already happened:

• On July 23, 1970, the President personally approved the "Huston plan" for political surveillance by such methods as burglary, wiretapping, eavesdropping, mail covers and spying on students by the CIA and other agencies. These methods were employed against dissenters, political opponents, news reporters, and government employees.

• In 1971, the President established within the White House a personal secret police (the "plumbers"), operating outside the restraints of law, and engaging in burglary, illegal wiretaps, espionage and perjury.

• While Daniel Ellsberg was facing trial, his psychiatric records were burglarized by White House aides and, at the direction of the President, a White House aide discussed the directorship of the FBI with the judge presiding over Ellsberg's trial.

• Private detectives were hired by White House aides to spy on the sex life, drinking habits and family problems of political opponents.

• Supporters of possible presidential opponents of President Nixon were marked as "enemies" on a special list, and targeted for harassment by the Internal Revenue Service.

• During three days in May 1971, over 13,000 people were illegally arrested in Washington, D.C. The dragnet arrests, unprecedented in American history, were declared unconstitutional by the courts. To justify the arrests, a White House spokesman, William Rehnquist, invented the doctrine of "qualified martial law."

• In 1973, the President bombed Cambodia, a neutral country, without the authorization of Congress. We learned later that he had been bombing Cambodia for three years and had deliberately concealed the bombing from Congress and from the people, thereby usurping the war-making powers of Congress. When the deception was revealed, the President said he would do the same thing under similar circumstances.

• The President has transformed grand juries into instruments of political surveillance and harassment, and caused politically motivated indictments to issue.

• The President has attacked the freedom of the press, and subjected news reporters to illegal wiretaps and harassing FBI investigations.

The doctrine of "inherent" power

Richard Nixon is not the first president to violate constitutional rights and he will not be the last. But no president has ever before systematically claimed that the Bill of Rights, which limits other government officials, does not limit the President or his agents.

When he wiretapped in violation of the Constitution he claimed an "inherent" power to do so.

When he secretly bombed Cambodia, he claimed an "inherent" power to do so.

When he directed the dragnet arrests of thousands of demonstrators in Washington, he claimed an "inherent" power to do so.

If the President is permitted to use the doctrine of "inherent" power to override the Bill of Rights anytime he pleases, civil liberties can be cancelled at whim.

The President of the United States should symbolize our system of individual rights under law. He sets the precedent for future presidents. As U.S. Supreme Court Justice Louis Brandeis said in a 1928 wiretapping case:

American Civil Liberties Union
323 W. Fifth St., Los Angeles, Calif. 90013

☐ Enclosed is my contribution of $________ to help the Impeachment Campaign.
☐ I am willing to write my Representative, and participate in the Impeachment Campaign. Please contact me.
☐ I want to join ACLU. Credit my contribution towards membership:
☐ $15 Individual ☐ $25 Joint ☐ More

Name________________
Address________________
City__________Zip________Phone______

ACLU of So. Calif.; Marvin Schachter, Pres.; Ramona Ripston, Exec. Dir.

In a government of laws, existence of the government will be imperiled if it fails to observe the law scrupulously. Our government is the potent, the omnipresent teacher. For good or for ill, it teaches the whole people by its example. Crime is contagious. If the government becomes a law-breaker, it breeds contempt for law; it invites every man to become a law unto himself; it invites anarchy. To declare that in the administration of law . . . the end justifies the means . . . would bring terrible retribution.

To preserve and protect our system of individual rights under law, to restore the integrity of the Bill of Rights for us and our children, and to make the lesson clear to all future presidents in whose hands we place our lives, Richard Nixon must stand trial before the Senate. If he does not stand trial, what he has done will be done by others.

How to impeach President Nixon

In order to stand trial before the Senate, where a two-thirds vote is necessary for conviction, the President must first be accused by a majority of the House of Representatives. This accusation by the House is called impeachment. Impeachment itself does not result in the removal of the President. Like an indictment, it merely begins a trial. Impeachment is what the House of Representatives does; the actual trial is held by the Senate. We believe such a trial must take place, however unpleasant.

The country can withstand the resignation of the Vice President.

The country can withstand the impeachment of the President.

The country cannot withstand a system of presidential power unlimited by the Bill of Rights.

If you believe that President Nixon should be brought to trial before the Senate for his violations of civil liberties, join in the campaign for impeachment. Make your voice count in defense of the Bill of Rights.

Write your Representative in Congress in support of impeachment. And, if you are not yet a member of ACLU, please use the coupon to join. We need your help in this extraordinary campaign for impeachment and in the day-in day-out defense of the Bill of Rights.

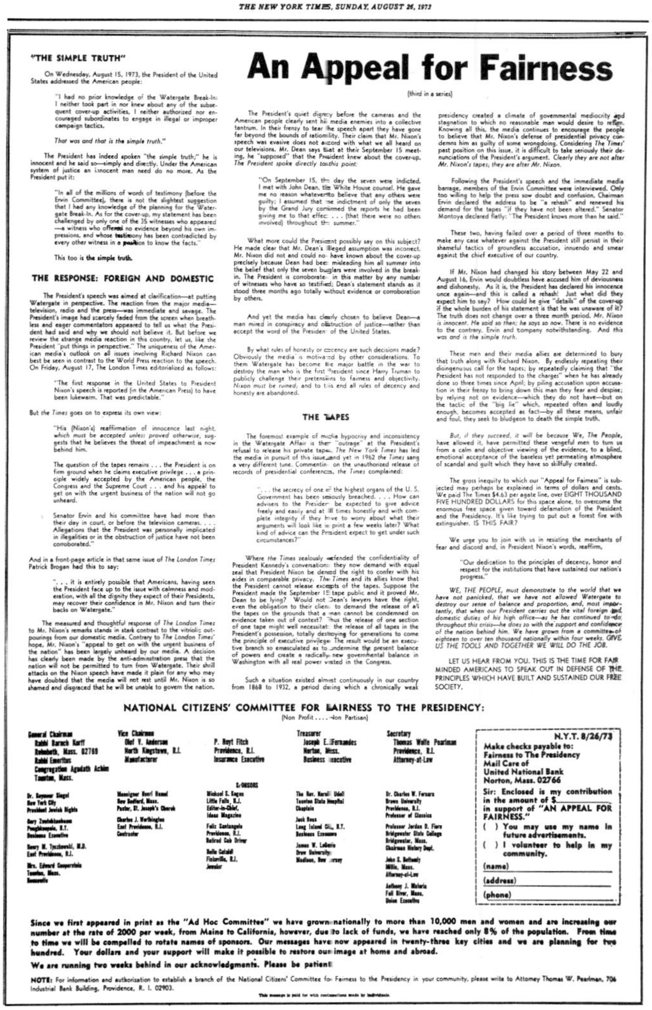

THE NEW YORK TIMES, SUNDAY, AUGUST 26, 1973

An Appeal for Fairness

(third in a series)

"THE SIMPLE TRUTH"

THE RESPONSE: FOREIGN AND DOMESTIC

THE TAPES

LET US HEAR FROM YOU. THIS IS THE TIME FOR FAIR MINDED AMERICANS TO SPEAK OUT IN DEFENSE OF THE PRINCIPLES WHICH HAVE BUILT AND SUSTAINED OUR FREE SOCIETY.

NATIONAL CITIZENS' COMMITTEE FOR FAIRNESS TO THE PRESIDENCY:

N.Y.T. 8/26/73
Make checks payable to:
Fairness to The Presidency
Mail Care of
United National Bank
Norton, Mass. 02766
Sir: Enclosed is my contribution in the amount of $________ in support of "AN APPEAL FOR FAIRNESS."
( ) You may use my name in future advertisements.
( ) I volunteer to help in my community.
(name)________
(address)________
(phone)________

Since we first appeared in print as the "Ad Hoc Committee" we have grown nationally to more than 10,000 men and women and are increasing our number at the rate of 2000 per week, from Maine to California, however, due to lack of funds, we have reached only 8% of the population. From time to time we will be compelled to rotate names of sponsors. Our messages have now appeared in twenty-three key cities and we are planning for two hundred. Your dollars and your support will make it possible to restore our image at home and abroad.

We are running two weeks behind in our acknowledgments. Please be patient.

NOTE: For information and authorization to establish a branch of the National Citizens' Committee for Fairness to the Presidency in your community, please write to Attorney Thomas W. Pearlman, 706 Industrial Bank Building, Providence, R. I. 02903.

Figure 12.11 Impeachment of a President is a rare and serious undertaking. To most citizens it is an unlikely and onerous option, given the weakening of the sense of secure authority that necessarily accompanies an attack on an incumbent President.

In the case of President Richard Nixon, certain political opponents, legal groups, and elements of the media presented a list of accusations to the people to focus public opinion on the question of impeachment. Unpopular actions by the President, by members of his Administration, and by persons associated with the Administration laid the groundwork for such accusations. The Watergate controversy and its perceived mishandling, suspicion over the possible concealment of evidence, the revelations of civil liberties violations by high Administration officials, unrest over economic problems and the conduct of foreign affairs—all contributed to a dramatic failure of public confidence in the conduct of White House duties, as documented by the results of public opinion polls through the months of 1973.

While the President was attacked by groups of opinion leaders and his popularity waned among the populace, groups such as the National Citizens' Committee for Fairness to the Presidency (the authors of the "appeal" shown above), as well as political supporters and personal friends, came to his aid. They marshalled arguments in his defense—such as President Nixon's defense of the integrity of his office, the political motivations of his accusers, and the lack of any evidence of actual wrongdoing. They also pointed to the dangers for the American national image abroad in allowing a continued undermining of the nation's leadership.

Both sides of the controversy attempted to mobilize public opinion—which had already risen to a level of awareness of the problems—and to focus it on actions of opposition or support. In future years, it may be safely said, the controversy over the impeachment of President Richard Nixon will be viewed as a political event of the greatest magnitude; the tides of public opinion during the controversy will provide political scientists with important material for the study of the dynamics of American public opinion vis à vis the Presidency and political authority.

of the American public to defer to supposed experts, and the tendency of experts to isolate themselves—and their information—from the public. Throughout the Vietnam debate, government representatives of various persuasions tended to argue that the President and his foreign policy advisers were better informed than anyone else and therefore the public, and even the Congress, simply had to defer to the President's judgment and accept presidential leadership. For many Americans, the argument held much sway. In 1964, when America's growing military forces in Vietnam were still called advisers, the minority of Americans who were interested in Vietnam had been about equally split between those who thought America was dealing with the situation about as well as could be expected and those who thought America was doing a poor job. But once full-scale military involvement in Vietnam became a reality, public opinion shifted massively; by 1965 the overwhelming majority had rallied to the President and his advisers in their support of the war effort (Gallup, 1972).

In 1966 and 1967, however, the sequence of obvious failures in Vietnam began to affect public opinion. When Americans viewed televised accounts of the furious Tet offensive in January 1968, it was apparent that the North Vietnamese had not been pounded into submission, as had been suggested by the experts. By March there were more "doves" than "hawks." Vietnam had demonstrated that the supposedly "best informed" had actually been insulated from the truth and thereby deceived about reality. The important question of the citizen's right to know, even about the most vital of foreign policy matters, had been raised afresh.

The case of the *Pentagon Papers* demonstrates these issues in a particularly intriguing and vivid way. Secretary of Defense Robert McNamara was one of the architects of the Vietnam involvement, but he had begun to have serious doubts about it. He therefore sought an analysis of the way the United States had become involved in the war. The study, which developed into the *Pentagon Papers,* was subsequently classified as secret and therefore not available to the public.

Daniel Ellsberg, who had once been a staunch supporter of the war and a Pentagon planner, had also changed his mind about the war. When he got hold

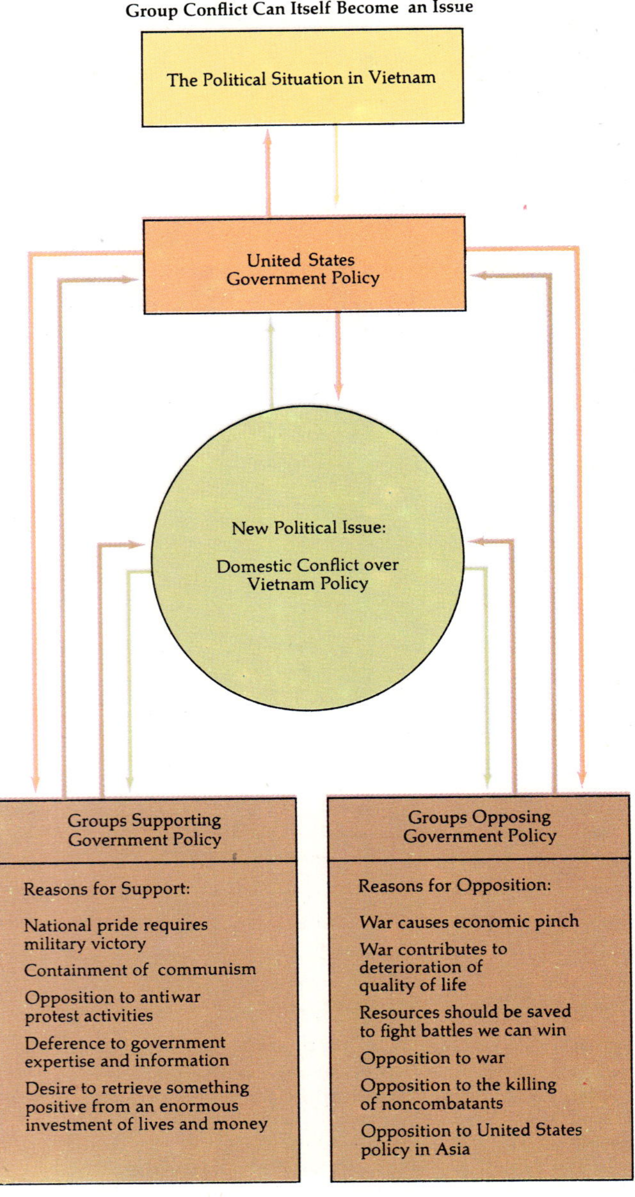

Figure 12.12 The conflict of opinion over a particular government policy has the capacity for itself becoming an issue of enormous magnitude—for example, the divisions of opinion regarding the Johnson and Nixon Administrations' conduct of the war in Vietnam. Wars and the diversity of opinions toward them have, in the past, been known to divide the nation: Benjamin Franklin's son was a Tory during the American Revolution, and the Civil War most notoriously set brother against brother. There was less dissension over the conduct of the World Wars of the twentieth century, but the war in Vietnam exploded into an issue of national polarization and internal strife.

of the "papers," he xeroxed them, and distributed them to the *New York Times* for publication. The government, in this case the Nixon Administration, tried to get the Supreme Court to halt publication of the papers on grounds that national security was involved. The Court, however, rejected the Administration's position.

Ellsberg was later indicted for copying the papers, but he maintained in his defense that the papers revealed nothing threatening to national security. The papers, he argued, simply informed the people about the history of America's choices in Vietnam and had been classified to avoid embarrassing the key decision makers involved. The Ellsberg position thereby attacked the whole system of government classification, under which thousands of documents had been kept from public view. The case was ultimately thrown out on the grounds that the government had obstructed justice by, among other acts, burglarizing the files of Ellsberg's psychiatrist's office. Although Ellsberg's challenge to the government system of classification was therefore never ruled on, the issues raised are bound to persist as long as the United States remains a world power. How is the public to judge wisely on matters of foreign policy unless it is adequately informed and given alternatives? Indeed, even with such information, how much can the public understand?

As has been shown in this chapter, people are neither adequately informed nor interested enough to fulfill the role assigned them in traditional democratic theory. Nor can experts be trusted implicitly— military and foreign affairs experts led America into Vietnam, experts designed and redesigned the welfare programs, and indeed, experts planned the Watergate break in. Must it be said, then, that democracy is merely a vision to strive after, that we shall always live in an imperfect world, and that there is no final answer?

Some political scientists put their hope in radical social reforms that will transform the political consciousness of the average citizen and instill in him political wisdom and democratic values. Others believe that the only real alternative to tyranny or anarchy is a society that is reasonably, fairly, and competently governed by a variety of elite groups. The fact that in a recent political science textbook one author supported the first of these positions, the other author the second, reflects the uncertain state of our understanding of the problem (Dye and Zeigler, 1971). Considering the fact that this uncertainty was shared by the ancient Greeks, it is not surprising that this chapter must also leave it unresolved.

SUMMARY

The development of public-opinion polling techniques in the 1930s has led to a dispute over what role public opinion should play in the formulation of government policies. It is evident that American public opinion is not well formulated; poll responses reflect a lack of understanding and interest. Only when politics affects people's lives directly are they generally interested. It is the informed minority of citizens that must be taken into account by politicians, for they are the ones who will vote and contribute time and money to campaigns.

The political socialization of children begins early, and the family plays a major role in establishing an individual's political choices. Although schools are a potentially important instrument of political socialization, only rarely do they expose children to argument about political values or policies. Like the schools, the media may increase knowledge of particular issues or candidates, but there is no evidence that it affects party affiliation or political outlook.

The majority of Americans do not have a particularly coherent and consistent political ideology. It is only when political actions exceed the broad limits the majority imposes on policy that the usually apathetic majority can be stirred to considerable concern and thus have an impact on policy.

SUGGESTED READINGS

Best, James J. *Public Opinion: Micro and Macro.* Homewood, Ill.: Dorsey Press, 1973.

Bogart, Leo. *Silent Politics: Polls and the Awareness of Public Opinion.* New York: Wiley, 1972.

Erikson, Robert S., and Norman R. Luttbeg. *American Public Opinion: Its Origins, Content, and Impact.* New York: Wiley, 1973.

Katz, Elihu, and Paul Lazarsfeld. *Personal Influence: The Part Played by People in the Flow of Mass Communications.* Glencoe, Ill.: Free Press, 1955.

13
PARTIES AND VOTING

Political parties promise the citizen an organized and legitimate means for exercising political power and influence. They also play the dominant role in selecting candidates for the voters to choose between, and party loyalty plays a major role in determining how people usually vote. In order to understand how and why certain candidates are elected to decision-making roles in American society, it is thus necessary to take a close look at the party system in the United States. Why does America have two parties instead of one, or four, or a dozen? What difference does it make? What do the parties do? What can they not do? After these questions have been examined, the chapter will turn to the relationship between the parties and the individual voter. Who votes? For whom do they vote and why?

PARTY SYSTEMS COMPARED

It is striking that America, with all of the diversity that characterizes its population, has been able to maintain a two-party system. Other nations have developed alternate party systems in order to better represent the diverse groups within their populations. Why has the United States chosen over the years to maintain a two-party system, and how does the system accommodate itself to the many social cleavages among its citizenry?

Coalition Government

Political systems can be classified according to the number of parties they have. Some nations have one-party systems, in which the party is often merely a vehicle by which rulers manipulate popular consent and by which they imply that democratic procedures are being followed. In such systems, political conflict is greatly muted because there is no legitimate vehicle for political opposition.

A second kind of party system, found in a number of Western European democracies, is the multiparty system, which consists of three or more competing parties. Each party in a multiparty system is awarded seats in the legislative body in proportion to the total number of votes it receives in the election—a system of *proportional representation*. Multiparty systems offer a wide range of political choices to the voters, and for reasons that will be discussed, political conflict is frequently quite intense. In nations that have multiparty systems, the voters choose among

Figure 13.1 The act of voting is the culmination of a process of interaction—with reason, passion, and interests all playing a role. Political parties strongly influence that process. Originating in the eastern states of the nation, the institution of the political party followed western expansion beyond the Appalachian Mountains and ultimately beyond the Rocky Mountains. But in expanding to new areas of the nation, the parties encountered novel groupings and conflicts. They took on new facets in their attempt to hold onto the maximum number of followers—to stretch as wide an umbrella as possible over as many voters as possible. Today's parties are the culmination of this expansion of the ideological and political umbrellas of the past.

any number of parties, each of which is struggling to gain power on behalf of the particular groups it serves. It is rare when any single party achieves majority support; therefore, governments in multiparty systems are characteristically based on coalitions of competing parties.

Coalition Parties

In terms of the degree of available political choice and the degree to which political conflict is lessened, the American two-party system falls in between the one-party and multiparty systems. One often hears complaints that there are no sharp ideological and programmatic differences between the Republican and Democratic Parties. Some even refer to them as Tweedledum and Tweedledee and claim that each is but an echo of the other and that Americans have no significant political alternatives. Although the two parties do not exactly echo each other, it is true that they both tend toward the middle of the road.

The reasons for this position are inherent in two-party systems.

Instead of a coalition government, the United States has two *coalition parties*. With only two parties, one party is bound to achieve majority support and thus to be able to govern without making deals with the other party. But to achieve a majority, bargains must still be struck among the many competing interest groups that make up American society (see Chapter 15). In other words, in two-party systems the necessary bargains and compromises among competing groups are struck within each party before the election instead of between the parties after the election.

Both the Republican and Democratic Parties are made up of coalitions among competing groups that have pooled their efforts in order to gain power. Obviously, no one party can be all things to all people. But to gain and to hold power, a party must offer enough things to enough people that it can maintain

Figure 13.2 What would the American ballot look like if a multiparty situation were suddenly fostered, if such devices as proportional representation or multimember districts were instituted? Consider the eight Italian political party symbols shown here, all of which symbolize parties that are listed on the Italian ballot. There could be advantages to a change in the electoral system in America: voters would be allowed a far greater choice and more representation of specific goals. But would America be able to avoid the disadvantages of multiparty systems—the difficulties of voter identification and the intense, many-sided conflicts?

Figure 13.3 When election strategists calculate their campaign goals and techniques, they first need to know how many electoral votes they need to win the election, and which states to aim for to gain that total. In a presidential campaign, the successful candidate must take a majority of the electoral votes of the states (each state's number of electoral votes being equal to the number of senators and representatives it sends to Washington). A majority of electoral votes, that is, the number needed to win the Presidency, is 270.

A state-by-state breakdown of electoral votes is given in the table to the right; it includes the three electoral votes from the District of Columbia. Strategists examine this table and try to decide which states to aim for in the campaign. The candidate who wins a majority of votes in a state, even if he or she wins by only one vote, wins the state's total electoral vote—the winner-take-all system. Clearly, setting sights for the more populous states seems a profitable strategy; however, campaigns in such states are expensive because of the large and diverse nature of their populations. Some candidates will aim at winning blocs of states, such as the southern or the rural bloc, which, in combination with certain large states, would bring the total above the needed 270 votes. The best strategy is obviously to put together winning combinations or coalitions of states that the candidate might win, put major resources into those states, and then use whatever resources remain in those states that are judged peripheral.

majority support. Thus, American parties are forever committed to a precarious balancing act: Each party seeks to reconcile the competing interests among its traditional supporters while it tries both to poach on the opposition's support and to gain enough support from the unaffiliated "independents" to win power.

Because so much political bargaining goes on *within* the structure of the parties, coalition parties tend to blur political conflicts and to prevent them from fully surfacing in ways that would stimulate voters to uncompromising and highly ideological positions. This muting of conflicts frequently makes for a more stable government and for a more tranquil society than is the case in multiparty systems where many conflicts of interest surface as disputes *between* political parties. As we will discuss later in this chapter, however, Americans pay for the stability and tranquility of the two-party system in that they are offered only limited political choices and they must choose between parties that are unable to achieve their political promises.

THE ORIGINS OF THE TWO-PARTY SYSTEM

The Constitution says nothing about political parties. In fact, the founding fathers were largely hostile to the idea of parties and made every effort to design a government that could never be dominated by any single faction or party (see Chapter 2). Nevertheless, the founding fathers, in their determination to ensure the indirect election of the President and the Vice-President, unwittingly paved the way for the emergence of a two-party rather than a multiparty system.

The Electoral College

Although the founding fathers recognized that all legitimate government must rest on popular consent, they were also very much concerned about the dangers of unlimited majority rule and the need for con-

---

Putting Together a Winning Presidential Coalition*

State Groups

Large Industrial States: California, Illinois, Massachusetts, Michigan, New Jersey, New York, Ohio, Pennsylvania, Wisconsin — **227**

Nonsouthern Rural States: Arizona, Colorado, Idaho, Indiana, Iowa, Kansas, Nebraska, Nevada, New Mexico, North Dakota, Oregon, South Dakota, Utah, Vermont — **81**

Southern States: South Carolina, Georgia, Alabama, Mississippi, Louisiana, Virginia, North Carolina, Tennessee, Arkansas, Texas, Delaware, Maryland, West Virginia, Kentucky, Missouri, Oklahoma — **161**

South minus border states: South Carolina, Georgia, Alabama, Mississippi, Louisiana, Virginia, North Carolina, Tennessee, Arkansas, Texas — **113**

Large States, with more than 10 electoral college votes: California, Florida, Georgia, Illinois, Indiana, Michigan, Missouri, New Jersey, New York, North Carolina, Ohio, Pennsylvania, Texas, Virginia, Wisconsin, Massachusetts — **332**

Large States with more than 20 electoral college votes: California, Illinois, Michigan, New York, Ohio, Pennsylvania, Texas — **211**

Small States, with 10 electoral college votes or less: Alabama, Alaska, Arizona, Arkansas, Colorado, Connecticut, Delaware, District of Columbia, Hawaii, Idaho, Iowa, Kansas, Kentucky, Louisiana, Maine, Maryland, Minnesota, Mississippi, Montana, Nebraska, Nevada, New Hampshire, New Mexico, North Dakota, Oklahoma, Oregon, Rhode Island, South Carolina, South Dakota, Tennessee, Utah, Vermont, Washington, West Virginia, Wyoming — **206**

***Total Electoral College Votes Needed to Win: 270**

State	Electoral Votes	State	Electoral Votes
Alabama	9	Montana	4
Alaska	3	Nebraska	5
Arizona	6	Nevada	3
Arkansas	6	New Hampshire	4
California	45	New Jersey	17
Colorado	7	New Mexico	4
Connecticut	8	New York	41
Delaware	3	North Carolina	13
District of Columbia	3	North Dakota	3
Florida	17	Ohio	25
Georgia	12	Oklahoma	8
Hawaii	4	Oregon	6
Idaho	4	Pennsylvania	27
Illinois	26	Rhode Island	4
Indiana	13	South Carolina	8
Iowa	8	South Dakota	4
Kansas	7	Tennessee	10
Kentucky	9	Texas	26
Louisiana	10	Utah	4
Maine	4	Vermont	3
Maryland	10	Virginia	12
Massachusetts	14	Washington	9
Michigan	21	West Virginia	6
Minnesota	10	Wisconsin	11
Mississippi	7	Wyoming	3
Missouri	12	**Total**	538

stitutional restraints. The Constitution reflects those concerns in its provision that the President and the Vice-President shall be elected by electors chosen within each state—as a group, these electors are known as the *electoral college.* Electors were originally chosen by the state legislators, and the number of electors was (and still is) equal to the total of the state's senators and representatives combined. In providing for the electoral college, the founders expected that each elector would exercise his own judgment in casting his vote, an expectation that was only rarely realized in fact.

The electoral college is still in force today. But the rise of political parties has resulted in the transformation of electors into party representatives who simply register the decision of the electorate. When a voter makes his choice on election day, he is actually choosing among slates of presidential electors. The electors then ceremoniously cast their ballots for their party's candidates, votes that are formally counted on January 6 by the House and Senate. The names of the victorious candidates are then solemnly, if anticlimactically, announced.

There have been many proposals for the reform of the electoral college and for the substitution of a more direct form of presidential selection. The critics of the present system cite the advantage it gives to the more populous and liberal-oriented states with their powerful voting blocs of urban and minority-ethnic interests. There are also recurring fears that the electoral system may result in the selection of a candidate for President who has not received the support of a popular majority. This situation may well have happened in 1968 had George Wallace, who ran as the candidate of the American Independent Party, received enough electoral support to deprive both Hubert Humphrey and Richard Nixon of a majority—a case that would have been thrown to the House of Representatives to decide.

In addition, the electoral college sharply influences presidential politics. In each state, the candidate who is victorious by even one popular vote wins all of the state's electoral votes. There is no system of proportional representation to ensure that a minority candidate gets credit for the percent of the vote that he does carry. Finishing second in such a race is as meaningless as finishing last. As a result of the "winner-take-all" nature of the system, there is a

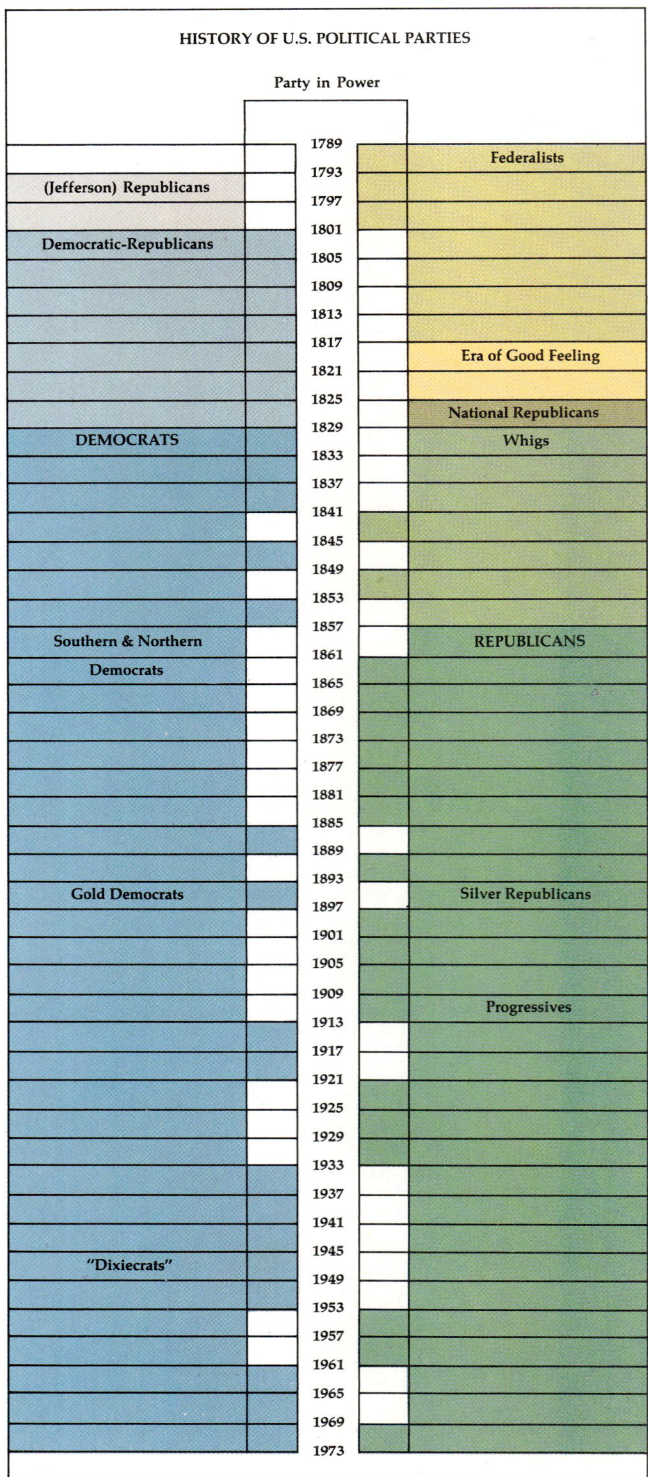

Figure 13.4 **The two major parties of the United States have changed names, splintered off smaller groups, and reabsorbed others. This chart (left) traces the complexities surrounding our two-party system (Madgic et al., 1971).**

Figure 13.5 **"Third parties" is a general term denoting parties of less strength than the two that have usually predominated in our history (under various names). This chart (below) indicates their year of origin and their latest appearance, up to 1968 (Madgic et al., 1971).**

MAJOR THIRD PARTY MOVEMENTS	First Appearance in National Election	Latest Appearance in National Election
Anti-Masonic	1832	1832
Liberty	1840	1844
Free Soil	1848	1852
Know Nothing (American)	1856	1856
Constitutional Union	1860	1860
Labor Reform	1872	1872
Prohibition	1872	1968
Greenback	1876	1884
Union Labor	1888	1888
Socialist-Labor	1892	1968
People's (Populist)	1892	1908
Socialist	1900	1956
Progressive: T. R. Roosevelt	1912	1912
R. M. La Follette	1924	1924
H. Wallace	1948	1948
Farmer-Labor	1920	1932
Communist	1924	1968
States' Rights	1948	1948
American Independent	1968	1968

strong geographical basis to presidential politics. The successful candidate neither wastes time in states he knows are traditional supporters of his party nor does he campaign in the smaller states whose electoral votes make little difference to the outcome of the election. Rather, he makes his appeal to the more populous states, such as New York, California, Pennsylvania, and Illinois, and he directs his message toward the urban and suburban groups within those states. He thus sacrifices many of the narrower issues in order not to antagonize the great masses of voters.

Third Parties

The winner-take-all nature of the electoral competition greatly deters parties that appeal to only one or a few interest groups, and it greatly favors parties that consist of coalitions of interests, parties that have broader bases of support. In other words, if one coalition party exists, the only reasonable hope of defeating it is for all opposing factions to band together in pursuit of a voting majority. The result is a strong tendency for there to be two dominant parties and for third-party efforts to be shortlived.

Yet pointing out the difficulties of third parties is not to suggest that significant third parties have never operated in American politics. Indeed, third parties have from time to time played a role in our politics. They have drawn attention to issues that the major parties have preferred to ignore.

Third parties have ordinarily depended on a regional base for electoral support. In some districts or regions they have been able to supplant one of the major parties or have even become the dominant party. For example, a Farmer-Labor Party was strong for a number of years in Minnesota, and George Wallace's American Independent Party won the presidential electors of the Deep South in 1968.

The need for third parties to have strong regional support is aptly illustrated in Strom Thurmond's try for the Presidency in 1948. In the election, Henry Wallace's Progressive Party received about as many votes as did Strom Thurmond's States' Rights Party. Because all of Thurmond's supporters were concentrated in a few states in the Deep South, he managed to win the electoral votes from those states. Henry Wallace's support was not geographically concentrated, however, and he failed to come within shouting distance of any electoral votes. Thurmond's regional base might well have put him into a strong bargaining position had Thomas Dewey, the Republican candidate, run a stronger race against Harry Truman, the Democratic candidate.

It is ironic, however, that this regional support has usually led to the ultimate failure of third parties. No regional party has ever had significant prospects of winning the Presidency or of winning control of Congress. The supreme prizes of political power are beyond their reach because their goals are too narrowly focused to appeal to a majority of voters. Their supporters are forever subject to appeals to not "waste" their votes but rather to back the least objectionable major party candidate.

For most of its history, America has been characterized by a two-party system. However, the two parties have not always been the same. Especially during the first century of the Republic, from time to time a new party would appear—a coalition of different groups within the population—and in several instances it was able to gain enough support to supplant one of the two major parties.

Contemporary Parties: Their Origins

In his Farewell Address in 1797, President George Washington called on the nation to be wary of the "baneful effects of the spirit of party." This warning resulted from events during his Administration that, much to his dismay, clearly signaled the emergence of political party divisions in the new nation.

Two main factions had been developing during Washington's eight years in office. Members of one faction called themselves the Federalists and were led by Secretary of the Treasury Alexander Hamilton (and by George Washington, despite his disdain for parties in principle). The Federalists were generally men of wealth and high social position. Members of the second group, the so-called Democratic-Republicans, were led by Thomas Jefferson and James Madison. They represented a coalition of small farmers, small property owners, and local political leaders in the southern and mid-Atlantic states. Jefferson's party soon dominated American politics, and the Federalists ceased to exist.

With the election of Andrew Jackson to the Presidency in 1828, the party of Jefferson and Madison—renamed the Democratic Party—was transformed into a mass membership party and became the dominant force in politics. Presidents Jackson and Van Buren reorganized their party to accommodate the new states admitted to the Union and to gain support from new voters who became eligible as the economic qualifications limiting the suffrage were eased.

Figure 13.6 The Republican Administrations at the turn of the nineteenth century show they have kept their political promises. Theodore Roosevelt (shown on the right), who succeeded the assassinated William McKinley as President, won the 1904 presidential election by two and a half million votes. Closely associated with the Spanish-American War, Roosevelt became associated with expansionism in the economy and in the world. The Democrats, who had until 1904 been led by the western populist element of the party under William Jennings Bryan, were accused by the Republicans of fiscal irresponsibility and isolationism.

In the growing sectional crisis that culminated in the Civil War, the Republican Party appeared on the scene. In 1860 its presidential candidate, Abraham Lincoln, won the election; the Democratic Party broke into two factions—the northern and the southern—each with a different view on the slavery issue and each with its own presidential candidate. The Republicans began as a somewhat radical party that was opposed to the further extension of slavery. But they quickly created a coalition of northern industrialists, merchants, and large numbers of workers, farmers, and freed slaves.

Although the Democratic Party survived the Civil War, the new Republican coalition won every presidential election for the next five decades except for Grover Cleveland's victories in 1884 and 1892 (he was defeated in his first try for a second term). As they monopolized presidential power, the Republicans slowly shifted their main support to businessmen and middle-class white Anglo-Saxon Protestants, whereas the Democrats attracted the new urban, Catholic immigrants and eroded Republican support among workers. With the advent of the Depression of the 1930s, the Republicans were discredited by President Hoover's failure to act decisively to counteract it. The Democrats, however, under President Franklin Roosevelt, had at last put together a winning coalition. They held the support of the farmer-labor-South coalition; when the urban-unemployed, the blacks, and the other ethnic minorities were added to it, the Democrats had a coalition that allowed them to dominate Congress and the White House for three decades.

In conclusion, it seems clear that the successful American party is the one that has been able to build a broad base of support.

THE STRUCTURE OF AMERICAN PARTIES

So far in this discussion we have broadly defined a *party* as a coalition of diverse interest groups that choose to unite once every four years to select a President and a Vice-President. But parties, of course, are far more complex affairs. There are really two types of party organizations. One is "inside" government and is composed of officeholders; it includes the President, the congressmen, and many state and local politicians. Within Congress there are caucuses, committees, and informal groups whose primary purpose is to attempt to pass legislation.

But it is the outside party organizations that are largely responsible for determining who gets into public office. The outside party organizations consist of the national party headquarters and state and local party organizations.

Just as the two major parties are loose coalitions of interest groups, the two national party organizations are loose coalitions of state and local party organizations. Much of the party power resides in the state and local party organizations because it is at these levels that many of the crucial party decisions are made: Who will be nominated for governor, mayor, representative, or senator is decided by state and local party organizations and not by the national party organization. Indeed, even the Presidency is primarily won or lost at the state level: Because of the electoral college system, the presidential candidate who wins in a given state receives all of that state's electoral votes. Therefore, to win the Presidency a candidate must win a sufficient number of majorities within states, regardless of the final count in the nationwide popular vote.

Local and State Party Organizations

At the grass-roots level of the party organization are the precinct or ward captains and the party workers. This is the level of party activity that most likely gets organized for only a few weeks preceding election day. Party supporters are registered and furnished with information on candidates and ballot proposals. Party volunteers make arrangements to transport party supporters to vote at the polls on election day.

At the county level, the central committee is responsible for raising money, for selecting candidates for county offices, and for coordinating countywide campaigns. Many observers believe that county party organizations are the most powerful units within either party. If so, the fact that there are about 3,000 counties in the United States gives some idea of how widely dispersed political power is within the party system.

At the top of the state party organization is the state central committee, headed by the state chairmen. Many state committees are not powerful—they are in many cases dominated by the governor or by a powerful senator, just as the President dominates his party's national committee. The state committee

Figure 13.7 (left) The Democratic convention of 1924 was the longest party convention in United States history. Split by religious issues and the question of supporting the Ku Klux Klan, the convention required 103 ballots to nominate William G. McAdoo for President. The formation of a new Progressive Party by Senator Robert M. La Follette took votes away from the Democrats, allowing the victory of Republican Calvin Coolidge, whose slogan was, "Keep Cool and Keep Coolidge."

Figure 13.8 Political party organization (right). Each of our two major political parties may be divided into two distinct parts: that which operates from inside the government (made up of elected or appointed officeholders) and that which operates outside government (includes national, state, and local party officials). In addition, distinctions must be made for the members of the "official" party organization (determined by law and by party rules) and the "unofficial" party organization (comprising all those who directly or indirectly affect the operations or goals of the parties); these additional distinctions characterize the party as it operates both inside and outside the government. It is important to note that the specifically party-oriented activities of most of the persons or groups on this chart occur primarily around election times and that the various components of the party organization influence, support, and oppose one another for control over such items as campaign funds and the statement of party goals.

serves the same functions as the county committee but at the statewide level.

National Party Organization

At the top of the party structure is the national committee—traditionally composed of one man and one woman from each state (although recent party reforms have expanded on this membership). An indication of the national party's lack of importance is the fact that national committeemen and women are ordinarily not very powerful in their home state party organizations (Cornelius Cotter and Bernard Hennessy, 1964). Many are given the position as a reward for many years of loyal service to the party. Their only formal responsibility is to attend two meetings a year and to ratify the decisions of the national chairman.

The national party really comes to life only once every four years when it holds conventions to nominate candidates for President and Vice-President and to adopt a party platform. Shortly after the convention, the national party again ceases to be important, largely because the presidential candidate creates his own campaign organization rather than relying on the national party organization to run his campaign.

This brief sketch of party organization suggests the great diffusion of party power throughout the hierarchy from the precinct level on up to the national level. Each stratum of the party has power within its own jurisdiction; but the boundaries of power are not well defined, and conflicts arise between party units over the uses of power. Furthermore, although those at the top may speak for the party, power is actually exercised by a variety of lower-level units, and actual control from the top is minimal (Samuel Eldersveld, 1964).

THE FUNCTIONS OF AMERICAN PARTIES

An understanding of party structure gives only a very superficial answer to the question: What is a party? A far better way to look at political parties is to look at what they do.

Political Party Organization: National, State, and Local

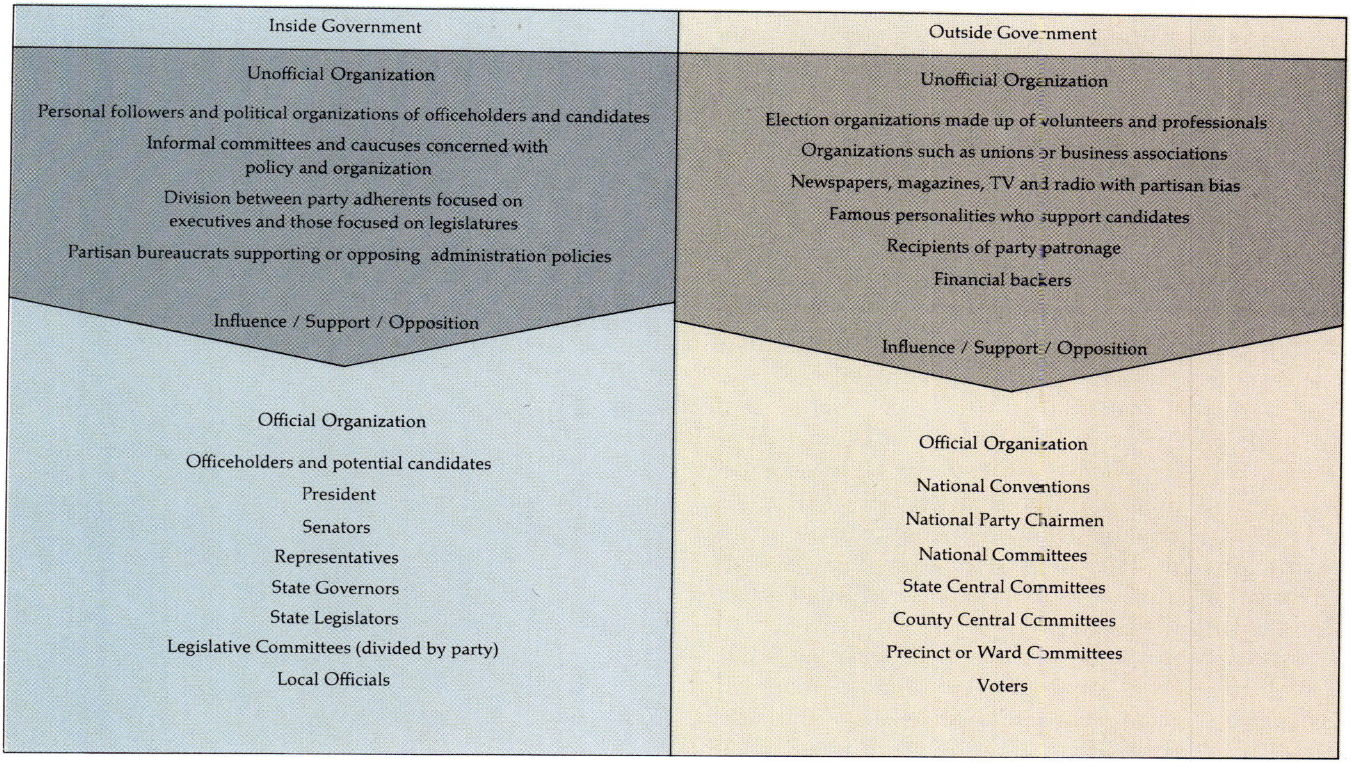

Inside Government	Outside Government
Unofficial Organization	**Unofficial Organization**
Personal followers and political organizations of officeholders and candidates	Election organizations made up of volunteers and professionals
Informal committees and caucuses concerned with policy and organization	Organizations such as unions or business associations
Division between party adherents focused on executives and those focused on legislatures	Newspapers, magazines, TV and radio with partisan bias
Partisan bureaucrats supporting or opposing administration policies	Famous personalities who support candidates
	Recipients of party patronage
	Financial backers
Influence / Support / Opposition	*Influence / Support / Opposition*
Official Organization	**Official Organization**
Officeholders and potential candidates	National Conventions
President	National Party Chairmen
Senators	National Committees
Representatives	State Central Committees
State Governors	County Central Committees
State Legislators	Precinct or Ward Committees
Legislative Committees (divided by party)	Voters
Local Officials	

Political parties were organized for the purpose of gaining power, and political power in America depends on winning elections. Political parties serve as the organizational framework within which many different interest groups combine in order to win elections, especially the Presidency. Thus, although parties serve several additional functions, their foremost reason for existing is to sponsor winning candidates for political office. As one observer has pointed out, "Whatever else they may or may not do, the parties must make nominations" (E. E. Schattschneider, 1948).

The Nomination Process

In nominating candidates for political office, parties are giving cues to the voters about which candidates best represent their interests. Without parties to screen and to select candidates, voters would be at a loss to choose among the helter-skelter of candidates who would offer themselves for election. In addition, to ensure that the representatives of important minorities or of certain sectional interests are not excluded from office, party tickets aim to provide a preselected reconciliation of competing interests. If the compromise is too neglectful of some interest within the party, those people who feel slighted may be drawn away by the opposition party. These aims and pressures are responsible for the evolution of the party nominating process.

Nomination by Caucus and by Convention

During the early years of the Republic, candidates were chosen in party meetings, or *caucuses,* which were composed of party leaders, legislators, and officeholders; the caucus met in order to maintain party control over those candidates who were running for office under the party label. This system, however unrepresentative, had the advantage of allowing the custodians of the party to select those who were to represent it. But in the 1830s and 1840s, when party members began to argue that it was wrong for candidates to be selected by those already in office, the caucus as a system of candidate selection fell into disrepute.

A more representative method of selecting nominees—the party convention—gradually emerged. Delegates selected from the lower levels of the party hierarchy convened to nominate candidates and to

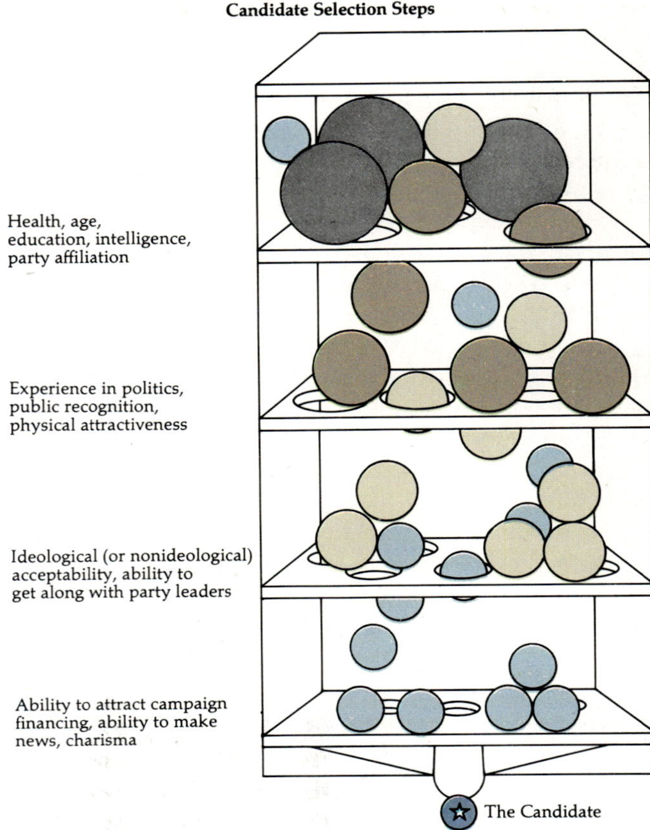

Figure 13.9 When parties informally endorse or formally nominate candidates to run in direct primaries, there must be a previous selection process by which the party organization makes its decision. Some of the main steps of the complex screening process by which party hopefuls are measured and selected are indicated above. It should be noted that these considerations do not exclude others, such as work in previous campaigns or special relationships with influential officeholders, nor is the order of the screening process fixed.

Figure 13.10 Mayor Richard Daley during the 1968 Democratic convention in Chicago. This convention received much attention because it pointed out the rift in the Democratic Party between the old-time party regulars and the younger, idealistic, party amateurs. Up until the party reform procedures of the McGovern-Fraser Committee went into effect during the 1972 Democratic convention, such officeholders as mayors, governors, and congressmen formed the hard core of the organized political parties and were thereby able to dominate conventions.

write a party *platform,* the body of promises and principles on which the party would make its appeal for voter support. Although it was an improvement, the convention system still excluded all but a few of the citizens from the nominating process. Reformers began casting about for an alternative method of making nominations that would be more responsive to the popular will.

The Direct Primary

The direct primary system of nomination first gained popularity in Wisconsin in 1904 and by 1915 had spread across the nation. It is a system that allows the voters from each party to choose the candidates that will be pitted against the opposition on the later general election ballot. But the primary system—still in effect in a number of states—has come under attack in recent years. Critics again point to the unrepresentative aspects of selection, but cite voter apathy as the culprit—in a sample of fifteen nonsouthern states, V. O. Key, Jr. found that less than 35 percent of the electorate voted in most primary elections (Key, 1964).

The low voter turnout in primaries often produces a slate of nominees who can muster only very limited popular support. But there is another disturbing aspect of the primary system—the removal of party influence has resulted in large numbers of self-starter candidates who owe little or nothing to the party. These self-starters decide on their own to run, do not seek party approval, and sometimes run "reform" campaigns against the very party organization under whose banner they march. Consequently, many argue that the direct primary has further eroded the concept of party responsibility and has greatly reduced the role of party leadership in the area of politics for which parties are most responsible—the nominating process. These criticisms have been partially overcome in some states by various kinds of endorsement procedures used to cue party members toward those primary candidates whose nomination is desired by the party leadership. For example, although a number of candidates may be contending for the same party's congressional nomination, the local and state party organization may officially endorse only one of them. Such endorsements usually have considerable impact on the decisions made by the voters.

The Organized Struggle for Power

Another important function of parties is to provide an organized continuity in the struggle for political power. Because of parties, those coalitions of interests that are defeated on election day have not lost everything, nor have they lost forever. The winners may take office, but the losers retain a party organization and a substantial base of supporters with which to resist policies contrary to their interests and from which to prepare to resume the competition for power at the next election. As Clinton Rossiter has noted: Each political party "... is a citadel that can withstand the impact of even the most disastrous national landslide and thus provide elements of obstinacy and stability in the two-party system" (Rossiter, 1960).

The Organization of Government

Parties also provide the resources for organizing the government. Although Presidents ordinarily appoint members of both parties to serve in the Administration, they rely primarily on fellow party members; in choosing which party members to appoint, they are to some extent guided by the particular coalition of interests predominant in their party. In similar fashion, it is on the basis of party that power in Congress is apportioned (see Chapter 8). For instance, the majority party (that party with the most seats in Congress) elects the Speaker of the House, the President Pro Tem of the Senate, and makes the major decisions regarding the choice of committee positions.

Although they are relatively effective as organizers, however, parties are not nearly so effective in guiding the policy decisions of either the Administration or of Congress. Party coalitions tend to come unglued in Congress, and it is commonplace for members to desert their party on important votes or for congressmen not to support the programs proposed by a President of the same party. Nevertheless, despite the lack of strong party discipline, parties are still the strongest determinant of a congressman's vote. Even though the average congressman is pulled in many directions by the various and often contradictory constituency interests that he represents, there is still an identifiable Democratic or Republican loyalty that shows up in his voting record. And party loyalty in Congress tends to be greatest in election

Figure 13.11 For many party delegates, the presidential convention is fun and hoopla or a moment in the sun to be remembered with pride. Many convention goers are amateurs and many of them never get behind the scenes of national politics even though they may be political notables in their home districts. Early in the nineteenth century, political parties began to mask the seriousness of their business with the frivolity of popular campaigns. The songs, drinking, camaraderie, and jokes give the professionals an image of fraternity with the ordinary folk, an image necessitated by the onset of universal suffrage and the distribution of power into the hands of the people. The donkey and the elephant, the celebrities, and the homespun humor make the momentous personnel and policy decisions of the transfer of power enjoyable to the many.

years when the lure of taking or holding control of Congress or the White House reinvigorates party members to work toward the primary goal of party politics: to conciliate the conflicts among a sufficient number of groups, sections, races, religions, classes, and ideologies to form an electoral majority in support of party-selected candidates.

WEAKNESSES OF AMERICAN PARTIES

The same features that make mass-based, coalition parties powerful in elections make them relatively weak in the governmental process. The strength of these parties comes from their diverse base and from the fact that they are built up from local organizations rather than down from a national leadership. Unlike members of most European parties, senators and representatives do not owe their positions to the national party—they were nominated and elected by state or district party organizations back home. (Strength is gained from this arrangement because it places decision-making power at the level where elections occur, a situation that maximizes the flexibility of parties and therefore increases their chances of winning elections.) Congressional parties are in this sense "pot luck," because they usually contain members with widely diverse, and sometimes antagonistic, political views. Thus some Republicans in Congress represent cities and suburbs concerned with keeping food prices down, and other Republicans represent farmers who are determined to get a better price for their meat and produce. Similarly, the Democratic membership of Congress includes representatives of black districts as well as representatives of districts composed primarily of southern segregationists.

Party Passiveness

Such diversity in the absence of national party power makes it difficult for either party to force its candidates to enact the campaign promises that were made as part of the party platform at the nominating convention. A member of a British or French party who habitually deserted his party and voted with the opposition would soon be expelled from the party and denied a seat in Parliament. Democrats and Republicans in Congress, however, can abandon party positions with impunity as long as the people back home continue to reelect them.

THE DEMOCRATIC PARTY REFORM MOVEMENT

Late on the second night of the 1968 Democratic national convention in Chicago, the forces committed to Robert Kennedy and Eugene McCarthy won their only important victory. By a roll-call vote the delegates adopted a reform resolution offered by the Ad Hoc Commission on the Democratic Selection of Presidential Nominees chaired by Governor Harold Hughes of Iowa. The late-night vote set in motion the most controversial and thoroughgoing review of the national convention process of nominating presidential candidates in American history.

To implement the resolution, National Chairman Fred Harris appointed two twenty-eight-member commissions in January 1969: The first was a commission on party structure and delegate selection to be headed by Senator George McGovern (who was later succeeded by Representative Donald Fraser), and the second was a commission on rules to be chaired by Representative James O'Hara. During the ensuing nine months a series of wide-ranging reforms were hammered out by the two commissions; the reforms were ultimately approved by the Democratic national committee and put into effect for the 1972 convention.

The McGovern-Fraser Commission produced eighteen specific changes in party rules and practices. They fell into three broad categories. First, the commission found that there was a wide range of procedures followed by the different states. No written party rules existed in at least ten states, and the delegate selection process was thus left to elected or appointed state officials. Furthermore, the "unit rule," an old practice by which a majority of a state's delegation could bind the minority to vote for the majority's choice, was widely used; proxy voting was permitted; and little public notice of delegate-selection meetings was provided.

The second area to be examined by the commission was the level of participation by black, female, and young delegates. In 1968 only 5.5 percent of the delegates were black, even though blacks made up 11 percent of the population; only 13 percent of the delegates were women even though over half the population was female; and only 4 percent of the delegates were under the age of 30 (and 16 delegations had no member at all within that age bracket).

The commission found other deficiencies of the party delegate selection process, deficiencies that it categorized as structural inadequacies. The commission noted, for example, that 38 percent of the 1968 delegates were selected before Senator McCarthy even announced his candidacy and that the choice was usually made by party committees that merely ratified delegate slates prepared and submitted by elected or appointed party or government leaders. Furthermore, it was found that fees had been assessed against delegates by state party organizations and that certain ex-officio delegates were not subject to any popular appraisal. There were many other practices that effectively excluded individuals from participation as delegates.

The McGovern-Fraser Commission proposed a series of guidelines for the state party organizations, and these were imposed by the Democratic national committee in an effort to correct the deficiencies. The guidelines urged the committee to:

1. *adopt explicit written party rules governing delegate selection;*
2. *adopt procedural rules and safeguards for the delegate-selection process in order to*
   - *forbid proxy voting;*
   - *ban the use of the unit rule;*
   - *require a quorum of not less than 40 percent at all party-committee meetings;*
   - *limit mandatory fees to no more than $10;*
   - *ensure, except in rural areas, that party meetings are held on uniform dates in public places;*
   - *ensure adequate public notice of all party meetings involved in the delegate-selection process;*
3. *seek a broader base for the party by*
   - *adding anti-racial-discrimination standards to state party rules;*
   - *encouraging representation on the state's convention delegation to minority groups, young people, and women in a reasonable relationship to their presence in the state's population;*
   - *allowing all persons eighteen years of age or older to participate in all party affairs;*
4. *make the following changes in the delegate-selection process:*
   - *select alternates in the same manner as delegates;*
   - *ban designation of ex-officio delegates;*
   - *conduct the entire process of delegate selection within the calendar year of the election;*
   - *select at least 75 percent of the total delegation at conventions at a level no higher than congressional districts, and follow apportionment formulas;*
   - *designate procedures by which delegate slates are prepared and may be challenged;*
   - *select no more than 10 percent of the delegates by the state committee.*

After a slow start, all the Democratic state parties began to carry out the mandate of the national committee by holding hearings, introducing bills, and amending party rules to accomplish the reforms. Ultimately, the performance of the states was mixed, but all made a minimal effort and, after many credentials challenges, had delegations seated that more nearly met the "anti-discrimination" guidelines. Under the new procedures, the 1972 convention delegations included 15.5 percent blacks, 40 percent women, and 21.4 percent who were under the age of 30. The unit rule was abolished in all states except California where party leaders flatly refused to comply. All delegates were chosen during the 1972 calendar year, and the selection process was broadened to include more local participation in delegate selection.

However, the events at the convention plus the landslide loss of Senator McGovern clouded the future of the Democratic reform effort. Old-line party regulars, who represented the old New Deal coalition, believed that they were the victims of discrimination and that their more practical approach to consensus politics was ignored. They contended that the reform elements practiced exclusionary politics and thus destroyed the well-established base of Democratic presidential politics.

The party reformers retorted that change was long overdue and that the old coalition was in a state of political decay and collapse. They argued that if the party were to survive it had to make special efforts to bring newly involved voters and workers into the party's fold.

While most attention was directed to the McGovern-Fraser Commission's efforts, the O'Hara Commission on Rules was preparing its proposals for procedural reform. Endorsed by the Democratic national committee, the new procedures provided for fewer and shorter speeches, abolished floor demonstrations, detailed means through which credentials challenges were to be decided, and ordered that housing, seating arrangements, and the order of roll-call votes be determined by lot.

Reform supporters believed that most of the procedural and delegate selection changes were long overdue and that they helped to democratize the national convention and the national committee. Critics contended that the changes went too far, that they excluded many of those who constituted the old Democratic Party, and that they were a contributing factor to the 1972 presidential defeat.

It is probable that the Democratic Party will temper the reform experiments. But the real question is whether the party reformers and the party regulars can reach a workable compromise on permanent party reforms. Will they be able to provide a home for the traditional elements of the Democratic Party as well as make room for the new participants who emerged in 1968 and 1972?

Because of the deep ideological divisions that lie submerged within mass coalition parties, party positions tend to be relatively nonideological in order to avoid alienating any particular group within the party. In consequence, parties are rather blunt instruments with which to carry out political promises.

This nonideological stance leads parties to act to preserve the status quo; their capacity to act boldly to meet popular needs with innovative policies is thereby greatly impeded. As Everett Ladd, Jr. has stated:

. . . this party passiveness before social change has probably had a salutary effect, contributing to the capacity of the parties to perform a "peacemaking" or "reconciling" function. But in a period of exceptionally rapid and extensive change—and none has been more pronounced in this regard than our own—it also has the adverse effect of heightening the sense of unresponsiveness in the political system. (Ladd, 1970)

Internal Conflicts and Limited Alternatives

The coalitional character of both parties also results in considerable internal conflict between party regulars (those the press often call the "political pros") and party activists. Party regulars work for the party as precinct captains and ward bosses and in many other organizational capacities; they do so to obtain power or an appointment to a government job. Because they are called on to work in support of candidates with quite diverse views, however, party regulars tend not to hold strong ideological positions.

Party activists are those who participate in campaign activities on the basis of their ideological commitments. They are particularly prevalent when there is an available candidate who represents a clearly defined political ideology. Thus, Barry Goldwater and George McGovern attracted large numbers of volunteer workers—party amateurs who felt strongly about the causes the candidates represent.

Because party activists tend to be committed to an ideological cause rather than to the more pragmatic goal of winning the election—the goal of party regulars—they frequently resist the compromises on which successful coalition parties are built. In both the Goldwater and McGovern cases, for example, the activists triumphed over the regulars

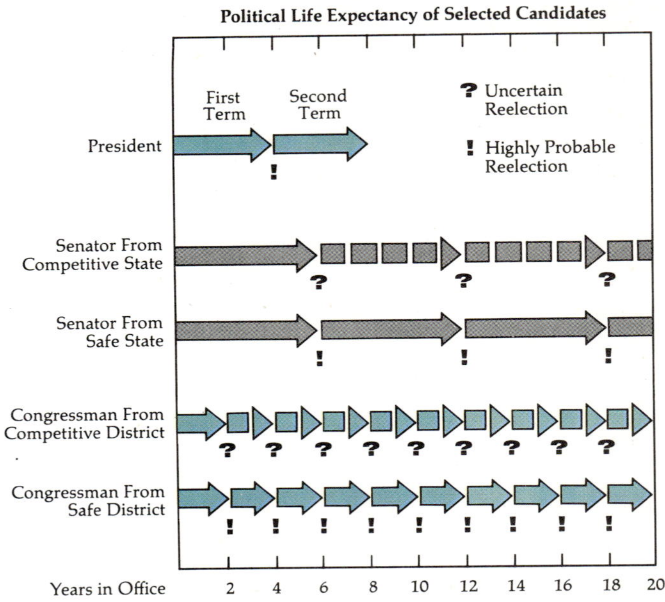

Figure 13.12 One of the primary factors affecting officeholders' chances for reelection is the party make-up of their constituencies. The above chart illustrates the differences between the comfortable outlook of an officeholder from a safe district or state (in which one of the parties consistently wins) and the not-so-comfortable outlook of an officeholder from a more competitive district or state. Most remarkable is the contrast between the long-term security of the senator from a safe state and the constantly running congressman (or representative) from a competitive district, whose incumbency is in doubt every two years. Such patterns of safety or insecurity influence party strategies and thus the political choices offered the voters.

and gained the presidential nomination for their man, but they met disaster at the polls (caused in part because many regulars "sat out" the election). Thus, although it may have been intellectually honest for McGovern activists to exclude Chicago Mayor Richard Daley and his Illinois delegation from the Democratic convention, it was also the best possible way to lose the election in Illinois to the opposition candidate, Richard Nixon.

Party regulars are generally more successful at winning power for their party than are activists; as a result, they usually are the ones who hold power within the party. Their nonideological stance, however, as well as their knowledge of what the voters will accept, leads them to select candidates with the broadest public appeal. The result is a narrowing of the range of political alternatives among which the American public is permitted to choose.

The two American parties thus cling to the center, because the margin of votes that either party needs in order to win lies in the middle. If either party moves very far to the left or to the right it invites the other to capture all of the middle-of-the-road political support—as was the case in Johnson's 1964 landslide when the Republicans moved to the right and in Nixon's 1972 landslide when the Democrats moved to the left.

But the two-party system must not be characterized as either wholly wonderful or wholly bad. It does serve to maximize government stability, for elections always produce a winner with an uncontested right to a specific term of office (in contrast with multiparty systems, in which the government frequently depends on coalitions among parties and can be removed from power whenever the coalition breaks up over some issue). The two-party system also mutes political conflict to such an extent that a transfer of power from one party to the other is tolerable to supporters of the other party. If ideological differences between parties became too sharp, it would become increasingly difficult for losing parties to accept the outcome of elections; the danger would thereby increase that they might turn to undemocratic means to seize or to maintain their hold on power.

On the other hand, as has been shown, the two-party system tends to be inefficient for translating programs into policy and for responding to public needs. Reforms come only very slowly, and groups with a special grievance may be frustrated in their efforts to gain redress (a process that is discussed in Chapter 16). Furthermore, the two-party system tends to greatly exaggerate the political power of moderate voters and candidates. Both parties are encouraged to take their habitual supporters for granted and to tailor their platforms, candidates, and campaigns to attract the minority of voters without a party affiliation.

Throughout this discussion of parties it has been necessary to bring in the voter because, in large part, parties do what they do in order to win votes. To fully understand parties, then, it is necessary to understand the voters.

THE AMERICAN VOTER

"American voters" and "the American public" are not synonymous terms. Even in presidential elections, only a bare majority of the public votes. In most off-year congressional elections—those that do not occur simultaneously with the presidential election—and in state and local elections, voter turnout is typically well below half (Robert Alford and Eugene Lee, 1968). To understand voting, one needs to know why more people do not vote and who the people are who do vote. Only then can the question of how people normally vote be discussed.

Barriers to Voting

Part of the reason for low voter turnout is that there are features of the law and of the election system that make it hard, or even impossible, for some people to vote. During the early decades of American history, for example, only white, male property owners who had lived in a community for a long time could vote. The first extension of *suffrage* (the right to vote) eliminated the property-owner restriction, giving the vote to virtually all white males over the age of twenty-one. Passage of the Fifteenth Amendment in 1870 extended suffrage to black males. Their right to vote was soon greatly restricted, however, so that just prior to World War II, only 5 percent of blacks in the South were registered voters (Donald Matthews and James Prothro, 1963). In 1920 women were finally given the vote through the adoption of the Nineteenth Amendment, but it took many years before eligible women came close to voting in the same proportion as men. Finally, the Twenty-sixth Amendment lowered the voting age from twenty-one to eighteen in time for the 1972 election.

In the South major barriers were erected to prevent blacks from voting. Poll taxes and literacy tests were put into effect; the tests were easily manipulated to prevent registration of blacks regardless of their actual level of literacy. (These rules kept down voting among poor whites as well.) The restrictions were removed by a series of voting rights acts passed by Congress between 1965 and 1970. In consequence, registration of blacks in Mississippi increased ten times, from 30,000 to almost 300,000 registered black voters within several years.

Residency requirements have also served to restrict voting. Most states required voters to have been residents for at least a year and to have lived in a county and precinct for several months in order to register. Because Americans move so often, it is estimated that perhaps as many as 5 million voters were barred from recent presidential elections on these grounds. Recent changes have reduced residency requirements for national elections.

Registration itself is a barrier to voting. In a number of European countries, a voter need only show up at the polling place on election day to automatically become registered. In many parts of the United States, however, registration is closed well before election day and thus before many potential voters have become sufficiently aware of an impending election to get registered. Some states require voters to reregister if they have failed to vote for two successive years.

Voting also tends to be curtailed in areas where the same party overwhelmingly wins election after election (one-party congressional districts or states). In such a situation, supporters of the excluded party tend not to vote because they believe their vote would be useless, and supporters of the dominant party tend not to vote because they feel their vote is not needed.

Disinterest

Even when all of these barriers to voting are taken into account, however, it remains that the overwhelming majority of Americans easily could vote, but a substantial proportion of them do not do so. As is mentioned in Chapter 12, most people simply

A sample of the 44 million nonvoters were asked: What was it that kept you from voting? (Gallup, 1972)

15 million were registered but were disinterested or did not like the candidates.
10 million could have registered but did not.
7 million were sick or disabled.
5 million were prevented from voting by residence requirements.
3 million were away from home.
3 million said they could not leave their jobs.
1 million did not obtain absentee ballots.

"Voting is the only way people like me can have a say about how the government runs things" (Survey Research Center, 1970).

1964	1966	1968	1970
73%	68%	57%	65%

POLITICAL PARTICIPATION

Generally speaking, how much interest would you say you have in politics—a great deal, a fair amount, only a little, or no interest at all? (Gallup, 1972)

	BY AGE 21–29 Years
Great deal	*18%*
Fair Amount	*48*
Little	*30*
No Interest	*4*

	30–49 Years
Great deal	*18%*
Fair amount	*52*
Little	*27*
No interest	*3*

	50 Years and Over
Great deal	*18%*
Fair amount	*46*
Little	*30*
No interest	*6*

Figure 13.13 Voting in New York City, 1915–1920. The appearance of women in the two bottom photos reflects the passage of the Nineteenth Amendment. In fact, the center picture displays the first votes cast by women in a New York City election.

are not very interested in politics; they are uninformed about issues and candidates and on many local and even statewide election days they do not even know that there is an election going on. The public's disinterest and lack of knowledge are reflected in the fact that voter turnout is greatly influenced by the scale of the election campaign. In the presidential election of 1972, for example, approximately 55 percent of American adults voted; in the 1970 midterm congressional elections, however, only 45 percent did so (Congressional Quarterly, 1970; 1972). The same disinterest is reflected in presidential primary elections in which only about 33 percent of the voters turn out (Austin Ranney, 1972) and in local elections, in which turnouts are even lower (Frank Sorauf, 1972). It seems that intense campaigning and the major issues of presidential elections reach only a bare majority of adults and get them interested enough to go to the polls.

Who Votes?

Not all groups or classes of Americans are equally likely to vote. In general, socially disadvantaged groups tend to be nonvoters, and the socially advantaged are the ones who show up at the polls regularly to cast their votes. The following factors influence who votes:

1. Income. The more money a person makes, the more likely he or she is to vote (Angus Campbell *et al.,* 1960).
2. Education. The higher a person's education, the more likely he or she is to vote.
3. Age. People between the ages of thirty-five and fifty-five are considerably more likely to vote than are younger and older persons (Campbell *et al.,* 1960). People do not seem to develop regular voting habits until they have established themselves in life. The fall off in voting among the elderly seems to be due to physical infirmities.
4. Sex. Men are more likely than women to vote. In recent elections, however, the voting gap between men and women has been getting smaller (Gallup, 1972).
5. Race. Whites are more likely than nonwhites to vote. Much of the large difference in past voting stemmed from discrimination against black voters. Remaining differences are primarily due to education and income differences between whites and nonwhites. Minority voter turnout rises greatly when a member of a minority is a candidate for office.

6. Party. Because (as is discussed later) Republican voters are more likely to be college educated and to earn high incomes than are Democratic voters, Republicans are more likely than are Democrats to vote.
7. Partisanship. Persons who identify themselves either as Republicans or Democrats are more likely to vote than are persons calling themselves independents (Campbell *et al.*, 1960).

A major reason for these differences in voting patterns is the degree to which people believe they can influence political decisions. Angus Campbell and his associates attribute these differences in voting patterns to people's sense of "political efficacy"—the degree to which a person believes "the affairs of government can be understood and influenced by individual citizens" (Campbell *et al.*, 1960). Campbell's findings showed that persons with a high sense of their own political efficacy virtually always vote.

It is hardly surprising that those groups most likely to vote—the educated, the well-to-do, the middle-aged, whites, and Republicans—are much more likely to believe in their ability to influence government. Indeed, one reason for their confidence is that by producing much higher voter turnouts, these groups do indeed have an impact on elections far out of proportion to their actual numbers in the population. A rich man's vote does not count for any more than a poor man's; but it does if the rich man votes and the poor man does not. Similar patterns are found in all forms of political participation, not just in voting. The socially advantaged are more likely to write letters to public officials, to contribute to campaigns, and even to display political bumper stickers (Bernard Berelson and Gary Steiner, 1964).

Which Candidates Do They Vote For?

Americans like to pride themselves on voting for the man rather than for the party. In election after election, however, at least half of the public votes a strict party line. As a farmer in a famous Bill Mauldin cartoon explained, "Me, I vote the man, not the party. Hoover, Landon, Dewey, Eisenhower, Nixon, Goldwater, Nixon." Somehow it just happened that each was a Republican.

Table 13.1 shows the degree of party regularity among voters. Although there are more Democrats than Republicans, the extent of this numerical ad-

vantage is not reflected in the vote because Democrats are less likely to actually vote than are Republicans (as is shown in the third column of Table 13.1).

Table 13.1   Voter Turnout

GROUP	PERCENT OF POPULATION	PERCENT THAT NORMALLY VOTE
Strong Democrats	20	72
Weak Democrats	24	61
Independents	29	57
Weak Republicans	16	72
Strong Republicans	11	84
Totals	100	65

Source: From Converse, Philip E. "The Concept of a Normal Vote," in Angus Campbell, Philip Converse, Warren Miller, and Donald Stokes, *Elections and the Political Order* (New York: Wiley, 1966), pp. 9–39.

Because of party-line voting, all candidates in partisan elections begin with an irreducible basis of voter support—no amount of campaigning can substantially cut into the other party's loyalist vote. Thus, elections are won or lost in accordance with the success of appeals to independents and to those voters who do not consistently vote with their party. Winning strategies therefore require that partisanship be deemphasized. Candidates who make their strongest campaign effort toward their own party loyalists make a serious error (except in one-party states or districts), because these votes can be counted on in any event. The votes needed to win lie in the uncommitted center of the political spectrum and among those voters of the opposition party with moderate views and less intense party loyalties. Thus, the voting habits of the American public greatly parallel the nonideological nature of the two major parties.

The Basis of Party Support

It is hardly accidental that some people are Republicans and others Democrats—party choice is not random.

Historic ties between a party and a region or a group account for many party loyalties. For decades following the Civil War period, for example, the "Solid South" voted only for Democratic candi-

□

PARTY REALIGNMENT

The alignment of groups within the American political party system is often an extremely delicate maneuver. During the days of Franklin Roosevelt's New Deal, the Democratic Party managed to attract blacks away from their traditional Republican affiliation (based on Lincoln's Republicanism) while still maintaining the solid Democratic votes of white southerners. After Roosevelt's death this coalition began to come unstuck. Southern resentment over a liberal civil rights plank in the 1948 Democratic platform led them to back the States' Rights third party. The Democratic candidate, Harry Truman, managed to win reelection anyway, despite the fact that the traditionally solid Democratic southern states voted for Strom Thurmond for President. Momentarily chastened when their defection proved an empty gesture, the white southerners returned to the Democratic Party—for awhile. But in 1964 they gave their support to the Republican Barry Goldwater, and in 1968 the states of the Deep South backed a maverick Democrat, George Wallace, again on a third-party ticket.

These defections of traditionally Democratic voters presented a tempting target to Republicans and led to the Nixon "southern strategy" (see Chapter 9). Gingerly the Republicans tried to realign their traditional supporters sufficiently to permit a strong appeal to the regional interests of the South. Their freedom to do so came in large part from their earlier loss of all but token black support. In 1972 the southern strategy appeared a success although it was obscured by the size of the Nixon landslide.

If the South is now Republican, then it would appear that over a period of nearly forty years, Republicans traded black support to the Democrats in return for the "Solid South." But meanwhile the Democrats replaced the Republicans as the majority party on college campuses (Gallup, 1972). And so it goes: give a little, get a little.

dates—they regarded the Republicans as the party of Lincoln and of the "Yankee Carpetbaggers" who had ruled the South during the postwar period of reconstruction. By the same token, blacks, when they were permitted to vote by the Fifteenth Amendment, overwhelmingly voted for the party of Lincoln and emancipation. This pattern has only recently broken down, with blacks becoming Democrats after the New Deal and the South going Republican in the 1960s (see □).

There is also a religious pattern to voting: Protestants have tended to be Republicans (except in the South), and Catholics have preferred the Democratic label. This religious partisanship partly accounts for the fact that the farm states of the Midwest have long been Republican country (Protestants are more numerous in small towns and on the farms), and large cities have been traditional Democratic strongholds (Catholics tend to outnumber Protestants in large cities). One reason for this religious pattern in voting is that during the major waves of Catholic immigration in the last part of the nineteenth century, the Republican Party contained a strong nativist, antiforeigner element. The Democrats, on the other hand, welcomed the Catholics (Seymour Martin Lipset, 1960). The only Catholics to have been nominated for President were Al Smith in 1928 and John Kennedy in 1960, and both were big-city Democrats.

In multiparty systems an obvious basis for political parties is social class: One party reflects the interests of the wealthy, for instance, another, the economic interests of the small shopkeeper, and another the interests of blue-collar workers. In America, however, parties are not nearly so representative of any one economic interest group. There are many wealthy Democrats, for instance, and many poor Republicans. But although the coalition character of both parties muffles their appeals to either advantaged or disadvantaged groups, they nevertheless do reflect somewhat different political ideologies and represent different groups of voters. The Republicans are the more conservative party and tend to draw their support from business and the well-to-do. The Democrats are the more liberal party and tend to draw their support from labor and the economically disadvantaged. Although the many factors discussed earlier limit the degree of class-based ideological politics that either party can engage in, the American two-party system does reflect the eternal conflict between the haves who want to keep what they have, and the have-nots who want to get more. The differences in the party's support are apparent in the following voting patterns taken from *The Gallup Poll,* 1972:

1. Race. In recent national elections as many as nine out of ten blacks have supported the Democrats—in the presidential election of 1968, 85 percent did so, whereas only 38 percent of whites voted for the democratic candidate.
2. Income. Whereas more than half of those Americans who earn less than $3,700 a year identified themselves as Democrats in 1969, only a third of those earning $10,000 or more chose the Democrats.
3. Education. In 1969, 52 percent of those persons with only grade-school education were Democrats, compared to 42 percent of those who had finished high school and 28 percent of those who had attended college.
4. Occupation. Only about 30 percent of those persons in the professions or in business called themselves Democrats in 1969, whereas almost 46 percent of the manual workers did so.
5. Sex. Although 30 percent of the men polled said they were Democrats in 1969, 44 percent of the women did so.

In each of these comparisons, those with less access to power, prestige, and the good life were more likely to be Democrats.

It must be recognized that these statistics suggest only *tendencies* and that no major category of Americans—neither the blacks, the workers, nor the uneducated—gives all its support to one party. Indeed, it is in the nature of coalition parties that groups do not become wholly polarized along party lines. Nevertheless, there are clear tendencies for such groups to follow their interests by supporting the party that is more responsive to their needs.

POLITICS OF THE CENTER

The discussion of parties and voting has thus come full circle. The fact that both parties gain significant support from all major interest groups and that victory in elections depends on gaining support from independents and from moderate members of the opposition party keeps both political parties

Figure 13.14 In the great game of politics, campaign buttons record the history of fierce political partisanship and the competition for votes.

anchored in the middle of the left-right political spectrum. Yet there is another way of looking at this situation: American voters tend to be concentrated in the middle of the political spectrum because that is the only range of plausible political alternatives available to them.

If, as was pointed out in Chapter 12, the majority of voters cannot correctly identify the liberal and conservative positions on many major issues, this inability partly results from the fact that they find it so hard to distinguish between Republican and Democratic positions on the issues. Although periodically one party or the other has shifted more noticeably to the left or to the right, the resulting political defeat has quickly checked the process.

As long as the two-party system endures, clearly differentiated political choices will be uncommon in American politics. In light of the structure of the American election system and of the nation's traditions, the two-party system is apt to be around for a long time to come, and American party politics will remain a politics of the center.

SUMMARY

American political parties cling to the ideological center of the political spectrum in order to appeal to the majority of voters. Differing from the multiparty systems of Western Europe, two-party systems tend to compromise differences within the parties prior to elections, rather than compromising differences between the parties afterwards. The United States thus has coalition parties rather than coalition governments.

Parties nominate candidates, promote continuity in the political struggle, provide the machinery for organizing government, and play a role in shaping policies and programs. Yet their diverse base of support and the fact that they are organized from the local level up (factors that facilitate their role in elections) prevent parties from exercising much control over the candidate once he is in office.

Because of voter apathy, lack of a sense of political efficacy, and residency requirements, only a bare majority of the American public votes. Political affiliation and voter turnout are strongly related to income and educational level. Voter loyalty to party tends to be high even though the coalitional nature of American parties makes them virtually indistinguishable on many issues.

SUGGESTED READINGS

Bachrach, Peter. *The Theory of Democratic Elitism: A Critique.* Boston: Little, Brown, 1967.

Broder, David S. *The Party's Over.* New York: Harper & Row, 1972.

Cotter, Cornelius P., and Bernard C. Hennessy. *Politics Without Power: The National Party Committees.* New York: Atherton, 1964.

Key, V. O., Jr. *Politics, Parties, and Pressure Groups.* 5th ed. New York: Crowell, 1964.

Pomper, Gerald M. *Elections in America.* New York: Dodd, Mead, 1968.

Sorauf, Frank. *Party Politics in America.* Boston: Little, Brown, 1968.

14
MONEY, MEDIA, AND CAMPAIGNS

Figure 14.1 From behind the scenes, many political campaigns give the impression that the electronic media, and especially television, have taken over the electoral system. Incredible sums of money are gobbled by the technology required to attach an impression of reasonableness, wisdom, even homey friendliness and sincerity to a candidate that may previously have been completely unknown to the public. The size of the country and a population accustomed to the simple, quick blandishments of television advertising have changed the American style of campaigning from communal fun to big business.

In and of themselves, elections neither guarantee nor necessarily indicate democracy. Many dictatorial regimes hold elections; however, the only vote permitted is a vote for the party in power. The fundamental feature of democratic elections is choice—voters are allowed to select among competing parties and candidates. Because political campaigns are simply the means by which choices are put before the voters, it follows that campaigning is fundamental to democratic elections. And fundamental to campaigning are money and media. This chapter is about the ways in which mass media campaigns and the need for large sums of money affect the political process in America.

Many Americans regard political campaigns at best as gaudy, partisan spectacles and at worst as immoral and wasteful deceptions. Every election year also brings complaints that candidates are sold like commodities, that image making degrades the democratic process, and that money plays too central a role in American politics. One way of answering these complaints would be to allow only very limited, low-key campaigns. Before opting for change, however, one should look carefully at the repercussions that any changes might have on the democratic system.

One possible result of drastically reducing campaigning is that elections would become correspondingly less democratic. Why is this so? For voting to be a meaningful exercise of choice, voters must first be informed about the options and candidates put before them. America, however, is no longer a nation of small towns and rural villages in which the issues are few and directly relevant and in which voters are personally acquainted with the candidates. Typically a candidate must gain support from thousands and even millions of persons who have never met him, who never will, and who, initially, have never even heard of him. Any steps to make campaigns low-key would simply increase the proportion of uninformed voters. Consider that in January 1971, little more than a year and a half before George McGovern became the Democratic nominee for President, 58 percent of American adults could not identify him (Gallup, 1972). Without a vigorous campaign to overcome his anonymity and acquaint the public with his views, McGovern could never have been considered as a possible political choice for the majority of voters.

In addition, if campaigning were reduced it is probable that elections would be dominated by the wealthy and highly educated, who are much more likely to get to the polls and vote than are lower-middle and working-class persons (see Chapter 13). Suppose, for example, that there were 50 educated and well-to-do voters who favored candidate Smith. Suppose also that there were 100 less educated and less wealthy voters who favored candidate Brown. If on election day all 50 of Smith's supporters voted and only 45 of Brown's supporters did so, Smith of course would win—the educated and wealthy would in effect determine the outcome of the election because they were the ones who actually voted.

The previous illustration is not so very far from the present state of affairs. In presidential elections it is seldom that more than half the eligible population votes, and it is primarily the less educated and less affluent who do not. Even with present levels of intensive campaigning, the middle and upper classes have an impact on voting quite out of proportion to their numbers. Seen in this light, it becomes obvious that the choice is not simply between having either restrained or wide-open campaigns, it is between having campaigns restricted to the informed and interested few and campaigns aimed at the mass of voters.

Because American campaigns are aimed at the mass of voters, they are necessarily somewhat gaudy and undecorous—they must attract the attention of people whose attention tends to be hard to gain. They also depend heavily on the mass media—the only feasible means for communicating with masses of people. Therefore, they are expensive.

THE COST OF CAMPAIGNS

The cost of winning and holding office has sky-rocketed in recent years. In 1956 all candidates for public office spent a total of $155 million trying to get elected. By 1968 the amount spent by all candidates had nearly doubled and the cost of presidential politics had almost quadrupled—to approximately $48 million (Herbert Alexander, 1971).

Much of this rise in spending came from the increased use and costs of TV and radio advertising. (On the average, a one-minute commercial on network television in prime evening time costs $50,000.) Some of the increase is simply the result of infla-tion—money buys a good deal less now than it did in 1956—and of population growth. However, the increase in the amount of money spent on elections is greater than these factors should dictate. Candidates are simply spending more money on their elaborate, more extensive campaigns.

Table 14.1   Presidential Election Spending, 1948–1972

YEAR	PARTY	AMOUNT SPENT	ONE PARTY OUTSPENT OTHER BY:
1948	Democratic	$ 3,557,574	
	Republican	3,686,775*	3.6%
1952	Democratic	7,192,048	
	Republican	12,299,239*	71.0
1956	Democratic	8,298,116	
	Republican	13,220,144*	59.3
1960	Democratic	14,251,923*	
	Republican	12,950,232	10.1
1964	Democratic	18,765,033	
	Republican	19,314,796*	2.9
1968	Democratic	19,819,244	
	Republican	29,592,832*	49.3
1972	Democratic	As of 1973, figures unavailable	
	Republican		

* Party spending most
Source: Congressional Quarterly Service, *Politics in America*, 1945–1968, 3rd Edition, May 1969, p. 114.

The many reforms of election spending and financing that have been proposed reflect the widespread feeling that elections have become too expensive—$48 million does indeed seem like a lot of money to spend to select someone to be President. On the other hand, a great deal more than that is spent in any given year to advertise soap and deodorants (and surely choosing a President is no less important than choosing a deodorant). Although the estimated $400 million seems a great deal to have spent in 1972 on all political campaigning, it represents less than a thousandth of 1 percent of the total GNP for the same year. Put another way, perhaps $400 million is little enough to spend to choose those public officials—local, state, and national—who are responsible for spending $276 billion in public funds every year.

To decide whether present levels of political spending are excessive, one must first examine what money does and does not buy in elections, where political

Figure 14.2 Contact with the voters is an indispensable part of political campaigns. Senator Warren G. Harding, campaigning for the Presidency (top left), addressed an audience of women voters on October 6, 1920, only six weeks after the Nineteenth Amendment had granted women the right to vote. Governor Franklin Roosevelt (top right) greeted New York farmers in a fact-finding and vote-getting trip through the state. In a classical whistle-stop campaign, President Roosevelt and Senator Alben Barkley (above) campaigned for the party in the congressional elections of 1938. One of Richard Nixon's self-proclaimed "crises" stemmed from his defeat in the 1972 campaign for governor of California (center right) against Edmund G. Brown. After losing the presidential election by a narrow margin to John Kennedy (right) two years before, former Vice-President Nixon hoped his successful election to the governorship would put him back in line for the White House. Instead, Nixon went into law practice in New York and waited until 1968 to make another, and successful, bid for the highest office.

money comes from, the effect the need for money has on potential and elected officials, and the relative merits and shortcomings of alternatives to present practices.

WHO NEEDS HOW MUCH MONEY?

A number of systematic attempts have been made to determine just how much advantage goes to the biggest spenders in elections, but the results have been somewhat inconclusive. It is known, however, that spending a lot of money does not necessarily bring positive results. If, for instance, a candidate spends a great deal more money than does his opponent, he may become vulnerable to charges that he is trying to buy himself into office. Massive spending by one candidate may also arouse strong support for the "underdog." Furthermore, there are limits as to how much money can be spent effectively. After a certain saturation point is reached in mass media exposure, for example, more advertising is unlikely to produce significantly more votes. In fact, the opposite may occur—the campaign may wear out the voters' tolerance.

Similarly, no amount of campaign spending could get a Republican elected in some districts or a Democrat in others. Nor could spending get an outspoken supporter of busing elected to public office in rural Alabama, and it could not get a segregationist elected in Harlem. As one researcher concluded: "Financial outlays cannot guarantee victory in elections" (Alexander Heard, 1960).

Once candidates have some money in their campaign coffers, there are various factors that determine how much more is needed and how it should be spent. The remainder of this section deals with some of these factors and briefly discusses some alternative campaign resources.

Anonymity, Incumbents, and Nonincumbents

Frequently the first major problem faced by politicians, and the one that is most costly to overcome, is anonymity. Because of his need to become known, a relatively unknown candidate must spend more money, at least initially, than does a well-known candidate (unless the well-known candidate has a bad image to overcome). Consider the fact that in 1963, only one year before the presidential nominations, more than 50 percent of the American public

Figure 14.3 (right) A breakdown of some of the advantages and disadvantages of being an incumbent or a nonincumbent as well as the advantages and disadvantages of running in a large versus a small district. Advantages and disadvantages are further broken down in terms of name recognition and media use, funds and workers, and issues. Thus, one could describe the advantage an incumbent might have with respect to media use in a large district or, conversely, the advantage a nonincumbent might have with regard to workers in a large district. As is evident from examining the chart, incumbents have a decided edge in campaigns, a conclusion that is borne out by election statistics.

did not know who Barry Goldwater was, and 78 percent *did* know of Nelson Rockfeller, another potential nominee. Clearly, Goldwater had to spend more money than did Rockefeller simply to become known (Gallup, 1972).

The problem of anonymity is particularly important in a race between an incumbent and a nonincumbent. As Table 14.2 indicates, incumbent members of the House of Representatives and of the Senate who choose to run for reelection have a much better chance of winning than do their nonincumbent challengers. Previous campaigns and the visibility of persons in public office give incumbents a considerable initial advantage over potential opponents. The usual advantages of the incumbent (which generally include having a staff and having access to low-cost printing and recording facilities), coupled with the advantage of already being well known, mean that a nonincumbent must be especially successful in raising money if he is to offer any effective opposition.

The natural advantages of well-known candidates help to explain why political parties are so prone to welcome such celebrities as sports stars, astronauts, war heroes, and actors as candidates for political office. Obviously, simply being well known is not enough to win, as the defeats of Shirley Temple Black, John Glenn, and other celebrities have demonstrated. Other things being equal, however, famous

Table 14.2 Reelection of Senators and Representatives, 1960–1970

YEAR	INCUMBENT SENATORS		INCUMBENT REPRESENTATIVES	
	Defeated	Successful	Defeated	Successful
1960	3.6%	96.4%	7.2%	92.8%
1962	17.6	82.4	5.6	94.4
1964	15.2	84.8	12.5	87.5
1966	12.5	87.5	10.6	89.4
1968	38.6	71.4	2.0	98.0
1970	23.3	76.7	5.3	94.8

Sources: Congressional Quarterly Almanac 1960, pp. 766–767; Congressional Quarterly Almanac 1962, pp. 1044–45; Congressional Quarterly Almanac 1964, pp. 1010, 1076; Congressional Quarterly Almanac 1966, pp. 1404–05; Congressional Quarterly Almanac 1968, pp. 958–969; Congressional Quarterly Almanac 1970, p. 1080.

Incumbent and District Advantages and Disadvantages

	Incumbent	Nonincumbent	Large District	Small District
Candidate Recognition and Media Use	Has already received media exposure, and has easy access to media for campaign purposes	Needs to make name known (assuming he or she has not previously held public office)	Requires large advertising expenditures	Media often cover more than one district, so candidate must purchase unnecessary coverage
Funds and Workers	Services provided while in office bring candidate into contact with many politically valuable groups and possible donors to campaigns	Needs to build up following and contributors Usually has not had access to sources required for favor-trading	Requires large expenditures for media Because there are many competing groups, resources are more easily available to nonincumbents	Advertising expenses can be small. Circulars, organizational activity, and word-of-mouth campaigning usually prove to be adequately effective Candidate can more easily monopolize support of most important political and economic groups
Issues	Has knowledge of politics and issues from experience in office and an established public record Can create issues by making official remarks, holding press conferences, proposing legislation	May have knowledge of politics and issues, but has no official record on which to run for office Needs to develop dramatic or timely issues with which he or she can be identified	Many issues available to select from especially if there are many different groups in the district Must find a few issues affecting most voters to emphasize in campaign Too varied a district may force campaign to concentrate on personal images rather than on issues	Issues are few and are well known to voters; candidates must evidence specific knowledge of district's problems Organizational support for candidates may become more important than the issues of the election

candidates at least do not need to spend enormous sums of money merely to get people to remember their names.

Precinct Spending

Differences in the amount of money that candidates must spend also occur at the precinct-worker level. Some candidates can attract droves of volunteers to work in their campaigns, whereas others have to hire people to do the work. Often the difference is not in the "attractiveness" of the candidates per se but in differences in their bases of support. For instance, students have the free time and often the inclination to work as campaign volunteers; therefore, candidates with special support among students have much less need to hire campaign help then do candidates whose support comes mainly from, for example, factory workers.

Ordinarily, Democratic candidates need to spend more money on precinct work than do Republicans. This need results from the fact that people who usually vote Republican are more likely to register and to vote than are people who normally vote Democratic (see Chapter 13). Accordingly, Democrats need to make greater efforts than do Republicans to get their supporters registered and to the polls on election day, efforts that usually require heavier spending on precinct operations.

State Versus National and Local Elections

The degree to which a candidate must actively seek contributions for his campaign depends in part on whether he is running for a national, local, or state office. Because presidential candidates are usually visible enough to attract the interest and money of a large number of citizens, they can usually raise the money needed to wage at least a minimal campaign. At the local level many campaign resources are not costly, and personal, face-to-face campaigning is often possible because of the relatively small size of districts.

Candidates in statewide races (for senator or governor), however, usually have to engage modern, high-cost campaign weaponry because they must make themselves known throughout the entire state. Unlike presidential candidates, candidates for state offices cannot count on receiving the funds necessary for even a minimum campaign. Indeed, when

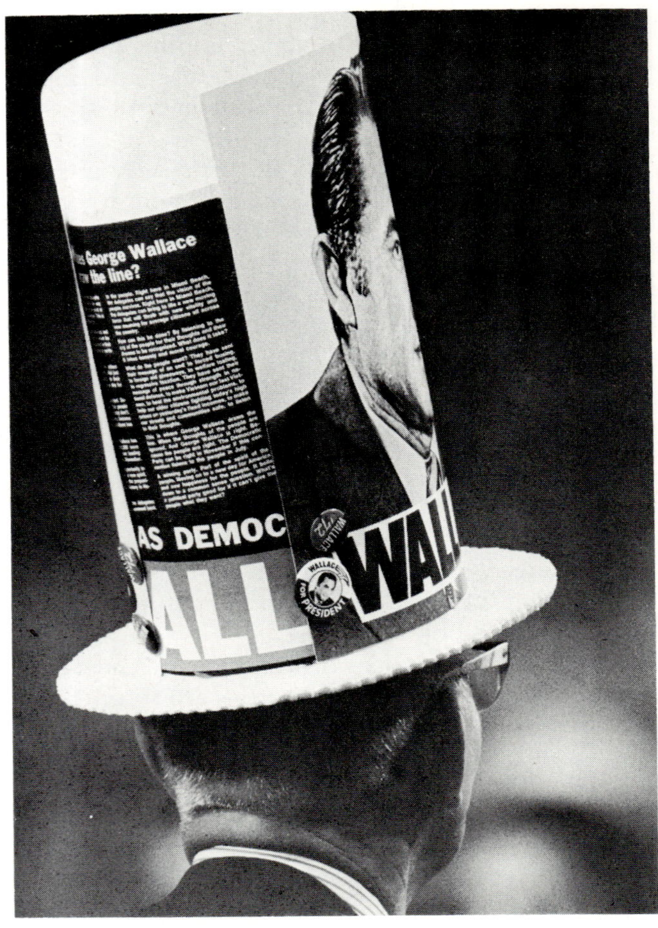

Figure 14.4 Who are they—the workers, contributors, enthusiasts? Under the gaudy hats are the persons who grease the complex wheels of political candidacies. They may be industrialists or clubwomen, officeholders or pensioners, small government advocates or civil servants. Some may contribute ten dollars once every four years, others one thousand dollars every two years. People are the resource behind money and advertising. The campaigner must capture the loyalties of a dedicated group of backers before the magic of word of mouth, of television image making, or of computerized mailings can ever begin.

state elections coincide with presidential elections, so much political money may be drained out of a state by a presidential candidate that state candidates face severe shortages. For example, many Republicans complained after the 1972 election that President Nixon's fund raisers had hurt them badly by monopolizing available Republican campaign donations.

Alternate Resources

As observers of the political scene have pointed out, perhaps no candidate is wealthy enough to hire the kinds of people who worked in John Kennedy's campaigns (Theodore White, 1961). Famous editors, scholars, executives, artists, and the like usually cannot be hired to work in campaigns; however, if they are sufficiently attracted to a candidate, they will volunteer. Money, it seems, is just one of many campaign resources.

Sometimes candidates hit on a gimmick that cannot be equaled by any amount of campaign spending. In 1970, for example, Lawton Chiles won election to the United States Senate from Florida against a much better financed opponent by taking a long walking tour of the state. As a result of the tour, he received so much news coverage in the mass media that he had little need to buy media advertising to get his name and his platform known to the voters. Such gimmicks will work, of course, only if they are unique and therefore newsworthy.

To sum up, the importance of money in any given election depends on a number of factors. Some candidates need much more money than do others. Resourceful or very attractive candidates can often find many substitutes for money, such as volunteers or ways of getting free media coverage. But all candidates need at least some money, and most need very substantial sums if they are to have any chance to win. Where does this money come from?

THE CONTRIBUTORS

Since April 1972, when the Federal Election Campaign Act of 1971 went into effect requiring public disclosure of the names of contributors to national election campaigns, Americans have finally gotten a look at how political campaigns are financed. The data shown in Table 14.3 indicate that only a small fraction of average Americans contribute any money to political campaigns. Such data reveal what many people have long assumed: Politics is paid for by a

Table 14.3   Political Campaign Contributors, 1968

INCOME	PERCENT WHO CONTRIBUTED
$0–2,999	2.9
3,000–5,999	4.1
6,000–8,999	7.1
9,000–11,999	7.6
12,000–19,999	12.0
20,000–more	36.7

Source: David Adamany, *Campaign Finance in America,* (North Scituate, Mass.: Duxbury Press, 1972), p. 83. The data were obtained from the University of Michigan Survey Research Center.

relatively small number of contributors who give very large sums of money. In the 1972 presidential election, for example, one contributor alone gave $2.1 million to Richard Nixon's campaign; another gave $1.0 million. In fact, the Nixon fund raisers were able to raise a total of $7.5 million from only eighteen contributors (Morton Mintz, 1973).

What causes contributors to give such huge sums of money to political candidates? There seem to be a number of motives. Some give so that they may claim the privilege of having senators as house guests, or they give in hopes of receiving such social favors as being invited to White House dinners. Others seek honors and status—it is not uncommon for large contributors to be appointed ambassadors to foreign nations.

Finally, most people give to a campaign because they strongly support the policy positions of a particular candidate. For example, several young millionaires have typically distributed their money in a kind of political philanthropy, much as their earlier counterparts contributed to more commonly recognized "good causes." One of the most visible of these contributors is Stuart Mott, heir to a General Motors fortune, whose contributions are clearly directed to liberal candidates with whom he is in ideological agreement. Indeed, any citizen who contributes may do so for similar reasons, even if his contribution is of somewhat lesser magnitude.

THE IMPACT OF CONTRIBUTIONS

In a very direct sense, people who contribute or fail to contribute to a candidate early in the office-seeking process play an extremely important role in deciding who gets to take his case to the voters. Aspiring candidates who can raise little or no money with which to seek nomination are often forced out of the race, even though they might have been able

Ambassadorial Donations to 1972 Nixon Campaign

Ambassador	Country	Amount
Walter H. Annenberg	Great Britain	$ 254,000
Henry E. Catto	El Salvador	25,000
Vincent de Roulet	Jamaica	28,000
Ruth L. Farkas	Luxembourg	300,000
John P. Humes	Austria	100,000
John N. Irwin	France	50,000
John V. Krehbiel	Finland	30,000*
Anthony D. Marshall	Trinidad and Tobago	48,505
Arthur K. Watson	France	300,000
	Total	$1,135,505

*Contributed to various Republican campaigns

Figure 14.5 Congress has recently been developing legislation to control the extent and the influence of large campaign contributions. Among its concerns has been the relationship between large contributions and the appointment of ambassadors. It has long been common practice for Presidents to reward large contributors with such appointments. This table (left) shows the contributions to the 1972 Republican presidential campaign (insofar as they were on record as of June 1973) made by men and women who were ambassadors before the election or who were appointed as ambassadors soon after the election (about half the list). Perhaps such contributions are not the only or the main qualification for ambassadorial appointments; yet there is sentiment in Congress against any future "buying" of ambassadorships, in view of the crucial nature of such positions in a time of world unrest (from Congressional Quarterly, 1973).

Figure 14.6 The sympathetic ear machine (right). The impact of political contributions on campaigners and political decision makers is usually indirect. Large campaign contributions ordinarily operate as a form of insurance policy, ensuring that in time of need one can get the ear of the officeholder, rather than operating as a form of direct bribery on specific matters. Such access to present one's case provides a distinct advantage to those who are able to make significant contributions.

to obtain sufficient funds had they managed to get nominated. During the 1972 presidential campaign, for instance, several contestants for the Democratic nomination dropped out of the race citing lack of financial support as the chief culprit. Among them were Senators Fred Harris and Harold Hughes. At the time they withdrew, their standing in the polls was similar to that of the eventual nominee, Senator George McGovern (who had secured the necessary funds to continue).

The impact of money on policy decisions is somewhat more indirect than its impact on election results. Although it is difficult to trace, the goal of getting elected or reelected might be so important to a potential candidate that he will tailor his platform to suit the needs and wishes of the people who contribute the most money. One political scientist, James Q. Wilson, fears that efforts to raise money to finance more costly campaigns cause candidates to increasingly play to a "liberal audience" or to a "conservative audience" of money givers, who tend to skew the positions of major party candidates away from the broad center (Wilson, 1971). Thus, political contributors may produce candidates who do not really reflect the political alternatives desired by most voters.

Because most campaign financing presently comes from a few large donors, the question is often raised whether this mode of funding leads to corruption. It is impossible to determine just how much influence generous contributors have on the behavior of elected officials. It is known, however, that the generous contributor can often gain access to the candidate once he is elected; it also usually means that the donor will receive at least a sympathetic hearing. And anyone who can gain access to a busy official with the assurance of a sympathetic hearing definitely has a head start in achieving some impact on the behavior of the official.

Perhaps the major opportunity for a contributor to influence an officeholder is on matters about which the officeholder is uncommitted. In these circumstances, officeholders might be especially receptive to overtures from those who are potential members of the money-giving alliance that must be forged to successfully contest for office again.

From time to time it has been revealed that officeholders have in fact been corrupted, and they have sometimes been convicted and sent to jail. Nevertheless, it is not clear that most elected officials are unduly influenced by their chief contributors. Even those contributors who hope to influence policy decisions frequently find themselves thwarted by political maneuvers and by the isolation of candi-

dates from donors through the middleman role of campaign finance chairmen.

On the whole, candidates try to avoid making explicit promises. Their fund raisers much prefer to make tacit promises ("You can be assured that candidate X will be your 'friend' if elected"), which leave candidates some room to maneuver later if necessary. It is important to realize, however, that elected officials often take positions in accord with the views of their major contributors out of conviction, not expediency. After all, a primary reason people support candidates is to elect those with whom they agree.

REFORM PROPOSALS

Because of the impact money has on elections, and through elections on public policy, several proposals have been advanced to neutralize its impact. The specific legislative proposals differ, but they basically follow several general lines.

Limiting Spending

Several proposals call for setting a maximum figure that candidates can spend; others stipulate the maximum amount that an individual can contribute, the purpose being to blunt the potential impact of large gifts on the candidate. Although these approaches appear to be attractive devices for neutralizing the impact of money, they have several drawbacks. If, for example, two candidates were limited to spending the same amount, other resources would simply take the place of money in terms of affecting the eventual outcome of the election. Practically stated, the advantages accruing to an incumbent (such as being well known) are usually so formidable that, in order for an opponent to have the same impact on the electorate, he must outspend him. Limitation legislation, by making it more difficult for challengers to mount effective campaigns, may thus result in the continual reelection of incumbents (see Chapter 8).

Despite the problems with laws entailing the limitation of campaign funds, such laws continue to be enacted. At times, the amount of money allowed has been unrealistically low, making the laws ineffectual. In other instances, various loopholes have made the laws easy to circumvent. Finally, laws that curtail the amount of money an individual can contribute have implications that go beyond practical, financial concerns. The First Amendment guarantees citizens certain rights of free speech. Such guarantees could seemingly be interpreted to mean that a person has the right to buy as much advertising or to give as much money as he wishes in

Figure 14.7 Senator George McGovern (left) works on a campaign speech with his advisers. The South Dakota senator's campaign for the Presidency in 1972 began unusually early because he was relatively unknown; victory in the state primaries was considered fundamental to his success because he had to convince early financial backers that his campaigning would be viable.

Figure 14.8 All campaigners need backers. The ideal situation is to find a backer who is in sympathy with one's own purposes. The "big givers" listed here (right) furnish some indication of the spread of interests and ideology among persons with money. There is also evidence here that big money goes to both parties—in fact, some of the same persons contributed to both parties. (These figures are based on voluntary disclosures made by candidates to the nonprofit Citizens' Research Foundation in October 1972.)

order to promote his ideas about various political candidates.

Providing Money or Services

Other proposals call for providing money or services (such as television time) to candidates. Many of these proposals aim to reduce the cost that must be borne by candidates and to reduce the chances that one candidate will win simply because his opposition could not raise enough money to field a minimal campaign. Some of these plans entail providing enough money at public expense to make it possible for a candidate to entirely shun privately raised money. Others, such as the tax "check-off" plan passed in the Revenue Act of 1971, entail creating a fund to provide at least partial support to candidates by permitting Americans to assign a dollar of their income taxes to the party of their choice. The Revenue Act of 1971 also includes a tax-incentive plan that allows citizens to take tax credits or deductions on money contributed to candidates (not parties) contesting for public office.

An alternative to giving money for campaigns is providing services. Such services might be television or radio time or mailing privileges. A wide array of such proposals has been introduced in past years. Some people envision providing such services to candidates entirely free of charge, whereas others would provide the services at reduced rates so that candidates could stretch their scarce dollars. To finance the cost of the services, some plans rely entirely on the government, some propose joint government-industry (usually the broadcasting industry) financing, and others envision relying entirely on industry to do the financing.

The temporary suspension of the equal-time section of the Communications Act provided an example of an industry-financed plan. The equal-time clause states that if a broadcaster grants time (either free or for a price) to a candidate, he must grant similar time to all of the candidate's opponents. If, for example, a network provides a program on which a major presidential candidate appears free of charge, it must give free time to all of the other candidates contesting for the Presidency. Because stations are limited in the amount of available time, and because it is costly for them to donate air time, they may opt not to give any time at all rather than be forced to give free time to a dozen or so candidates. In 1960 the networks were freed from the restrictions of the equal-time clause, which meant that they could provide free time to major candidates without having to worry about the demands of minor candidates. The 1960 debates between presidential candidates

---

Who's Who Among the Big Givers, 1971-1972

Walter T. Duncan, 45, a Texas real estate developer with an aversion to publicity and photographers. Gifts: Hubert Humphrey, $300,000; Nixon, $257,000. "McGovern goes too far," said Duncan in explaining his post-primary Republican switch.

W. Clement Stone, 70, Winnetka, Ill., chairman and chief executive officer of Combined Insurance Co. of America (assets: $319,725,000). Gifts: Nixon, $25,000; Republican National Committee, $11,000. Stone, who was Nixon's biggest financial backer in 1968, said that he had given $500,000 to Nixon by October 1972, the bulk of it before the Federal Election Campaign Act went into effect in April 1972.

Ray A. Kroc, 70, Chicago, chairman and chief executive officer of McDonald's Corp., Oak Brook, Ill. Gifts: Nixon, $255,000.

Max Palevsky, 48, Los Angeles, founder of Scientific Data Systems, largest single stockholder in Xerox, interests in films (*Marjoe*) and publishing, chairman of Straight Arrow Publishers (*Rolling Stone*). Gifts: McGovern, $126,852; McCloskey, $9,825. Loans: McGovern, $230,000.

Dr. Alejandro C. Zaffaroni, 48, president of Alza Corp., a Palo Alto, Calif., pharmaceutical firm. Gifts: McGovern, $226,000; McCloskey, $11,000. Zaffaroni, a developer of contraceptives and a drug researcher, is also a Uruguayan citizen and thus unable to vote in the presidential election.

Stewart Rawlings Mott, 34, New York City philanthropist, son of the General Motors pioneer and major stockholder Charles Stewart Mott. Gifts: McGovern, $212,361; Lindsay, $5,000; McCloskey, $5,500. Loans: McGovern, $377,500.

Foster G. McGaw, 75, Evanston, Ill., honorary chairman and founder of American Hospital Supply Corp. Gifts: Nixon, $196,298, and $3,000 to a Republican Party committee

Mr. and Mrs. Joseph Irwin Miller. Miller, 63, is chairman of Cummins Engine Co., Columbus, Ind. Gifts: Lindsay, $150,000; McCloskey, $18,500.

Joseph M. Segel, 41, Merion, Pa., president of the Franklin Mint, Inc., a manufacturer of commemorative coins and medals. Gifts: Nixon, $114,000.

Evan P. Helfaer, 74, Milwaukee, major stockholder in Colgate-Palmolive Co. Gifts: Nixon, $110,261.

Anthony T. Rossi, 71, Bradenton, Fla., chairman and president of Tropicana Products Inc. Gifts: Nixon, $100,000.

Dwayne O. Andreas, 54, Miami Beach, chairman of First Interoceanic Corp., chairman of the executive committee of Archer-Daniels-Midland Co. (flour and soybean products). Gifts: Humphrey, $75,000; Nixon, $25,000. His money earmarked for the Nixon campaign was later found by the FBI in the bank account of one of the original Watergate Five.

Martin Peretz, 32, an assistant professor of social studies at Harvard whose wife has holdings in the Singer Company. Gifts: McGovern, $76,000. Loans: McGovern, $114,000.

Henry L. Kimelman, 51, chairman of the West Indies Corp. and various other corporations in the Virgin Islands, and McGovern's national finance chairman. Gifts: McGovern, $76,740. Loans: McGovern, $290,000.

John Kennedy and Richard Nixon resulted from this decision.

Only two of all of these alternate proposals have the status of law (tax incentives and the check-off plan), and neither has been operating long enough to indicate clearly what the impact might be. Most of the proposals, however, would probably accomplish at least part of two goals: If enacted, the proposals would make it more likely that candidates would have sufficient resources to wage a campaign in which they could communicate effectively with voters; the proposals would also make it more likely that some of the pressures for financing campaigns would be reduced, thereby making the candidates less indebted to the preferences of contributors.

All of the proposals mentioned here have their limitations. Most of them cover only candidates for federal office, and some limit themselves only to the Presidency. In addition, several of the money or service proposals direct their benefits to candidates rather than to party organizations. Those who believe that strong party organizations have positive benefits fear that such proposals may weaken the already enfeebled American parties. A difficulty of service plans in particular is that the services they provide may not be needed or used by all candidates. It would be difficult, for instance, for a con-gressional candidate to utilize free television time if there were no television stations in his district. What he may need is newspaper, radio, billboard, or direct-mail services.

Throughout this discussion of campaign funding, the mass media have been referred to repeatedly because it is primarily the cost of media exposure that makes campaigns so expensive. But the media influence many aspects of politics other than expense. Indeed, to understand why candidates spend millions of dollars on TV and radio time and newspaper ads, it is necessary to know what they hope to get for their money. The following section examines the role of the mass media in contemporary American politics. Major attention will be focused on the role of television because TV time is both so costly and so effective—TV is the medium most Americans (65 percent) report as the primary source of their impressions about candidates (Burns Roper, 1969).

THE IMPACT OF THE MASS MEDIA

In February 1973, CBS televised a production of Shakespeare's *Much Ado About Nothing*. The rating services estimated that 11.1 million viewers tuned in—a rather weak rating for a show in prime time. Yet, as the producer of the show pointed out, probably more people saw this classic play on that

one night than had seen it in its thousands of live stage performances since it was first staged in London in the late 1500s. Similarly, anyone who appears on a network news broadcast is likely to be seen by more people than ever saw Queen Victoria, Julius Caesar, or Napoleon Bonaparte.

The development of mass communications media has altered politics as greatly as it has altered American society in general. News, information, ideas, styles—the whole panoply of our culture is now transmitted to virtually everyone almost simultaneously. Marshall McLuhan's claim that television and the news media have turned the earth into one huge "global village" is, in some respects, not a great exaggeration; when major events occur, virtually the whole world is watching.

Not so long ago, fads, styles, and popular songs took many months or even years to spread across the nation; now they spread in days. And observers have not yet even begun to understand the implications of the fact that civilians can now sit in their living rooms and *watch* a war (in Vietnam, for example) as it happens.

Campaigning for the Media

In the nineteenth century, after a candidate was nominated for President, he ordinarily retired to his home and entertained a series of visiting dignitaries while around the nation his supporters made speeches in their home communities on his behalf. Then, a few days after the election, he would find out whether or not he had won. Today the life of a presidential candidate is a desperate physical ordeal—hands become raw and puffy from shaking thousands of other hands each day, cracking voices are kept audible by constant medical treatment, and there is little sleep, constant travel, and a routine of twenty or thirty speeches a day. At first glance it would seem that the mass media should have made such campaigns unnecessary, that candidates should be able to stay in one place and campaign over television and through the newspapers. Just the opposite is the case, however.

The first rule in modern campaigning is that several minutes on the evening news are worth more than a whole blitz of paid political ads. Before candidates can get news coverage, however, they must do or say something that TV news (and newspaper) editors consider newsworthy. Modern campaigns are therefore designed to create newsworthy statements and events.

It is important for a candidate to get newstime for several reasons: It is free, it reaches many people who ignore political commercials, it gives a news label to

Figure 14.9 Campaigns create their own momentum and their own chemistry. And sometimes the results are tragic. One can only speculate about the motivations of Sirhan Sirhan, the man who assassinated Senator Robert Kennedy (left), while he campaigned for California primary votes in 1968. We know for sure, however, that every major candidate is catapulted by the media into the glare of the public stage before an audience of two hundred million. No money can buy perfect protection, for campaigning needs audience contact if for no other reason than to make it believable on the television news broadcasts. Perhaps physical courage and a certain degree of fatalism are ingredients that must be added to the already unusual composition of the candidate for American political office.

a political statement, and it reaches all voters, not simply those already supporting the candidate. The result is that candidates do such things as rise at dawn to shake hands at factory gates in hopes that TV and newspapers will show them doing so, and they travel across the country because their appearance in a particular city is certain to be treated as newsworthy by the press and television of that city. Thus, during the last week of the 1968 California presidential primary, Robert Kennedy campaigned every day in San Francisco, Los Angeles, and San Diego—the three media markets that together reach 80 percent of the state's voters—in order to get daily news coverage in each city. This grueling procedure involved packing more than 100 reporters and campaign aides on jets several times a day, but it succeeded. Senator Kennedy received news coverage on the media of the three cities each day, and the tide that was carrying voters from Kennedy to Eugene McCarthy was reversed.

An additional feature of campaigning for media attention involves the content of political speeches and statements. Candidates have had to learn that the live audiences they address are merely part of the stage props for their media performance. Although highly partisan attacks may be popular with live audiences (which tend to consist mainly of supporters), such attacks are ill-suited for attracting support from independents and voters affiliated with the opposition party—and these are the voters often needed to win. Thus, speeches must be designed to appeal to the mass of voters, who constitute, through the media, the real audience of political speeches. By the same token, candidates no longer have the luxury of saying different things to different audiences—a strong civil rights speech given in Harlem is just as likely to be heard in Georgia.

Candidates do not depend on mass media campaigns simply because the media exist; they do so because in many parts of the nation—especially in major urban areas—the only way to reach the mass of voters is through the mass media. In the first part of the 1900s political campaigning in many urban areas was based on party organizations. The primary elements in these organizations were ward bosses and precinct captains. These party functionaries made it their business to keep in close touch with the residents of their assigned neighborhoods. They saw to it that supporters of their party were registered, they campaigned door-to-door to ensure sup-

port for the party's slate of candidates, and they got their voters to the polls on election day. Because of the present mobility of Americans—in many cities and suburbs the average family moves every three years—this kind of campaign organization has become impractical in most large communities. The close personal ties that a precinct captain must have with local voters is impossible in neighborhoods always filled with newcomers. The only practical way to reach such mobile voters is through the mass media, particularly television and radio. (Indeed, candidates prize whatever radio time they are able to buy on radio commuter shows because masses of voters can regularly be found in their autos with their radios on for long periods in the morning and late afternoon.)

Media Candidates

The importance of television and radio in the modern campaign has led to the creation of a new kind of political professional as a replacement for the old-time ward boss—the media specialist, or image maker. The purpose of media specialists is to help candidates win elections by creating media ads and managing television and public appearances in ways designed to show their clients in their best light.

Much has been written about candidates who tend to "come over" well or poorly on television. It has frequently been noted that Richard Nixon was probably defeated in 1960 because he looked sinister on TV as a result of inadequate make-up or that much of John Kennedy's "magic" was a result of the family's good looks. In reality, however, it simply is not known how much difference such things actually make with the voters—there is no sound basis for comparison. It is known, however, that most party politicians *think* such things matter, and therefore they take TV image into account when they choose the party's candidates.

Interestingly, many image makers argue that candidates do not lose elections because of bad TV "images"; rather, they lose because TV shows them as they really are. They argue that in being able to see candidates close up, hear them, watch them, and see how they act and react, the public forms a fundamental impression of the real person whose name is on the ballot. Many observers claim, for instance, that the intimacy created by television was the cause of the demise of Senator Joseph McCarthy—when the American public actually saw on TV the way in

Figure 14.10 (left) Before the advent of the electronic media, personal appearances were the mainstay of political campaigns. However, for a modern candidate to depend solely on the dramatic impact of public appearances would be political suicide. Thus, most candidates' campaign strategies include a mixture of public appearances and media coverage. In fact, public appearances are often simply a device for getting news coverage.

Figure 14.11 Although many criticize the expense and superficial quality of television coverage, television is still the primary means by which people acquaint themselves with political candidates. As indicated here (right), television was used as a source of information in the 1972 elections twice as often as were newspapers, the next in line. (The total equals more than 100 percent because respondents were allowed to list more than one source.)

"During the last election campaign, from what source did you become best acquainted with the candidates for national offices—the Presidency, the Senate, and the House of Representatives?" (The Roper Organization, 1973)

Source	Percentages Applicable to 1972 Election
Television	65%
Newspapers	29
Radio	8
Magazines	5
People	6
Other	2

Figure 14.12 Democratic and Republican nominating conventions—Miami, Florida, 1972. Although the real work of lining up delegate votes is done behind the scenes, the revelry of the presidential nominating convention captures the eye of the media and signals the public that the race for the Presidency has officially begun. Senator George McGovern (above) rode a tide of antiwar feeling and the excitement of real change in the air to nomination by the Democratic convention. A quota system for ethnic minority and female representation resulted in a dramatically variegated and exciting convention, while the Republican convention, with its anticlimactic renomination of President Nixon, had to work hard to manufacture a note of spontaneity. Governor George Wallace (lower right), whose candidacy had been an early threat to Nixon's "southern strategy," was paralyzed from a would-be assassin's bullet in May 1972.

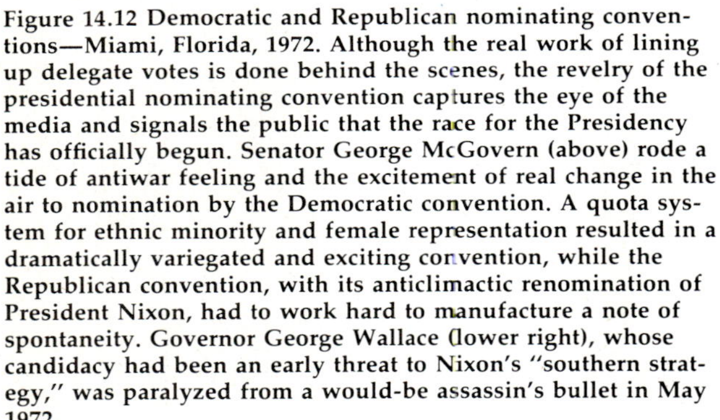

which he conducted himself during the 1954 Senate hearings, instead of simply reading about his efforts against "communists," McCarthy was finished as a national figure. Similarly, Senator Howard Baker's questioning of witnesses during the televised Senate hearings on the Watergate conspiracy in 1973 boosted him into the national limelight.

Campaigning for the media has also made campaign coordinators especially important. These individuals are responsible for, among other things, seeing that large crowds turn out to see their candidate. Such crowds are important, not because they mean more people will see the candidate in person, but because the film on the evening news will give the impression of enthusiastic popular support. Similarly, it is considered vital that coordinators choose halls and auditoriums that are too small for the anticipated crowd so that the press will report that "Candidate Smith addressed an overflow crowd," and the TV film will show a crowded hall. Candidate Smith's opponent could have twice as many people come to see him, but if the hall was too large and the TV film showed many empty seats, his appearance would be considered a disaster (Jerry Bruno and Jeff Greenfield, 1971).

The Media Voter

In his best seller, *The Selling of the President 1968*, Joe McGinniss discusses the effects he believes television has had on how voters judge candidates. McGinniss argues that television is a test of a candidate's personality, not of his ideas. "Print is for ideas," he writes, but on television "style becomes substance." Furthermore, on TV a candidate

. . . is measured not against his predecessors—not against a standard of performance established by two centuries of democracy—but against Mike Douglas. How well does he handle himself? Does he mumble, does he twitch, does he make me laugh? Do I feel warm inside? (McGinniss, 1969)

Many scholars who have examined the impact of the 1960 Kennedy-Nixon debates agree with McGinniss. After carefully examining the reaction of individuals to this feat of television, it was concluded that the mass audience was left with "some very distinct impressions of the capabilities of the two men as debaters and as persons, but . . . with very

Figure 14.13 Vice-Presidential candidates add scope to a presidential campaign. In most cases, they are relative unknowns who have been chosen because their regional or religious background or their political outlook helps to balance the presidential ticket. Once in office, many a Vice-President has remarked on the insignificance of the office. To John Nance Garner, Franklin Roosevelt's first Veep, the Vice-Presidency wasn't worth "a pitcher of warm spit." To Spiro Agnew in 1969, the Vice-Presidency showed him "what a turkey feels like before Thanksgiving," a sentiment he probably reiterated on his resignation from the office in 1973.

little idea of what the debate was about'' (Elihu Katz and Jacob Feldman, 1962).

Despite the strength of television in transmitting "images" rather than "substance," there is evidence that today's voters are better informed about candidates and issues than they were before the advent of television. Several days before the election in 1944, for example, only 55 percent of those who planned to vote for President Franklin Roosevelt could name his vice-presidential running mate, Harry Truman. In 1956, after television had entered the scene, 60 percent of voters who were shown a picture of the Democratic vice-presidential candidate could correctly identify the man as Estes Kefauver. By 1971, 76 percent of Americans could identify Edmund Muskie, who unsuccessfully ran for Vice-President in 1968 (George Gallup, 1972).

Although the questions asked in these polls are not entirely comparable, the Gallup results do suggest that since the advent of television the average voter has become better able to identify candidates for high political office. In contrast, voters have not become more aware of those candidates who receive relatively little TV exposure. In 1942, before television, about half of the public could name their district's congressman; by 1966 the proportion had not increased (Gallup, 1972). It seems possible to conclude from these statistics that the increased voter awareness of candidates for high political office is a result of the television coverage they receive.

MEDIA AND PUBLIC POLICY

As has been shown, the mass media have changed campaigns, campaigners, and voters. But these changes are only part of the story, for the influence of the mass media has extended into the very nature of the policy-making process. Two of the most obvious ways in which the media have influenced policy making have been by increasing the amount of information available to politicians and to the public and by creating issues.

Increasing Information

A constant theme of Unit III is that no single political institution or individual has the ability to give the final "answers" regarding the formulation and execution of policy. The decision maker needs the cooperation of others (and thus must often accommodate them or anticipate their reactions) if he is to perform his work and achieve his goals. Through the media, an official can learn of the plans and proposals of others that might have some relevance for his own work. This knowledge can assist him in the very difficult art of timing—by using information available in the media an official can ascertain the climate of support prevailing at a given moment and decide whether he should push a proposal at that time or wait until more favorable conditions prevail.

Officials also follow the media to see how it relays news about the government. Viewing the news in this way gives them some idea, they believe, of how their constituents (who may be groups inside or outside government) view a situation. In other words, the media serve as a kind of "instant" public opinion poll. Editorial reactions in newspapers and on television and radio stations or the reactions of individuals or groups that make the news are helpful in this kind of measurement of public opinion.

On many issues, politicians deal with only those people who represent the concerns that will be directly affected by an issue. If an issue is made public through exposure in the media, however, other persons may feel that their concerns, too, should be considered, and they may begin to make their positions heard. The result may well be a policy decision that reflects a far more inclusive mix of constituent concerns.

Creating Issues

In April 1973 the *Wall Street Journal* reported the results of a public opinion poll: 91 percent of voting-age Americans were aware of the Watergate scandal, and many independents and Republicans said it might cause them to vote against the GOP in the next election. The Watergate case aptly demonstrates a number of the ways in which the mass media influence political issues. Without dogged investigations and reporting by the mass media, the scandal probably would have remained buried; without the blitz of mass media coverage, the issue would probably not have achieved as rapid, widespread, nor as deep an impact on the public

The mass media, especially the mass news media, are able to generate widespread awareness and concern about events or conditions—to bring matters before the public so that they become "issues on the agenda" (see Chapter 9). Furthermore, the speed of mass media transmission makes it possible for political movements concerned with particular issues to grow with unparalleled rapidity. An obvious case in point is the meat boycott of April 1973. Meat prices had been rising very rapidly, and consumers were growing upset about the increases. Shoppers who might have been slow to notice how much and how rapidly meat prices were rising were kept well informed by constant reports over the mass media. A small group of consumers decided to attempt a one-week meat boycott in order to bring pressure to bear on government and on the food industry to curb rising prices.

Without the mass media, it would have taken months to spread the word about the boycott across the country, and the whole undertaking would have been futile. In several minutes of TV news coverage, however, the plans became known nationwide. Overnight, groups supporting the boycott appeared across the nation, leading to continuing media coverage and increased public awareness. There is little doubt that the Nixon Administration's announcement of a freeze on meat prices occurred in response to the boycott and publicity surrounding it. In sum, the mass media were the key to the entire enterprise.

Aside from any specific complaints an Administration might have about the news media, however, it should be recognized that conflict between the news media and political leaders is probably unavoidable and even to be desired. It is in the interest of political leaders to put the best possible face on their performances—to proclaim their successes and bury their failures; it is in a reporter's interest to dig out the failures. No one becomes a famous reporter or wins a Pulitzer Prize for repeating government press releases—big stories are usually those somebody has tried to hush up. Because of this inherent tension between government and the news media, Douglass Cater has described the press as "the fourth branch of government" (Cater, 1959). He argues that along with the Congress, the courts, and the Administration, the press plays a fundamental role in the checks-and-balances system beloved by James Madison and written into the Constitution.

Whether or not the mass media should be considered a fourth branch of government, it is obvious that newsmen are a fundamental part of American

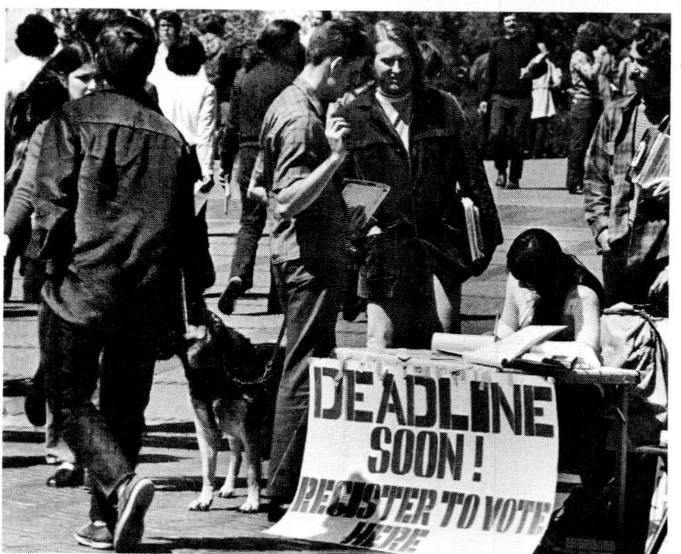

Figure 14.14 Kaleidoscope of a campaign. The campaign of Wisconsin Senator Eugene McCarthy to capture the 1968 Wisconsin nomination attracted an army of young volunteers. These energetic though inexperienced workers were attracted by McCarthy's thoughtful approach to politics, by the senator's early fight against the war in Vietnam, and by his surge from underdog to real contender. Many of the same young people rang doorbells for George McGovern in 1972.

TOPICAL INSERT

THE ART OF THE PRIMARY: WEST VIRGINIA, 1960

by T. H. White

Tired from his exertions in Wisconsin, tired from his efforts in the meaningless District of Columbia primary, tired from his travels (flying by commercial airliners and carrying his own bags through the airgates), half of Hubert Humphrey's time was spent in raising money to continue, the other half barnstorming in his lonesome bus.

Strangled for lack of money (Humphrey's expenditures in West Virginia were to total only $25,000— nothing, in the scale of American politics), knowing himself in debt, aware of the nature, depth, and resources of this final drive by John Kennedy, as the final weekend approached Humphrey became a figure of pathos. He needed advertising, he needed workers, above all he needed TV.

I remember the final Saturday morning. One of Humphrey's assistants informed him that the TV stations that had booked him for a Sunday night half hour were threatening to cancel unless they were paid that day.

"Pay it!" snarled Humphrey. "Pay it!" I don't care how, don't come to me with that kind of story!" Then, realizing that his crestfallen aide was, like himself, destitute, Hubert pulled out his checkbook and said, "All right, I'll pay for it myself."

Mrs. Humphrey watched him do so, with dark, sad eyes, and one had the feeling that the check was money from the family grocery fund—or the money earmarked to pay for the upcoming wedding of their daughter.

What happens when a man goes on cold on TV with such a grocery-money investment was grotesquely shown by Humphrey's final appeal to the voters of West Virginia on that day before the election. A telethon is a political gimmick in which a candidate, theoretically but not actually, throws himself open to all questions from any voter who cares to call the broadcasting station. A good telethon requires good staff in order to screen questions and artfully sequence them

so they give the illusion of spontaneity yet feed the candidates those pretexts on which he can masterfully develop his themes.

But Humphrey demonstrated what happens when such a telethon is authentic. For when authentic, unscreened questions are fed to the candidates, the effect is comic. Except that, watching Hubert Humphrey fight his last national battle with family grocery money, the effect was more sad than comic.

The telethon opened with Humphrey sitting alone at a desk, with a telephone. The first question was a normal mechanical question: "What makes you think you're qualified to be President, Senator Humphrey?"

Then came a rasping voice over the telephone, the whining scratch of an elderly lady somewhere high in the hills, and one could see Humphrey flinch (as the viewers flinched), and the rasp said, "You git out! You git out of West Virginia, Mr. Humphrey!" Humphrey attempted to fluster a reply and the voice overrode him. "You git out, you hear! You can't stand the Republicans gitting ahead of you!"

Humphrey had barely recovered from the blast before the next call came: What would he do about small-arms licensing for people who like to hunt? Then, what would he do about social security? None of the questions were hitting anywhere near the target area of Humphrey's campaign program, and then a sweet womanly voice began to drawl on the open switch: "How about those poor little neglected children, Mr. Humphrey, I mean how can we lower taxes like you say and take care of all those little children who need more schools . . ." On and on she went, as Humphrey (his precious, costly minutes oozing by) attempted to break in and say that he too was for the poor little neglected children.

From that point on the telethon lost all cohesion—proving nothing except that TV is no medium for a poor man.

politics. They serve as an important link between government and the people, and they are the primary vehicle for political campaigns; indeed, candidates run their campaigns for mass media consumption. And only those who can raise the large sums of money necessary to buy mass media advertising have a chance of being successful in their campaigns. The mass media are also the primary source of mass political awareness and have probably made the modern voter better informed than his nineteenth-century forebears. In modern American politics, money, campaigns, and the mass media are inseparably linked.

SUMMARY

Election campaigns are the means by which choices are put before the voters. Because campaigns are aimed at the masses of voters, they are necessarily gaudy in order to attract the attention of the usually unattentive. Low-key campaigns would lower the degree of popular participation and would thereby facilitate dominance by a wealthy and educated elite. Campaigns must rely on the mass media—expensive, yet the only feasible means of mass communication.

Campaigns at national, state, and local levels cost $400 million in 1972. Yet it must be remembered that large sums do not guarantee victory and that it is primarily the wealthy few who contribute to campaigns (and thereby gain access to elected officials). Reform proposals suggest spending limitations or providing campaign services to candidates so as to reduce costs.

Campaigns are geared to catch the attention of the media. The media specialist or image maker has emerged as an essential member of the campaign team. The media influence public policies by raising the public's level of awareness, by indicating the state of public opinion to politicians, and by critically evaluating the operation of government. In so doing, the media serve an essential check-and-balance function.

SUGGESTED READINGS

Adamany, David. *Campaign Finance in America*. North Scituate, Mass.: Duxbury Press, 1972.

Cater, Douglass. *The Fourth Branch of Government*. New York: Vintage Books, 1959.

Dunn, Delmer D. *Public Officials and the Press*. Reading, Mass.: Addison-Wesley, 1969.

————. *Financing Presidential Campaigns*. Washington, D.C.: The Brookings Institution, 1972.

Heard, Alexander. *The Costs of Democracy*. Chapel Hill: University of North Carolina Press, 1960.

Nimmo, Dan. *Newsgathering in Washington*. New York: Atherton Press, 1963.

AMERICAN PETROLEUM INSTITUTE, 1801 K St. NW, Washington, D.C.

Lobbyist—Carl F. Arnold, 1100 Connecticut Ave. NW, Washington, D.C. Filed 4/4/73.

Legislative interest—"Legislation affecting the petroleum industry."

CONGRESS WATCH, 2000 P St. NW, Washington, D.C.

Lobbyist—Richard Morgan Downey, same address as employer. Filed 6/18/73.

Legislative interest—"Matters concerned with consumer, environmental, transportation, congressional reform, health, safety, energy, elections and criminal law."

NATIONAL FEDERATION OF INDEPENDENT BUSINESS, 921 Washington Building, Washington, D.C.

Lobbyist—Frederick L. Williford, 10010 Green Forest Drive, Adelphi, Md. Filed 4/13.

Legislative interest—"All bills affecting small business."

SPORTSMAN'S PARADISE HOMEOWNERS ASSOCIATION, Route 2, Box 228, Blythe, Calif. Filed for self 6/25/73.

Legislative interest—"To clear and settle title to certain real property located in the vicinity of the Colorado River, known as 'Sportsman's Paradise,' in Imperial County, Calif. HR 2218 and other pending legislation. For enactment."

WASHINGTON OFFICE ON AFRICA, 110 Maryland Ave. NE, Washington, D.C. Filed for self 6/29/73.

Legislative interest—"Legislation affecting Southern Africa: a. bill to restore U.N. sanctions against Rhodesia, S 1868, HR 8005, for, b. fair employment practices of U.S. corporations in South Africa and Namibia, H J Res 269, for."

15
INTEREST GROUPS AND PRIVATE GOVERNMENTS

Figure 15.1 Interest groups and lobbyists are required by law to publicly identify themselves and their goals. There are hundreds of organizations and individuals in Washington who represent one or more interests on a full- or part-time basis. They range from extremely well-financed organizations such as the American Petroleum Institute, involved in worldwide affairs and supported by thousands of engineers, lawyers, and public relations experts, to small, single-issue groups such as the Sportsman's Paradise Homeowners Association. The importance of interest groups, large and small, in the formulation and implementation of public policy has led to significant questions regarding the extent to which private concentrations of power should be made accountable to the American people.

As previous chapters have discussed, traditional Liberalism represented the interests of the rising middle classes during the early days of the industrial revolution. Confronted with governments whose decisions greatly affected their lives, the new middle classes in Europe found they had no say in political decisions. Their demands for liberty and for the democratization of political power were protests against governments that were repressive and unresponsive.

The essence of tyranny is a government that need answer to no one for its actions, whose rulers cannot be called to account for their policies by those whom the policies affect. The Liberal-minded founding fathers of the United States were determined to avoid such a situation when they wrote the Constitution. The design of the government, based on Madison's fragmentation model, reflected their intentions to make each part of the government subject to the approval of many other parts and to make the government as a whole free from tyranny (see Chapter 2).

From the point of view of the eighteenth-century middle classes, power was primarily governmental power; liberty was primarily escape from government repression. Clearly, Liberalism was correct in identifying government as a major threat to liberty. However, early Liberal thought failed to concern itself with other potentially powerful influences on policy, such as great concentrations of *private* power. The founders regarded government as an arena within which powerful private factions contended over matters of public policy, but they gave little attention to how these factions were to be made accountable to the people.

This oversight was in many ways understandable. Liberal political doctrines arose in societies in which power resided in the hands of a small ruling elite—political power was virtually synonymous with the state. Large corporations, big unions, professional associations, and the like did not exist. Liberal thinkers were not worried about how to ensure that what was good for General Motors was also good for the nation because they had no grounds for anticipating the formation of such huge concentrations of private power. At the time the Constitution was written, industries in both Europe and America were characterized by innumerable small firms. Similarly, such organizations as unions or trade associations were local in scope when they existed at all. It is really only in the twentieth century that huge organizations of any kind have come into being. Yet Americans have already come to take these large concentrations of power for granted.

Observers have begun to recognize that many major policy decisions that greatly influence the national welfare are made primarily or entirely by organizations and groups whose activities are not subject to public accountability. As Chapters 3 and 4 point out, corporations and other private groups in the United States determine many policies that in other nations are made by the government. For instance, the number of cars General Motors makes in a given year is decided by G.M. management and is subject to market conditions, not to government economic planning. Often, American corporations even maintain their own foreign policies substantially independent of (and sometimes contrary to) the policies of the State Department. Decisions such as these have considerable impact on the lives of all Americans, but they are rarely taken to the public for consideration.

Large private interests also often play the major part in determining government policies that affect them. For instance, labor unions greatly influence labor legislation and Department of Labor policies, and the American Medical Association is the most influential group in determining government health policies and programs. The decisions and activities of such groups as these greatly influence the lives of all Americans, but the groups are accountable to the public only in very limited ways.

This chapter examines the impact of interest groups on public policy. What are interest groups? Who belongs to them? How do they influence, or even *make,* public policy? In what ways do they constitute private governments? And to what extent is American government a private rather than a public institution?

AMERICANS AND GROUPS

Americans are joiners. To confirm this statement the average citizen has only to look in his wallet. Chances are he will find membership cards for such organizations as the Elks, a state automobile club, a trade union, a civic association, the Kiwanis, an outdoor club, the YMCA, or maybe an acknowledg-

ment for contributions to a church. The individual who does not belong to one form of association or another, formal or informal, is rare indeed.

Foreigners visiting the United States have often marveled at this quality of American life. In the early 1800s Alexis de Tocqueville remarked:

The Americans make associations to give entertainments, to found seminaries, to build inns, to construct churches, to diffuse books, to send missionaries to the antipodes; in this manner they found hospitals, prisons and schools. If it is proposed to inculcate some truth or to foster some feeling by the encouragement of a great example, they form a society. Wherever at the head of some new undertaking you see the government in France, or a man of rank in England, in the United States you will be sure to find an association. (Tocqueville, 1840, p. 107)

Some claim this national trait is a mark of the loneliness of American life; others claim it is a reflection of the American genius for self-help and the sign of a drive for democratic solutions to mutual problems. Both sides may well be correct.

Americans learn by training and experience, usually at an early age, the arts of taking part in meetings, of speaking and listening, and of reaching agreement for common action; the skill of working in committees for all manner of ends is widespread. Often the purposes of such meetings and groups are immediate and specific—the saving of a local landmark, perhaps, or the exploitation of some business opportunity. But there are also many groups with more general goals, such as the reduction of the strains of modern life (as in the giving of mutual help for escape from alcoholism) or the gaining of better understanding of oneself and one another (as in an encounter group).

The American tendency to form and to join groups is a political factor of much importance. If an individual has taken part in, for example, meetings of a school club, it will not be a wholly strange experience for him to participate in a town meeting or in union affairs. Moreover, the very idea of seeking out like-minded individuals to band together to promote or oppose some action of government will come more readily to people who have had the experience of working in a group. In one degree or another, every unit of government in America is aware of this fact and is sensitive to the possibility

Figure 15.2 Americans as "joiners." Whether sparked by loneliness, self-help, or clannishness, Americans of all ages have a varied organizational life open to them. Boy Scouting (top left) provides youth with the opportunity for organized group outings and nature study. The Ku Klux Klan (top center), born to protect white power in the post-Civil War Reconstruction, still lives in the South and North. Masonic and other fraternal and veterans' organizations and their female auxiliaries (right) mix fun and charity with interest-group support for favored legislation. The "Jesus freak" phenomenon of the late 1960s and 1970s (above) is a reaction away from the disorders and dangers of the drug scene toward the mass therapy of crowd-supported enthusiastic religion—a kind of reaction to social ills that has reappeared often in American and world history.

that it can find itself in trouble with an organized band of citizens.

POLITICAL RAMIFICATIONS OF GROUPS

On considering the political ramifications of groups, some social scientists—the *pluralists*—have concluded that the existence of a great number of organizations in America, particularly the private (nongovernmental) associations, protects the nation against the rise of mass movements that might lead to dictatorship and totalitarianism. This belief rests on the conviction that individuals involved in relatively small associations of different sorts will not be easily mobilized into mass movements or mobs. Why should such involvement have this effect?

For one thing, people in groups are not simply a mass of individuals. They are connected with one another in a variety of ways. Rather than each person responding to mass appeals for support on the basis of his private sentiments or judgments, his response is mediated through the group. Group leadership and decision making, and peer pressure thus stand between many Americans and potential demagogues.

Furthermore, few groups or associations command the exclusive loyalty of their members. Because most members belong to a number of different groups and associations, the degree to which any given group or association can take extreme positions is limited. For example, delegates at an American Legion convention may have many other equally compelling commitments to other groups and organizations— some are Catholics, some are Protestants or Jews; some are Democrats, some are Republicans; some belong to unions, others are businessmen. The list of additional organizational and group claims on a gathering of legionnaires could be extended almost

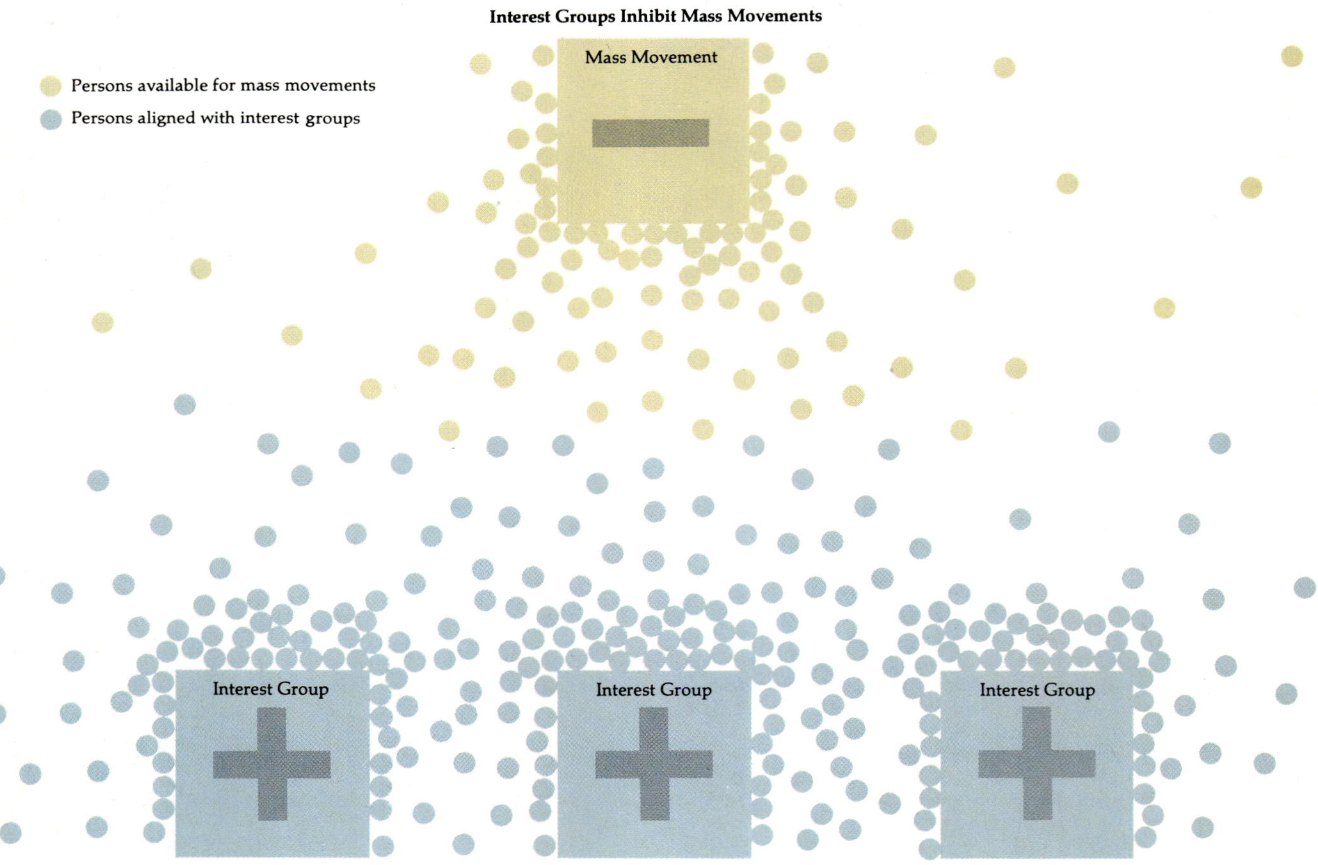

indefinitely. It is evident that the American Legion is constrained in the positions it can take because it does not command exclusive loyalty: Positions repugnant to the Catholic Church, to Republicans, or to labor, for example, are likely to face opposition.

This inability to command exclusive loyalty tends to encourage groups and associations to focus their goals and activities quite narrowly. Such focusing not only reduces the potential for conflict with other groups to which members may also belong, but it makes groups distinctive and gives them a competitive advantage in gaining and holding members. For example, craft unions—labor unions limited to those sharing a common occupation, such as plumbing or carpentry—have been more successful in maintaining member support than have industrial unions—those including all persons working in a given industry, such as auto manufacturing—or large general labor groups, such as the Knights of Labor, an organization that sought to represent all workingmen in the 1880s. It has proved far easier to get a group of people mobilized to seek better wages for themselves than to enlist their support for better wages for "everybody." Presumably a totalitarian movement would also face the difficulty of trying to mobilize support for very general goals in the face of competition from smaller groups and associations offering more specific and concrete benefits.

In addition, narrowly based and highly selective organizations have consistently proved to be more effective in getting their way with government than have those with broader and more inclusive memberships because they can maintain greater unity and can focus their demands more precisely. An outstanding example is the contrast in effectiveness between the Farmers Alliance of the late nineteenth

Figure 15.3 A major hypothesis concerning American political life is that the great number of private associations serves to protect the nation against mass movements that might lead to totalitarianism. This belief views private associations or interest groups as filtering devices, in that the individual's sentiments and judgments are mediated through the outlook of the group. The hypothesis is illustrated here (left): the attraction of magnetic poles portrays the inhibiting effect of interest groups on the attraction of mass movements or mob action.

Figure 15.4 Interest groups' relations with the government are often convoluted. Here (top right), a Senate Judicial Subcommittee interviews ITT corporation lobbyist Dita Beard, in a Denver hospital, with regard to her memo that indicated ITT had contributed to the 1972 Republican campaign in return for favored treatment in antitrust proceedings. The National Rifle Association executive pictured here (bottom right), spends much of his time directing pressure on Congress to promote marksmanship training in schools and to defeat all gun-control laws.

century, which sought to include practically everyone associated with farming, and the modern, powerful American Farm Bureau Federation, which has been highly selective in choosing members. The Farmer's Alliance was short-lived and ineffectual, whereas the Farm Bureau has long played a powerful role in governmental agricultural policy decisions.

One of the individuals with whom the pluralist stance is most frequently associated is James Madison. In a brief but cogent article, *Federalist Paper No. 10,* written to persuade the voters of New York to ratify the Constitution, Madison argued that to try to suppress the disputes and demands of different groups seeking their own advantage (he called them "factions") would destroy not just the freedom of people in those groups but everyone's freedom. In fact, as is shown in Chapter 2, Madison argued that liberty could best be served by having many different groups struggling with one another—the more, the better.

Modern American pluralists, most notably Robert Dahl, have partly followed Madison, but some of them have gone on to argue that there is no reason to restrict the political activities of the groups, however selfish the groups may be, as long as they do not actually cheat by bribery or violence or otherwise violate the "rules of the game." The reason given for this argument is that it is impossible to define what is in the public interest and what is not. Politics, accordingly, is viewed as a struggle among selfish interests that are all equally good because there is no way to prove what is or is not in the public interest.

INTEREST GROUPS AND POLITICAL POWER

Private associations that seek to be influential in the policy process have been termed *pressure groups* because of their determined and unrelenting tactics. Because this term is so value laden, however, and because it is now considered difficult to say just what is wrong (if anything is) about the objectives of the groups, the more neutral term *interest groups* is now used. This term also has the merit of referring to the groups' ends rather than to their means.

It is one of the curiosities of American life that a feature of such size and of such importance to the political system as interest groups should be widely regarded as mysterious. Interest groups cover the entire range of common activities from the respectable to the disreputable, and their existence is familiar to everyone. Yet, when they take steps to influence the decisions of government, more frequently than not by the most simple and direct of methods, they become part of that sinister entity that has variously

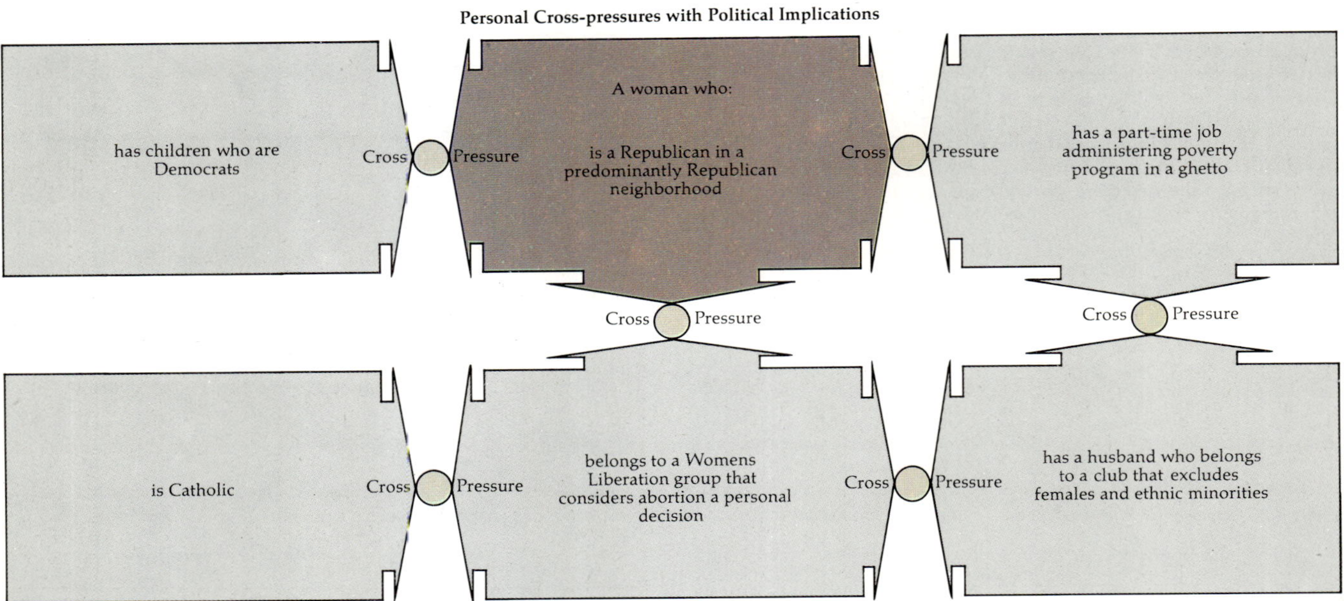

Personal Cross-pressures with Political Implications

been termed "the secret government," "the hidden government," and "the invisible government."

Occasionally, of course, there are scandals, or hints of scandal, as when International Telephone and Telegraph (ITT) was accused of attempting to influence the Republican Party by giving generous contributions to the party at a time when the corporation was facing possible antitrust difficulties with the government. Doubtless, ITT would not wish to be considered an interest group—it contended that its generosity to the party was unconnected with the antitrust matter.

The ordinary working of interest groups, however, seldom constitutes the material for a scandal. In truth, there is little about this aspect of politics that is invisible to those who care to look. The advice and requests of these groups are abundantly familiar to legislators and administrators. The apparent shock with which the activities of these groups are discovered is less a result of the secrecy of their operation than of the media's lack of interest and therefore the blindness of the public.

How Many Interest Groups Are There?

The number of interest groups in the United States is very difficult to estimate for several reasons. One reason is that it is difficult to know which groups to count. Is General Motors an interest group? It obviously is deeply concerned with government regulations on automobile exhaust fumes, highways, and tariffs, and its representatives maintain close contact with the parts of government that they seek to influence. Accordingly, should any or all of the other major corporations listed by *Fortune* magazine as the 500 largest be considered interest groups? Probably none on this list can afford to be indifferent to what government does. And what about the Boy Scouts? This organization has laudable, almost public, purposes but often quite special demands to make. Should a sports club be included as the kind of demand that only an interest group would make? What about a request for a stadium?

Another difficulty in trying to determine the number of interest groups is that new groups are constantly forming while others are disappearing. In addition, a group that is politically active at one moment may at another moment lapse into minor, less visible activities. For example, at various times the American Medical Association has been the largest spender in efforts to sway Congress, but these times have been those when bills to create a system of government-supported health insurance (which many doctors fear would cut into their profits) have been before Congress.

Figure 15.5 When one refers to a particular group for approval or adopts a role and becomes significantly committed to the norms of that role, such references and commitments can set up great pressures. Many such commitments or identifications are or can become political. In this diagram (left) we see a number of a hypothetical woman's commitments, many of which conflict with one another, setting up cross-pressures that she must either resolve or learn to live with.

Figure 15.6 Differing from interest groups, which maximize their power by narrowing the interests they represent, political parties are "umbrella parties" that attempt to be as representative as their most basic commitments will allow them to be. Thus we find (right), under the Republican "umbrella," an interesting mixture of moral, economic, and political associates, who play down ideological, sectional, and class differences in order to achieve party goals.

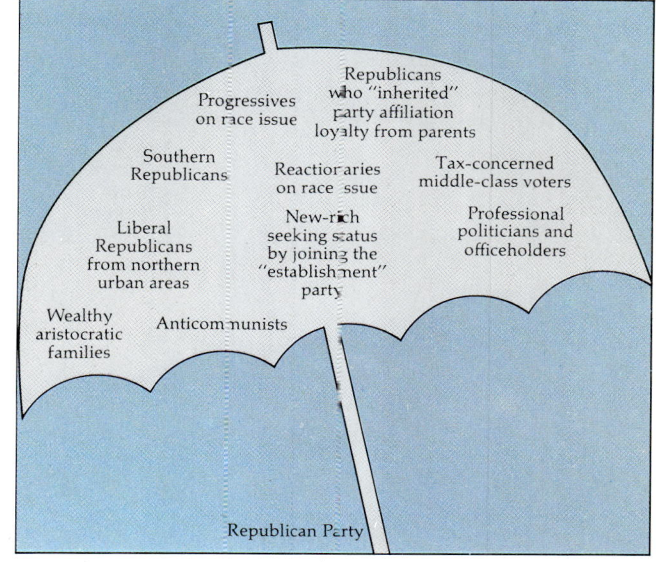

Still another problem is that there are many organizations with imposing titles—the National Association of . . ., the American Institute of . . ., and so on. Not infrequently, however, these seemingly impressive bodies consist of little more than a small office with maybe half a dozen such titles on the door and a single person inside. (The opportunities are vast for an entrepreneur to try to persuade small businessmen or others that they should have a "Washington representative" and should therefore subscribe to his services.) Whether a grandiosely named organization is more than a ghost may not be immediately apparent.

With these cautions in mind, it can be noted that the *Encyclopedia of Associations* lists the associations in the United States. The entries include many recognizable names: the United Auto Workers, the National Farmers Union, the Chamber of Commerce of the United States, and others that frequently make the news. The list also includes other, less famous names, such as the United States Duffers' Association, the Gourd Society of America, and the Northwest Cherry Briners Association. Even so, there is no entry for "the highway lobby," but such a group is indeed a reality. It is a loose but highly effective alliance of automobile, trucking, oil, and highway-construction interests that is responsible for creating the highway trust fund, whose large resources go into the building of the vast Interstate system of highways (see Chapter 10).

Interest groups are usually regarded as selfish—with some justification. The very word "interest" suggests that the ends sought will primarily benefit only a segment of the nation. Still, not all of the groups that attempt to influence government are obviously selfish in nature. There are quite a number of groups that claim to represent the public—Ralph Nader's Center for Responsive Law, for example, or John Gardner's Common Cause, the Sierra Club, the League of Women Voters, the John Birch Society, and various peace groups. Should these groups be regarded in the same light as, for example, the United Auto Workers or the Gourd Society of America? The problem is not an easy one.

Lobbies

Interest groups take part in one way or another in almost every stage of the political process. One of the major ways in which interest groups are active is through *lobbying*. The term lobbying is derived from the practice of individuals who waited in the lobbies of government buildings for congressmen, senators, and other legislators in hopes of being able to influence them for a given cause.

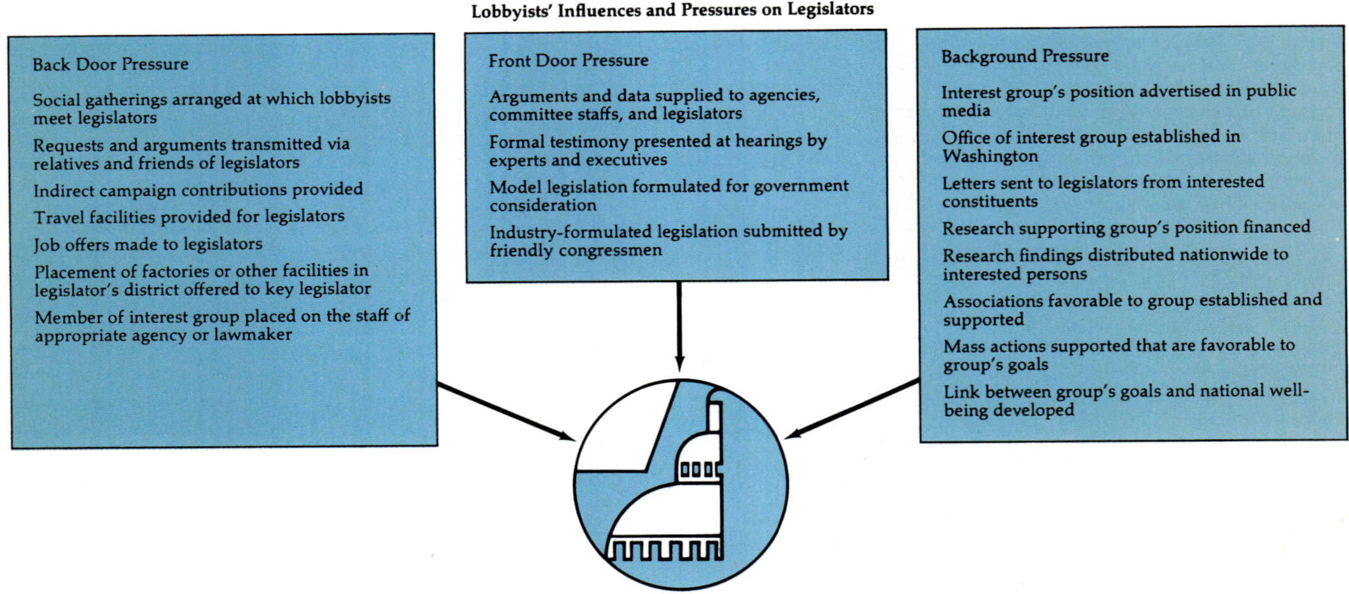

Lobbyists' Influences and Pressures on Legislators

Although attention is usually focused on lobbying activities within the federal government, lobbying also occurs at the state and local levels. In California, for example, it could be said that on two occasions lobbying machines (as contrasted with party machines) exerted more influence on policy than did elected public officials. The first instance was in the 1890s when the Southern Pacific Railroad was reputed to run the state, including much of the official government and both political parties (Walton Bean, 1968). The second instance was during the 1940s when much of the work of the legislature was orchestrated by a political genius named Arthur Samish, the "secret boss of California." His clients included a number of the most important large interests of the state; it was reputedly necessary to lobby him rather than lobby the elected assemblymen or senators.

Arthur Samish's career prospered for many years despite the California constitution's definition of lobbying as any attempt to "influence the vote of a member of the legislature by bribery, promise of reward, intimidation or any other dishonest means." Any such attempt was punishable as a felony. The flamboyant Samish once commented on this provision, stating that such methods were for amateurs, and that he did not need them, his own technique being simply to "select and elect" the right individuals to the legislature, which he was well able to do. As Samish wrote:

My method of delivering votes was the soul of simplicity. It was merely this:
Select and Elect.
That was all. I simply selected those men I thought would be friendly to my clients' interests. Then I saw to it that those men got elected to the legislature.
Select and Elect.
In that way I made certain that the bills I wanted for my clients won a friendly reception in the legislature. Sometimes an assemblyman or a senator might have disappointed me. Maybe he voted the wrong way on a bill I wanted. Too bad for him. I did my best to see that he didn't return to the legislature after the next election. And most times I was successful in that endeavor.
Select and Elect.
I didn't care whether a man was a Republican or a Democrat or a Prohibitionist. I didn't care whether he voted against free love or for the boll weevil. All I cared about was how he voted on legislation affecting my clients. (Samish and Thomas, 1971, pp. 34–35)

Restrictions on Lobbying

In 1946 the United States Congress, in an attempt to control lobbying activities, passed the Federal Regulation of Lobbying Act. This act requires that persons

Figure 15.7 **(left) Lobbyists work through the front door, through the back door, and sometimes from a position of some distance. They know that there is no one best way to assure the passage or defeat of a piece of legislation. Lobbyists worth their salt to their clients are capable of using a variety of persuasive techniques on legislators, on their staffs, and on relevant bureaucrats buried within the recesses of the federal agencies. They are also prepared to develop mass public relations campaigns timed to coincide with important governmental decisions, if necessary.**

Figure 15.8 **Political philosophers have recognized for ages that the definition of the concept "public interest" involves complex and subjective arguments. Our entire system of representation is designed both to protect the debate over the definition of the public interest and to create at least temporary answers to that elusive question. On the question of government regulation of production (right), we see three views, each recommending itself as an adequate definition of the public interest. Government is the name of the game by which such disparate perspectives are accommodated to one another.**

who are paid to influence legislation be registered and disclose the source and use of their pay (of sums more than $500) to the clerk of the House of Representatives and the secretary of the Senate. The theory is that the legislators and the public will thereby be informed as to the interested nature of some of the "advice" they receive from lobbyists. Accordingly, there exist regular lists of lobbyists and the amount of money they are willing to state as having passed through their hands for lobbying.

Because of loopholes in the act, however, the financial reports do not necessarily reflect reality. For instance, the act states that a report must be given to the proper authorities by those who pay or receive money for the "principal purpose of influenc(ing), directly or indirectly, the passage or defeat of any legislation by the Congress of the United States." Some important lobbying groups quite le-

gally insist that because their activities do not "principally" consist of lobbying, they need not give the information sought. (There is virtually no attempt or machinery available to check on the information that *is* submitted.) Because of this and other loopholes, it is extremely difficult to get an accurate picture of exactly who is spending how much money for lobbying activities. In addition, the newspapers tend to be only slightly interested in lobbying activities; only in the case of an unusual or conspicuous lobbying campaign do they bother to print stories on the matter.

Because it is so difficult to control lobbyists and their influence over legislators, people have periodically suggested that all forms of lobbying be forbidden and stiff penalties be enforced for noncompliance. Unless Americans are prepared to amend the United States Constitution in an especially im-

Top Spenders for Lobbying, 1972 (of those recorded)	
Common Cause	$558,839
AFL-CIO	216,294
Veterans of World War I of the U.S.A. Inc.	213,743
American Postal Workers Union	208,767
United States Savings & Loan League	191,726
National Council of Farmer Cooperatives	184,347
American Farm Bureau Administration	180,678
Disabled American Veterans	159,431
National Association of Letter Carriers (AFL-CIO)	154,188
American Trucking Association Inc.	137,804
Farmers Educational Cooperative Union of America	113,156
United Mine Workers of America	110,045
American Nurses Association Inc.	109,643
National Association of Home Builders of the United States	99,031
American Medical Association	96,146
Brotherhood of Railway, Airline and Steamship Clerks	88,540
Recording Industry Association of America Inc.	88,396
American Insurance Association	82,259
National Federation of Federal Employees	82,080
National Housing Conference Inc.	77,906
International Brotherhood of Teamsters	76,897
National Limestone Institute Inc.	75,777
American Civil Liberties Union	73,131
National Association of Real Estate Boards	70,941
Liberty Lobby Inc.	70,019

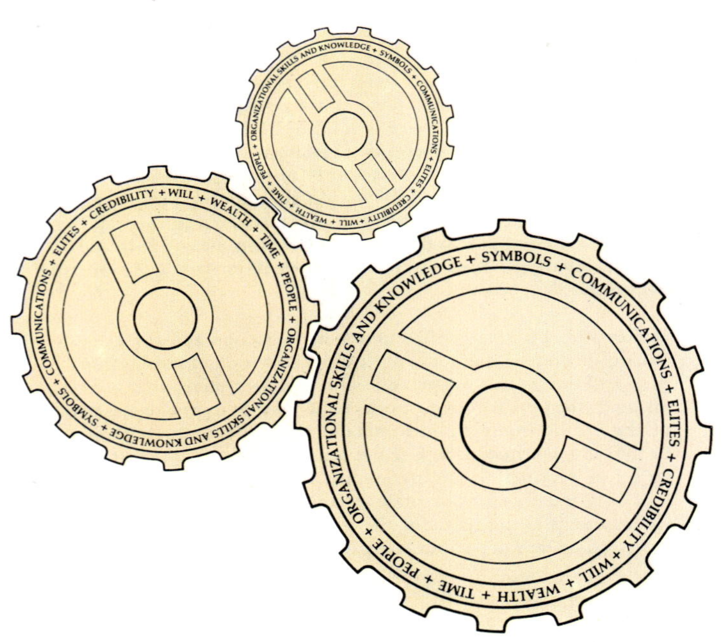

portant respect, however, such an idea must be immediately rejected. The First Amendment explicitly states that Congress shall make no law prohibiting the right of the people "to petition the Government for a redress of grievances." This provision, together with the same amendment's guarantee of free speech, virtually prohibits any outright attempt to abolish the practice of lobbying.

The Pervasiveness of Lobbyists

Even if some ingenious method were found to circumvent the provisions of the First Amendment, however, it is unlikely that lobbying could be discontinued. The reason is that many members of Congress, probably all at some time, are themselves lobbyists. As is shown in Chapter 8, the average congressman spends much of his time responding to the demands of his constituents. He inevitably has some group that is especially important in his district or state, and his reelection may well depend on the success with which he urges passage of measures designed to benefit the particular members of that group. This situation need not imply dishonesty on the part of the legislator. Senator Henry Jackson of Washington, for example, is a well-known defender of the interests of Boeing and of the aircraft industry in general. Although Senator Jackson has a strong record on environmental matters, he has strongly supported the attempt to build a supersonic aircraft, which has been vigorously opposed by numerous environmentalists. Given the fact that Boeing, the prospective builder of such a machine, is the major employer in the most populated region of Jackson's state, he needs no reminder of what might happen next election day were he to support the withdrawal of government support of the project.

Figure 15.9 Lobbying groups are required to report their annual expenditures (far left). Until recently, however, there has been little effort to research the accuracy of such reports or to estimate the indirect expenditures of such lobbying groups and their associated organizations. The citizens' lobbying group, Common Cause, claims that its top position as big spender of 1972 is the result of its meticulous reporting of every penny spent, as opposed to the alleged discrepancies in the reports of other groups. A glance at similar lists for a number of years will show that the ranking tends to change depending on the critical legislation on the docket in any one year and the particular groups affected by it.

Figure 15.10 Components of power (left). Wheels of power interlock to create a system of power, or coalition. Within the nation there are a multitude of such power coalitions that operate in all spheres of social, political, and economic life. Examine the elements that make up these wheels of power: Wealth, Time, People, Organizational Skills, and so forth. Some individuals or groups have more of these elements than do others. For example, one group may have superb financial and organizational resources, whereas another may have many more people and access to powerful symbols. These groups may use their unique resources in battling one another, or they may cooperate and dovetail their advantages in opposition to other groups or to the government itself.

Figure 15.11 Senator Henry Jackson of Washington attempts to keep his balance at a Dade County, Florida bicycle meet (right). Jackson regularly walks a tightrope in his attempts to maintain the support of big business in the Pacific Northwest while keeping his strong pro-environmentalist reputation. In 1972 Jackson tried to parlay his middle-of-the-road, northern Democrat status into a presidential bid, but he failed to gain enough backing from war-weary voters to make a successful campaign.

In one sense, even the executive branch of the government engages in lobbying activities. According to a publication of the Congressional Quarterly Service, the President, particularly since World War II, has applied significant pressure on Congress

. . . for enactment of legislation he favored and for defeat of legislation he opposed. He operated both through his capacity to influence public opinion and through direct contacts with Members of Congress. . . . probably all Presidents in U.S. history used the power and prestige of their office to pressure Congress . . . (Congressional Quarterly, 1968, p. 65)

Lobbies and Political Parties

Another form of political power in America is the political party. It is not easy to specify precisely what the relationship is between parties and interest groups. In one sense, there is some truth in the statement that to the extent that parties are powerful, interest groups are weak, and vice versa. When an interest group looks only to one party for furtherance of its purposes, the party can take that group's support for granted and assist it to only a minimum degree. If, however, the interest group can play one party off against the other, it is in a much better bargaining situation and, as a result, is more powerful. When a party can ignore interest groups generally and persuade voters as a whole to think of the national interest instead of their own separate and group interests, the party is powerful. Hence, interest groups can be seen as being engaged in a quiet contest with parties for the loyalties of citizens. In general, given the common distrust of "politics," which Americans tend to associate merely with parties, interest groups at many points are more powerful, in terms of citizen support, than are parties.

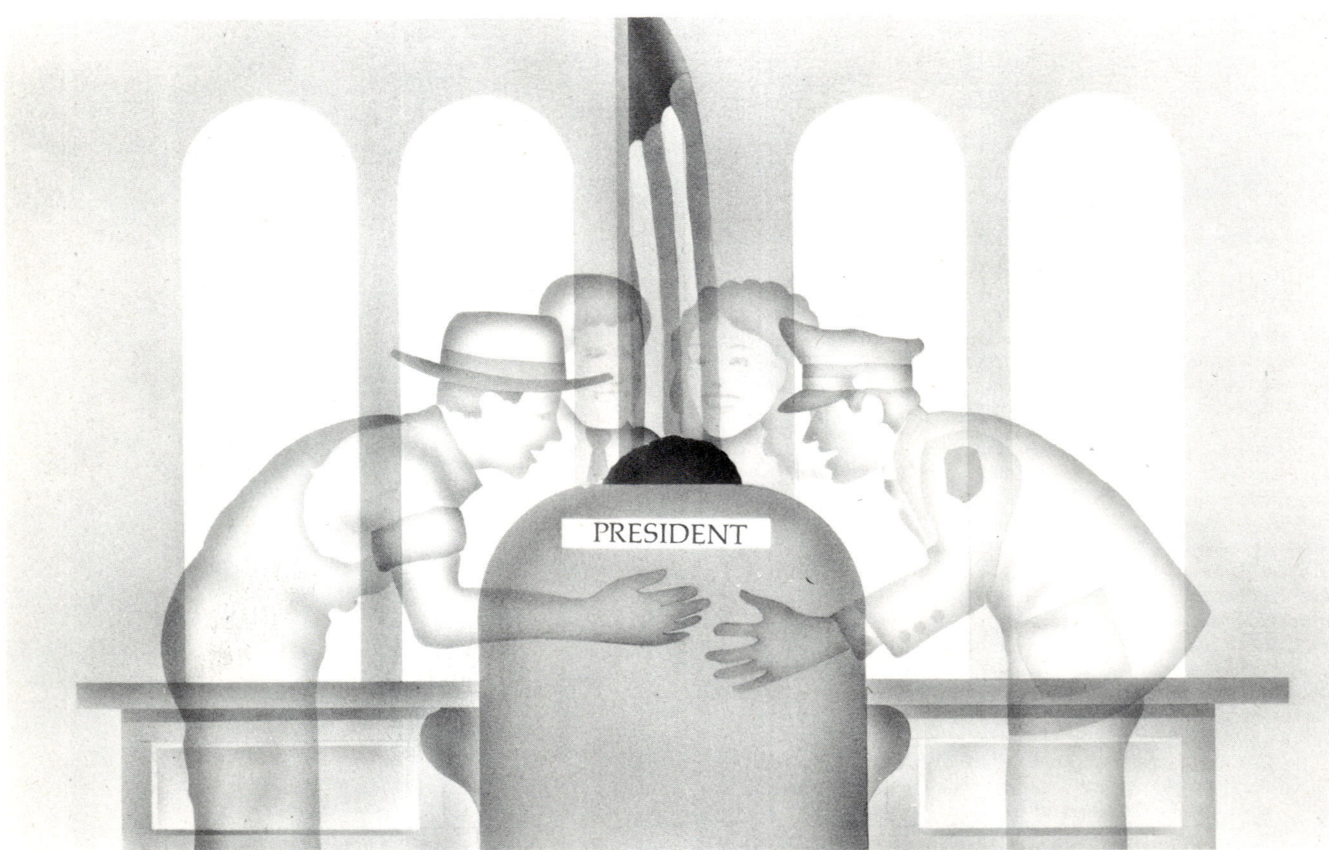

Another aspect of the relationship between parties and interest groups is that, in a very broad sense, parties are concerned with personnel, whereas interest groups are concerned with policies; parties are preoccupied with getting candidates elected to office, and interest groups are preoccupied with the outcomes of what government does. In detail, however, they often trade roles, for parties draw up platforms and take policy positions designed to attract voters for their candidates, and interest groups find they frequently can best secure their favored policies by gaining the election of the most friendly candidates.

Clearly, there are other areas of concentration of political power. From time to time, for instance, a few families have had very large shares of power, but this concentration is definitely the exception, not the rule. It is also possible to discover inequalities of power on the basis of class, but this kind of analysis frequently becomes vague and difficult to follow in more than a very broad sense. The existence of a "power elite" has also been asserted, as is seen in Chapter 2, but the term needs much care in interpretation; it will be discussed later in this chapter. For the present, it is sufficient to consider the hypothesis that interest groups seem to be the most characteristic form of political power in the United States.

THE GROWTH OF ORGANIZATIONS

Although no statistical measure of the growth of interest groups in general is possible, it is certain that it is one of the important developments of the twentieth century. Farm organizations, for example, did exist before 1900, but they have been most effective since World War I. Trade associations and employers'

Figure 15.12 **The President is never alone (left). Many of the hopes and fears of all Americans, of farmers, of the military services, and of the minority interests, are focused on this pinnacle of American power. Through their representatives they hope to demonstrate their powers to hurt or to help the President, his party, and his ideals and thus to influence decisions favorable to their interests. For better or for worse, lobbying is an intended consequence of our system of checks and balances, and the Presidency is one point of access into that system.**

Figure 15.13 **Perhaps one of the last of the militant mass-union organizations, the United Farm Workers (right), led by Cesar Chavez, is trying to bring major California fruit and vegetable growers under union contracts. Previously known as the United Farm Workers' Organizing Committee (UFWOC), the UFW uses the black eagle banner and is a member of the AFL-CIO. Until recently it was locked in bitter battle with the non-AFL-CIO Teamsters Union, the most powerful single union in the nation, over representation of the migrant farm workers. The workers' position on the nation's economic ladder is incredibly low because they have been excluded from the protections given most other workers by the National Labor Relations Act. Because most of these workers are of Mexican extraction, the UFW movement is characterized by Latin symbology, language ("huelga" means "strike"), and appeals to cultural consciousness.**

associations also originated in the nineteenth century, but the most dramatic growth came in the twentieth century. The American labor movement began shortly after 1800, but its most important growth occurred in the 1930s and early 1940s.

The growth in strength of interest-group organizations is particularly related to the professionalization of leadership and to the adoption of modern management skills, in sum, to the *bureaucratization* of organization. The simple device of maintaining a regular office staffed by paid employees who are on the job five days a week, month in and month out, is a great advance over relying on part-time amateurs. Maintaining files of members and correspondence and memoranda also gives an organization a great advantage over a rival that fails to do so.

Many groups have developed *in reaction* to governmental intervention in matters of concern. However, many other organizations have come into being *with* the active assistance of government. Not the least of the reasons for the latter pattern is that government officials have wanted citizen guidance in the development of policy. In one sense this desire represents the laudable wish of officials to be democratic; in another sense it is a wish to escape criticism and to build political support for particular governmental agencies. Both aspects can be seen in, for example, the strong assistance and initiative of public officials in the formation of the Chamber of Commerce of the United States and the American Farm Bureau Federation.

CONSPIRACY AND CORRUPTION?

It is tempting to regard the closeness of relations between agencies of government and private interest-group organizations as a form of conspiracy. The word conspiracy, however, is too vivid; the usual lack of secrecy alone makes it unjustified. Moreover, the participants in the sometimes very close and cordial relationships between officials and private-group leaders are likely to insist that there is nothing wrong in what they do. They state that the specialized knowledge possessed by the group leaders is invaluable to government. Furthermore, they state, because an interest group may have a particular stake in the actions of a given agency, it is all very correct that the group's leadership should get a special hearing.

Figure 15.14 The history of the United States labor movement is long, dramatic, and even violent. During its early period the act of organizing workers was considered a crime and the Supreme Court negated all attempts to ameliorate labor conditions, even for children. The Industrial Workers of the World (I.W.W.) was founded in 1905 as a reaction to the complacency of the old craft unions, which numbered few members and looked down on the incoming, unskilled immigrants. I.W.W. efforts to organize industrial workers were met with violence and imprisonment of "wobbly" (slang for I.W.W.) speakers. The current successful years of organized labor—here represented by a gathering of union presidents with AFL-CIO president George Meany (left foreground)—were preceded by generations of very lean and violent years.

Nevertheless, a serious problem remains. What is one to make of a situation in which some expert on the payroll of a private industry is allowed (or encouraged) by his employers to serve the government as a WOC (*without compensation*) for an extended period of time and then return to his private post? He may well have knowledge that is otherwise unavailable to the government and may be completely honest, yet he knows that his public service is temporary and that his future lies with the company that is still paying him. What of the situation in which a high government official is in charge of regulating matters affecting a major corporation? He knows that, as a government official, he is likely to be replaced when a new Administration is voted into office, yet he will have acquired valuable knowledge in the course of his service that he will be reluctant to see go to waste. As he takes positions affecting the corporation, he may receive praise for his judgment from the corporation. As it becomes apparent that he is highly regarded, the thought of a subsequent career with the corporation may be difficult for him to dismiss.

Although it would be difficult to impugn the integrity of the particular individuals in either of these instances, it has to be recognized that a serious problem of persistent and insidious bias exists. There is no conspiracy, and there is no corruption in the common sense, but the public may well have suffered.

An admiral in charge of procuring great quantities of steel retires and becomes head of a steel company; a famous general leaves the federal service to head a corporation with important military contracts; a civil aviation administrator resigns to become head of a major airline—these are cases that have occurred in the not-too-distant past. There are many others that are less well known. At a minimum, the web of personal, social, professional, and even financial relationships may prove significant in the subsequent contacts between private and public bodies, especially where there is a conflict of interest (see the Perspective on the military-industrial complex).

PRIVATE GOVERNMENTS

In an important sense, many interest groups are themselves forms of government. They are usually not parts of the official structure of either the federal, state, or local governments, but, as will be discussed, many of them have significant power in the making and administration of official policies.

The powers that private organized groups exercise over their members vary widely, but some are very important indeed. For instance, if a man moves to a town where trade unions are strong, he may be required to join a union before he can work at a given craft, such as bricklaying or printing. Similarly, it is often vital that medical doctors be members in good standing in the local medical association before they are allowed hospital-access for their patients. Or a rancher's request for use of federally owned grazing land for his cattle may be examined in light of the respect with which he is held by the ranchers' association.

There are also various ways in which regulations drawn by private groups control entry into professions or businesses. These regulations may include apprenticeship or other educational requirements, or they may call for tests of "character," such as those administered by bar associations. Other restrictions may include requirements that certain kinds of work be done only by licensed workers, the granting of licenses being done by boards over which unions or professional associations have control.

Because of these powers, it is possible for many associations to enforce rules (sometimes they are even termed "laws") for the regulation of their members. The enforcement of such rules may be—and often is—backed up with penalties of fines, suspension, or expulsion. In some associations, such as many unions, expulsion may involve the loss of rights to pensions and other benefits that members generally regard as having been important parts of their earnings.

Because of these restrictions, it is insufficient to say, as various writers have, that the way in which a private association is governed internally does not matter, because an aggrieved member can always resign. Resignation that costs the individual the right to make a living in a chosen field (in a position that may have required years of training) or that forces his moving to another area is a very costly recourse and one not to be taken lightly. Resignation would be a meaningful solution only if alternative and rival organizations were available to join. Alternatives are only rarely available, however; in fact, most organizations such as unions and professional associations jealously seek to destroy incipient rivals.

The "Iron Law of Oligarchy"

Because there are so many associations that have significant power over their members, it is important to understand how they are governed. Without question, there are many variations in the governments of private associations; the system existing in one cannot be assumed to prevail in the others. Is it possible, however, to discover any common pattern in a substantial number of these associations?

In 1914 Robert Michels, a German sociologist, wrote about the pattern he perceived in the governments of private associations. According to Michels, such organizations are run by "the iron law of oligarchy." According to this law, "[he] who says organization says oligarchy."

Michels looked at the organizations that had the greatest professed devotion to democracy, the Social Democratic parties of Europe, and looked at how they were governed internally. What he discovered was that, in their own affairs, these parties were invariably dominated by a few leaders and that oligarchy (rule by the few) was their persistent condition. He observed that differences of interest and outlook developed in these parties between the leaders and the led and that these differences sometimes amounted to conflicts of interest within the organization. In such conflicts, moreover, all the advantages lay with the leaders, who necessarily knew more about the affairs of the organization and had control of the files, the membership lists, the treasury, and the hired staff (the bureaucracy) of the organization. By contrast, the membership was ignorant, generally incompetent in organizational affairs, and usually apathetic. The result was that the leadership consistently won whenever there was a conflict, except in the rare instances when a rival set of leaders overthrew the existing leaders and became leaders themselves, resulting once again in oligarchy.

Michels' argument is very disturbing to many who believe in democracy, and there have been many efforts to disprove it. Disproving the argument depends in part on how "oligarchy" and "democracy" are defined and in part on the importance that is given to the "iron," or the invariable, part of the argument. Without arguing the theoretical case, however, it remains true that many illustrations of this law of oligarchy are to be found among the private associations of America.

The Government of Trade Unions

Among the American associations there are probably none that profess a stronger commitment to democracy than the trade unions. Following Michels, they are probably the most appropriate private governments to examine. Despite some important variations among them, their features tend to be as follows.

The source of authority in unions is, like that in the United States as a whole, the members (or the citizens). Membership, however, is not something that comes with birth; members must apply and be accepted, sometimes having to pass tests and take oaths. The highest body of government is the entire membership. The membership, however, frequently numbers in the thousands, and all members cannot assemble in town-meeting fashion to conduct organization affairs. The nearest approximation—the convention—has accordingly been adopted. The yearly conventions of many associations consist of more than a thousand delegates and may last for five days, seldom longer. The delegates are chosen in local units by any of a number of ways; usually, they are elected.

It is tempting to compare a union convention to a meeting of the United States Congress, but there is one difference between the two that prohibits such a comparison: Convention delegates are present as substitutes for the whole body of union members—they are not representatives as are members of Congress. The difference may appear subtle, but it is important. Delegates at a union convention are not expected to act on their own judgment, but are expected to do as they have been instructed—in a large and short-lived assembly, the practical difficulties of rational discussion are great. The delegates (who are, for the most part, ordinary members) are neither experts nor necessarily well informed. Moreover, the official leadership, having made all the arrangements for the convention and appointed all the crucial committees, will be in firm control of what goes on. The presiding officer is usually the president of the association and is able to choose from among the individuals wishing to speak. Should some dissident nevertheless attempt to seize a microphone, the presiding officer has only to turn a switch to silence that microphone. A convention, then, is more likely to be a device for generating a show of enthusiasm than to be a deliberating body as is Congress (Grant McConnell, 1958).

Given this characteristic of conventions, it is evident that there is nothing in union governments akin to the separation of powers in the United States government. The official leadership is supposedly a mere agent of the convention and general membership, but in reality it is apt to have firm control. Moreover, there are none of the other checks and balances designed to limit leaders' powers that are taken for granted in public government. The judicial system of unions typically consists of a trial committee of a local union and includes provisions for appeal to the leadership of the local; appeals go from there to the national leadership and then to a vote of the convention. This system ultimately reduces the internal legal system to at best a popularity contest or at worst a pattern of political decisions firmly in the hands of the established leaders. Opposition to such leaders can be dangerous.

These official arrangements would perhaps be less dangerous to dissidents if anything like a party system were to arise, which might provide protection for individuals who want to voice complaints and who are willing to replace the existing leaders. Although many unions have internal factions, they are generally deplored. (Only the International Typographical Union has had a genuine system of political parties that contest to provide alternative leaders.) It is usually argued that there are no reasons for unions to allow for rival parties, there being no grounds for differences. This argument is false, however, because any union will have differences between young and old, between employed and unemployed, and between workers in different types of plants—to say nothing of all the differences of opinion any group of humans will display. The unfortunate fact, however, is that virtually all organizations seek a degree of unity—or appearance of unity—that amounts to unanimity.

The lack of a party structure would be of less importance if unions guaranteed the basic liberties of

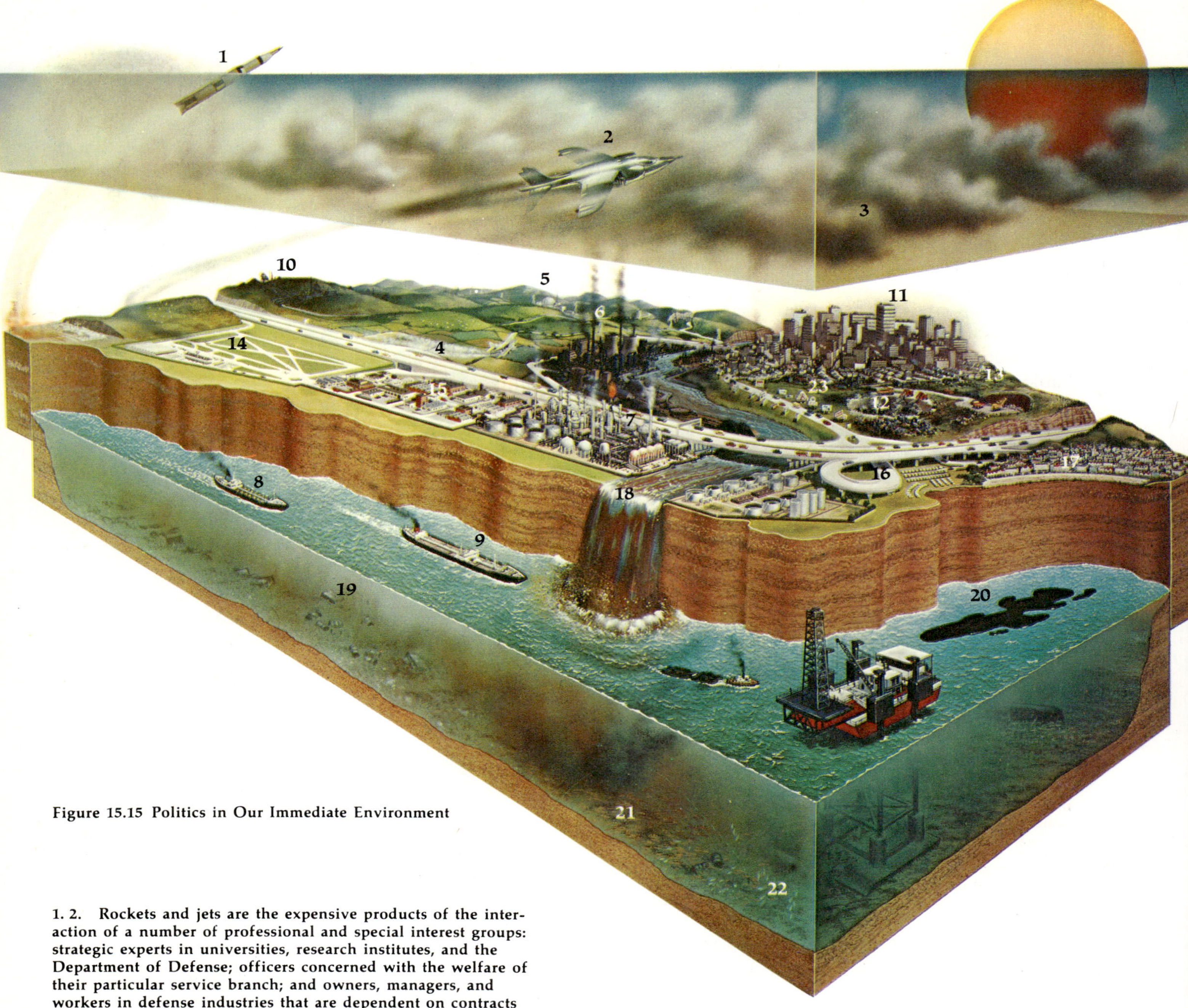

Figure 15.15 Politics in Our Immediate Environment

1. 2. Rockets and jets are the expensive products of the interaction of a number of professional and special interest groups:
strategic experts in universities, research institutes, and the
Department of Defense; officers concerned with the welfare of
their particular service branch; and owners, managers, and
workers in defense industries that are dependent on contracts
and the security of government purchasing.

3. Pollutants trapped in the atmosphere create a problem that
extends beyond the boundaries of any particular city or suburb. Regional planning is necessary to develop effective population and transportation policies for the purpose of controlling
wind-distributed air pollution.

4. Associations of farmers and of aerial spraying companies
attempt to obstruct state and national government policies that
limit the kind and scope of pesticide use.

5. With the advent of nuclear power, an entirely new industry has arisen that exerts pressure on government for favorable
treatment.

6. Power utilities are legal monopolies whose rate structures
are decided by utilities commissions, which are, in turn, the
focus of tremendous pressures to allow expansion and higher
rates for the benefit of managers and investors.

speech and expression and provided devices for protecting those willing to dissent. Union constitutions rarely contain anything like the Bill of Rights, however. On the contrary, they frequently carry penalties for offenses vaguely described as "slandering an officer" or "conduct unbecoming a union man." It is not surprising, then, that protection of individual rights in unions has had to come through legislation by Congress (McConnell, 1958). In 1959, for example, Congress passed the Landrum Griffin Act, which guarantees fair elections and a few other rights in unions. Scandals have occurred since, however, the most notorious being the 1970 murder of Joseph Yablonski, an opposition contender for the post of president of the United Mine Workers (see the Perspective on Appalachia).

The Government of Corporations and Associations

If union governments have serious shortcomings by democratic tests, the governments of corporations are ridiculous when similarly measured. Although shareholders are the presumed source of authority, their votes are weighted according to how many shares they hold. Moreover, most stockholders consistently authorize others to cast their votes for them (that is, they vote by proxy). Because the corporate leadership controls the proxy machinery and the list of stockholders, opponents are at a great disadvantage in any attempt to challenge the leadership. In addition, stockholders are generally ill-informed and apathetic about corporation affairs. The consequence is that management is as likely to control the choice of directors as the other way around. Either way, any presumption of democracy in corporations is unwarranted.

Other private associations have varying devices for governing themselves; however, few of them could be considered truly democratic bodies. Most of them are wary of the rise of internal opposition to leaders and seek to suppress its expression, if by no other means than strong social disapproval. Ironically, this social disapproval may be strongest and

7. Oil companies regulate refinery output to maintain prices, and they lobby government representatives for favorable tax policies.

8. 9. United States shipbuilders and the National Maritime Unions win direct and indirect subsidies from Congress in the guise of national defense requirements.

10. Coal mining spoils the landscape and pollutes the watersheds; yet mineral extraction continues because of energy demands and the influence of mining lobbies at state and national levels.

11. Large corporate headquarters govern far-flung national and international operations, making government regulation difficult because of the complexity of corporate activities; the incremental nature of most "big" decisions means that negative results are frequently unforeseen by corporate decision makers.

12. 13. The sites within city environs of waste disposal and quarrying activities have usually been established before the spread of urban dwellings made land-use planning by government agencies an urgent necessity.

14. Airport landing procedures, passenger ticketing conditions, fares, routes, and specifications for airplane performance and maintenance are all regulated by the Federal Aeronautics Administration and the Civil Aeronautics Board.

15. Open space, even scarce agricultural land, is often turned into facilities such as industrial parks by entrepreneurs who regard immediate profit as a higher social priority.

16. Highway building contractors, land speculators, trucking and automobile industries, construction unions, and local, state, and federal highway-planning agencies form a large interest community with much political clout.

17. Suburban sprawl is facilitated by bank lending policies and by the activities of land developers.

18. Federal and state regulations are directed to cleaning up the nation's rivers, yet local interests often pressure government to slow down enforcement efforts.

19. The disposal of radioactive wastes from nuclear power stations is the focus of struggle among government agencies (such as the Atomic Energy Commission) and private contractors on the one side, and environmentalists and independent scientists on the other, over how much government regulation and limitation is necessary to maintain public health and safety.

20. 21. Water pollution, caused by decaying industrial and organic wastes and oil spills, leads citizens and their representatives to turn to government for regulation of private interests.

22. The struggle over fishing rights has been influential in our relations with such nations as Japan, Peru, and Iceland. Fishing companies successfully influence treaty negotiations among nations with strong fishing enterprises.

23. Advertising firms are politically active in protecting billboards from environmentalist legislation, which classifies billboards as visual pollution.

most effective in the smaller organizations, which would at least seem to offer the best opportunity for genuine discussion and compromise.

Private Government and Public Policy

If the nature of private government in associations is important to their members, it is also important to members of the public outside. The reason, entirely aside from the stake everyone has in the development of a pervasive democratic spirit, is that these associations have a large influence over particular segments of public policy.

A significant development within this realm of influence is that policy on matters of sometimes vital concern—the quality and availability of medical care, the price and production of food, the supply of fuel for heating and industry, to cite but a few examples—has become firmly established in the hands of a few producers or providers of services. As mentioned in Chapter 2, proponents of the power-concentration hypothesis contend that this concentration of power is simply an aspect of something more general: the existence of a well-coordinated "power elite" made up of the highest leaders of government, industry, and the military, most of whom have ties with one another of family, education, and social standing. They supposedly meet frequently and informally, and they tend to think alike; together they make the "big decisions" affecting all the nation. In a very general sense this picture is correct, for if one were to seek out the very highest leaders of affairs, one would find that many of them know one another and have many of the same characteristics and backgrounds. Such information, however, would be neither surprising nor interesting.

"Big decisions" are few, and those that can be named usually turn out on close examination to have been influenced by many groups and individuals and brought about by accidents, unforeseen events, and misunderstandings. In general, they tend to be made gradually, step by step, in which each step is a small decision taken without thought of the larger consequences. These smaller decisions (the decision to restrict the imports of oil, for example) may be made within a small circle of leaders from industry and Congress, but the long-range results may be neither intended nor expected (such as environmental destruction). The consequences of such lesser

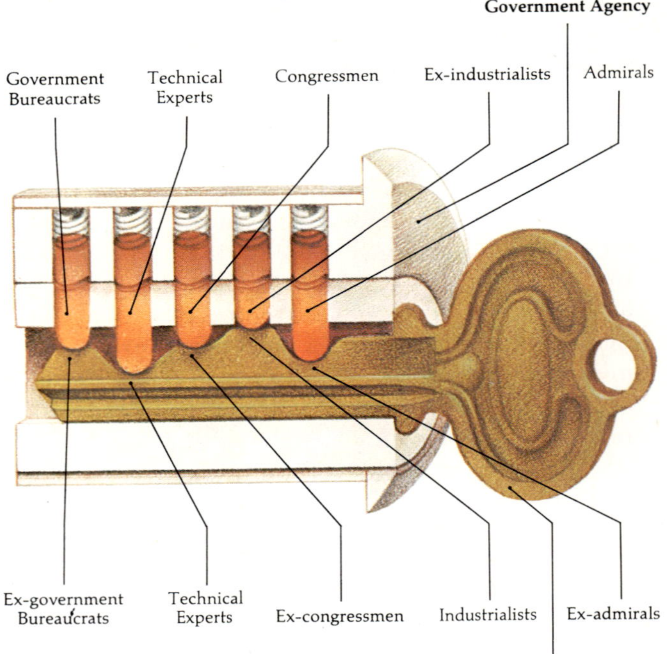

Figure 15.16 (above) Just as the notches on a key must be finely tooled to fit a particular lock, so it might be said in a colloquial way that the successful lobbyist must be able to "fit in." That is, he or she must share the jargon, the informal mores, or the point of view of the government agency or operation to which the interest group is orienting its message. Clearly, if the interest group representative—the lobbyist—has a similar background of experience and training with the government people he or she deals with, there is a better chance of proper "fit." Thus we find many former government employees, elected officials, and technical experts who assume the position of go-between, communicating the preferences, abilities, needs, and information from interest groups to those persons and offices in the government that are responsible for making decisions.

decisions may extend very far indeed, to the continuation of prosperity or not, or to the improvement or worsening of our foreign relations.

The basic problem with interest groups and their private governments, then, is not so much that they are selfish or that occasionally some form of corrupt behavior occurs, but that too frequently they have successfully isolated segments of public policy and its administration and made them responsive solely to particular interest-group constituencies. For example, the making of agricultural policy has long been contained within the circle of a few congressmen and senators from farm states, a few leaders of farm organizations and food-processing corporations, top officials of the Department of Agriculture (carefully chosen to please the farm leaders), and carefully chosen experts from agricultural colleges. Although it should be obvious that everyone has an interest in food and the policy concerned with its production, the participation of the general public in farm and food policy has been slight. Day-to-day administration of this policy has been contained within even narrower bounds, and things are much the same in other fields of policy.

Interest groups, then, can be seen to form one of the really fundamental problems of American democracy. There is no easy answer to be found in attempting to abolish or silence them. They serve some positive functions, and, much more important, it would restrict liberty for everyone were they restrained. But to say this is not to deny that American policy in many areas has served narrow groups to an excessive degree. The worst part of the problem is that parts of government are so inextricably mixed with politically powerful and narrowly based private groups that the distinction between what is public and what is private is frequently lost. This distinction is vital to the nation and to democracy; without it, we can have only a system of every group for itself, and the devil take the hindmost.

SUMMARY

The framers of the Constitution identified government as a major threat to liberty yet failed to concern themselves with other potentially powerful influences on policy: great concentrations of private power.

It is politically important that Americans join and form groups. To the pluralists, groups perform a check-and-balance function on government activity, they guard against mob action, and they serve to focus citizen demands. The terms "pressure group" and "interest group" are used to denote groups that seek to influence the policy process. Those attempting to abolish interest groups' primary technique—lobbying—fail to realize the pervasiveness of lobbying and its basis in the Constitution.

Interest groups are a characteristic form of political power in the United States. Group organization and activity tends to intensify in times of crisis—war and depression—when government intervention in economic affairs has been greatest.

To some, the close relations of interest groups and government agencies suggest conspiracy. Although an overstatement, the liaison may well be against the public interest. Many interest groups, such as unions and corporations, are themselves forms of *private* government, with significant power to make and to administer official policies. This concentration of power partially supports the power-elite thesis, although the incremental nature of the "big" decisions suggests otherwise. The basic issue is not interest-group corruption; rather, it is the isolation of policy making and administering to suit the interests of the few.

SUGGESTED READINGS

Herring, Pendleton. *The Politics of Democracy.* New York: Norton, 1965.

Lowi, Theodore J. *The End of Liberalism.* New York: Norton, 1969.

McConnell, Grant. *Private Power and American Democracy.* New York: Knopf, 1966.

Seidman, Harold. *Politics, Position and Power.* New York: Oxford, 1970.

Truman, David. *The Governmental Process.* New York: Knopf, 1951.

Zeigler, Harmon. *Interest Groups in American Society.* Englewood Cliffs, N.J.: Prentice-Hall, 1964.

16

MASS POLITICAL PARTICIPATION: MOBILIZATION, PROTEST, AND VIOLENCE

It is hardly news that the 1960s were years of protest, violence, and social turmoil. The decade began with civil rights marches and protests in the South. It ended in an uproar of antiwar demonstrations. In between came the assassinations of Malcolm X, John Kennedy, Martin Luther King, and Robert Kennedy. Watts burned, as did black ghettos in many major cities.

The relevance of these events for this chapter is that in some ways they all may be thought of as *political* acts—protest, demonstration, and even rioting may represent efforts by particular groups to influence public policy.

This chapter takes up where the previous chapter left off. The focus remains on the political impact of interest groups. But whereas Chapter 15 discusses the abilities of such familiar groups as General Motors and the Boy Scouts to influence and in some respects to make public policy, this chapter turns the lens a bit. It focuses on groups outside the ordinary political process, groups whose political participation often takes place outside traditional political institutions. For we could hardly come to grips with recent American politics if we did not study the ways in which citizens attempt to affect political events by working outside formal structures of power.

As is pointed out in Chapter 15, interest groups use a great variety of tactics to influence policy. For analytic purposes we may label some tactics as *formal* because they seek to exercise influence through the formally authorized, constitutional structures of authority by which the society is governed. For example, formal political participation can take such forms as bloc voting, contributing time and money to political campaigns, and even running candidates for office. But groups may also participate in politics in ways that we may label *nonformal*—that is, they may attempt to gain political ends by methods outside the formal constitutional structures of governance.

The broad range of nonformal ways of participating in politics is suggested in Figure 16.2. Nonformal participation includes many activities that are completely conventional. This is particularly true for legitimate, individual activities suggested in the upper-left corner of the figure. Privately consulting with elected officials, doing research on policy, and attempting to persuade others of the significance of

Figure 16.1 Courage of opinion knows no age. Here, police arrest an old couple during an antiwar sit-in at an Oakland, California military induction center.

policy positions are activities that are necessary to representative government. The activities of trade unions and professional associations and special-interest lobbying are also common to modern democratic political systems. Thus, in some respects, there is nothing unconventional about nonformal political participation.

What distinguished the decade of the 1960s, however, was the influence of nonformal political participation characterized by (1) mass action, and (2) the threat or reality of illegitimate tactics. Large numbers of people were willing to engage in, or they at least threatened to engage in, tactics at odds with the basic norms or rules that have been developed in American society for political behavior.

No political system of any size can hope to provide in practice a governmental structure resembling "pure" representative democracy, in which each citizen is represented equally by freely elected represent-atives. However, if representative governments are to flourish, ways must and will be found to express the interests and views of various groups within the population. People will also find ways to make their views known as forcefully as possible in an attempt to have their position reflected in law and procedure.

GROUPS AND DEMOCRATIC THEORY

The importance of *groups* in the American political process has long been acknowledged by political theorists. In a complex society it may be impossible to represent adequately the interests of each citizen. But this "defect" of the system may theoretically be compensated for by the active political participation of groups of individuals whose needs or goals are similar. Thus, associations develop to represent agricultural interests, the American Medical Association seeks to secure the interests of doctors, and the American Legion acts as a watchdog over veterans'

Nonformal Political Participation and Activity			
	Legitimate	**Borderline Legitimacy**	**Illegitimate**
Individual	Private advising to elected officials Conducting research on public policy Rabble-rousing, speech-making Joining politically-oriented interest groups	Legislators' interceding in administrative decisions Spreading negative rumors about a firm or officeholder	Assassination Bribery Extortion
Small Group	Working for a public-interest law practice Conducting consumer-oriented investigations Lobbying Publishing periodicals, newspapers, and reports	Overloading bureaucracies with requests	Disrupting opposition's political campaign Contributing to campaigns in direct exchange for favorable governmental action Terrorism
Collective Action	Participating in a community organization Trade union organizing and negotiating; research and publications Conducting ad hoc pressure (such as, for POWs) Conducting legal boycotts Participating in protest marches and demonstrations	Mass protests blocking normal activities Illegal boycotts	Strikes by public employees Rioting

benefits. The system of group representation, far from being irrelevant to the functioning of democratic institutions, is actually crucial to those institutions. In theory and in practice, group representation serves to link individuals and political institutions.

Influencing the System: The Basic Tools

In previous chapters we have observed that formal political institutions tend to underrepresent the poorer members of American society. In voter registration, in voting rates, in participation in electoral campaigns, and in holding office there is a relationship between the relative wealth of individuals and the degree of their political participation. There is similar bias in the system of group representation. The influence that interest groups are able to exercise tends to depend on their command of certain resources, the status of their individual members (and thus of the group itself), and the degree of group cohesion.

Resources

Other things being equal, the greater the resources commanded by a group the more likely it is to be successful. Group resources include the personal wealth of the members as well as the size of the group's treasury. Another resource that is vital to the success of the group is the *skill* or political competence of the people who staff the organization. If tactical success depends on writing effective news releases and contacting newspapers, the effectiveness with which the job is done may well depend on the sophistication and educational background of the members.

Status

The higher the status and reputation of groups the more likely they are to succeed. They are more likely

Figure 16.2 (left) The problem of long-term strategy and short-term tactics confronts the group or individual whose resources or ideology require that they work outside the formal structure of a given political system. To some, working from the "outside" may suggest actions that are still within the framework of legally sanctioned (legitimate) action; others may see the situation as unyielding or crucial enough to seek opportunities for actions considered to be in a gray area (borderline legitimacy) of acceptability or justifiability in the political community. When a political actor sees little chance of affecting political outcomes through acceptable or partially acceptable action, and yet the need appears overwhelming as compared even to the risk of punishment, extreme action of an "illegitimate" nature may be resorted to and possibly justified outside the normal codes of the society.

Figure 16.3 (right) Rumors were common that the Watts riot in Los Angeles, in August 1965, was the result of a planned conspiracy. But a great deal of investigation showed evidence only of a contagious flare-up of black frustration. The Watts riot represented the first in a series of "long, hot summers" of the mid-1960s, during which blacks in many cities across the nation rose in rebellion against symbols of white controlled economic and law-enforcement systems.

to gain the attention of others, and their views are more likely to be listened to and given weight. Such factors as the social status and expertise of the individual members are two important factors that determine the reputation of the group. It is for these reasons that doctors' organizations have such extraordinary influence: They are composed of members of the highest social standing, whose expertise in their field is almost impossible to challenge successfully. However, a group may enjoy high status independent of the status of members. By developing a reputation for honesty and thoroughness, for example, a group may gain a reputation for reliability regardless of the status of members.

Cohesion

Group influence is significantly affected by the extent to which members are willing to act together and to stay together in the face of opposition or hard times. Particularly if a group's identity is dependent on its demonstration that it has a large following, members' willingness to display solidarity is critical. For example, a Massachusetts prison reform group that claimed the support of thousands of citizens found it critical to show a large turnout at a meeting of the membership; it felt its continued effectiveness depended on its ability to show the governor's staff that it indeed enjoyed the support it had claimed. The organization that fails to display this cohesion may in fact be positively ineffective; its lack of solidarity demonstrates to its opponents that the members have no clear ideas about what they want or that the members are unwilling to act together to achieve collective ends.

The Potential for "Illegitimate" Actions

This brief discussion of group characteristics suggests why certain groups may find it necessary to resort to illegitimate actions to gain their ends. For the poorer the group's members are, the less likely they are to command personal and organizational resources, the less likely they are to command status and respect, and the less likely they are to be experienced in or optimistic about the uses of collective action. The importance of potentially illegitimate tactics becomes greater when command of other aspects of group strength is relatively low.

In this chapter we seek to understand why certain groups resort to tactics that society has labeled illegitimate. The importance of this consideration is, as already noted, that groups are necessary to the functioning of representative democracy. Furthermore, the potential for disruption and threats to the established norms of society represent some of the few tactical advantages that disadvantaged groups in American society may command. This consideration of the issue of tactics and illegitimacy focuses an assessment of the potential for such groups to affect the political process. We first examine an essential prerequisite to political success—organization. We then examine both the problems and the potential of protest activity and end the chapter with a discussion of the problem of violence in political activity.

THE PROBLEM OF ORGANIZATION

In American society those people who are most in need of group representation are often those that are least represented. In an open society all people are free to meet and organize: It therefore seems ironic that the most disadvantaged people—those who get the least from politics—are also least likely to organize. Why wouldn't those groups with the most grievances have the most incentive to organize and thus to develop organizations to push for satisfaction of their needs?

The substandard conditions under which people live is only one of many factors that should promote the emergence and persistence of organizations. In this section we examine other problems of relatively powerless groups (that is, groups that are relatively lacking in resources, status, and cohesion) that affect their likelihood of organizing. This is done under three headings: creating organization; maintaining organization; and acting in the political process.

Creating Organization

People often have the impression that organizations abound in minority ghettos, rural poverty areas, and other economically disadvantaged places. The newspapers and televised news programs are filled with reports of the activities of organizations dedicated to defending the interests of these communities or to securing changes in public policy in response to the needs of these communities. Obviously, such organizations do exist; in the past fifteen years, groups have organized to obtain changes in many areas, such as schools, health care, housing, and police protection; groups have also organized around the needs of neighborhoods and the problems of minority racial and ethnic communities.

But the amount of publicity given to such organizations says nothing about the total number of organizations compared to the proportion in more affluent communities. Nor does it say anything about their numbers relative to the perceived need nor about their actual incidence of success. To say that blacks are well organized because one has heard of the NAACP, or that Mexican-Americans are well organized because one has heard of the farmworkers' union headed by César Chavez, has the same validity as saying that Americans tend to be rich because one has heard of the Rockefellers. On the contrary, the development of effective organizations among the least advantaged members of society is relatively exceptional and often rare indeed.

An organization must show that it has a chance to be effective, or to win. However, the place of relatively powerless groups in American society strongly suggests that organizations of politically or socially disadvantaged people have not been effective in the past and thus are not likely to be effective in future ventures. The cynicism of potential members regarding a group's chances for success represents a major organizational problem not encountered by more affluent groups.

Another necessity of successful organization—particularly necessary in appealing to poor people—is the offering of material benefits to potential members. A potential member must be convinced that he or she will materially gain from joining the organization in order to make up for his or her doubt that the organization can be successful in substantially achieving its overall objectives. For it is "irrational" for people to join organizations when they can receive the benefits of the organization without joining (Mancur Olson, 1968). Why, for example, should a person campaign for a neighborhood health center when it is likely that he or she will be able to use the facility once it is built even if he or she has not worked for it? This obstacle is particularly formidable when an individual feels that the contributions of any one additional person would make no difference in the outcome.

The same dilemma characterizes the act of voting: It is unlikely that the fortunes of any given candidate will be affected by the decision of any single voter. Then why do people vote? Presumably the answer lies in their socialization toward the act of voting and in the satisfaction they receive from acting in the way they think responsible citizens should act (see Chapter 12). But in a community or in a racial or ethnic group with a history of neglect, a different socialization process may be at work. Indeed, in some communities it may be regarded as foolish to work in community organizations; a community activist may be laughed at if he or she suggests that group efforts will be rewarded.

One way of overcoming the effects of these obstacles is by making available benefits that can be enjoyed by and be distributed to individual members, even though the organization continues to work for collective goals. For example, the National Welfare Rights Organization (NWRO) was able to overcome the reluctance of potential members to join by showing that members could gain increases in their welfare payments through NWRO strategies.

The long history of failure in attempts to develop meaningful organizational efforts results in a reinforcement of cultural biases against organizational activity. As Lee Rainwater has suggested:

The most pervasive fact about lower class people as organizational participants is that they are not socialized either within the family or in their outside lives to work towards the solution of their problems on the basis of organization. (Rainwater, 1968, p. 31)

As we have suggested, the inclination not to join organizations may be related to the implicit calculation of high cost (both in time and money) and the low benefits of joining.

The actual cost of participating in organizations may be quite high. There may be monetary costs: days lost from jobs, carfare, babysitting money, helping to defray organizational expenses. In addition, lower-income people tend to hold the kinds of jobs that do not permit them free time for organizational activity. Of course, there are time and energy costs that discourage organizational involvement at all income levels; but when compared to the free time available to many students, lawyers, and middle-income housewives, the obstacles to participation do seem greater to lower-income individuals.

Another factor that works against organizational participation in working-class communities is the active antagonism of other interests. Managers may look unfavorably on union activities of workers, particularly in small work places or in jobs organized around a "helping" ethos—for example, teachers are supposed to be "above" union involvement, and hospital workers are supposed to forego union involvement for the sake of contributing to (other people's) health care. Civil rights organizing in the South in the early 1960s was severely hampered by the antagonism of the local white population—antagonism that in some cases led to the murder of some of the participants. The potential for brutal confrontations restricts the number of people willing to engage in demonstrations. Considering less violent sanctions, students may think twice about protesting on their college campus when they are likely to be observed by administrators who do not share either their views on policy or their recommendations as to the way the institution should be run.

Maintaining Organization

All organizations, including those in disadvantaged communities, require basic resources in order to manage their daily affairs. Political campaigns may be won or lost on the basis of the availability of office workers, telephones, and mimeograph paper. But there are special reasons why organizations composed of relatively powerless constituents have difficulty maintaining themselves.

Such organizations must continually demonstrate that they are alive and well. The precarious position of community groups creates a demand for continual expressions of strength. Organizations may be challenged to show that they are in fact representative of large numbers of people. They may also have to demonstrate strength and to convince skeptical potential members, potential allies, and future "targets" that they are a force to be reckoned with. Saul Alinsky, at his death in 1972 the foremost American community organizer, has written that one of the primary tasks of a community organization is to select a vulnerable target and to mount a quick campaign against it in order to obtain a quick victory for the organization. Thus, with a successful battle under its belt, the organization would be able to recruit new members more easily. In one of his early campaigns, for example, Alinsky selected a large, chain department store as the organization's first target. He apparently made this selection because he felt the store's concern for its national image would make it give in quickly to the organization's

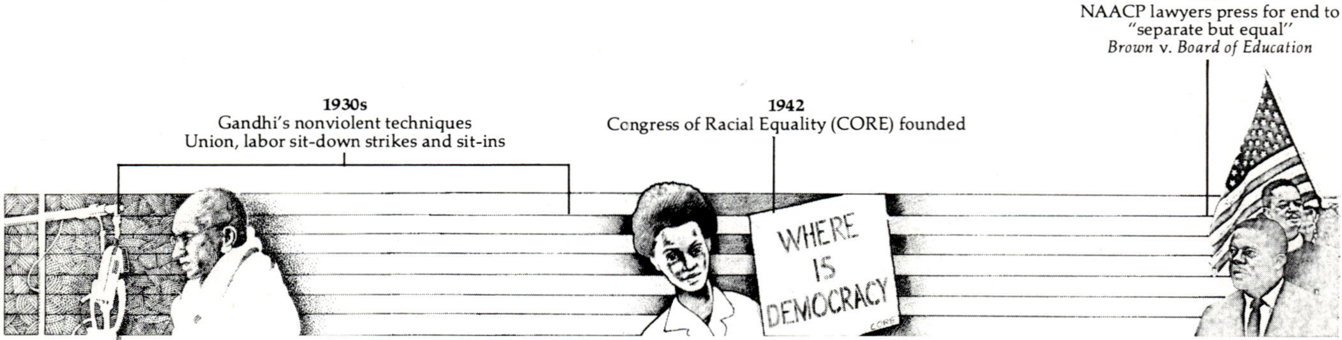

Figure 16.4 Any continuing movement provides an informative study for the evolution of organizing and pressuring tactics. The civil rights movement in the United States, like all movements, derived ideas from similar preceding movements, such as Mahatma Gandhi's in South Africa and India and labor struggles dating back to the nineteenth century in both Europe and the United States. Various organizations and leaders of the black movement have worked toward such diverse goals as voter registration, higher employment, improved housing and education, and the development of favorable legal precedents; their tactics have included court litigation, boycotts, civil disobedience, moral appeals to white sympathizers, the advocacy of separate power bases and cultural institutions, and the intimidation of opponents by threat and by violence. Some of these tactics were used simultaneously, while others seemed to predominate during certain periods of the 1950s and 1960s. Each strategy had its unique effect on sympathetic groups, on opposition groups, and on public opinion.

demands. It was not selected because of its particular importance to the organization's goals.

But where is the energy for such tactics to come from? And if the energy is found, perhaps it could be better used for other purposes. Quick campaigns may be useful in overcoming the skepticism of potential members, but it may also focus attention on secondary (rather than primary) goals in exchange for short-run success.

Because they lack the usual resources that contribute to a group's ability to effect real change, relatively powerless groups may resort to *threat* in order to gain their ends. A group may call attention to its needs by threatening to strike, boycott, protest, picket, or by any other form of disruptive action. But it is significant that even here this apparent tactical resource is severely compromised.

Many disruptive tactics may turn out to be counterproductive because they involve high risks for a group's members. As a result, community organizations must often appear to threaten whereas they are actually designing tactics with little risk for members. This balancing act is required by the decidedly *conservative* orientation of members; that is, members want to risk as little as possible by their actions. For example, tenants are afraid of eviction no matter how angry they may be over housing conditions.

Similarly, welfare recipients are very concerned over the possibility that they may be cut from the welfare rolls if they protest against new regulations, no matter how much their rights to criticize the welfare system are theoretically protected by the Constitution. Demonstrations must appear to be militant, whereas in fact they may paradoxically have to be conservative in the risk to members. Sometimes, demonstrations are carefully negotiated with law enforcement or other public officials so as to reduce or to minimize the possibility of violence and arrests.

The most significant mass demonstrations of the past fifteen years can be usefully analyzed from this perspective. The climactic civil rights March on Washington, D.C. in August 1963 and peace demonstrations in later years were all highly symbolic expressions of concern that were relatively free from significant risk. The National Welfare Rights Organization, perhaps the most broadly based grass-roots organization of poor people in recent years, followed a strategy that symbolically seemed highly threatening to public order. It tried to project an image of threat to the welfare system, with coordinated demonstrations at welfare offices around the country. But the primary tactic was to inspire welfare recipients to make legitimate claims for additional funds, claims that were well within their rights.

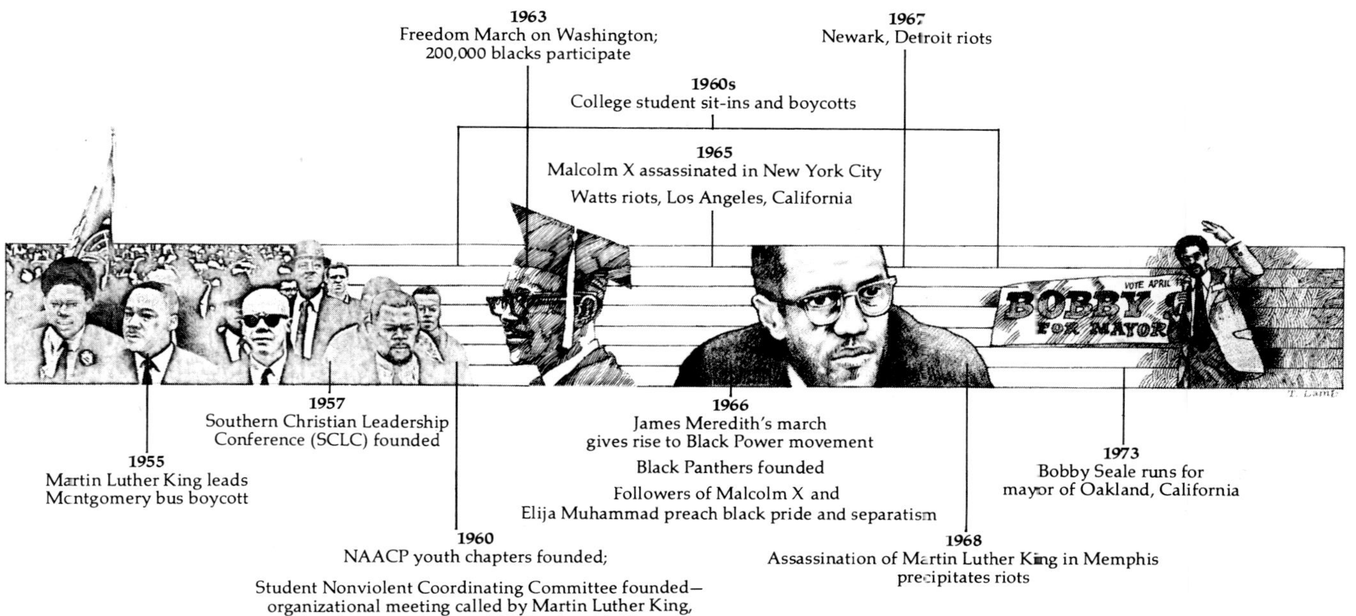

At times, the possibility of threat to an organization's members results in greater sympathy for the demonstrators. For example, when the Reverend Martin Luther King, Jr. led civil rights demonstrators through the streets of Cicero, Illinois, the marchers were regarded as courageous by some (and foolish by others) because of their willingness to confront angry white residents of that suburban Chicago community. Similarly, the use of cattle prods and high-pressure water hoses on civil rights demonstrators in Birmingham, Alabama in 1963 has been widely credited with focusing sympathetic attention on the plight of southern blacks and on the brutal nature of the opposition. As in most instances of protest and demonstration, much depends on the way the news media communicate the events. A peaceful demonstration at a welfare office can be viewed as a riot and thereby in a sense *can become* a riot in the minds of the public. Violent police suppression of disorder can be viewed by the media as justified or unjustified, and so the public will perceive it.

Community Organizations in the Political Process

The relative weakness of community organizations is finally apparent in their interactions with government agencies or private institutions from which they seek political rewards. Here we focus on the fact that the targets of community organizations have substantial abilities to undermine strategies of such organizations. The *ordinary* channels of access available to more affluent organizations are ordinarily closed to members of community organizations because they often lack familiarity, experience, or "contacts" that are associated with government programs. Such contacts help more affluent organizations solve what is often a major strategic concern—to pinpoint responsibility for specific policies or programs. As a result, community organizations may have difficulty in "targeting" their demands, to say nothing of the difficulties in gaining satisfaction once they do manage to fix responsibility. As noted already, the necessity for successful response is of paramount importance because community organizations need to show their ability to succeed. In contrast, more stable organizations can persist for a long time without receiving immediate returns on their tactical investments. The public interest organization Common Cause, for example, with an upper-middle-class

Legal and Institutional Resources for Environmental and Industrial Groups	
Environmentalists' Resources	**Industry's Resources**
"Right to petition" (lobbying) promotes favored bills and obstructs anti-ecology action	"Right to petition" (lobbying) provides legal protection for presenting needs and arguments to legislators
"Freedom of association" protects organization of groups	"Freedom of association" provides foundation for laws protecting privacy and continuity of probusiness groups
Many conservation and purification laws provide guidelines for limiting pollution and punishments for polluters	Certain laws allow industrial use of public lands and natural resources (forests, minerals, waterways)
Class-action suits can attack resource misuse that affects large segments of the population	"Due process" requirements protect private property in litigation and government action
Federal, state, and local agencies have been created that decide questions pertaining to the use of land and other resources	Representation on public regulatory agencies usually includes industry representatives
"Fairness doctrine" allows ecologists to present their views on television	"Fairness doctrine" allows probusiness publicity on television
Some laws reward informants who report polluters	Congress and state legislators must balance environmental needs against needs for food, energy, and economic stabilization

Figure 16.5 The first step in organizing is to calculate one's present and potential resources with reference to one's goals. The public is commonly aware of money and people as resources, but laws and the rules of operating political institutions can act as resources also (above). Both sides of a conflict, such as the environmentalist-industry example shown here, can make use of the laws favoring their cause to conduct a series of legal battles that may go on for years. The intricate nature of conflict in the courts, deriving from the use of such legal resources, sometimes frustrates participants to the point where they are driven to the use of other tactics, including corruption or mass mobilization, to achieve their goal of influencing public policy.

Figure 16.6 Two different concepts of organizing the poor are represented here. VISTA (Volunteers in Service to America) is a government-sponsored organization that recruits and trains volunteers (top) to help fight poverty, disease, and lack of education; volunteers live in distressed areas, teach practical skills, and assist in medical care and in the development of a sense of community. Until 1971 VISTA was under the Office of Economic Opportunity, but it was then placed under Action, a federal agency charged with the supervision of all federally sponsored volunteer programs. Saul Alinsky (bottom) was the founder and director of the Industrial Areas Foundation in Chicago; the foundation was set up to train community organizers of the poor in tactics that Alinsky had derived from labor union organizing ideas as well as from practical experience in organizing the Chicago poor during the 1930s and 1940s. Supported by private foundations, by a few sympathetic industrialists, and by many church organizations, Alinsky trained the poor for direct confrontations with controlling elites; he sought to develop the necessary leadership skills among his trainees and taught the art of prolonged and tough negotiation. One graduate of Alinsky's training was Cesar Chavez, organizer of the United Farm Workers.

constituency, has been able to persist for several years without demonstrating immediate or substantial successes. It is doubtful whether an organization devoted to and supported by a less affluent constituency could survive for as long with a similar record of success relative to goals.

Government agencies can and do avoid accepting responsibility in a variety of ways and for a variety of reasons. First, responsibility for policies and programs is often *in fact* diffuse and elusive. (Public agencies are often happy to take credit for successful programs, but when they come under attack, the responsible parties are difficult to find.) The decentralization of the American governmental bureaucracy imposes an often difficult environment from which to try to get a response—as a result, the "buck" may be passed indefinitely (see Chapter 10). The frustration that results from efforts to locate the responsible person or agency in turn contributes to the fragmentation of the community organization.

Second, the structure of the political system, discussed in Chapter 2, affects the potential strength of community organizations because of the gap between responsibility for decision making and responsibility for policy implementation. Community organizations may try to put pressure on city agencies that implement policies (for example, urban renewal agencies) only to be told that true responsibility for the policy rests with the federal government (for example, the Department of Housing and Urban Development—HUD). In the unlikely event that the group manages to send a delegation to the regional office of a federal agency, it may be told that the agency's Washington office truly holds responsibility for this policy. In the still less likely event that meaningful communication with Washington is established, the group may finally be told that pressure on congressmen or pressure exerted on the local level of government is the most effective way to achieve change—thus bringing the advice full circle. The elusive nature of policy-making and policy-implementing responsibility seriously affects the organization's ability to demonstrate success.

At times community organizations do manage to achieve meaningful relationships with government agencies. The agencies may in effect recognize the organizations as spokesmen for a given neighborhood or community in a particular policy area. For example, HUD officials have at times shown an interest in meeting with the National Tenants Organization. Other agencies dealing with various social-welfare programs, such as poverty, housing, and community health, often depend on community organizations to recruit clients, pass along information, and promote the services that the programs provide. Although at times community organizations may abandon or distort some of their goals when they enter such relationships, nonetheless these relationships do represent a significant achievement of some status and influence.

But in these relationships, the position of community organizations is precarious at best. For example, President Nixon's unilateral decision to eliminate the Office of Economic Opportunity (OEO) in March 1973 not only threatened to eliminate a large number of programs that had served poor people, but it also threatened to disrupt one of the few programs that had successfully developed channels of communication between community groups and government agencies.

Indeed, it is important to note that the most significant criticisms of OEO antagonists have been over the agency's programs that help to assist in *community* development. The unique aspect of the OEO poverty program—as well as its most controversial program area—has been the encouragement of community action and citizen participation. Similarly, the legal services program has gained the antagonism of poverty program opponents because of the fact that poverty lawyers, often in conjunction with community organizations, litigate for the *general* rights of poor people—so-called *class-action* suits—rather than restricting themselves to the representation of individual clients. (Opponents of the program of legal services for the poor have particularly objected to the class-action suits against the policies of government agencies. They assert it is inappropriate for one government agency to be in effect subsidizing a lawsuit against another.)

PROTEST IN THE POLITICAL PROCESS

The decade of the 1960s has been characterized as the age of protest. The number of sit-ins, demonstrations, and marches protesting policies as diverse as lunch-counter racial segregation, the war in Indochina, oil spills, inadequate ethnic studies programs

Figure 16.7 The women's liberation movement has discovered the difficulties of raising the consciousness of targeted audiences and motivating them to action without overstepping the invisible line that separates motivating tactics from alienating tactics. Unity marches, such as this one in New York City, may well focus attention on a problem, raise the expectations of onlooking women, and give courage to the timid with a show of members. However, organizers must carefully style the march to maximize effectiveness and to lower the risk that the overall impression might dissatisfy potential adherents.

▢
"THIRD PARTIES"

Used in this context, the term "third parties" refers to interest groups that might be motivated to participate in controversy in ways favorable to protest goals.

in colleges, and the lack of equal educational opportunity testifies to the broad range of citizen concerns that have found expression in protest tactics.

Protest tactics are among the primary resources of relatively powerless groups. Often lacking sufficient resources to enter into effective arrangements within the conventional political arena, relatively powerless groups may try to strengthen their bargaining position by activating other groups on their behalf. This is the essence of protest.

Arousing Public Interest

Protest is more than the mere voicing of objection to policies or conditions. It is a political process designed to activate others, particularly when other groups or individuals would not be inclined to form alliances. Activating "third parties" (see ▢) can generally be accomplished by appeal, by threat, or by a combination of the two.

Appeals to Public Concern

By *appeal* we mean that protest can call attention to injustice, suffering, or deprivation in such a way that outside groups or individuals are moved to express their concern in politically relevant ways. (An important variant of this theme is noted in Chapter 9. Politicians may sense public sympathy to the goals of protest groups and so their response may actually *anticipate* overt expressions of public concern.) However, the extent to which appeals will generate public concern, the expression of which activates government officials, depends on many factors. Among these factors are: the actual degree of injustice, exploitation, or suffering; the extent to which the public perceives this suffering and regards it as unjust; the extent to which the protesting group is regarded as "worthy" of social concern; and the extent to which the public perceives that the system has available resources that might be applied to the satisfaction of these concerns.

Threat as Political Leverage

The number of "ifs" that these factors represent lead us to consider the great significance of *threat* as a component of protest. By literally threatening, and thereby significantly discomforting others, protest groups may be successful in getting others to intervene in the conflict in order to stop the threatened activity. The group's bargaining resource then becomes its willingness to stop doing something. Of course, the nature of the threat may vary considerably: Protest groups may threaten to disrupt government operations by sitting for long periods in public officials' offices; they may threaten to demonstrate in front of the house of a prominent citizen to show that slum conditions exist in buildings he owns; or they may threaten to have group members drive their cars through major tunnels at five miles an hour in order to bring traffic to a halt.

Appeals and Threats Combined

Protest appeals and threats may be combined. During the period (1960–1966) when civil rights groups were dedicated to the use of nonviolent tactics to overturn the legal basis of discriminatory and segregated practices in the South, groups threatened civic order by disrupting various public facilities. Most prominent among these groups were the Student Non-violent Coordinating Committee (SNCC), the Southern Christian Leadership Conference (SCLC), and the Congress of Racial Equality (CORE). By virtue of their discipline, nonviolence, respectable appearance, and courage in the face of hostility, the civil rights groups sought to appeal to the public's sense of justice. The nonviolent nature of their "civil disobedience" was expressly meant to show their willingness to defy laws that they considered unjust. The significance of civil disobedience as a tactic was not only that protesting groups objected to unjust laws; it was also that they chose to disobey the law.

Here was a paradox that received wide attention. Whereas *government by law* was perceived to be the key to protecting blacks against racist lawlessness, here were blacks demonstrating that the law was their oppressor. Most significantly, ordinary men and women were clearly willing to deliberately break the law rather than to accept the political processes by which they might hope to have the laws changed. At least for this group of Americans, here was a declaration that the formal political process was inadequate. It is a commentary on the sanctity of the idea of government by law that black civil disobedience, expressed in nonviolent form, was to many Americans as shocking as it was.

Protest and Legitimacy

This discussion of civil disobedience illustrates a more general point concerning the relationship between protest and *legitimacy* (see ☐). So many of the tactics usually associated with groups of poor people or disadvantaged citizens compel attention

☐

LEGITIMACY
Legitimacy refers to the quality of being considered right and proper according to social norms in a given context. Accordingly, a law may be "illegitimate" if it offends the norms of society (a point that is discussed in the Perspective on Marijuana and Civil Liberties). Thus, sabotaging a political campaign may be considered illegitimate even though no law has been broken. Some activities, such as sit-ins, were considered legitimate by supporters of civil rights and considered illegitimate by opponents. Action may be considered illegitimate at one point in time and legitimate in another.

precisely because society brands the actions "illegitimate." As a result, most protest tactics either appear to be semi-illegitimate or they are in fact illegitimate from the point of view of the dominant society.

There are a number of reasons why protest tactics border on the illegitimate. First, laws are often constructed, consciously or unconsciously, to restrict the opportunities of less powerful groups within the population. For example, many cities developed trespass laws in the early 1960s to use against protest demonstrations. And even if the laws have not been developed for this purpose, they are often applied or enforced by the police or the courts so as to achieve this result. Public nuisance laws, for example, have been used by police against deviants or people regarded as undesirable. Courts have held, indeed, that these laws are often so loosely written, and permit such broad discretion by law enforcement officers, that they are unconstitutional. As a result, protesters frequently come into conflict with the law. Second, willingness to risk criminal penalties for acts of principle is a powerful demonstration of dedication. In pleading their case, community groups may use illegitimate tactics in order to show their resolve. Third, willingness to defy law or to act illegally in and of itself powerfully threatens a society in which (like all modern societies) civil order depends on self-regulation and acquiescence to the regime. Fourth, the threat to defy the law (if properly announced and publicized) brings the protesting group into public confrontation with public authorities, and thus accords them media coverage in a way that might not be achieved through the use of more conventional political channels.

In short, the use of illegitimate tactics cloaks the demands of the users with an urgency that other political tactics cannot summon. The point can be made by considering a protest march by antiwar veterans. They may seek to gain legitimacy by displaying the flag and thus signaling the essential patriotism of the group. But exactly the same march that displayed the flag upside down would gain far more publicity and notoriety. It is a strategic question whether the circumstances would dictate the milder patriotic march or the more offensive one.

The Limitations of Protest Tactics

The fact that effective protest is usually uneasily balanced on the borderline of legitimacy and illegitimacy indicates the *fragile* nature of protest tactics. Because of this balancing act, protest demonstrations often run the risk of alienating potentially sympathetic groups and of arousing opposing groups to

Figure 16.8 **Every group engaged in political action is aware of the advantages that come from achieving outside support and even from building coalitions with other groups, if not too many values or important tactics need be compromised. Picture yourself on the strategy-forming committee of a political organization. You are in a political confrontation. Which tactics of those listed here would you choose? Whom would you alienate? Whom attract? What are your own goals and values in relation to these tactics? What are the pros and cons of taking the middle ground?**

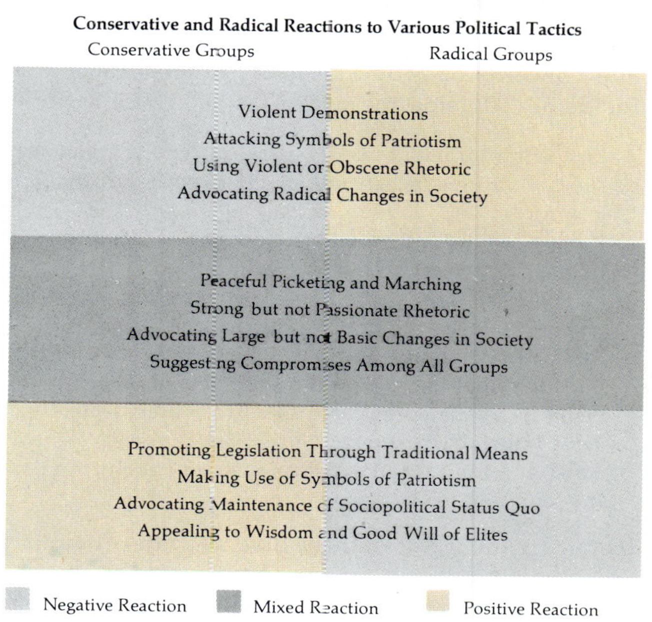

action. Again it is a matter of strategy (rarely an easy calculation) to anticipate whether any given protest tactic may have costs greater than it has benefits. Decisions regarding protest strategy are particularly delicate to those groups that have begun to gain some success—the wrong choice may cause the group to lose the "alliances" it has been building. This reluctance to alienate supporters and sympathizers may account in part for the tendencies of protest groups to become more cautious and restrained as they grow in power and status. (Community organizations may also become more conservative if they are given responsibilities for operating governmental programs or granted an influential role in policy development.) The calculation to try protest tactics and to risk the possible alienation of newly developed allies is less risky for protest groups with relatively little power, because they have little to lose.

The risk of alienating possible supporters is only one of the reasons that protest is at best an uncertain opportunity. Other reasons include the following. First, relatively powerless groups lack stable resources on which to organize protest campaigns. The need of such groups for at least minimal organizational capability may even place protest beyond their reach, for without an organization there can be no protest campaign.

A second factor that often prevents the use of protest tactics is that groups must balance the interests and concerns of people in many diverse roles both inside and outside the organization. These include:

1. Protest group members, who are concerned about the risks of various tactics and skeptical of the utility of joining;
2. Protest group leaders, whose flow of rewards from this activity must be maintained;
3. Communications media personnel, who can appreciably influence the group's impact;
4. Sympathetic groups and individuals and other "third parties" who, because of the problems of illegitimacy, could be alienated by "excesses" in protest tactics;
5. The "targets" of protest, whose basic interests lie in satisfying their usual constituents and in returning the situation to the status quo.

Balancing the needs of these diverse actors obviously is extremely difficult.

Third, protest success depends on gaining coverage in newspapers and television, because protest depends on activating outside groups to enter the conflict on the protesters' behalf. Without publicity, protest tactics are meaningless. The most successful protest leaders in the recent past have been those who have raised the ability to gain publicity to an art. They know how to time and to style their tactics and public appearances so as to maximize media coverage. For example, the skillful leader plans to conduct demonstrations early enough on Saturdays to meet the deadlines to gain publicity in widely read Sunday newspapers. However, because government offices (the sites of much protest activity) are usually not open on weekends, the leader must choose time and place very carefully.

The news media not only report the news; they also significantly *determine* it. Protest leaders design tactics in response to their understanding of what editors will consider newsworthy. Tactics often escalate in severity or militance for the simple reason that what is news on one day will be "old hat" the next week. In terms of membership commitment, few protest tactics have been as impressive as the Milwaukee NAACP Youth Council marches led by Father Groppi that occurred in protest over the city's refusal to pass an open housing ordinance. The marches began in September 1967 and continued for a remarkable 240 straight nights. Yet the tactic's ultimate failure occurred in part because of the media's lag in interest in reporting the marches day after day.

Fourth, protest campaigns are political struggles in which the targets of protest command significant resources that can limit or undermine protest strategies. These include:

1. Delay—appointing a commission or relegating a problem to study;
2. Tokenism—conceding a tiny fraction of what is desired but giving the impression that it is a significant concession;
3. Discreditation—attempting to damage a group's credibility or legitimacy in the public arena; and
4. Suppression—utilizing police actions of various kinds.

Protest is one of the few resources available to relatively powerless groups, but, except in rare instances, its potential is highly limited. Protest *can* call attention to the intensity of a group's feelings and to its commitment to values or goals. Thus, protest is one of the ways that issues get defined, their importance gets heightened, and they thereby get placed on the public agenda (see Chapter 9).

Contexts for Effective Protest

There are two instances when protest tactics seem particularly effective. One such instance is when other, more powerful groups in the society are available to be mobilized in behalf of protest objectives. Another is when protest tactics coincide with the objectives of influential politicians or public officials. Early protest over civil rights, for example, contributed substantially to policy development because at that time liberal northern public officials could gain credit with their constituents by giving civil rights issues high priority.

Protest tactics can sometimes force recognition that groups have a claim to be heard in the political process. But once they gain that hearing the group will be forced to rely once again on influence of a more routine kind. In sum, protest may raise issues to the public agenda, it may help provide a group with higher standing in public controversies, or as noted earlier, it may enhance organizational development. But by itself, protest must be considered a somewhat fragile tactical tool on which relatively powerless groups cannot rely.

THE PROBLEM OF VIOLENCE

Violence may be a political tactic. This view is often disputed by those who would maintain that destructive behavior may only properly be regarded as illegitimate, usually criminal; and that violence therefore cannot properly be labeled political. But we have already seen that protest tactics border on the illegitimate and in an important sense must be either illegitimate or must threaten illegitimacy if they are to succeed. In this section we take up nonformal political participation mechanisms that are no longer on the borderline of illegitimacy but that depend for their success, if any, precisely on their destructive nature or on the threat of destruction.

Political violence may be regarded as destructive acts or acts that threaten destruction through the use of force. The goal of political violence may be to affect the distribution of benefits in the society or the ways in which policy decisions about such benefits are made. Political violence may be direct in its

methods, or it may be primarily expressive. It may be supportive of the status quo, as when white rioting erupted on the University of Mississippi campus to prevent the enrollment of a black student, James Meredith; violence may also be opposed to the status quo, as in the ghetto riots in Plainfield, New Jersey in 1967, which researchers for the National Advisory Commission on Civil Disorder called a focused political rebellion.

An important consideration affecting our understanding of political violence is that it is not the people doing the violence who get to define the meaning of their acts. For example, the labeling of windowbreaking by young people engaged in antiwar protest as either vandalism or as frivolous youthful exuberance may deprive the activity of the political meaning that the youth sought to give the events. This labeling was particularly apparent during the civil disorders of 1967 when politicians and the media tended to view the disorders as perpetrated by the "riff-raff" of the ghetto or by a small band of conspirators going from city to city. Later evidence indicated that these riots were fairly well supported by a large sector of the ghetto population and indicated that conspiracy was clearly not a factor in these events. Nonetheless, these early "labels" may have prevented the general public from fully perceiving ghetto revolts as expressions of opposition to the status quo.

However, it would be misleading to say that violent political activities are always deliberate. But then, to what extent is any political activity always deliberate? Voting, for example, can only be considered partially rational; in many ways it is a political reflex composed of unconscious motivations that stem from socialization, mimicry, and the approval of one's peers (see Chapter 12). Similarly, political violence may sometimes be deliberate and may sometimes be composed of both deliberate and unintentional components. Violence may also be completely lacking in political orientations—for example, it might focus on the distribution of society's values, in which cases the action would not be regarded as political.

Figure 16.10 summarizes the distinctions between deliberate acts of violence and those that have both deliberate and unintentional components. (Note that if the figure were focused on violence *per se*, rather than on political violence, a third vertical column would be devoted to the unintentional components of violence.)

Figure 16.10 also categorizes acts of political violence as to the nature of their targets and the degrees of violence employed. Thus, political violence is focused against property, as in the destruction of draft records or the "liberation" of Indian treaty documents; it is directed against persons where the intention is to threaten the use of force but hopefully not to employ it, as in the physical blocking of access to buildings; or it is directed against persons with the intent to harm. Figure 16.10 also suggests, although the idea is not developed there, that political violence may under some circumstances be engaged in by authorized forces of the state—for example in the Chicago police suppression of the crowd during the 1968 Democratic convention.

As we have already noted, political violence through the use of threat may increase public attention to grievances and the concerns of the groups involved. But again, there are two considerations that affect the success of these political tactics. First, the greater the threat the greater the attention; but the likelihood is also greater that other elements of society will be alienated. Among the factors affecting opposition and disapproval of violence are the extent to which the violence is deliberate and therefore pre-

sumably controllable and the extent to which it is directed at property or people. The rankings provided in Figure 16.10 for different kinds of political violence are intended to suggest the degree of opposition that will be aroused by different kinds of violent acts. That is, the more deliberate the acts are and the more threatening they are to people's lives, the greater the opposition they will receive.

These rankings, however, fail to include a most important consideration. The status of both the victims and the instigators of violence plays an important part in determining whether the society will condemn or ignore the violence. A recent example of this distinction is provided by American concerns over violence on campuses. When the National Guard shot into a crowd at Kent State University in May 1970 and killed four students, a great amount of public attention was focused on the event. However, similar events involving black students at South Carolina State University in Orangeburg, at Jackson State College in Mississippi, and at Southern University in Baton Rouge in the last ten years received nowhere near the same degree of publicity.

The Suppression of Political Violence

Although violence at times heightens public awareness of groups and their demands, it also permits public officials to use military or police personnel

Figure 16.9 (left) What will drive the average middle-class person to political action? And what is effective political action for someone who feels the necessity of personal restraints and who is basically committed to the system? Political officeholders began to see answers to these very crucial political questions in 1973 when the increases in food prices motivated numbers of middle-class persons, especially women, to engage in political pressuring through petitions and consumer boycotts.

Figure 16.10 (right) Political violence occurs in many forms, which can, at a basic level, be analyzed by target and by motivation. The rankings (in parentheses) suggest the degree of opposition, on a scale of one to five, that might be aroused by such acts.

to contain or suppress the violence; and usually such intervention has the support of the general public. Public opposition develops in part because most citizens generally object to violent public behavior no matter how unjust or oppressive the target of that behavior may be. Opposition also develops because the intervention of the police or the army results in the defining of violent acts as *criminal* and hence not worthy of respect or sympathy.

Because intervention by police or military personnel severely discredits or directs attention away from the political concerns of a protest group, public officials have been known to create a public impression of impending violence whether or not dissident groups are actually planning to use it. This tactic has been used frequently in the case of marches protesting the Vietnam War. Police officials begin by telling the newspapers that antiwar groups intend to promote violence. Then, in response to the apprehension that they themselves have generated, massive troops of police or National Guard are sent into the area. When violence does not result, law officials take credit for having prevented the predicted violent activity. The fact that violence did not occur is explained by the presence of troops; but an equally plausible explanation is that no violence was intended in the first place. Because police intervention is only justified by the existence of criminal or dis-

orderly behavior, police have a major stake in influencing the public to believe that such behavior was about to occur. In recent years we have learned from a number of sources that political leaders often subsidize violent activity through the use of *agents provocateurs,* or undercover agents, either to entrap political dissidents or to discredit the movement that would be linked publicly with the violence.

Like protest, political violence may at times combine with other strategies to play a role in the achievement of certain goals. Particularly when other groups are concurrently attempting through legitimate means to achieve similar goals, political violence can heighten public awareness. It can also signal to the public the potential costs of continuing inequitable policies. All in all, however, violence and protest activities come up against the barrier represented in the phrase "I will not give in to threats." The response to both forms of political activity has at times been a hardening of the opposition.

The Responsiveness of Political Structures

This chapter has indicated that many aspects of political participation occur through nonformal institutional mechanisms. We have suggested that these mechanisms are critical to the development of democratic systems; they are critical particularly in a society that is too complicated for formal representative

Political Violence		
Primary Targets	**Deliberate**	**Mixed (both deliberate and unintentional components)**
Property	Vandalism of draft records (1) Invasion of Bureau of Indian Affairs; stealing of documents Farm protest (example: dumping milk)	Trashing in antiwar protest (3) Civil disorders (1967)
Persons (with intent to threaten)	Hijacking; taking hostages (2) Physically blocking access to buildings, construction sites	
Persons (with intent to harm)	Assassination, lynching, sniping (4)	Civil disorders (pre-1960s) (5) Police crowd control and riot suppression

institutions to adequately represent the wide range of existing social interests and in which social, economic, and political inequalities are widespread. We have focused attention on the politics of relatively powerless groups in order to assess the extent to which nonformal participation may be able to compensate for the inadequacies of the formal structures.

The era of the 1960s is widely regarded as an activist decade. Politics seems to have been governed by protests and by violence; the era was marked by the mobilization of poor communities and of ethnic interest groups and the reawakening of interest in the rights and status of American women. These are a part of the legacy of American protest activity in the past decade. Other contributions include the incorporation in many public programs of mechanisms to seek out and to acquire citizen perspectives on policy making, and the development of public-interest pressure groups to pursue in an *institutionalized* way what relatively disadvantaged political organizations were able to achieve on an ad hoc basis. It is, of course, difficult to assess the results of the decade of protest. Although for any individual protest movement or organization the results may be dismal and disappointing, it remains true that the net impact of protest activity may be to make an unmeasurable but real contribution to political forces that are otherwise in motion. Efforts to transcend the status quo—as illustrated by the civil rights movement with respect to opening up public accommodations and extending voting rights in the South—may require the expressions of popular discontent whose only realistic vehicle is protest and large-scale demonstrations. As such, these tactics may be necessary, however insufficient, for accomplishing significant change.

Yet the persistence into the 1970s of the problems that this text has identified—those problems that effectively define American politics—provides little evidence that the activities of the 1960s were suc-

cessful. It does not seem that the volume of organization, protest, and violence promoted by relatively powerless groups in those years has made an independent substantial contribution toward resolving these problems. That is, in the absence of more stable and effective political power, it seems that nonformal political participation has little substantial impact. Yet these tactics and opportunities represent some of the few ways in which relatively powerless groups can develop the capacities needed to enter and to influence the political process. If this is indeed the case, the conclusions presented in this study of nonformal political participation serve as a severe commentary on the openness and inclusiveness of American political structures.

SUMMARY

This chapter deals with the abilities of protest groups to affect the political process, the problems and potentials of protest activities, and the specific problem of violence in political action.

Collective action is necessary in a complex society; effective group action depends on resources—money, skill, status, and cohesion. The 1960s were distinguished by the large numbers of people that were willing to engage in political actions on the assumption that all groups, not only those whose resources afford them easy access to power, must have their views heard.

There are many obstacles to the organization of protest groups. Cynicism of success discourages support and membership; many lower-income people are not socialized to organize for the solution of their problems; organizations frequently lack "contacts" with the formal political process that might afford them the success with which to attract membership.

Protest is a primary resource of the relatively powerless group. Although it may mobilize the support of other groups and raise the salience of an

Figure 16.11 The self-fulfilling prophecy of predicted violence. Here, Century City plaza in Los Angeles in June 1967 on the occasion of one of President Johnson's last major public appearances before deciding he would not run for a second full presidential term. The escalation and conduct of the Vietnam War was accompanied by mass demonstrations and riots that put great pressures on the unprepared police and National Guard units. 1967 saw the peak of such demonstrations, and police attempted to match demonstrators and rioters with intimidation and, in some instances, with a massive show of force. These tactics horrified some of the bystanders and some of those who followed media reports, while others applauded police actions in giving the demonstrators "what they had coming to them."

The Washington Post
Largest Rally in Washington History
Demands Rapid End to Vietnam War
Militants Resume
Evening Violence
Apollo 12 Switches
To Riskier Course
White House:
A Display
Of Normality
Thousands at Justice Dept.
Gassed in Radicals' Assault
News Stories
On the Inside

VETERANS FOR PEACE
VIETNAM VETS FOR PEACE
NOT ONE MORE DEAD!
bring ALL the GIs home NOW!
bring ALL the GIs home NOW!

I WON'T FIGHT IN VIETNAM

issue, the inherent risks may outweigh the benefits. Political violence is another tactic used to influence political decisions. In combination with other strategies, it may play a role in the achievement of certain goals; but, as with protest, it may also result in a hardening of the opposition.

SUGGESTED READINGS

Alinsky, Saul. *Reveille for Radicals.* New York: Random House, 1969.

Alinsky, Saul. *Rules for Radicals.* New York: Random House, 1971.

Lipsky, Michael. *Protest in City Politics: Rent Strikes, Housing and the Power of the Poor.* Chicago: Rand McNally, 1970.

Lipsky, Michael, and Margaret Levi. "Community Organizations as a Political Resource" in Harlan Hahn (ed.), *People and Politics in Urban Society.* Vol. 6, Urban Affairs Annual Reviews. Beverly Hills, Calif.: Sage Publications, 1972.

Morlan, Robert. *Political Prairie Fire: The Nonpartisan League, 1915–1922.* Minneapolis: University of Minnesota Press, 1955.

Olson, Mancur. *The Logic of Collective Action.* Cambridge, Mass.: Harvard University Press, 1965.

Figure 16.12 How effective were antiwar demonstrations in mobilizing public opinion and influencing the government? On November 15, 1969 more than 250,000 Americans of all ages converged on Washington, D.C. in the largest antiwar demonstration in the nation's history. The month before, Moratorium Day had been observed across the nation, marked by work stoppages, teach-ins, rallies, and marches. To what extent should the antiwar movement be credited with this massive coalescing of sentiment? Data prepared for the National Commission on the Causes and Prevention of Violence (the Violence Commission) suggested that the growth of protest had little or nothing to do with the antiwar movement itself, with its pronouncements, or with the aims of its leaders. Although the movement had provided the opportunity for active commitment by sympathizers, public attitudes on the war were instead the result of events taking place in Washington and Vietnam. President Nixon responded to the demonstrations of antiwar sentiment by calling on the "great silent majority" to continue to support his program to end the war.

WHICH POWER TO WHICH PEOPLE?

The wild populism of the 1960s has given way to the quieter politics and startling corruptions of the 1970s. But what can we make of that assertive slogan "Power to the People" that is one of the legacies of the last decade? What can we make of it when there are so many forms of power? Will it be power to federal court judges to integrate school districts, or power to local school boards to resist integration; power to Cesar Chavez to organize migrant farm workers, or power to the California growers to resist the black eagle unions; power to the Pentagon to maintain or expand its budget, or power to the liberal senators who want it cut; power to pot smokers through the legalization of marijuana use, or power to those who would repress it; power to the people of Appalachia to find jobs and improve their life chances, or power to those who would strip the land and ignore the poverty of its people? And then there are also so many people; so many varied majorities and minorities, so many arenas of political combat and competition. so many stone walls.

Which power to which people? We can look back now on what we have talked about in this book and see how conservative, liberal, and radical perspectives on politics try to cope with this question. We can assess the possibilities that confront us as a society and try to judge the usefulness of these schools of political ideas. In summarizing and synthesizing the ideas of conservatives, liberals, and radicals, we are not attempting to do full justice to the ideas of any one thinker. Rather, we want to point out the central tendencies and problems of these doctrines.

Conservatism, or what happens when "tradition" means power to those who already have power:

Conservatism in one form or another remains one of the staples of the American political diet. It consists of one helping of respect for authority, one bowl of skepticism about innovation, one portion of national pride plus military power, and a sprinkling of rhetoric about "free enterprise." American conservatism had a spectacular revival in the 1960s with the presidential nomination of Barry Goldwater and the election of Richard Nixon. Yet conservatives were disappointed in Nixon, the cold warrior and right-winger who traveled to Communist China and the USSR, imposed domestic price and wage guidelines, and proposed some liberalizing changes in the welfare system. But such reversals are the stuff bad dreams are made of.

American conservatism can always count on several important sources of support: on big money (especially from the newly rich); on the puritanical streak that runs like a two-lane blacktop country road through the mind of America; and on those who wish to resist change or hold onto the privileges they have. Yet conservatism does not feed exclusively on fear and the pleasures of inequality. Conservatives are common in every society because, by temperament and by training, many of us prefer established usage to change. Conservatism also has a way of putting things in what appear to be their proper places. It has a weighty quality, something like the monarchical tradition from which it is descended.

But in a society like our own, conservatism usually means power to those who already have power. Conservatives prefer to talk of principles, but what those principles frequently mean is that those who want to alter the distributions of power and privilege had better wait in the anteroom until they are politely asked in, or more likely, asked to leave. The conservative is likely to find women's rights a bit curious, to be temperamentally hostile to unions, to doubt the capacity of minority groups to play responsible roles in politics and social life, and to distrust freedom (at least in any sphere but the economic).

Conservatism faces two dilemmas that its supporters are often insensitive to, but that cut to the very heart of conservative doctrine. First, insistence on maintaining traditions and opposing politically induced change (as in racial integration and anti-poverty efforts) may mean that large portions of the population remain alienated from their own society. Their frustration and fear means that there is always an explosive potential, which conservatives usually expect the police to repress. The more the need for such repression, the more a society wastes its energies on holding people down rather than on allowing them to join the community.

Conservatives also fail to realize that rapid change is unavoidable in modern society. The automobile, for example, has led to radical change in American life in the last fifty years. It has affected family patterns, helped create the modern suburb, opened up many new possibilities for mobility, and been in-volved in the development of awesome problems of land use, pollution, and fuel consumption. The conservative is inclined to let such matters go their way. He figures that whatever people are willing to pay for, they should have (except for prostitution, marijuana, or gambling, of course). Yet these economic innovations may undermine traditional values more seriously than what he considers "moral vices."

There is a final and most vexing problem for the conservative: how to feel free to criticize the very authorities he wants to see respected. He is likely to be the first man to rally around the flag and the last to leave it. But what if the flag is in the wrong place or at the wrong time? He is not likely to admit it. Therefore he is frequently caught with blinders on, unable to see what is by now obvious to everyone else, that the emperor has no clothes on.

Liberalism, or what happens when the best intentions do not help:

In America, modern liberalism gained its identity in the thirties, with Roosevelt's New Deal. Since then it has stood for reform of a sort that aids those who are losers in the marketplace struggle for success. It has employed the tools of economic regulation, bureaucratic planning, and social services. It is strongly internationalist in commitment and civil libertarian by temperament. Generally, liberalism is open to change, forever listening to the critics.

Liberals want to set the world straight—a laudable desire, since the world is so obviously tilted. But how is this to be accomplished? There are several central ideas. First, liberals want to supplement the current capitalist system with some reforms. These include social security, unemployment insurance, the right to unionize, medicare, and so on—humanitarian efforts that lower the risks of losing out in the competitive struggle. Liberals also want to reform the structure of power. The direct influence of business should diminish while unions grow more powerful. Liberals like to see new groups become politicized; blacks, youth, and women are therefore encouraged. Pluralism, the group struggle, represents for liberals the guarantee of a reasonably equitable politics.

Two other aspects of liberal thought and practice deserve mention. Liberals, because of their interest in reform, have turned to the federal government as their main vehicle. They have created new departments and bureaucracies to develop and to administer new programs, a practice that often puts them at odds with defenders of local powers and initiatives. Liberals are also strongly committed to avoid any return to America's isolationist past. International life beckons with challenges and problems. Liberals are often ready to take up the cudgels on behalf of those they see as threatened peoples.

The 1960s were tragic years for American liberals, years during which the New Deal coalition, which somehow had held such a diverse group together for so long, seemed finally to be breaking apart. The Vietnam troubles pointed up several of the problems liberalism ran into in the sixties and that persist for liberals today. Many came to see that the power of the United States was not purely benign in its consequences, but that American power could also have malevolent results. Why? Perhaps the national security apparatus, which liberals had helped create, had gone out of control, a bureaucracy running for its own sake, without adequate criticism or democratic regulation. Other governmental organs and programs, even those that liberals had hoped would provide a basis for social reform, had become independent sources of power and sometimes of oppression. The welfare system was a notorious example of humanitarianism gone sour. Urban renewal had turned into Negro-removal. And even the school, that best hope of long-term liberal reform, was attacked as oppressive and regimenting. So liberals had to face the fact that the government they turned to as a source of reform could itself be a source of resistance to change. Perhaps they had created too much bureaucracy; perhaps local initiative had been too thoroughly stifled.

Liberals ran into another problem too. Though they wished to reform capitalism and the American political process, they were actually deeply tied to these very systems. After all, the New Deal, reformist as it was, helped to save American capitalism and the prevailing forms of politics. Liberals tried to create a more equitable system, but their loyalties to capitalism often ran deeper than they acknowledged. The stirrings of the downtrodden and disenfranchised during the sixties were disturbing to many liberals who hoped most of all for a politics that was smoothly managed and efficient, even more than for one that was just and open.

The pluralistic group struggle that liberals looked to as the appropriate way of distributing the spoils of power and privilege was never as satisfactory as liberal theory claimed it was. Some groups always had enormous advantages. Business, for example, started out with its considerable financial capabilities and its legal expertise. The oilmen knew how to do the job of persuading. The big unions also could mount an effective lobbying effort. Liberal theory somehow could not cope with these enduring realities. For liberals, all groups were equally legitimate, if not equally laudatory. The very system of group conflict that liberals endorsed had distributed the spoils very unequally, because the social system on which it was based provided unequal resources to start with. One solution some liberals tacitly endorsed was a system that has been characterized as "universal ticket-fixing." Each group gets its way under some circumstances, even if the rules have to be changed. So, the accommodating liberal lets the big farmers eat at the federal trough, the ghetto blacks bully the school teachers, the oilmen get their depletion allowance, the suburban whites stay lilywhite. Everybody gets a piece of the action. Is such an arrangement politically healthy? What about the public interest, and what about the rule of law? Don't there have to be some limits to pressure group politics? If so, who sets those limits? Is it to be Congress or the courts?

What was probably the most enduring success of liberalism in the sixties has a strong element of irony to it—the Supreme Court's championing of civil liberties and due process. The Court is, of course, a kind of elite institution, insulated from immediate majorities. Liberals attacked just such elitism in the 1930s when the Court struck down New Deal legislation concerning the management of the economy. In the fifties and sixties, however, the Court came to support liberal ideas at a time when popular majorities probably would not have. The New Burger Court may modify some of the Warren Court decisions, but most will probably stand, unexpected monuments to an elitist liberalism.

Radicalism, or what happens when most of the people don't like the slogan "Power to the People":

American radicalism has had many bad days. As we explained in Chapter 1, the Left has always had difficulties establishing itself in American politics. But the sixties saw the birth of a new wave of American radicalism, one that contained many rather exciting and courageous elements. Radicals contributed both to the sanity and to the madness of that decade. It is certain that America would have been considerably diminished without them.

The brands of radicalism that emerged in an evolutionary fashion during the sixties included many strange and diverse types: from the puritanical discipline of the Progressive Labor group, to the anarchist freaks of portions of Students for a Democratic Society (SDS), to the deeply serious and committed young people who chose to blow up buildings, occasionally also people, and also occasionally themselves. The most significant and effective of the radicals, however, were 'morally concerned protesters, of various left-wing and liberal persuasions, who risked jail, personal injury, and sometimes the loss of careers, in order to try to change public policies. They were draft resisters, sit-iners, marchers—all of those who dared to say things out loud that most Americans were not ready to hear. Most notably, many of the things these people were attacked for saying at one point, later became sentiments that large portions of the American public and major segments of the political elite came to accept. In this respect, radicalism was often proven right, as well as politically meaningful in the sixties.

Radicals, in America as elsewhere, had long been critics of capitalism and had argued that "democracy" did not mean enough if it did not include more social and economic equality than existed in societies like ours. This sort of criticism, important as it was, was nothing new in the 1960s. The added element, beginning with the early years of the SDS, was the emphasis on "participatory democracy." The political parties, the argument asserted, could not be trusted truly to represent majority sentiment. The system was rigged to favor the rich and powerful, with a few sops to the common man from time to time. It was the corporations and their allies in government who shaped policy in America, not the public. Even more equality was not enough. What was needed was the chance for people to have a voice in decisions that affected their own lives. Such a theory ran counter to some of the tendencies of liberals at that time, tendencies toward managerialism, or getting things running more smoothly and thereby helping folks at the grass-roots level. In some ways the new radical approach, with its focus on localism, had something in common with conservative thought—although, in practice, conservative localism frequently was a mask for the oppression of some by others, particularly blacks by whites.

In its initial manifesto, the later-to-be-famous Port Huron Statement, SDS declared a concern that working people, blacks, youth, and others ought to have more of a voice in policy making. This rallying cry was to be heard throughout the next ten years, but it was often spoken by those with goals strongly opposed to those of the Left. Here was one of the ironies of left-wing ideas, that anyone could preach participatory democracy, but the consequences were very different depending on who did the participating. "White power" meant one thing in Cicero, Illinois and "Black power" quite another. Also, in a predominantly middle-class society, it became harder and harder to talk about the working class as the vanguard of social change, even though the unions often supported progressive domestic legislation. Most Americans did not feel exploited in the sense that Karl Marx or other radicals had expected, although more subtle forms of dehumanization might make themselves felt. To this obvious problem, some members of the Left had a reply: Those who resisted change had been confused by capitalist propaganda and racist socialization. Often this assertion was true enough, but it did not alter the basic reality that the "people" were far from a unified group, and that many of the "people"—perhaps most of them, most of the time—were likely to resist the changes that radicals favored and to support the wars that radicals opposed. This problem of the Left led to another: how to institutionalize and somehow to stabilize its potential power. Throughout the sixties, radical and opposition political movements sprang up, at universities, in ghettos, among women or Chicanos or young workers, only to fade away after having some initial impact.

The Left seemed to have a permanent problem about making itself permanent. This problem was partly because of the temperament of the most involved left-wingers. But it was also because left-wing politics only became respectable for most Americans from one emergency to another, meaning that the Left would have great difficulty gaining any enduring base of power.

THINKING FORWARD: THE NEXT POLITICAL IDEAS

Political theories arise from the problems of social life. Liberalism became the fighting creed of the new middle class in Europe in its attempt to diminish the power of the feudal aristocracy. Conservatism arose, at first, as the defense of some aspects of the same aristocratic society. Radicalism opposed both, calling Liberalism to task for its failure to make men truly free. But the quarrels and circumstances that gave rise to these ideologies are long past, and nowadays even the more recent conflicts between capitalists and socialists seem a bit outdated.

What are the sorts of political ideas we need to deal with the realities and prospects of today's situation? No doubt we can put to use the inheritance we have, that amalgam of liberal, conservative, and radical ideas that is our usual guide. But the world of the last third of the twentieth century requires us to develop our own distinctive ways of coping with its distinctive conditions. It is true that much of what we live with now has grown out of the past and is not basically new. Poverty, after all, is not new. Corruption is not new. The issues of personal freedom are not new. The problems of power, of foreign affairs, of national security, are not new. Nor is America's great wealth new, nor are her political institutions and practices, nor her diverse population, nor her racial problems, nor her prominent place in the world.

But many things have been added, and in some cases they have altered entirely the prospects before us. Pollution and environmental issues generally are something radically new and require a thorough rethinking of our ways of living and using our resources. Poverty also begins to look somewhat different if seen in the larger context of the overall distribution of wealth and management of the economy. Now that even conservatives have accepted some form of government economic planning (as the Nixon years have shown), the United States is likely to face the sorts of income-distribution issues many European societies have been coping with for some time. What share of our national income should go to what groups? Should the market be allowed to decide? Should our tax system make significant changes in the market distribution?

What will we learn from the Vietnam War? More generally, what has recent history taught us about our role in the world and the role of the military within that role? We have suffered terrible losses of our own and inflicted even more terrible losses on others. The military budget is enormous and may continue to be so. Our policies in the developing world have been only moderately successful. At our worst we have acquired a well-deserved reputation for being the world's main counterrevolutionary power (although the USSR, as in Czechoslovakia in 1968, showed it too was in the running for that dubious honor).

At the minimum, we may have learned that the world is more complicated than our theories about it allowed us to see. The revolutions and changes that take place in the developing areas do not fit very neatly into communist/anticommunist categories. There was a leftward-moving government in Chile, for example, that was democratically elected. What attitude might we have taken toward it? Is socialism something we should always oppose, and must we carry any anticommunist government piggy-back whenever it wants our assistance? We seem to be pulling back from world-policeman role in the aftermath of Vietnam. But there are more choices than to police or not to police. How can we expand our store of political ideas to deal with the more complicated and open world that is truly out there and in which most of the world's people reside? The issues of hunger and development are the key ones for most of humanity and will remain so for our lifetimes. How will we relate most meaningfully to such matters as the world's richest nation?

Then there is the issue of *liberty* and its meaning in modern life. A hundred years ago, Liberalism had a clear meaning for it: freedom from governmental restraint, freedom to buy and sell and work, freedom to speak one's mind. In the catastrophic days of the Depression, in the 1930s, it also had a clear meaning, which Roosevelt articulated concisely: "freedom from fear." But what does liberty mean now? Most of us no longer need worry about a job, nor about having enough to live on. Although there are still some rather serious threats, our society has become freer and more open in recent decades. Perhaps we now need to turn our attention to the development of the very self that is to enjoy freedom. After all, freedom is not an external matter alone; it must also be an inner achievement. It ought to involve a capacity for individuality, for making one's own choices; a capacity to experiment; a sense of self-development encouraged by one's society; an inner psychological balance. In our society it would mean the encouragement of just such traits. No doubt if we did this there would soon develop more *anarchists* among us, people like Henry David Thoreau, who went off by himself to Walden Pond and kept a famous diary, in which he included the well-known passage about the man who does not march to the same beat as his fellows because he may hear a different drummer. Maybe there would be more such anarchists, and if there were, their rallying cry would be: Power to the inner man.

POWER, COMMUNITY, AND AMERICA'S FUTURE

But although the inner man may be an anarchist, even a healthy anarchist who looks with a very skeptical eye at the rules of the body politic, *someone* must also make those rules, form the groups, create the communities, fashion the loyalties, and deal with the issues that perpetually involve us collectively. Thoreau, after his night in jail for refusing to pay his taxes (in protest against slavery and the Mexican War), went berry-picking with a group of his friends. When they climbed a hill in the country, he reported in his essay on Civil Disobedience, for him "the state was nowhere to be seen." But, as we have emphasized throughout this book, *government* is to be seen almost everywhere either by commission or by omission. That is what we have written about: war, economics, race, and liberty—the policies the American government pursues or fails to pursue and how they affect us.

One of the underlying themes in our treatment of American politics has been the structure of power in American society. We have seen that many groups and individuals have great difficulty in making themselves felt in the political process, certainly in any consistent fashion. Our chapter on mass political participation pointed out that disadvantaged groups in our society have persistent troubles getting themselves organized and attaining some political clout.

The distribution of political resources is radically unequal, and as long as it remains so there will be a bitter, unresolvable quality about the political and social conflict in our society. For this reason, if for no other, the issues connected with race and poverty will continue to be painful parts of our national life. Worse yet, many just grievances that might be remedied will never become part of the public agenda. Instead they will fester and contribute to the crime, decay, and political cynicism that are already much in evidence. In these unresolved grievances we see one of the primary threats to the creation of a genuine political community in the United States.

Another theme running through this book has been an attempt to evaluate the quality of political decision making in America. We have seen, for example, that most Americans are not well informed about the political issues of the day and that, moreover, many simply care too little to bother finding out more. Of course, people do come to care about politics when it begins to affect them directly, or when they perceive its subtle connections with their lives. But then it is often too late to try to change policies that have already been made. If fewer citizens are informed and interested, politics becomes more of an elite matter. There is no guarantee, of course, that either masses or elites will make just and reasonable policies. However, it is worrisome in a democratic society when political participation remains low and public sophistication about political life is so sharply limited.

And finally, what is a political community anyway? We have flag-wavers in America and others who wear the flag as a shirt; we have Archie Bunker and Benjamin Spock; we have the peace symbol and "America: Love it or Leave it." In the last decade we have seen American social life torn apart by a fierce series of conflicts springing particularly from issues of foreign affairs and race. We have tried to argue in this book that it is in these two areas, plus the areas of economic management and civil liberties, that are to be found the central problems of political life. The community we create will depend largely on how sensibly we deal with these areas: whether we are symbolized by the B-52, the two-car garage, the Constitution, or the vitality and imagination of our national life.

L.L.

THE CONSTITUTION OF THE UNITED STATES OF AMERICA[1]

We the People of the United States, in Order to form a more perfect Union, establish Justice, insure domestic Tranquility, provide for the common defence, promote the general Welfare, and secure the Blessings of Liberty to ourselves and our Posterity, do ordain and establish this Constitution for the United States of America.

ARTICLE I

Section 1. All legislative Powers herein granted shall be vested in a Congress of the United States, which shall consist of a Senate and House of Representatives.

Section 2. The House of Representatives shall be composed of Members chosen every second Year by the People of the several States, and the Electors in each State shall have the Qualifications requisite for Electors of the most numerous Branch of the State Legislature.

No Person shall be a Representative who shall not have attained to the Age of twenty-five Years, and been seven Years a Citizen of the United States, and who shall not, when elected, be an Inhabitant of that State in which he shall be chosen.

[Representatives and direct Taxes[2] shall be apportioned among the several States which may be included within this Union, according to their respective Numbers, which shall be determined by adding to the whole Number of free Persons, including those bound to Service for a Term of Years, and excluding Indians not taxed, three fifths of all other Persons.][3] The actual Enumeration shall be made within three Years after the first Meeting of the Congress of the United States, and within every subsequent Term of ten Years, in such Manner as they shall by Law direct. The Number of Representatives shall not exceed one for every thirty Thousand, but each State shall have at Least one Representative; and until such enumeration shall be made, the State of New Hampshire shall be entitled to chuse three, Massachusetts eight, Rhode-Island and Providence Plantations one, Connecticut **five**, New York six, New Jersey four, Pennsylvania eight, Delaware one, Maryland six, Virginia ten, North Carolina five, South Carolina five, and Georgia three.

When vacancies happen in the Representation from any State, the Executive Authority thereof shall issue Writs of Election to fill such Vacancies.

The House of Representatives shall chuse their Speaker and other Officers; and shall have the sole Power of Impeachment.

Section 3. The Senate of the United States shall be composed of two Senators from each State, chosen by the Legislature thereof, for six Years; and each Senator shall have one Vote.

---

[1] This version, which follows the original Constitution in capitalization and spelling, was published by the United States Department of the Interior, Office of Education, in 1935.

[2] Altered by the Sixteenth Amendment.

[3] Negated by the Fourteenth Amendment.

Immediately after they shall be assembled in Consequence of the first Election, they shall be divided as equally as may be into three Classes. The Seats of the Senators of the first Class shall be vacated at the Expiration of the second Year, of the second Class at the Expiration of the fourth Year, and of the third Class at the Expiration of the sixth Year, so that one-third may be chosen every second Year; and if Vacancies happen by Resignation, or otherwise, during the Recess of the Legislature of any State, the Executive thereof may make temporary Appointments until the next Meeting of the Legislature, which shall then fill such Vacancies.

No Person shall be a Senator who shall not have attained to the Age of thirty Years, and been nine Years a Citizen of the United States, and who shall not, when elected, be an Inhabitant of that State for which he shall be chosen.

The Vice President of the United States shall be President of the Senate, but shall have no vote, unless they be equally divided.

The Senate shall chuse their other Officers, and also a President pro tempore, in the absence of the Vice President, or when he shall exercise the Office of President of the United States.

The Senate shall have the sole Power to try all Impeachments. When sitting for that purpose, they shall be on Oath or Affirmation. When the President of the United States is tried, the Chief Justice shall preside: And no person shall be convicted without the Concurrence of two thirds of the Members present.

Judgment in Cases of Impeachment shall not extend further than to removal from Office, and disqualification to hold and enjoy any Office of honor, Trust, or Profit under the United States: but the Party convicted shall nevertheless be liable and subject to Indictment, Trial, Judgment, and Punishment, according to Law.

Section 4. The Times, Places and Manner of holding Elections for Senators and Representatives, shall be prescribed in each State by the Legislature thereof; but the Congress may at any time by Law make or alter such Regulations, except as to the Places of Chusing Senators.

The Congress shall assemble at least once in every Year, and such Meeting shall be on the first Monday in December, unless they shall by Law appoint a different Day.

Section 5. Each House shall be the Judge of the Elections, Returns and Qualifications of its own Members, and a Majority of each shall constitute a Quorum to do Business; but a smaller number may adjourn from day to day, and may be authorized to compel the Attendance of absent Members, in such Manner, and under such Penalties, as each House may provide.

Each House may determine the Rules of its Proceedings, punish its Members for disorderly Behaviour, and, with the Concurrence of two thirds, expel a Member.

Each House shall keep a Journal of its Proceedings, and from time to time publish the same, excepting such Parts as may in their Judgment require Secrecy; and the Yeas and Nays of the Members of either House on any question shall, at the Desire of one fifth of those Present, be entered on the Journal.

Neither House, during the Session of Congress, shall, without the Consent of the other, adjourn for more than three days, nor to any other Place than that in which the two Houses shall be sitting.

Section 6. The Senators and Representatives shall receive a Compensation for their Services, to be ascertained by Law, and paid out of the Treasury of the United States. They shall in all Cases, except Treason, Felony, and Breach of the Peace, be privileged from Arrest during their Attendance at the Session of their respective Houses, and in going to and returning from the same; and for any Speech or Debate in either House, they shall not be questioned in any other Place.

No Senator or Representative shall, during the Time for which he was elected, be appointed to any civil Office under the Authority of the United States, which shall have been created, or the Emoluments whereof shall have been increased, during such time; and no Person holding any Office under the United States shall be a Member of either House during his continuance in Office.

Section 7. All Bills for raising Revenue shall originate in the House of Representatives; but the Senate may propose or concur with Amendments as on other bills.

Every Bill which shall have passed the House of Representatives and the Senate, shall, before it become a Law, be presented to the President of the United States; If he approve he shall sign it, but if not he shall return it, with his Objections, to that House in which it shall have originated, who shall enter the Objections at large on their Journal, and proceed to reconsider it. If after such Reconsideration two thirds of that House shall agree to pass the bill, it shall be sent, together with the objections, to the other House, by which it shall likewise be reconsidered, and if approved by two thirds of that House, it shall become a Law. But in all such Cases the Votes of both Houses shall be determined by Yeas and Nays, and the Names of the Persons voting for and against the Bill shall be entered on the Journal of each House respectively. If any Bill shall not be returned by the President within ten Days (Sundays excepted) after it shall have been presented to him, the Same shall be a Law, in like Manner as if he had signed it, unless the Congress by their Adjournment prevent its Return, in which Case it shall not be a Law.

Every Order, Resolution, or Vote to which the Concurrence of the Senate and House of Representatives may be necessary (except on a question of Adjournment) shall be presented to the President of the United States; and befor the Same shall take Effect, shall be approved by him, or being disapproved by him, shall be repassed by two thirds of the Senate and House of Representatives, according to the Rules and Limitations prescribed in the Case of a Bill.

Section 8. The Congress shall have Power To lay and collect Taxes, Duties, Imposts and Excises, to pay the Debts and provide for the common Defence and general Welfare of the United States; but all Duties, Imposts and Excises shall be uniform throughout the United States;

To borrow money on the credit of the United States;

To regulate Commerce with foreign Nations, and among the several States, and with the Indian Tribes;

To establish an uniform Rule of Naturalization, and uniform Laws on the subject of Bankruptcies throughout the United States;

To coin Money, regulate the Value thereof, and of foreign Coin, and fix the Standard of Weights and Measures;

To provide for the Punishment of counterfeiting the Securities and current Coin of the United States;

To establish Post Offices and post Roads;

To promote the Progress of Science and useful Arts, by securing for limited Times to Authors and Inventors the exclusive Right to their respective Writings and Discoveries;

To constitute Tribunals inferior to the Supreme Court;

To define and punish Piracies and Felonies committed on the high Seas, and Offenses against the Law of Nations;

To declare War, grant Letters of Marque and Reprisal, and make Rules concerning Captures on Land and Water;

To raise and support Armies, but no Appropriation of Money to that Use shall be for a longer Term than two Years;

To provide and maintain a Navy;

To make Rules for the Government and Regulation of the land and naval forces;

To provide for calling forth the Militia to execute the Laws of the Union, suppress Insurrections and repel Invasions;

To provide for organizing, arming, and disciplining the Militia, and for governing such Part of them as may be employed in the Service of the United States, reserving to the States respectively, the Appointment of the Officers, and the Authority of training the Militia according to the discipline prescribed by Congress;

To exercise exclusive Legislation in all Cases whatsoever, over such District (not exceeding ten Miles square) as may, by Cession of particular States, and the acceptance of Congress, become the Seat of the Government of the United States, and to exercise like Authority over all Places purchased by the Consent of the Legislature of the State in which the Same shall be, for the Erection of Forts, Magazines, Arsenals, dock-Yards, and other needful Buildings;—And

To make all Laws which shall be necessary and proper for carrying into Execution the foregoing Powers, and all other Powers vested by this Constitution in the Government of the United States, or in any Department or Officer thereof.

Section 9. The Migration or Importation of such Persons as any of the States now existing shall think proper to admit, shall not be prohibited by the Congress prior to the Year one thousand eight hundred and eight, but a tax or duty may be imposed on such Importation, not exceeding ten dollars for each Person.

The privilege of the Writ of Habeas Corpus shall not be suspended, unless when in Cases of Rebellion or Invasion the public Safety may require it.

No bill of Attainder or ex post facto Law shall be passed.

No capitation, or other direct, Tax shall be laid unless in Proportion to the Census or Enumeration herein before directed to be taken.

No Tax or Duty shall be laid on Articles exported from any State.

No Preference shall be given by any Regulation of Commerce or Revenue to the Ports of one State over those of another: nor shall Vessels bound to, or from, one State, be obliged to enter, clear, or pay Duties in another.

No Money shall be drawn from the Treasury, but in Consequence of Appropriations made by Law; and a regular Statement and Account of the Receipts and Expenditures of all public Money shall be published from time to time.

No Title of Nobility shall be granted by the United States: And no Person holding any Office of Profit or Trust under them, shall, without the Consent of the Congress, accept of any present, Emolument, Office, or Title, of any kind whatever, from any King, Prince, or foreign State.

Section 10. No State shall enter into any Treaty, Alliance, or Confederation; grant Letters of Marque and Reprisal; coin Money; emit Bills of Credit; make any Thing but gold and silver Coin a Tender in Payment of Debts; pass any Bill of Attainder, ex post facto Law, or Law impairing the Obligation of Contracts, or grant any Title of Nobility.

No State shall, without the Consent of the Congress, lay any Imposts or Duties on Imports or Exports, except what may be absolutely necessary for executing its inspection Laws: and the net Produce of all Duties and Imposts, laid by any State on Imports or Exports, shall be for the Use of the Treasury of the United States; and all such Laws shall be subject to the Revision and Control of the Congress.

No state shall, without the Consent of Congress, lay any duty of Tonnage, keep Troops, or Ships of War in time of Peace, enter into any Agreement or Compact with another State, or with a foreign Power, or engage in War, unless actually invaded, or in such imminent Danger as will not admit of delay.

ARTICLE II

Section 1. The executive Power shall be vested in a President of the United States of America. He shall hold his Office during the Term of four years, and, together with the Vice-President, chosen for the same Term, be elected, as follows:

Each State shall appoint, in such Manner as the Legislature thereof may direct, a Number of Electors, equal to the whole Number of Senators and Representatives to which the State may be entitled in the Congress: but no Senator or Representative, or Person holding an Office of Trust or Profit under the United States, shall be appointed an Elector.

[The Electors shall meet in their respective States, and

vote by Ballot for two persons, of whom one at least shall not be an Inhabitant of the same State with themselves. And they shall make a List of all the Persons voted for, and of the Number of Votes for each; which List they shall sign and certify, and transmit sealed to the Seat of the Government of the United States, directed to the President of the Senate. The President of the Senate shall, in the Presence of the Senate and House of Representatives, open all the Certificates, and the Votes shall then be counted. The Person having the greatest Number of Votes shall be the President, if such Number be a Majority of the whole Number of Electors appointed; and if there be more than one who have such Majority, and have an equal Number of Votes, then the House of Representatives shall immediately chuse by Ballot one of them for President; and if no Person have a Majority, then from the five highest on the List the said House shall in the Manner chuse the President. But in chusing the President, the Votes shall be taken by States, the Representation from each State having one Vote; a quorum for this Purpose shall consist of a Member or Members from two-thirds of the States, and a Majority of all the States shall be necessary to a Choice. In every Case, after the Choice of the President, the Person having the greatest Number of Votes of the Electors shall be the Vice President. But if there should remain two or more who have equal votes, the Senate shall chuse from them by Ballot the Vice-President.]⁴

The Congress may determine the Time of chusing the Electors, and the Day on which they shall give their Votes; which Day shall be the same throughout the United States.

No person except a natural-born Citizen, or a Citizen of the United States, at the time of the Adoption of this Constitution, shall be eligible to the Office of President; neither shall any Person be eligible to that Office who shall not have attained to the Age of thirty-five years, and been fourteen Years a Resident within the United States.

In Case of the Removal of the President from Office, or of his Death, Resignation, or Inability to discharge the Powers and Duties of the said Office, the same shall devolve on the Vice President, and the Congress may by Law provide for the Case of Removal, Death, Resignation, or Inability, both of the President and Vice President, declaring what Officer shall then act as President, and such Officer shall act accordingly, until the disability be removed, or a President shall be elected.

The President shall, at stated Times, receive for his Services a Compensation, which shall neither be increased nor diminished during the Period for which he shall have been elected, and he shall not receive within that Period any other Emolument from the United States, or any of them.

Before he enter on the execution of his Office, he shall take the following Oath or Affirmation:—"I do solemnly swear (or affirm) that I will faithfully execute the Office of President of the United States, and will, to the best of my Ability, preserve, protect, and defend the Constitution of the United States."

---

⁴ Revised by the Twelfth Amendment.

Section 2. The President shall be Commander in Chief of the Army and Navy of the United States, and of the Militia of the several States, when called into the actual Service of the United States; he may require the Opinion, in writing, of the principal Officer in each of the executive Departments, upon any subject relating to the Duties of their respective Offices, and he shall have Power to Grant Reprieves and Pardons for Offenses against the United States, except in Cases of Impeachment.

He shall have Power, by and with the Advice and Consent of the Senate, to make Treaties, provided two thirds of the Senators present concur; and he shall nominate, and by and with the Advice and Consent of the Senate, shall appoint Ambassadors, other public Ministers and Consuls, Judges of the supreme Court, and all other Officers of the United States, whose Appointments are not herein otherwise provided for, and which shall be established by Law: but the Congress may by Law vest the Appointment of such inferior Officers, as they think proper, in the President alone, in the Courts of Law, or in the Heads of Departments.

The President shall have Power to fill up all Vacancies that may happen during the Recess of the Senate, by granting Commissions which shall expire at the End of their next Session.

Section 3. He shall from time to time give to the Congress Information of the State of the Union, and recommend to their Consideration such Measures as he shall judge necessary and expedient; he may, on extraordinary occasions, convene both Houses, or either of them, and in Case of Disagreement between them, with respect to the Time of Adjournment, he may adjourn them to such Time as he shall think proper; he shall receive Ambassadors and other public Ministers; he shall take care that the Laws be faithfully executed, and shall Commission all the Officers of the United States.

Section 4. The President, Vice President and all civil Officers of the United States, shall be removed from Office on Impeachment for, and Conviction of, Treason, Bribery, or other high Crimes and Misdemeanors.

ARTICLE III

Section 1. The judicial Power of the United States, shall be vested in one supreme Court, and in such inferior Courts as the Congress may from time to time ordain and establish. The Judges, both of the supreme and inferior Courts, shall hold their Offices during good Behaviour, and shall, at stated Times, receive for their Services, a Compensation, which shall not be diminished during their Continuance in Office.

Section 2. The judicial Power shall extend to all Cases, in Law and Equity, arising under this Constitution, the Laws of the United States, and Treaties made, or which shall be made, under their Authority;—to all Cases affecting ambassadors, other public ministers and consuls;—to all cases of admiralty and maritime Jurisdiction;—to Controversies to which the United States shall be a Party;—to Controversies between two or more States;—between a State and Citizens of another State;[5]—between Citizens of different States,—between Citizens of the same State claiming Lands under Grants of different States, and between a State, or the Citizens thereof, and foreign States, Citizens or Subjects.

In all Cases affecting Ambassadors, other public Ministers and Consuls, and those in which a State shall be Party, the supreme Court shall have original Jurisdiction. In all the other Cases before mentioned, the supreme Court shall have appellate Jurisdiction, both as to Law and Fact, with such Exceptions, and under such Regulations as the Congress shall make.

The trial of all Crimes, except in Cases of Impeachment, shall be by Jury; and such Trial shall be held in the State where the said Crimes shall have been committed; but when not committed within any State, the Trial shall be at such Place or Places as the Congress may by Law have directed.

Section 3. Treason against the United States, shall consist only in levying War against them, or in adhering to their Enemies, giving them Aid and Comfort. No Person shall be convicted of Treason unless on the Testimony of two Witnesses to the same overt Act, or on Confession in open Court.

The Congress shall have power to declare the Punishment of Treason, but no Attainder of Treason shall work Corruption of Blood, or Forfeiture except during the Life of the Person attainted.

ARTICLE IV

Section 1. Full Faith and Credit shall be given in each State to the public Acts, Records, and judicial Proceedings of every other State. And the Congress may by general Laws prescribe the Manner in which such Acts, Records and Proceedings shall be proved, and the Effect thereof.

Section 2. The Citizens of each State shall be entitled to all Privileges and Immunities of Citizens in the several States.

A Person charged in any State with Treason, Felony, or other Crime, who shall flee from Justice, and be found in another State, shall on demand of the executive Authority of the State from which he fled, be delivered up, to be removed to the State having Jurisdiction of the crime.

No Person held to Service or Labour in one State, under the Laws thereof, escaping into another, shall, in Consequence of any Law or Regulation therein, be discharged from such Service or Labour, but shall be delivered up on Claim of the Party to whom such Service or Labour may be due.

Section 3. New States may be admitted by the Congress into this Union; but no new State shall be formed or erected within the Jurisdiction of any other State; nor any State be formed by the Junction of two or more States, or parts of States, without the Consent of the Legislatures of the States concerned as well as of the Congress.

---

[5] Qualified by the Eleventh Amendment.

The Congress shall have Power to dispose of and make all needful Rules and Regulations respecting the Territory or other Property belonging to the United States; and nothing in this Constitution shall be so construed as to Prejudice any Claims of the United States, or of any particular State.

Section 4. The United States shall guarantee to every State in this Union a Republican Form of Government, and shall protect each of them against Invasion; and on Application of the Legislature, or of the Executive (when the Legislature cannot be convened) against domestic Violence.

ARTICLE V

The Congress, whenever two-thirds of both Houses shall deem it necessary, shall propose Amendments to this Constitution, or, on the Application of the Legislatures of two-thirds of the several States, shall call a Convention for proposing Amendments, which, in either Case, shall be valid to all Intents and Purposes, as part of this Constitution, when ratified by the Legislatures of three-fourths of the several States, or by Conventions in three-fourths thereof, as the one or the other Mode of Ratification may be proposed by the Congress; Provided that no Amendment which may be made prior to the Year One thousand eight hundred and eight shall in any Manner affect the first and fourth Clauses in the Ninth Section of the first Article; and that no State, without its Consent, shall be deprived of its equal Suffrage in the Senate.

ARTICLE VI

All Debts contracted and Engagements entered into, before the Adoption of this Constitution, shall be as valid against the United States under this Constitution, as under the Confederation.

This Constitution, and the Laws of the United States which shall be made in Pursuance thereof; and all Treaties made, or which shall be made, under the Authority of the United States, shall be the supreme Law of the Land; and the Judges in every State shall be bound thereby, any Thing in the Constitution or Laws of any State to the Contrary notwithstanding.

The Senators and Representatives before mentioned, and the Members of the several State Legislatures, and all executive and judicial Officers, both of the United States and of the several States, shall be bound by Oath or Affirmation to support this Constitution; but no religious Test shall ever be required as a qualification to any Office or public Trust under the United States.

ARTICLE VII

The Ratification of the Conventions of nine States shall be sufficient for the Establishment of this Constitution between the States so ratifying the same.

Done in Convention by the Unanimous Consent of the States present the Seventeenth Day of September in the

Year of our Lord one thousand seven hundred and Eighty seven, and of the Independence of the United States of America the Twelfth. In Witness whereof We have hereunto subscribed our Names.

. . .

[The first ten Amendments were ratified in 1791 and form what is known as the Bill of Rights.]

Amendment 1

Congress shall make no law respecting an establishment of religion, or prohibiting the free exercise thereof; or abridging the freedom of speech, or of the press; or the right of the people peaceably to assemble, and to petition the Government for a redress of grievances.

Amendment 2

A well regulated Militia, being necessary to the security of a free State, the right of the people to keep and bear Arms shall not be infringed.

Amendment 3

No Soldier shall, in time of peace, be quartered in any house, without the consent of the Owner, nor in time of war, but in a manner to be prescribed by law.

Amendment 4

The right of the people to be secure in their persons, houses, papers, and effects, against unreasonable searches and seizures, shall not be violated, and no Warrants shall issue, but upon probable cause, supported by Oath or affirmation, and particularly describing the place to be searched, and the persons or things to be seized.

Amendment 5

No person shall be held to answer for a capital or otherwise infamous crime, unless on a presentment or indictment of a Grand Jury, except in cases arising in the land or naval forces, or in the Militia, when in actual service in time of War or public danger, nor shall any person be subject for the same offence to be twice put in jeopardy of life or limb; nor shall be compelled in any criminal case to be a witness against himself, nor be deprived of life, liberty, or property, without due process of law; nor shall private property be taken for public use, without just compensation.

Amendment 6

In all criminal prosecutions, the accused shall enjoy the right to a speedy and public trial, by an impartial jury of the State and district wherein the crime shall have been committed, which district shall have been previously ascertained by law, and to be informed of the nature and cause of the accusation; to be confronted with the witnesses against him; to have compulsory process for obtaining witnesses in his favour, and to have the Assistance of Counsel for his defence.

Amendment 7

In suits at common law, where the value in controversy shall exceed twenty dollars, the right of trial by jury shall be preserved, and no fact tried by a jury, shall be otherwise reexamined in any Court of the United States, than according to the rules of the common law.

Amendment 8

Excessive bail shall not be required, nor excessive fines imposed, nor cruel and unusual punishments inflicted.

Amendment 9

The enumeration in the Constitution, of certain rights, shall not be construed to deny or disparage others retained by the people.

Amendment 10

The powers not delegated to the United States by the Constitution, nor prohibited by it to the States, are reserved to the States respectively, or to the people.

Amendment 11
[ratified in 1795]

The Judicial power of the United States shall not be construed to extend to any suit in law or equity, commenced or prosecuted against one of the United States by Citizens of another State, or by Citizens or Subjects of any Foreign State.

Amendment 12
[ratified in 1804]

The Electors shall meet in their respective States and vote by ballot for President and Vice-President, one of whom, at least, shall not be an inhabitant of the same State with themselves; they shall name in their ballots the person voted for as President, and in distinct ballots the person voted for as Vice-President, and they shall make distinct lists of all persons voted for as President, and of all persons voted for as Vice-President, and of the number of votes for each, which lists they shall sign and certify, and transmit sealed to the seat of the government of the United States, directed to the President of the Senate;—The President of the Senate shall, in the presence of the Senate and House of Representatives, open all the certificates and the votes shall then be counted;—The person having the greatest number of votes for President, shall be the President, if such number be a majority of the whole number of Electors appointed; and if no person have such majority, then from the persons having the highest numbers not exceeding three on the list of those voted for as President, the House of Representatives shall choose immediately, by ballot, the President. But in choosing the President, the votes shall be taken by states, the representation from each state having one vote; a quorum for this purpose shall consist of a member or members from two-thirds of the states, and a majority of all the states shall be necessary to a choice. And if the House of Representatives shall not choose a President whenever the right of choice shall devolve upon them, before the fourth day of March next following, then the Vice-President shall act as President, as in the case of the death or other constitutional disability of the President.—The person having the greatest number of votes as Vice-President, shall be the Vice-President, if such number be a majority of the whole number of Electors appointed, and if no person have a majority, then from the two highest numbers on the list, the Senate shall choose the Vice-President; a quorum for the purpose shall consist of two-thirds of the whole number of Senators, and a majority of the whole number shall be necessary to a choice. But no person constitutionally ineligible to the office of President shall be eligible to that of Vice-President of the United States.

Amendment 13
[ratified in 1865]

Section 1. Neither slavery nor involuntary servitude, except as a punishment for crime whereof the party shall have been duly convicted, shall exist within the United States, or any place subject to their jurisdiction.
Section 2. Congress shall have power to enforce this article by appropriate legislation.

Amendment 14
[ratified in 1868]

Section 1. All persons born or naturalized in the United States, and subject to the jurisdiction thereof, are citizens of the United States and of the State wherein they reside. No State shall abridge the privileges or immunities of citizens of the United States; nor shall any State deprive any person of life, liberty, or property, without due process of law; nor deny to any person within its jurisdiction the equal protection of the laws.
Section 2. Representatives shall be apportioned among the several States according to their respective numbers, counting the whole number of persons in each State, excluding Indians not taxed. But when the right to vote at any election for the choice of electors for President and Vice-President of the United States, Representatives in Congress, the Executive and Judicial officers of a State, or the members of the Legislature thereof, is denied to any of the male inhabitants of such State, being twenty-one years of age, and citizens of the United States, or in any way abridged, except for participation in rebellion, or other crime, the basis of representation therein shall be reduced in the proportion which the number of such male citizens shall bear to the whole number of male citizens twenty-one years of age in such State.
Section 3. No person shall be a Senator or Representative in Congress, or elector of President and Vice-President, or hold any office, civil or military, under the United States, or under any State, who, having previously taken an oath, as a member of Congress, or as an officer of the United States, or as a member of any State legislature, or as an executive or judicial officer of any State, to support the Constitution of the United States, shall have engaged in insurrection or rebellion against the same, or given aid or comfort to the enemies thereof. But Congress may by a vote of two-thirds of each House, remove such disability.
Section 4. The validity of the public debt of the United States, authorized by law, including debts incurred for payment of pensions and bounties for services in suppressing insurrection or rebellion, shall not be questioned. But neither the United States nor any State shall assume or pay any debts or obligation incurred in aid of insurrection or rebellion against the United States, or any claim for the loss or emancipation of any slave; but all such debts, obligations, and claims shall be held illegal and void.
Section 5. The Congress shall have the power to enforce, by appropriate legislation, the provisions of this article.

Amendment 15
[ratified in 1870]

Section 1. The right of citizens of the United States to vote shall not be denied or abridged by the United States or by any State on account of race, color, or previous condition of servitude—
Section 2. The Congress shall have power to enforce this article by appropriate legislation.

Amendment 16
[ratified in 1913]

The Congress shall have power to lay and collect taxes on incomes, from whatever source derived, without apportionment among the several States, and without regard to any census or enumeration.

Amendment 17
[ratified in 1913]

The Senate of the United States shall be composed of two Senators from each State, elected by the people thereof, for six years; and each Senator shall have one vote. The electors in each State shall have the qualifications requisite for electors of the most numerous branch of the State legislatures.

When vacancies happen in the representation of any State in the Senate, the executive authority of such State shall issue writs of election to fill such vacancies: *Provided,* That the legislature of any State may empower the executive thereof to make temporary appointments until the people fill the vacancies by election as the legislature may direct.

This amendment shall not be so construed as to affect the election or term of any Senator chosen before it becomes valid as part of the Constitution.

Amendment 18
[ratified in 1919]

Section 1. After one year from the ratification of this article the manufacture, sale, or transportation of intoxicating liquors within, the importation thereof into, or the exportation thereof from the United States and all territory subject to the jurisdiction thereof for beverage purposes is hereby prohibited.

Section 2. The Congress and the several States shall have concurrent power to enforce this article by appropriate legislation.

Section 3. This article shall be inoperative unless it shall have been ratified as an amendment to the Constitution by the legislatures of the several States, as provided in the Constitution, within seven years from the date of the submission hereof to the States by the Congress.

Amendment 19
[ratified in 1920]

The right of citizens of the United States to vote shall not be denied or abridged by the United States or by any State on account of sex.

Congress shall have power to enforce this article by appropriate legislation.

Amendment 20
[ratified in 1933]

Section 1. The terms of the President and Vice-President shall end at noon on the 20th day of January, and the terms of Senators and Representatives at noon on the 3d day of January, of the years in which such terms would have ended if this article had not been ratified; and the terms of their successors shall then begin.

Section 2. The Congress shall assemble at least once in every year, and such meeting shall begin at noon on the 3d day of January, unless they shall by law appoint a different day.

Section 3. If, at the time fixed for the beginning of the term of the President, the President elect shall have died, the Vice-President elect shall become President. If a President shall not have been chosen before the time fixed for the beginning of his term, or if the President elect shall have failed to qualify, then the Vice-President elect shall act as President until a President shall have qualified; and the Congress may by law provide for the case wherein neither a President elect nor a Vice-President elect shall have qualified, declaring who shall then act as President, or the manner in which one who is to act shall be selected, and such person shall act accordingly until a President or Vice-President shall have qualified.

Section 4. The Congress may by law provide for the case of the death of any of the persons from whom the House of Representatives may choose a President whenever the right of choice shall have devolved upon them, and for the case of the death of any of the persons from whom the Senate may choose a Vice-President whenever the right of choice shall have devolved upon them.

Section 5. Sections 1 and 2 shall take effect on the 15th day of October following the ratification of this article.

Section 6. This article shall be inoperative unless it shall have been ratified as an amendment to the Constitution by the legislatures of three-fourths of the several States within seven years from the date of its submission.

Amendment 21
[ratified in 1933]

Section 1. The eighteenth article of amendment to the Constitution of the United States is hereby repealed.

Section 2. The transportation or importation into any State, Territory, or possession of the United States for delivery or use therein of intoxicating liquors, in violation of the laws thereof, is hereby prohibited.

Section 3. This article shall be inoperative unless it shall have been ratified as an amendment to the Constitution by conventions in the several States, as provided in the Constitution, within seven years from the date of the submission hereof to the States by the Congress.

Amendment 22
[ratified in 1951]

No person shall be elected to the office of the President more than twice, and no person who has held the office of President, or acted as President, for more than two years of a term to which some other person was elected President shall be elected to the office of the President more than once.

But this Article shall not apply to any person holding the office of President when this Article was proposed by the Congress, and shall not prevent any person who may be holding the office of President, or acting as President, during the term within which this Article becomes operative from holding the office of President or acting as President during the remainder of such term.

This article shall be inoperative unless it shall have been ratified as an amendment to the Constitution by the legislatures of three-fourths of the several states within seven years from the date of its submission to the states by the Congress.

Amendment 23
[ratified in 1961]

Section 1. The District constituting the seat of Government of the United States shall appoint in such manner as the Congress may direct:

A number of electors of President and Vice-President equal to the whole number of Senators and Representatives in Congress to which the District would be entitled if it were a State, but in no event more than the least populous State; they shall be in addition to those appointed by the States, but they shall be considered, for the purposes of the election of President and Vice-President, to be electors appointed by a State; and they shall meet in the District and perform such duties as provided by the twelfth article of amendment.

Section 2. The Congress shall have power to enforce this article by appropriate legislation.

Amendment 24
[ratified in 1964]

Section 1. The right of citizens of the United States to vote in any primary or other election for President or Vice-President, for electors for President or Vice-President, or for Senator or Representative in Congress, shall not be denied or abridged by the United States or any state by reason of failure to pay any poll tax or other tax.

Section 2. The Congress shall have the power to enforce this article by appropriate legislation.

Amendment 25
[ratified in 1967]

Section 1. In case of the removal of the President from office or of his death or resignation, the Vice-President shall become President.

Section 2. Whenever there is a vacancy in the office of the Vice-President, the President shall nominate a Vice-President who shall take office upon confirmation by a majority vote of both Houses of Congress.

Section 3. Whenever the President transmits to the President Pro Tempore of the Senate and the Speaker of the House of Representatives his written declaration that he is unable to discharge the powers and duties of his office, and until he transmits to them a written declaration to the contrary, such powers and duties shall be discharged by the Vice-President as Acting President.

Section 4. Whenever the Vice-President and a majority of either the principal officers of the executive departments or of such other body as Congress may by law provide, transmit to the President Pro Tempore of the Senate and the Speaker of the House of Representatives their written declaration that the President is unable to discharge the powers and duties of his office, the Vice-President shall immediately assume the powers and duties of the office as Acting President.

Thereafter, when the President transmits to the President Pro Tempore of the Senate and the Speaker of the House of Representatives his written declaration that no inability exists, he shall resume the powers and duties of his office unless the Vice-President and a majority of either the principal officers of the executive departments or of such other body as Congress may by law provide, transmit within four days to the President Pro Tempore of the Senate and the Speaker of the House of Representatives their written declaration that the President is unable to discharge the powers and duties of his office. Thereupon Congress shall decide the issue, assembling within forty-eight hours for that purpose if not in session. If the Congress, within twenty-one days after receipt of the latter written declaration, or, if Congress is not in session, within twenty-one days after Congress is required to assemble, determines by two-thirds vote of both Houses that the President is unable to discharge the powers and duties of his office, the Vice-President shall continue to discharge the same as Acting President; otherwise, the President shall resume the powers and duties of his office.

Amendment 26
[ratified in 1971]

Section 1. The right of citizens of the United States, who are eighteen years of age or older, to vote shall not be denied or abridged by the United States or by any State on account of age.

Section 2. The Congress shall have the power to enforce this article by appropriate legislation.

REFERENCES*

A

Abrams, Charles. *The City Is the Frontier.* New York: Harper & Row, 1965. [6a]

Adams, John. "Letter to Hezekiah Niles, February 13, 1818," in Charles Francis Adams (ed.), *The Works of John Adams.* Boston: Little, Brown, 1856. [1]

Adelson, Joseph, and Robert P. O'Neil. "Growth of Political Ideas in Adolescence: The Sense of Community," *Journal of Personality and Social Psychology,* 4 (July 1966), 295–306. [12]

Agricultural Economic Report No. 73. *Employment, Unemployment, and Low Incomes in Appalachia.* Washington, D.C.: Government Printing Office, May 1965. [4a]

Alexander v. Holmes, 396 U.S. 19 (1969). [6a]

Alexander, Herbert E. *Financing the 1968 Election.* Lexington, Mass.: Heath, 1971. [14]

Alford, Robert R., and Eugene C. Lee. "Voting Turnout in American Cities," *American Political Science Review,* 62 (September 1968), 796–813. [13]

Alinsky, Saul. *Rules for Radicals.* New York: Random House, 1971. [16]

Almond, Gabriel A. *The American People and Foreign Policy.* New York: Praeger, 1960. [1]

Almond, Gabriel, and Sidney Verba. *Civic Culture: Political Attitudes and Democracy in Five Nations.* Princeton, N.J.: Princeton University Press, 1963. [12]

Amalgamated Food Employees Union Local 590 et al. v. Logan Valley Plaza, Inc., et al., 425 Pa. 382, 227 A. 2d 874 1968. [7]

Anderson, James E. *Politics and the Economy.* Boston: Little, Brown, 1966. [4]

Anderson, John W. *Eisenhower, Brownell, and the Congress.* University, Ala.: University of Alabama Press, 1964. [6a]

Annual Report of the Appalachian Regional Commission for Fiscal Year 1968. House Document 91-59. January 23, 1969. Washington, D.C.: Government Printing Office, 1969. [4a]

Anslinger, H. J., and Courtney R. Cooper. "Marijuana: Assassin of Youth," *The American Magazine,* 124 (July 1937). [7a]

Arizona Daily Star. "Youth Risk $5 to Smoke Pot," September 24, 1972. [7a]

Arizona Daily Star. "Pot Problem Is Insolvable, Concert Officials Say," September 24, 1972. [7a]

Arizona Daily Star. "Pot Statute with $5 Fine Shattered by Court Ruling," September 30, 1972. [7a]

Arnold, Thurman. *The Folklore of Capitalism.* New Haven, Conn.: Yale University Press, 1937, chap. 9. [4]

Auerbach, Stuart. "Drug Panel Says U.S. Response Tends to Perpetuate Problem," *Los Angeles Times,* March 23, 1973. [7a]

B

Bailey, Stephen K. *Congress Makes A Law.* New York: Columbia University Press, 1950. [4]

Banfield, Edward C. *The Unheavenly City.* Boston: Little, Brown, 1968. [4]

Baran, Paul A., and Paul M. Sweezy. *Monopoly Capital.* New York: Monthly Review Press, 1966. [3]

Barber, Richard J. *The American Corporation.* New York: Dutton, 1970, chap. 3. [4]

Barnet, Richard J. *The Economy of Death.* New York: Atheneum, 1969. [5a]

———. *Roots of War.* New York: Atheneum, 1972. [5]

Barrett, Laurence. "The Military: Servant or Master of Policy," *Time* (April 11, 1969), 20. [5a]

Barron v. Baltimore, 7 Peters 242; 8 L. Ed. 672 (1833). [7, 11]

Baumol, William. "Macroeconomics of Unbalanced Growth: The Anatomy of Urban Crisis," *American Economic Review* (June 1967), 415–426. [4]

Bean, Walton. *California, An Interpretive History.* New York: McGraw-Hill, 1968, 299–310. [15]

Beard, Charles A. *An Economic Interpretation of the Constitution.* New York: Macmillan, 1913. [2]

Becker, Theodore L. (ed.). *The Impact of Supreme Court Decisions.* New York: Oxford University Press, 1969. [6a]

Bell, Daniel. *The End of Ideology.* 2nd rev. ed. New York: Collier Books, 1962. [1]

Berelson, Bernard. "Democratic Theory and Public Opinion," in Bernard Berelson and Morris Janowitz (eds.), *Reader in Public Opinion and Communication.* 2nd ed. New York: Free Press, 1966. [12]

Berelson, Bernard, and Gary Steiner. *Human Behavior: An Inventory of Scientific Findings.* New York: Harcourt, Brace & World, 1964. [13]

Berelson, Bernard, Paul Lazarsfeld, and William N. McPhee. *Voting: A Study of Opinion Formation in a Presidential Campaign.* Chicago: University of Chicago Press, 1954. [12]

---

*Figures in brackets following references indicate chapter(s) in which reference is cited.

Berle, Adolf A. *The American Economic Republic.* New York: Harcourt, Brace & World, 1963. [4]

Bickel, Alexander. *The Least Dangerous Branch.* Indianapolis, Ind.: Bobbs-Merrill, 1962. [11]

Black, Charles. *The People and the Court.* Englewood Cliffs, N.J.: Prentice-Hall, 1960. [11]

Black, Hugo. "The Bill of Rights," *New York University Law Review,* 35 (1960). [7]

Blau, Peter, and Otis Dudley Duncan. *The American Occupational Structure.* New York: Wiley, 1967. [3]

Blumberg, Abraham S. (ed.). *The Scales of Justice.* Chicago: Aldine, 1970. [7]

Bowman, Mary Jean, and W. Warren Haynes. *Resources and People in East Kentucky.* Baltimore: Johns Hopkins Press, 1963. [4a]

Boyd, James. "A Senator's Day," in Charles Peters and Timothy J. Adams (eds.), *Inside the System.* New York: Praeger, 1970. [8]

Brown v. Board of Education of Topeka, Kansas, 347 U.S. 483 (1954). [6, 6a]

Brown v. Board of Education of Topeka, Kansas, 349 U.S. 294 (1955). [6a]

Brown, Dee. *Bury My Heart at Wounded Knee.* New York: Bantam, 1972. [6]

Brown, Robert E. *Charles Beard and the Constitution.* Princeton, N.J.: Princeton University Press, 1956. [2]

Bruno, Jerry, and Jeff Greenfield. *The Advance Man: An Offbeat Look at What Really Happens in Political Campaigns.* New York: Morrow, 1971. [14]

Bryce, James. *The American Commonwealth.* New York: Putnam's Sons, 1959, II, 341–350; first published, 1888. [1]

Budd, Edward. *Inequality and Poverty.* New York: Norton, 1967. [3]

Bunzel, John. "Comparative Attitudes of Big Business and Small Business," *Western Political Quarterly,* 70 (March 1955), 658–675. [4]

Burns, James M. *The Deadlock of Democracy.* Englewood Cliffs, N.J.: Prentice-Hall, 1963. [2]

Business Week. "A Plan of Attack on the Energy Crisis," June 30, 1973, 26. [10]

C

Campbell, Angus. *White Attitudes Toward Black People.* Ann Arbor: University of Michigan Institute for Social Research, 1971. [6]

Campbell, Angus, Philip E. Converse, Warren Miller, and Donald E. Stokes. *The American Voter.* New York: Wiley, 1960. [9, 12, 13]

Canterberry, E. Roy. *Economics On a New Frontier.* Belmont, Ca.: Wadsworth, 1968. [4]

Cantril, Albert H., and Charles W. Roll, Jr. *Hopes and Fears of the American People.* New York: Universe Books, 1971. [12]

Canty, Donald. *A Single Society: Alternatives to Urban Apartheid.* New York: Praeger, 1969. [6]

Carroll, Holbert N. *The House of Representatives and Foreign Affairs.* Boston: Little, Brown, 1966. [8]

Casper, Jonathan. *American Criminal Justice: The Defendant's Perspective.* Englewood Cliffs, N.J.: Prentice-Hall, 1972. [11]

Cater, Douglass. *The Fourth Branch of Government.* New York: Vintage, 1959. [14]

Caudill, Harry M. *Night Comes to the Cumberlands.* Boston: Little, Brown, 1963. [4a]

Civil Rights Cases, 109 U.S. 3 (1883). [11]

Clarke, James W., and E. Lester Levine. "Marijuana Use, Social Discontent and Political Alienation: A Study of High School Youth," *American Political Science Review,* 65 (March 1971), 120–130. [7a]

Cochran, Thomas C., and William Miller. *The Age of Enterprise.* Rev. paper ed. New York: Harper & Row, 1961, chaps. 7 and 8. [4]

Coles, Robert. *Migrants, Sharecroppers, Mountaineers.* Boston: Little, Brown, 1967. [4a]

Collier, John. *Indians of the Americas.* New York: (Mentor Books) New American Library, 1952. [6]

Commonwealth v. Leis. 243 N.E. 2d 898 (1969). [7a]

Congressional Quarterly. *Global Defense.* Washington, D.C.: Congressional Quarterly Service, 1969. [5]

———. *Legislators and the Lobbyists.* 2nd ed. Washington, D.C.: Congressional Quarterly Service, May 1968. [15]

———. *Weekly Report.* Washington, D.C.: Congressional Quarterly Service, November 6, 1970. [13]

———. *Weekly Report.* Washington, D.C.: Congressional Quarterly Service, November 11, 1972. [13]

Congressional Record, October 19, 1971. [6a]

Converse, Philip E. "The Nature of Belief Systems in Mass Publics," in David E. Apter (ed.), *Ideology and Discontent.* New York: Free Press, 1964. [1, 12]

Converse, Philip E., Warren E. Miller, Jerrold G. Rusk, and Arthur C. Wolfe. "Continuity and Change in American

Politics Parties and Issues in the 1968 Election," *American Political Science Review,* 63 (December 1969), 1103–1104. [12]

Cooper v. Aaron, 358 U.S. 1 (1958). [6a]

Cotter, Cornelius, and Bernard Hennessy. *Politics Without Power: The National Party Committees.* New York: Atherton, 1964 [13]

Cronin, Thomas E. "The Textbook Presidency and Political Science." Paper prepared for delivery at the 66th Annual Meeting of the American Political Science Association, 1970. [9]

D

Dahl, Robert A. *A Preface to Democratic Theory.* Chicago: University of Chicago Press, 1956. [2, 7]

———. "The Supreme Court as a National Policy-Maker," *Journal of Public Law,* 6 (1958), 279–295. [11]

Danelski, David. *A Supreme Court Justice Is Appointed.* New York: Random House, 1964. [11]

Davidson, Roger H. *The Role of the Congressman.* Indianapolis: (Pegasus Books) Bobbs-Merrill, 1969. [8]

———. "Public Prescriptions for the Job of Congressman," *Midwest Journal of Political Science,* 14 (November 1970), 648–666. [8]

Democratic Study Group. *Voting in House.* (March 10, 1969.) [8]

Dennis v. United States, 341 U.S. 494 (1951). [11]

Dickens, Charles. *American Notes.* New York: Dutton, 1934, 242ff. [1]

Dolbeare, Kenneth M., and Murray J. Edelman. *American Politics: Policies, Power and Change.* Lexington, Mass.: Heath, 1971. [4]

Doloria, Vine. *Custer Died for Your Sins.* New York: Avon, 1970. [6]

Domhoff, G. William. *Who Rules America?* Englewood Cliffs, N.J.: Prentice-Hall, 1967. [2]

Donovan, John C. *The Politics of Poverty.* Indianapolis: (Pegasus Books) Bobbs-Merrill, 1967. [4]

Downie, Leonard. *Justice Denied.* New York: Praeger, 1971. [11]

Downs, Anthony. *Who Are the Urban Poor?* Rev. ed. New York: Committee for Economic Development, 1970. [3]

Dred Scott v. Sandford, 19 How. 393 (1857). [6, 11]

Drucker, Peter. *The Age of Discontinuity: Guide Lines to Our Changing Society.* New York: Harper & Row, 1969. [10]

Drury, Doris. *The Accident Records in

Coal Mines of the United States. Bloomington: Indiana University, April 1964. [4a]

Dulles, John Foster. "The Goal of Our Foreign Policy," *Department of State Bulletin,* 31 (December 13, 1954a), 892. [5]

———. "The Evolution of Foreign Policy," *Department of State Bulletin,* 30 (January 24, 1954b), 108. [5]

Dunning, William A. *Reconstruction: Political and Economic.* New York: Harper & Row, 1968. [6]

Dye, Thomas R. *Politics, Economics, and the Public.* Chicago: Rand McNally, 1966. [2]

Dye, Thomas R., and L. Harmon Zeigler. *The Irony of Democracy: An Uncommon Introduction to American Politics.* Belmont, Ca.: Wadsworth, 1970. [12]

E

Easton, David. *A Systems Analysis of Political Life.* New York: Wiley, 1965. [9]

Easton, David, and Jack Dennis. *Children and the Political System: Origins of Political Legitimacy.* New York: McGraw-Hill, 1968. [12]

Eckstein, Otto. *Public Finance.* Englewood Cliffs, N.J.: Prentice-Hall, 1964. [4]

Economic Opportunity Act, 88th Congress, March 1964. [4a]

Edelman, Murray. *The Symbolic Uses of Politics.* Urbana: University of Illinois Press, 1964. [2]

Eldersveld, Samuel J. *Political Parties: A Behavioral Analysis.* Chicago: Rand McNally, 1964. [13]

Erikson, Robert S., and Norman R. Luttbeg. *American Public Opinion: Its Origins, Content, and Impact.* New York: Wiley, 1973. [12]

Evans, Rowland, Jr., and Robert D. Novak. *Nixon In the White House: The Frustration of Power.* New York: Random House, 1971, chaps. 7, 12, and 13. [4]

Everett, Robinson O. (ed.). *Anti-Poverty Programs.* Dobbs Ferry, N.Y.: Oceana Publications, 1966. [4a]

Eyestone, Robert. *Political Economy: Politics and Policy Analysis.* Chicago: Markham, 1972. [4]

F

Fenno, Richard F. *The President's Cabinet.* Cambridge, Mass.: Harvard University Press, 1959. [9]

Ferman, Louis A., Joyce L. Kornbluh, and Alan Haber (eds.). *Poverty in America, A Book of Readings.* Ann Arbor: University of Michigan Press, 1965. [4a]

Filler, Louis, and Allen Guttmann (eds.). *Removal of the Cherokee Nation: Manifest Destiny or National Dishonor.* Lexington, Mass.: Heath, 1962. [6]

Fine, Sidney. *Laissez-Faire and the General Welfare State.* Ann Arbor: University of Michigan Press, 1969, chaps. 4 and 5. [4]

Finer, Joel J. "Psychedelics and Religious Freedom," *Hastings Law Journal,* 19 (March 1968), 667–758. [7a]

Fisher, Douglas Alan. *The Epic of Steel.* New York: Harper & Row, 1963. [4a]

Fiske, John. *The Critical Period in American History, 1783–1789.* Boston: Houghton Mifflin, 1916. [2]

Flanigan, William H. *Political Behavior of the American Electorate.* 2nd ed. Boston: Allyn and Bacon, 1972. [12]

Fortune. "What They Believe: A *Fortune* Survey," January 1969. [12]

France, Anatole. *Crainqueville.* Winifred Stephens (tr.). Freeport, N.Y.: Books For Libraries, 1922. [3]

Fremantle, Anne. *Mao Tse-tung: An Anthology of His Writings.* New York: (Mentor) New American Library, 1954. [7]

Friedman, Milton. "The Role of Monetary Policy," *American Economic Review,* 58 (March 1968), 1–17. [4]

———. "The Poor Man's Welfare Payment to the Middle Class," *Washington Monthly,* 4 (May 1972), 11–16. [3]

Froman, Lewis A. *Congressmen and Their Constituencies.* Chicago: Rand McNally, 1963. [8]

G

Galbraith, John K. *American Capitalism: The Concept of Countervailing Power.* Boston: Houghton Mifflin, 1956, chaps. 9 and 10. [4]

———. *The New Industrial State.* 2nd ed. Boston: Houghton Mifflin, 1971, chaps. 2 and 3. [4]

Galloway, George B. *History of the United States House of Representatives.* New York: Crowell, 1962. [8]

Gallup, George H. *The Gallup Poll: Public Opinion 1935–1971.* New York: Random House, 1972, Vol. 3. [6a, 7, 10, 12, 13, and 14]

Gallup Poll. April, 1973. [12]

Gardner, John. "A Formula for Reform of the Political Process," *Los Angeles Times,* May 13, 1973. [13]

Gautreaux et al. v. Chicago Housing Authority, 296 F. Supp. 907 (1969). [6]

Gideon v. Wainwright, 372 U.S. 335 (1963). [7]

Gitlow v. New York, 268 U.S. 652 (1925). [7]

Gladwin, Thomas. *Poverty U.S.A.* Boston: Little, Brown, 1967. [4a]

Glock, Charles Y., and Rodney Stark. *Religion and Society Tension.* Chicago: Rand McNally, 1965. [1]

Goldston, Robert. *The Great Depression.* Indianapolis: Bobbs-Merrill, 1968. [4a]

Goode, Erich. "Marijuana and the Politics of Reality," *Journal of Health and Social Behavior,* 10 (June 1969), 83–94. [7a]

———. *The Marijuana Smokers.* New York: Basic Books, 1970. [7a]

Gorer, Geoffrey. *The American People, a Study in National Character.* Rev. ed. New York: Norton, 1964. [1]

Greeley, Andrew M., and P. B. Sheatsley. "Attitudes Toward Racial Integration," *Scientific American,* 225 (December 1971), 13–19. [6a]

Green v. School Board of New Kent County, Virginia, 391 U.S. 430 (1968). [6a]

Griswold v. Connecticut, 381 U.S. 479 (1965). [7a]

Grossman, Joel. *Lawyers and Judges.* New York: Wiley, 1965. [11]

Gruchy, Alan. *Comparative Economic Systems.* Boston: Houghton Mifflin, 1966. [3]

Grund, Francis J. *The Americans.* Boston: Marsh, Capen, and Lyon, 1837, 202–204. [1]

Guttmann, Allen (ed.). *Korea and the Theory of Limited War.* Lexington, Mass.: Heath, 1967. [5]

H

Halberstam, David. *The Best and the Brightest.* New York: Random House, 1972. [4, 8, 9]

Hamilton, Alexander. "No. 78," in Alexander Hamilton, James Madison, and John Jay, *The Federalist.* Benjamin F. Wright (ed.). Cambridge, Mass.: Harvard University Press, 1961; first published, 1788. [11]

Harrington, Michael. *The Other America.* New York: Macmillan, 1962. [4a]

Harris, Louis. "Political Labels Depend on Who Applies Them," *St. Petersburg Times,* January 18, 1971, A10. [12]

Harris Poll. *Washington Post.* October 23, 1972. [9]

Hartz, Louis. *Economic Policy and Democratic Thought: Pennsylvania 1776–1860.* Cambridge, Mass.: Harvard University Press, 1948. [4]

———. *The Liberal Tradition in America.* New York: Harcourt, Brace & World, 1955. [1]

———. *The Founding of New Societies.* New York: Harcourt, Brace & World, 1964. [1]

Hays, Samuel P. *The Response to Industrialism, 1885–1914.* Chicago: University of Chicago Press, 1957. [4]

Heard, Alexander. *The Costs of Democracy.* Chapel Hill: University of North Carolina Press, 1960. [14]

Heath, Jim F. *John F. Kennedy and the Business Community.* Chicago: University of Chicago Press, 1969, chaps. 3, 5, 8, and 13. [4]

Heilbroner, Robert. "The Roots of Social Neglect in the United States," in Eugene Rostow (ed.), *Is Law Dead?* New York: Simon & Schuster, 1971. [3]

———. *The Economic Problem.* 3rd ed. Englewood Cliffs, N.J.: Prentice-Hall, 1972. [3]

Hess, Robert D., and Judith V. Torney. *The Development of Political Attitudes in Children.* Chicago: Aldine, 1967. [12]

Hess, Stephen. "Foreign Policy and Presidential Campaigns," *Foreign Policy,* no. 9 (Winter 1972–73), 3–22. [9]

Hinckley, Barbara. "Incumbency and the Presidential Vote in Senate Elections: Defining Parameters of Subpresidential Voting," *American Political Science Review,* 64 (September 1970), 836–842. [8]

———. *The Seniority System in Congress.* Bloomington: Indiana University Press, 1971. [8]

Hirschi, Travis, and Joseph Zelan. "Class, Status, and Politics: The Case of Student Activism." Report to the Carnegie Commission's National Survey of Higher Education, 1973. [12]

Hofstadter, Richard. *The American Political Tradition.* New York: Knopf, 1948, chaps. 1, 2, and 3. [4]

Holland, Robert. "Views of Candidates Differ on Support for Education," *Richmond Times-Dispatch,* November 3, 1968, F4. [7a]

Howe, Mark DeWolfe. *The Garden and the Wilderness: Religion and Government in American Constitutional History.* Chicago: University of Chicago Press, 1965. [7]

Huitt, Ralph K. "Democratic Party Leadership in the Senate," *American Political Science Review,* 55 (June 1961), 333–345. [8]

Humphrey's Executor v. United States, 295 U.S. 602 (1935). [9]

Hyde v. United States, 225 U.S. 347 (1912). [7]

I

In re Gault, 387 U.S. 1 (1967). [7]

Institute for Strategic Studies. *The Military Balance, 1970–1971.* London: Institute for Strategic Studies, 1971. [5]

J

Jennings, M. Kent, and Richard G. Niemi. "The Transmission of Political Views from Parent to Child," *American Political Science Review,* 62 (March 1968), 169–184. [12]

Joint Committee on the Organization of the Congress. *Organization of the Congress, Final Report.* 89th Congress, 2nd Session, 1966. [8]

Joint Economic Committee, Congress of the United States. Report of the Subcommittee on Economy in Government. *The Economics of Military Procurement.* Washington, D.C.: Government Printing Office, May 1969. [5a]

Jordan, Winthrop D. *White Over Black.* Baltimore, Md.: Penguin, 1969. [6]

K

Kaplan, John. *Marijuana—The New Prohibition.* Cleveland, Ohio: World Publishing, 1970. [7a]

Katz, Elihu, and Jacob J. Feldman. "The Debates in the Light of Research: A Survey of Surveys," in Sidney Kraus (ed.), *The Great Debates.* Bloomington: Indiana University Press, 1962. [14]

Keller, Morton (ed.). *The New Deal, What Was It?* New York: Holt, Rinehart and Winston, 1963. [4a]

Keniston, Kenneth. "Introductions," in H. H. Nowlis (ed.), *Drugs on the College Campus.* Garden City, N.Y.: Doubleday, 1969. [7a]

Kennan, George F. "The Sources of Soviet Conduct," *Foreign Affairs,* 25 (July 1947), 566–582. [5]

Kennedy, John F. "Inaugural Address, January 20, 1961," *Public Papers of the Presidents of the United States, John F. Kennedy, 1961.* Washington, D.C.: Government Printing Office, 1962. [5]

Key, V. O., Jr. *Politics, Parties and Pressure Groups.* 5th ed. New York: Crowell, 1964. [13]

Kohlmeier, Louis M., Jr. *The Regulators: Watchdog Agencies and the Public Interest.* New York: Harper & Row, 1969. [4]

Kuhn, James W. "The Riddle of Inflation," *The Public Interest,* no. 27 (Spring 1972), 63–77. [4]

L

Ladd, Everett C., Jr. *American Political Parties: Social Change and Political Response.* New York: Norton, 1970. [13]

———. *Ideology in America: Change and Response in a City, a Suburb, and a Small Town.* New York: Norton, 1972. [1]

Laird, Melvin R. *Toward a National Security Strategy of Realistic Deterrence.* Statement of Secretary of Defense Melvin R. Laird on the Fiscal Year 1972–1976 Defense Program and the 1972 Defense Budget. Washington, D.C.: Government Printing Office, 1971. [5]

Lane, Robert E. *Political Ideology.* New York: Free Press, 1962. [1, 3]

Lang, Kurt, and Gladys E. Lang. *Collective Dynamics.* New York: Crowell, 1961. [7a]

Larner, Jeremy, and Irving Howe (eds.). *Poverty: View from the Left.* New York: Morrow, 1968. [4a]

Leary v. United States, 383 F. 2d 851 (5th Cir. 1967). [7a]

Leary v. United States, 395 U.S. 6 (1969). 7a]

Lenski, Gerhard. *Power and Privilege: The Theory of Social Stratification.* New York: McGraw-Hill, 1966. [7]

Leonard, William N. *Business Size, Market Power and Public Policy.* New York: Crowell, 1969. [4]

Leuchtenburg, William E. *Franklin D. Roosevelt and the New Deal 1932–1940.* New York: Harper & Row, 1963. [4]

Levitan, Sar A. *Federal Aid to Depressed Areas.* Baltimore, Md.: Johns Hopkins Press, 1964. [4a]

Levy, Leonard. *Freedom of Speech and Press in Early American History: Legacy of Suppression.* New York: Harper & Row, 1963. [7]

Lewis, Anthony, and The New York Times. *Portrait of a Decade.* New York: Bantam, 1965. [6a]

Lewis, Oscar. *La Vida.* New York: Random House, 1965, xlii–lii. [4]

Lindesmith, Alfred R. "The Marijuana Problem—Myth or Reality?" in *The Addict and the Law.* Bloomington: Indiana University Press, 1965. [7a]

Link, Arthur. *Woodrow Wilson and the Progressive Era.* New York: Harper, 1954. [6]

Lipset, Seymour Martin. *Political Man.* Garden City, N.Y.: Doubleday, 1960. [13]

———. *The First New Nation.* New York: (Anchor) Doubleday, 1967. [1, 2]

———. *Rebellion in the University.* Boston: Little, Brown, 1971. [12]

Lipsky, Michael. "Protest as a Political Resource," *American Political Science Review,* 62 (1968), 1144–1158. [16]

———. *Protest in City Politics: Rent Strikes, Housing and the Power of the Poor.* Chicago: Rand McNally, 1970. [16]

Lipsky, Michael, and Margaret Levi. "Community Organizations as a Political Resource," in Harlan Hahn (ed.),

People and Politics in Urban Society. Vol. 6, Urban Affairs Annual Review. Beverly Hills, Ca.: Sage Publications, 1972. [16]

Littauer, Raphael, and Norman Uphoff (eds.). *The Air War in Indochina.* Rev. ed. Boston: Beacon Press, 1972. [5]

Lochner v. New York, 198 U.S. 45 (1905). [7]

Logan, Rayford W. *Betrayal of the Negro.* New York: Collier, 1965. [6]

M

McClosky, Robert. *The American Supreme Court.* Chicago: University of Chicago Press, 1960. [7]

McColley, Robert M. *Slavery in Jeffersonian Virginia.* Urbana: University of Illinois Press, 1965. [6]

McConnell, Grant. "The Spirit of Private Government," *American Political Science Review,* 52 (September 1958), 754–770. [15]

————. *Steel and the Presidency—1962.* New York: Norton, 1963. [4, 9]

McCulloch v. Maryland, 4 Wheat. 316 (1819). [2, 11]

MacEwan, Arthur. "Comment on Imperialism," *American Economic Review,* (May 1970). [3]

McGinnis, Joe. *The Selling of the President 1968.* New York: Trident, 1969. [14]

McLaurin v. Oklahoma, 339 U.S. 637 (1950). [6]

Madison, James. "Number 10," in Alexander Hamilton, James Madison, and John Jay, *The Federalist.* Benjamin F. Wright (ed.). Cambridge, Mass.: Harvard University Press, 1961; first published, 1788. [3, 15]

————. "Number 54," in Alexander Hamilton, James Madison, and John Jay, *The Federalist.* Benjamin F. Wright (ed.). Cambridge, Mass.: Harvard University Press, 1961; first published, 1788. [6]

Malcolm X and Alex Haley. *The Autobiography of Malcolm X.* New York: Grove Press, 1966. [7]

Mandel, Jerry. "Who Says Marijuana Use Leads to Heroin Addiction?" *Journal of Secondary Education,* 43 (May 1968), 211–217. [7a]

Manley, John F. *The Politics of Finance.* Boston: Little, Brown, 1970. [4]

Mapp v. Ohio, 367 U.S. 643 (1961). [7]

Marbury v. Madison, 1 Cranch 137 (1802). [11]

Marshall, George C. "European Initiative Essential to Economic Recovery," *Department of State Bulletin,* 16 (June 1947), 1160. [5]

Mason, Alpheus T., and William M.

Beaney. *American Constitutional Law.* 5th ed. Englewood Cliffs, N.J.: Prentice-Hall, 1972. [7]

Masters, Nicholas. "Committee Assignments in the House of Representatives," *American Political Science Review,* 55 (June 1961), 345–357. [8]

Matthews, Donald R. *The U.S. Senators and Their World.* Chapel Hill: University of North Carolina Press, 1960. [8]

Matthews, Donald R., and James W. Prothro. "Political Factors and Negro Voter Registration in the South," *American Political Science Review,* 57 (June 1963), 355–367. [13]

Matthews, Donald R., and James A. Stimson. "Decision-making by U.S. Congressmen: A Preliminary Model," in Sidney Ulmer (ed.), *Political Decision-Making.* Princeton, N.J.: Van Nostrand, 1970. [8]

Mead, Margaret. *And Keep Your Powder Dry.* New York: Morrow, 1943. [1]

Meiklejohn, Alexander. *Political Freedom: The Constitutional Powers of the People.* New York: Oxford University Press, 1965. [7]

Melman, Seymour. *Pentagon Capitalism: The Political Economy of War.* New York: McGraw-Hill, 1970. [5a]

Michels, Robert. *Political Parties.* Eden Paul and Cedar Paul (trs.). Glencoe, Ill.: Free Press, 1949. [15]

Miller, Warren E., and Donald E. Stokes. "Constituency Influence in Congress," *American Political Science Review,* 57 (March 1963), 45–56. [6a, 8]

Mills, C. Wright. *The Power Elite.* New York: Oxford University Press, 1956. [2]

Mintz, Morton. "Large Contributors to GOP in '72 Listed," *Washington Post,* May 13, 1973, M7. [14]

Mintz, Morton, and Jerry S. Cohen. *America, Inc.: Who Owns and Operates The United States.* New York: Dial Press, 1971. [4]

Miranda v. Arizona, 384 U.S. 436 (1966). [7, 11]

Mosca, Gaetano. *The Ruling Class.* New York: McGraw-Hill, 1939. [1]

Mosher, Frederick E. *Democracy and the Public Service.* New York: Oxford University Press, 1968. [10]

Moynihan, Daniel P. *Maximum Feasible Misunderstanding.* New York: Free Press, 1969. [4]

————. *The Politics of a Guaranteed Income: The Nixon Administration and the Family Assistance Plan.* New York: Random House, 1973. [3]

Mueller, John E. *War, Presidents and Public Opinion.* New York: Wiley, 1973. [9]

Murphy, Walter. *Congress and the Court.* Chicago: University of Chicago Press, 1962. [11]

Muse, Benjamin. *Virginia's Massive Resistance.* Bloomington: Indiana University Press, 1964. [6a]

Musolf, Lloyd D. *Government and the Economy.* Chicago: Scott, Foresman, 1965. [4]

N

NAACP v. Button, 371 U.S. 415 (1963). [7]

Nadel, Mark V. *The Politics of Consumer Protection.* Indianapolis: Bobbs-Merrill, 1971, 3–22. [4]

National Commission on Marijuana and Drug Abuse. *Marijuana: A Signal of Misunderstanding.* The Official Report of the National Commission. New York: New American Library, 1972. [7a]

Neustadt, Richard E. *Presidential Power.* New York: Wiley, 1960. [9]

Newby, Idus A. *Development of Segregationist Thought.* Homewood, Ill.: Dorsey Press, 1968. [6]

New Republic. "Nixon Replies," October 26, 1968, 11–15. [6a]

Niebuhr, Reinhold. *The Irony of American History.* New York: Scribner's Sons, 1952. [1]

Nigro, Felix A. *Modern Public Administration.* New York: Harper & Row, 1970. [10]

Nixon, Richard M. *United States Foreign Policy for the 1970's: A New Strategy for Peace.* Washington, D.C.: Government Printing Office, 1970. [5]

Nossiter, Bernard. [Defense Contracts.] *Washington Post,* December 8, 1968 and December 9, 1968. [5a]

O

Oelsner, Leslie. "Scales of Justice," New York Times News Service, printed in *The Daily Enterprise,* September 28, 1972. [3]

Olson, Mancur. *The Logic of Collective Action.* Cambridge, Mass.: Harvard University Press, 1965. [16]

Orfield, Gary. *The Reconstruction of Southern Education: The Schools and the 1964 Civil Rights Act.* New York: Wiley, 1969. [6a]

P

Packer, Herbert. *The Limits of the Criminal Sanction.* Stanford, Ca.: Stanford University Press, 1968. [11]

Pechman, Joseph. "The Rich, the Poor and the Taxes They Pay," *The Public*

Interest, no. 17 (Fall 1969), 21–43. [4]

Peltason, Jack W. *Fifty-eight Lonely Men.* New York: Harcourt, Brace & World, 1961. [6a, 11]

People of the State of Michigan v. Sinclair, 387 Mich. 91, 194 N. W. 2d (1972). [7a]

People v. Stark, 157 Colo. 59, P. 2nd 923 (1965). [7a]

People v. Woody, 394 P. 2d 813 (1964). [7a]

Phelan, William, Jr. "The Authoritarian Prescription," *Nation,* 209 (November 3, 1969), 467–473. [5a]

Phillips, Kevin. *The Emerging Republican Majority.* New Rochelle: Arlington House, 1969. [9]

Pierce, Lawrence C. *The Politics of Fiscal Policy Formation.* Pacific Palisades, Ca.: Goodyear, 1971. [4]

Plessy v. Ferguson, 163 U.S. 537 (1896). [6, 11]

Posner, Richard A. "Power in America," *The Public Interest,* no. 25 (Fall 1971), 114–121. [4]

Potter, David M. *People of Plenty.* Chicago: University of Chicago Press, 1954. [1]

President's National Advisory Commission on Rural Poverty. *Rural Poverty in the United States.* Washington, D.C.: Government Printing Office, May 1968. [4a]

Purcell, Edward A., Jr. "Ideas and Interests; Businessmen and the Interstate Commerce Act," *Journal of American History,* 54 (December 1967), 561–578. [4]

Pusey, Merlo J. *The Way We Go to War.* Boston: Houghton Mifflin, 1969. [5]

R

Race Relations Law Survey. Vanderbilt University School of Law, 2, no. 6 (March 1971), 207–214. [6a]

Rainwater, Lee. "Neighborhood Action and Lower-class Life Styles," in John Turner (ed.), *Neighborhood Organization for Community Action.* New York: National Association of Social Workers, 1968. [16]

Ranney, Austin. "Turnout and Representation in Presidential Primary Elections," *American Political Science Review,* 66 (March 1972), 21–37. [13]

Reedy, George. *The Twilight of the Presidency.* New York: Norton, 1970. [9]

Rees, David. *Korea: The Limited War.* Baltimore, Md.: Penguin, 1970. [5]

Riker, William. *Federalism.* Boston: Little, Brown, 1964. [2]

Ripley, Randall B. *Party Leadership in the House of Representatives.* Washington:

The Brookings Institution, 1967. [8]

Robinson, James A. *The House Rules Committee.* Indianapolis: Bobbs-Merrill, 1963. [8]

Robinson, John P., Jerrold G. Rusk, and Kendra B. Head. *Measures of Political Attitudes.* Ann Arbor, Mi.: Survey Research Center, Institute for Social Research, 1968. [12]

Roche, John P. "The 'Tradition' of Freedom," in Milton Konvitz and Clinton Rossiter (eds.), *Aspects of Liberty.* Ithaca, N.Y.: Cornell University Press, 1958, 129–162. [1]

Rogers, Harrell, and Charles M. Bullock. *Law and Social Change: Civil Rights Laws and Their Consequences.* New York: McGraw-Hill, 1972. [2]

Rogin, Michael Paul. "Liberal Society and the Indian Question," *Politics and Society,* 1, no. 3 (May 1971), 269–312. [1]

Roper, Burns W. *A Ten Year View of Public Attitudes Toward Television and Other Mass Media 1959–1968.* New York: Television Information Office, 1969. [14]

Rose, Peter I. "The Myth of Unanimity: Student Opinions on Critical Issues," *Sociology of Education,* 37 (Winter 1963), 137. [12]

Rossiter, Clinton. *The American Presidency.* New York: Harcourt, Brace & World, 1960. [9]

———. *Parties and Politics in America.* Ithaca, N.Y.: Cornell University Press, 1960. [13]

Rothman, David J. *Politics and Power: The United States Senate, 1869–1901.* Cambridge, Mass.: Harvard University Press, 1966. [8]

Rothman, David J. (ed.). *Rural Poor in the Great Depression, Three Studies.* New York: Arno Press and *The New York Times,* 1971. [4a]

Rourke, Francis E. *Bureaucracy, Politics and Public Policy.* Boston: Little, Brown, 1969. [10]

Runyon, Trod. "Marijuana Blues," Letter to the Editor, *Playboy* (April 1968), 66. [7a]

S

Salisbury, Robert. *Governing America.* New York: Appleton-Century-Crofts, 1973. [12]

Salpukas, Agis. "Freed Poet Hails Michigan Ruling," *New York Times,* March 12, 1972, 35. [7a]

Samish, Arthur H., and Bob Thomas. *The Secret Boss of California.* New York: Crown, 1971. [15]

Samuelsen, Paul A. *Economics: An Introductory Analysis.* 5th ed. New York:

McGraw-Hill, 1961, chap. 14. [4]

Sanford, Terry. *Storm Over the States.* New York: McGraw-Hill, 1967. [2]

Schattschneider, Elmer E. *The Struggle for Party Government.* College Park: University of Maryland, 1948. [13]

Schenck v. United States, 249 U.S. 47, 51–52 (1919). [7]

Schlesinger, Arthur M. *A Thousand Days: John F. Kennedy in The White House.* Boston: Houghton Mifflin, 1965. [4, 5a]

Schlesinger, Joseph A. *Ambition and Politics.* Chicago: Rand McNally, 1966. [8]

Schmidt, Dana. "Government Study Urges Eased Laws in Marijuana," *New York Times,* February 12, 1972. [7a]

School of Abington Township, Pennsylvania v. Schempp, 374 U.S. 203 (1963). [11]

School Segregation Cases, 347 U.S. 483 (1954). [11]

Schubert, Glendon A., Jr. *The Presidency in the Courts.* Minneapolis: University of Minnesota Press, 1957. [9]

Schwartz, Bernard. *The Professor and the Commissions.* New York: Knopf, 1959. [10]

Sears, David O. "Political Behavior," in Gardner Lindzey and Elliot Aronson (eds.), *Handbook of Social Psychology.* Reading, Mass.: Addison-Wesley, 1969, Vol. 5. [12]

Selznick, Gertrude, and Stephen Steinberg. *The Tenacity of Prejudice.* New York: Harper & Row, 1969. [7]

Sharkansky, Ira. *The Maligned States.* New York: McGraw-Hill, 1972. [2]

Sherbert v. Verner, 374 U.S. 398 (1962). [7]

Sherman, Howard. *Radical Political Economy.* New York: Basic Books, 1972. [3]

Sherrill, Robert. "Before You Believe Those Exercise and Diet Ads Read the Following Report," *Today's Health,* 49 (August 1971), 34 –36+. [3]

———. *Why They Call It Politics.* New York: Harcourt, Brace, Jovanovich, 1972, chap. 8. [4]

Skolnick, Jerome. *Justice Without Trial.* New York: Wiley, 1967. [11]

Slaughterhouse Cases, 16 Wallace 36 (1873). [7]

Smith, Alexander, and Harriet Pollack. "Crimes Without Victims," *Saturday Review,* 54 (December 4, 1971), 27–29. [11]

Smith, Russell E., and Dorothy Zietz. *American Social Welfare Institutions.* New York: Wiley, 1970. [4a]

Sorauf, Frank J. *Party Politics in America.* Boston: Little, Brown, 1972. [13]

Sorenson, Theodore. *Kennedy.* New York: Harper & Row, 1965. [9]

Spence v. Sacks, 183 N.E. 2d 634 (1962). [7a]

Stanley, David, et al. *Men Who Govern.* Washington, D.C.: The Brookings Institution, 1967. [5a]

Stark, Rodney. *Police Riots.* Belmont, Ca.: Wadsworth, 1972. [3]

Stein, Herbert. *The Fiscal Revolution in America.* Chicago: University of Chicago Press, 1969. [4]

Steiner, Stan. *The New Indians.* New York: Delta, 1968. [6]

Sundquist, James L. *Politics and Policy: The Eisenhower, Kennedy, and Johnson Years.* Washington: The Brookings Institution, 1968. [4, 9]

Sundquist, James L. (ed.). *On Fighting Poverty.* New York: Basic Books, 1969. [4a]

Swann v. Charlotte-Mecklenburg, 402 U.S. 1 (1971). [6, 6a]

Sweatt v. Painter, 339 U.S. 629 (1950). [6]

T

Tabb, William K. *The Political Economy of the Ghetto.* New York: Norton, 1970. [3]

Thompson, James D. *Organizations in Action: The Social Science Bases of Administrative Theory.* New York: McGraw-Hill, 1967. [10]

Tocqueville, Alexis de. *Democracy in America.* 2 Vols. Phillips Bradley (tr.). New York: Knopf, 1945; first English edition, 1835. [1, 3, 5a, 6, 15]

Townsend, Robert. *Up the Organization.* New York: Knopf, 1970. [10]

Truman, Harry S. "Special Message to the Congress on Greece and Turkey: The Truman Doctrine, March 12, 1947." *Public Papers of the Presidents of the United States, Harry S. Truman, 1947.* Washington, D.C.: Government Printing Office, 1963. [5]

The Trustees of Dartmouth College v. Woodward, 4 Wheaton 518 (1819). [11]

Turner, Julius, and Edward Schneier. *Party and Constituency: Pressures on Congress.* Rev. ed. Baltimore, Md.: Johns Hopkins University Press, 1971. [8]

U

United States Agency for International Development. *U.S. Economic Assistance Programs Administered by the Agency for International Development and Predecessor Agencies, April 30, 1948–June 30, 1970.* Washington, D.C.: Government Printing Office, 1971. [5]

United States Bureau of the Census. *Historical Statistics of the United States, Colonial Times to 1957.* Washington, D.C.: Government Printing Office, 1960. [1]

United States Bureau of the Census. *Statistical Abstracts of the United States: 1972.* 93rd ed. Washington, D.C.: Government Printing Office, 1972. [1]

United States Commission on Civil Rights. *1964 Staff Report: Public Education.* Washington, D.C.: Government Printing Office, October 1964. [6a]

————. *Public Knowledge and Busing Opposition.* Washington, D.C.: Government Printing Office, 1973. [6a]

United States House of Representatives. Subcommittee of the Committee on Ways and Means. *Hearings, Control of Narcotics, Marijuana, and Barbiturates.* 82nd Congress, 1st Session, 1951. [7a]

United States Senate. Committee on Foreign Relations. *Some Important Issues in Foreign Aid.* 89th Congress, 2nd Session, 1966. [5]

United States Senate. Committee on Rules and Administration. *Report, 1956 General Election Campaigns.* 85th Congress, 1st Session, 1957. [4]

United States v. O'Brien, 376 F. 2d. 538 (1968). [7]

United States Senate. Subcommittee to Investigate Juvenile Delinquency, Committee on the Judiciary. *Hearings, Narcotics Legislation.* 91st Congress, 1st Session, 1969. [7a]

United States v. Butler, 297 U.S. 1 (1936). [11]

United States v. Curtiss-Wright, 299 U.S. 304 (1936). [11]

V

Valentine, Charles A. *Culture and Poverty.* Chicago: University of Chicago Press, 1968. [4]

von Hoffman, Nicholas. "The Press Conference," *Washington Post,* May 11, 1970. [9]

W

Wald, Michael, et al. "Interrogations in New Haven: The Impact of Miranda," *Yale Law Journal,* 76 (July 1967), 1521–1648. [7, 11]

Walls, David S., and John B. Stephenson. *Appalachia in the Sixties.* Lexington: University Press of Kentucky, 1972. [4a]

Warren, Charles. *The Supreme Court in United States History.* 2 Vols. Boston: Little, Brown; Vol. I, 1922, Vol. II, 1926. [6]

Watts, William, and Lloyd A. Free. *State of the Nation.* New York: Universe, 1973. [6]

Waxman, Chaim Isaac (ed.). *Poverty: Power and Politics.* New York: Grosset & Dunlap, 1968. [4a]

Weber, Max. *The Protestant Ethic and the Spirit of Capitalism.* London: Allen & Unwin, 1930 (English translation); first published, 1904. [1]

Wesberry v. Sanders, 376 U.S. 1 (1964). [8]

White, Theodore H. *The Making of the President 1960.* New York: Atheneum, 1961. [14]

————. *The Making of the President 1968.* New York: Atheneum, 1969. [9, 14]

Wiebe, Robert H. *Businessmen and Reform: A Study of the Progressive Movement.* Cambridge, Mass.: Harvard University Press, 1962. [4]

Wilcox, Clair. *Public Policies Toward Business.* 4th ed. Homewood, Ill.: Irwin, 1971, chaps. 3, 5, and 11. [4]

Wildavsky, Aaron. *The Politics of the Budgetary Process.* Boston: Little, Brown, 1964. [10]

————. "The Two Presidencies," *Trans-Action,* 4 (December 1966). [9]

Williams, William Appleman. *The Contours of American History.* Cleveland, Ohio: World, 1961. [4]

Wilson, James Q. "The Bureaucracy Problem," *The Public Interest,* No. 6. (Winter 1967), 3–9. [4]

————. "Crime and the Liberal Audience," *Commentary,* 51 (January 1971), 71–78. [14]

Wilson, Woodrow. *Congressional Government.* New York: Meridian Books, 1956; first published in 1885. [8]

Wolf, Thomas W. *Soviet Power in Europe, 1945–1970.* Baltimore, Md.: Johns Hopkins Press, 1970. [5]

Wolfinger, Raymond E. (ed.). *Readings on Congress.* Englewood Cliffs, N.J.: Prentice-Hall, 1971, 286–305. [8]

Woodward, C. Vann. *Origins of the New South.* Baton Rouge: Louisiana State University Press, 1951. [6]

————. *Reconstruction and Reaction.* Boston: Little, Brown, 1966. [6]

Wright v. Council of the City of Emporia, 407 U.S. 451 (1972). [6a]

Wukasch, Barry C. "Marijuana and the Law: An Analysis of Evolving Federal Drug Policy." (Unpublished Dissertation, University of Arizona, 1972.) [7a]

Y

Youngstown Sheet & Tube Co. et al. v. Sawyer, 343 U.S. 579 (1952). [9]

Z

Zeigler, Harmon, and Wayne Peak. "The Political Functions of the Educational System," *Sociology of Education,* 43 (1970), 115–142. [12]

ADVISERS AND CONTRIBUTORS

Richard J. Barnet, cofounder and co-director of the Institute for Policy Studies, was educated at Harvard College and Harvard Law School. In the Kennedy Administration he was an official of the State Department and the United States Arms Control and Disarmament Agency and was a consultant to the Department of Defense. He has been a visiting professor at the National University of Mexico and at Yale. His books include *Who Wants Disarmament?*, *Intervention and Revolution*, *The Economy of Death*, and *Roots of War*. He is coauthor of the forthcoming book, *The Earth Managers: The Power of the Global Corporation*. Professor Barnet is responsible for the Perspective on The Military-Industrial Complex.

Edward N. Beiser, associate professor of political science at Brown University, graduated from the City College of New York and earned his Ph.D. at Princeton University. His particular fields of interest are American politics, judicial behavior, constitutional law, and civil liberties. His published works have appeared in various political science and legal journals, including *The American Political Science Review, Polity, Law and Society Review,* and the *Social Science Quarterly*. Professor Beiser is responsible for the Civil Liberties chapter.

Jonathan D. Casper received his B.A. from Swarthmore College and his M.A. and Ph.D. from Yale University. Formerly a research fellow in government at The Brookings Institution and assistant professor of political science at Yale University, he is currently assistant professor of political science at Stanford University. His particular interest is in the perceptions of criminal defendants in the judicial system. He is the author of *American Criminal Justice: The Defendant's Perspective, Lawyers Before the Warren Court,* and *The Politics of Civil Liberties*. Professor Casper is responsible for the chapter on the Courts.

Harry M. Caudill, a lawyer in Whitesburg, Kentucky, received his law degree from the University of Kentucky and was presented Honorary Doctor of Law Degrees by Tusculum College, Berea College, and the University of Kentucky. He is President of the Letcher County Bar Association and has served as Representative in the State Legislature and as Chairman of the Congress of Appalachian Development. He is particularly concerned with the problems of the people of the Appa-

lachian counties. Author and historian of the Cumberland Mountain region, his works include *Night Comes to the Cumberlands, Dark Hills to Westward,* and *My Land Is Dying*. He is responsible for the Perspective on Appalachia.

James W. Clarke is associate professor and chairman of the department of government at the University of Arizona. He received his B.A. at Washington and Jefferson College and his Ph. D. at Pennsylvania State University. His articles on American political behavior have been published in the *American Political Science Review, The Journal of Politics, The American Journal of Political Science, Trans-Action,* and several books in the fields of political science, sociology, and psychology. Professor Clarke is responsible for the Perspective on Marijuana Laws and Civil Liberties.

Roger H. Davidson, professor of political science at the University of California, Santa Barbara, received his A.B. at the University of Colorado and his Ph.D. at Columbia University. He previously taught at Dartmouth College and was Scholar in Residence with the National Manpower Policy Task Force in Washington, D.C. He has served as consultant to the White House on reform of grant-in-aid programs, consultant to the National Commission on the Causes and Prevention of Violence and the National Commission on Population Growth and the American Future, and he was a Professional Staff Member of the Select Committee on Committees, United States House of Representatives. He is the author of *The Role of the Congressman* and the coauthor of two books: *Congress in Crisis* and *On Capitol Hill: Studies in Legislative Politics*. His most recent book is *The Politics of Comprehensive Manpower Legislation* Professor Davidson is responsible for the Congress chapter.

Barbara Deckard is assistant professor of political science at the University of California, Riverside. She received her B.A. from Rice University, and after completing her Ph.D. at the University of Rochester, she was a postdoctoral fellow at the University of Texas at Austin. She is interested in American politics generally and Congress and methodology in particular. She has had articles published in *The Journal of Politics* and *Polity*. Professor Deckard contributed to the chapter on Wealth and Its Distribution.

Delmer D. Dunn received his B.A. from Oklahoma State University and his M.S. and Ph.D. from the University of Wisconsin, Madison. Previously a research associate at The Brookings Institution, he is presently associate professor of political science at the University of Georgia. His publications include *Public Officials and The Press, Financing Presidential Campaigns,* and articles in the *Public Administration Review* and the *Social Science Quarterly.* Professor Dunn is responsible for the chapter on Money, Media, and Campaigns.

George Frederickson, associate dean of the school of Public and Environmental Affairs at Indiana University, received his Ph.D. from the University of Southern California. He is the coauthor of *Power, Public Opinion, and Policy in a Metropolitan Community* and editor of the book *Neighborhood Control in the 70's.* He is also the research and reports editor of the *Public Administration Review* and the editor of *Sage Professional Papers in Administrative and Policy Studies.* Professor Frederickson contributed to the Bureaucracy chapter.

Paul Halpern is a graduate of Cornell University and holds a Ph.D. from Harvard University, where he was formerly a teaching fellow. He is presently assistant professor of political science at the University of California, Los Angeles. He is currently completing a study of the response of the American automobile industry to consumerism. In addition to his work on corporate politics, he has done research in the areas of urban politics, organizational behavior, and the American Presidency. Professor Halpern is responsible for the chapter on Management of the Economy.

Robert J. Huckshorn, professor of political science at Florida Atlantic University, received his Ph.D. at the State University of Iowa. Previously, he was associate director of the National Center for Education in Politics in New York and has taught at the University of California, Los Angeles and at the University of Idaho. He has been particularly active in national Republican politics. He is the author of numerous articles and essays and coauthor of *Republican Politics: The 1964 Election and Its Aftermath for the Party; The Politics of Defeat: Campaigning For Congress;* and *Current Politics: The Way Things Work in Washington.* Professor Huckshorn contributed to the Parties and Voting chapter.

Everett C. Ladd, Jr. is professor of political science and director of the Social Science Data Center at the University of Connecticut. He received his A.B. from Bates College and his Ph.D. from Cornell University. Besides his Connecticut position, he is Research Fellow in the Center for International Affairs, Harvard University. His research interests are in the areas of American political thought and ideology, public opinion, political parties, and social change and political response. He has published numerous books and articles and most recently has coauthored *Academics, Politics, and the 1972 Election,* and *Professors, Unions, and American Higher Education.* Professor Ladd is responsible for the chapter on American Ideology.

Harlan Lewin, associate professor of political science at California State University, San Diego, received his A.B. in experimental psychology from Harvard University and his Ph.D. in political science from the University of California, Berkeley. His particular field of interest is modern political thought and American government and politics. He has written an article that appears in *American Government and Politics: A Reader* and has presented papers before the American Political Science Association. Currently, he is doing research on the relationship of ideologies and participation in the United States. Professor Lewin served as graphics consultant and contributed to the captions.

Robert L. Lineberry received his B.A. from the University of Oklahoma and his Ph.D. from the University of North Carolina at Chapel Hill. He is associate professor of government at the University of Texas at Austin. His major teaching and research interests are in urban politics, public policy, and American national politics. He is coauthor of *Urban Politics and Public Policy* and his principal works have been published in the *American Political Science Review, Georgetown Law Review,* and the *Journal of Politics.* Professor Lineberry is responsible for the chapter on Interests and Institutions.

Lewis Lipsitz, formerly an instructor at the University of Connecticut, is presently a professor of political science at the University of North Carolina at Chapel Hill. He received his B.A. from the University of Chicago and his M.A. and Ph.D. from Yale University. Political philosophy and American politics are his major areas of interest. He is the author of numerous articles and is the editor of *American Government: Behavior and Controversy* and *The Confused Eagle: Readings in American Politics.* Also a poet, his works have been published in various magazines and anthologies, and he is the author of *Cold Water,* a book of poems. Professor Lipsitz is responsible for the Prologue, Epilogue, and Unit Introductions. He was a primary contributor to the formulation of the book and provided continued guidance, with special emphasis on Unit I.

Michael Lipsky, associate professor of political science at M.I.T., received his B.A. from Oberlin College, his M.P.A. from the Woodrow Wilson School of Public and International Affairs at Princeton University, and his M.A. and Ph.D. from Princeton University. He has previously taught at the University of Wisconsin and at Princeton University. He has written numerous articles on urban politics and political strategies of politically subordinate groups, and he is the author of *Protest in City Politics,* and coauthor of the forthcoming book, *Riot Commission Politics.* Professor Lipsky is responsible for the chapter on Mass Political Participation: Mobilization, Protest, and Violence. He also participated in the formulation of the book and served as one of the principal advisers who guided the development of the book, with special emphasis on Unit II.

Norman R. Luttbeg, professor of government at Florida State University, received his doctorate from Michigan State University. His research and publication has been in the area of understanding how public opinion relates to public policy. He is the author of *Public Opinion and Public Policy* and the coauthor of *American Public Opinion: Its Origins, Content, and Impact.* He has published in the *American Political Science Review,* the *Midwest Journal of Political Science,* the *Public Opinion Quarterly,* the *Social Science Quarterly,* and the *Journal of Politics.* Professor Luttbeg contributed to the Public Opinion chapter.

Donald R. Matthews is professor of political science at the University of Michigan and faculty associate at the Institute for Social Research. He was formerly a Senior Fellow in governmental studies at The Brookings Institution and has taught at the University of North Carolina and at Smith College. Interested in American politics generally, with special interest in Congress and legislative behavior, in the politics of race, and in the nominating process, he is currently doing a study on presidential nominating politics for The Brookings Institution. He is author of *U.S. Senators and Their World* and coauthor of *Negroes and the New Southern Politics*. Professor Matthews was a primary contributor to the formulation of the book and to the guidance and review of its progress, with special emphasis on Unit III.

Grant McConnell received his B.A. from Reed College, was a Rhodes Scholar to Oxford University, and earned his Ph.D. at the University of California, Berkeley. He has been a member of the faculties of Mount Holyoke College, University of California, Berkeley, and University of Chicago, where he was chairman of the department of political science. He is currently at the University of California, Santa Cruz. He has held temporary and visiting appointments at the University of Washington, Cornell University, and Makerere University College in Uganda. His publications include *The Decline of Agrarian Democracy, Steel and the Presidency, The Modern Presidency,* and *Private Power and American Democracy*. Professor McConnell is responsible for the chapter on Interest Groups and Private Governments.

Mark V. Nadel, assistant professor of government at Cornell University, received his B.A. from the University of California, Berkeley and his M.A. and Ph.D. from Johns Hopkins University. He has also been a Brookings Institution Research Fellow. His teaching and research has been in the areas of the Presidency, regulatory politics, and business-government relations. He is the author of *The Politics of Consumer Protection* and coeditor of *American Democracy: Theory and Reality*. Professor Nadel is responsible for the chapter on the Presidency and also contributed to the Congress and Bureaucracy chapters.

James K. Oliver is assistant professor of political science at the University of Delaware. He received his undergraduate degree in Asian Studies and his M.A. in government at Florida State University. He received his Ph.D. in International Studies from the American University. He is currently completing a coauthored book on American foreign and defense policy and has been a participant in the Department of State's Scholar-Diplomat program in the Bureau of Politico-Military Affairs. Professor Oliver is responsible for the chapter on Foreign Affairs and National Security.

Gary Orfield is a Research Associate at the Brookings Institution. He has taught at Princeton University and the University of Virginia and served as Scholar-in-Residence at the United States Civil Rights Commission. He received his B.A. from the University of Minnesota and his M.A. and Ph.D. from the University of Chicago. He founded the Movement for a New Congress in 1970, has worked with Ralph Nader, and has written on Indian affairs. His works have been published in *Saturday Review, New Republic, Nation,* and *Washington Post*. He is the author of *The Reconstruction of Southern Education* and forthcoming books on Congress and on federal urban policy. Professor Orfield is responsible for the chapter on Race and Government and for the Perspective on Desegregating the Schools.

John C. Pierce is associate professor at Washington State University. After receiving his undergraduate degree from the University of Puget Sound and his graduate degrees from the University of Minnesota, he taught at Tulane University. He has published in several scholarly journals and is coeditor of two books: *Readings on the American Political System* and *Cross-National Micro-Analysis*. Professor Pierce contributed to the Parties and Voting chapter.

Douglas D. Rose is assistant professor of political science at Tulane University. He received his undergraduate degree at Williams College and his graduate degrees at the University of Minnesota. His particular interest is mass political behavior, such as voting and tax-paying. His publications have appeared in several scholarly journals. Professor Rose contributed to the Parties and Voting chapter.

William A. Schultze, associate professor of political science at California State University, San Diego, has previously taught at Rutgers University, Valparaiso University, and Kansas State University. He received his B.A. from Nebraska Wesleyan University and his M.A. and Ph.D. from Rutgers University. His particular areas of interest include urban government and politics, political leadership, American national government and politics, and political theory and philosophy. He is coeditor of *American Government and Politics: A Reader* and author of *The Process of Urbanization: The Political Aspects* and the forthcoming text, *Urban Politics and Policy: The Search for Community*. Professor Schultze provided advice to the editors on several chapters and is responsible for the chapter summaries.

Rodney Stark, professor of sociology at the University of Washington, worked as a newspaper and magazine writer before earning his Ph.D. at the University of California, Berkeley. He is the coauthor of five books that deal with religious behavior. His most recent book, *Police Riots,* was published in 1972. Professor Stark contributed to many chapters in this book, especially Wealth and Its Distribution, Bureaucracy, Public Opinion, Parties and Voting, and Money, Media, and Campaigns.

Jack Walker, professor of political science at the University of Michigan, was formerly an instructor at Furman University and at Boston University. He received his Ph.D. from the University of Iowa. His major concentration has been on policy making and public administration in American state and city governments. He has been most directly concerned with racial politics in America, problems of democratic theory, and theories of policy change and the diffusion of innovations. He has published numerous articles in scholarly journals and is author of *Sit-Ins in Atlanta* and coauthor of *Race In the City: Political Trust and Public Policy in the New Urban System*. Professor Walker was a principal contributor to the formulation of the book and to its guidance and review, with special emphasis on Unit IV.

INDEX

Italic numbers refer to illustrations.
c   refers to caption.
m   refers to marginal note.

A

A & P, 66
Abrams, Charles, 199
absolutist position, 217
    See also civil liberties
abundance, American, 19–20, 29
    See also Potter, David
ACLU. *See* American Civil Liberties Union
Adamany, David, 418, 433
Adams, John, 17, 40, 342, 342m
Adams, Sherman, 301c
Addams, Jane, 212m
Adelson, Joseph, 372
administration. *See* bureaucracy
AFL-CIO, 447c, 448c
Age of Discontinuity: Guidelines to Our Changing Society
    (Drucker), 331
Agnew, Spiro, 428c
agricultural price supports, 103–104
agriculture, 103–104
Agriculture, Department of, 37, 85, 104, 317, 320m,
    322, 455
aid. *See* economic aid; foreign aid; military aid
Alabama, 47, 108, 176–177, 178
Alaska, 181–182
    pipeline, 320m
Albuquerque, N.M., 242
Alcatraz Island, 181
Alexander, Herbert, 412
Alexander v. *Holmes* (1969), 198, 199
Alford, Robert, 403
Algeria, 19
Alien and Sedition Acts, 276
alienation in American life, 22
Alinsky, Saul, 462, 465, 477
Allende, Salvador, 42, 275c
Alliance for Progress, 137
Almond, Gabriel, 22, 26, 27–28, 370
Alternative Society, An, 64–65
Amalgamated Food Employees Local 590 v. *Logan Valley
    Plaza, Inc.* (1968), 215m
amendments, constitutional. *See* each amendment
    by name; i.e., First Amendment
America, Russia, and the Cold War, 1945–1971 (La
    Feber), 148
American Bar Association, 347
American Battle Monuments Commission, 319
American Civil Liberties Union (ACLU), 212m
American Commonwealth (Bryce), 30
American Constitutional Law (Mason and Beaney), 243
American Criminal Justice: The Defendant's Perspective
    (Casper), 359
American Democracy: Theory and Reality (Weissberg
    and Nadel, eds.), 298
American Farm Bureau Federation, 440, 448
American Federalism: A View from the States (Elazar), 51
American Foreign Policy Since World War II (Spanier),
    148
American Independent Party, 391
American Indian Movement, 181
American Legislative Process: Congress and the States
    (O'Keefe and Ogul), 277
American Medical Association, 436, 441
American Public Opinion: Its Origins, Content, and Impact
    (Erikson and Luttbeg), 385
American Rifle Association, 382
American Security Council, 155
American Socialist Party, 18c, 18–19
American Supreme Court, The (McCloskey), 359
Americanism, 18, 21–22, 29
amnesty, 219, *219*
anarchism, 207, 484
Anderson, James, 84, 98, 104, 105
Anderson, John, 194
Ann Arbor, Mich., 242
Anslinger, H. J., 229
antitrust laws, 104–105
Anzus Pact, *126*
apologies for delays in congressional responses, 318
Appalachia, 100–101, 107–121, 178, 479

Appalachia in the Sixties (Walls and Stephenson), 121
Appalachian Regional Development Act (ARDA),
    100, 116
    See also regional development
ARA. *See* Area Redevelopment Act
ARDA. *See* Appalachian Regional Development Act
Area Redevelopment Act (ARA), 100, 108, 113–114,
    273–274
    See also regional development
Area Redevelopment Administration, 114
    See also regional development
Arizona Daily Star, 242
Arkansas, 193
Army Corps of Engineers, 313, 320m
Army Scientific Advisory Committee, 155
Army Special Forces, 136
Arnold, Thurman, 104
Articles of Confederation, 39
    See also Constitution; constitutional convention
Ash, Roy, 153
assassination, 2–3
Atlanta, Ga., 201
Atomic Energy Commission, 151, 153, 320m
Attorney General, 40
    civil rights and, 178, 300, 302
    judicial recruitment and, 347
    state election laws and, 185
Auerbach, Stuart, 241
Australia, 48

B

Bacall, Lauren, 302c
Bachrach, Peter, 409
Bailey, Stephen, 91
Baker, Howard, 428
balancing approach, 217
    See also civil liberties
Baltimore, Md., 201
Bancroft, George, 38
Banfield, Edward, 101
Baran, Paul, 60
Barber, Richard, 105
Barkley, Alben, 413c
Barnet, Richard, 149, 160
Barnett, Ross, 47
Barrett, Laurence, 149, 151, 156
Barron v. *Baltimore* (1833), 210, 211, 346
Barron's 119
Baumol, William, 100
Bay of Pigs invasion, 2, 135c, 140, 140m, 152–153,
    298
Bean, Walton, 443
Beaney, William, 224, 243
Beard, Charles, 38, 39, 41
Beard, Dita, 439c
Beer, Samuel, 17m
belief systems. *See* ideologies
Bell, Daniel, 14, 106
Berelson, Bernard, 368, 376, 406
Berle, Adolf, 91, 105
Berlin, 125–127, 127c, 135, 137–138, 140, 246–247
Berman, Daniel M., 203
Best, James J., 385
Beth-Elkhorn, 119
Bethlehem Steel, 109, 119
Betrayal of the Negro (Logan), 188
Bickel, Alexander, 340m, 344
Big Sandy Corporation, 109
Bilateral Treaties, *126*
Bill of Rights, 206, 210, 211–212, 346, 490
    See also amendments, constitutional
Binkley, Wilfred E., 309
Birmingham, Ala., 177, 195, 464
Black, Charles, 340m, 344
Black, Hugo, 212, 217, 353
Black, Shirley Temple, 415
Black Muslims, 225
Black Panthers, 185c, *463*
black power movement, 3, 183, 225, 248

CREDITS AND ACKNOWLEDGMENTS

Special thanks are extended to the following persons for their help in providing and developing graphics: Terry Lamb, Ignacio Gomez, and Dick Oden, artists who have contributed their creativity; Mona El Khadem for her help in creating line mechanicals; Nancy Brown and Gary Sawade for their help as graphic researchers; Nona Remos for her help in retouching the black and white photographs; Miriam Wohlgemuth, Louis Neiheisel, and Steve Harrison for doing most of the production art on charts, graphs, and diagrams; Brad Ensminger and Tom Rago for their roles as production artists in preparing camera-ready art; Lyn Smith for her in-house photo research assistance; Ed Yotka, Thomas J. Yotka, and Vincent Di Prima of UPI-COMPLEX for extensive photo research. We also wish to extend special thanks for editorial contributions and help to the following individuals: Leslie Bolinger for her help as a rewriter and editorial researcher; Marion Fusco, for proofreading the text; Davey Estrada, Elaine Kleiss, and Bill Schultze, who developed the index; Beverly Cefaratti, Amy Barnett, Rolande Angles, and all the other typists, who helped with the manuscript.

Contents
viii to xi—Tom Lewis

Prologue. Politics in Everyday Life
xii—Charles Gatewood

Unit I. What is "American" Politics?
6—designed by Tom Lewis, art work executed by Ignacio Gomez and Nona Remos

Chapter 1. The American Ideology
12—Charles Gatewood; 15—after Harlan Lewin, 1974; 19—Brown Brothers; 23—(top) Marc Riboud/Magnum Photos, (bottom) Phil Stotts; 25—(top and bottom left) Brown Brothers, (left center) George Hall, (center) General Cable Corporation, (right center) Burk Uzzle/Magnum Photos, (bottom right) Roger J. Adams; 26—Dick Oden; 27—Ignacio Gomez

Chapter 2. Interests and Institutions
32—Phil Stotts; 35—Ignacio Gomez; 38—Terry Lamb; 39—The Granger Collection; 41—Louie Neiheisel after Harlan Lewin, 1974; 43—(left) Louie Neiheisel after Robert Lineberry, 1974, (right) Louie Neiheisel and Patti Ortega after Harlan Lewin, 1974; 44—Terry Lamb; 46—Louie Neiheisel after R. F. Madgic, S. S. Seaberg, F. H. Stopsky, and R. W. Winks, *The American Experience*, copyright © 1971 by Addison-Wesley Publishing Company, Inc., reprinted by permission.; 48—Patti Ortega after Harlan Lewin, 1974; 50—Ignacio Gomez.

Chapter 3. Wealth and Its Distribution
52—Dennis Brack/Black Star; 54—Ignacio Gomez; 55—Miriam Wohlgemuth; 56—(top) Louie Neiheisel adapted from the Bureau of Economic Analysis, Social and Economic Statistics Administration, (bottom) Louie Neiheisel adapted from U.S. Department of Commerce, *Pocket Data Book, USA 1971*, Table 263 ; 57—(bottom) Louie Neiheisel adapted from U.S. Department of Commerce, Bureau of the Census, *Current Population Reports*, 1972; 59—Miriam Wohlgemuth after Harlan Lewin, 1974; 60—(left) Brown Brothers, (top center and right) The Bettmann Archive, Inc., (bottom center) Wells Fargo Bank History Room; 61—(top) courtesy Chase Manhattan Bank, (bottom) United California Bank; 67—Wilson McLean; 68—(top left) George Hall, (left center) George Hall/Woodfin Camp, (bottom left) R. Bruegel/Chaos Travels Ltd., (right) John and Bini Moss/Black Star; 70—(top) Enrico Natali/Rapho-Guillumette, (bottom) Victor Friedman/Rapho-Guillumette; 71—Ken Heyman; 73—(left) Bruce Davidson/Magnum Photos, (top right) Elihu Blotnick/BBM Associates, (right center) Daniel Brody, (bottom right) Bruce Davidson/Magnum Photos.

Unit II. What Is the Government's Agenda?
76—designed by Tom Lewis, art work executed by Ignacio Gomez and Nona Remos

Chapter 4. Management of the Economy
82—Brown Brothers; 84—Union Pacific Railroad Museum Collection; 86—(top left) The Bettmann Archive, Inc., (top right) Brown Brothers, (bottom) after The Cleveland Trust Company for "Rise and Fall in American Business," 87—(top) Brown Brothers, (bottom) UPI-COMPIX; 90—Ignacio Gomez; 95—after Harlan Lewin, 1974; 96—Louie Neiheisel after Harlan Lewin, 1974; 97—UPI-COMPIX; 103—Ignacio Gomez; 104—Dick Oden

Chapter 4a. Perspective: Appalachia
107—courtesy OEO; 109—(left) UPI-COMPIX, (right) George Hall; 110—(left) Earl Dotter/BBM Associates, (right) courtesy OEO; 111—Terry Lamb; 112—Dick Oden; 114—(top left) Brown Brothers, (bottom left and right) UPI-COMPIX; 115—UPI-COMPIX; 116—Miriam Wohlgemuth after Harlan Lewin, 1974; 117—Arthur Sirdofsky; 118—(top left and right) Arthur Sirdofsky, (bottom left and right) courtesy OEO; 119—(left) Earl Dotter/BBM, (right) UPI-COMPIX; 120—UPI-COMPIX

Chapter 5. Foreign Affairs and National Security
122—Magnum Photos; 125—Bundesarchiv, Koblenz; 126—Dick Oden and Miriam Wohlgemuth; 127—UPI-COMPIX; 128—Louie Neiheisel after Harlan Lewin, 1974; 129—UPI-COMPIX; 130—(top) Library of Congress, (bottom) UPI-COMPIX; 132—Ignacio Gomez; 133—UPI-COMPIX; 134—Dick Oden; 135—UPI-COMPIX; 137—Ignacio Gomez; 138—Observer; 139—(all but bottom left) UPI-COMPIX, (bottom left) Library of Congress; 141—(left) Louie Neiheisel, (right) POPPERFOTO; 142—from U.S. Department of State, Agency for International Development, 1972; 143—UPI-COMPIX; 145—after Harlan Lewin, 1974; 146—(top) Louie Neiheisel after Harlan Lewin, 1974, (bottom) Library of Congress.

Chapter 5a. Perspective: The Military-Industrial Complex
149—UPI-COMPIX; 150—(left) Cornell Capa/Magnum Photos, (center) Charles Moore/Black Star, (right) Bob Van Doren; 151—Bob Van Doren; 153—reprinted with permission from *The Washington Monthly*, copyright © 1970 by The Washington Monthly Company, 1028 Conn. Ave. N.W., Washington, D.C. 20036; 154—Miriam Wohlgemuth after Harlan Lewin, 1974; 155—from M. Barone, G. Ujifusa, D. Matthews, *The Almanac of American Politics*, Gambit, Inc., Boston, 1972; 156—Mona El Khadem after Harlan Lewin, 1974; 157—Louie Neiheisel from the U.S. Department of Defense, Office of the Assistant Secretary of Defense for International Security Affairs, *Military Assistance and Foreign Military Sales Facts*, p. 21 ; 159—Terry Lamb; 160—Ignacio Gomez.

Chapter 6. Race and Government
166—Fred Ward/Black Star; 168—Dick Oden; 171—UPI-COMPIX; 175—(left) Elliott Erwitt/Magnum Photos, (right) UPI-COMPIX; 177—(top) Claus Meyer/Black Star, (left and right center) UPI-COMPIX, (bottom left) Jeffrey Blankfort/BBM Associates, (bottom right) Charles Moore/Black Star; 180—UPI-COMPIX; 181—Roger Malloch/Magnum Photos; 182—(top) Louie Neiheisel after U.S. Bureau of the Census, 1971, (bottom) Louie Neiheisel after *Black Americans: A Chartbook*, U.S. Bureau of Labor, Bureau of Labor Statistics, Bulletin No. 1699, 1971; 183—Louie Neiheisel after U.S. Public Health Service, *Vital Statistics of the United States*, annual; 184—(left) Dennis Brack/Black Star, (right) Jeffrey Blankfort/BBM Associates; 185—Stephen Shames/Black Star; 187—(top left) Cheste Higgins, Jr./Rapho-Guillumette, (all other photos) UPI-COMPIX, (bottom) Louie Neiheisel after U.S. Department of Commerce, Bureau of the Census, *Pocket Data Book U.S.A. 1971*, figure 4.

Chapter 6a. Perspective: Desegregating the Schools
189 and 190—UPI-COMPIX; 191—Terry Lamb;
192—Louie Neiheisel after Harlan Lewin, 1974; 193
to 195—UPI-COMPIX; 197—Ignacio Gomez; 199 to
201—UPI-COMPIX; 202—Arthur Sirdofsky; 203—
Louie Neiheisel after David H. Soule, *Task Force
Report on Pupil Transportation*, U.S. Department of
Transportation, 1973.

Chapter 7. Civil Liberties
204—Nacio Jan Brown/BBM Associates; 207—UPI-
COMPIX; 209—Ken Heyman, courtesy *Time
Magazine*; 210—Louie Neiheisel after Congressional
Quarterly, Inc., Washington D.C.; 211—Dick Oden;
213—(left) Dorthea Lange, courtesy of National
Archives; (right) Phil Stotts; 214—UPI-COMPIX;
215—Terry Lamb; 216—Dick Oden; 217—Eve
Arnold/Magnum Photos; 219—reprinted from *U.S.
News & World Report*, copyright © March 12, 1973,
U.S. News & World Report, Inc.

**Chapter 7a. Perspective: Marijuana Laws and Civil
Liberties**
228—"Penalty for Possession of Marijuana (First
Offense)," a PLAYBOY Poster, reproduced by
special permission of Playboy, copyright © 1969,
1971, 1972 by Playboy; 229—courtesy of Roninfilm,
Inc.; 230 to 232—UPI-COMPIX; 234—Culver
Pictures; 235—California Historical Society; 237—
Miriam Wohlgemuth after Harlan Lewin, 1974;
239—John Dawson; 240—Dick Oden.

Unit III Who Runs the Government?
244—designed by Tom Lewis, art work executed by
Ignacio Gomez and Nona Remos.

Chapter 8. Congress
250—Don Peterson; 253—Fred Ward/Black Star;
255—Miriam Wohlgemuth after Congressional
Quarterly, Inc., Washington, D.C., 1973; 256 and
257—Terry Lamb after Harlan Lewin, 1974; 258—
Miriam Wohlgemuth; 259, 261, and 262—Miriam
Wohlgemuth after Harlan Lewin, 1974; 263—Louie
Neiheisel after Harlan Lewin, 1974; 264—Miriam
Wohlgemuth after Harlan Lewin, 1974; 265—after
Harlan Lewin, 1974; 266 and 267—Mona El Khadem
and Miriam Wohlgemuth after Harlan Lewin, 1974;
269—(left to right, top to bottom) courtesy of the
following congressional members: Louis C.
Wyman, George Mahon, John A. Ashbrook, Shirley
Chisholm, Ogden Reid, John E. Moss, Wilbur Mills,
Joel Broyhill; 273—Dick Oden; 275—(all but
bottom) Jason Lauré, (bottom) UPI-COMPIX.

Chapter 9. The Presidency
278—Don Peterson; 280—after Congressional
Quarterly, Inc., Washington, D.C., 1972; 281—Dick
Oden; 282—Louie Neiheisel after *U.S. Government
Organization Manual 1972-1973*; 283—UPI-
COMPIX; 285—Dick Oden; 287—Louie Neiheisel
after Harlan Lewin, 1974; 290 and 292—UPI-
COMPIX; 293—after Harlan Lewin, 1974; 295—UPI-
COMPIX; 297—Fund for New Priorities, courtesy of
Calderhead, Jackson, Inc.; 298—UPI-COMPIX; 299—
(top) UPI-COMPIX, (bottom) Magnum Photos; 301
and 303—UPI-COMPIX; 305—(top left and right)
UPI-COMPIX, (bottom left) Jason Lauré; 306—
Louie Neiheisel after Harlan Lewin, 1974; 307—(left
to right, top to bottom) art by Aaron Majers, Patti
Orozco, Paul Rios, and James Holman, courtesy of
Sunnyside Elementary, Chula Vista, California;
308—after Congressional Quarterly, Inc.,
Washington, D.C., 1973.

Chapter 10. The Bureaucracy
310—John Oldenkamp; 313—courtesy of The New
York Historical Society; 314—Louie Neiheisel after
U.S. Government Organization Manual 1972-1973; 315—
after Harlan Lewin, 1974; 316—Louie Neiheisel
after *U.S. Government Organization Manual 1972-1973*;
321—U.S. Department of Transportation; 323 and
329—Louie Neiheisel after Harlan Lewin, 1974.

Chapter 11. The Courts
332—Fred Ward/Black Star; 335—Dick Oden; 336—
Louie Neiheisel; 337—Louie Neiheisel after James
MacGregor Burns & J. W. Peltason, *Government by
the People* (8th ed.), © 1972, redrawn by permission
of Prentice-Hall, Inc., Englewood Cliffs, N.J.; 341—
Ignacio Gomez; 343—Patti Ortega after Harlan
Lewin, 1974; 345—(top) after Harlan Lewin, 1974,
(bottom) UPI-COMPIX; 348—Miriam Wohlgemuth
after Harlan Lewin, 1974; 349—Library of Congress;
358—UPI-COMPIX.

Unit IV. Where Do We Come In?
360—designed by Tom Lewis, art work executed by
Ignacio Gomez and Nona Remos.

Chapter 12. Public Opinion
366—George Gardner; 368 and 369—Ignacio Gomez;
370—Bruce Davidson/Magnum Photos; 371—UPI-
COMPIX; 372—Dick Oden; 373 and 374—after
Harlan Lewin, 1974; 375—Louie Neiheisel after
Harlan Lewin, 1974; 378—(left to right) UPI-
COMPIX (6), courtesy of the Governor's office of
New York, Jan Lukas/Rapho-Guillumette, courtesy
of the Governor's office of California, UPI-COMPIX
(2); 380—after Harlan Lewin, 1974; 383—(left)
American Civil Liberties Union, (right) National
Citizens' Committee for Fairness to the Presidency,
618 Industrial Bank Bldg., Providence, Rhode Island
02903; 384—Louie Neiheisel after Harlan Lewin, 1974.

Chapter 13. Parties and Voting
386—The Bettmann Archive, Inc.; 388—Italian
Embassy; 389—after Harlan Lewin, 1974; 390 and
391—Louie Neiheisel after R. F. Madgic, S. S.
Seaberg, F. H. Stopsky, and R. W. Winks, *The
American Experience*, copyright © 1971 by Addison-
Wesley Publishing Company, Inc., reprinted by
permission.; 393—Janet Lanphier; 394—Library of
Congress; 395—Louie Neiheisel after Harlan Lewin,
1974; 396—Mona El Khadem and Miriam
Wohlgemuth after Harlan Lewin, 1974; 397—Burt
Glinn/Magnum; 398—Vaccaro; 399—George
Gardner; 402—Mona El Khadem and Miriam
Wohlgemuth after Harlan Lewin, 1974; 404—(top
and bottom) American Institute of Public Opinion
(Gallup Poll), (center) Center for Political Studies,
University of Michigan, Ann Arbor, Michigan;
405—(top and bottom) Brown Brothers, (center)
UPI-COMPIX; 408—reprinted from *American
Government 73-74*, The Dushkin Publishing Group,
Inc.

Chapter 14. Money, Media, and Campaigns
410—Jan Lukas/Rapho-Guillumette; 413—UPI-
COMPIX; 415—after Harlan Lewin, 1974; 416—Dan
McCoy/Black Star; 417—Lawrence Frank/Rapho-
Guillumette; 418—after data from Government
Accounting Office; 419—Ignacio Gomez; 420—Burt
Glinn/Magnum Photos; 421—reprinted by
permission from *Time*, The Weekly Newsmagazine,
copyright © Time Inc., 1972. 422—© Alan R.
Hipwell; 424—Dick Oden; 425—after Television
Information Office, New York; 426—(top left) Fred
Ward/Black Star, (top right) Dan McCoy/Black
Star, (bottom) Dennis Brack/Black Star; 427—(top
and center) Ken Heyman, courtesy *Time* Magazine,
(bottom left) Elliott Erwitt/Magnum Photos,
(bottom right) UPI-COMPIX; 428—UPI-COMPIX;
429—(top) UPI-COMPIX, (bottom) Paul Sequeira;
431—(left center) Doug Wilson/Black Star, (bottom)
Bob Fitch/Black Star, (all other photos) Charles
Harbutt/Magnum Photos.

**Chapter 15. Interest Groups and Private
Governments**
434—from Congressional Quarterly, Inc.,
Washington, D.C., 1973; 437—(top left, center right,
and bottom) Bob Van Doran, (top center) The
Bettmann Archive, Inc., (top right) UPI-COMPIX,
(left center) W. Stanton/Magnum Photos; 438—
Louie Neiheisel after Harlan Lewin, 1974; 439—
UPI-COMPIX; 440—Mona El Khadem after Harlan
Lewin, 1974; 441—Miriam Wohlgemuth after
Harlan Lewin, 1974; 442—Louie Neiheisel after
Harlan Lewin, 1974; 443—Ignacio Gomez; 444—
(left) from Congressional Quarterly, Inc.,
Washington, D.C., 1972, (right) Patti Ortega after
Harlan Lewin, 1974; 445—UPI-COMPIX; 446—
Ignacio Gomez; 447—Bob Van Doran; 448—(top and
center) Brown Brothers, (bottom) UPI-COMPIX;
452—illustrations © Mitchell Beazley, Ltd. 1971;
454—Dick Oden.

**Chapter 16. Mass Political Participation:
Mobilization, Protest, and Violence**
456—Bob Fitch/Black Star; 458—after Michael
Lipsky, 1974; 459—Library of Congress; 462 and
463—Terry Lamb; 464—after Harlan Lewin, 1974;
465—(top) Joan Larson, courtesy of VISTA, (bottom)
Arthur Siegel; 467—Ken Regan/Camera 5; 469—
Louie Neiheisel after Harlan Lewin, 1974; 472—
George Gardner; 473—after Michael Lipsky, 1974;
474—American Civil Liberties Union; 476—(top
left) Library of Congress, (top right) Peter Lake/
Black Star, (left center) Flip Schulke/Black Star,
(center) Andrew Rakoczy/Black Star, (right center)
Charles Harbutt/Magnum Photos, (bottom left)
Michael Abramson/Black Star, (bottom right) Ken
Heyman, Courtesy *Time* Magazine.

Epilogue. Which Power to Which People?
478—Charles Gatewood.

Cover—designed by Tom Lewis, art work executed
by Ignacio Gomez and Nona Remos.

American Government Today, Book Team

Roger G. Emblen, *Publisher*
Rose Fujimoto, *Publishing Coordinator*
Karen W. Key, *Senior Editor*
Janet Lanphier, Bobbie Savitz, *Associate Editors*
Patricia Campbell, *Editorial Assistant*
Mike Mendelsohn, *Designer*
Dale Phillips, *Associate Designer*
Phyllis Barton, *Production Supervisor*
Nancy Hutchison Sjöberg, *Rights and Permissions Supervisor*
Alison Harding, *Photo Researcher*
Howard Smith, *Social Science Marketing Manager*

CRM Books

Richard Holme, *President and Publisher*
Russ Calkins, *Marketing Manager*
Roger G. Emblen, *Publishing Director*
Arlyne Lazerson, *Editorial Director*
William G. Mastous, *Director of Finance and Administration*
Trygve E. Myhren, *Vice-President, Marketing*
John Ochse, *Sales Manager*
Henry Ratz, *Director of Production*
Tom Suzuki, *Director of Design*